DEAN ACHESON

DEAN ACHESON

THE STATE DEPARTMENT YEARS

BY

DAVID S. McLELLAN

ILLUSTRATED WITH PHOTOGRAPHS

DODD, MEAD & COMPANY

NEW YORK

Library of Congress Cataloging in Publication Data

McLellan, David S
  Dean Acheson: the State Department years.

  Includes index.
  1. Acheson, Dean Gooderham, 1893–1971.
2. United States—Foreign relations—1945–1953.
E748.A15M32   973.918′092′4 [B]   76–8482
ISBN 0–396–07313–1

To my wife—Ann Handforth McLellan

ACKNOWLEDGMENTS

A study of this length depends upon the support and assistance of many people whom I would like to thank. Many of Dean Acheson's former colleagues and many foreign ambassadors and political figures accorded me interviews or discussed various parts of this study with me. Among those I would like especially to thank are Clement R. Attlee, Lucius Battle, Henri Bonnet, McGeorge Bundy, General of the Army Omar Bradley, Edmund B. Burling, Sir Anthony Eden, Edgar Faure, André François-Poncet, Felix Frankfurter, Sir Oliver Franks, Dorothy Fosdick, Paul G. Hoffman, Loy Henderson, Patrick J. Hurley, Philip C. Jessup, Louis Johnson, Joseph Jones, Senator William F. Knowland, Wilmarth Lewis, David Lloyd, Archibald MacLeish, Charles Burton Marshall, René Massigli, Herbert Morrison, Richard Neustadt, Paul Nitze, John Lord O'Brian, Dean Rusk, Harry S Truman, Robert Schuman, Marshal D. Shulman, and Sir William Strang. Joseph Lawton provided a wealth of information about Acheson's boyhood years. Gaddis Smith, whose own biography of Dean Acheson set a high standard; Robert Ferrell, editor of the American Secretary of State series; and Richard Loss were also helpful.

I would also like to thank Barbara Evans, Dean Acheson's secretary of many years, for her help in guiding me through the various files of Mr. Acheson's papers. The Acheson family has very graciously responded to a number of inquiries and also made available family and official photographs.

The manuscript could not have achieved its final form without the outstanding editorial help of Ruth Limmer, Chairman of the English Department at Goucher College.

A considerable debt is also owed to various institutions that supported me during the course of researching and writing this biography. The

foundations of the study were laid during a sabbatical leave that I spent
as an Associate at the Washington Center of Foreign Policy Research.
At this time Mr. Dean Acheson gave me a number of interviews and permitted me access to his papers. The Truman Library Institute provided
a summer stipend that enabled me to examine the documents in the
Truman Library as well as to meet with other scholars working on the
history of the Truman Administration. I wish to thank Dr. Philip Brooks
in particular for his help and interest. The Faculty Research Committees
of the University of California, Riverside, and of Miami University, Oxford, Ohio, have been most helpful in financing my travel and typing
expenses. Finally, I would like to thank the Trustees of the Rockefeller
Foundation for providing me and my wife with a valuable interlude for
writing at the Villa Serbelloni, Bellagio. William C. Olson, its present
director, has given me encouragement in this endeavor for longer than
I can remember.

Within the Department of Political Science at Miami University I
wish to thank in particular the chairman, Herbert Waltzer; William D.
Jackson; and Ronald Stupak. I was fortunate to be able to draw upon
interviews conducted by Dr. Stupak which explored Mr. Acheson's relationship with the members and staff of the Senate and House Foreign
Relations Committees.

Secretaries Jean West and Elizabeth Pantle were unstinting in their
willingness to type endless drafts of many of the chapters. Betty Marak's
typing of the final draft of the manuscript drew praise from everyone
connected with the enterprise.

Finally, I would like to acknowledge the major role played by my
wife, Ann, in the production of this study. Without her encouragement
and support, and without her willingness to make suggestions, the book
would never have been written.

—DAVID S. McLELLAN
Miami University
Oxford, Ohio

CONTENTS

ILLUSTRATIONS

DEAN ACHESON

CHAPTER

1

EARLY YEARS

ONLY CHANCE MADE Dean Gooderham Acheson an American and not a British subject. Both of his parents—Edward Acheson and Eleanor Gooderham—were Canadians who moved to the United States only a year before their first son's birth, on April 11, 1893. After a few months at St. George's Church in New York City, the senior Acheson accepted the position of rector at Holy Trinity Church in the quiet university town of Middletown, Connecticut.

The Acheson family had it roots in the tangled history of Scottish–Irish relations. After centuries in Scotland, principally in the city of Edinburgh, the Acheson family migrated to Ulster at the time of James I. Alexander Acheson, Dean's Ulster grandfather, joined the British army shortly before the Crimean War and apparently participated in the Battle of Balaklava. Upon his return, Alexander married Mary Campion, daughter of a family which had come to south Ireland at the time of the early settlements about Cork. Their son, Edward Acheson, was only fourteen when he emigrated alone to Toronto, Canada, where he worked in a millinery warehouse. He must have been a young man of remarkable resolve, because he put himself through school and the University of Toronto. While still a student at the University of Toronto, he joined the Queen's Own Rifles, a militia regiment. A month later, in May 1885, his regiment was sent to Saskatchewan to subdue an Indian uprising; and in a sharp engagement with the Indians at Cut Knife on May 22, 1885, Acheson's father, together with Rifleman G. E. Lloyd, later Bishop of Saskatchewan, distinguished himself by bringing in the wounded under fire. Although listed as a rifleman, Edward Acheson also reputedly conducted the first church service west of Winnipeg at Fort Qu'Appelle en route to Swift Current.

Upon his return from military service, Edward Acheson completed his education at Wycliffe Theological Seminary in Toronto and was or-

1

dained a minister of the Episcopal faith. Why Edward Acheson chose the ministry may have had to do with his military service. His army experience was a signal influence on Acheson's father, reinforcing in him appreciation for the virtues of order and discipline. It would not have been unusual for a young Britisher (and Canada was after all still very British) with an education and a sense of social duty to go into the government, the military, or the ministry, and the idea of service figured strongly in Edward Acheson's thinking. Shortly after he was ordained he married Eleanor Gooderham, one of eight or nine children of a wealthy Canadian family. One story has it that while attending the seminary he had seen her going by in a carriage. Turning to a fellow seminarian, Edward Acheson said, "I'm going to marry that girl." He subsequently met her through the church and did.[1]

The Gooderham family, prosperous millers, had come out from Norfolk, England, and in 1832 settled in Toronto, where they established themselves in the same business. The Gooderham windmill, preserved by the City of Toronto as a historic monument, serves as a testament to the milling enterprises of the original Gooderhams. In due time the processing of grain as a beverage supplanted the milling of flour, and distilling became the mainstay of the family's prospering enterprise. By the time Edward Campion Acheson married Eleanor Gooderham, the Gooderhams were one of the leading business and banking families in Toronto.

The Gooderhams were such valuable citizens that one of Acheson's mother's brothers was elected mayor of Toronto and another was knighted by King George V at the time of his coronation. Acheson's mother had been sent to England for her schooling and returned an ardent Anglophile. "My mother's enthusiasm for the Empire and the Monarch," Acheson writes, "was not diluted by any corrupting contact with Canadian nationalism."[2] Having a daughter married to a minister verged on the irresponsible, so upon her marriage Eleanor was given enough money not to make her penurious, but not enough to tempt irresponsibility. Quite by chance the young minister's first call came from a church in New York from which they removed a year later to Middletown, Connecticut.

The first rectory in which the Achesons were ensconced was an old, inadequate, early nineteenth-century house. Not long after the family had settled in Middletown, they had a visit from Mrs. Acheson's father. Mr. Gooderham was shocked to see how inadequate the house was and whisked his daughter off to New York to buy new furniture with which to equip the old rectory. Later, about the time Dean went away to prep school, a new rectory was built for the Achesons. It still stands, a red brick Georgian-style building of spacious dimensions.

Middletown, at the time of Dean Acheson's birth, was still very much a part of rural America. Acheson remembered walking to the post office each morning with his father past the harness-maker's store, through a town still making use of a livery stable and a blacksmith, and waiting while his father passed the time of day with his fellow townsmen.

Despite their British and Canadian antecedents, the Achesons settled down to become Americans first and foremost. Although Mrs. Acheson was very British and the rector flew a green flag on St. Patrick's Day, they quickly adapted themselves to their new country, became American citizens, and made Connecticut the center of their family life.

In due time the Acheson family achieved a very special place in Middletown. Although comparatively well off for those days,* the Achesons were not part of the old established gentry—the Russells, the Hubbards, the Alsops, and so forth. The status they did enjoy was derived in part from his father's position as a rector of the Episcopal Church but more especially from the impact his father's strong, warm, and tolerant personality exerted upon the community.

As rector of the Holy Trinity Church, Acheson's father counted among his parishioners such members of the social elite as the Alsops and the Russells,** textile manufacturers who had lived in Middletown for generations and who constituted a virtual aristocracy. But the Achesons were not in the least "society" minded. Church work was the center of both parents' life. Rector Acheson did a great deal in the parish for the sick and the poor. And Mrs. Acheson, despite her qualities of elegance, worked hard for the church. Both contributed to the community as well, quite outside the church. Mrs. Acheson was the prime mover in raising the funds to build the Red Cross building in Middletown. But the rector and, later, bishop is best remembered for his ability to meet people of all social levels. Joseph Lawton, who was Acheson's closest boyhood friend, remembers how scandalized the neighbors were when the Irish Catholic Lawtons moved onto the fashionable street near the Achesons. Yet the Achesons welcomed Joe into their home, and he and Dean became the closest of companions. Even after Dean had gone away to Groton and Yale, Joe frequented the Acheson house, and he remembers the warmth and naturalness with which Acheson's father carried on a conversation.

---

* The first thing Joseph Lawton, a boyhood chum, had to say about Dean was that he owned a pony and a pony cart—and this put him above everyone else. Interview, March 6, 1970.

** The Alsop in question is John Alsop, the uncle of Joseph, Stewart, and John. Wilmarth Lewis writes that John Alsop "lived in the family's large 1840 house that was filled with family possessions, but he was hampered by an inadequate income." Wilmarth Sheldon Lewis, *One Man's Education* (Knopf, 1967), p. 187. The Russells owned one of the local textile mills that harnessed a fast-flowing tributary of the Connecticut River and that still stands, gaunt and inactive, today.

Dean Acheson's father was amazingly articulate—an outgoing, raconteur type of person.

The same common touch and democratic attitude attended Rector Acheson's relations with the community. He was an easy mixer and got along well with everyone, although his paternal interest in others sometimes gave him an embarrassing moment. He once stopped to admonish an obstreperous child who was giving its mother a hard time only to have the boy's mother tell him to mind his own business.* But contretemps aside, he is better remembered for the quiet commonsense quality of his sermons, which was just the opposite of the hell-and-damnation doctrines prevalent at the turn of the century. What a relief it was, the daughter of a Methodist minister still remembers, to hear Bishop Acheson preach.[3] It was not at all a theology of hopelessness and despair, but of hope and redemption. Given the quality of his ministry and the general esteem in which he was held in Middletown, it was not surprising that Edward Campion Acheson should have been elected the Episcopal Bishop for Connecticut.[4]

If the memory of Acheson's father among those who attended Holy Trinity when he was the rector or who knew him later when he was bishop is that of a warm, friendly man, the same is less true of Acheson's mother. Eleanor Acheson is still remembered in Middletown as a tall, handsome woman, exceedingly graceful and distinguished, regally dressed in clothes especially made for her. Mornings she would often be seen riding horseback. She was also among the first in town to own a car. She was a very astute, intelligent woman and, like Acheson's father, a first-rate organizer. She was more reserved than Acheson's father, and that may explain why she shone a little less warmly in the firmament of Middletown.

Acheson resembled his mother not only in his striking carriage, but in his taste for beautiful clothes and in his elegant presence. Because of her marked English accent and style, she was somewhat intimidating. People felt that she dominated too much.** "Everybody loved the Bishop. Mrs. Acheson did not receive the same warmth of treatment."[5] But she was also a sensible mother with time to give to Dean and the two younger children.

---

* Interview with Mrs. Richter. Mrs. Richter, who came with her father to Middletown from Fall River, Massachusetts, in 1914, remembers how impressed she and her father had been when Bishop Acheson called upon them not long after their arrival in Middletown on nothing more than a note from their Fall River minister. Mrs. Richter also remembers how thoughtful the rector was in his presentations to whatever group he happened to be addressing.

** Joseph Lawton remarks that "certain groups did not like her because she dominated—she took over everything she went into."

Dean adored his mother and they always had great fun together. She had a wonderful sense of humor which she passed on to her son. Joseph Lawton remembers the delight with which both engaged in humorous repartee at the other's expense. Acheson's wife remembers the first time she visited the Acheson household with Dean's sister with whom she roomed at Wellesley. "We got out of the car and started up the walk, and Dean was standing just behind his mother in the open doorway, the two of them laughing over some mutually shared point of humor." [6] Acheson had an exuberant sense of humor.

His later training in law led Acheson to emphasis upon method and order, but he loved all things that were the very opposite. With all his later austerity he still loved to be amused and to amuse others, and there was often a certain sense of mischief in his humor. His personal affection went to people who did things in an outrageous, flamboyant style. He liked his life to have fun and sparkle in it and often would provide it himself. He was not beyond bringing a perfect stranger home if he found him sufficiently entertaining. His favorite authors were Mark Twain and Anthony Trollope and his own humor ran to that vein. It is not difficult to understand how Acheson and Truman, another public figure with a splendid sense of humor, took to each other. They both had a rollicking sense of humor which may have gotten them through some really bad moments together.

While very proper, the home atmosphere was easygoing and relaxed. The care of the Acheson children while they were still young was left to a Miss Sinclair, a "very happy-go-lucky, very cheerful person" called "Sin," [7] a friend whom Mrs. Acheson had brought with her from Toronto. Dean felt very close to his sister Margot, who was two years younger, but less close to his brother Edward, who was considerably younger. Later Dean and his sister attended Miss Patton's School in Middletown.

Joe Lawton does not remember Acheson's father ever becoming really angry with his son, even when the neighbors complained about his leading the neighborhood kids in some mischief like throwing pebbles on the roof of someone's house. Whatever Dean did, it was rarely serious enough to provoke his father, who seemed to expect a certain amount of high jinks from his son. Later, however, when he was a student at Yale, Acheson had a falling out with his father and was banished from the household for an entire year. Of course, as with most upper-class families, the burden of raising young Acheson was passed on at a tender age to the prep schools of the day. But while he was at home Dean enjoyed the freedom and security of a warm, tolerant, and affectionately disciplined home life.

Dean Acheson was not the only American statesman of the first half of the twentieth century whose father was a minister. Both Woodrow

Wilson and John Foster Dulles had Presbyterian ministers for fathers, with important consequences for their lives. In Acheson's case the relationship between father and son appears to have been an altogether happier and less oppressive one than that between young Wilson and his father. The Calvinist strain, which in Woodrow Wilson's case seems to have led his father to establish "intellectual and moral goals beyond human achievement in his zealous and sensitive son," [8] was fortunately not present in Bishop Acheson. Acheson's father was more of a humanist than a moralist and certainly did not impose any stultifying moral perfectionism upon his son. Lawton remarks that Dean never cared much about religion. He had to attend Sunday worship and usually sang in the choir. That was about all that was expected of him. "My father," Acheson writes, "at a very early date took the view that his jurisdiction was limited. He would read to us, teach us verse, occasionally discipline us (on reference from lower authority), but there he stopped." [9] He never subjected his son to the kind of personal regime and inquisition that inspired in young "Tommy" Wilson a fear of personal inadequacy which he would spend much of his life overcoming. Every Fourth of July, Acheson writes, "my father performed his one child chore of the year. . . . The eight children of our block on Broad Street climbed into an express wagon, with the rest of their explosive equipment [firecrackers] and a picnic lunch to be carried by him to a pond on the edge of town," there to shoot up toy boats and hear Indian stories.[10] Otherwise Acheson senior seems to have preserved his "Olympian detachment," breaking it only from time to time to provide young Acheson with a collie pup or a pony or to take the whole family off to the Connecticut seashore or to Round Mountain Lake in the Maine woods.[11]

In the wilderness setting of Maine, Bishop Acheson appears to have played his most active role in the formation of his son. He taught the boy the arts of trout fishing, canoeing, and camping and expected everyone to carry his own pack and put up with the rigors of the trail. "A tendency to whine or grouse resulted in ignominious dismissal to the end of the line." [12] This was the Bishop's way of telling his son that: "Much in life could not be affected or mitigated and, hence, must be borne. Borne without complaint, because complaints were a bore and nuisance to others and undermined the serenity necessary to endurance." [13]

It was only later, after he had moved "through the novitiate of the woods," that Acheson began to understand the more serious lessons which his father had to impart.

As a prelate he was a baffling man, widely read in theology and Christian doctrine, yet rarely speaking of either, privately or in his sermons. . . . But no conviction could have been deeper than his in a code of conduct, based on perceptions of what was decent and civilized for man inextricably caught up in social relationships.[14]

The religious influence, while it was there, was not the "overwhelming, immutable component of everyday existence" which it was for the other statesman of the manse, Woodrow Wilson. There was no undue moralizing and catechizing in the Acheson household and certainly no scarifying vision of the fires of eternal damnation. "If his goal was the salvation of his soul," Acheson writes of his father, "it was a salvation by works performed with charity and humor as well as by zeal." [15]

Life in the rectory was more of a frame within which the essential drama of growing up took place. Acheson was later wont to say that with his father a minister and his mother the daughter of a distiller, he knew good and evil at an early age. It is equally plausible, if less witty, to posit that from the moral homilies of his father Dean acquired a sharp sense of right and wrong and that the words of the Collect and the *Book of Common Prayer* made an enduring contribution to his thought.

Acheson has written with sparkling affection of growing up in Middletown at the turn of the century. The excitements of small-town New England were all there—the horse-drawn fire engines surging into the street, the coming and going of the steamers on the Connecticut River, the "ghost train" which came through every evening from New York to Hartford, and above all the small-town atmosphere in which Dean obviously felt himself the center of a secure and wonderful world. His status and general qualities as a person gave him a close circle of friends—in addition to Joe Lawton, there were the Ruble boys whose father ran the department store just around the block from the rectory and Mansfield Craig who added glamour because his great uncle was a Union general killed in the Civil War. With Dean's pony and pony cart at their disposition, the boys ranged far and wide in the environs of Middletown.

Compared with home life, going off to prep school was something of an ordeal. At nine Dean was sent to Hamlet Lodge, a boarding school in Pomfret, Connecticut, where he prepared for Groton. The prep school regime came as a shock, and he notes with a certain bitterness the loss of freedom and privacy which he suffered both at Pomfret and later at Groton.

Pomfret was within easy visiting distance of Middletown. Joe Lawton remembers accompanying the rector on one of his periodic visits to see Dean there. When they reached the top of the long steps that led up to the school, they encountered a boy walking smartly up and down. The rector asked him what he was doing. The boy explained that he was being disciplined. After admonishing him, Acheson's father asked where he might find Dean and the boy replied: "He's over there being punished too." [16]

Groton

Two years later, in 1905, Dean entered Groton. Among Acheson's schoolmates one finds Averell Harriman (Franklin Delano Roosevelt had graduated a few years earlier), but Acheson was definitely not among the scions of the rich and well-to-do with whom Americans later came to identify Groton.

Groton had been founded by Endicott Peabody in 1884 on the English public school model. Foremost among Peabody's aspirations for his school was that it produce a spirit of noblesse oblige and a dedication to public service in its graduates. Public service, it was understood, did not extend to electoral politics. Dean Acheson was one among several dozen graduates including Franklin D. Roosevelt, Sumner Wells, and Harriman who went on to achieve conspicuous responsibility.* The conservatism of the students to which Acheson was an exception is indicated by the fact that Dr. Peabody had to threaten his alumni with excommunication to get them to tolerate President Roosevelt's appearance at Groton after his inauguration!

Of his experience at prep school Acheson records only his resentment at his loss of freedom and privacy. One classmate has testified that Acheson did not relish the constant exhortation to participate and conform, to be "one of the boys," and that he was less than an enthusiastic participant in school activities. But a master who knew him at the time reports simply that he was just another of the boys, neither outstanding nor a problem.

Acheson entered Groton in 1905 and graduated in 1911. I was a master here during all his Groton years and knew him well. He was a very nice boy, with good manners and a pleasant twinkle, a good scholar without being brilliant and in my memory not particularly athletic, aside from rowing.[17]

The 1910–1911 *Grotonian* contains the English prize essay for that year, entitled "The Snob in America," and signed D.G.A. He participated in his share of activities, did his studies, and seemed to fit in without any difficulty.[18]

Acheson claims that he found the prevailing social and political attitudes at Groton stuffy. The students looked upon unrest among the American working classes as a piece of ingratitude and cheek. None of them had firsthand knowledge of the desperate economic plight of the masses (of course neither had Acheson) and most were devoid of either sensitivity to or sympathy for their plight. William Jennings Bryan was looked upon as a demagogue and a public menace, and Teddy Roosevelt as a

---

* In his book *Philadelphia Gentlemen*, Digby Baltzell remarks upon how few Grotonites ever amounted to anything: F.D.R., Harriman, Acheson. This seems a somewhat excessive judgment.

traitor to his class. But like his father, Dean supported Teddy Roosevelt in the struggle within the Republican Party and was mildly conscious that this preference set him apart from most of his classmates, who were staunch supporters of William Howard Taft.

While Dean may have been more conscious of the hardships of the times and sensitive to the call for reform by Teddy Roosevelt and Woodrow Wilson, he was still far removed from the hardships of the working class. While Dean was still at Groton the Achesons had a racing car built for him. Because he was still too young to drive it himself, Mrs. Acheson obtained a license for Joe Lawton, three years Dean's senior, and the boys had a grand time spinning around town. In the summer of 1907, when Dean was fourteen, Bishop Acheson took him for a travel vacation in Europe. (Joe Lawton, who had just graduated from high school, was invited to go along, expenses paid, but he had just received an offer of a job in the Middletown bank and his parents expected him to take it; so Joe missed out.)

The summer Acheson graduated from Groton marked an important event in his early years. Like many a youngster, Dean yearned to prove himself as a man. That summer—the year was 1911; he was eighteen—Dean persuaded his parents to let him join a work gang building the railroad across western Canada. Through the family's connections in Toronto, Dean soon had the job arranged and spent the summer getting to see what hard work was about and learning something about the immigrants and laborers with whom, until then, he had come into very little contact. With his earnings he bought his mother a beautiful platinum and pearl brooch.

Yale

The next step in Acheson's educational progression was Yale. There were only about 300 in his class, and while not all held upper-class pedigrees, nearly three-quarters had attended prep schools. "Although it made no difference whether you had money or not (few knew who were rich unless they had famous names) . . . Yale was anything but 'democratic.' " [19] It was democratic in the sense that "Yale was a place where the highest undergraduate social honors were attainable by boys without money or 'family.' " [20] It was not democratic in that it demanded a high degree of conformity to accepted standards of dress and manner. Either one competed for prestige or one cultivated a dilettante social life in which one's reputation as an attractive social figure won one the all-important laurels of social success and election to one of the exclusive secret societies. Either one adapted to the environment or found oneself an outsider.

Once he had taken the measure of Yale's not very taxing educational demands, Acheson apparently settled down to enjoying life. His classmate Archibald MacLeish did not know him well at the time, but what he does remember of young Acheson is revealing. "He was the typical son of an Episcopal bishop—gay, graceful, gallant—he was also socially snobby with qualities of arrogance and superciliousness. Dean led a charming social existence at Yale." [21] Acheson's own recollection is that "The years at Yale were squandered in learning things that were meaningless. You memorized more facts about subjects you had already memorized in school. There was no point in it—Greek, chemistry, biology—all those subjects had either been learned enough or they were not worth continuing." [22]

Of education at Yale, Wilmarth Lewis writes:

Learning was not fashionable at Yale. . . . A few courses were "hard" and their instructors were respected accordingly, but the average student . . . quickly sized up how much time was required to "get by" in the others. . . . Although now and then members of the faculty made little speeches on the desirability of study, no one, not even the speakers, took them seriously. What Yale really believed was painted on the proscenium over the stage in Lampson Lyceum: *Non Studiis Sed Vitae Discimus.* At Yale we learned life, not studies. "Life" was primarily finding out how to get on with one's fellows and to advance in the never-to-be-relaxed struggle for the first prize—which was . . . election to a Senior Society.[23]

Still there were a few professors who inspired an intellectual zest in their students, and one of these was Chauncey Tinker, whose English courses Acheson attended. Acheson became enamored with English literature and for a while even thought of going in for writing.

Where Yale had something to offer, Acheson seems to have found it, but he did not care to waste his time on boring subjects. He preferred to have a good time and only where his gifts were challenged gave his studies serious attention. Otherwise Dean led a grand social life at Yale. He made the freshman crew; and although he did not make the varsity, he continued to take an active part in rowing, which, together with football, was the prestige sport. He accompanied the crew to Henley in the summer of 1913 and had a splendid time. He also joined Delta Kappa Epsilon (Deke), one of the most social and elegant of the Yale fraternities, and by his senior year he had attained the magical aura of a big man on campus. "How did the 'big men' differ from the lesser? They had an air of well-being, their walk was confident, they had prevailed, and life was good to them." [24] Although four of the leading seniors—Dean Acheson, Norman Donaldson, Archibald MacLeish, and Douglas Moore—were later to become his intimate friends, Wilmarth Lewis was only a freshman and could only gaze down on them from the chapel gallery each morning as President Hadley rushed through divine service.

On weekends Acheson would go home to Middletown accompanied

by his friends. Although MacLeish perceived Acheson to be something of a snob and a smart aleck, Dean continued to treat Joe Lawton and his other Middletown chums as equals. Joe was often invited to the Achesons for the weekend festivities, and he was there when Acheson met Alice Stanley, his wife-to-be. Margot Acheson had brought her Wellesley roommate home for the weekend, and Dean was immediately attracted—so much so that Joe found himself with Dean's original date on his hands. Dean's friendship with Alice Stanley developed hand in hand with his success at Yale. In his junior year Acheson was tapped for Scroll and Key, the epitome of success.

Clearly Yale was not an experience that was critically significant to Acheson's development, unless being a young patrician and having a good time at an age when others must look for work can qualify. Unlike Wilmarth Lewis, Archibald MacLeish, and others who cultivated their literary talents and formed intellectual associations, Acheson's days were spent in enjoying himself. At graduation, the class historian, in an obvious swipe at Acheson's reputation as a bon vivant and good-time Charlie, predicted that "Dean Acheson leaves next week to do mission work in British East Guatemala." There were certainly few indications that Acheson would soon embark upon a law school career that would quickly bring him to the center of American jurisprudence. That summer Acheson visited Japan, the first of a number of experiences that were to open important windows on the larger world beyond New England and even beyond America.

Harvard Law School

Acheson graduated from Yale in June 1915 and entered Harvard Law School the following September. Although the war had begun in Europe, it was not as yet occupying the center of American minds.

Other than to make him work harder, Harvard made little impact upon Acheson at first. Archibald MacLeish, who also graduated from Yale in 1915 and who entered law school along with Acheson, does not remember Acheson showing any unusual affinity for his legal studies during the first year or two. MacLeish, however, left Harvard at the end of his second year for military service in France and did not have a chance to see Acheson's intellectual development come to fruition. At Harvard the ruthlessly logical mind which was to cut down so many opponents and completely reorient American foreign policy in the years after World War II had it first training and testing. Years later, when others had doubts or turned away from the implications of the Cold War for America's traditional international principles and freedom from responsibility, the power of the logic which Acheson had first discovered at Harvard would impel him to stick to the facts. One might not agree with it, but there was rigor to Acheson's view of the Cold War, a rigor which reflected a training in logic that made certain moves, unpalatable though they might be, mandatory.

To say that Acheson received his first training in this kind of logic at Harvard does not, however, do justice to the significance which the study of the law had for Acheson. Training in the law was an intellectual awakening for him. It not only afforded an intellectual challenge hitherto missing, but more importantly it provided him with a socially sanctioned mode of excelling and of achieving personal distinction which was destined to become a crucial goal in his life.

When Acheson arrived, Harvard was in a period of intellectual brilliance. Christopher C. Langdell had introduced the Socratic method to the instruction of the law, replacing rote learning. The faculty included the most brilliant legal minds of the age: Roscoe Pound, Albert Martin Kales, Zechariah Chafee, Jr., Edward H. Warren, Samuel Williston, Joseph H. Beale, and of course Felix Frankfurter. Acheson responded powerfully to the teaching of these men, and they inevitably responded to this bright, eager, and attractive young man. Felix Frankfurter in particular was taken with him. Acheson had his first course with Frankfurter during his second year; it appears to mark Acheson's takeoff point.

Although still comparatively young, Frankfurter had behind him a brilliant career as a young assistant to Henry Stimson when the latter was United States Attorney for the southern district of New York. Invited to join the Harvard Law School faculty in 1913, he quickly established himself as an outstanding teacher and person.[25] Like the rest of the students, Acheson was naturally attracted to the brilliant young professor around whom hung an aura of success in the glamorous world of the New York Bar. Frankfurter, who had a wonderful facility for friendship, made it a practice to know the brighter and more attractive students in his classes, and Acheson was just the sort of bright, ambitious young man in whom Frankfurter took pleasure. Besides being smart, Acheson was witty and socially attractive—not unimportant virtues in Frankfurter's scale of things. Their friendship, which began like so many others, with Frankfurter's interest in a protégé, flowered into something vastly more enduring and important to both men.* Frankfurter was to play an important role in Acheson's career, and the two men were to be lifelong intimates.

While slow in starting, Acheson's reputation was such by the end of

---

* Personal interview, June 17, 1960, Washington, D. C. They visited back and forth and exchanged messages daily. Acheson represented Frankfurter in the difficult Senate Hearings following his nomination by F.D.R. to the Supreme Court. Frankfurter provided Acheson with a total, enduring friendship based upon intellectual and personal affinities of the most human sort.

his second year that he was elected to the board of the *Harvard Law Review*. It is no wonder that when MacLeish returned from France to resume his studies in January 1919 he was astounded to discover that Acheson had become a remarkably accomplished student, possessed of a surer grasp and deeper interest in the law than MacLeish had imagined possible.[26]

The war, meanwhile, had finally caught up with Acheson. Upon graduation in June 1918, he enlisted as an ensign in the Navy and served a brief stint at the Brooklyn Navy Yard. Before he had any direct experience with the war, it was over and he had his discharge.

Another event of critical importance in Acheson's life took place at about this time. He and Alice Stanley were married May 5, 1917. Following his discharge from the Navy, Acheson returned to Harvard Law School while Alice went to live with his parents in Middletown to await the birth of their first child.

Alice Stanley was from Michigan, the daughter of a lawyer for the Grand Trunk Railroad. Like Acheson, she was tall and comely, and she shared his growing liberalism and sense of excitement about law and politics. In addition to raising a family, Alice Acheson became a professional painter. Although Dean had little interest in art, he always encouraged his wife's interest. Like Dean, she was also very early committed to the liberal ideals of the Democratic Party and remained so all her life. Most of her time was taken up with raising their family—a son and two daughters—and managing their home in Georgetown. Of Alice Acheson's relation to her husband, MacLeish remarks that she was a continually steadying breeze blowing from a fixed corner which he could always count upon.

Acheson had returned to Harvard in January 1919, intending to do graduate work, but his stay lasted only six months. Louis D. Brandeis, whom Woodrow Wilson had appointed to the Supreme Court over the outraged cries of the business community, was looking for a clerk. Did Frankfurter know of anyone? Frankfurter did indeed. Acheson left Harvard in June 1919 to take up his first appointment as clerk to Justice Brandeis.*

Harvard was a crucial phase in Acheson's development. The law school settled him down and gave him a serious purpose in life. It stimulated his mind and gave him a powerful tool through which his mind would henceforth operate. It also gave him a reputation for intellectual

---

* MacLeish remarks of the Acheson he encountered upon his return to Harvard in 1919: "The Acheson who had been scornful of zeal, was now full of zeal—zeal for the law. One can see in retrospect that his friendship with Frankfurter had begun to work its influence. His years with Brandeis and through Brandeis with Holmes completed this apprenticeship."

brilliance which he would take care to enhance. And it gave him the backing of a powerful sponsor and the chance to begin his career as a clerk to a Supreme Court justice—that is, at the very top of a new lawyer's professional ladder. More subtly, Acheson's Harvard experience established a connection between his high self-esteem and unwillingness to be judged by others and his tremendous drive to excel.

The security of his early life provided Acheson with an emotional balance. There was no compulsive need to get ahead, for the Achesons were well established in Middletown society, and Dean passed through Groton and Yale with a minimum of difficulty.

The stability and harmoniousness of his childhood accounts, at least in part, for his remarkable self-confidence. If his upbringing also stressed the need to keep his emotions under control, the principal lesson his father inculcated seems to have been the need to meet life with a certain stoicism. As we shall attempt to show later on, one of the most salient features of Acheson's performance as Secretary of State was the remarkable stoicism he seemed to achieve in the face of the most extreme personal and public crises. It is also plainly evident that his record as a Democrat and New Dealer, in contrast to the Republicanism of most Americans in his social class, reflects a remarkable ability to accept social change with equanimity. Change which others would view as a threat to their pocketbook and social values, Acheson accepted quite philosophically.

2

LAW: PATH TO PUBLIC SERVICE

ONE WRITER observes that "The apprenticeship to Brandeis was a profoundly moving influence in Acheson's life. It meant a continuation of the active intellectual life begun at Harvard, and contact with the great men who moved in the Brandeis orbit." [1] Brandeis's career as the champion of the people against entrenched economic interests, combined with the powerful acumen of his legal reasoning, had made of him a living legend. One can well imagine with what anticipation Acheson approached his clerkship. Brandeis, at the height of his powers, was making judicial history. Acheson gives us an intimate picture of one aspect of their working relationship:

Generally I came down to the Justice's office on Sunday morning. [Saturday was the Court's conference day.] The Chief Justice's messenger brought around the assignment slips fairly early. These were printed slips bearing the names of the justices with blank spaces to the right of them, into which the Chief Justice wrote the numbers of the cases which he had assigned to Justice Brandeis for opinion. The same was done with each of the justices. Brandeis would instruct me to begin work on certain of the numbered cases and would say what others he would start on. At this time we rarely had much discussion about the cases or the opinion, although he would answer any questions or discuss any point which I wished to discuss with him. Usually, however, I knew very little about the case except that it was to be affirmed, reversed, or dismissed, and I would go to work on the record and briefs to find out about it. He did not look with much favor on his law clerks spending time in the court room listening to arguments, although on a case of outstanding interest he was broadminded on this. [2]

As clerk, Acheson's task was to prepare preliminary drafts of opinions for Brandeis.

My work usually was cast in the form of a draft opinion, since he found this the most helpful way to get it. When he finished his preliminary work on opinions which he took, he would give me the material to check, criticize, or rewrite, as I thought best. In those days he wanted a good deal more rigorous criticism from his law clerks than I think he regarded as necessary later in his judicial career. When I finished my work on a draft which had been assigned to me or got as far as I could, I gave it to him. As you know from the files, he tore it to pieces, sometimes using a little, sometimes none.[3]

One can also well imagine the demanding character of Acheson's apprenticeship to Brandeis. With Brandeis, "perfection was the norm and you went up from there. The fact that you did something carelessly or made a mistake was a shock to Brandeis. He didn't get angry or nasty; he was just plain shocked and surprised that anyone could have the temerity to make a blooper or be careless. Brandeis possessed an almost stultifying sense of perfection." [4] In later years Acheson rarely wrote a deliberative sentence without the sense of Brandeis watching over his shoulder.

During Acheson's first year as clerk, Brendeis's wife had a nervous breakdown. The illness drew the jurist and his young clerk closer together. In that period of intense strain and sorrow, the iron man found an outlet for his emotion in simple talk and gossip with his clerk, who became one of the very few persons to whom Brandeis ever opened the citadel of his privacy. "In short," Acheson wrote many years later, "Brandeis was not an institution or an enigma, but a man albeit a magnificently disciplined and able one. Humor could come through and fire could come through, and so could affection." [5] It was no surprise therefore that toward the end of Acheson's first year Brandeis should have made him the unusual request of staying on for a second year.

As Brandeis's clerk Acheson became acutely aware of many of the brutal social conditions of the era. The postwar years witnessed a resurgence of labor violence as workers tried to protect their wartime gains and employers marshalled union-busting forces in arrogant and callous disregard for human lives.

There was, I believe, a Congressional committee or commission sitting in Washington in 1920, inquiring into conditions in the coal industry. Many miners came to town to testify or to work on the testimony of others. Several times I met groups of them at the home of Mr. William Hard, who was then a journalist in Washington. From these conversations I got a vivid impression of conditions in the coal fields and of the state of severe repression under which the miners lived, in which the authority of the state government and the power of the mine owners seemed to combine to block any efforts that they made to improve their conditions. I remember specifically listening to groups from Harlan County and from Pennsylvania, who talked about the state police to whom they referred as "Cossacks." [6]

The Coronado Case, with Brandeis dissenting, provides a good illustration of the perspective from which Acheson viewed the desperate labor struggles of the day. The Coronado Case involved a conflict between the union miners of the Coronado Mine and the employers, in the course of which the mine owner's attempts to work the mine with nonunion labor brought on open warfare. The case eventually came before the Supreme Court and was given to Brandeis, who had his clerk, Acheson, undertake the initial draft of an opinion.

"The facts," Acheson wrote in his preparation for Brandeis, "present a picture of a primitive struggle clothed in the forms of industry." In the owner's decision to discontinue relations with the union,

> There was no conference with the men, nor was there any process of law to determine the justice of this proposal to sacrifice standards of work and living in order that operation might continue at a profit. . . . There is a refreshing absence of hypocrisy about this matter; both sides understood clearly that the conflict between cheap labor and union standards was to be settled on the basis of power—physical, economic and legal—with no interference from principle. . . . Conditions became like those in a country occupied by a small invading force. . . . Engagements took place between small parties of the invading forces and the inhabitants. . . .[7]

In refuting the charges of the company, Acheson conceded that the object of the union's actions was to "prevent competition in the standards of living" of the miners. The Sherman Act, he agreed, forbade restraints on trade in the articles of commerce; and when the union, by a boycott, imposed such a restraint, the act applied. "But the conditions of life and the labor of a human being are not articles of commerce," Acheson continued. "This is not a matter of law or fact, but of the culture of a people. It seems to me to be one of the fundamental conceptions of our political philosophy and not to rest for its truth either on the Civil War or the Clayton Act." [8] As was called for, Acheson's memorandum supported a decision in favor of the union. But behind the thrust of Acheson's legal reasoning, one senses the indignation of a nature offended by the unnecessary brutality and waste of unregulated labor relations. Given the rule of claw and fang, how could the best interests or intents of either side achieve recognition? The experience with Brandeis, combined with his own openness of spirit, sharpened Acheson's awareness of the dangers into which unregulated social conflict threatened to plunge American society. Unlike most of the bright young men who were heading for Wall Street or Main Street to earn their fortunes and to have their minds closed once and for all, Acheson had the fortune of serving his apprenticeship under Brandeis, the unsleeping watchdog of the American conscience for three decades.

Among the other justices, Acheson was naturally most taken by Oliver Wendell Holmes, Jr. Holmes would hold open house each week and invite clerks and other bright young men in for tea. Acheson became a favorite on whom the old man enjoyed trying out his glib lines and cynical witticisms. While Holmes was a model of greatness from whom Acheson drew much, his withering cynicism reinforced Acheson's burgeoning tendency not to suffer fools lightly.

"Holmes possessed a caustic intellectual stringency," one intimate of Acheson's writes, "which when passed on to younger people was not always admirable." [9] But it would not do to exaggerate the philosophic influence that Holmes exerted on Acheson.

The concentrated exposure to Brandeis and to some extent Holmes made a deep and lasting impression upon Acheson. Both were austere skeptics who held to the belief that civilization depended upon the wisdom, industry, and courage of a small number of its members. In an analysis of Brandeis, written at Frankfurter's behest in the autumn of 1920, Acheson recorded that the justice had no faith in mass salvation through "universal Plumb Plans."

People haven't the intelligence for that sort of thing. They have only the intelligence to operate in small personal groups which deal with things with which they are intimately acquainted . . . he [Brandeis] can believe that all through this mass of blubber, society, there are individual minds which are working and which may be able to guide a handful of followers out of the wilderness, if they are let alone. But that "if" is a very big one. No one is ever let alone. The capacity for stupid, wasteful, ruinous interference seems to be infinite in these masses of blubber. His goal seems to be by the use of intellect to gain a purely negative freedom from interference for people who want to use their intellects.[10]

Obviously, these lines express but one facet of Brandeis's outlook, but it is interesting that it is the one that Acheson chose to stress.

The impact of his mentor's skepticism was doubtless reinforced by the pitiless mediocrity and willful stupidity of the times. The League of Nations had gone down to defeat. Harding sat in the White House, soon to be engulfed in a wave of scandal. Palmerism, the McCarthyism of the post–World War I era, was rampant. The courts were confronted by cases involving the claims of women and children to be protected against exploitation. Working-class rights, recognized in most civilized countries as essential to the social order, were being fought by management. In the privacy of his chambers, Brandeis commented scathingly to his clerk upon the intelligence of the employers:

We are being governed by a set of insane men—insanity is not the word for this sort of thing. They have lost all power to see and weigh consequences.[11]

Given the temper of the times, it was easy for a young man of spirit and passion to fall in with the skepticism of his mentors and to adopt an elitist point of view, for what had been Acheson's felt sense of natural superiority was now given wider scope and sanction. If American civilization was to be saved from disaster it would have to be saved by those few persons who had the wisdom, and the courage, and the tenacity to do it.

Another latent dimension in Acheson's personality was reinforced by his exposure to Holmes and Brandeis, both of whom moved in a kind of stoic grandeur. Their lives had some ultimate meaning which, unfathomable though it might be, Acheson had an obligation to strive for. Again describing to Frankfurter what he believed to be an intimate portrait of Brandeis, Acheson wrote:

Instead—as I see him—he thinks that the great end in life lies with the individual mind, in its building up its own worlds, in its explorations and darings and triumphs over weaknesses and fears and laziness, and perhaps something more—but that I don't even guess at.[12]

In his hero worship, the moral grandeur of Brandeis loomed very large. Acheson admired his devotion to duty, his rigorous integrity, and the simplicity of his life, relieved as it was by the civility of culture and humor.* Increasingly at the core of Acheson's conduct would be the conviction that how a man lives his life is the most important thing. Not merely does it set the gentleman off from more common clay, but it gives life its very meaning. According to Frankfurter, Acheson was convinced that "a code makes a man meaningful and organic; a whole man, a living civilized and free being. Otherwise one is a flaccid and vacillating creature."[13] "The elements of Acheson's code: loyalty, essential truth, not pretending to be better than you really are" would play a potent role in Acheson's career.[14] The code would make it impossible for him even to contemplate those many compromises which a politician must make if he is to be elected; it would make him critical of those whom he considered to be knowingly and willfully trifling with the public trust; and it would lead him, in an agony of conscience, into refusing to turn his back on Alger Hiss. Such a code produces men who hold to their principles no matter what the opposition—men of conviction.

Having set enormously high standards for himself, Acheson became merciless in judging others. He all too readily forgot that those who made it in elective politics had to make it by another code. He overlooked that success in elective politics, while not so dignified or noble perhaps, was just as demanding and just as necessary to the life of a democracy as his own brand of skill and energy.

---

* Mrs. Acheson vividly remembers the spartan simplicity of the Brandeis household. The Brandeises held open house on Monday afternoons. The Achesons frequently stayed for dinner which was served on a bare mahogany table. Personal interview, February 21, 1975.

When after two years Brandeis was ready to let him go, Acheson could take pride in a task well done. His apprenticeship had not only broadened him, it had given him new proof of his intellectual powers and the confidence to strive for even greater successes. Everything had so favored Acheson that a mere six years after leaving Yale he had the esteem and backing of Frankfurter, Brandeis, and Holmes. He had what every young man longs for—a sense of destiny—the knowledge that one has been tested and that the gods have looked favorably.

If the apprenticeship with Brandeis had the effect of bringing out the liberal and humanistic strain in Acheson, it did not make him into a crusader. Although he was passionately interested in fair labor laws and even wrote a book (never published) on the subject during his last months at Harvard Law School, he never got a chance to follow it up. Upon completion of his clerkship he applied for a post as counsel to a Boston labor union, but the position never materialized. When the chance came to join the rising Washington law firm of Covington and Burling, Acheson accepted with alacrity.

The job did not pay very much, and the Achesons still had to struggle to make ends meet. In 1922 they bought a modest home in Georgetown that had no furnace and only one bathroom. They later enlarged it, but at the time it provided rather cramped quarters for a family with young children. In 1924 they acquired a farmhouse in Sandy Spring, Maryland, where the family could go in the summers to get away from the heat.

But the decision to join Covington and Burling had important implications for Acheson's later career. In the first place it brought him into a firm whose senior partners had been active in politics: Judge Covington in Maryland politics, where he had represented the Democratic Party in Congress, Edward Burling and George Rublee in the Bull Moose movement to get Teddy Roosevelt re-elected in 1912 and restore Progressivism to the Republican Party. Their previous political services gave them important connections which led to the firm's handling of a number of cases involving the federal government. In the course of his legal work, Acheson now developed close relations with key people in the important federal departments.

The original partners gave the firm a breadth and tolerance which it still possesses. "We have always had different points of view in our firm on economic and political matters," one partner remarked, "which has made it a more interesting and exciting place." * They point to Acheson as someone who contributed to this eclectic and tolerant situation as it

---

* Personal interview with Edward Burling, Sr., Washington, D. C., April 17, 1963. This viewpoint was also expressed by other younger partners in the course of interviews.

continued during the years after he joined. John Lord O'Brian, for example, a member of the firm somewhat senior to Acheson, was the Republican candidate for the U.S. Senate from New York in 1938. Burling was active in Roosevelt's 1932 campaign, and Rublee had drawn Acheson into supporting the Republican Dwight Morrow in his successful bid for the Senate from New Jersey in 1930.

The firm opened its doors January 1, 1919, and Acheson was the third young lawyer to be hired. There was never any question in the partners' minds that anyone who had served two years as Justice Brandeis's law clerk must be a good man indeed.[15] As for Acheson, he once again found himself with brilliant prospects. The federal government was not yet involved in regulatory activities on the scale it would be under the New Deal, nor in disbursing scores of billions of dollars. Hence it was still not the mecca of the great legal firms engaged in defending their clients against or extracting favors from Uncle Sam. But World War I had stimulated the government's role in the economy, and those who were in on the ground floor for what litigation there was stood in a favored position later on.

Everything in Acheson's relationship with Covington and Burling helped to mature him at an early age. One of his first cases was as counsel to the Norwegian government in a suit against the United States government for damages and claims involved in the American government's requisition of Norwegian ships during World War I. It was heard by the Court of International Justice at the Hague. Acheson and his senior partner, Burling, won the case. Burling, like Brandeis, treated Acheson as an equal. There was no master–neophyte relationship. The volume of business obliged Acheson to assume responsibilities that would normally have been reserved to an older and more experienced lawyer; success in these ventures contributed to Acheson's unusual sense of independence and confidence. He soon emerged as one of the leading advocates before the United States Court of Appeals in Washington, D. C., where many important cases involving the federal government were heard. According to Frankfurter's recollection of this period, "Dean was a hot-house product in the best sense of the word. Everything conspired to enhance his reputation and position in Washington during those early years. He and his wife were a socially attractive couple. Both had poise and brains; both were charming and exciting people." [16] Their circle of friends included, besides Brandeis and Edward Burling, Stuart Chase and Sinclair Lewis as well as such leading lights in the political life of Washington as Senator Robert M. La Follette. Most of the people whom they knew were liberals and activists who had fought for the League of Nations and were busily engaged in calling for reform of the economic system. Acheson admired their purposes but not their zeal.

There were now, or soon to be, three children, Jane, David, and Mary. Acheson was an excellent father. His natural athletic interests inclined him toward the out-of-doors life. The farm in Sandy Spring meant that the family got away each weekend as a unit to enjoy the simple kind of rural life that he had enjoyed as a boy growing up in Middletown. Acheson acquired a horse from Justice Brandeis, and soon horseback riding was an important part of weekends at the farm. One of the mares had a foal and David Acheson was told that when he could break the growing steed he could have it. During the next few years, while Acheson's life was bound up in the legal practice of his law firm and in his family, there was little on the surface to suggest that he would become something other than an eminently successful partner of an eminently successful Washington law firm.

The streak of romanticism in Acheson and his zest for the droll found an outlet in the Penguin Club, which brought together a group of young Washington spirits for an occasional evening of mirth and entertainment. R. M. Boeckel, who for years was associated with the *Congressional Quarterly*, remembers Acheson's participation until about 1925. The Penguin Club had a diverse list of guests. Boeckel's two most vivid memories were of "Senator La Follette's charming us for two hours or more with Irish fairy tales. This was during the 1924 campaign for the Presidency. And the other of Mademoiselle Lillian Lietzel, leading star at the time of Ringling Brothers and Barnum and Bailey Circus, who after a brilliant performance under the big top came to our quarters late at night and gave a piano recital." *

Washington was far from being the provincial capital that it had been before the war. The war had made America turn outward; and even though the Senate had rejected the Versailles Treaty, the United States remained too important not to be involved in the international arena. In 1921 the Washington Arms Conference was held; a few years later the Kellogg–Briand Pact was signed. Europe's economic and financial dependence upon the United States also contrived to make Washington an important world center. At first hand Acheson observed the evil results of America's failure to accept responsibility for its new economic status as a creditor nation, first by loaning out money under unsound circumstances and then by driving up tariffs, thereby rendering it practically impossible for the European nations to repay their debts. The education which Acheson received in the utter madness of the economic policies of successive Republican administrations later made him a fervent

---

* Personal letter from R. M. Boekel, March 31, 1964. "Other guests I remember with pleasure were Eamon De Valera, Norman Thomas, Roger Baldwin, Morris Ernst, and Monsignor John Ryan."

backer of Cordell Hull's reciprocal trade agreements program. But even more importantly it prepared him to be an architect of the Bretton Woods agreement and other postwar economic policies to ensure the healthy development of the world economy.

At the same time as he was an observer of the political scene, the growth of his legal reputation also put Acheson in touch with influential Washington legal and political circles. And his home in Sandy Spring gave him roots in the Maryland Democratic Party. He became active in Montgomery County Democratic politics in the mid-twenties, participating in meetings and campaigns, but he had neither the inclination nor the aptitude for the glad-handing performance which was expected of an active politician. He could campaign for others, but not for himself. When he attended the 1932 Democratic nominating convention he found it "a mad and not a little degrading spectacle," [17] and dealing with Congress a number of years later, he wrote to his daughter Mary, was "a low life but a merry one." [18]

In effect Acheson was saying that he did not want to be in the position of having to justify or defend himself to the masses, but in point of fact he made a valiant effort to educate them. The repugnance Acheson felt at seeming in any way to be appealing to the judgment of the electorate can only be regarded as a manifestation of his underlying personality or of his conditioning at Groton. Either it was the personality of a highly defended person who cannot recognize any faults within himself and who, therefore, while exceedingly competent and of excellent character, simply will not let himself be judged by others, or it manifested a consciousness of excellence and superiority which finds catering to the masses demeaning and degrading. Whatever the reason, it put an absolute bar to Acheson's ever running for public office and also subtly shaded his respect for congressmen and senators. It had one further effect: by barring himself from elective office, Acheson closed off an avenue of political experience and denied himself the political base in state or congressional politics which so often serves as a constituency for those who later in their career come to high appointive office.

Alfred E. Smith's 1928 campaign in particular enlisted Acheson's support. The Democratic candidate against Hoover was something of a litmus test for liberals. As governor, Al Smith had provided New York with a practical program of administrative and social reform. Besides being a tested political leader, Smith had an attractive and buoyant personality. Above all, he seemed like a refreshing breeze to a generation parched from Prohibition and the windiness of moral platitudes. But Smith was a Catholic, a condition then as later destined to arouse considerable prejudice and misgivings about the candidate. Acheson campaigned hard for Smith in eastern Maryland. Although Smith failed to

win the Presidency, the campaign found Acheson more completely engaged than ever in Democratic politics.[19]

Nineteen thirty-two found Acheson at the Democratic National Convention, not an important figure but with access to the immediate circle
of the leading candidate—Franklin Delano Roosevelt. That autumn he
took an energetic hand in directing the Roosevelt campaign in Montgomery County, Maryland.

The campaign confirmed Acheson in his distaste for a career on the
hustings. In the course of the campaign he found the writing of political
tracts preferable to the task of glad-handing and making speeches. Once
again there reappeared the unresolved tension between the patrician, for
whom the task of vote-getting is a distasteful and demeaning business,
and the analyst, who apprehends the necessity for political skills and
bargaining if his party and government are to succeed. Yet without having to engage in politicking, it is clear that Acheson now wanted access
to public office. And with Roosevelt's election there would be posts in the
new Democratic administration for just such talented people as himself.

Soon after Roosevelt's inauguration on March 4, 1933, Acheson was
invited to attend meetings at the White House where the President's
legislative program was being put together. Acheson regarded this as a
good omen. His heart was set on the post of Solicitor General in the
Justice Department. Acheson was characteristically attracted to this post
by virtue of its high standing in the eyes of the legal profession. Ever
since the Teapot Dome Scandal had revealed the weaknesses of the Attorney General's office, appointments to the office of Solicitor had gone
to men of outstanding integrity and legal talent.

Roosevelt first offered the post to Felix Frankfurter, who turned it
down partly because of his disinterest in a political career and partly because of his appointment to the Eastman Professorship at Oxford. Frankfurter recommended Acheson for the position. But it was not to be. When
F.D.R. asked his Attorney General, Homer Cummings, if the appointment of Acheson would be all right, Cummings said, "No, it's not all
right." * Rather than endeavor to rally Brandeis, Frankfurter, and other
influential friends to his support and get Roosevelt to overrule Cummings,
Acheson preferred not to seek the post unless it was offered to him on his
merits. Bitterly disappointed at the failure to secure the appointment,

---

* Acheson later learned the reason for Cummings's opposition. Cummings, from
Connecticut, had been married a number of times, and Acheson's father, the Episcopal
Bishop of Connecticut, had finally refused church sanction. The post of Solicitor Gen-
eral went to an "estimable but ineffectual old gentleman from North Carolina named
J. Crawford Biggs. From the first, Biggs showed his unfitness for the responsibility
by losing ten of seventeen cases in his first five months." Arthur M. Schlesinger, Jr.,
The Politics of Upheaval (Boston: Houghton Mifflin Co., 1960), p. 261.

Acheson left for an extended motor trip in late April 1933 with Mrs. Acheson and Hume Wrong, a young Canadian diplomat on duty in Washington.

A few days after his return from the vacation trip, Acheson was asked to lunch with William Woodin, Roosevelt's recently appointed Secretary of the Treasury. The invitation had been arranged by Arthur Ballantine and James Douglas, Undersecretary and Assistant Secretary respectively in the Hoover Treasury, who had been held over to effect the transition to the Roosevelt Administration. These men wanted the new Secretary of the Treasury to meet Dean Acheson, with whom they were friends and whom they regarded as a cohort. No sooner had Acheson returned to his office, following lunch, than Woodin called up to ask him to be Undersecretary of the Treasury. Acheson readily accepted and was formally appointed on May 19, 1933.

The appointment is an interesting one from several points of view. Acheson's inexperience with Treasury matters, while a very real problem, was a no more glaring defect than that suffered by many other lawyers appointed to posts in government. The *Baltimore Sun* noted approvingly that by contrast with the complaints then arising about "academic theorizing by professors in government" and against "practical" businessmen and bankers tainted with conservatism, "Mr. Acheson, a lawyer . . . has offended neither by making profound academic studies of Treasury finance nor by following its ramifications extensively in a practical way."

Nevertheless, his appointment was bitterly assailed in the course of Senate hearings by Senator James Couzens, an anti–Wall Street Republican from Michigan. Because of his law firm's clientele, Acheson's nomination was attacked as a concession to reactionary financial interests. Senator Couzens criticized Acheson's legal connections in particularly vehement terms:

I know that Mr. Acheson and Mr. Woodin are going to be just as much the agents of the Morgan house as anybody we could possibly put in the Treasury Department.*

It is worth noting that Senator Couzens was anxious to explain that nothing in the record reflected upon the personal integrity of Mr. Acheson, a refrain which would echo years later through McCarthy's attacks. Mr. Acheson, Couzens declared, was simply the neutral instrument of the occult forces of the House of Morgan. Put Acheson in a position of public trust and he would be the abject servitor of the Morgan interests, a spine-

---

* *Congressional Record*—Senate, 1933, p. 1337. The *American Business Journal* commented on Acheson's appointment as follows: "In extending to him [Acheson] our sincere congratulations . . . the editor of the *American Business Journal* feels that we are voicing the sentiments of the entire legal and business world."

less agent of the monstrous Morgan money conspiracy. After a strong speech from Millard Tydings (D–Md.), the Senate brushed aside Couzens's criticism and confirmed Acheson's nomination.*

Once in office and under the pressure of the economic crisis gripping the country, Roosevelt's economic ideas underwent a rapid evolution; a schism quickly emerged between those to whom radical monetary reform seemed the only solution and those for whom a stable dollar tied to gold was the foundation stone of the republic. As Acting Secretary of the Treasury (Woodin suffered an incapacitating illness shortly after his appointment), Acheson found himself at the very center of the controversy.

In this debate between the two groups of advisers, Acheson generally sided with the monetary conservatives who in the end were routed. But it would be wrong to attribute Acheson's break with Roosevelt to the monetary aspect of the situation. The significance of Acheson's conflict with Roosevelt deserves analysis under three headings: ideological, legal, and personal.

Acheson's economic views, which were largely derivative, were neither as rigid nor as conservative as those held by Lewis Douglas, director of the Bureau of the Budget, or by James Sprague and James Warburg, two other Treasury advisers. His view of the economic order was not an ideological commitment vested with moral overtones; he did not see devaluation as "the end of Western civilization" or as comparable to the Oath of the Tennis Court in the French Revolution. Acheson, like Brandeis, was too much of a reformer and humanist to adopt a posture of ideological opposition to the New Deal. But like many people not directly confronted by the political crisis facing Roosevelt, Acheson was reluctant to believe that devaluing the dollar in order to raise prices was either desirable or necessary. Nevertheless, Acheson's quarrel with Roosevelt was not on strictly economic grounds.

A second issue raised by Roosevelt's monetary policies was that of legality. In the first place, the gold content of the dollar had been established by Congress, and it was questionable whether the President had the power to change it without congressional authorization. Secondly, many people held bonds, including government bonds, whose value would be cut in the proportion that the dollar was devalued. Roosevelt had been persuaded by Professor George F. Warren of Cornell University that the road to recovery lay in the direction of a price increase that would aid the farmer and stimulate business. The way to do this, Warren

---

* *Congressional Record*—Senate, May 16, 1933, p. 3484. Seventeen years later a Senate subcommittee headed by Tydings would be engaged in examining Joseph McCarthy's charges that Acheson was part of a Communist conspiracy which was coddling known Communist agents in the State Department.

advised Roosevelt, was by controlling the gold value of the dollar and forcing it downward. This adjustment would have the salutary effect of inducing inflation and thereby raising prices. The question then was did the President have the requisite authority to do so on his own? Roosevelt expected his associates to figure out a legal loophole to get around congressional authority, so it would not obstruct his course of action.

The Treasury itself was obliged by law to pay only $20.67 per ounce for gold. The President wanted to pay between $30 and $40. Herman Oliphant, a counsel in the Farm Credit Administration headed by Henry Morgenthau, Jr., argued that the Reconstruction Finance Corporation had the legal power to pay *steadily increasing* prices for gold under a complicated scheme that circumvented the congressionally fixed price. This procedure certainly raised some difficult legal questions, but faced with 15,000,000 unemployed and many citizens in an insurrectionary state of mind, the government would have been unreasonable not to have put legal scruples aside if it felt that by doing so it might improve the situation. Seven years later Acheson would offer the Roosevelt Administration, faced with a similar legal dilemma, a similar legal loophole enabling Roosevelt to order the transfer of fifty overaged destroyers to the British home fleet. But at this time Acheson revealed a remarkably delicate legal sensibility. Despite the opinion of Homer Cummings, Stanley Reed (then general counsel for the Reconstruction Finance Corporation and later Mr. Justice Reed), and others that the Oliphant plan was legal, Acheson refused to go along. Rejecting the validity of the legal advice, he informed Roosevelt that unless *ordered in writing* by superior authority to take the action required of the Secretary of the Treasury to implement the gold purchase plan, he would not do so.

The crisis came with shattering rapidity. Until he had the Attorney General's concurring opinion, Acheson refused to sign the order to make devaluation of the dollar legal. Roosevelt turned upon him indignantly: "Don't you take my word for it that it will be all right?" By now Acheson's grip on his temper was slipping, and he defied Roosevelt by remonstrating that it was he, not Roosevelt, who had to put his actual signature on the order. "That will do!" Roosevelt commanded. A few days later, Secretary Woodin, who had been ill, told Acheson, "Look here, son, you're in terrible trouble. The President has a paper on his desk firing you. If he does, I've told him that I'll resign. You'd better resign gracefully yourself." [20] Before Acheson could act on his superior's advice, Roosevelt himself announced Acheson's "resignation" to the press. Thus Acheson's first venture into government was abruptly terminated before it had really begun.

Acheson's abrupt dismissal appears to have been precipitated by the belief that he had leaked a memorandum or "opinion" opposed to that of the President to Eliot Thurston of the *New York Tribune.* According to Grace Tully the President later learned that the "break in secrecy had come through Lewis Douglas but it was too late for corrective action to be taken with regard to Acheson." [21] The President, she says, "acted impulsively and later regretted it." [22] This puts a different light on Roosevelt's later readiness to welcome Acheson back into his administration. Acheson appears to have believed that Adolf Berle had something to do with his dismissal, and years later there would be bad blood between the two in the State Department.

His "resignation" made a lasting impression upon Acheson. Years later he had occasion to remark:

My troubles with F.D.R. had a very deep and very lasting effect on my judgment in many things. I wasn't particularly well satisfied with my performance in it. It wasn't that what I had done was wrong . . . [but] I did not have enough consideration for the problems of the President. . . . Whether I was all right or not it warned me that there are terrible problems that an assistant to the President can get into by allowing things to get to the point where trouble occurs, and that, therefore, you ought to be very alert and watchful to consider his position and interests twice as much as your own.[23]

As a result of this chastening experience, Acheson was later to approach the Truman relationship with a keen sense of the President's problems and the delicacy of his prestige. But he may also have felt more at ease with Truman's orderly procedures and with the businesslike and dignified way in which Truman conducted relations with his lieutenants.

Finally, Acheson's break with Roosevelt may well have been contributed to by the latter's "arrogant and condescending manner." [26] To be called to an early morning conference in Roosevelt's bedroom and to have Roosevelt's grandchildren cavorting about was more than Acheson's pride could take. An officer of the government, Acheson expected to be treated not as an employee but as a social equal. To an individual of Acheson's patrician and personal sensibilities, Roosevelt's behavior was degrading and therefore intolerable. But Acheson never ceased to admire Roosevelt's political powers. "He was strong willed, ruthless, and powerful. A man whom I could respect but never particularly liked. . . . I respected his ability to rule, but I did not like him." [27] As Acheson says, he learned a great deal from the episode, but it would not be the last time that he would risk his political career by taking a highly unpopular position.

Although outsiders, especially critics of Roosevelt, were quick to applaud Acheson for his act of independence and moral courage in resigning, their approbation hardly consoled Acheson for his banishment from government. Unlike most men of his generation and class, Acheson viewed a life of public service as the only possible outlet for the nagging sense that how one lived one's life was important and that government offered the greatest scope for a life of excellence. According to McGeorge Bundy and Frankfurter, Acheson took his banishment from government extremely hard but was careful not to allow his break with Roosevelt to turn him against the New Deal or the Democratic Party. When in 1936 Lewis Douglas and James Warburg—two other apostates from Roosevelt's administration—proposed that he join them in forming a Democrats-for-Landon movement, Acheson publicly dissociated himself from the enterprise. In a letter to the *Baltimore Sun,* Acheson let it be known that far from opposing Roosevelt, he could not support Landon. In addition to his disappointment with Landon's program and his attacks upon the Reciprocal Trade Agreements program, Acheson objected to the charges of Communism which the Republican National Chairman, John Hamilton, had seen fit to throw at the New Deal. "It seems to me utterly fantastic to suggest that Communism is in any manner involved in this campaign. It serves only to arouse a spirit of bigotry. . . ." [24]

On the positive side, Acheson affirmed his admiration for Secretary of State Hull's tenacious efforts to revive international trade. His policies, Acheson concluded, "are among the most constructive acts of any government in the post-war period" and "when they are attacked I must be on his side." [25]

CHAPTER

3

RETURN TO THE LAW

IT WOULD BE a long time before Acheson returned to government, and, in the meantime, he turned to his law practice. Business was better than ever and Acheson's financial situation prospered. The firm was now known as Covington, Burling, Rublee, Acheson, and Shorb. By the mid-thirties, the New Deal was working a revolution in the relationship of the federal government to the American economy, and being one of the few big firms in Washington gave Acheson's law firm an immense volume of business. Acheson once again took his place as one of the foremost practitioners before the Federal Court of Appeals in Washington. He assumed more and more of the responsibility for running the firm. He was also much sought after as a public speaker and a trustee for various institutions. He agreed to serve as a trustee of the Brookings Institution, and in October 1936 he was elected a Senior Fellow of the Yale Corporation, the governing board of Yale University. It is amusing to note that he beat out Robert Alphonso Taft, class of 1910, for the post. Senator Taft may have become Mr. Republican, but in 1936 Dean Acheson was Mr. Yaleman, his break with F.D.R. no doubt having enhanced his appeal to the Yale alumni.

These were also years when his children were growing up. He appears to have been a more than satisfactory father. Alice Acheson had principal responsibility for the children until they went off to college or, in the case of David, to Groton and Yale. But Acheson took his share of the responsibility and seems to have had the love and esteem of his children. While not given to strong emotional display, Acheson elicited from his daughters, judging from their letters, a spirit of "wry, puckish humor."

His enforced retirement from public life also gave Acheson the leisure to read widely in English history and biography. He acquired a great admiration at this time for the Victorian period. He saw it as a period when the British managed their world role with great responsibleness. The willingness of the British to transfer great amounts of capital over-

30

seas Acheson saw at the root of England's greatness and the basis for a prolonged era of world peace and stability. The role that Britain had played would be at the forefront of Acheson's mind in 1945 when America faced the choice between exercising a constructive role in the world or returning to isolationism.

While his law practice and family kept Acheson busy, it did not afford him the satisfaction that it had prior to his government service. There is considerable agreement that Acheson was not content simply to pursue his practice and accept his exile from government as final. "The heady experience of being in on big political decisions," Frankfurter commented, "was like getting used to French cuisine. Once Dean had dined on such rare meat it was painful to return to the hardtack of the law." [1] A law partner remarks of this period that Acheson "no longer had the stomach for the tedious details. The law did not consume his devoted interest." [2]

Nevertheless, it was the law in its larger sense that provided him an outlet for his energies and intellectual restlessness. And by a curious inversion of circumstances, instead of drifting away from the New Deal, Acheson's writings and utterances after 1935 reveal a steady growth of respect for what the New Deal had wrought, so that by the end of the thirties he had come to accept its basic premises. In settling in his own mind the arguments for and against the burning issues of social change, of public versus private rights, of personal freedom and public power raised by the Great Depression and the New Deal, Acheson also clarified his thinking on matters which would have an important bearing upon his performance as Secretary of State.

On July 4, 1936, in an address to the Maryland Bar Association on the occasion of the hundredth anniversary of Roger Taney's appointment to the Supreme Court, Acheson devoted his speech to the issue of judicial restraint.[3] The regularity with which the Supreme Court was striking down legislation designed to ameliorate the ravages of the Depression and correct the abuses of unregulated corporate power was about to precipitate a decision on Roosevelt's part calling for radical reform of the Court. In recalling that Justice Taney had urged judicial restraint upon a Court faced by legislation and litigation born of the Jacksonian upheaval and of the impending crisis over slavery, Acheson drew his listeners' attention to the sound intuition which had led Taney to *refuse* to substitute the opinion of the Court for the common sense and good faith of the other branches of the government. To do so, Taney had reasoned, would not only be to misread the essential freedom which the Constitution intended for legislatures and executives in the exercise of their judgment, but would disarm government "of the powers necessary to accomplish the ends of its creation and see the functions it was designed to perform transferred to the hands of privileged corporations." [4]

Acheson's statement of the case for judicial self-restraint is less note-worthy for its ideological congruity with the New Deal than for its tren-chant defense of the power of government to act when the need arises, lest all be lost through fatal paralysis of the public power. Acheson's address caught the attention of Norman Hapgood, former editor of *Har-per's,* who sent it along to F.D.R. with the following comment:

Referring back to our talks about the Supreme Court: it is just possible that you may not have seen notices of Acheson's address on Taney, so I enclose one, with parts marked, showing how strongly he takes the Holmes–Stone view. As he is about 40, I suppose, and has the solid court behind him as a lawyer accustomed to put cases before them, I should think he might well be con-sidered when the time comes.[5]

"Keep on keeping me posted," the President urged.

Statement of Philosophy

Other than to declare himself for Roosevelt, Acheson took no part in the 1936 campaign. But a few months later, in an address to the Chicago Law Club, he gave a more fully developed statement of his political philosophy. Like a sound Madisonian, Acheson found the essence of the political and social transformation sweeping America to lie in the ex-istence of new interests pressing for recognition. There had grown up in the twentieth century, Acheson declared, a proportion of the American people whose relationship to property was not that of ownership and whose interests in property "were not recognized in any way in our legal order." [6] With the maturing of the industrial revolution, the right of un-limited freedom in property had assumed destructive propensities. The bulk of the population, whose relationship to property was not protected by the laws of ownership, were now demanding protection as a result of the catastrophe wrought by the Depression. They were determined to use their political power to right the social imbalance. The most pressing legal and political problem of the age, Acheson declared, is the people's de-mand that those "who are not owners, as well as those who are owners, have interests in property and in the use of property which must be con-sidered and protected." To achieve these protections and rights, govern-ment must possess the right to investigate and regulate the uses of eco-nomic power, to occasionally establish active competition "where there is a widespread popular belief that an industry has been particularly re-sistant to control," and to compel big business and unions alike to observe certain rules of organization and collective bargaining.[7]

No one can doubt the strength of Acheson's pro-union sentiment at that time. He was extremely active as counsel for the International Ladies Garment Workers Union, defending the minimum hours and wages law which various states had instituted. His sympathy for labor was tempered nevertheless by the injunction of reciprocal responsibility and discipline. In the same speech, Acheson admonished his listeners with a characteristic analogy from Justice Holmes to remember that all parties "are little ganglions within and not little gods outside the industry." [8]

The greatest danger to the fabric of society lay, he continued, in letting industrial disputes degenerate to the point at which all parties to the dispute lost their sense of common interest in its settlement. Collective bargaining, he declared, afforded a method "more fruitful than focusing the efforts of all upon the politics of power. The road leads only to a conflict of increasing bitterness, in which finally all objectives disappear except the extermination of the opponent." [9] This, of course, would be the dilemma that Acheson would face in his efforts to contain the Soviet Union without giving in to those who called for extermination of the opponent.

The premises of his social thought confirmed Acheson in a number of political positions which were to become salient in his performance in the State Department. In the first place, his deprecation of the utopian strain in the New Deal in no way weakened his faith in the efficacy of human reason. As frail a reed as it is, reason is one of the few means in man's possession which enables him to cope with his destiny. The New Deal only served to confirm Acheson in his earlier conviction that by the steady application of intelligence and self-discipline man has a fighting chance to avoid the worst disasters of a largely unpredictable future. In this same philosophy were nurtured Holmes, Brandeis, and F.D.R.

In the same liberal tradition, Acheson was neither wedded to an egoistic psychology nor beguiled by a formal individualism into denying that man's problems are social or collective in nature and that government affords an engine whereby man's intellect can be pitted against those collective problems. Like Brandeis, Holmes, and F.D.R., Acheson developed a deep aversion to all attempts to shackle human behavior with immutable laws, ". . . whether they are the laws expounded in the *Social Statics* of Herbert Spencer or those in *Das Kapital* of Karl Marx." [10]

Later, when he became Assistant Secretary and then Undersecretary of State, Acheson was subject to fits of irritation and exasperation about the chaotic and ineffectual way in which the Department of State functioned. On several occasions under Secretary James F. Byrnes he was on the point of resigning, and much of his towering admiration for General George C. Marshall seemed to derive from Marshall's actions in bringing order into the running of the Department. Acheson's striving for order and rational mastery must be seen as one of the most powerful expressions of his personality. Deeply affected by the breakdown of society caused by the Depression, Acheson continued to favor techniques designed to overcome the crisis of social collapse and human waste. His deep-felt need for order prompted in Acheson a predisposition in favor of change.

While others of his class were breaking with the New Deal, Acheson found in it precisely the traits which appealed to his personality: imaginative and legal mastery of chaos, avoidance of wasteful social conflict through mediation and collective bargaining, and strong rational action by the government to get things done. Acheson was a strong respecter of the belief that larger forces usually direct affairs and people, but he believed that within the interstices of these movements it was possible for people, provided they were well led, to master their fate, at least to some extent.

An address to the Bar and Officers of the Supreme Court in 1938, in memory of Justice Benjamin N. Cardozo, reveals another facet of Acheson's maturing political philosophy. Significantly, he chose to speak of "Cardozo and the Problems of Government." In his remarks, Acheson eulogized Cardozo's frank acceptance of the right of government to assert itself in a rough and ready way, so long as it did so in "the pursuit of legitimate ends by methods honestly conceived and rationally chosen." [11] In the words of Cardozo: ". . . more will not be asked by those who have learned from experience and history that government is at best a make-shift, that the attainment of one good may involve the sacrifice of others, and that compromise will be inevitable until the coming of Utopia." [12]

Acheson heartily endorsed the presupposition of good faith which Cardozo extended to the acts of legislatures and executive officers alike: ". . . no one was less moved by dialectics designed to prove that an honest attempt to remedy an evil had no reasonable relation to the end sought. He had no sympathy with judicial attitudes which, while charged with no duty or power to initiate solutions, condemned on *a priori* reasoning the efforts of puzzled men as lacking any rational foundation and as purely fanciful." [13]

In later years Acheson's impatience with Congress would spring from precisely the sense that while Congress felt no duty or responsibility to initiate foreign policy solutions, it condemned on a priori and constitutional grounds the efforts of the Executive to do so.

The difficulty comes in the application of the principle. It comes from the resistance of the human mind to the conclusion that what it disapproves of can be reasonable, and from its inability to find in considerations which are beyond its experience the basis of honest belief and rational action on the part of others. Only a mind rigidly disciplined by humility and restraint and gifted with imagination can surmount these obstacles.[14]

Acheson was also quick to note the generous latitude which Cardozo extended to the public servant and his "deep respect for the integrity and intelligence of officers whose work he reviewed." [15]

In these attitudes we see anticipations of Acheson's later affinity for the creative use of governmental power in solving problems of foreign policy and of his impatience with congressional attempts to interpose constitutional dogma between the Executive branch and its solution of those problems. In espousing the right of government to a larger role in the social order, Acheson looked further than immediate goals of humanitarianism and meliorism. Beyond the instant necessity of recovering from the wreckage of the Great Depression, Acheson saw looming up the whole question of American society adjusting to a new economic and social order which would supersede that of individualistic liberalism. Here we see in full flowering the Acheson ideal of a government manned by wise, masterful, and dedicated public servants who, by virtue of their willingness to grapple with the great problems of society and apply the canons of experience and reason, make it possible for society to succeed.

Acheson's idealization of the virtues of strong government in no way weakened his respect for the importance of Congress and public opinion. *svrc!* On the contrary, their relationship was indispensable to the proper functioning of strong government. The Constitution intended that government in America should work by virtue of the clash of power on power. Nevertheless, anyone who interfered with the realization of this ideal or who would thwart the execution of its principles Acheson tended to perceive as wholly petty and irresponsible, worthy only of contempt. Not unlike Woodrow Wilson, who imputed meanness of motives and virtual immorality to anyone who challenged him on issues he conceived himself to be uniquely competent at, Acheson reacted, albeit with lesser compulsiveness, toward anyone who appeared, for partisan or any other motives, to challenge self-evident facts upon which Acheson was determined to base policy.

Acheson "was deeply impressed by the intricate problems thrown up by industrial civilization; merely to analyze these issues requires a vast body of technical knowledge." [16] Not simply expertise was needed, but servants with the broadest vision of the requirement of social action and the largest talents. But the vision of the good society which had animated Brandeis's commitment to positive government and which had seemed so radical in its day, was subtly displaced in Acheson's mind by another vision in which the role of government would be both greater and more systematic.

Return to Active Service

The development of Acheson's intellectual affinity for the New Deal was accompanied by a gradual healing of the breach with Roosevelt. And by 1939 Acheson was named chairman of the Attorney General's Committee on Administrative Procedure. As its title implies, the committee's task was to establish procedures assuring fair treatment for persons or concerns falling afoul of the numerous federal regulatory laws. Because New Deal legislation had greatly extended the scope of bureaucratic jurisdiction in the administration of regulatory and other government functions, this expansion of administrative jurisdiction and discretion inevitably required a better quality of performance in adjudicating the complaints of private citizens and firms than had been previously necessary.

Existing procedures were proving inadequate, particularly in view of the separation that existed between the hearing officer who took evidence and the executive officer who rendered the final decision. "Almost invariably," Acheson's committee found, "the agency heads rely heavily upon subordinates other than the hearing officer to digest the record [of the hearing] and to draft the findings and opinions in accordance with the directions of the agency," so "the conduct of the hearing becomes divorced from responsibility for decision." [17]

Acheson's deep respect for government had as its concomitant a lively sense of obligation to act so as to preserve the fundamental right of the private citizen to a scrupulously fair and intelligent hearing. The latter was as vital a part of Acheson's idea of positive government as the need for strong government to act as an agent for creative control and management of the economy. He also believed in the right of a government employee to a fair hearing, something that he would not always succeed in securing for State Department employees under attack by the McCarthyite inquisitors a decade later.

The failure of government to act sensibly, where a modicum of intelligence would improve the quality of its performance in the life of the citizenry, prompted Acheson's committee to propose a profoundly sweeping reform of administrative procedures. The Acheson Report recommended that each agency be given a corps of judges, to be called "hearing commissioners. . . . These officials should be men of ability and prestige, and should have a tenure and salary which will give assurance of independence of judgment." [18] These hearing commissioners would become the fulcrum of a reformed administrative system. They would have full authority to preside at hearings and to "make findings of fact, conclusions of law, and orders for the disposition of matters coming before them. Subject only to higher appeal and review, decisions of these officials would be final." [19]

A minority of the authors of the Acheson Report felt that it did not go far enough and that in cases where it was practicable the deciding officials should be completely divorced from the investigating and prosecuting agencies. Acheson opposed the division of the regulatory agencies into completely separate entities for prosecution and adjudication on the grounds that it would seriously hamper informal negotiations and settlements, which are "the life blood of the administrative process."[20] The majority adopted Acheson's reasoning. As well as giving to Americans the sort of procedural guarantees which they needed against "big government," Acheson acquired familiarity with governmental and administrative processes which would prove a hallmark of his career at State.

Acheson and Frankfurter

Acheson's long-standing friendship with Felix Frankfurter next brought him into the limelight in connection with F.D.R.'s nomination of the Harvard law professor to the Supreme Court. The nomination blew up a storm of prejudice against the nominee, partly for his New Deal affiliations and partly because he was a Jew. A Senate Judiciary Subcommittee dignified the charges against Frankfurter by hearing testimony of maliciously hostile witnesses. Frankfurter at first refused to appear in person, saying he had no wish to testify to his own qualifications, but asked Acheson to be his personal representative. Following a spirited defense of his qualifications by two veteran "irreconcilables" of the Senate, the Republican William Borah of Idaho and the Independent George Norris of Nebraska, Frankfurter appeared on his own behalf.

Shortly after Frankfurter's confirmation by the Senate, Roosevelt informed Acheson that he was sending his name up to the Senate for appointment to the Washington, D. C., Circuit Court of Appeals. Acheson, whose interest in a judicial career had never been great, remonstrated: "Would you like to be a judge?" F.D.R. admitted with a chuckle that he would not. Acheson retorted, "Well, neither would I," and with that he bespoke his commitment to the life of political action.

Despite his reconciliation with Roosevelt, what Acheson's political future might have been without the advent of war in September 1939, we will never know. While there was no longer a barrier of temperament and political philosophy between Acheson and the works of the Roosevelt Administration, it is not at all clear whether Acheson's style could have been fittted into a peacetime New Deal. With the advent of war in Europe, however, the emphasis within the Administration shifted radically to foreign affairs, where Acheson's style and background were invaluable assets.

War broke out in September 1939. Almost immediately Acheson showed himself concerned with the dark and somber issues which international conflict always raises—the use of power, the willingness to act expeditiously and with the minimum of delay, and the need to take risks. These were the very issues which Americans had been ducking for twenty years. His speech to a Yale audience on November 28 was not only rooted in the power realities of international politics, but it showed remarkable insight into the new problems which were being generated by the twentieth century and the new forms of power that would be called upon if the problems were to be overcome.

In order to understand the march of the dictators, he informed his audience, one must take a long view; one must go back beyond World War I and into the last century. The financial power with which London organized the international life of the nineteenth century had broken down.

This Nineteenth Century world economy was far from perfect. It contained within it injustices which demanded correction. Nevertheless, it brought about an enormous increase of the human population . . . and at the same time a standard of living never before thought possible.

. . . We can see that the credits which were once extended by the financial center of London no longer provide the means for the production of wealth in other countries. . . . We can see that British naval power can no longer guarantee security of life and investment in distant parts of the world and a localization of conflict nearer home.[21]

The rise of the dictators "is the response of Asia and a large part of Europe to the failure of some of the vital mechanisms of the Nineteenth Century world economy. Both the failure and the response constitute those 'foreign affairs' toward which we are asked to frame an American attitude."

The United States, he said, faces nothing less than the need to reconstitute an effectively functioning international system. To do this the country must first make itself "so strong that we shall not be caught defenseless or dangerously exposed in any even possible eventuality." More than that, "a realistic American policy should have two aspects—one we may call the prophylactic side; the other, the therapeutic. One should attempt to check the disintegration of the world, in which our national life and individual lives are rooted, by strengthening the forces opposing disintegration; the other should attempt a cure."

Rather than wait around until the war came to the Western Hemisphere, the United States should see to it that those nations already forced to fight aggression "have the weapons and supplies with which to fight." [22]

If I am told that what I suggest is unneutral and amounts to acts of war, I answer that I am not interested in the words or epithets applied to it.

But a mere attitude of negation is not enough. The world order, which is so vital to us, will continue to disintegrate, even without the bludgeoning of revolutionary attack, unless vigorous reconstruction is undertaken. We cannot stand aloof from this effort if we are alive to our own interest.[23]

Then, in a statement rich with implications for the future, Acheson advanced the thesis that the United States must join "with other financially strong nations" in making industrial capital available to the underdeveloped parts of Europe, even if that meant accepting some limitations and sacrifices.

Meanwhile, the opening phase of the war in Europe had witnessed the extinction of Poland, smashed to the ground by the combined German and Russian assault. The onset of the "phoney war" following the defeat of Poland did not significantly alter the balance for or against active American intervention. And although the astonishing collapse of French armies before the onslaught of Hitler's blitz did make an impact upon American thinking, and the German campaign against Britain during the summer of 1940 appeared particularly menacing, there was still no pronounced desire in the country to become involved in the struggle. The most that the country seemed willing to do was to permit the President to extend assistance to the British in their hour of need. In mid–May 1940, the British requested the loan or lease of fifty overaged American destroyers. The British needed these ships desperately because of the one hundred destroyers they had available in home waters, almost half had been lost or damaged. Now with the Germans poised for a cross-channel invasion additional destroyers were indispensable.

Desperate though Britain's plight might be, Roosevelt felt constrained from releasing the vessels. In the first place, he had to consider their value to America's own defense should war approach American shores. Secondly, under the Act of June 28, 1940, only such equipment could be released for foreign sale as had first been certified nonessential to national defense. Certification was a complicated process.

So many influential people were stirred by Britain's plight that the President was swamped with proposals suggesting how he might ignore or circumvent the statutory prohibition and at the same time escape the obligation to secure congressional approval. Within the Administration Benjamin Cohen, one of the President's assistants, and Harold Ickes were actively preoccupied with the matter. Outside of government, William Allen White, editor of the Emporia *Gazette* and founder of the Committee to Win the War by Aiding the Allies, and members of the influential Century Group were active. The latter came up with the exceedingly seductive proposition that the government would be justified in turning over the destroyers in return for American bases in British possessions in the Western Hemisphere. Roosevelt was unresponsive.

Under the circumstances the Century Group felt that its only remaining recourse was to appeal to Wendell Willkie, the Republican nominee

for President, to join with Roosevelt in establishing political support for
such a move. Roosevelt warned the delegation that it would not be enough
just to have Willkie's personal support but that he would need Willkie's
influence with Republican congressmen if he were to win congressional
approval for such an exchange. What counted, Roosevelt declared, was
not Willkie's attitude but that of the Republicans in Congress. But when
they turned to Willkie, members of the Century Group found that although he personally favored a destroyer–bases exchange, he was unwilling to put pressure on the congressional branch of the Republican
Party. He had so recently won the nomination that he was not willing to
appear to poach upon congressional Republican terrain or to affront the
isolationists in the party. Meanwhile, the President and his advisers were
more than ever convinced that the transfer of destroyers to Britain would
require congressional action—that is, the amendment of the June 1917 and
June 1940 laws forbidding such a transaction.

Acheson, who strongly believed in the absolute necessity of Britain's
getting the destroyers, would have no hesitancy this time about helping
F.D.R. get around the legal obstructions to Executive action. He and Ben
Cohen got together privately and examined the various statutes and decisions of the courts bearing upon the President's power to make the
transaction without congressional sanction. They finally managed to demonstrate to their own satisfaction that the sale of the destroyers could be
fitted into the existing legal framework if the Acts of June 15, 1917, and
of June 28, 1940, were properly construed. Such an interpretation, they
believed, would relieve the President of any obligation to secure congressional amendment of the law. They next drafted a brief to that effect, and
Acheson persuaded two prominent members of the New York bar, C. C.
Burlingham and Thomas Thatcher, as well as his law partner, George
Rublee, to sign it.

Because time was of the essence, Acheson determined that their four
signatures were enough to obtain respectful attention; in any event the
opinion would stand or fall on its merits. He next got in touch with
Charles Merz, a former Yale classmate who had charge of the editorial
page of the *New York Times*. Merz agreed to publish the opinion in the
form of a letter to the *Times*.

The letter made an immediate impact. Secretary of War Henry Stimson immediately drew it to the British ambassador's attention as providing a means of avoiding congressional conflict and solving the problem of
executive action. At the time Secretary Stimson wrote to Mr. C. C. Burlingham,

Sometime I hope I shall have a chance to tell you what a part your opinion
. . . played in world politics. The job is not yet finished, for it is a tough one,
but I think it will come out all right. And if it does I believe it will mark a

real turning point in the war and the relations of the U.S.A. and Great Britain. . . .[24]

It still remained for the President to decide that the legal opening which the opinion purported to demonstrate was sufficient to enable him to bypass Congress. Roosevelt had his Attorney General, Robert Jackson, provide him with his own opinion; it came to the same conclusion by a somewhat different route. But even before he had received Jackson's opinion, the President had determined that he had sufficient legal leeway, based upon the Cohen–Acheson brief, to act.

Roosevelt immediately sought and secured Churchill's agreement to authorize the use of Newfoundland, Bermuda, the Bahamas, Jamaica, St. Lucia, Trinidad, and British Guiana as naval and air bases by the United States. With this string of Atlantic bases in hand, the President was in a strong position vis-à-vis public opinion because the isolationists had for years been clamoring for the acquisition of these very bases in return for the cancellation of Britain's war debts, "arguing that such a deal would not be unneutral, because it would be designed exclusively for the strengthening of national defense." [25]

By showing the Administration that it had the legal right to exchange the destroyers without the necessity of congressional action, Acheson spared Roosevelt the embarrassment of a full-scale debate which, coming in the late summer of an election year, might have damaged his claim to have kept the nation out of war. In responding to criticisms of the manner in which he had enabled the Administration to circumvent congressional authorization, Acheson revealed a point of view at odds with the scruples which he had shown about devaluing the dollar without congressional sanction.

Acheson remonstrated:

I continually hear people saying that the President should have gone to Congress. This seems only another way of saying that the transaction was impossible, and I have very little patience with people who insist upon glorifying forms on the theory that any other course is going to destroy our institutions. The danger to them seems not in resolving legal doubts in accordance with the national interest but in refusing to act when action is imperative.*

Acheson responded in a similar vein to Quincy Wright's criticism that the destroyer transaction was an unneutral act by first stressing the difference of opinion among international lawyers as to the extent of the obligation resting on neutral states to avoid unneutral acts and concluding with a strong affirmation of *raison d'état*:

---

* Letter, Acheson to John McCloy, September 12, 1940. A decade later Acheson's failure in a similar situation to secure congressional approval for the country's entry into the Korean War would get him into greater difficulty.

. . . close questions of interpretation have always been and should be resolved in consonance with the vital public interests of the sovereign whose laws are construed.*

This is a far cry from the concern with legalism that characterized Acheson's earlier performance. In place of dubiety about the legitimacy of action, Acheson now testified to his robust faith in the capacity of American institutions to respond to the needs of the times without being sapped in their essential function. At the same time he stressed the primacy of action. The necessity of state was carrying Acheson away from the Brandeis emphasis upon the danger of centralized power.

Acheson would come increasingly to see the fate of nations as imperiled by the inhibitions which democratic leaders felt against taking this or that action lest it breach some legality or disturb popular opinion. His own proclivity was to view the life of the law as what it was intended to preserve or to do; it was not meant to obstruct action necessary to the preservation of the society which gave it life. The circumstances of the war in Europe appeared to free Acheson from traditional scruples and to inspire in him a confidence in his insights into power politics. In the meantime the war was also stimulating his latent desire to return to public life and to exercise his ample capacity for action.

By the middle of October Willkie's campaign was beginning to generate concern in the White House where the President had hoped to have a relatively easy time of it. Some of Roosevelt's advisers thought that Acheson, having just helped them with the destroyer–bases deal, might contribute a filip to Roosevelt's increasingly worrisome campaign.

Whatever reservations Acheson may still have held about Roosevelt as a person were easily offset by his growing respect for Roosevelt's approach to the war. Whatever line of policy Roosevelt took promised to be more active and decisive than that of a Willkie hamstrung by a party whose main force was resolutely isolationist.

The call to join the inner circle of the President's advisers had a symbolic connotation about it. Acheson had come full circle in the seven years since leaving office and was now returning as his own man to the antechambers of power.

Not content with providing the President with a spark of confidence

---

* Twenty-three years later the author was sitting in Acheson's office when Acheson returned from participating in a panel of the American Society of International Law concerned with legal aspects of President Kennedy's Cuban Blockade. Mr. Acheson was livid with indignation. Mr. Quincy Wright and the other scholars had just tried taking him over the coals for the counsel which he had given President Kennedy's decision: "What a commentary," he spluttered. "There they sit claiming that a nation does not have the right to resort to self-help when its national existence is at stake. Have they never read Coke's response . . . ?"

and helpful speech memoranda, on November 1 Acheson delivered a withering radio attack upon Willkie's claims to the White House. To Willkie's claim that the war required a production engineer and not a politician in the White House, Acheson replied:

Government is not a branch of manufacturing. The leadership of a people is not learned by designing an assembly line. Churchill has never produced anything, if by "anything" Mr. Willkie means electric current or business deals. . . . We are not voting for a production manager; we are voting for a President.[26]

Acheson then concluded in that vein of withering sarcasm:

But, even if Mr. Willkie were right, even if we were looking for a production manager, would Mr. Willkie qualify? I am afraid he has not been very candid about what he has produced. Mr. Willkie is a lawyer and has produced talk. He has even written a book.

He became the president of a holding company, specialized in its public relations, and produced more talk. For many months he has gone from one end of the country to the other and produced still more talk.

This is all right. I have no fault to find with that. But I want him to take off those stage overalls and let us have a real look at him. When we look at Mr. Willkie without the overalls we see clearly that he is not the man who is needed to guide America in the next four years.[27]

On November 4 Roosevelt was re-elected to an unprecedented third term; three months later Acheson was appointed Assistant Secretary of State for Economic Affairs. After seven years he was at last returning to public service. Although the invitation emanated from Cordell Hull, the decision was doubtless Roosevelt's. No appointment of the Assistant Secretary rank was ever made without Roosevelt's personal judgment and decision. Nor did Frankfurter's influence have much bearing on it. Frankfurter may have broken the ice with Roosevelt and reintroduced Acheson to the good graces of the White House, but it was the mutuality of their views on the war that appealed to Roosevelt.

CHAPTER

4

WARTIME SERVICE

THE FUNCTIONS to which Acheson had been appointed as Assistant Secretary of State for Economic Affairs in January 1941 seemed so ambiguous and ill-defined that he immediately set about defining and enlarging them. "In accepting Mr. Hull's invitation to enlist, I had a much clearer idea of what I wanted to do than he had of what he wanted me to do. . . . At any rate, I did not come back to dream in a somnolent office." [1] Acheson immediately set about the task of becoming effective by doing two things: he got rid of the Foreign Service officers assigned to him and brought in his own people. He brought Donald Hiss—a lawyer and member of the State Department staff who was temporarily serving in the Office of Production Management—back to the department as his executive assistant. Heading the several departments in economic affairs reporting to him were Charles Taft,* a Cincinnati lawyer and brother of the senator; Emilio Collado (later vice-president of Standard Oil of New Jersey); and Thomas Finletter (later Secretary of the Air Force in the Truman Administration). Although Acheson found Secretary of State Hull a somewhat pathetic and ineffective operator, he did his best to support him and Hull later repaid his loyalty by defending Acheson when the McCarthy attacks began. The State Department itself Acheson found to be essen-

---

* Of this experience, Taft writes: "I worked for Dean for about a year when I was head of the Office of Wartime Economic Affairs, from about the middle of January 1944 to somewhere along in December. I was very fond of Dean and very strong for him as a person. When Gene Rostow, who was his assistant, with whom I worked closely also, was attacked so violently by Pat Hurley, the 'globaloney general,' who had made a study of Iran for President Roosevelt, Dean defended Gene warmly as he always stood up for his employees, especially when they were right." Personal letter to the author, September 24, 1970.

tially ineffective, "breathless and bewildered like an old lady at a busy intersection during rush hour." *

It was a frustrating situation but Acheson saw no one to blame but the department itself. The President, who shared Acheson's view of the department as fusty and ill-equipped to play a significant role in wartime operations, was fed up with Hull; and to the extent that it was impossible for Roosevelt to enjoy a satisfactory relationship with his Secretary of State, it was obviously not possible for the department to perform the role which by any definition should have been its.

As a result of this internecine warfare, the State Department was constantly bested or excluded in the struggle for influence and control over wartime decision making. By an Executive Order of April 13, 1942, for example, the Board of Economic Warfare, under its able executive director, Milo Perkins, succeeded in having Roosevelt transfer to the board the power and the funds to buy abroad materials for production; succeeded also in making the board the State Department's adviser on Lend–Lease; and, worst of all from Acheson's viewpoint, succeeded in getting for itself the authority to conduct for the President negotiations with foreign nations concerning economic matters. This order, Acheson wrote, was "a painful, bitter, and humiliating defeat." [2] Similar defeats met the State Department all along the line, to the point at which its role in political and diplomatic planning was reduced to individual members of the State Department consulting with the President and his staff, but the department itself having no systematic role in the determination of wartime policy. Acheson even wondered if Roosevelt's intention in having Hull sponsor studies on postwar planning was not simply a means of taking the department's attention away from its immediate ineffectuality by giving its leading lights the impression that they were preparing for the peace. Despite the ineffectuality of the department, however, public service still provided Acheson with a means to embellish his self-esteem and an outlet for his competitive striving. Despite frustrations and setbacks, he persisted in his efforts to enhance the influence and effectiveness of his own section and to some not inconsiderable extent succeeded in doing so. By the end of his period as Assistant Secretary for Economic Affairs, Acheson was playing a role of increasing importance. He participated in all Lend–Lease decisions of policy significance, chaired the United Nations Relief and Rehabilitation Agency (UNRRA) planning

---

* Acheson, *Present at the Creation, op. cit.,* p. 39. Acheson refers again to the department as "the little old lady," "shaking her umbrella as threateningly as anyone," but essentially impotent.

committee, and represented the State Department at the Bretton Woods Conference of 1944.

As for policy matters, Acheson's attention for the first half of 1941 was taken up with the question of how far the United States should go in restricting Japanese access to American strategic materials by subjecting them to licensing procedures. Acheson was almost alone in the State Department hierarchy during that period in favor of applying the export freeze to all the Axis countries even at the risk of war. After the German attack upon the Soviet Union in June 1941, the embargo was extended to Japan, and Acheson watched with satisfaction the gradual drying up of trade between the United States and that country.

Once hostilities broke out, Acheson's task was to secure strategic materials for the United States and deny them to the enemy. Much of his time was spent in getting Switzerland, Sweden, Spain, and other neutrals to cease and desist from exporting or transshipping strategic materials to supply Hitler's war machine.[3] It was a frustrating business, involving as it did the need to make a determination as to when neutral claims were valid—when not to export *would* risk German occupation—and when such claims were merely excuses for continuing a profitable trade with the Germans. Acheson was all for assuming that the Nazis were bluffing and that the United States therefore ought to go to the extreme in pressuring the neutrals. In each case he was convinced that his calculations of German strength and intentions were accurate, and he was much chagrined to find even the British frequently siding with the neutrals. From this, as well as from the Japanese case, we see strong evidence of Acheson's "optimizing" as opposed to "satisfying" policy. In each instance Acheson was determined to push to the limit in order to extract the maximum advantage even at some risk. From this experience, Acheson claimed to have drawn the lesson that even a neutral or a "relatively weak ally by determined, sometimes reckless, decisions can change and even prevent action by a much stronger power with ultimate responsibility."[4]

Another matter with which Acheson became involved—Lend–Lease— revealed Acheson's distinctive breadth of comprehension.

The Lend–Lease act was signed into law on March 11, 1941. It authorized the President to sell, lease, or lend, under such terms as he thought proper, arms, munitions, food, and other defense articles to any country whose defense he deemed vital to the United States. These were to be paid for at the end of the war in goods and services on an agreed upon basis that did not compromise economic recovery and international trade as had happened with the war debts after World War I.

When it came time to negotiate the Lend–Lease Agreement, Britain revealed acute distrust of the American provision calling for an end to all discriminatory trading practices, which would mean an end to imperial preference. The depth of American feeling about imperial preferences can only be understood if one recognizes the importance that the principle of nondiscriminatory trading relations has assumed in the American mind. Conversely, the depth of British feelings can only be understood if we recognize that every diminishment of Britain's trading position was felt to be a nail in the British coffin. To the traditional British desire for maximizing its trading opportunities in order to sustain its domestic industry, wartime planning had added a new dimension. British planners and economists anticipated that for Britain to obtain the goal of full employment after the war would require that the government retain absolute control over the workings of the British economy. If another setback to domestic life such as the Depression were to be avoided, the British government had to retain not only its ability to make whatever deals it could on the outside, but it must not tie its economy to the unpredictable swings of the American economy. This view was an article of doctrinal faith with British Laborites who were an influential part of Churchill's wartime Cabinet. Added urgency came from the fact that all indications by British economists pointed to a disastrous postwar fall in Britain's trade and overseas investment income. The retention of imperial preference was therefore viewed as a matter of life and death.

The American position, which from the President on down was regarded as a model of generosity, stipulated that Britain would be freed of all Lend–Lease debts and obligations incurred to the United States in the course of the war, provided it agreed to abandon imperial preference. American self-satisfaction rested on the premise that it was not going to repeat the fiasco after 1918 of trying to collect war debts from economically depressed allies, and also that with Britain's abandonment of imperial preference markets would be available to American traders.

The draft of the Lend–Lease Agreement which Acheson was assigned to produce did at least recognize the dilemma which Britain would face after the war. Acheson made Article VII, calling for the abolition of imperial preference, conditional upon both countries working out measures which would "eliminate all discrimination and would provide for mutually fair and advantageous relations." [5]

John Maynard Keynes arrived in Washington to negotiate the agreement. In early July 1941, Keynes, Britain's greatest economist, was burdened by a particular sense of responsibility for his country's economic fate. He distrusted America's intentions with every fiber of his being. His distrust sprang in part from the terrible misgivings and forebodings he had about Britain's future. It sprang also from his belief that the Americans, neither knowing nor caring about the dire peril in which the world economy would stand at the war's end, were not prepared to do anything about it. Finally, Keynes's distrust sprang from his forebodings about the kind of mentality—bred of laissez-faire chauvinism—that would take over the United States government when the war emergency passed.

In a letter half apologizing for the vehemence with which he had attacked Acheson's formulation of Article VII of the Lend–Lease Agreement, Keynes bared his concern to Acheson that if all the Americans had in mind was the most-favored-nation clause and a return to the nineteenth-century model of free trade, with everyone for himself and the devil take the hindmost, "it would be a cover behind which all the *unconstructive* and *truly reactionary people* of both our countries would shelter. We must be free to work out new and better arrangements which will win in substance and not in shadow what the President and you and others really want." [6] This was the man with whom Acheson had to deal and with whom he had to reconcile British and American interests. Acheson, unlike most Washington officials, found Keynes's imperiousness and abrasiveness tolerable—Keynes was, after all, a brilliant and cultivated gentleman—and the two soon got on famously.

Had Acheson remained unresponsive to the difficulties Keynes was alluding to or unresponsive to the British economist's desire for arrangements which would guarantee the substance and not just the shadow of a multilateral trading world, then negotiations might have gone much worse and deepened rather than eased the rancor and distrust. As it was, Acheson learned from the encounter. He did not need to be converted to the case for giving the international economy more powerful institutional supports than it had had in the past. He shared Keynes's vision of an expanding world economy based upon practical multilateral arrangements. Unlike Harry Dexter White, the Treasury negotiator who continued to press for concessions from the British, Acheson saw that it was no longer a question of forcing a competitor to give ground; it was necessary that Americans assume a direct responsibility in order to avoid a postwar economic collapse. Exposure to Keynes alerted Acheson to the awesome responsibility looming up for the United States in managing postwar economic problems. The subsequent American draft of December 2, 1941, went even further in the direction of reassuring the British about the future by phrasing Article VII in terms of a mutual obligation to reach agreement "directed to the expansion, by appropriate international and domestic measures, of production, employment, and the exchange and consumption of goods." But the British Cabinet still stuck stubbornly to the conviction that the mere signing of the Lend–Lease Agreement itself abrogated imperial preference tariffs. And it was not until February 1942, after F.D.R. had sent a personal cable to Churchill making it clear that the United States was asking not for any advance commitment on Empire preference but essentially for a commitment to discuss its elimination as part of a general agreement on the economy, that the British agreed to sign.

Acheson now learned firsthand just how painful it is for foreign governments to negotiate with the United States. They must first meet the terms of the Executive branch, which usually insists upon conditions designed to mollify congressional opinion in advance; but foreigners have no assurance that what they agreed to will, in fact, be acceptable to the congress. Either they must concede their negotiable points to the Executive with no assurance that more will not be extracted from them in the course of Senate ratification, or they must hold back, seeking to protect themselves against precisely such congressional upsets.

Despite Acheson's solicitude, uncertainty and strain clouded these delicate wartime negotiations. Acheson could not avoid being impressed with the necessity that the Executive impart to its partners the absolute certainty that whatever was agreed upon would not be altered and weakened by the Senate. In turn, this assurance implied that the President and the Secretary of State must take an unyielding line with the Congress when it came to ratification or else see their power of negotiation "go aglimmering." It was to overcome the distrust of the Congress by foreign governments that Acheson justified his insistence upon Executive supremacy.

When in July 1944 an international conference was convened at Bretton Woods, New Hampshire, to formulate proposals of a definite character for an international monetary fund, Acheson was a member of the United States delegation. His role at the conference was a modest one; he was neither an economist nor a banker. But he was pre-eminent among the lawyers about whom Keynes said in his farewell address ". . . they have turned our jargon into prose and our prose into poetry." Acheson devoted most of his attention to the charter of the Bank for Reconstruction. As the British economist Roy Harrod records, the charter "was drawn up, not by the formal committees, but by Professor J. W. Angell and Mr. Emilio G. Collado, working on successive days into the small hours; they referred difficult points to Mr. Dean Acheson and sometimes to Mr. E. E. Brown, prior to the assimilation by the British." [7] Acheson's greatest contribution to the establishment of the Bretton Woods agreements, however, came later when the agreements were before Congress for ratification.

Acheson's support for the broader principle of America's responsibility for the postwar economic situation did not extend to the United Nations Charter. While Acheson, like other high officials, made a number of speeches envisioning a better postwar world, nowhere did he extol the United Nations or give it anything but the most perfunctory support. Acheson believed that the war revealed the collapse of the whole structure of utopianism based on the concept of the harmony of interests of which the United Nations was another example. He was not a cynic or pessimist but he did not believe Americans could afford to exaggerate the United Nations as a panacea for the problems that would face America at the war's end.

In a public address after the war, at a time when most public officials were shouting hosannas to the United Nations, Acheson made only the tartest of references to it:

I am told that the way to solve this or that problem is to leave it to the United Nations. But it seems to me inescapable that if they are . . . united, they are still nations; and no more can be expected of this forum for political adjustment than the sum total of the contributions. . . . In the Arab proverb, the ass that went to Mecca remained an ass, and a policy has little added to it by its place of utterance.[8]

In later years, he said of the United Nations: ". . . its presentation to the American people as almost holy writ and with the evangelical fervor of a major advertising campaign seemed to me to raise hopes which could only lead to bitter disappointment."

It was impossible for Acheson to let his mind fly in the face of facts. The elements of force, power, conflict, and war are the "real" facts of international relations; they cannot be wished or moralized away. Acheson had not served his apprenticeship under Brandeis, the most bedrock judicial empiricist of his age, for nothing. Besides, respect for the facts was part of Acheson's personality. The facts were what told him that the world was hard and that man's sojourn was not intended to be an easy one. Disrespect for the facts was dishonest—a means of deceiving oneself which is just as much a violation of one's integrity as any other form of dishonesty; it can never be productive of worthwhile results. Hence while Acheson might have gone along with the United Nations Organization had its utility been kept in perspective, the more its virtues were exaggerated, the more Acheson reacted against it. Furthermore, the United States was paying a price for its obsession with the United Nations. The President and his advisers were bartering away points because of the exaggerated importance which they gave to procedural questions in the United Nations.

A good deal can be inferred about Acheson's personality from his views of the United Nations. His views were so strong and pungent that we cannot afford to overlook them. The principal things Acheson seemed to have had against the United Nations were its function as a cynosure of uncritical idealism, the assumption that all nations were equally important, the assumption that a natural harmony of interests existed which only goodwill was required to discover, the assumption that the institutions and practices of legislative procedure in liberal democracy could be extended to international relations, the assumption that the United Nations was preferable to diplomacy (by popular definition tricky and insincere) because it reached through a façade to "the people." Acheson had no faith in such abstractions as "the people." It was one of those pernicious abstractions like sovereignty and self-determination that lead to trouble.

As early as June 1946, Acheson warned the American people and its statesmen that they must change their perceptions about the nature of international politics. Involvement in foreign affairs, he declared,

. . . is a long and tough job and one for which we as a people are not particularly suited. We believe that any problem can be solved with a little ingenuity and without inconvenience to the folks at large. We have troubleshooters to do this. And our name for problems is significant. We call them headaches. You take a powder and they are gone. These pains about which we have been talking are not like that. They are like the pain of earning a living. They will stay with us until death.[9]

In the words of Oliver Wendell Holmes, "Man is not foreordained for repose." * For Acheson there were no panaceas and no institutions or mechanism that could produce easy or automatic solutions to man's problems. Only work—the active occupation with the real, the immediate, the possible—could be crowned with success. If only Americans would make a start toward attacking those problems which "through hard and intelligent work can be reduced to manageable dimensions. . . . Problems which are difficult against a background of confusion, hesitation, and disintegration may well become quite possible of solution as national and international institutions become healthy and confident and vigorous in a large part of the world." [10]

We see in Acheson's dismissal of the United Nations an attitude of mind that was hostile to trumpery and ballyhoo. As Acheson saw it, all those things which were not real and substantial, which did not accord with the political essences of reality, but which were cooked up to serve man's vanity or to divert him from the real essences of politics—all found expression in the campaign for the United Nations. People who could not face the truth about human nature were for the UN; people who fairly squished with the juice of human kindness but who had a pretty soggy brain were also for the UN; people who preferred to preserve their illusions intact favored the UN. Later, after he had retired, the UN and people like Adlai Stevenson who chose to treat it seriously became the

---

* "For my part, I believe that the struggle for life is the order of the world, at which it is vain to repine." O. W. Holmes in *The Mind and Faith of Justice Holmes,* edited by Max Lerner (Boston: Little, Brown, 1943), p. 19.

object of considerable emotional animus on Acheson's part. Nevertheless, Acheson took the United Nations seriously in his dealings with it as Secretary of State. Where it could be employed as a forum or negotiating place between East and West, it was so employed; where, as in the case of the Truman Doctrine, the Soviet veto threatened to obstruct action, it was not employed.

While Acheson labored to defeat the Axis powers, his duties did not give him any direct voice in the decisions which directly affected the conduct of the war and the United States's policy toward those powers. Only an incident at the very end of the war against Japan tells us something about Acheson in this regard. Joseph Grew, the former ambassador to Japan, had been selected for the post of Undersecretary upon Hull's departure and Stettinius's brief appointment as Secretary. Grew's determination to modify the unconditional surrender terms for Japan to the extent of retaining the emperor drew "a violent reaction on the part of Mr. Acheson and Mr. MacLeish." * Grew's proposal appealed to them "neither on grounds of political inclination nor in relation to their functions in the State Department." Acheson pointed out, "The institution of the throne is an anachronistic, feudal institution perfectly adapted to the use of anachronistic, feudal-minded groups within the country." [11] Acheson also reported that Congress would react strongly to any suggestion that Hirohito be allowed to remain as emperor.

Although Grew finally got his way, the strength of Acheson's opposition is significant.** At the time it was cited as an additional reason for identifying Acheson with the "liberal" clan in the State Department; later

---

* Eugene Dooman testimony cited in Len Giovanitti and Fred Freed, *The Decision to Drop the Bomb* (New York: Coward, McCann, 1965), p. 93. Dooman's testimony before the Senate Judiciary Committee a few years later formed part of the case against Acheson's alleged mishandling of Far Eastern policy. Dooman was in the Far Eastern Division at a time when lines were forming among Foreign Service officers concerning United States policy toward Nationalist China.

** Like other episodes of this period, Acheson's opposition to Grew would figure prominently in the later campaign by Joseph McCarthy and others to get rid of Acheson. In his Wheeling, West Virginia, speech first attacking the State Department for harboring Communists, McCarthy charged that Joseph Grew, who as Undersecretary favored prosecuting John Service for his involvement in the Amerasia case, was opposed by Dean Acheson and forced to resign. "Two days after Grew's successor, Dean Acheson, took over as Undersecretary of State, this man—John Service—who had been picked up by the F.B.I., and who had previously urged that Communism was the best hope of China, was not only reinstated in the State Department but promoted, and finally, under Acheson, placed in charge of all placements and promotions." Acheson's opposition to Grew on the matter of the emperor was held against him by more conservative types in the department and became the basis for the charge that Acheson had master-minded Grew's ouster as part of a plot to install a soft if not pro–Communist orientation on the department.

it was used against him by Senator Pat McCarran in the Senate Judiciary Committee hearings into the Amerasia Case. Upon his return from duty in China, Foreign Service Officer John Stewart Service unwittingly loaned copies of his diplomatic cables to Philip Jaffe, editor of *Amerasia,* a left-leaning magazine on Asian affairs. When the FBI raided the offices of *Amerasia,* Service became implicated and was later arrested, only to have the charges against him dismissed. But the consequences of this case for Acheson were in the future. At the time Acheson shared the wartime conviction, which was certainly not limited to liberals, that the emperor was as much of an instigator of aggression as Hitler, and that he ought to be permanently removed from a position in which he could again do harm. However, the vehemence with which Acheson clung to his position in the face of reasoned arguments for retaining the emperor under American control may be indicative of the presence of strong emotional feelings about "the enemy." It also suggests a lack of knowledge or intuitive feeling for Asia which stands out by contrast with his instinctive grasp of European diplomacy.*

These are good examples of Acheson's willingness to defend positions he thought to be right. Issues which a more discrete or compromising person would have avoided were occasions for the sharp assertion of Achesonian will. Doubtless there were many issues on which he had to defer to others, but there were a sufficient number of showdowns to indicate that we are dealing with a leader who had not yet achieved the ability to control or subdue his emotions. The sense of challenge or provocation seemed to arise with startling rapidity, reach a climax, and then pass. He did not let go aggressively in ways that were obviously or seriously detrimental to his success, but he made enemies who were to come back to haunt him.**

---

* He may also have learned something from this episode. When he became Undersecretary scarcely two months later, he did not automatically align himself with the anti–Soviet hardliners. He was among those who supported Henry Stimson's recommendation that the United States must try to reach some kind of atomic control agreement with Russia before a nuclear arms race took over.

** Another such episode involved Pat Hurley. After being invalided out of active military service in 1944, Hurley was attached to the Middle East Supply Center. He returned to Washington bitterly condemning British imperialism and urging that the U.S. dissociate itself from Britain and espouse democracy. Acheson admitted that he may have been too brusque with Hurley's proposal, describing it in the phrase of one of his assistants as "messianic globaloney." At a subsequent meeting, Hurley accused Acheson's assistant of putting that phrase in a memorandum to the Secretary. Acheson brusquely rebuked Hurley for implying that a memorandum Acheson had written was the responsibility of a junior officer. The fat was in the fire. A bitter row ensued between the two men. Eighteen months later, upon his return from China, Hurley accused the Department of State, the Foreign Service officers, and by implication

Assistant Secretary of State for Congressional Relations

The second area in which wartime service gave Acheson a chance to develop his experience was, by one of those strokes of irony less rare than people imagine, in his relations with the Congress. On November 27, 1944, Hull resigned as Secretary of State, bringing to an end a long and increasingly unhappy relationship with the President. In his place, Roosevelt nominated Edward Stettinius, former vice-president of General Motors and chairman of the board of United States Steel.

Stettinius was determined to reshuffle the department hierarchy and Acheson's post as Assistant Secretary for Economic Affairs was assigned to Will Clayton, chairman of the board of the Texas-based cotton firm of Clayton, Anderson. Acheson was told that he could have the post of "congressional relations and international conferences" with the implication that he would probably rather resign. Rather than go out of office in a departmental reshuffle, Acheson masked his chagrin and accepted the offer, but when it came time for the swearing-in ceremony for Stettinius and the other six new appointees, Acheson gave malicious vent to his pique. It happened at a press conference after the ceremony when Stettinius introduced each of the new recruits to the newsmen. Last, Stettinius introduced Dean Acheson, who had been sworn in four years earlier. The next thing Acheson heard himself saying into the microphone was: "These little pigs went to market, but this little pig stayed home." [12] Stettinius was not amused.

In spite of his dissatisfaction, Acheson poured into the assignment on the Hill all of the energy and skill with which he formerly tackled more legal and bureaucratic functions. The first thing Acheson did was to establish a system in the Department of State whereby all congressional requests for help of any kind would be funneled through his staff. In this way, as well as by encouraging a judicious amount of overseas junketing by important committee members, Acheson soon built up a reservoir of goodwill. Next Acheson assigned important State Department bills to each staff member to be watched over as they progressed through Congress.

Acheson reserved for himself the task of working with the leading foreign-policy figures in the House and Senate and, in Woodrow Wilson's phrase, applying the "oil of government" to the legislative machinery. Perhaps because the policies which he had to sell were not his own, and therefore he was more at ease, or because the times and the men were propitious to what had to be accomplished, Acheson soon found himself

---

Acheson and Secretary of State Byrnes of selling him and China out. In a certain sense, this was the opening gun for the soft-on-Communism campaign against Acheson.

enjoying the give and take of congressional relations. For once dealing with the political realities of the Congress did not impair his effectiveness.

Doubtless, too, this was a situation in which his untiring efforts and gentlemanly style paid off. He was soon consorting with the Senate and House pachyderms at their favorite waterhole—the liquor-lined office of the Senate secretary, Les Biffle. There the legislative calendar was fixed, the nose counts taken, and the anticipated necessary deals worked out. "The effectiveness of the decisions by this group," Acheson later recorded, "came not from its sheer power to put them through the Senate but from its knowledge of how to put them through and the willingness to put its knowledge to work." [13]

When Roosevelt died on April 12, 1945, Acheson was in a position to guide the remaining legislation through the Congress for the new President, Harry S Truman. His first impressions of Truman were highly favorable but he was not a member of the President's immediate circle of advisers. His job was to get the mass of legislation on which the postwar peace was to be built through the Senate.

The intense satisfaction that he obtained from mingling on equal terms with leaders of the Senate and House power structure more than made up for the psychic cost of scurrying around plying his wares to the lesser lights. Here was a situation closer to his heart than ever he had anticipated—that of associating with a relatively small number of dedicated lawmakers doing the work of the world in an urbane and civilized style. Acheson's letters to his daughter Mary suggest, in a combination of uneasiness and disbelief, that he might actually be enjoying the debauch. "I had a fine lunch today in the office of the Secretary of the Senate with Senators and House members. A real Texas ham was offered and whisky. I am getting to be a real politician." [14]

We have already noted an earlier comment to his daughter on the same subject: "This is a low life but a merry one." [15] But on June 25, after a day of glad-handing and bonhomie attendant on the passage of one of his bills, he wrote: "This business of talking to everyone and attending meetings all day is a shiftless way of conducting oneself." [16]

Perhaps the most delightful passage of all is his account of dining with Congresswoman Jessie Sumner with whom he had just had some sharp exchanges.

I was asked to sit at a table with Jessie Sumner of Illinois, the worst of the rabble-rousing isolationists. . . . We got along famously. She is a grand old girl. . . . We became great friends and are going to lunch again. I often wonder whether I have any principles at all.[17]

So we see Acheson's hauteur melting just enough for him to enjoy those he once would have scorned and to achieve a string of smashing congressional successes. The Trade Agreements Act, the Bretton Woods Agreements, the Food and Agriculture Bill, the United Nations Charter, and a number of lesser items were all passed by solid majorities during his tenure.

It had been agreed that Acheson would be free to resign his post upon completion of the war against Japan. The President and his Secretary of State returned from Potsdam on August 7. On August 8 Acheson submitted his resignation, which was accepted in a warm letter from the President on August 9. That night he dined at the home of Eugene Meyer, publisher of the *Washington Post*, with Fred Vinson, Secretary of the Treasury and a close friend of Truman's, and with Wayne Coy, an assistant editor of the *Post*. Two days later the Achesons left Washington for Saranac Lake, where their daughter Mary Bundy was convalescing from tuberculosis.

If the last six months had been better and more satisfying than the previous years, they had still not led anywhere. Little did he suspect, however, that even before he had arrived at Saranac Lake, Byrnes would be telephoning him to return as Undersecretary in place of Joseph Grew.

CHAPTER

5

UNDERSECRETARY OF STATE: 1945–1947

ACHESON LEFT the State Department on August 9, 1945, fully believing that another phase of his career as a public servant was at an end. When Joseph C. Grew had resigned as Undersecretary of State following Potsdam, Acheson's name had not figured in speculation about his successor because it was believed that Acheson was bent on returning to private law practice. Actually, James Byrnes had been too busy to give the appointment of a new Undersecretary much thought.

No sooner had Acheson left than Byrnes realized how sorely the department would miss his experience and skills. Byrnes had found it easy to get along with Acheson, and he became increasingly aware that if he, as Secretary, were to be in attendance at foreign ministers' meetings for extended periods of time he would need someone in Washington to run the department and maintain the routine planning. Acheson had also come to President Truman's attention for his successful liaison work with the Congress on behalf of the United Nations Charter and the Bretton Woods agreements.

Acheson and his wife had barely arrived at Saranac Lake when a call came from Byrnes. Would Acheson return as Undersecretary? The promotion which had eluded him when Stettinius had appointed Grew to the post was now offered to him.

Acheson's initial reaction was one of uncertainty. Experience told him that the task would be a frustrating one, and he had no illusions about the troubles and inefficiencies prevailing within the department. While the subsequent frustrations were all that he expected them to be, Acheson later considered the decision to return to State to have been "one of the most fortunate of my life." [1] The deep underlying desire to make an impact upon his times was not easily resisted.

Acheson's appointment was scarcely noticed in the swirl of excitement and exultation surrounding the Japanese surrender. Byrnes was due to leave for the London Foreign Ministers' Conference on September 5 (a departure postponed until the 18th), and Acheson had to be ready to step into his shoes. One comment on the appointment is interesting because it came from I. F. Stone, who was almost ecstatic about the choice.

He has been pro–de Gaulle, anti–Franco, strongly opposed to the admission of Argentina to the U.N., and friendly to the Soviet Union . . . of all the men now in the department, Acheson was by far the best choice for Undersecretary, and it is no small advantage to pick a man who already knows a good deal about the inner workings.[2]

Acheson was Acting Secretary even before he had received Senate confirmation as Undersecretary. Confirmation would have been a routine matter had not Acheson's outspokenness involved him in a contretemps with Senator Kenneth Wherry (R–Neb.), a senator with whom he was destined to have some very bitter exchanges. It came about in the following manner. General MacArthur, from his post as Supreme Commander in Tokyo, let it be known that because the Japanese were behaving with such admirable docility, American occupation forces could soon be cut to 200,000 men. The circumstances at the time were such that every congressman was under pressure to "bring the boys home." MacArthur's statement had the effect of contributing to this pressure and thereby undermining the policy of the government. The Pentagon prudently ignored MacArthur's statement, and Truman was careful to avoid criticizing MacArthur publicly. By contrast, Acheson held a press conference at which he criticized MacArthur's statement and noted that occupation policy was being made in Washington, not in the field.[3] When Senator Wherry demanded that Acheson retract his criticism of MacArthur, he got a curt letter of rebuttal from the still unconfirmed Undersecretary of State. For this rather imprudent performance, Acheson earned Wherry's lifelong enmity. When Acheson's nomination came before the Senate on September 24, Wherry succeeded in rallying eleven Senate Republicans to vote with him on a motion to return Acheson's name to the Foreign Relations Committee. On the actual vote to confirm, only Wherry voted against him, but in an unusual move, Tom Connally (D–Tex.), chairman of the Foreign Relations Committee, declared that the Senate would "never have voted for Mr. Acheson's confirmation unless it had been implicitly understood that he would not have a predominant voice in foreign policy."[4]

The unusual influence which Acheson as Undersecretary exerted upon foreign policy between August 1945 and June 1947 was due in part to his personal qualities and in part to the consequence of special circumstances. With Byrnes and his successor, George Catlett Marshall, gone from Washington during much of their tenure as Secretaries of State, it fell to Acheson to advise the President, to administer the Department of

State, and to oversee the day-to-day conduct of American foreign policy. President Truman, unlike Roosevelt, did not consider himself a ready-made expert on international affairs. He needed steady, informed advice, for which he turned increasingly to Acheson. The forcefulness and clarity of Acheson's thought appealed to the President's penchant for quick, clear decisions, and the two men soon established a congenial working relationship. Acheson also fitted in with Truman's conception of the Presidency.

Byrnes's casual way of administering the department and his necessarily frequent and extended absences from Washington (he was away for 350 of his 562 days in office) created special difficulties. Furthermore, because Byrnes operated with a small staff almost independent of the department, it was frequently difficult to get him to give his attention to policy problems within the department or to pay attention to the President's wishes—especially because Byrnes considered himself more qualified than Truman to be President and frequently failed to communicate to Truman his plans and decisions. As a result Acheson frequently had to witness and temper the President's exasperation without being disloyal to Byrnes. Despite the potential for ill feelings that the situation posed, Acheson managed to retain the confidence of both men. The responsibility that he now shared for the direction of America's affairs brought out a patience and control that he had not always previously exercised. His gay and irreverent wit still sparkled over the dinner table, but he showed more willingness to suffer fools if not gladly then at least patiently. According to Archibald MacLeish, it was only after Acheson became Undersecretary that a "remarkable personal growth occurred. Dean rapidly took on a style and stature which I had not expected." Part of this growth was accounted for by a greater control over his temper and a more philosophic approach in his dealings with others.

Acheson was more at ease with himself because he was increasingly at the center of power and exerting an unprecedented influence on a historic transformation in America's world situation.

One of the first things Acheson did to get the department to run more efficiently and to make it more responsive to the needs of the President was to set up a daily 9:30 A.M. meeting with all the assistant secretaries and bureau chiefs. This gathering provided him with a means, which he later developed in many other ways, of making assistant secretaries responsive to the need for action and aware of the whole range of problems confronting the department. At the end of his term as Undersecretary, those who participated in the nine-thirty meetings presented Acheson with a silver carafe and tray from the "officers who have enjoyed and benefited from participation in that uniquely Achesonian organization, the Nine-thirty Club—or Prayer Meeting." [5] It was signed among others by Charles Bohlen, Will Clayton, George Kennan, Alger Hiss, and Dean

Rusk. The nine-thirty meeting began a career-long effort by Acheson to make the Department of State the most potent force possible in the design and execution of American foreign policy. He never fully succeeded, but he came as close as any Undersecretary and Secretary of State ever came to making the department an effective and responsive instrument of the President's will and of information and expertise in the conduct of U.S. foreign policy.

The Atomic Bomb

One of the great issues facing the United States was what to do about the atomic bomb. It was part of man's unenviable lot that the weapon which brought the war to an end should also open a new era in world politics—one fraught with the knowledge that man had given birth to a form of power which could destroy civilization.

Human nature had not been transformed by the unlocking of the secret of atomic energy. Two attitudes toward the bomb immediately manifested themselves. Within the United States a large number of people immediately saw the bomb as giving the United States a miraculous guarantee of its future peace and security. Even President Truman shared the wonderfully reassuring conviction that what America had wrought no other nation could conceivably duplicate. In an old-fashioned bull session with newsmen on October 7, 1945, near the little Tennessee resort town of Tiptonville, where he had spent the day fishing, the President gave vent to that innocent pride in the superiority of the American productive system which had produced the bomb. "It was idle," Truman declared, "to talk of withholding the scientific knowledge. . . . But engineering secrets were something else again. The United States could not share them. As a matter of fact, no other country could use them. Only the United States had the combination of industrial capacity and resources necessary to produce the bomb." [6]

The second view held that the production of the bomb showed that man was becoming a menace to himself. His moral and political capacities were being outstripped by his scientific and technological genius. Unless statesmen transferred control of the bomb to some international agency, it would become the cause of a nuclear arms race which would put civilization in jeopardy. The nuclear scientists who had developed the bomb were especially determined to use their influence to overcome nationalistic inhibitions against sharing the secret of the bomb. And on September 9, 1945, a month after Hiroshima, James Franck and sixty-four other Chicago-based scientists released to the press a petition urging the President to share the secrets of the bomb with other nations to avoid an atomic armaments race. [7]

Within the government Secretary of State Byrnes, Secretary of the Navy James Forrestal, and others constituted a dominant view that the United States should hold on to the monopoly of both the bomb and its know-how. In Byrnes's case the difficulties which he was experiencing in negotiating with the Russians prompted a negative view of both the likelihood and the desirability of trying to negotiate an atomic control agreement with the Soviet Union.[8] By contrast, Henry Stimson, retiring Secretary of War, presented to the President a three-page memorandum on September 12 proposing that the United States and Britain make a direct offer to Russia of full partnership in further developing and controlling atomic energy.

When the Cabinet met on September 18, Acheson, as Acting Secretary, heard Stimson, speaking extemporaneously, argue that the scientific and, by implication, the technological secrets for the development of atomic energy could not be kept secret; therefore, the United States had little to lose and everything to gain by making a direct offer of an atomic partnership to Russia. In the ensuing discussion on the Stimson proposal, the Cabinet was divided. Partly out of conviction and partly out of loyalty to Stimson, Acheson supported the principle of Stimson's proposal. Most of the Cabinet, however, opposed giving away anything to the Russians. Forrestal put it succinctly: "The Russians, like the Japanese, are essentially Oriental in their thinking, and until we have a longer experience with them . . . it seems doubtful that we should endeavor to buy their understanding and sympathy." [9]

Despite the negative response from the majority of the Cabinet, the debate over what America's policy should be had at least been opened. And moderate and cautious though Acheson's position was, it put him, in effect, in favor of some approach to the Soviet Union, a position which was not shared either by his superior, Byrnes, or by a majority of the President's top advisers.*

Stimson's message had called forth a policy discussion but it was still not a policy. And Acheson's immediate attention was too taken up with preparing legislation for domestic control of atomic energy to give much

---

* This does not mean that they had a plan for employing the atomic bomb for some form of diplomatic leverage or blackmail. As Lynn E. Davis observes: "The successful testing of the bomb did not produce a new or tougher policy of opposition to the Soviet Union's Eastern European policy at Potsdam." *The Cold War Begins: Soviet American Conflict over Eastern Europe* (Princeton: Princeton University Press, 1974), fn. p. 297. See also John Lewis Gaddis, *The United States and the Origins of the Cold War 1941–1947* (New York: Columbia University Press, 1972), pp. 248–252. Martin J. Sherwin, *A World Destroyed: The Atomic Bomb and the Grand Alliance* (New York: Alfred A. Knopf, 1975) reports that the bomb was seen all along as an American advantage that would only reluctantly be given up but was not actively brandished as an instrument of U.S. diplomacy.

time to the international side.* With congressional interest mounting as various senators fought for priority of place on the prestigious committees that would be charged with legislating on atomic energy, and with the scientists more waspish and distrustful than ever, the Administration was under urgent pressure, even if Truman did not know it, to come up with a comprehensive plan for domestic controls.

Under Stimson the War Department had already prepared a bill authorizing creation of a nine-man commission to oversee the management of America's atomic energy resources, but because its terms were weighted in favor of military security, the bill was under fire from the scientific community and others opposed to the threat of American militarism.

Because Stimson was retiring and because, following Hiroshima, virtually all discussions of the bomb had been cast in an international context, the State Department had agreed to sponsor the Administration's draft of the bill. Acheson as Acting Secretary quickly found himself at the center of the bitter debate over domestic control. In the absence of Byrnes, Acheson held back from committing the department as much as possible, but it soon became apparent that unless Truman translated his own thinking and that of Secretary Stimson into some concrete form linking both domestic and international programs, Presidential freedom of action would become severely limited. Acheson found the President beset by all the other complications facing the nation and still without any clear sense of what he wanted to do.[10] It was characteristic of Truman's performance at this time that having originally supported the War Department's plan, he now discovered that the bill would make the proposed Atomic Energy Commission virtually independent of Presidential control, and now he had to fight to have the bill changed.

Sensing the dilemma in which the President found himself, Acheson threw aside his hesitations about acting. Along with Robert Patterson, who had replaced Stimson as head of the War Department, Acheson joined forces with Robert Oppenheimer and with George L. Harrison, former president of the New York Life Insurance Company and a wartime consultant to Stimson on the Manhattan Project, to clear the way for legislation governing the atomic establishment that was more weighted in the direction of civilian and Executive control. Moving at forced draft and with the aid of Herbert Marks, a bright young State Department

---

* Because whatever form domestic control took would have a bearing on international control, Acheson was assigned the task of working with the White House and the Army in preparing the Administration's legislative proposals for atomic energy control. Richard G. Hewlett and Oscar E. Anderson, Jr., *A History of the United States Atomic Energy Commission,* Vol. I, *The New World, 1939–1946* (University Park: Pennsylvania State University Press, 1962), p. 423.

legal adviser, Acheson reached agreement with Patterson and Harrison on a Presidential message which would put Congress on the desired track.

The message affords a good insight into Acheson's thinking. In addition to calling for a civilian commission to control all domestic sources and uses of atomic energy, it also recognized that atomic energy involved "forces of nature too dangerous to fit into our usual concepts." [11] Acheson emphasized the scientists' conclusion that "what we know [about] the bomb is not a secret which we can keep to ourselves." [12] There could be little doubt that the Russians were working on nuclear weapons:

The joint development of this discovery with the U.K. and Canada must appear to the Soviet Union to be unanswerable evidence of an Anglo–American combination against them. . . . It is impossible that a government as powerful and power conscious as the Soviet Government could fail to react vigorously to this situation. It must and will exert every energy to restore the loss of power which this situation has produced.[13]

Under the circumstances, the message continued, "the advantage of being ahead in such a race is nothing compared with not having the race."

Acheson recognized that his suggestion would encounter political difficulties at home. The public and Congress might be unprepared to accept a policy involving substantial disclosures of atomic secrets to the Soviet Union. But Acheson saw no alternative. The United States had to find a way of assuring the Russians that it did not intend to keep a monopoly of atomic weapons while at the same time educating the American people to the fact that the atomic secrets could not be kept indefinitely. Acheson's attitude of mind contrasted strongly with that of Forrestal, Bernard Baruch, and others who preferred to regard the bomb as a form of private property owned collectively by the American people, to be licensed out only to private firms for capitalist purposes.

On the basis of Acheson's recommendation, the President's message to Congress of October 3 contained the strong suggestion that the very "hope of civilization" depended upon "a satisfactory arrangement for control of this discovery," and that a satisfactory arrangement for control "can no longer rely on the slow progress of time to develop a program of mutual control among nations." [14] Additionally, the President's message informed Congress that he would "initiate discussions first with our associates in this discovery, Great Britain and Canada, and then with other nations," by which Acheson meant the Soviet Union.

While Congress proceeded to get into a wrangle with both the scientific community and with the President over the extent of the plenary power to be vested in the domestic Atomic Energy Commission, progress on international control bogged down completely. Instead of proceeding immediately to examine the feasibility and practicality of establishing an international control system that would protect American interests, nothing was done. The failure to initiate studies was due in part to Truman's assumption that the American monopoly of the industrial know-how could not be broken and therefore that haste was not necessary, and in part to the disorganized state of Administration planning in which the separation of diplomatic and military problems defeated any concerted approach to such a new and complex matter as atomic control. The lack of an adequate Executive study left Truman at a disadvantage in dealing with a Congress that had very definite views. A poll of congressmen in late September showed fifty-five out of sixty-one responding senators and representatives unequivocally opposed to sharing knowledge of the bomb with *any* country.[15]

The public, just as firmly opposed to sharing America's atomic know-how, was occupied with two contradictory notions: (1) that international control was feasible and desirable, and (2) that the United States need not give up any element of its security to attain it. While backstopping the President's campaign for civilian control of atomic energy at home, Acheson was also casting about for some means of bridging this gulf. Unfortunately, Secretary Byrnes, returning from a futile Foreign Ministers' Conference in late October and exasperated by weeks of wrangling with Molotov, still had no taste for or confidence in negotiating an arms-control agreement with the Russians. Whatever benefits Byrnes had expected from the A-bomb to improve America's bargaining position had been proved illusory: the American delegation had run into a stone wall at the London meeting of the Foreign Ministers' council. The new weapon may have impressed the Kremlin leaders—they apparently ordered a quick acceleration of Russia's atomic development program—but Molotov successfully avoided any outward show of concern, and Soviet diplomats showed only the most perfunctory interest in American plans for international control of atomic energy.

But if the Soviet Union was holding firm, and the American government was wrangling, other governments were not prepared to procrastinate. The bomb was too frightening a thing to be left untended; and just as nature abhors a vacuum, so other nations abhorred a monopoly of atomic power, especially if they thought they had some claim to a voice in its development and control. The British government believed that by right of its wartime pooling of its nuclear effort with America it had acquired the right of access to America's atomic technology. Now, just when Britain was ready to embark on its own atomic development program, this access was somehow being denied them.

New Labor Prime Minister Clement Attlee demanded a meeting to discuss the situation. Truman had no choice but to acquiesce, and on

October 31 the White House announced that the prime minister would arrive in time for talks to begin on November 11.

With Attlee and his entourage due to arrive in ten days, Acheson still could not get Byrnes interested in the issues. Fortunately, Vannevar Bush, president of the Carnegie Institution and former director of the Office of Science Research and Development, took the initiative and prepared a memorandum which emphasized the need to conduct the negotiations with the British in such a way as to open the door simultaneously for step-by-step negotiations with the Soviet Union. Unless the Administration took immediate cognizance of the temptation facing the hostile and distrustful Russians to develop their own atomic capability, Bush explained, it would be too late to avert a nuclear arms race. The Bush memorandum, which proposed giving foreign scientists access to America's basic research labs as a means of inducing Russia to start collaboration, was very much in line with Stimson's and Acheson's views, and with the gist of the President's October 3 announcement that as soon as negotiations had begun with Britain and Canada, they would be extended to include other nations, the intention being not to isolate Russia.

But when Attlee, Truman, and Mackenzie King, the Canadian prime minister, met in Washington on November 10, they were immediately caught up in the frenzied need of every summit conference to arrive at an agreed-upon declaration in the quickest possible time. As a consequence, Truman agreed to a course of action that Stimson had specifically disapproved and that the President had agreed was the wrong one. Instead of providing for a direct approach to Russia, which had previously been considered essential, the three Anglo–Saxon leaders agreed that atomic control should be handled through the United Nations before "a large group of nations that included many small ones of no demonstrated power." [16] Acheson was dismayed. Had it not been agreed that the only hope of inducing the Russians to cooperate lay in treating them as the only other significant bargaining partner? Yet here they were adopting an exactly opposite course of action, which could only deepen Soviet determination to get on with its own atomic bomb!

The other concern which Acheson, Bush, and others had had was that the *wartime* basis of Anglo–American atomic collaboration be amended so as *not* to have it impair American chances of negotiating successfully with the Soviet Union on the all-important question of international control. Logically any new agreement with the British should have been held off pending negotiations with the USSR so as to avoid creating the impression of an atomic bloc being formed at Russia's expense. Such negotiations were no task for a hastily convened one- or two-day summit conference. But in order to placate the British, whose prime minister was

more interested in what Britain was to get than in the adverse impact
upon the ever-suspicious Russians, the United States acquiesced, in principle at least, in continuing the preferential arrangement whereby Britain
—but not Russia—benefited from a full and effective exchange of scientific
(but not industrial or commercial) information. To top off this fiasco,
Truman's failure to include representatives of the Senate in the discussions gave rise to bitter and suspicious resentments in senatorial minds
that the President was indeed giving away America's atomic secrets. If
any more was needed, this meeting permanently convinced Acheson that
diplomacy required careful preparations and that summit meetings were
the height of folly.

Perhaps these events help to explain the blunt and unsparing criticism
of American policy-making to which Acheson gave vent a few nights later
in an address to the Maryland Historical Society. In a speech remarkable
for its brutal candor, Acheson declared that American policy was failing
because public officials were not explaining and sponsoring a foreign
policy with appropriate vigor. It was their responsibility to "put forward
a program they believe in." They "cannot merely look around and try to
find out what the people want and set that up in a program for them
to approve." Yet that was what the leadership was doing. "I venture to
say," Acheson continued, "that I can state in three sentences what the
undercurrent is as the 'popular' attitude toward a foreign policy today.
Here they are:

> (1) Bring the boys home
> (2) Don't be a Santa Claus
> (3) Don't be pushed around." [17]

Acheson did not believe that America could play its part in international
affairs if it completely scrapped its military establishment, refused to use
its tremendous economic power for constructive purposes, and then proceeded to be truculent and uncompromising. Either the Administration
would have to educate the American people, or it would have to ignore
the people, which he believed to be an improper approach to policy-making in a democracy. He feared the emotional reaction that was building
up in America against Russia, an emotional reaction that was not leading
to any constructive change in American policies. "Emotional reactions
cannot change facts." Secondly, "there is no possible sense in the United
States undertaking to play a Machiavellian game of slick horse trading.
. . . We should not think that the smart thing to do is to engage in secret
pacts with the United Kingdom, or the Soviet Union, or France. . . . We
must have an intelligent . . . foreign policy which will stress the interests of the United States." [18] Specifically, Acheson urged that the American people get behind the loans to Britain and France and international

agreements designed to support peace and economic recovery. For the time his was a pretty progressive and drastic speech.

Up until now Acheson had not had to take a public position on the burning issue of Soviet–American relations. He had shown himself strongly in favor of reaching agreement with the Soviet Union on international control of atomic energy and on other issues, including possibly some form of credits. But he was also aware from the cables and newspaper reports reaching the department that Soviet authorities were behaving in a heavy-handed and repressive way throughout their zone in Eastern Europe.[19] What were Soviet intentions and what ought the United States do about them? Neither American policy nor the American people had been prepared for what was happening. If Roosevelt had understood that Soviet occupation meant Soviet dictation, he had not explained it to the American people. If the United States did not approve of what the USSR was now doing, what could it now do about it? In point of fact, very little. It could protest and object, as Byrnes had done at the Foreign Ministers' meetings in London, but that had gotten nowhere. It could refuse to approve or give economic backing, as George Kennan recommended, to the regimes which were being imposed on the peoples of Eastern Europe. But Washington had neither the means nor the will to contest militarily what was being done. In fact it was not at all clear in the Department of State or in the White House what significance should be put upon Soviet actions because it was not yet entirely clear how they affected American strategic interests.

There were, of course, the Admiral Leahys, the Vandenbergs, and the Forrestals, whose stock in trade was to reinforce the President's own initial inclination to brand the Soviets as aggressors and to label anyone who disagreed with them appeasers. Acheson did not agree. Like Truman, Acheson was prepared to follow the line traced out by Roosevelt with the same growing uneasiness that Roosevelt had felt about Soviet intentions shortly before his death. But unless the U.S. had a policy and the means of policy implementation, a break with the Soviet Union over these matters would accomplish nothing. Until the Administration could determine the strategic significance of what was going on in Eastern Europe and define a policy to cope with Soviet intentions, policy had to be made from day to day on the basis of the diplomatic cables. And that was about all Acheson was doing.

The one situation in the autumn of 1945 in which Acheson was directly responsible involved Czechoslovakia, which had been jointly occupied by Soviet and American forces at the war's end. In July, Jan Masaryk, the Czechoslovakian foreign minister, reflecting what appeared to be Soviet pressure, asked for the withdrawal of United States forces. Ambassador Lawrence Steinhardt opposed the demand and recommended that American forces be withdrawn only in line with Soviet withdrawals. Acheson supported Steinhardt, noting in a memo to Secretary of War Stimson that the presence of American forces was "the most concrete and telling evidence of our interest in the restoration of stable and democratic conditions in Czechoslovakia" and would have a "beneficial political effect on other countries in the region." [20] Following Acheson's advice, Truman suggested simultaneous Soviet and American withdrawals, a proposal with which Stalin fortunately concurred. A democracy was installed with a Communist premier, but this would only last as long as Czechoslovakia showed complete subservience to Moscow's wishes.

Actions such as these, while indicative of Acheson's growing awareness of the crisis in our relations with Russia, in no way reflected a clear and unambiguous design for frustrating Soviet plans for Eastern Europe. Quite the contrary. The Administration was still probing for the significance of a range of Soviet activities that had hardly been anticipated when postwar plans and agreements were being made at Teheran and Yalta.

The uncertainty of Acheson's own thinking was evident when he agreed to speak before an American–Soviet Friendship Rally in Madison Square Garden on November 14. Had he known how pro–Soviet the audience was going to be, he might have thought twice. Acheson admitted that Soviet–American relations were deteriorating.[21] Nevertheless, Acheson did not start out remembering all the evils associated with Stalinism, such as the great purges, nor did he analogize so readily as some between Hitler's Germany and Stalin's Russia. He was still hopeful that the past history of Russian–American friendship might deter tension from turning into hostility.

We understand and agree with [the Soviet Union] that to have friendly governments along their borders is essential both for the security of the Soviet Union and for the peace of the world. . . . But it seems equally clear to us that the interest in security must take into account and respect other basic interests of nations and men, such as the interest of other people to choose the general surroundings of their own lives and all men to be secure in their persons.[22]

Acheson's reasoning seemed to be taken straight from the text of Roosevelt's Four Freedoms. The United States could not feel secure while, with no indication of where they would end, undemocratic changes were being imposed in violation of the Atlantic Charter. "We believe that the adjustment of interests should take place short of the point where persuasion and firmness become coercion, where a knock on the door at night strikes terror into men and women." [23]

Boos and hisses greeted these lines. But Acheson went on to explain the dilemma of American foreign policy. Since it was obvious that a contradiction existed between the right of a great power to define its sphere of influence and the right of other peoples to be free from coercion, this contradiction had to be resolved by each side agreeing to adjust its particular interest in security "to the general interest in security" and "to the principles and organizations which have been agreed upon to ensure it." * This may sound excessively one-sided in view of America's relative immunity from danger and the more difficult circumstances under which Russia has had historically to labor in guaranteeing its existence. No doubt Acheson was being somewhat naive in believing that the general principles of the United Nations could afford the same assurance to the Soviet Union as they did to the United States, but if they could not, the United States then faced the problem of not knowing on what principles its interests should be founded. Was there to be one rule for the Soviet Union and another for everyone else?

Reflected in what Acheson said was the dilemma facing American foreign policy as he and others in the State Department saw it. "Once committed to the Atlantic Charter principles, State Department officials [including Acheson] saw only costs—in terms of American public opinion, the reconstruction of postwar peace, and the possibility of success for other United States goals—in not maintaining the integrity of these principles in Eastern Europe." [24] Either the Soviet Union would have to show that America's present reliance upon the United Nations was workable or the United States would have to find some other alternative. Here Acheson was voicing the deeper significance of the Soviet–American disagreement over the principle of self-determination for the peoples of Eastern Europe. The continued demobilization of American armed forces and the signing of the peace treaties depended upon the guarantee that the principles of the UN Charter were going to be made to work.** If these were

---

* Department of State *Bulletin*, November 18, 1945, pp. 787–798. Revisionist critics ignore the logic of the choices that faced the Administration. If it was wrong to expect the Soviet Union to conform to the principles of self-determination enunciated in the Yalta Declaration on liberated Europe and in the UN Charter to the detriment of *their* security interests, then the U.S. was inevitably bound to reconsider whether those same principles were an adequate basis and whether the UN was a sufficient guarantee of American interests. Henry Wallace and Robert Taft offered one logical alternative: the entire liquidation of American involvement in Europe. But then why had we fought the war in the first place? And if Europe succumbed to chaos and if Communism was clearly a possibility, would we not face the necessity of liberating it all over again?

** These were the terms Roosevelt had in mind when he said that United States forces would not remain in Europe more than two years beyond the war's end. But these were not the conditions emerging. For the importance of the provisions of the Atlantic Charter and the UN Charter together with the wartime statements by Presi-

not to be operative, the United States would soon be driven to look for other bases for its foreign policy. The handwriting was on the wall. Given massive uncertainties about Soviet intentions, the situation in Europe could not be allowed to deteriorate indefinitely. Too much was at stake to let American foreign policy take its traditional course into isolationism and neglect.

The British Loan

Acheson was already acting upon his determination to do whatever necessary to prevent an additional area of international deterioration—that in European economic affairs. Roosevelt had assumed that by providing our allies with Lend–Lease we would not be repeating the mistake we had made after World War I—that of expecting our allies under straitened economic circumstances to repay their wartime loans and obligations. Like generals who are always prepared to fight the last war, not the one they actually face, Lend–Lease would have been a fine solution to the World War I situation from which the allies emerged basically intact; but no one had anticipated the utter destruction and debilitation with which Europe emerged from World War II. Even Britain was ruined, in debt to the tune of tens of billions of dollars. There was no way Europe could recover from the war and meet its indebtedness without massive financial assistance from the United States.

Between the governments of Britain and America, or more especially between the economic specialists on both sides of the Atlantic, there had been slowly emerging an expectation that Britain would need some form of financial assistance after the war. But this nexus of understanding did not extend to the American people or even to the Congress. Furthermore, this understanding, to which Acheson was privy, was complicated by radically opposed British and American ideas for solving the crisis. On the American side, rabid distrust of Britain's imperial preference system, combined with a crude determination in certain quarters to secure an abolition of Britain's restrictive trading and financial practices, produced an attitude of mind holding that if Britain wanted a loan it would have to denude itself of all economic protectionism and put itself at the mercy of America. According to one British writer, this was an attitude "which for its ruthless and Olympian incomprehension of the real issues," could

---

dent Roosevelt concerning the creation of representative governments in Eastern Europe, see Lynn E. Davis, *The Cold War Begins: Soviet-American Conflict over Eastern Europe* (Princeton, N.J.: Princeton University Press, 1974), pp. 372–388.

"only be compared with the attitude adopted by President Wilson in the rather similar circumstances of 1918." *

The principal American negotiators for the British Loan were Will Clayton and Fred Vinson. For passion and obduracy in the cause of free trade, Cordell Hull had found his heir in Will Clayton, Assistant and later Undersecretary for Economic Affairs. Like Hull, Clayton was convinced that war sprang from colonial-style imperialism and that open markets and multilateral trade were panaceas for war. Clayton's business background, as head of the largest firm of cotton brokers in America, had a lot to do with his zeal for free trade.

The other negotiator, Secretary of the Treasury Vinson, was what one writer has called a "homespun alumnus" of the House of Representatives. He was not one of Truman's better appointments. His experience in international financial matters was virtually nil. And while he was not a vindictive or unreasonable man, his background had not prepared him to think in anything but the narrowest and most conventional terms. By background he was more prepared to follow public opinion than to lead it. Acheson was the only one among ranking American officials *not* imbued by the good old American "get Britain" mentality.

Hostility within the Administration to the loan has led one authority to write:

Nothing is harder to reconcile with the notion of the British Loan as a symbol of Anglo–American solidarity than the tone of discussions in Washington. The State Department was quite willing to use these meetings as a lever for its free-trade enthusiasts. . . . It is one of the ironies of Cold War history that this fixation on free trade should be interpreted as a clear sign of hostility when it was applied to the Russians. But somehow it would fail to shake the image of an Anglo–American entente when it was pressed against the British.[25]

Acheson could not have agreed more. Acheson feared that the loan would prove insufficient,** and he did not share the mordant satisfaction that Truman and his other advisers took in imposing American terms on the British. It was characteristic of Acheson's pragmatic outlook on economic matters that, despite worsening political relations, he also favored extending credits to Russia and the East European countries.

---

* D. C. Watt, "American Aid to Britain and the Problem of Socialism," *The American Review*, Spring, 1963, p. 48. Raymond Aron notes: Criticism of the American action in Europe on the assumption that it derives from the 'Open Door' [and hence imperialist] ideology seems in the circumstances [of a world facing collapse] pointless, almost absurd." *The Imperial Republic* (Englewood Cliffs, N.J.: Prentice-Hall, 1974), p. 38.

** The need for Marshall Plan assistance within eighteen months of the loan proved him to be right.

The abrupt cessation of Lend–Lease in August permitted the British Cabinet but two courses of action: either it must prepare its people for radical alterations in Britain's national life or it must try to secure American aid. Once Britain's situation was understood, so the Cabinet thought, Washington would grant Britain the money in the form of an outright gift or an interest-free loan. Lord Keynes, the chief British negotiator, let his faith in logic and reason get the better of his judgment to such a degree that he assured the Cabinet that a grant-in-aid of $6 billion could be virtually counted upon. But when negotiations opened in Washington in October the Cabinet was shocked to learn that America not only refused to make an interest-free loan but even insisted upon dictating terms that trespassed upon Britain's cherished financial freedom.

Acheson came into the negotiating picture directly on November 29 with his release from the atomic energy matters. His presence was felt immediately and in a most positive way. After several concessions designed to ease the British position, the Loan Agreement was signed on December 6: Britain would receive $3.75 billion at 2% interest, the interest charge to be waived when Britain earned an inadequate amount of foreign exchange. But the worst trouble did not arise over the loan itself; the most desperate disagreements arose over Clayton's insistence on the abandonment of imperial preference, over free convertability of the sterling to dollars one year after the loan came into effect, and over American efforts to force London to oblige its creditors to scale down their wartime accumulation of sterling advances. Hugh Dalton, then chancellor of the exchequer, writes of the Cabinet reaction to all this: "We came nearest to breaking the negotiations on this point [convertability]." [26] Acheson, too, opposed the one-year deadline for convertability on the grounds that Britain's recovery was too uncertain a proposition to saddle it with a rigid deadline. He pointed with little effect to the interest which the United States had in a strong Britain as a trading partner and, although he did not say it, as a strategic partner as well. On convertability he and the British were overruled. Within months of its coming into effect the run on the British exchequer by its debtors and sterling bloc partners converting pounds to dollars had ruined the loan and virtually bankrupted Britain overnight. It was this emergency that prompted the need for the Marshall Plan.

Once the Loan Agreement was signed, Truman forwarded it to the Congress with an appeal for fast action. But public opinion polls had shown from the outset that almost a majority of the American people opposed it.

As with so many other aspects of postwar American policy, Acheson would find it difficult to convince people of the necessity for the British Loan because the Roosevelt Administration had oversold the nation on the efficacy of multilateralism and of the Bretton Woods institutions. Why, it was now asked, since the World Bank and Monetary Fund had been set up at Bretton Woods, was it necessary to make additional loans?

But the main seat of resistance to the loan lay in the Congress, where the notion of international involvement and responsibility was anathema to a whole host of influential congressmen and senators. Many of these were prewar isolationists, but others were minions of that part of the American business community that believed perfervidly in the virtues of free enterprise and wanted nothing to do with loans to socialist governments or restraints on American freedom of action. Acheson's fight for the loan lay in the future. More immediate problems had suddenly arisen, caused by Secretary of State Byrnes's unexpected decision to convene another meeting of the Council of Foreign Ministers.

Atomic Matters Again

On November 23, 1945, Byrnes, on his own initiative and without consulting Truman, cabled Moscow to arrange another Foreign Ministers' meeting, this time in Moscow.* The cable did not mention atomic energy. The conference was set for December 15, but it was not until November 29 that Byrnes, prompted by Vannevar Bush, took the first step toward enlisting Soviet cooperation in the atomic field by suggesting to the British that the Moscow agenda include a proposal for a United Nations commission to study control of the atom. That the coming conference was to include discussion on atomic matters was announced on December 7 along with announcement of the conference itself.

Reaction from the public and scientific community was favorable. But just as deterioration in Soviet–American relations had produced a hardening of Soviet official attitudes, so too had it produced a hardening of congressional attitudes against concessions which might in any way detract from America's atomic monopoly before a foolproof inspection system was established and operating.

In an effort to allay congressional suspicions, Byrnes met with the leadership from the Foreign Relations and Foreign Affairs committees two days prior to his departure for Moscow. When he announced that he intended to *suggest* the exchange of scientific information with the Soviet Union, suspicion flared anew. Vandenberg declared that "His [Byrnes's] plan was a great shock to the entire Committee." Had the congressmen and senators read the Agreed Declaration of the Truman-Attlee-King meeting carefully and paid attention to Bush's explanatory testimony of

---

* Byrnes has explained that the meeting was the fruition of his inspiration during a Thanksgiving Day reflection on Soviet–American disagreements. James F. Byrnes, *All in One Lifetime* (New York: Harper & Brothers, 1958), p. 326.

December 4 before the Senate Special Committee on Atomic Energy, they would have had no reason to have been shocked by the proposal because both document and speech described the exchange of scientific information as first priority in negotiating international control.

In the absence of any authoritative study, however, it is not surprising that the senators responded as they did. Vandenberg reported that the members of Congress who met with Byrnes were opposed to giving away any atomic secrets "unless and until the Soviets are prepared to be 'policed' by the United Nations" to ensure "absolute and effective . . . inspection and control." Challenging Byrnes's assumption that the Soviets would cooperate on controls, the members of Congress insisted that no further secrets, scientific or otherwise, be revealed until the international plan as a whole had been worked out.

The Administration's haphazard plan for opening atomic negotiations by talking frankly about the exchange of scientific information (which, on the assumption prevalent at the time, the Soviets would soon acquire anyway) was now challenged, and the failure of the Administration to explain and secure congressional endorsement for its proposals was once again producing needless confusion and opposition. Senator Vandenberg and his colleagues believed that there should be absolutely no atomic energy disclosures until a rigid system of international control had been devised and until Congress had given its approval.*

Two days later Byrnes left for Moscow. And Vandenberg, still dissatisfied with Byrnes's explanation, demanded to see the President. Acheson, who was present at Vandenberg's request, was now treated to the painful spectacle of an ill-informed President being dragooned by a senator into reminding his Secretary of State of what should have been understood from the beginning: that Byrnes was to merely open the subject pending detailed negotiation of the modalities. Truman, whom Acheson found to be clearly unfamiliar with the issues at controversy, agreed to instruct Byrnes that he "had no intention whatever of disclosing any scientific information," but was "intended primarily to discuss with Moscow the matter of securing Soviet support for the establishment of the United Nations Commission on Atomic Energy Control." [27]

Unfortunately, confusion and a lack of understanding continued to plague the subject. From Moscow Byrnes replied that he did "not intend presenting any proposal *outside the framework* of the three-power decla-

---

* Oppenheimer has testified that in discussions about the Agreed Declaration at the State Department prior to Byrnes's departure it became apparent that "we didn't have a very well thought through notion of what international control was or what we could say to the Russians," and that the decision was, therefore, to ask them "to subscribe to the three-power declaration." U.S. Atomic Energy Commission, *In the Matter of J. Robert Oppenheimer*, 1954, p. 36.

ration . . ." [28] of the previous November. This was hardly an answer to Vandenberg's objections, which were precisely to the provision in the three-power declaration that provided for the exchange of scientific information prior to the existence of a foolproof inspection system. Truman heard no more from Byrnes following this December 17 assurance until December 24, when Byrnes cabled that Molotov had objected "to any reference to control plan being developed by stages" (thereby allaying senatorial fears) and had insisted on "complete subordination of the Atomic Energy Commission to the Security Council." In the end Byrnes succeeded in persuading Molotov of the merit of proceeding by stages, the first stage to be exchange of scientific information in the hope of building Soviet confidence to accept foolproof international control. This was just what Truman had wanted to avoid.*

On December 27 Truman finally received a text of the State Department communiqué on the conference. It appeared that Byrnes *had* made some agreements, especially on Eastern Europe, without first consulting the President. In light of the caveat in the Acheson cable to Byrnes "that any proposal advanced would be referred here [to the President] before agreement was reached," Truman was very angry.[29] He did not relish being taken for granted. The part of the communiqué dealing with atomic energy had *not* been cleared with the White House and it appeared to confirm Vandenberg's notion that the disclosure of scientific information would precede the creation of a system of safeguarded inspection. The senator was so upset, he wrote, that "I very nearly resigned" from the United States Delegation to the United Nations "when the Moscow Communiqué came out, because I could not possibly subscribe to what it said about the atomic bomb." ** Vandenberg again demanded to see Truman. Once again accompanied by Acheson he marched to the White House.

---

* Hewlett and Anderson, *op. cit.*, p. 470. Gaddis, *op. cit.*, p. 379 Once again the United States found itself committed, this time without the explicit consent of the President. The Soviets, Truman learned, had withdrawn their objections to proceeding by stages and Byrnes had accepted the Soviet suggestion on the role of the United Nations Security Council. Because congressional objections had focused the President's attention upon the exchange of scientific information, the Soviet agreement to proceed by stages, potentially quite significant in light of U.S. desire for a foolproof inspection before giving up its monopoly, was lost from sight. This was the occasion for a sharp breach between Truman and Byrnes, a breach which might have been avoided had there been an adequate policy-formation process on atomic energy.

** Arthur H. Vandenberg, Jr., ed., *The Private Papers of Senator Vandenberg* (Boston: Houghton Mifflin Company, 1952), pp. 230–232. Vandenberg was habitually "very near resigning." He never did. He was not above using his presence at these conferences to puff up his standing back home, usually by posturing as the guardian of America's vital interests which others (principally Byrnes) were ever ready to throw away. He put a lot of unfortunate pressure on the Administration to adopt a tougher line. Gaddis, *op. cit.*, pp. 292–296.

Once again the President assured Vandenberg of his determination not to share atomic information until "proper safeguards" had been established, and that the order of the items presented in the Agreed Declaration and the Moscow communiqué were to be read together as a whole. Private assurances were not sufficient. Vandenberg extracted a humiliating public statement from the President to the effect that the separate stages were not to be considered in the order presented in the Declaration and the communiqué, but "that the whole is to be read together" and that "complete and adequate 'security' must be a part of each 'stage' of disclosure." [30] Acheson and the senator went to the State Department, where a draft statement to this effect was prepared; then they returned to the White House, where the President read and approved the statement before it was issued by the senator himself.

To Acheson, acting as intermediary between the President and Vandenberg and between the President and Secretary Byrnes, the whole situation was exceedingly painful. Vandenberg was virtually dictating atomic policy to the President, who was going along because he had had no adequate briefing from his Secretary of State.

Another official might have taken the philosophic view that it was nothing to him that his two superiors were getting themselves into a mess. Until becoming Undersecretary, Acheson had been too remote to feel any responsibility for administrative failures outside of his own area, but now he felt a sense of chagrin at the shambles into which policy had fallen. He was incensed at seeing the President reduced to ineffectuality because Byrnes had failed to achieve a clear understanding with him as to what he intended doing in Moscow. Perhaps Acheson felt vindicated in his own intensity of feeling about the necessity of intelligence and communication to effective administration. But Acheson's feelings were peculiarly affected by the spectacle of Truman's embarrassment. Here was the President, upon whom everything depended for whatever order might be attainable under the American system of government, reduced to embarrassed impotency because of Byrnes's failure to plan and communicate.[*]

Part of Acheson's drive for administrative order lay in his profound, almost obsessive concern for the consequences which follow from disorder and policy failure. Policy-making in a democracy was difficult enough, he felt, without the failure to communicate adding to the con-

---

[*] This would not be the last time that Acheson would feel exasperated by Byrnes's insouciant handling of the policy procedures. The delicacy of his situation as Undersecretary would become further complicated by Truman's decision to replace Byrnes at some suitable moment in the future—a decision about which Acheson learned in relaying instructions to Eisenhower, about to depart for a tour of American installations, of the intent to secure Marshall's agreement as Byrnes's replacement.

fusion. Any system gives to a few men responsibility for making it work, and as Acheson saw it, any failure on their part represents an intolerable betrayal of trust.[31] Acheson believed that for any social system to work somebody must assert leadership; somebody must bring about action. And when duly constituted leadership defaulted in its responsibility— whether through lack of will or negligence—it failed in its highest duty. In the years ahead, avoiding this kind of failure became an obsession with Acheson. Only the growing importance of his own responsibilities and a growing respect for Truman appear to have kept him from resigning at this time.[32]

The results of the Foreign Ministers' Conference in Moscow, while superficially encouraging in that they resolved the impasse over Romania and Bulgaria so that work on peace treaties with Germany's former satellites could begin, did not achieve much progress on the issues that were disturbing Truman. It seemed too much as if Stalin were simply delaying things, waiting for events to take their course. Nor was the President immune to those in the White House who, like Admiral William Leahy, were sharply critical of Byrnes, or to influential senators like Vandenberg, who feared Byrnes was giving away too much.*

The Acheson–Lilienthal Plan

Early in January 1946, Acheson had a more promising opportunity to contribute to policy on atomic energy. Byrnes asked him to assume the chairmanship of a committee—consisting of Vannevar Bush, James B. Conant, Leslie R. Groves, and John J. McCloy—whose function was to devise a system which would make effective international control possible while satisfying those in Congress and the country who were deeply concerned about the need for national security.

At Acheson's instigation, the committee agreed to create a panel of qualified persons to ascertain the basic facts which any policy maker would have to know in order to recommend strategies for the inspection and control of atomic energy. Arguing that at least one member of the panel "should be experienced in statecraft as well as familiar with technological and scientific matters," ** Acheson within a few days recruited

---

* Leahy's strictures were particularly bitter. The Moscow communiqué, Leahy confided to his diary, was "an appeasement document that gives the Soviet everything and preserves to America nothing . . . (and proves that Byrnes was not immune to the communistically inclined advisers in the State Department)." Entries in the Leahy Diary December 26 and 28, 1945. Cited in Herbert Feis, *From Trust to Terror: The Onset of the Cold War, 1945–1950* (New York: Norton, 1970). See also Gaddis, *op. cit.*, pp. 286–287.

** In his diary entry for January 22, David Lilienthal reports how Acheson pointed out to Truman how significant it was to have men trained in government and statecraft

a board of consultants consisting of David E. Lilienthal of the Tennessee Valley Authority, with fifteen years of government experience; J. Robert Oppenheimer, the atomic physicist; Charles A. Thomas, vice-president of the Monsanto Chemical Company; Harry A. Winne, vice-president in charge of engineering for General Electric; and Chester I. Barnard, president of the New Jersey Bell Telephone Company.

The prospect of at last getting a handle on the question of whether it was feasible to get the atomic genie back in the bottle exhilarated Acheson. By conveying to Lilienthal and his associates the real extent of the Administration's interest in achieving an analysis of the feasibility and practicality of devising a control system, Acheson inspired in them an attitude of mind unique in committees of that sort.[33]

Before the board's investigation, everyone had taken it for granted that international control would mean that somewhere along the line each nation would have its production and utilization of atomic energy subject to some form of international inspection. Moreover, such inspection was assumed to require an inordinate number of highly trained personnel who would serve as an army of snoopers, whose function was deemed likely to weaken the system by creating mutual distrust. As the inadequacy of conventional inspection revealed itself, the members of the Acheson–Lilienthal study group embraced an ingenious and radically different concept of control. Why not go back to the mines where the flow of atomic energy had its sources? Such mines would be few in number and not easily hidden. Why not, in place of an army of snoopers, establish an International Atomic Development Authority which would *own* the mines and *operate* all those activities declared to be dangerous. All *nondangerous* activities would be left to national ownership and operation; for such purposes—industrial, scientific, and medical—the Authority would license the use of various atomic elements, and activities with a potential military application would be entirely in its hands. Since the Authority "would always know just where its ores were, and in what quantities, and to what purposes they were being put," the Lilienthal board concluded that management of dangerous operations would require far fewer scientists and far less direct inspection than a plan relying exclusively upon inspection. The additional security in such a plan would lie in the fact that any ag-

---

learning the facts for once, so that "the facts about atomic energy could be translated into terms of public policy." Without such men, Acheson had said to the President, it would be "as if one called in a very intelligent and well intentioned South Sea Islander and said 'There are too many cows being killed on railroad tracks and I want you to do something about it.' But the South Sea Islander, although smart and meaning well and wanting to be helpful, has never seen a cow or a railroad." David E. Lilienthal, *The Journals of David E. Lilienthal*, Vol. II, *The Atomic Energy Years, 1948–1950* (New York: Harper & Row, 1964), p. 12.

gressor nation illegally seizing facilities for the production of fissionable materials would require no less than a year to produce a significant atomic capability, thereby allowing sufficient time for counteraction by the other nations of the world.*

The facts led these hard-headed men to espouse the first form of international authority which would actually do things other than simply administer and regulate. Acheson recognized that the plan might not meet with the acceptance of the parent committee or of the President and the Congress, but it was an exercise in sheer reason and logic that he could not resist, and his obvious delight with the report was evident in his unstinting praise of it both in private and in public. He immediately became the plan's staunchest defender within the parent committee where, for a time, it had its skeptics, its critics, and its detractors. But Acheson insisted that the logic of the board's proposal came as close to what the President wanted as they could hope to come. Nor was there any available alternative that would both safeguard American security and provide for international control in a form likely to be acceptable to the Soviet Union. By dint of his forceful logic and persuasiveness, Acheson persuaded the committee to endorse it as a basis upon which to formulate U.S. policy.

There still remained one hurdle. How was the plan to explain the transitional steps necessary in the period of moving from national to international control? Acheson joined with his committee in asking the board of consultants to produce a "last and rather delicate chapter" on the problem of transition.

This chapter, which Lilienthal and his group were reluctant to undertake, would clearly go beyond the scientific and technical considerations of a reliable control system. Nevertheless, upon Acheson's insistence, the board loyally met the new charge. In the last chapter the board acknowledged the right of the United States to the retention of a position of relative security during the transition, but sought to put at rest once and for all the illusion that the United States held a permanent advantage. The loss of our atomic monopoly "cannot be indefinitely postponed." Nevertheless, the board held out assurance to the Congress in particular that the balance of advantage during the transition period would be with the United States and concluded that the continued location of atomic production facilities in the United States assured that in the event of a breakdown during the transition, the United States would be in a favorable position

---

* In an otherwise favorable commentary on the Acheson–Lilienthal Report, scientists Edward Teller and H. C. Urey warned that the degree of safety provided by denaturing of materials was overstated in the report. Edward Teller, "The State Department Report—'A Ray of Hope,'" *Bulletin of the Atomic Scientists* (April 1, 1946), 13; "H. C. Urey on State Department Report," *Ibid.*, p. 13.

to recommence weapons production. The point was hardly likely to win the plan support in Moscow.

The weighting of the last chapter and the Letter of Transmittal in favor of American discretion and security would afford little inducement to other countries to forego production of atomic weapons. Nevertheless, the plan was a step in the right direction: it laid the basis for development of American policy on atomic energy, and there was no prohibition against suitable adjustments in the stages by which the United States relinquished its monopoly.

Next Acheson took a calculated risk in recommending that the report be made public:

. . . it would seem desirable that the report be made available to broader circles both within and without the government. It appears to us the most suitable point now available for further study and the wide discussions that are necessary in developing a sound solution.[34]

Even before formal authorization was given, the report had found its way into the public domain. The *New York Times* printed it in its entirety and it was issued in an inexpensive paper edition. The enthusiastic reception which it received indicated that the public was hungry for information and leadership. It would appear that it also attracted support, because it rekindled the nation's flagging confidence in the efficacy of internationalism.

The adverse side of its publication was that despite qualifications as to its incomplete and tentative nature, the report was immediately considered authoritative and regarded as the official position of the United States.

Both in his foreword to the report and in the Letter of Transmittal, Acheson had been careful to recognize that the proposals ought to be studied by those "who must assume responsibility for political action" and that the plan was not the final word. Much of the care with which he approached the whole question of negotiation and implementation of the plan was dictated by the sober realization that there was a considerable gap between an abstract plan, however intellectually sound, and the policy which must eventually reconcile it with the national interest of the United States and of fifty other nations. Nevertheless, Acheson had no reason to expect what happened next.

Without consulting the State Department, Secretary Byrnes recommended to the President the appointment of retired financier Bernard Baruch to be America's chief delegate to the United Nations Atomic Energy Commission. Lilienthal's diary entry for March 19, 1946, pretty well sums up the feeling of those, including Acheson, who had labored so long:

When I read this news [Baruch's appointment] last night, I was quite sick. We need a man who is young, vigorous, not vain, and who the Russians could feel isn't out simply to put them in a hole, not really caring about international cooperation. Baruch has none of these qualifications. And this morning comes the list of men who will, as he says, really do the work—which is substantially true. It is the old crowd: Hancock, Eberstadt, Swope (Herbert Bayard), and that familiar bull in the china closet, Searls. God! Isn't *this* something." [35]

In addition to his friendship with him, Byrnes was obviously prompted by the knowledge that Baruch's prestige with Congress would make somewhat easier the adoption of America's atomic energy policy. But that did not make the appointment any easier for Acheson to accept. To select a complete outsider, someone who had not had the benefit of the intensive education which had gone into the report and who had no sense of America's diplomatic position, was incomprehensible. Acheson never felt more bitter about Byrnes's handling of the department. Discouraged by the trend of events, Acheson made his resignation available to the President on April 17, 1946.*

So jealous was Baruch of prerogative that his first demand was that the President agree to regard the Acheson–Lilienthal report as only a "working paper" and not an official document. One after another, all the virtues that orderly policy procedures had built into the Acheson–Lilienthal plan were struck down. Baruch had a legitimate point that the public release of the report committed him prematurely to policy positions which in the light of subsequent study might not prove feasible. But only arrogance, ignorance, or perversity could have prompted Baruch to do what he did to the report. Taking advantage of Truman's inexperience and gullibility, and Byrnes's failure to protect the President, Baruch secured practically carte blanche to determine United States atomic policy.

On April 18, Baruch told Byrnes that when he and his group were finished with their own report, "we want to take it to the President because, since you're busy, the report would probably be received and reviewed by someone in the State Department unacquainted with the issue." [36] Byrnes so far yielded to Baruch that the coordination of scientific, military, and political considerations, essential to the development of policy decisions, was to be accomplished, if at all, by Baruch, rather than by responsible governmental departments. [37]

While the Acheson–Lilienthal approach merely sought to promote the control of atomic energy to prevent the clandestine production of atomic

---

* This is brought out in the President's letter of May 12, 1947, accepting Acheson's resignation as Undersecretary of State: "I can easily appreciate the reasons which impelled your desire to return to private life as embodied in your letter written as long ago as April 17, 1946. . . ."

energy, Baruch wished to include in his approach methods for invoking punishment and sanctions against any nation caught violating the control system. The Acheson–Lilienthal plan assumed that upon notification that one of their number was in violation, the other nations would reassume their right to manufacture atomic weapons, taking for granted that each nation under the principle of self-help would do what was necessary to protect itself against a deliberate violator. Baruch's objectives went beyond the mere prevention of surprise attack: he wanted the control of atomic energy to serve as a means of eliminating war. Baruch envisaged an Atomic Energy Authority empowered to undertake enforcement measures, free of any veto, and authorized to drop atomic bombs if necessary to forcibly restrain a country engaged in an operation declared illegal by the treaty. I. F. Stone writes: "The Baruch plan, as it became known when it was submitted to the UN, must have seemed to Moscow the blueprint for a world capitalist superstate in which the US would retain its atomic monopoly behind the facade of an international organization under US control." In *Present at the Creation*, Acheson disclosed publicly for the first time that he felt the plan as transformed by Baruch contained provisions "almost certain to wreck any possibility of Russian acceptance," because Moscow would see them "as an attempt to turn the United Nations into an alliance to support a United States threat of war against the USSR unless it ceased its efforts" to develop an atom bomb.[38]

The struggle over sanctions and penalties, over ownership and inspection, and over the preliminary raw-material survey waged back and forth between Acheson and the Baruch group all through May and early June of 1946. On June 4 the Baruch group presented Byrnes with a memorandum containing its essential positions. Acheson red-penciled and deleted the section specifying penalties against crimes in favor of "a clear statement of the consequences of violations of the system of controls, including definitions of the acts which would constitute such violations. . . ."[39] He also fought for the principle that the Authority must have control of all atomic energy activities intrinsically dangerous and over all sources of uranium and thorium. On June 6, Acheson completed a revision of the Acheson–Lilienthal report; it now contained carefully guarded concessions to the Baruch position which, Acheson felt, offered the best hope of getting their original report accepted.

On June 7, Baruch's group completed a draft "statement of United States Policy," apparently in the form to be presented at the United Nations a week later, and when Baruch arrived at Byrnes's office with this document, Byrnes immediately accompanied him to the White House where he, Byrnes, laid the two drafts—the Baruch memorandum and the Acheson revision of the original report—before the President. Unless the President had seen the Acheson draft earlier in the day, he apparently had no opportunity to read and digest it in the course of Baruch's appearance. In any event, Truman and Byrnes were now prisoners of their previous commitments to Baruch. Lilienthal reports Byrnes as saying at this time, "This is the worst mistake I have ever made. But we can't fire him now with all the other trouble." [40] Instead of a step-by-step examination of the wisdom of Baruch's proposals, the President merely read the document and initialed each paragraph in Baruch's presence. Whatever reservations Truman may have harbored and which might have come into the open under different circumstances were now suppressed; according to Baruch, Truman appeared "absolutely firm" on the question of the veto.[41] Acheson had lost. But so, in effect, had Baruch. Not one of America's allies was prepared to go along with the Baruch proposals concerning the veto. M. Parodi, the French delegate to the Atomic Energy Commission, warned against raising the issue at all. He noted that a country could always have recourse to "individual measures" if dissatisfied with the operation of the control system or if a veto should be employed in the Security Council to prevent investigation. By presenting the Soviet Union with an issue on which Western agreement had not been worked out beforehand, Baruch's proposals enabled the Soviet Union to divert debate away from the merits of the control plan to the issue of the veto on which the United States found itself virtually isolated.

When in the course of the ensuing debate, which stretched over several weeks, it became apparent that his interpretations had no support, Baruch lost his head. He complained that he was not being understood, and he warned his fellow delegates that they must either vote in America's favor or the American people "would—and they should—withdraw their support from this organization. . . ."

The upshot of Baruch's inept diplomacy was to leave the United States in the hole.* The towering national interest in establishing an effective international control system had been sacrificed to the blind pursuit of an impractical objective.

In one of his strongest efforts to avoid the Cold War, Acheson was defeated by a Secretary of State who unwisely recommended to Truman

---

* Another more Machiavellian interpretation is that American policy-makers, anxious to retain the U.S. monopoly of atomic weapons, had to convince American and foreign opinion of their commitment to the principle of outlawing the bomb. The Baruch proposal afforded such a gesture. It was widely regarded at the time as an imaginative and magnanimous act on the part of the United States government. In short, having proposed a seemingly reasonable and generous plan, the American government was able to depict Soviet intransigence on the issue as the only obstacle to a world freed from the threat of atomic war. John P. Lovell, *Foreign Policy in Perspective* (New York: Holt, Rinehart and Winston, 1970), p. 107. John W. Spanier and Joseph L. Nogee, *The Politics of Disarmament* (New York: Praeger, 1962), pp. 56–57.

the appointment of an unprepared person and who failed to counsel Truman of his Presidential prerogatives. Acheson was again reconfirmed in his conviction that a Secretary of State must plan carefully and brief the President fully. His obsession for administrative order arose out of demonstrations of dramatic disorder.

6

ACHESON AND THE CRISIS IN
THE EASTERN MEDITERRANEAN

THE PATTERN of Soviet intentions in Eastern Europe had been pretty well set by 1946. Bulgaria, Romania, and Poland were already under de facto Communist control. In Poland, where the Soviets were pledged to hold free elections as soon as possible, the opposition forces led by Mikolajczyk were under extralegal and extraparliamentary attack. No Polish government other than one which had the Lublin faction as its nucleus was going to be permitted to prevail in Poland. And when it became apparent that the non–Communist opposition might prevail, "free" elections were postponed long enough to get the leadership of that opposition out of the way. A not negligible part of Acheson's time during 1946 would be spent dealing with Ambassador Arthur Bliss Lane's outrage at the cavalier and all-too-often murderous fashion with which the Kremlin dealt with the Polish opposition. Elections held in Hungary and Czechoslovakia produced non–Communist majorities. But that did not mean that they were free of Soviet dictation. In Hungary the future was already clear. The government of Premier Imré Nagy, which included a number of Communist ministers, was forced to pursue a course that was not only friendly to the Soviet Union but one that would make it impossible for Nagy to govern except on terms laid down by the Communists.[1]

The case of Czechoslovakia was somewhat distinct because Eduard Benes had adopted a pro–Soviet orientation while in exile and the population was more favorably disposed toward their Soviet liberators. But this did not mean that the Soviet Union did not exert considerable pressure on Prague or that the Western-style democracy would be permitted to prevail should its sentiment turn against the Soviet interests. As Benes reported to Ambassador Steinhardt late in 1946: ". . . if Secretary [Byrnes] had had to deal with [the] Soviet Government as a representative of a small, contiguous country, he would appreciate [the] necessity of doing voluntarily what the Soviet Government was in a position to coerce in the absence of voluntary action. *"

Each side's design for the postwar world had been tied to differing interpretations of the accords signed at Yalta. Roosevelt had acceded to Soviet terms only reluctantly, on the assumption that rather than disagree prematurely we would wait and see how the Soviet Union observed the agreements.**

The failure of the Kremlin to observe even the spirit of the agreements as it was understood in the United States and Great Britain was a signal for revision of American assumptions about the postwar world.† Naturally

---

* FR:1946, VI, p. 240. Steinhardt to Byrnes. Benes added, "Czechoslovakia had been so dependent on the good will of the Soviet Union . . . that to have voted against [the] Soviet Union on any occasion that Poland and Yugoslavia voted with [the] Soviet Union would have been to invite serious reprisals. . . ." *Ibid.* A similar pattern of pressure was exerted on the democratically elected Imré Nagy government in neighboring Hungary all through 1946, designed to make it impossible to govern. *FR:1946*, VI, pp. 291–295, 344–373.

** A perfect diagnostic of this attitude is found in a letter Charles Bohlen wrote to George Kennan from Yalta. Kennan had written that Roosevelt's approach was worse than futile. It was a travesty. Bohlen, obviously disturbed, wrote back:

> I can't say I have given your letter the attention it deserves, but there is simply not time. As you know, there is a very great deal in your expositions that I agree with. You should know that in this connection the U.S. government is following admittedly a policy of no small risk. But have you ever seriously thought through the alternatives? The 'constructive' suggestions that you make are frankly naive to a degree. They may well be the optimum from an abstract point of view. But as practical suggestions they are utterly impossible. . . . Furthermore, I don't for one minute believe that there has been any time in this war when we could seriously have done very differently than we did. It is easy to talk about instruments of pressure that we had in our hands. But the simple fact remains that if we wished to defeat Germany we could never have even tried to keep the Soviet armies out of Eastern Europe and Germany itself. . . . Either our pals intend to limit themselves or they don't. I submit, as the British say, that the answer is not yet clear. But what is clear is that the Soyuz [Soviet Union] is here to stay, as one of the major factors in the world. Quarreling with them would be so easy, but we can always come to that.

Taken from Charles E. Bohlen, *Witness to History 1929–1969*, ed. by Robert H. Phelps (New York: W. W. Norton & Co., 1973), p. 176.

† Maxim Litvinov, pre-World War II Soviet Foreign Minister, later remarked upon the unnecessary secrecy and callousness with which the Kremlin conducted its policies. Soviet "diplomacy might have been able to do something to avoid [misunderstanding] if we had made our purposes clear to the British and if we had made clear the limits of our needs, but now it is too late. . . ." And again: the Foreign "Commissariat is run by only three men and none of them understand America or Britain." Quoted in Vojtech Mastny, "The Cassandra in the Foreign Commissariat: Maxim

Stalin would view Western protests as fraudulent and guileful; first, because he had entered into the agreements on the basis of the Soviet definition of its interests (and of the meaning of terms like "freedom" and "democracy"), and second, because, given the sentiments of the people involved, acceptance of Western terms would have produced anti–Soviet governments which were intolerable to the Kremlin. From Stalin's viewpoint, Soviet actions were necessary and right given the circumstances. American protests (and they were no more than that) did *not* cause the Soviet Union to impose Communist-type dictatorships on the countries of Eastern Europe; except for Czechoslovakia, their fates were sealed by January 1946.*

Frustrated by Soviet delays in getting the peace that he expected and chafed by his critics for being too easy in his dealings with the Soviets (Republican criticism was intensifying), Truman poured his dissatisfaction into a letter, supposedly written as a combined chastisement and directive, to the errant Byrnes. In it Truman noted:

I do not think we should play compromise any longer. We should refuse to recognize Rumania and Bulgaria until they comply with our requirements; we should let our position on Iran be known in no uncertain terms and we should continue to insist on the internationalization of the Kiel Canal, the Rhine–Danube waterway, and the Black Sea Straits and we should maintain complete control of Japan and the Pacific. We should rehabilitate China and create a strong central government there. . . . I'm tired of babying the Soviets.[2]

Truman's views were not given a public airing, but the months that followed were marked by a rhetorical escalation that all but doomed hope of East–West understanding. On February 9, 1946, Stalin gave an election-eve speech that was interpreted in some quarters as a declaration of World War III. As reported from Moscow by George Kennan, Stalin had stressed the incompatibility of communism and capitalism and had called upon the Soviet people to consolidate their victory in war "through restoration and increase of [the] economic might of [the] USSR." These pre-election statements by Stalin and other Soviet leaders called forth much comment within the department and led to a series of studies designed to analyze their policy significance.[3]

The speech, which did little more than spell out the operating assump-

---

Litvinov and the Cold War" *Foreign Affairs*, Jan. 1976, vol. 54, no. 2, p. 371. This article is the first time that the Kremlin's failure to deal more insightfully and intelligently with the Western powers has been raised. Over and over Anglo-American statesmen were left in the dark as to Stalin's intentions.

* The Soviet argument that they were affording the Western allies as much of a say in Eastern Europe as had been accorded Soviet representatives in Italy and Japan overlooks the point that the Communist Party was allowed to flourish in those countries and that U.S. forces were soon withdrawn from Italy, France, etc.

tions of Soviet foreign policy, was given an even more sensational interpretation among the public at large, especially by the press, which played
an important role in stimulating anti–Soviet feeling,[4] because it came at a
tense moment in Soviet–American relations: less than a week later, on
February 16, 1946, news of the Canadian spy case broke with the announcement from Ottawa of the arrest of twenty-two persons on charges
of trying to steal atomic secrets for the USSR. The Canadian case, which
shocked Americans with its evidence that the Russians had obtained
secret data on the bomb, stimulated pressure for vigilance against Communist espionage within the United States.

On March 5 Churchill made his famous Iron Curtain speech at Fulton,
Missouri. The Fulton speech painted a much darker picture of Soviet
actions in Eastern Europe than that to which Americans were accustomed.
With Truman sitting in the audience, Churchill asserted that the Russians
did not want war, but they did want "the fruits of war and the indefinite
expansion of their power and doctrines." Drawing upon his wartime experience, Churchill stressed that the Kremlin only respected military
strength and called for the formation of what some observers, including
the Kremlin, regarded as an Anglo-American alliance. Acheson considered
Churchill's speech an unmitigated disaster. Once again the President had
been led into seeming to endorse a position which was neither helpful nor
appropriate to the complicated state of United States policy. In an effort
to dissociate U.S. policy from the speech, Acheson was ordered by Byrnes
to absent himself from the New York reception to be accorded Churchill.[5]
Although Churchill's speech reflected what many in the Administration
thought privately about Soviet behavior, Acheson certainly was not convinced that the situation called for an anti–Soviet alliance. The State Department still preferred to work through the United Nations, as it was
intending to do in the Iranian case, and to see if the Kremlin's "expansive
and proselytizing tendencies" were as real as Churchill made out.*

More influential on department thinking than Churchill's speech was
Kennan's long cable from Moscow on the nature and motives of Soviet
foreign policy. Wartime collaboration had collapsed, Ambassador Harriman was on his way home, and Kennan, temporarily in charge of the
Moscow embassy, had been asked his opinion on why the Russians behaved as they did. Kennan's response, which was received on February
22, was a long and compelling analysis that was to crystallize official

---

* More representative of State Department views was Byrnes's speech of February 28, 1946, delivered to the Overseas Press Club. In it Byrnes pointed out that
Americans had welcomed Russia into the family of nations as a power second to none,
but that there were limits as to how far the U.S. could put up with violations of the
United Nations Charter.

thinking about the impossibility of achieving satisfactory relations with the Kremlin. Of this cable Acheson wrote:

It had a deep effect on thinking within the Government, although Government response with action still needed a year's proof of Soviet intentions as seen by Kennan. . . . His recommendations—to be of good heart, to look to our own social and economic health, to present a good face to the world, all of which the Government was trying to do—were of no help; his historical analysis might or might not have been sound, but his predictions and warning could not have been better.[6]

All these statements marked a new stage in American attitudes toward the Soviet Union. They constituted a de facto recognition that Soviet–American relations were in a state of conflict. But it was still far from clear what the United States should do, what American strategy should be, and what concrete means should now be employed to neutralize Soviet actions or delaying tactics. Even the Administration's definition of the adversary's strategic goals remained ambiguous: did the Kremlin have definite designs for further expansion? Was it simply behaving in a difficult and unfriendly fashion out of internal political compulsions characteristic of a totalitarian regime, as Truman continued at times to believe? Certainly there was no attempt to undertake a major redefinition of American strategy outside the context of insisting upon respect for the principles of the United Nations Charter.

Those responsible for day-to-day relations with the Soviet bloc had their hands full figuring out what to do. Typical of the ambiguity that still marked policy were certain of the issues that Acheson had to wrestle with. Byrnes had hardly returned from his December trip to Moscow than he was due to leave as head of the American delegation for the opening of the United Nations Organization in London. One of the problems he was leaving behind for Acheson's attention was the growing crisis with Russia over its refusal to evacuate its troops from the northern provinces of Iran; another was the still pressing need for the Administration to devise a plan for international control of atomic energy. One involved confrontation and the other the pursuit of agreement with Russia. The atomic matter was due to come before the United Nations sometime in the first half of the year and the American government had as yet not the slightest idea of what recommendations to make.

Iranian Crisis—Winter 1946

Unlike the Soviet occupation of Eastern Europe, which could be considered part of the legacy of the war itself, Soviet pressure on Iran represented an entirely new manifestation of Soviet intentions.

Under a wartime agreement with Great Britain and the United States, the Soviets had been allowed to occupy the northern half of Iran to fore-stall German intervention and to facilitate transshipment of American Lend–Lease goods to the Russian front. The agreement called for the evacuation of Soviet forces within six months after the war's end. As the date agreed upon approached, it became more and more evident that So-viet authorities were determined to prolong their stay; the proof was that an indigenous regime in Azerbaijan had set up a movement for autonomy, which Moscow denied having anything to do with although Soviet forces prevented the Iranian army from re-entering the area. The Soviet position, as stated by Andrei Vyshinsky, was that there was nothing untoward about a local population setting up an autonomous state (as if it hap-pened every day in the Soviet Union). There was no question in Ache-son's mind that these actions were not only a violation of the principles of the United Nations but a threat to the stability of other regimes in the area. Just as Russia had as its objective a security belt in Eastern Europe, so the American leadership believed that the best warranty of American postwar interests lay in the existence of a system of formally sovereign and independent states. Roosevelt had said specifically that he regarded a strong and independent Iran as "something of a testing ground for the Atlantic Charter and the good faith of the United Nations."[7] Conflicts of interest were bound to arise if the more powerful states insisted upon unilaterally changing the status quo at the expense of their weaker neigh-bors. The United States had not involved itself twice in European wars to preserve the balance of power to see it destroyed by a new menace. The fact that Iran was closer to Russia than America really did not mat-ter, because, under the Rooseveltian formula, peace was universal. Ache-son saw the situation in more practical terms as a threat to the stability of a part of the world in which the United States had a genuine economic interest.*

---

* *FR:1943*, IX, pp. 131–136. Jernegan Memorandum. *FR:1946*, VII, pp. 515–530. George V. Allen (unpublished memoir). Papers of George V. Allen, Harry S Truman Library. Bohlen has put the American motives in a somewhat different order. *Witness to History: 1929–69*, *op. cit.*, p. 251:

> While it is often difficult to determine motives in diplomatic situations, it is simple when narrowly defined national interests are involved. In the case of Iran, the full motivation of the United States is not easy to put on paper. There was unquestionably a feeling that in this first important case before the Security Council the United States should demonstrate that one of the great powers should join the other nations in a group action against a recalcitrant great power. Soviet moves in Iran were a clear violation of United Nations principles. If the test had not been met, the United Nations would have been a dead letter when it had no more than started.

> While Iran could be viewed as a clear-cut issue of principle, power considera-

Unable to gain access to that part of its territory occupied by Soviet forces and facing the prospect of seeing Azerbaijan detached from Iran and incorporated into Soviet Azerbaijan, the Iranian government determined to present its complaint to the Security Council of the newly formed United Nations. On January 3, 1946, Acheson urged Byrnes to support Iran in putting the issue on the Council agenda on the grounds that Moscow had not shown itself responsive to the proposal made in December in Moscow for a tripartite commission to look into the matter.

Asked by Acheson to comment from Moscow on Soviet intentions in Iran, Kennan replied that he did not think the Soviet leaders would risk war but that they were determined "to bring into power in Iran a regime prepared to accede to major immediate Soviet demands, particularly continued maintenance of Soviet armed forces in Iran and granting of oil concessions. . . . Soviet forces in Iran will serve this scheme by sheer force of intimidation." [8] On March 17, 1946, as if to underline his worry, Kennan cabled from Moscow that the

Soviet Government has no intention of withdrawing its troops from Iran. On the contrary, reinforcements . . . have been sent in. . . . I find it hard to conceive that [the] Soviet Government could be planning overt aggression against Turkey at this juncture. . . . This is not to say that smashing of Turk power, achievement of Soviet bases on straits and establishment of "friendly" regime in Ankara may not be objectives of Soviet policy to be pursued in due course and time.[9]

Some indication of the uncertainty that may have existed in the Kremlin can be gleaned from Ambassador Smith's report of a meeting with Stalin on April 5. Stalin spoke bitterly of Anglo–American actions in denying Russia the delay that it had asked for on the Iranian issue, but he readily admitted that the United States had not opposed Soviet efforts to obtain concessions for Iranian oil. Smith also observed that it was ludicrous to think that the United States intended to or would ever support an attack in the direction of the Baku oil fields, which was the reason Stalin gave for Soviet troops remaining in Azerbaijan. Despite the efforts of Smith to explore as frankly as possible the issues that were dividing Russia and America, he elicited very few concrete results. Stalin then concluded by stating that despite East–West differences we "should not be alarmed or apprehensive . . . because with patience and good will these differences would be reconciled." [10] But this was just the problem. Little

---

tions also entered into our decision in that we took a stand in an area remote from normal United States national interests because of the realization that if we did not, we would have to do so someplace much closer to our shores.

if anything came of Stalin's reassurances, and the future remained shrouded in obscurity.

The date for the withdrawal of the Soviet forces (March 2, 1946) came and went. The Iranians brought their complaint before the Security Council of the United Nations. The Soviet Union agreed to bilateral discussions with Teheran to settle the issue, and there followed a two-month-long war of nerves. Then, at dinner in Paris on April 28, Byrnes explained to Molotov that if only the Soviet troops were removed, the United States would drop the entire case.* Shortly thereafter Soviet troops were withdrawn, although Soviet pressure was far from ended. The Soviet-sponsored regime in Azerbaijan continued to resist incorporation into Iran, and it looked for a time as if Premier Qavam's government would accede to Azerbaijan independence rather than risk a showdown with the Russians and possible collapse of the government itself. At one point, the cables from Rossow, American vice-consul in Soviet-occupied Tabriz, and from Ambassador Murray, reporting Soviet troop movements, became so ominous that the department had to consider the possibility of war. Undersecretary of State Acheson, who was more or less responsible for orchestrating American policy, eased past the issue by saying that we ought to "let the USSR know that we are aware of its moves, but 'leave a graceful way out' if it desired to avoid a showdown." [11]

The uncertain effort to shore up Iran's territorial integrity gave Acheson his first real experience with a crisis situation. He recognized that its success may have been due as much to surprise and uncertainty in the Kremlin as to any real American power to influence the situation. Nevertheless the Iranian situation demonstrated to Acheson the political and strategic importance of an area where American interests had previously been essentially economic.

The British Loan—Spring 1946

In addition to wrestling with policy for the international control of atomic energy and toward Eastern Europe and the Middle East, Acheson carried the brunt of the struggle to secure passage of the British Loan.

Hearings on the loan opened on March 13, 1946, before the Senate Committee on Banking and Currency. In his testimony Acheson sought to overcome the prejudices of his listeners by appealing to their instinctual support for anything that had the label "free enterprise" attached to it.

---

* FR:1946, VI, p. 441. Byrnes concluded from his failure to get anywhere at this time that "the observations of Molotov and Vyshinsky again reveal the Soviet thesis that the relations between the great powers were more important than the strict [observance] of the charter."

"We believe passionately that only by continuing a system of free enterprise and having other nations in the same state, that we can continue the same sort of world in which the United States has lived in the past." Revisionist historians often point to such statements as evidence that capitalistic America was in dire need of overseas markets and that Acheson was nothing more than a mouthpiece for big business. To be sure, a capitalist economy functions best in the context of a multilateral trading world, and the American economy, being the most powerful, would benefit disproportionately from such a context. But, paradoxically, Acheson's arguments were an attempt to convince the representatives of the capitalist system, Republican and Democrat alike, that America had a stake in restoring the conditions of a multilateral trading world and that the loan was indispensable to that end. This approach was necessary because their opposition to the loan was based on concerns about the propriety of the United States supporting a "socialist" government in power, about the failure of Britain to repay its World War I debts, and about the motives of our ally in asking for a loan at all. The loan was also opposed by part of the business community and by their spokesmen in Congress because it was a derogation from the capitalist principle of self-help and free enterprise. Certainly opponents did not fear that American capitalism was in danger of collapse unless it acquired Britain's overseas markets, although there was a smug undercurrent of satisfaction both in Truman and in the Administration over mastering the British economically.

Acheson's defense of the loan was nothing more than a recognition that unless America accepted its economic responsibilities it would face the collapse of Europe or a repetition of 1929. The year 1929 did not sound the death knell of capitalism; instead it saw the onset of the Great Depression and the rise of Nazism and Japanese militarism. The loan was primarily intended to avoid their happening again. Should Congress not approve the loan, he foresaw:

. . . much that is disturbing—import prohibitions and restrictions, quotas, discriminatory measures and bilateral deals. . . . [American] suspicion and resentment would be fed on Britain's need to eat and work, for she can do neither adequately without imports, and she would be forced to get those imports by whatever shifts would deliver the goods. I see no hope to useful international cooperation in such a prospect.[12]

Naturally Acheson stressed that by passing the loan and committing the United Kingdom to the abolition of certain kinds of tariff and exchange restrictions, the United States stood to gain economically. What would one have expected him to say? Senators like Taft, who still believed in isolationism, were not convinced that the loan was justified on either economic or strategic grounds.*

Fortunately not all American economic interests were opposed to the loan. American bankers and traders, still smarting from the interwar experience, were acutely aware that failure to ratify the loan would leave us vulnerable to "the worst depression that we have ever known, even worse than 1932 and 1933." Acheson marshaled his forces well. The leading bankers—Randolph W. Burgess, W. L. Hemingway, William McChesney Martin, and others—were brought in to testify.[13] And in an effort to offset isolationist and ideological opposition, they deprecated the charge that we were supporting British "socialism" and even argued that the loan might be able to help the conservatives in England by relieving Britain of the pressure of austerity.

Preaching anti–Communism at this point might have assured speedy passage of the loan, but the Administration still did not care to make anti–Communism the basis of its foreign policy. The loan was justified on economic grounds, and that was the basis on which Acheson strove to carry it through Congress.** But when the Senate hearings ended in April, the loan's chances for passage still remained glum, and in order to improve its prospects, Byrnes reassured Vandenberg that the United States intended to maintain its policy of firmness at the forthcoming Foreign Ministers' Conference in Paris. Reassured, Vandenberg warned his colleagues (invoking the anti–Soviet bias for the first time): "If we do not lead some other and powerful nation will capitalize on our failure and we shall pay the price of our default." [14] Acheson regarded it as unfortunate that the loan had to be justified with veiled allusions to the Soviet threat, but he accepted it as a price that had to be paid to secure the support needed. In a more perfect world there would be neither a Soviet problem nor an economic problem. In the meantime, given the choice between offending the Kremlin, which was making the postwar situation so difficult, or losing the loan, Acheson had regrets but few illusions.

On April 24 the *New York Times* declared editorially that it was "to be hoped" that Vandenberg's support "will line up proportionately as many Republican votes as there are Democratic votes." [15] That was just about what happened. The loan passed the Senate on a bipartisan basis

---

* Acheson's exchanges with Taft were already extremely abrasive. For a typical exchange see *Anglo–American Financial Agreement,* Hearings before the Committee on Banking and Currency, U.S. Senate, 79th Congress, 2nd Session, March 13, 1946, pp. 336–337.

** In order to envenom Soviet–American relations unnecessarily by making anti–Communism the vehicle for getting the loan passed, the Department of State agreed to justify the loan on economic grounds. *FR:1946,* VI, p. 824. Unfortunately, sooner or later someone was bound to underscore its obvious political implications.

in late April by a vote of 46 to 32, but it still faced an uphill fight in the House, where it was not approved until July 13.

Although Acheson had initially hoped that the British Loan could be debated without getting involved in the question of a loan to the Soviet Union, he was doomed to be disappointed. Before the House Committee first one witness and then another found it expedient to strengthen the case for the British Loan by underlining its significance as a bulwark against Communism. And this debate, with its stress upon bolstering an anti–Communist ally, all but doomed the prospects for a similar loan to Russia, even had the Kremlin been willing to accept the American terms. As a State Department economic analyst wrote on May 23:

The British Financial agreement secured senatorial approval only after an acrimonious debate and it appears that part of the support for this loan came from those who felt it would strengthen the political position of the United States in relation to the U.S.S.R. . . . There is [therefore] reasonable doubt whether Congress would approve additional funds for the Ex–Im bank that were clearly intended for the U.S.S.R.[16]

Two alternatives were still open: either to take advantage of the Soviet failure to respond favorably to U.S. terms in order "to break off gracefully loan negotiations" or to hold off asking Congress for the $1.25 billion "until we get a clearer picture of Soviet intentions." [17] Under the circumstances Acheson agreed that a loan for Russia was impossible. Still and all, Acheson could not help but feel that this was an awful way to do business. One constructive action could only be gained at the expense of constructive alternatives foregone in another direction.

Dismayed by the delays and aberrations in policy formation, Acheson was convinced that policy could only be effective if it were energized and directed from a single source—the President. This did not mean that Congress or public opinion was not to be consulted; it meant that the President should have a unified policy which everyone in the Executive would support. As part of this philosophy, Acheson was a lion in defense of the President. Fierce to the point of recklessness in defending the President's program before Congress, he always made it clear that it was the President's program. And Truman, who was conscious of how history would judge his Presidency, fully appreciated that his authority was being actively asserted by Acheson and not permitted to lie fallow. As a result, Acheson's standing with Truman was steadily rising.

After two years in office, Truman's Presidency had all the appearance of the martyrdom of St. Sebastian with the arrows of adversity sticking out everywhere. It seemed that he could do nothing right and what he did right appeared inept. Many of his Cabinet members, carry-overs from Roosevelt, felt little loyalty to the new President and thought nothing of airing their disagreements in public. Others, like the Secretary of the Navy, James Forrestal, were more subtle in their contempt or misreading of Truman. Forrestal had taken to holding informal luncheon meetings of Cabinet members for the purpose of discussing broad governmental policies without the President's knowledge. Although these meetings were convened, as Acheson says, "in all innocence and complete loyalty," [18] it soon became evident to him that a sinister interpretation might be put upon them, especially if they became known to the President from some outsider. "It seemed clear to me that the meetings should end and that the ending should come from a friendly suggestion of the President before and not after any sinister purposes should be attached to them." [19] He and James Webb, then Director of the Bureau of the Budget, took their concern to Truman, who tactfully let it be known at the next Cabinet meeting that there should be no more group discussion of government business outside his presence.

Acheson pleased Truman in other ways as well. His powers of logic and exposition were unexcelled, and the President reportedly took an unfeigned delight in hearing Dean lay out a problem or take up the advocacy of some course of action. After the fiascos of his first year in office, Truman sensed that in Acheson he had someone who knew what he was talking about, someone who could unobtrusively redeem his own inexperience and lack of knowledge, and someone who would defend his policies brilliantly and effectively. By the end of the summer of 1946 James Reston's observant eye had caught the developing rapport between the President and his Acting Secretary of State. Nothing can be more appealing to the President, Reston noted, than Acheson's "gift of negotiation and debate" which are "probably his greatest contributions to the formation of our foreign policy today. He plugs away, with great powers of definition, for a steady, consistent policy, based on the facts . . . and despite the limitations, his job, his intelligence, his knowledge, and capacity of definition are sufficient to be effective, if they are not—and many times they are not—decisive." [20]

By the whole thrust of his personality Acheson was the President's man. Elitist by temper, thirsting for action, and preoccupied with the danger of yet another breakdown in world politics, where else could Acheson's loyalties lie but with strong Presidential leadership? Acheson was the king's man par excellence, in the tradition of Coke's lions under the throne. He had no political career of his own to attend to and no roots in the Legislative branch. He was there to serve the President. This was both a strength and a weakness. No one could be such a firm and unbending defender of Presidential power and still find a warm welcome with the Congress, however much they might be predisposed to respect his talents.

Acheson's view of the importance of the State Department also contributed to the strength of his relationship with Truman. If the President is the decider-in-chief, it is to the interest of the Secretary of State that he be the principal source of the President's advice on foreign policy matters. But because the Department of State was not the sole competitor for the President's ear, Acheson could hope to win that influence for his department only if it was the best organized and most efficiently run agency, capable of providing the President with the most accurate information and the soundest advice available. Upon becoming Undersecretary Acheson had immediately sought to coordinate policy-making within the department so as to enable it to compete effectively with its rivals.

Acheson's unceasing campaign, often frustrated, to bring the department under the unified control of the Secretary and the Undersecretary reflected his instinctive linking of knowledge and power.* "For five years," Acheson later remarked, "the conviction had been growing upon me that what the Department needed most was a disciplinary innovation which would convince its members that in fact as well as in theory 'control' and all that that implied and required resided in the Secretary of State as the President's chief secretary. However, that would have to await the arrival of General Marshall." [21] This was not entirely true. Acheson had already succeeded in imparting an intellectual direction and distinction to the department. The nine-thirty meetings with the principal department officers were only part of it. They in turn were expected to coordinate operations with each other and by imparting to their subordinates the sense that what they were doing was important thereby to elicit their best efforts and loyalty. By utilizing the department in this way, Acheson gained for it the President's respect and thereby enhanced its influence with him. Acheson had often disparaged the Foreign Service officers until he became their boss; then, knowing how to get the best out of them, he couldn't say enough good things about them. Kennan, who had for years condemned the diffuse authority and ineffectiveness of the department, unconsciously paid a tribute to Acheson when called upon to prepare recommendations for the Marshall Plan. He remarked, "To the ex-

---

* Byrnes's cavalier treatment of the department annoyed Acheson, all the more so when Byrnes allowed unworthy charges by Congressman Andrew Jackson May, chairman of the House Committee on Military Affairs, relayed to him by none other than Joseph Panuch, security officer for the department, against individuals in the O.S.S. to be the basis for rejecting the annexation of the government's intelligence function to the State Department. Acheson regarded Byrnes's ill-considered and craven capitulation to the forces within the department opposed to the intelligence function, as a mistake. He feared that some other agency, less honest and more likely to emerge as a rival to the department, would exercise it. He was right. Within two years the CIA would be created.

tent that the fortunes of this American policy may be said to have rested
on us, at that particular moment, they rested on the general level of
competence of people of our rank and reputation in the department and
Foreign Service." *

The Turkish and Yugoslav Crisis—Summer 1946

Although the crisis over the Dardanelles had been building up for
some time, it suddenly broke like a summer storm in the months of July
and August 1946. It passed almost as quickly as it came, but the postwar
landscape was never to be the same.

The war in Europe had hardly ended when the Soviet Union made
known its wish that the Montreux Convention of 1936, governing ingress
and egress to the Black Sea, be revised in such a way as to allow the
Soviet Union occupation of bases in Turkey and possible joint control
of the Dardanelles in time of war. On June 7, 1945, Moscow also called
for revision of the Soviet–Turkish frontier in the regions of Kars and
Ardahan in Eastern Turkey. (The current frontier had been agreed upon
in 1922 by none other than the Soviet Commissar for Nationalities, Joseph
Stalin, who had agreed that if Turkey would give up Batum, Russia would
surrender the area adjacent to Kars.) [22] Moscow justified its present
demands for sweeping revision of the Montreux Convention on the
grounds that Turkey, although neutral, had permitted Axis ships of war
to pass through the strait. In point of fact several small Axis ships had
been permitted through because they were not specifically covered by the
Montreux Convention; Turkey's intention was to be "stiffly correct,"
thereby enabling it to refuse passage of any and all larger German warships that might have done Russia serious harm.

At the Potsdam Conference, the United States and Britain went so
far as to endorse the Soviet request for revision of the Montreux Convention. On November 2, 1945, the United States presented the Turkish
government with a note embodying suggestions for revision. Among the
principles proposed was one which read: ". . . except for an agreed
limited tonnage in time of peace, passage through the Strait be denied
to the warships of non–Black Sea powers at all times except with the
specific consent of the Black Sea powers." This was deemed to go such
a long way toward meeting Soviet complaints that its security was not

---

* George F. Kennan, Memoirs, 1925–1950 (Boston: Little, Brown, 1967), p. 345.
They rested also upon the department's reputation for effectiveness which Acheson
had been able to establish during the preceding eighteen months as Undersecretary.
It was fortunate that this effort was succeeding because foreign policy was about to
meet a severe test.

adequately guaranteed. The Turkish government, although inclined to view this proposal as an unwarranted concession, indicated willingness to go along.* But it quickly became apparent that the Soviet Union was not to be satisfied with anything less than Kars and Ardahan and joint Soviet military occupation of the strait.** The heavy-handedness with which the Soviets launched their campaign gradually convinced the British and Americans of the validity of the Turkish claim that Moscow was aiming at nothing less than Soviet domination of Turkey. Over the next six months, the Kremlin mounted a war of nerves against Turkey. Reports reached Washington and London of warnings and threats by Soviet Ambassador Vinogradov to officials of the Turkish foreign ministry of what would happen if they did not yield to Soviet demands.[23]

The Turkish government viewed the Soviet campaign, in conjunction with what was going on in Iran, as nothing less than an attempt to bring Turkey into the same relationship with Russia as Poland. And as Soviet pressure on Ankara mounted, cables from the American ambassador increasingly stressed that "the real Soviet objective towards Turkey is not a revision [of the Montreux Convention] but actual domination of Turkey," a view vehemently shared by the Turkish government and Turkish opinion.[24] The Truman Administration took the occasion of the Turkish ambassador's death to convey his coffin home on the U.S.S. *Missouri* as a gesture of support to the Turks. It was rather showy and old hat, but it was about all the United States could do under the circumstances. Turkey did not make public the Soviet demands of June 1945 in the hope that Moscow would withdraw them; that Moscow knew how injurious to Turkish–Soviet relations its demands were is indicated by the fact that as late as June 26, 1946, the Soviet ambassador still insisted that the Turkish government not confirm publicly that such demands had been made.[25]

In August the war of nerves which had been flashing on and off behind the scenes was suddenly allowed to come out into the open. A Soviet note of August 7 reiterated the demand that a joint Turkish–Soviet

---

* At the outset, Turkey distrusted U.S. efforts to meet the USSR halfway on revision of the Montreaux Convention (*FR:1946*, VII, p. 805). As with the case of Iran, the Turks feared that the great powers would strike a bargain at Turkey's expense.

** Sometimes the Soviet demand for Kars and Ardahan was dropped, but only in the context of reinforcing the claim for agreement by Turkey "regarding the Strait" (*FR:1946*, VII, pp. 812, 816). At the close of one meeting Soviet Ambassador Vinogradov reportedly warned the Turkish foreign minister: "We waited a long time regarding arrangements we wanted with Poland and finally got it; we can wait regarding Turkey."

regime be instituted for control of the Dardanelles. A copy of the note was handed to Acheson by the Soviet chargé d'affaires, Orekhov.*

Although the Turkish government was not unduly alarmed, since a copy of the note had been delivered to London and Washington, Ankara made clear that, while it was trying to be reasonable toward Russia and agreeing to a conference, it was counting on the United States. The chargé d'affaires Elbridge Durbrow also reported from Moscow on August 12 that Stalin had told a visiting Czech delegation that the USSR "had no intention of attacking Turkey."[26] But if this was true it was not entirely reassuring in context of the crisis that was arising over the shooting down by Yugoslavia of two unarmed American aircraft and the war of nerves being played out along the Morgan Line separating Yugoslavia from the contested territory around Trieste.

Moved by the urgency and uncertainty of the situation, on August 15 Acheson convened a State-War-Navy meeting which agreed upon one of the strongest policy memos yet prepared for the President. The memo read in part as follows:

In our opinion, the primary objective of the Soviet Union is to obtain control of Turkey. . . . If the Soviet Union succeeds in obtaining control over Turkey it will be extremely difficult, if not impossible, to prevent the Soviet Union from obtaining control over Greece and over the whole Near and Middle East.[27]

Exaggerated though this view may appear, it rested upon great uncertainty about Soviet intentions and upon a pattern of Soviet threats that were playing like St. Elmo's fire along the entire northern tier of the Middle East from Trieste on the Yugoslav frontier to Azerbaijan in the east.

Previous experience with Soviet obduracy was now invoked to justify the opinion that appeals to reason would not work. The Acheson memo for the first time openly acknowledged that "the only thing which will deter the Russians will be the conviction that the United States is prepared, if necessary, to meet aggression with force of arms." There was, Acheson continued, "a strong possibility that if the Soviet Union is given clearly and unequivocally to understand the United States' position it will cease and desist." [28] But in carrying out this policy, our words and acts would only carry conviction to the Soviet Union "if they are formulated against the background of an inner conviction and determination on our part that we cannot permit Turkey to become the object of Soviet aggression."[29] On the basis of this opinion Acheson recommended, and the President approved, that the United States "must resist with all

---

* FR:1946, VII, pp. 827–828. Commenting on the Soviet note from Moscow, the embassy noted: "We do not believe that an attack on Turkey will be made at present, although possibility of such action exists."

means at its disposal any Soviet aggression and in particular . . . any Soviet aggression against Turkey." [30]

The President agreed that he was prepared to pursue the matter "to its end," and the Soviet, British, and Turkish governments were notified that the United States intended to back Turkey in resisting any changes in the Montreux Convention beyond those agreed to at Potsdam. The British were so stunned that they came by the department to find out if the Administration really meant it. Acheson informed the British ambassador that we meant every word of it, that by appreciating the "seriousness of the step which we were taking, we and the others involved in this matter would conduct ourselves with restraint and seriousness, doing everything in our power to bring about a peaceful solution of the mater. . . ." [31] In notifying the United States ambassador to Turkey of the President's decision, Acheson advised him to tell the Turks that when replying to the Soviet note they should assume "a reasonable, but firm attitude." [32] On August 19 Acheson handed the Soviet chargé d'affaires the American reply, which expressed United States willingness to participate in a conference called to revise the Montreux Convention *but only for revision along the lines previously agreed to,* lines which did not impair Turkey's responsibility for the defense of the strait. [33]

Right in the middle of the strait crisis another crisis broke, this time involving the downing of two American transport planes by Yugoslav fighters. In order to understand the really tense atmosphere that action created it must be remembered that the United States and British forces had for a number of months been menaced by the eruption of Yugoslav forces into the contested zone of Trieste.

Even if Tito was not acting as a puppet of the Kremlin, and Acheson knew that Tito had every reason for acting on his own account, his actions were sufficiently threatening to the Western position in the area that they could not be completely separated from what was going on at the Dardanelles and in Greece.* At the war's end this area of mixed ethnic stock had been declared an international zone pending political

---

* Ernest R. May has written that "Truman and the men around him ascribed to Soviet machinations developments which might with equal plausibility have been explained in other ways." And he cites Yugoslav actions as an example of actions that Truman and his advisers took to be simply those of a Soviet puppet. Some, including George Kennan, did explain it that way but Acheson did not need to view Tito as a puppet of Moscow to recognize that what he was doing also served the general interest of Moscow in weakening Western positions and was part of a general phemonenon that the United States was ill-prepared to deal with. Ernest R. May, *"Lessons" of the Past* (New York: Oxford University Press, 1973), p. 45. The trouble with May and other scholars of a more revisionist cast is that they never tell us how things might have been done differently. The memory of Munich was strong in Acheson's mind but the problems were real and threatening too.

resolution of the boundary problem by the foreign ministers. Tito's frustration with not achieving immediate control of Trieste was so intense that it was feared he might resort to force to make good his claims. Meanwhile demobilization had so reduced the British and American garrisons in Trieste that their weakness was seen as a great temptation to Tito. From a military view the Allies' position was so precarious that General William Morgan, the British commander, had asked for permission to withdraw from Pola, an exposed point, and to turn it over to the Yugoslavs rather than risk having his garrison overrun and annihilated. By the summer of 1946 the situation had become so tense that there was imminent danger of an incident touching off full-scale hostilities. Secretary Byrnes in Paris had twice called in Edward Kardelj, the Yugoslav foreign minister, to remonstrate with him. In an effort to dampen down the panic that seemed to grip the Anglo–American command facing the Yugoslav army, Byrnes and Ernest Bevin, the British foreign minister, relayed instructions to the garrison commander in Trieste that "in event of a general attack by the Yugoslav army, while making every effort to hold in general the status quo . . . your course of action should be consistent with maintaining the Allied Forces tactically intact." [34] To his credit, Byrnes considered a Yugoslav attack unlikely, but he did not rule out local incidents. At the same time, the Yugoslav government was carrying on a war of nerves and harassment against United States embassy personnel in Belgrade. Yugoslav employees of the embassy were being arrested, charged with espionage, and either imprisoned or executed.* Acheson had to deal almost weekly with some threat or indignity to American personnel.

At this juncture Tito's government began complaining about alleged overflights of Yugoslav territory by American planes enroute between Vienna and Rome, and on August 9, a C-47 was forced to land by Yugoslav fighter craft. The first thing Acheson did was to tell the American embassy to notify the Yugoslav government that the United States "regretted that [the plane] had inadvertently passed over Yugoslav territory despite standing instructions to avoid such territory," and that on the basis of information available the plane had lost its way. Hardly had that incident begun to be settled when, on August 19, a second aircraft was actually shot down.

At his press conference that day Acheson opened up all stops. Even if our planes had overflown Yugoslav territory, it was not a matter "which in normal circumstances and in other parts of the world leads to friction

---

* *FR:1946*, VI, pp. 911–912, 913–914. The treatment was so much in excess of that being meted out to United States representatives in other Communist capitals that it was probably not being directed from Moscow but to Tito's own account. But this made it no less ominous.

between governments. . . . Nobody shoots down planes that are lost . . . that isn't the ordinary aid to navigation with which they are familiar."[*] Acheson characterized the actions as "an outrageous performance." On August 22 Acheson notified Byrnes that, on the advice of the Joint Chiefs, the President was approving the use of bombers to fly the Vienna-to-Rome route. Byrnes concurred.

Tito finally expressed his regrets for the incident, while still insisting that American planes were continuing to violate Yugoslav airspace.

More than any other postwar incident, the forcing down of unarmed planes aroused the anger of the American people. Since Yugoslavia was receiving $429,000,000 in UNRRA assistance, 73 percent of which was being financed by the United States, many people naturally demanded that Washington cut off such aid to Yugoslavia. The Secretaries of War and Navy, Patterson and Forrestal, insisted that unless the State Department took energetic action by either protesting to UNRRA or cutting off UNRRA funds to Yugoslavia they would take it up with the President. Acheson demurred from this course of action on the grounds that the United States should not attempt to use UNRRA, an independent international agency, for purely national ends, justified though such action might be. In the end, representations were made to Fiorello La Guardia, head of UNRRA, complaining that while Yugoslavia received vast sums of American aid, it maintained an excessively large military force that directly menaced the Morgan Line, which the United States was trying to guard pending a settlement in Paris, and was giving support to the Greek guerrillas under Markos Vafiades. Aid to Yugoslavia was not cut off, but as in the Turkish crisis, Acheson was becoming increasingly concerned by the intransigence of the other side and by the paucity of American means to influence the situation.

The impact of these events left neither Acheson nor American foreign policy unaffected. The first fact soon to be made plain by the 1946 election results was that Congress would no longer accept the administration of large-scale American relief funds through the United Nations. Either the Administration would have to forego economic aid as an instrument of postwar American foreign policy or it would have to come up with a new approach that put far more stress on American national interests. Furthermore, whether intended or not, the United States had now acquired an acute interest in the Eastern Mediterranean. This second fact was summed up in a Joint Chiefs of Staff memorandum delivered to Acheson on August 23.

---

[*] *FR:1946*, VI, pp. 923–924. A subsequent exchange between the embassy and the department suggests that United States pilots may have gone out of their way to provoke the Yugoslav riposte. But United States officials, including Acheson, tried to meet Yugoslav demands as reasonably as possible.

Strategically Turkey is the most important military factor in the Eastern Mediterranean and Middle East. If Russia attains military dominance . . . by political concessions, her military threat is projected so that there is grave doubt that, in case of a major world crisis, the Middle East and Eastern Mediterranean could be considered militarily tenable for the non–Soviet powers.

In spite of the written word of the United Nations' Charter, many and major indications point to a calculated Soviet policy of expanding Soviet de facto geographical and political control.[35]

While the crisis with Yugoslavia was being played out, that over the Turkish strait gradually began to run its course too. On August 22 the Turkish government sent what Ambassador Wilson called a "reasonable and firm" answer to the Soviet demand for sweeping revision by agreeing to attend a conference but not to accept any terms which would alienate Turkish sovereignty. The United States stand must have done its work because a leisurely Soviet reply came back on September 25 reaffirming Soviet demands but in a softer tone.[36] It was viewed "as extraordinarily mild" [37] and gradually nothing more was heard about the Dardanelles.

These successive crises made real to Acheson, if that was still necessary, the responsibility that the United States held for the fate of certain parts of the world. Regardless of what Soviet intentions were, its actions and those of its associates had had the effect of posing threats to third countries which, if permitted to go unchecked, would have unpredictable and potentially disastrous political and strategic consequences for the United States. Up until 1946 Soviet activities in Eastern Europe and the zone occupied by Soviet forces in Manchuria could be viewed as "consolidationist" in nature. Russian armies were there, after all, as a result of the battle to defeat the Hitlerian and Japanese enemies. But the pressure upon Iran and Turkey, however much an expression of traditional Russian national interest, constituted a new and ominous problem, one which Acheson recognized could not be handled through the United Nations.* It was no longer a question of theorizing, à la George Kennan, about Soviet intentions, but a question of hard cold realities to which the American government had to react or risk the consequences.

All that spring and summer American and British embassy people as well as specialists in the department struggled to decipher the riddle of Soviet intentions. (On one visit to the Kremlin, Ambassador Bedell Smith even asked Stalin if he intended going much further, and Stalin replied, "No, not much further." But how could anyone know?) It was perfectly apparent that the USSR was facing terrible problems at home as a result

---

* Ironically, it is possible to view the crisis in the Eastern Mediterranean as marking the end of America's reliance upon the universalistic strategy of the United Nations and the embarking of the Administration upon a strategy of spheres of influence with all the conflict that such a strategy traditionally entails.

of the war. Was the campaign of fear and threat which Stalin and Andrei Zhdanov initiated that summer designed to mobilize the long-suffering Soviet people or was it to prepare them for possible war against the West? The notion that American authorities inaccurately perceived the extent of Soviet weakness and therefore overestimated the Soviet threat is only partially valid. Neither Durbrow nor Smith reporting from Moscow took Stalin's world revolution rhetoric entirely at face value, nor did Truman or Acheson regard ideology as the motive force behind Soviet expansionism. Neither man stayed up nights reading Lenin (as Dulles is reported to have done) or pouring over exegeses of the Bolshevik operational code, nor were they personally likely to be influenced by theories of Communist conspiracy such as appear to have influenced Forrestal, Leahy, and others.

The problem was that Soviet weakness did not seem to be an obstacle to its exerting pressure on its weaker neighbors. And it was feared that the delays in resolving such critical issues as the economic recovery of Europe, and of Germany in particular, would sooner or later play into Soviet hands. If Stalin was not deliberately delaying the settlement of these critical issues, just what was he up to? * Whatever Soviet intentions, the crises of that summer convinced Acheson that the United States could not just sit by and let situations go by default. They also made him keenly aware of how insubstantial America's capacity to influence Soviet behavior really was. These considerations would be decisive to Acheson's recommendations in the months and years ahead.

The crises of that summer having passed, Acheson departed with Mrs. Acheson for a September holiday in the Canadian Rockies. But while they were gone the President was destined to be engulfed by another of those Cabinet squabbles that marked his first years in office. This time it involved America's policy toward the Soviet Union on the eve of the 1946 congressional elections and in a very political way. Henry Wallace, Roosevelt's Vice-President from 1940 to 1944 and Truman's Secretary of Commerce, had written Truman a letter earlier in the summer taking issue with the pro–British, anti–Soviet tone of American foreign policy. Now he wanted to make a speech on the subject. Wallace was disturbed that American policy toward Russia was too hostile and was being unduly warped in an attempt to appease the Republican Party. As we have noted, there was something to these charges, although

---

* In Stalin's infrequent meetings with Byrnes and the new American ambassador, Bedell Smith, he would exhort them to be patient—that things would straighten themselves out. After a while that kind of advice was as useless and disturbing as Stalin's favorite metaphor of capitalist encirclement. Stalin never evinced an interest in coming to grips with the issues dividing the two powers in a concrete way. He listened, he was reasonable, but nothing much came of these meetings.

by themselves they did not explain the shift in American foreign policy. Before giving his speech, Wallace showed it to Truman, and in characteristic fashion Truman seems either not to have read it or to have failed to gauge the import of certain passages. In the speech Wallace warned that "the tougher we get, the tougher the Russians will get. . . . We must not let our policy be influenced by those inside or outside the United States who want war with Russia, but this does not mean appeasement." [38]

If Wallace's words were intended to strike at Republicans and British imperialists, they caromed off and hit Secretary of State Byrnes. Byrnes, negotiating in Paris, was irate at having his policy criticized by another Cabinet member and, egged on by Vandenberg and Dulles, who were members of the American delegation, threatened to resign. The issue was magnified out of all proportion by the press and by critics of Wallace in and out of government. Given the way the American Cabinet system functions, disagreements over policy often break into print; as long as the President backs the Cabinet member responsible, there is usually little trouble. But this time too many people, including Republicans prepping for the upcoming elections and those out to get Wallace, made their opposition to Wallace a matter of principle. Byrnes insisted that Truman either fire Wallace or he would resign. Feeling he had no choice, Truman asked for and received Wallace's resignation.

The reaction to Wallace's speech was symptomatic of the growing intolerance many Americans were expressing toward anyone who failed to see total evil in the Soviet Union. It is important to note that this emotion existed without the Administration having engaged in any deliberate or recklessly irresponsible anti–Soviet rhetoric. Whatever their private views, Truman, Byrnes, Acheson, and others had been fairly circumspect in their public characterizations of Soviet behavior. It does not do to overlook the impact which the Canadian espionage case and the crises of that summer, sensationally reported, had had upon the average American. The demand for anti–Communist conformity was beginning to set in.

The struggle to define United States policy in terms of the new situation was to continue behind the scenes, but the need to secure public backing for what was a rapidly evolving shift in the assumptions underlying foreign policy was soon to eventuate in the Truman Doctrine. That too was bound to arouse the latent emotions of Americans who preferred not to be bothered.

Acheson returned from his vacation refreshed but confronting the same basic set of problems. By this time the focus had shifted somewhat to the civil war in Greece, where until now the United States had played second fiddle to Britain.

CHAPTER

7

THE GREEK CRISIS AND THE TRUMAN DOCTRINE

THE GREEK civil war presented a still more complicated situation for Truman and his advisers. In the bargain struck between Churchill and Stalin in Moscow on October 9, 1944, Greece had been allotted to the British sphere of influence.[1] In the final months of World War II, strife broke out between the British-backed government-in-exile, committed to the restoration of the monarchy, and various resistance groups opposed to the monarchy. Among the resistance groups, the Communist-led Popular Army of Liberation (E.L.A.S.), the military arm of the National Liberation Front, was by far the most significant.

The British, Churchill in particular, were committed to the restoration of the monarchy and to the support of the government-in-exile. When, therefore, fighting broke out in December 1944 between the pro-royalist government and E.L.A.S., Churchill favored vigorous action by the Greek government, with the support of British troops, to suppress the insurgency. The rebellion was put down, and a cease-fire was worked out [2] that restored an uneasy peace to the scene; but in no way was the bitterness and hostility among the competing political factions ended.

The American government had not approved of Churchill's handling of the situation, and, with the advent of the Labor government, Washington made a concerted effort to correct the worst abuses of Greece's centrist and reactionary government. The crux of the problem was seen to be the need to end the persecution of the opposition and to reintegrate the disaffected sectors of Greek society into the political system. On January 11, 1946, the American ambassador to Greece, Lincoln MacVeagh, warned the Secretary of State that

If we fail to deal with the Greek problem with imagination and understanding at this moment it's our view that the present democratic government will certainly fall and probably be succeeded by a regime of the extreme right which in turn could scarcely fail to produce in due course a Communist dictatorship.[3]

Acheson was acutely aware of the unrepresentative and repressive nature of the Athens regime.* During the first half of 1946 he opposed extending the Greek government additional economic aid until it mended its ways.[4] He was also opposed to the precipitate restoration of the monarchy which had never shown itself to be a particularly worthy representative of the Greek people. It was Acheson's hope, expressed through department policy, that the right-wing government of Premier Constantine Tsaldaris would hold off a plebiscite on the monarchy until passions had died down and some semblance of economic and political normalcy had been achieved.[5] All to no avail. The plebiscite was held on September 1 amid mounting tension along the northern frontier where Greece's Communist neighbors were aiding and abetting the guerrilla movement of General Markos. The result was a victory for the return of the monarchy (1,666,000 for, 525,000 against).**

Acheson was also outspoken in his criticism of Greek border claims against Albania, Yugoslavia, and Bulgaria. He regarded them as fatuous and mischief-making under the circumstances, and he minced few words in telling Tsaldaris that he would be a lot better advised to concentrate on the economic and political rehabilitation of the country. Greek officials seeking United States aid continued to find Acheson one of the hardest

---

* Critics have written that "the possibility that men [referring to the Greek resisters] had taken to the hills of their own and not as agents of a foreign power was never seriously considered." Richard J. Barnet, *Intervention and Revolution* (New York: World Publishing, 1968), p. 121.

This is simply not true. The State Department and Acheson were fully cognizant of the fact that the resisters were disaffected opponents of the regime, driven to resort to guerrilla activities when they could not win power themselves as Tito's forces had done in Yugoslavia. But against the legitimacy of their activities had to be weighed the possible consequences for American interests in the Mediterranean and Europe of the fall of the Athens government; and the example afforded by Soviet actions in Eastern Europe and of neighboring Communist support could not be overlooked in any assessment of the total picture. Secondly, critics have said that "'Democracy' and 'economic stability' never implanted themselves in Iran, Greece, or Turkey after 1945. . . ." Certainly by English or American standards this is probably a true statement, but political conditions did improve in Greece after 1948—political prisoners were gradually released, and parliamentary government, elections, and a modicum of prosperity were realized until the Colonels' Coup of 1968.

** The election was not entirely fair—the pro-government forces mobilizing the vote for the king and obstructing the opposition. But at least it was supervised by an Allied Mission to Observe the Elections, which reported that while "the party representing the government view exercised undue influence," even without that influence "we are satisfied that a majority of votes for the King would have been obtained." *FR:1946*, VII, p. 206.

people to deal with well into the summer.* On August 7 Acheson notified Truman that it was the feeling of the department (and needless to say himself) "that it would be unwise for this Government to commit itself to extend any additional Export–Import Bank credits to Greece until the Greek government has shown that it is taking the measures within its own power to deal with its economic problems." ** Acheson continued to tax the Greek government with its barbaric and repressive policies until well into the fall. When Ambassador Lincoln MacVeagh wired Acheson that he had told the newly enthroned king that certain policies of his present defense minister, Mavromichalis, might be tending toward fascism, and recommended that the king end the government's persecution of the Greek people who had gone into the mountains and whose wives and children were being treated as hostages, Acheson wired back that he should inform the king that the United States government "is in full agreement with ideas expressed." [6]

However much Washington deplored the stupid and repressive policies of the Greek government, it was not prepared to let events take their course. Whatever reservations the United States may have had about supporting Athens in the first half of 1946, they were removed by the incessant attacks upon Greece coming from the Communist bloc. While it was true that the Greek civil war had its roots in an indigenous situation, it was not true that Stalin practiced a hands-off policy after 1945. In discussing the 1946 outbreak, General Markos, leader of the Communist guerrillas, has admitted that Albania, Yugoslavia, and Bulgaria had provided him with arms and ammunition on instruction from Moscow. Markos described Stalin's modus operandi very well: in order to increase support for his guerrillas, Markos agreed to territorial concessions to Greece's Communist neighbors. "In this way Comrade Stalin achieved his aims with regard to Albania, Yugoslavia, and Bulgaria, giving them what they wanted at our expense, so that we might get what we needed to achieve power." [7] The fact that Markos did not receive all that he hoped for and needed does not do away with the charge that Stalin and Greece's Communist neighbors contributed to the threat which the Soviet Union constituted to its immediate neighbors, as well as Greece. A United Nations Inquiry Commission with representatives from a number of countries, including the United States and the USSR, was in Greece investi-

---

* *FR:1946*, VII, pp. 190–191; Acheson to MacVeagh and Acheson to Byrnes. Acheson to MacVeagh, pp. 193–194, pp. 201–202. "I said frankly that U.S. can do little toward long-term aid to Greece if Greek Government unwilling or unable to take measures in order to conserve Greek resources and lay basis for immediate economic reconstruction . . . to prevent profiteering and to tax profiteers. . . ."

** *FR:1946*, VII, pp. 187–188; Acheson to Truman. He told MacVeagh to discourage any Greek mission from coming to the United States and wanting funds.

gating charges by the Greek government at the time of the Truman Doctrine decision. The commission's report, adopted by the Security Council in April 1947 over protests of the Soviet and Polish delegates, indicted Yugoslavia, Albania, and Bulgaria for interfering in Greek internal affairs. So it is not entirely valid to say that the Greek civil war served only as the excuse for instituting the Truman Doctrine. As one shock followed another along the northern tier of the Middle East, the Department of State, whose principal advisers to the President were Byrnes and, more especially, Acheson, could no longer forebear drawing certain conclusions about Soviet motives and intentions. On September 12 it was proposed that, in light of Russia's determination to create instability in the Near East and Eastern Mediterranean, the United States reverse its policy of refraining from the sale of any military equipment to the countries of that area.[8]

On September 24 Byrnes wired Acheson that, given world developments and the hardening of Soviet attitudes on certain issues, the United States should be prepared to extend such economic assistance to Greece and such military assistance to Turkey "as we reasonably can." [9] On September 27 the first big United States credit was extended to Greece.[10]

Soviet intervention in Iran and Turkey was dissipating but the damage to peaceful relations had been done. Acheson shared the view that the area was vital to American strategic interests and was determined to do whatever possible to salvage it.

In Iran, Premier Qavam, still temporizing with the pro–Soviet forces in Teheran, hesitated to risk Soviet displeasure by sending Iranian troops into the territory evacuated by the USSR. Acheson, Loy Henderson, head of the Near Eastern Division of the State Department, and the new ambassador, George V. Allen, were genuinely worried that if Qavam temporized too much by admitting Tudeh party representatives to his Cabinet and failing to assert control over Azerbaijan he might again lose control of the situation. Convinced now of the strategic importance of the northern tier, Acheson ordered Allen to warn Qavam that if he continued to placate Communist forces both internally and externally he would at some point fall victim to their domination. Acheson to Ambassador Allen: "In your conversation with Qavam you should continue to impress upon him that, if his foreign policy persists in preference for a single great power and apparent disregard for those powers which are truly interested in . . . Iran, there is a dangerous possibility that Iran will be deprived of its status as an independent nation. . . ." [11]

To make good on convincing Qavam of United States disinterest and to allay any suspicion of United States support for Britain, Acheson ordered Allan not to make any joint Anglo–American representations to Qavam, but to act entirely on his own initiative. On October 1, Acheson recommended to Byrnes in Paris that "the best hope [of] preserving Iranian independence would be to strength Qavam's hand by [a] positive show [of] U.S. interest in Iran through full implementation [of] our declared policy of economic assistance." On October 5, Byrnes wired his concurrence.* On October 12 the Joint Chiefs of Staff gave its first appraisal of United States strategic interest in Iran. Naturally it viewed Iran as strategically important to the defense of the Middle East and especially to "the military implications of the current Turkish situation." [12] On October 15 the Iranian ambassador formally requested Acheson that Iran be given $10 million credit. On October 18 the Office of Near Eastern Affairs recommended to Acheson that in order to salvage Iran the United States must make economic and military assistance available *immediately*. On October 19 Qavam purged his Cabinet of pro–Soviet elements. On November 14 Acheson notified Allen that the Iranian request for $10 million in military aid would be approved and, on November 22, that an Export–Import Bank loan for Iran was being actively sought by the department. Largely on the basis of this American backing, Qavam finally sent Iranian forces into Azerbaijan; the autonomous regime collapsed.

The importance which the Near East had assumed in Acheson's thinking as a result of the crises of the previous spring and summer now prepared him to overlook the failings of the Greek government if that was necessary to salvage it from collapse. Helping it to survive now outweighed his distaste for its cruelty and stupidity.

In early October Acheson directed the Office of Near Eastern Affairs to examine America's strategic interest in the Greek situation. Even though Greece was still viewed as primarily a British responsibility, Acheson wanted to know what we should do about it should Britain waver. On October 21 Loy Henderson responded with a memorandum that clearly anticipated the main outlines of the Truman Doctrine:

The strategic importance of Greece to U.S. security lies in the fact that it is the only country in the Balkans which has not fallen under Soviet hegemony. Greece and Turkey form the sole obstacle to Soviet domination of the Eastern Mediterranean which is an economic and strategic area of vital importance. . . . We cannot afford to stand idly by in the face of maneuvers and machinations which evidence an intention on the part of the Soviet Union to expand its power. . . . In the broader political sense . . . it may also be pointed out that: It has become clear and indisputable that the national security of the U.S. rests, to a degree which can hardly be over-emphasized, on maintenance of the principles of the United Nations. . . . This requires that those key nations not already under the control of the U.S.S.R. should be confirmed in their faith

---

* *FR:1946*, VII, pp. 520–521; Acheson to Byrnes. "While Qavam has pleaded for U.S. economic assistance . . . Allen has so far been unable to give effective assurances due to our hitherto narrow concept of economic aspects [of] our Iranian policy."

that the U.S. will give complete support to the U.N. principles. . . . The moral strength imparted by high principles and the conviction that the U.S. is defending not only its own cause but that of all free nations is a tremendous factor in world affairs. . . . We should not, therefore, endanger our moral standing nor allow it to appear that the situation has degenerated into an ideological duel solely between the U.S. and the U.S.S.R.[13]

In enunciating four months later the doctrine that bears his name, Truman would put less emphasis on the United Nations. The logic of the situation left no doubt in Acheson's mind that America alone would have to do whatever was needed to keep Greece from going under.

Under Acheson's direction the Department of State now began to take a far more active interest in the fate of Greece. On October 15 Acheson directed that henceforth United States policy be one of positive support for Greece on all fronts—diplomatic, economic, political, and military—on the grounds that the United States could no longer risk the downfall of the government while it was under direct attack by Communist forces supported from Yugoslavia and Albania.[14] But at Byrnes's direction it was decided to continue to rely on Britain to supply Greece with arms lest the United States create the impression of carrying on a provocative policy in Greece with regard to the Soviet Union and its Balkan puppets.[15] Acheson still sought to pressure the Tsaldaris government into reforming its ways by actively recruiting the king's disapprobation of the government's cruel and illegal methods.[16] At the same time Acheson notified the Greek government in no uncertain terms that the United States still had no intention of supporting its exaggerated territorial claims against Bulgaria.*

By late November the Greek economy was about to go on the rocks and guerrilla forces in northern Greece had become so threatening that Acheson had orchestrated a two-pronged strategy (1) of bringing the Greek complaint before the United Nations Security Council and proposing that Secretary General Trygve Lie appoint a commission to investigate Greek charges, and (2) of preparing to supplement the British role as principal backer of Greece if the need arose.** Anticipating the eventual

---

* Minutes of a conversation between Acheson and the Greek ambassador, November 4, 1946, FR:1946, VII, pp. 258–259. Acheson made it clear that the United States was limiting its support to resistance to aggressive action against the territorial integrity of a state—not to a disputed and dubious boundary.

** FR:1946, VII, p. 283. A United Nations Commission of Investigation was established by the Security Council on December 19, 1946. Mark Etheridge was the American member. The Soviet and East European members did all they could to delay and to divert the Commission's attention to the faults of the Greek government. Etheridge's findings were another source of information about the calamitous state of affairs in Greece, and his findings soon convinced Acheson that time was running out. It is noteworthy that the British government, which until now had played down the seri-

responsibility that Washington would have for Greece, Acheson recommended to Truman that some form of economic fact-finding commission be sent to Greece. On December 11 Truman named Paul Porter to head such a commission. On December 28 Acheson could sufficiently anticipate the direction of United States policy to notify MacVeagh that relief was coming in the form of an economic aid program being prepared for authorization by the Congress. Thus the program of United States aid to Greece and Turkey was in the works even before the British formally abdicated responsibility.*

At home the Administration was at the nadir of its political fortunes. The Republicans had scored heavily in the congressional elections of that year (two men, Richard Nixon and Joseph McCarthy, who would become the twin nemeses of the Administration in its problems with Communism, had been elected). The public continued to view Truman as the wrong man in the wrong place (and he enlisted very little popular esteem), an attitude that prevailed to some degree among his principal Cabinet officers.

The Republican victory had a strangely invigorating effect on Truman. Knowing that he had a fight on his hands, Truman seemed to take charge of the situation as he had never done before. He seemed surer of himself and more willing to assert his will against his challengers. He would have to do something because the Joint Congressional Committee on the Budget was recommending a budget ceiling of $31.5 billion, and he was asking for $37.7 as a bedrock minimum, of which $11.2 billion was for national defense.

By late December the situation in Greece was visibly crumbling. All the manifestations of a regime in the last stages of decay were appearing. The civil service, notoriously corrupt and inefficient, was now in a state of paralysis. Greek political leaders were more intent upon sabotaging each other than in leading the country. The British were too far sunk in their own difficulties to have any energy or resources to spare in meeting Greek needs. The promised British re-equipment of the demoralized Greek army was lagging abysmally.[17] Suddenly it became apparent that the rot of years had undermined the whole edifice.

Whether the extent of the crisis would have been discovered in time had not Mark Etheridge and Paul Porter both been there is a moot point. Their diagnoses and warnings, added to those of MacVeagh, hit the de-

---

ousness of the Greek crisis, began to reverse itself rather precipitously. *FR:1946,* VII, p. 264. It was the specter of what it would cost to salvage Greece that led Britain to abruptly terminate its role.

* "For your confidential information program under preparation in Dept. contemplates such aid, but minimum of 2 or 3 months required. . . ." Acheson to MacVeagh, *FR:1946,* VII, p. 286.

partment broadside in January and February. It was no longer a question of eventual American aid to Greece; the question now was would Greece still be a non–Communist country in five, six, or seven weeks. Hundreds of millions of dollars were needed—and needed immediately—sums way beyond Britain's capacity to provide.

Greece was not the only point of decay and collapse. Marshall's mission to China had failed, and that country was on the way to civil war. Europe was ending the winter of 1946–1947 in worse shape than ever. Acheson intended to get action. He warned Truman and the incoming Secretary of State, General Marshall, that a crisis situation was likely to face the Administration within weeks. The millions now earmarked for Greece as a supplement to British aid were not sufficient; what was now needed was a special request to Congress "on an urgent basis for a special loan to Greece." [18] Meanwhile he set Loy Henderson's staff to work collating the reports from Etheridge, Porter, and MacVeagh; ". . . their combined judgment [was] that unless Greece received immediate assurance of large-scale military and financial aid, the last vestiges of the authority of the Greek Government would disappear within a few weeks. . . ." [19] It was also their judgment that the aid "should be administered on the spot by an American mission large enough, expert enough, and exercising sufficiently direct participation in and sanctions over the Greek Government to bring about a thorough reorganization of the Greek economy and administrative system." [20] Consequently, the crisis which broke with the delivery of the British notes,* announcing that Britain was unable to continue to support Greece and would have to abdicate its role within thirty days, was not entirely unexpected. The British may even have decided that American interest afforded an opportune moment to lay down a burden which had become financially unsupportable.

Because Marshall was still taking hold as Secretary and was due to leave the following week for Moscow, the formulation of a new American policy for Greece and Turkey fell to Acheson. A sense of drama attended the ensuing meetings, not because the United States had decided to oppose Soviet moves—that was already being done—but because everyone felt that for once the department was prepared to do something quickly, efficiently, and decisively, and because everyone knew that this time Congress and the American people would be asked to underwrite the policy and, therefore, to understand its necessity.

Efforts to elicit Soviet intentions or to find some diplomatic basis for accommodation had consistently failed. The struggle over Greece was

---

* The British *aide-memoire* notifying the department of its decision was delivered unofficially on Friday, February 21, and officially on Monday, February 24.

shaping up as part of a great power struggle for control of an area strategically important to the United States. Acheson recognized that the Eastern Mediterranean held the key not only to vast reserves of oil (which might someday be vital to Western economies), but also that its fall to the Soviet Union would deliver a shock to the morale and security of Western Europe from which it might not recover. Whatever the legitimate interests of the Soviet Union in the area, Acheson was determined not to let the fate of the area be sealed by Soviet threats and blackmail. "To dawdle over pros and cons and be delayed by qualms about the unsavory character of the Greek Government or fear of being associated with British imperialism or of seeming to threaten Russia was absurd and dangerous." Because Acheson admired the stability and order which Britain had given to international relations for almost a century, he had no misgivings about America stepping into Britain's place in those parts of the world on which the freedom and security of the West clearly seemed to depend. (By contrast he was not nearly so disturbed by the possible fall of Nationalist China because events there seemed less important and less amenable to American influence.)

Over the weekend Loy Henderson in consultation with Acheson worked out a general plan for a major program of economic and military aid to Greece and to Turkey. Shortly before noon on Monday, February 24, Marshall reported to Truman the gist of the problem and the recommendations that would soon be forthcoming. The essential decision to ask Congress for a full-scale aid program was approved by Marshall on February 25 and by President Truman on February 26. With that, responsibility for planning was turned over to Acheson.

The problem was not with turning aid to Greece to good effect; the problem lay in getting the American Congress and the American people to accept the necessity for such a program. The tide of withdrawal, which Roosevelt had prophesied would see American forces gone from Europe within two years, was flowing as strongly as ever. Republican majorities had just taken control of both houses of Congress and, according to Speaker Joe Martin, were determined to fulfill election promises for a 20 percent across-the-board reduction in income taxes with a collateral reduction in government spending. On the foreign front, Europe was just simply not recovering from the war, and to make matters worse it had just been struck by one of the worst winters in living memory. The British Loan was being spent with no evidence that it was stemming Britain's disastrous balance-of-payments problem. Cables were pouring in from all parts of Western Europe warning that economic breakdown and chaos were likely unless something was done immediately.

At home, the Republicans were using the crisis in postwar relations to sow dissatisfaction with the Administration's efforts to preserve even a modicum of normalcy in its dealings with the Soviet Union and to undermine confidence in its plans to help Europe recover. Senators like Vandenberg were playing a double game—holding the Administration responsible for not making Russia adhere to the letter of the agreements signed at Yalta and Potsdam and at the same time rejecting the Administration's arguments that only a larger, more concerted economic and political effort by the United States could save Western Europe and such other parts of the world as were threatened by starvation and chaos.

Clearly the Greek crisis provided a situation in which it might be possible to reverse popular attitudes and get the American people to do something before it was too late. Acheson was well aware that in trying to decide what to do in difficult situations "too frequently the mind vacillates between unpleasant choices and escapes through procrastination." [21] That had to be avoided.

But the country was far from ready to accept any new sacrifices. It was all the more critical, therefore, that congressional leaders be convinced of the validity and necessity of the Administration's program of economic and military assistance to Greece. Only then would there be any hope of winning over the rest of the Congress and of rallying popular support. According to Joseph M. Jones,[22] Secretary Marshall's opening statement to the congressional leaders asked to gather at the White House on February 27 was strangely lacking in force, and Acheson, who had accompanied him to the briefing, asked to speak. Familarity with the situation permitted Acheson to speak in bold and ominous terms.

What Acheson had to say was said with the deliberate intention of stimulating his listeners; but it was also an expression, somewhat dramatic in formulation, of a conviction that the values of western civilization—individual freedom versus the corporate or totalitarian state—were at stake. Coming on the heels of Nazi Germany, what was happening in Eastern Europe seemed ominous.

Only two great powers remain in the world . . . the United States and the Soviet Union. We have arrived at a situation unparalleled since ancient times. . . . Not since the period of Athens and Sparta and of Rome and Carthage has there been such a polarization of power. . . . We have also in the world today the same challenging problem which existed in the period of ancient history of one great power being a democracy, laying its stress upon the worth of the individual . . . while the other great power is a police state exerting rigid control over the individual.[23]

Perhaps Acheson was seeing things too much through the eyes of an American reared and educated on the virtues of Anglo-American democracy and committed to the system that brought him success. But his convictions about individual freedom were salient and vital and not simply an ideological mask for economic or elite interests. He saw the collapse of Western Europe as a probability that, should it occur, would either close an all-too-brief chapter in the history of human progress or lead to another war. Admittedly Acheson's class background and his powerful belief in the sanctity of individual conscience and freedom are not separable and clearly distinguishable sources of motivation, and one may argue that, in justifying the Truman Doctrine, Acheson was also defending capitalism. But he was also defending something that he considered more important than capitalism—namely the necessity for individual freedom and democracy to survive against a tyranny not unlike the one from which Europe had just been rescued. He did not hide that, in defending Europe and the Middle East, America was also intent upon its own security and its own access to vital resources but these were means to the end not the end in itself. For the United States to take steps to strengthen countries threatened with Communist subversion, Acheson told the congressmen, was not to pull British chestnuts out of the fire; it was to protect the security of the United States. Stakes in the Middle East were so high that failure of the United States to act decisively would open three continents to Soviet penetration and have an injurious psychological effect on Europe, which was facing critical economic and political difficulties of its own. It was a matter of building our own security and safeguarding freedom by strengthening free peoples against Communist aggression and subversion. We have the choice, Acheson concluded, "of acting with energy or losing by default."

Never, Acheson recalled later, had he spoken "under such a pressing sense that the issue was up to me alone." [24]

In casting relations in such a stark context, Acheson said nothing more than what Soviet leaders and propagandists had been saying all along; therefore, that Acheson and the United States should be picked out as the initiators of the Cold War has always been a mystery. Had Acheson understood as much as we do about the mirror-image effect of one country's words or actions engendering a similar response in the other, he might well have tempered his strictures, but that would not have changed the starkly bipolar and conflict-ridden nature of the situation. The impervious and enigmatic nature of the other side seemed only to add point to the belief expressed by Acheson that two different ways of life were being contested.

Acheson's statement had its desired effect. "Mr. President," said Vandenberg, now chairman of the Foreign Relations Committee, "if you will say that to the Congress and the country, I will support you and I believe most of its members will do the same." But the effort to educate the American people was far from over. Like human beings everywhere, Americans were not interested in doing things for other people unless they

could be moved to believe that some vital principle or interest was at
stake. A great deal of effort, therefore, went into determining just what
Truman should say. Acheson set the tone for those in the department
charged with drafting the President's message by "repeating the exposition that had so impressed the legislators." [25]

Right from the outset Acheson had perceived of the Truman message
as much a call to action as a diplomatic announcement. Why should it
be kept from the American people that there was a conflict? Why should
it be kept from the American people that if the United States did not do
something to save Greece and other parts of the world threatened by
starvation and chaos, hostile forces would take over and add to the
already tense situation prevailing in Europe and the Middle East? For
better or for worse, United States foreign policy turned on the right of
other states to realize their political independence and sovereignty; that
was the principal reason why the United States had fought in both world
wars. If it was wrong, then American intervention in both those wars
was wrong. Given the spectacle of what was happening in Eastern
Europe and in Russia itself and the fact that Soviet pressure on Iran and
Turkey was very much like the pressure Hitler had exerted on his prospective victims, what else could one assume but that there existed a
conflict between two different ways of life? The more reasonable Soviet
attitudes toward Finland and Czechoslovakia were lost from sight when
contrasted with what was happening in Poland, Hungary, Romania,
Turkey, Iran, and Greece.

In the sense that the Soviet and Western political systems were fundamentally different, and if one triumphed the other would disappear, it
was a contest between two different ways of life. It wasn't only American
capitalists who believed this; a majority of people in other countries,
including the European democracies, felt the same way. If that view was
true—and the only way to arouse the American people was by telling them
it was true—then Acheson was determined to do so. Not to stress what
was self-evident would deprive the policy of its only acceptable justification to the American people.

Hence, in drafting the President's speech, Acheson took over, almost
intact, the passage in the State Department working paper which began:

One of the primary objectives of the foreign policy of the United States is the
creation of conditions in which we and other nations will be able to work out
a way of life free from coercion.

And he included the following passages:

At the present moment in world history nearly every nation must choose between alternative ways of life. The choice is too often not a free one.
One way of life is based upon the will of the majority, and is distinguished

by free institutions, representative government, free elections, guarantees of individual liberty, freedom of speech and religion, and freedom of political expression.

The second way of life is based upon the will of a minority forcibly imposed upon the majority. . . . I believe that it must be the policy of the United States to support free peoples who are resisting attempted subjugation by armed minorities or by outside pressure.

Then, to take the provocative and threatening edge off of the policy, Acheson declared that American help "should be primarily through economic and financial aid. . . ." From the perspective of a quarter of a century these words may sound piously self-serving and moralistic, but in the context of the time, people quarreled not so much with the truth they were expressing as with the possibility that they might exacerbate Soviet–American relations.

There were two kinds of objections to the speech, both of which Acheson brushed aside. Kennan objected to the tone and ideological content of the message. "The Russians might even reply by declaring war!" [26] This was the kind of objection that always came from Kennan because he could not understand that to be successful any American foreign policy required the backing of the American people, and if the American people were to be supportive, a deliberate appeal had to be made to their moral as well as their intellectual sense.

The other complaint, more of a recommendation, came from Clark Clifford, who, reflecting the White House desire to cast its appeal as widely as possible, wanted to include a passage not only lamenting the worldwide trend away from the system of free enterprise but also linking its gradual disappearance to the threat to democracy at home. Acheson rebuffed Clifford's recommendation even more summarily than Kennan's. That a Labor government in Britain was asserting state control over the economy had nothing to do with the principle of the Truman declaration because it came into power through democratic means.

On March 10, in anticipation of what he was going to say, Truman, with Acheson backing him up, held a meeting with an enlarged congressional delegation that now included Senator Taft. There was considerable discussion and many questions were asked, but no opposition was registered. According to Reston, who had a close relationship with Vandenberg, the latter made it clear that he was in favor of moves to block Soviet expansion at key points and that "he insisted that the President was obligated to explain in the most direct terms to the Congress and to the country why it was the United States was moving into these areas." The President assured his listeners that he intended to lay the facts on the line.

On March 12 the President addressed a joint meeting of Congress.

Contrary to some critics, he did not ignore the role of the United Nations or play down the corruption of the Greek regime; neither did he ignore the role which the British government had been playing nor the need to send large numbers of American personnel, including military. He acknowledged that Turkish needs were different from Greek needs but that both countries shared the same general problem: the need to shore up national strength. In all, Truman asked for $400,000,000, a sizable sum in those days. Republicans now recoiled in horror.

The public reaction to the speech was all that Acheson could have hoped for. The *New York Times* said:

The epoch of isolation and occasional intervention is ended. It is being replaced by an epoch of American responsibility. Our aim must be to establish conditions under which the United Nations and our own principles have a chance to survive.[27]

Everywhere, Truman's address was received as a historic declaration—something of a break with past American efforts to avoid power politics, but nonetheless necessary.

Some like Walter Lippmann, who supported the principle of direct action in Greece and Turkey, were disturbed by the open-endedness of the commitment and the bypassing of the United Nations. Lippmann conceded that there was not much the United Nations could do, but unilateral action was bad business; we should have informed the UN Secretary General and brought our actions as much into line as possible with the principle of collective security.

Immediately following his address, Truman departed for Key West, leaving Acheson behind to defend it. In the weeks that followed Acheson testified before the House and Senate Foreign Relations committees. Acheson rejected the charge that the United States was embarked upon an ideological crusade.

There have been various statements in the press that this was an ideological crusade. That is not what the President is talking about. He is talking about [situations] where a free people is being coerced to give up its free institutions. . . .

The element of subversion was evident in the Greek situation a year later when Tito's defection from the Soviet bloc dried up external support for the Markos forces (by then headed by Nikoz Zacharides) in the north. Acheson could have pointed to the Chinese civil war as an example of an ideological conflict from which the Administration was endeavoring to disentangle the country, but he did not want to arouse the pro-Chiang lobby in the Congress. Acheson went on to say that Truman did not intend to imply "one must react to [threats] in exactly the same way. The situations of different cases are utterly different, and what you do in one case you cannot do in another case." Clearly Acheson had not thought through the implications of the sweeping language he had used to mobilize public opinion. He was both annoyed and provoked by those who, like Congressman Walter Judd, wanted to know why if aid to Greece was justified, aid to Nationalist China was not. Had Acheson been better positioned to engage in a debate on China, he might have explained that the political and logistical conditions of China did not justify additional American support, whereas the strategic and political situation in Greece did. Such a response would not have pleased Judd and others of the China lobby, but it would have clarified the strategic calculus implicit in Acheson's thinking at the time. Although Acheson did not like being caught in such logical contradictions, they were clearly the price of his desire to mobilize public opinion and not of a secret desire to involve America in a policy of worldwide interventions; Acheson had no intention of letting the United States become involved in China or anywhere else where conditions were hopelessly inimical to American success.

Despite his impatience with some of the criticisms levied against it, Acheson worked with Vandenberg to make Truman's proposal more palatable by promising that its global scope would be limited in practice and by tying the program more closely to the United Nations. As a result it was passed in the House by a large majority, 333 to 66, and in the Senate, 79 to 4. So it is hard to say that Acheson lacked the tactical and political skills for getting along with Congress.

Despite later criticism, the Truman Doctrine was widely supported at the time, both at home and in Europe. In taking the lead in proposing the Truman Doctrine, Acheson was acting in accordance with both American and European sentiment and the traditional imperatives of equilibrium." [28] In reacting to the sphere of influence which the Soviet Union had carved out for itself in Eastern Europe, Acheson was acting according to the logic of the situation. The peace and security of Europe had always depended upon some form of the balance of power. Traditionally, the balance had been maintained by the European system. But with the eclipse of the European system and the emergence of a global system, it was inevitable that the United States, supported by its European allies, should take the lead in reconstituting the balance. As Aron observed, "The Americans were responding to an appeal from the Europeans and replacing Britain at its own request." [29] Why should Washington have been expected to show more forebearance than Moscow when the issues were so clearly posed? In his conversations wtih the Yugoslav Communist Djilas, Stalin as much as admitted that he would have been surprised had Washington behaved differently. Nor will it do to make too much of the style and rhetoric of the actual declaration except insofar as it stimulated a crisis atmosphere at home.

The Truman Doctrine was a defensive policy dictated by the uncertainties of Soviet intentions in an area of the world vital to Western interests and by the opportunities for effective action within a limited and definable situation. While Acheson had taken the lead in packaging the Truman Doctrine in the universalistic rhetoric essential to winning public support, its actual scope and intent were designed to serve an essentially defensive and prophylactic policy objective. Once the situation in the area stabilized it remained a purely secondary area of Acheson's interest until after the Korean attack. But henceforth and in other places the Kremlin would be confronted by a set of precisely formulated policies. It still had time to make some adjustments, but the interregnum of American powerlessness and withdrawal was about to undergo a rapid reversal.

CHAPTER

8

THE MARSHALL PLAN

ACHESON KNEW for some time that the aid to Greece and Turkey was only an advance installment on a much larger problem—that of European economic recovery. Despite the earlier loans to Britain and France and other forms of aid to destitute countries, Europe was not recovering. Like an automobile engine on a cold day, the European economy was sputtering but so far it had failed to ignite. The critical levels of production and exchange needed to make the economies work had simply not been achieved. Unless something drastic was done, people would simply lose hope, and the struggle to survive would degenerate into civil war—at least in France and Italy where the hostility between the Communists and their enemies was open and naked.

Acheson had warned earlier against excessive optimism about Europe's recovery and against the assumption that Britain was just another untrustworthy economic competitor. Now the winter of 1946–1947, the severest within memory, had dealt a stunning blow to Britain's recovery plans.* Beyond a shortage of coal and steel, Britain was suffering from wartime obsolescence of its industry and the deferment of maintenance. The resultant losses were proving far greater than had been anticipated. Britain's sources of supply in Southeast Asia and elsewhere had not recovered to anywhere near the levels anticipated. ("The world food situation has hardly eased at all; the raw material situation has become worse rather than better.") [1] The lifting of price controls in America and the pent-up demand for supplies everywhere had shot prices up by 40 percent and thereby reduced not only the value of the American loan but of British currency holdings by 40 percent. The continuingly disrupted and de-

---

* "The February coal and power crisis—the result of unprecedented weather conditions impinging upon a critically low stock position—has set this process of recovery back. It has left in its wake a continuing shortage of coal and steel, which will continue to hamper output for the rest of the year." FR:1947, III, p. 20.

pressed state of world trading relations was denying Britain a return to its normal markets and forcing upon it an unprecedented dependence on American and Canadian imports without any compensating dollar flow from sales to third-world countries with whom Britain normally enjoyed a favorable balance of payments. To make matters worse, Britain had incurred a net wartime indebtedness to many parts of the world which it was both morally and legally bound to repay. It had been hoped that, as a result of the American loan, Britain would be able to negotiate agreements with Egypt, India, and other countries to whom it owed sizeable sums, which would permit Britain to repay them over time and, in the interim, enable it to return to free convertibility of its gold, dollar, and other holdings on current account. Nothing had worked out as anticipated.

The situation on the continent, if not worse, was no better, and there it was complicated by a high degree of political disunity and disorder. Although the Communist parties of France and Italy were not actively opposing those governments, there was a lack of confidence in the ability of the existing governments to solve their problems. In France, for example, de Gaulle was threatening to return to the political arena with the intent of overthrowing the incumbent Third Force government and, at the risk of a showdown with the Communists, of seizing power.

All the parts of the problem were interrelated. Unless Germany recovered and was able to end the increasing drain which it made upon Britain's dollars, it would not be possible for Europe to recover, and unless Britain recovered the world economy would not recover.* A sense was growing that if recovery was to be achieved, greater attention to the interdependence of all parts of the world economy was absolutely essential.

No one as familiar with international economic and monetary problems as Acheson could ignore the meaning of all this. Already Britain was having to abdicate its role in Greece. What would happen if it had to do the same in Germany, Palestine, India, Malaya? Yet that was precisely what the logic of Britain's situation implied. Where would America be then? Acheson knew that the crisis over Greece was only part of a much larger and equally urgent problem that the United States had been avoiding. Even if the Soviet Union had not existed, the problem would still have been there; Roosevelt's optimism had been self-deceiving when he be-

---

* The dependence of the rest of the world upon the British economy was underscored in their many Treasury and Cabinet reports to Washington. There could be no doubt that Britain's economy and financial system constituted the linchpin of a worldwide structure of delicate interdependence. Everywhere—in Africa, Asia, and Latin America—financial arrangements were like a house of cards. Should Britain fail to master its problems, situations everywhere would become difficult if not unmanageable.

lieved that postwar collaboration between the United States and the Soviet Union under the aegis of the United Nations would suffice. The problem had always been far more fundamental and the demands upon the United States far greater than Roosevelt had allowed for. The fact that Soviet–American cooperation had failed to materialize did not create the economic crisis; it only made it more difficult.

People often debate the genesis of the Marshall Plan. The origin is very clear. On March 5 Acheson met with Truman to discuss the upcoming program of aid to Greece and Turkey. At the end of their hour-long discussion, Acheson issued a memo:

In the course of our discussions on the Greek and Turkish problem, frequent reference was made to the fact that this is only part of a much larger problem growing out of the change in Great Britain's strength and other circumstances not directly related to this development. I believe it important and urgent that study be given by our most competent officers to situations elsewhere in the world which may require analogous financial, technical and military aid on our part.

I have asked Assistant Secretary Hilldring [Major General John Hilldring] . . . to direct attention . . . to this important problem and, in consultation with the Treasury Department, undertake a thorough study to be submitted to me or Secretary Marshall as soon as possible.[2]

Instead of pursuing trade and investment policies designed to give United States business the maximum advantage, the Truman administration felt America would prosper in a prosperous world: American private enterprise would be encouraged to export capital, technology, skills, and management to foster economic growth. It was Acheson's economic policy to see that Europe and other countries were endowed with the capacity to compete with the United States economically, which they eventually did, as a means of making them stronger, more prosperous allies and trading partners.

Following several discussions with Acheson, John Hilldring, the State Department member of the Ad Hoc Committee of the State-War-Navy Coordinating Committee, defined the tasks as follows:

. . . incident to possible requests which may be made to the United States by foreign governments for substantial economic, financial, or technical assistance, or for military equipment,
a) What are the countries to which, within the next few months, we may find it necessary to give . . . aid
b) What are the relevant considerations of United States national security and interest
c) . . . What . . . should be the character of such assistance
d) What arrangements should be made with foreign governments . . . to as-

sure to the maximum practical extent the accomplishment of our objectives . . .[3]

In its report of April 21 the Ad Hoc Committee already stressed the global nature of the problems which any future aid program must meet. Perhaps more heavily than later reports, it also stressed containment: any future U.S. aid program should "support economic stability and orderly political processes throughout the world and oppose the spread of chaos and extremism, . . . prevent the growth or advancement of national or international power which constitutes a substantial threat to U.S. security and well-being, . . . orient foreign nations toward the U.S. [and] toward support of the U.N. . . ." [4]

The report also urged that we act only if the problem at hand "is one within our economic, technical, and financial capabilities," that the United States have full knowledge "of the manner in which the means provided are distributed and used," and that the country being aided "proceed with the development and support of free and democratic institutions." [5]

The Economic Aid Group of the Ad Hoc Committee, recognizing the great economic interdependence of all European countries, emphasized that recovery should be continent-wide, even to including the Soviet satellites. (This suggestion would have an important bearing on the subsequent decision to entice the USSR into participating in what became known as the Marshall Plan.) But it placed particularly heavy emphasis on the revival of German production and trade, because the recovery of Europe had always been predicated upon the recovery of Germany. This piece of realism had not been ignored at the war's end, as the struggle over the Morgenthau Plan makes clear, but it had been played down, and occupied Germany had been treated as a separate economic and political problem from the rest of Europe. Contrary to intentions, however, the occupation zones of Germany had also become economically separate entities, each power taking from its zone and bargaining for what it could get from the other zones. Now, as Europe continued to languish and even decline, the importance of Germany came rushing back to the foreground.

During all these deliberations Secretary of State Marshall was in Moscow trying to negotiate peace treaties for Germany and Austria, and Acheson was left to run the department. The success or failure of Marshall's mission would be very important, because with the recognition that there could be no economic recovery of Europe without Germany, it was determined that either Germany would participate as a unified economic entity under four-power control or, failing that, its Western zones would be given back their independence and enabled to play an integral role in Europe. (The merger of British and American zones had already occurred that winter.)

The second part of the problem facing Marshall had been the question of reparations, first discussed at Potsdam. Conscious of the friction that would later arise should the American people discover that they were being taxed at one end of the German cow to subsidize reparations at the Russian end, Byrnes had proposed that the United States would agree to the line of the Oder and Western Neisse Rivers for the western boundary of Poland *if* the Soviets would agree to the principle that payments for imports should constitute the first charge on German production and that reparations should only come *after the Germans had enough resources to subsist without external assistance.* Despite, or perhaps because of, the unresolved ambiguities of the Potsdam agreement and the fact that Germany was never brought under a unified administrative system, friction quickly developed over reparations. The Russians were determined to enforce their reparations policy at any cost and insisted that reparations must not be relegated to second place as a charge on the German economy. Under the circumstances of the occupation, part of these costs would have to be shifted to the Western powers, and the United States was equally determined not to subsidize Soviet reparations. A great deal had changed in the intervening years since Potsdam, and just as the United States could not expect to undo anything that had been done in Eastern Europe, Moscow should not have expected to alter the pattern in the Western zone. As Hadley Arkes has observed, "In the end, the Soviets could not evade the consequences of their . . . past. Given the character of the Soviet regime, given the peculiar quality of its ties to foreign parties and subversive movements, the burden of proof [of its good intentions] by 1946 had to rest with the Soviet Union. If the evidence was no more than evenly balanced, one could not expect responsible men to put history out of mind or forget the few reliable things they knew." [6] In May, 1946, General Lucius Clay ordered a halt to the removal of American plants from the American zone on the grounds that "we were being placed in the position not only of financing reparations to the Soviet Union but also of agreeing to strip our own zone . . . without getting the benefits which would come from the amalgamation of all zones." [7] Although Clay's decision had not sealed the division of Germany, in the absence of any new agreements the division of Germany *was* being sealed and quickly becoming an issue in the East–West confrontation.

A point had been reached in the spring of 1947 where either Germany had to be restored as an integral part of Europe's economic recovery or there would be no recovery, and the Moscow Foreign Ministers' Conference of March–April 1947 represented the last chance Russia would have to influence choices involving the Western zone. Despite all the ballyhoo over the Truman Doctrine, the Kremlin did not seem to have understood the critical nature of the economic problems facing British and American authorities. Had the Soviets been more aware of what the Western economic crisis portended, they might have been more flexible. Instead the Moscow Conference soon degenerated into the same old wrangles. The Soviets rejected American proposals for a federated Germany on the grounds that the rights accorded the individual states and provinces would favor ex–Nazis and reactionaries and preserve intact the German trusts and industries which had dealings with American and British business and financial groups. The Kremlin favored ties to a centralized German state based on "democratic" elections, which Marshall and Bevin took to mean that only parties approved by the Kremlin could take part.

The Soviets also failed to get the message about reparations. They seemed completely oblivious to the United States' determination not to renege on the terms established at such a high price at Potsdam—namely that reparations would be made only after an unsubsidized minimal standard of life had been established for Germany. Since the Western zones of Germany were still little more than rubble-strewn charnel houses, Molotov might have done better than to insist upon terms which Russia was obviously not going to get, any more than the United States was going to undo the situation in Eastern Europe. Whatever the merits of the Soviet case for reparations or, for that matter, of Soviet claims to participation in the Ruhr as opposed to its exclusive development for the benefit of the West, a more realistic Soviet bargaining position might have made a difference at this point, especially because Marshall and Bevin were as yet not so unalterably anti–Soviet that they would have been closed to negotiation. But the Kremlin seemed to have been only superficially aware of the magnitude of the economic crises facing capitalism; either that or it was confident that the West would not surmount the crisis and Russia need merely hold firm. Making a final courtesy call on Stalin, Marshall and his translator, Charles Bohlen, were keenly struck by Stalin's seeming indifference to what was happening in Germany.

During our visit, which lasted about an hour and a half, Stalin took a relaxed attitude toward the failure of the conference to achieve any results. Doodling the inevitable wolf's heads . . . [Stalin] asked what difference it made if there was no agreement. "We may agree the next time, or if not then, the time after that." To him there was no urgency about settling the German question. We should be detached and even relaxed about the subject. This was his main thesis, and he answered almost all of Marshall's questions with similar responses.[*]

---

[*] Charles E. Bohlen, *Witness to History 1929–1969* (New York: W. W. Norton, 1973), p. 263. Bohlen continues: "Stalin's seeming indifference to what was happening in Germany made a deep impression on Marshall."

In many ways, the failure of these meetings contributed directly to the Marshall Plan. Marshall came away convinced that Stalin, looking over Europe, saw that the best way to advance Soviet interests was to let matters drift. But the Truman Doctrine had already given evidence of the American government's unwillingness to let that happen. Was not the Kremlin aware that a similar active American response might attend delays over Germany? On the way back from Moscow, Marshall stopped in Berlin for a hurried meeting with Clay, who was given authorization on the spot "to proceed vigorously with the strengthening of the bizonal organization," for both Marshall and Bevin were resolved that any "further delay would serve no purpose." [8]

Immediately upon his return, Marshall discussed the problems of European reconstruction in a radio address to the American people. He presented the problems of effecting a peace settlement for "the vital center of Germany and Austria—an area of large skilled population, of great resources and industrial plants." He next observed that the complex character of the problems should be understood "together with their immediate effect on the people of Europe in the coming months . . . *we cannot ignore the factor of time here* [emphasis added]. The recovery of Europe has been far slower than had been expected. Disintegrating forces are becoming evident. The patient is sinking while the doctors deliberate. . . . Whatever action is possible to meet these pressing problems must be taken without delay." [9]

Then Marshall called in Kennan, director of the newly established Policy Planning Staff, and ordered him to study the problem of *Europe's* need for American aid. Kennan's first memorandum stressed many of the principles that gave the Marshall Plan its distinctive character. He agreed with his chief that the Communists were exploiting the economic and political dislocation of Europe and that America must embark on a comprehensive economic strategy to overcome those weaknesses. But the program should be as much as possible a result of European initiatives; it should be a grant program and not a loan program, and the program "should be designed to encourage and contribute to some form of regional political association of Western European States." [10]

The urgency of Europe's economic recovery still took precedence over any fear Kennan may have harbored against dividing Europe: "Our occupational policies in Germany and Austria must be shaped toward enabling the Western zones of those countries to make the maximum contribution to economic restoration in Western Europe in general." [11] Kennan also endorsed the principle that was later adopted of extending the program "to Czechoslovakia and other states within the Russian orbit" provided they can give guarantee "that their participation will be constructive."

Acheson echoed Kennan in arguing, "It would be a colossal error for the U.S. to put itself in the position where it could be blamed for the division of Europe." [12] Not even Russia was to be excluded if it wished to participate.

Much has been made of the conditions attached to the Marshall Plan as evidence of ulterior motives. Certainly the time was long past when the Administration could talk of Soviet–American friendship and still hope to get anything accepted by the Congress or by the American people. And no government has ever acted without some ulterior purposes in mind. The question is: what ulterior motives did the Administration harbor in extending the invitation to the Soviet Union? The primary interest of the Administration in pushing for the Marshall Plan was to bring about European recovery. As one authority has written, "The urgency of recovery justified whatever efficiency demanded, and what efficiency demanded . . . was a very high level of coordination among the Europeans themselves. At the very least, coordination would involve a vast exchange of information . . . and comprehensive data on national development plans and the state of capital and consumer needs. To reveal information of this kind to other nations was to lay bare the strengths and weaknesses of a national economy." [13]

The European states were accustomed to having their economic situations known, and there was little feeling, except perhaps among local Communists, that joint planning would lead to American intervention and imperialism. (Later on the French resented the pressure put upon them through the Marshall Plan to accept the creation of the West German republic.) But the Soviet Union was in a different position. Traditionally secretive and morbidly suspicious of outside influences, Russia could easily view the Marshall Plan as a threat to its grip on Eastern Europe. Yet given its political situation at home the Administration was unlikely to secure passage of any grandiose spending program that did not give evidence of providing a final and absolute answer to Europe's economic recovery. Hence, ulterior motives were inherent in the logic of the situation. The Administration could not hope to secure passage of a program that did not require some degree of concession from the Soviets; and the Soviets could not participate in a program that might weaken their grip on Eastern Europe or involve a break with their traditional suspicion and fear of Western influences.

That did not mean, however, that the invitation was deceptive. The Soviet Union and its satellites were important producers of food and raw materials that Western Europe needed. A revival of East–West trade could have reduced the burden on the United States and relieved some of the pressure on the Europeans for exports to the dollar area. . . . Thus Kennan urged Marshall to "play it straight"—to make the offer an open one and then, if necessary, see how the Soviet Union could fit in.[14]

Acheson's role with regard to the Marshall Plan now became that of directing public attention to the issues and building support for a program in congressional and media circles. Profiting from the backlash of criticism following the Truman Doctrine speech, which had accused him of being too negative and ideological, Acheson carefully tailored his statements to the economic and practical nature of the problem.[15]

So great was Truman's confidence that he virtually left to Marshall and Acheson the drafting of the initiative and the means by which it would be developed and presented to the American people. But of course Truman was being kept abreast of developments, and Acheson did secure the President's approval of the sweeping statement about the economic problems facing both the United States and Europe when he agreed to speak in the President's place to the Delta Council in Cleveland, Mississippi.

Asked by Truman to substitute for him, Acheson agreed to do so provided he could use the occasion to lay out the dimensions of the European recovery problem and set off a public discussion that would stimulate Administration efforts to come up with a program. Truman agreed.

No attempt was made to build up public expectations in connection with the speech, but Acheson knew that the press, already stimulated by discussions of Europe's economic crisis, would pay attention. On May 8, 1947, speaking to a shirt-sleeve crowd of farmers and businessmen in the agriculturally rich delta region of Mississippi, Acheson laid it on the line. He described in broad detail the destruction wrought in Europe and elsewhere by the war; Europe's failure to recover due to natural disasters but also due to the absence of Germany and Japan as productive partners; Europe's acute dollar deficit which, unless overcome, would reduce its ability to finance its imports from the United States; and the fact that all our economic efforts up until then had been unsuccessful because we had failed to recognize the magnitude of the problems facing the world. While Acheson defended the concept of foreign aid in terms of "our duty and privilege as human beings," he was even more emphatic in pointing out that the Administration was pursuing the policy "chiefly as a matter of national self-interest." And while conscious of criticism leveled against the Truman Doctrine, he had no intention of disowning the future Marshall Plan's paternity; so he did not obscure the fact that a program of economic aid to Europe would be in keeping with the policy announced by President Truman in his message on aid to Greece and Turkey.

. Acheson told his audience that the United States was "going to have to undertake further emergency financing of foreign purchases if foreign countries are to continue to buy in 1948 and 1949 the commodities which they need to sustain life and at the same time rebuild their economies," and that such financing would call for sacrifices.[16] He went on to indicate that what the Administration was considering was substantially more vast and ambitious than any existing programs.

Requests for further U.S. aid may reach us through the International Bank or through the Export–Import Bank, or *they may be of a type which existing national and international institutions are not equipped to handle.* . . . [Emphasis added.] [17]

If Acheson's speech was intended as a trial balloon, it had its desired effect. While it provided a stimulus to press discussion of the immediate need for a comprehensive new foreign-aid program, Senator Vandenberg and his fellow Republicans hit the ceiling. "Alarmed Senator Vandenberg telephoned both Acheson and Marshall, and a meeting of the three took place at Blair House. The Senator was excited: Acheson had publicly said we were going to entertain enormous requests for foreign aid! . . . What was going on? . . . Secretary Marshall assured him that he had no intention of presenting any further legislative requests at this session," but went on to explain why, sooner or later, "we were going to have to undertake a very large program of foreign aid." [18] Mollified by the promise that Congress would not be ignored in the planning, Vandenberg cooled down and became interested. But Vandenberg's response was a warning to Acheson that the Administration would have to proceed with the utmost care if the whole proposal was to enlist the total support of the country, regardless of economic or political differences. Acheson was now the most insistent advocate of a much larger role for Congress.

The decisive meeting at which the Marshall Plan was decided occurred on May 28, 1947; Marshall, Acheson, Clayton, and Kennan were all in attendance. Oddly, President Truman was not. Kennan drove home his point that the initiative for the new program should come from Europe and that the plan should be presented in such a way as not to exclude Eastern Europe. Acheson addressed the major problem of timing. He recommended that over the next four to six months the Administration prepare Congress and the public for new foreign-aid legislation that might be presented in the fall or in the new session beginning in January 1948.

That noon Acheson lunched with a dozen senators wanting to be informed about the Administration's plans. Brien McMahon (D–Conn.) warned that he would vote against another fait accompli handed him by the Administration. Others expressed similar reservations.[19] Impressed, Acheson urged Marshall to make a speech on the subject as soon as possible.[20] The next day Marshall decided to accept the invitation to speak at the Harvard commencement on June 5. So great was Marshall's assurance about what he was doing that he did not deem it necessary to clear his Harvard address with Truman; and so great was Truman's confidence in Marshall that he did not ask him to do so.[21]

In the meantime Acheson was employing his reputation around Washington as a mover and shaker to direct press (and especially European press) attention to the need for Europeans to come up with some proposals for their own salvation and not just wait for the United States to to propose something.

On June 4 Acheson lunched with Leonard Miall of the BBC, Malcolm Muggeridge of the *Daily Telegraph,* and Stewart McCall, another British journalist, informing them that Marshall's speech was intended to elicit a European response and that they should be certain to urge Ernest Bevin to pick up the initiative.*

Bevin did just that, launching the idea that if the United States would agree to support it, the Europeans would come up with a comprehensive plan for the integration and recovery of their lagging economies.

Without entirely knowing it, Acheson's public relations efforts were leading American diplomacy in a new direction. Until then American foreign policy, except in time of war, had rarely involved the American people. America had not had to fight many wars, it had virtually no security problem, and not much money had needed to be spent on armaments. Now all that was changing. The country was being asked to assume a role of major responsibility; it was being asked to spend hundreds of millions of dollars in foreign assistance and to support its government in difficult situations overseas on a permanent basis. Changes of such magnitude could not take place in a democracy like America without involving the people and their representatives in the broadest sense. The United States was not a country that had a tradition of *raison d'état* in which even parliamentary primacy gave way to executive management of foreign affairs; nor was it a country in which the people had become inured to the endless deceptions and setbacks that are the concomitants of great-power diplomacy. Even less were they prepared for the revolutionary upheavals that were beginning to occur in many parts of the world. The necessity of citizen involvement was occurring at a time when Americans were ill-prepared for the costs, both economic and psychological, of world responsibility. As the tide of involvement rose, so did people's belief that something or someone had to be blamed for all the

---

* It was part of the strategy to keep Marshall's Harvard proposal low-keyed, so as not to have it appear that the Administration was deciding everything and telling the Europeans what they should do—a good practice later abandoned as Washington got into the bad habit of proposing and deciding everything.

pain it was causing. There had to be a villain, a scapegoat. In the absence of any experience with the discouraging workings of the international system, the natural tendency of Americans was to reduce the conflict to a struggle between democracy (good) and communism (bad). Acheson and Truman had not intended to light the fires of this Manichean drama, but in their efforts to overcome isolationism and partisanship, they had certainly contributed a stick or two.

It was completely out of character for Acheson knowingly to arouse an emotional storm in people by demagogic means. He had always deplored Roosevelt's use of the press and radio to exploit popular opinion, and he had forewarned of the coming of a demagogue who would exploit the fears and frustrations of the American people to rout the forces of reason and tolerance. He could hardly have believed, therefore, that through his speeches and policies calling upon the American people to resist the threat of aggression and chaos by opposing those forces in a peaceful and organized way, he would be accused of consciously and deliberately creating an anti-Communist hysteria in the country and preparing the way for McCarthyism.

Having abandoned his view that postwar conflict with Russia was avoidable, provided both sides tried to be reasonable, he now found himself obliged to move from being the impatient critic of American opinion to the active molder of that opinion. But he had made these shifts first and foremost in response to what he considered powerful evidence that, unless something was done, a much worse disaster impended. Two years of fruitless negotiation and wrangling had led Acheson to doubt the sincerity of Soviet intentions. And two years marked by further erosion and decline prompted him to wonder if Americans were fully aware of the threat to Western civilization posed by Europe's inability to recover. Contrasted with the Soviet emphasis upon the state and the right of a small clique of men in the Kremlin, imbued by a messianic creed, to dictate the destiny of 300,000,000 Soviet citizens and other people, the Western emphasis on the rights of the individual seemed to pose the conflict in starkly moral and ideological terms. Acheson was all too conscious of the forces of self-interest as well as idealism that marched behind the American banner. But alongside the claim to absolute control over people's lives maintained by the Kremlin, the greed and disorder characteristic of the West did not seem so bad. Acheson once said:

This belief in the individual is in our blood. It is our most fundamental characteristic. It gives a certain typical disorderliness to our behavior which baffles some foreign observers. But it can no more be separated from us than our sense of humor. . . . We have no desire to force our behavior and ideas on other people. If, for reasons incomprehensible to us, they want to act differently and—to us quite misguidedly—that is their affair. But we don't like them to push other people around—particularly when those other people are trying to live as we think all decent people should live.[22]

In such a struggle Acheson was less concerned about changing the nature of the other system than in rallying Americans to an appreciation of the value of their own. "Citizens," Acheson quoted Milton, "it is of no small concern what manner of men ye be whether to acquire or to keep possession of your liberty." To move the American people he believed he had no choice but to arouse them to the threat posed to their liberties. But it was not his intention to launch them on an anti–Communist crusade.

It had been agreed when Marshall took office that after a suitable period Acheson would be allowed to return to private life; the date generally agreed upon was July 1. Upon his return from Moscow, Marshall suggested Robert A. Lovett as a replacement. Lovett was very much in the "establishment" mold, although the term had not been thought of in those days. He was a fellow graduate of Acheson's at Yale and had spent his life with Brown Brothers, Harriman, the quintessential model of the Wall Street investment house. Lovett had served as civilian organizer of the Army Air Corps in World War II and was well known to General Mashall. Like Acheson, "he knew Europe well," which may have been part of the later trouble that confronted the Administration in dealing with the Far East. In any event, his nomination as Acheson's successor was unanimously confirmed by the Senate (Lovett's being a Republican no doubt helped). Acheson immediately invited him to move into his office and begin learning the ropes. A smooth transition was assured. On Monday, June 30, Acheson's last day in office, a pleasant ceremony was held in the Rose Garden of the White House at which Truman conferred upon him the Medal of Merit. Then he met for the last time with the Cabinet, to bid them good-bye, and that evening he was once again a private citizen. As Acheson notes in his memoirs, it was only after he had stepped down that he appreciated the stress and fatigue under which he had been operating.

Happily, Acheson's partners invited him to rejoin the law firm, and after a vacation in the Canadian Rockies, he returned to the "hardtack" of the law. But he would rarely be far from public life. That summer he took on operational responsibility, together with former Secretary of War Robert Patterson, for the Citizens' Committee for the Marshall Plan and spent much of his time speaking in various parts of the country on its behalf.

These long-forgotten meetings and speeches have no importance in themselves, but are illustrative of the efforts of hundreds, perhaps thousands of other speakers and workers who by their sweat and tears reached the minds, or at least the attention, of innumerable others . . . to affect the several hundred people in Washington who would write and enact the European Recovery Program into law.[23]

Less than a year later, on Sunday, April 4, 1948, Truman telephoned Acheson. Would he consider returning to public life as administrator of the Marshall Plan? Acheson was aware that the choice of the administrator was a long and complicated political decision, intimately tied to a vision which Senator Vandenberg and others had for the plan. Aside from the fact that Vandenberg, as well as many other Republicans and Democrats, wanted the program administered by a businessman as a symbol of its immaculately nonpolitical and nonpartisan character, there was in the Congress a fanatically anti–Acheson faction led by his old nemesis Senator Wherry, who would have made Acheson's appointment a matter of personal privilege. Acheson warned Truman against nominating him and recommended Paul Hoffmann. "Paul was a good man; the President would do well to accept him and, by so doing, irrevocably commit Vandenberg to the support of an adequately financed program. If I was wrong and the Senator accepted me, I would do it." [24] Hoffmann was nominated.

Acheson did accept one appointment. The Congress had created a Commission on the Organization of the Executive Branch to study ways of improving the performance of its various departments and bureaus. Former President Hoover had been designated chairman, and Truman wanted Acheson as second-in-command to "act as Democratic watch-dog lest the Commission be used for partisan political purpose." [25] Despite an occasional set-to, Acheson got along superbly well with the ex–President, discovering in him a capacity for humor and irony that he had not suspected. Involvement gave Acheson a chance to view the operation of the State and Defense departments in a more detached light. In only two respects did the Commission's work have a bearing on his later role as Secretary of State. He was among those favoring the strengthening of the office of the Secretary of Defense so as to make it an effective counterpoise to a more unified Joint Chiefs of Staff. He was also instrumental in pushing through, and later putting into effect, a proposal for the amalgamation into a single foreign service of both State Department and Foreign Service personnel above a certain rank.

These deliberations got Acheson into the tortured area of Foreign Service organization and morale which would become an even more critical and consuming problem in the years to come. But as 1948 wound to its end, Acheson was enjoying the solaces of a certain amount of private life, obliged to follow the desperate course of events surrounding the Berlin blockade, the schism between Yugoslavia and the Kremlin, and the civil war in China only as a private citizen.

9

EUROPEAN DIPLOMACY, 1949:
THE FOUNDATIONS

TRUMAN'S UPSET VICTORY in the 1948 election provided the President with and additional term in office with the need to select a new Secretary of State, for General Marshall, nearing seventy, wanted to retire. Truman considered W. Averell Harriman, European chief of the Marshall Plan; Lewis Douglas, ambassador to the United Kingdom; Chief Justice Fred M. Vinson; Associate Justice William O. Douglas, and Dean Acheson. There is very little doubt that Acheson was his first choice.

In mid–November, Truman invited Acheson to stop off for a few moments at Blair House where President and Mrs. Truman were staying while the White House was being repaired. The two men discussed the appointment. Acheson modestly suggested some other names. Truman replied that there might be many others better suited to be Secretary of State—or for that matter President—but he did not know who they were. He was President and he wanted Acheson. That night Acheson discussed it with his wife; the next morning he accepted. The naming of Acheson as Secretary of State—one of Washington's better kept secrets—was not announced until January 7, 1949.

The temper of politics, both domestic and international, had changed greatly in the eighteen months Acheson had been out of office. The Marshall Plan, the fall of Czechoslovakia, the defection of Yugoslavia from the Communist bloc, the Berlin blockade, and the impending fall of Nationalist China had all worked to polarize the international scene. At home the Hiss trial and a series of espionage revelations had served to sharpen an already acute anti–Communist psychosis. Loyalty checks and security clearances had been introduced, and no one was immune to the charge of being soft on Communism. Although it would be a year before Joe McCarthy spoke his piece, hysteria was already abroad in the land.

Lashed by Soviet actions in Europe and outraged by revelations of espionage in high places, the country was in a truculent mood, ready to take out its wrath on whoever fell afoul of its suspicions. Right-wing politicians, columnists, and publishers, fed up with twenty years of Democratic rule, were only too happy to pander to the all-too-human need Americans felt for some explanation of how Roosevelt had lost the peace and how America had been deceived. The basis of accusations was often as mysterious as charges of witchcraft or the evil eye. For no rhyme or reason one suddenly acquired the reputation of being a "Com-Sym"; judgments and associations formed a decade or more earlier could suddenly be raised as evidence of disloyalty.

Due to a combination of circumstances, anyone associated with the State Department was especially fair game, and Acheson had made enough enemies to be a prime target for charges of all sorts. Consequently much of the Senate hearing on his nomination as Secretary of State was taken up with questions designed to clarify his position and disembarrass him of certain unfavorable accusations.

Two charges against him seemed to fit the accusation of being soft on Communism. Adolf Berle, with whom Acheson had served in the department during the war, had only recently testified before the House Un-American Activities Committee that Acheson had been derelict in investigating charges against Donald and Alger Hiss linking them with a Communist espionage network in the Department of State. Berle charged that after hearing from Whittaker Chambers about the Hiss brothers, he had gone to Acheson for whom they worked: "Specifically, I checked with Dean Acheson, and later I checked when Acheson became the Assistant Secretary of State, and Alger Hiss became his executive assistant. . . . Acheson said that he had known the family and these two boys from childhood, and could vouch for them absolutely." [1]

In replying to this charge Acheson was able to show that Alger Hiss had never been his executive assistant, had in fact not worked in any branch of the department that reported to Acheson until *after* the war. He was also able to explain that he had met Donald Hiss when Donald had served as law clerk to Justice Holmes and, again, through two of his senior law partners with whose sons Donald Hiss was friendly. Upon being appointed Assistant Secretary in 1941 (not in 1939 as Berle implied), Acheson had asked to have Donald made his personal assistant; and when, a few weeks later, Berle came to him with a report of derogatory information against one of the Hiss boys, Acheson was unable to get from Berle a clear identification of which brother he was referring to. Nonetheless, Acheson questioned Donald Hiss, asking him "to take time to reflect and let me know whether he had any associations which would embarrass me. He did take time to reflect. He told me he had no such associations," but if Acheson had any reason to feel embarrassment about him, "he would go back to his other work." [2] Acheson accepted Donald Hiss's testimony then and never afterward had any reason to doubt his veracity. Subsequently Donald left Acheson's office for military duty and other services, and at the time of the Senate confirmation hearing was serving as a member of Acheson's law firm. (At that same time Alger Hiss stood accused of having transmitted copies of State Department documents to Whittaker Chambers sometime in the mid-thirties and was on trial for perjury in connection with those charges.)

Berle had also made a gratuitously prejudicial charge by identifying Acheson as the leader of a pro–Soviet group in the State Department. "The opposite group in the State Department [to the hard-line anti–Soviet group with which Berle identified himself] was largely the men in Mr. Acheson's group, of course, with Mr. Hiss as his principal assistant in the matter. . . ." [3] Under the circumstances of the time a charge like that was devastating. As with other charges of a similar ilk, the truth would never catch up.*

Berle's accusations were essentially the product, as Berle himself half admitted, of rancor at having been bested in bureaucratic infighting. Berle was wrapping a combination of personal and bureaucratic grudges in the mantle of an ideological conflict over how far Russia was to be trusted. Fortunately Acheson succeeded in convincing the committee that neither he nor Donald Hiss had been part of any pro–Soviet group in the department, but the charges were useful in blackening Acheson's reputation.

Acheson also had to counter vague allegations that his law firm had been improperly involved with the Polish government while he was Undersecretary of State and that he had personally authorized a loan to the Communist government of Poland over the objections of the ambassador, Arthur Bliss Lane. Acheson defended his role in the loan by making clear that it was a decision supported by the relevant divisions within the department and one which he personally approved, despite the undemocratic character of the Polish government, because it would facilitate the supply of Polish coal, vitally needed at the time, to Western Europe.

In the course of the hearing, Acheson had to defend the integrity of

---

* It was a little like the unspecified charge that Hurley, following his tumultuous resignation as ambassador to China in November 1945, made against Acheson that he had not been sufficiently vigilant in pursuing American economic interests in the Middle East against the British. Ironically, Hurley was airing resentments incurred when Acheson refused to reprimand his assistant, Eugene Rostow, for notations on a Hurley memo unflattering to Hurley's extreme ambition to see American oil interests triumph in the Middle East at the expense of the British.

his record on a number of other issues that were becoming the touchstone of who was and who was not to be trusted to hold government employment. Specifically he agreed that Assistant Secretary of State John Peurifoy should have his unstinting support in his duties as security affairs officer for the department in eliminating any subversive personnel.

Acheson hastened to have read into the record evidence from his speeches of his long-standing opposition to totalitarianism and to aggression, and to explain to the committee that his opposition to the Soviet Union was of a piece with these statements. The whole performance was climaxed by having Acheson recite a statement drafted for him by Senator Vandenberg. "It is my view that communism as a doctrine is economically fatal to a free society and to human rights and fundamental freedom. Communism as an aggressive factor in the world conquest is fatal to independent government and to free peoples." Such a pledge, while not incompatible with Acheson's views, was hardly congenial to his temperament. It was stated and accepted like a ritual incantation to drive away whatever suspicions might exist that Acheson was fixed by the evil eye of Communism.

Although the committee vote to confirm Acheson and his nomination was approved by the Senate by a vote of 83 to 6, an attitude of hostility toward Acheson remained. A dozen or so senators would use Acheson as a scapegoat to hinder the movement toward internationalism.

One critic of the appointment argues that Acheson was a bad choice: his overwhelming personal identification with Truman and his lack of personal political support made him extremely vulnerable to attack. Acheson had an unusual record of diplomatic and administrative experience, Bradford Westerfield, professor of political science at Yale University writes, but he began as Truman's creature and never rose much above that status.[4] Truman and Acheson were so closely linked, Westerfield argues, that "in their growing political weakness they seemed to undermine one another." The only trouble with this theory is that more systematic analysis does not bear it out. In the first place, others besides Acheson were the target of Republican attack. Senator William Jenner's attack upon General Marshall, a figure of towering national stature, was probably the most excoriating one ever launched upon a public figure. Secondly, a comparison of the accusations against Acheson and John Foster Dulles show that both were attacked, in part at least, as a function of their party affiliation—that is, Democrats supported Acheson and attacked Dulles, and Republicans attacked Acheson and supported Dulles. The adequacy of their political base in the country at large had very little to do with it. Finally, another scholar has carried the analysis a step further and shown that senators supported or attacked Acheson far more on the basis of their belief sets than on the basis of their party preference.* Had Acheson been from the Senate he might have been shielded against some of the more extreme personal attacks, but after his experience with Byrnes, Truman was not about to make any senator Secretary of State. While Acheson was certainly not a popular figure, the source of his troubles was not in the weakness of his position as a political figure nor in his personality—astringent though it might have been—but in the policies he espoused and in the courage with which he faced down those who aspired to use the specter of Communism at home to divert attention away from the real issues.**

Although Truman's unexpected victory permitted Acheson to become Secretary of State, it was to have profound and disturbing consequences for the rational conduct of foreign policy. Walter Lippmann had argued in favor of Dewey's election on the grounds that after sixteen years of Democratic Presidencies, only a Republican Presidency would restore

---

* The fifteen senators who attacked Acheson most violently were precisely those most isolationist in their preferences and most opposed to what was at the time perceived to be Acheson's refusal to espouse a more systematically anti–Communist foreign policy. Those senators most critical of Acheson for getting us involved in NATO and for not attacking Russia with sufficient zeal made an astonishing 1,286 statements hostile to Acheson and seven statements cordial to Acheson. By contrast those senators, including several Republicans, favorable to Acheson's alliance policy and moderate on the Cold War were consistently supportive of him. Professor Stassen found that the senators who showed the most indiscriminate hostility toward Acheson were Republican isolationists and Cold War extremists "whose personal policy beliefs were so strongly opposed to the postwar extension of American commitments that they could not contain their discontent within the requirements of their party role." Quoted in Glen H. Stassen, "Individual Preference Versus Role-Constraint in Policy Making: Senatorial Responses to Secretaries Acheson and Dulles," *World Politics*, Vol. XXV, No. 1, October, 1972, p. 115. Whatever may have been Acheson's political weaknesses, the attacks mounted against him were almost entirely by those who had an almost unreasoning hostility toward his policies and who used the hysteria over Communism and the fall of China to erode popular confidence in his performance. Those senators, including Republicans from the East and West coasts, who agreed with Acheson's policies were far less critical and far more cordial and supportive of Acheson. The one Democrat who opposed Acheson, Senator McCarran, was an isolationist but a moderate on the Cold War. His mind set prevailed over his Democratic Party role in attacking Acheson. Every articulate senator on the Foreign Relations Committee, including four Republicans, supported Acheson. Only one, who was somewhat more of a Cold War hawk than Acheson, was less than totally supportive, and again it was not because of Acheson's personality or political deficiency but because he generally disagreed with his policies.

** Fortunately, Acheson inherited a soundly organized Department from his predecessor, General Marshall. He wisely delegated the administering of the Department to James E. Webb, whom Truman had asked to be made Undersecretary. Webb, who had been serving as Director of the Budget, enjoyed Truman's confidence and gave Acheson a second-in-command with government-wide knowledge and ability in administering large organizations.

Republicans to a sense of responsibility out of the sobering obligation to meet the needs of the country with something more than destructive criticism. In retrospect Lippmann's analysis certainly seems to have been right, because the 1948 defeat so outraged and envenomed the conservative and isolationist wing of the party that it lost all restraint in its attacks upon the Administration, and in its attacks in particular on the delicate issues of foreign affairs and Communists in government. Ronald J. Caridi, in his book *The Korean War and American Politics*, sums up the consequences of the election as follows:

Dewey's surprise defeat at the hands of the underrated Truman precipitated a movement within the party to reject bipartisanship, both in domestic and foreign affairs. It was assumed by those in revolt that the party in power would reap the credit for successful legislation despite the aid rendered by the minority party. Leaders of the GOP's orthodox wing—particularly Senators Taft, Wherry, and Bridges—were now of the opinion that the most politically expedient policy to follow was to oppose Administrative proposals and in the process develop an alternative program.[5]

To complicate matters for Acheson, within a year of his appointment Vandenberg was stricken with cancer, and his moderating influence was effectively removed as a restraint upon the orthodox faction.*

The choice of Acheson as Secretary of State was part of Truman's view of his second Administration. He was determined to be his own man. He wanted a Secretary who would be loyal, who would not upstage him, and who would bring to foreign policy the utmost competence and brilliance. Further, Acheson probably approximated more closely the requirements of the office than any previous Secretary of State in this century.[6] In his two years as Undersecretary he had worked easily with the President—no small matter when two men are forced to preside over so many difficult and vexatious problems. One cannot overestimate even at this early date the mutual affection which each inspired in the other. "One can see at a glance," Acheson subsequently wrote, "that if these two men [President and Secretary of State] are going to do their work properly, they have got to spend a lot of time together, much of which may not be pleasant. The problems are frustrating. They are sure to provoke controversy. . . . So the Secretary of State has the makings of an unwelcome visitor."[7] But Truman had the greatest admiration for Acheson's judgment and acumen, was at ease with him, and could express his

---

* Dulles's defeat too in a special New York election to fill the Senate seat of the late Robert F. Wagner also gave orthodox Republicans one more example that "their party could not win by associating itself with the program of the opposition." Ronald J. Caridi, *The Korean War and American Politics: The Republican Party as a Case Study* (Philadelphia: University of Pennsylvania Press, 1969), p. 4.

views on the political angles without the sense of constraint that may have inhibited his relations with the more austere Marshall.

If the personal relationship was congenial, the situations the two men had to deal with were not. The period after July 1947 marked a critical turning point in the Cold War. Acheson had left office with East–West relations deadlocked; the lines were drawn but the battle had not yet been engaged. In the intervening eighteen months the Marshall Plan had been enacted into legislation and Western Europe saved from economic collapse, but the Marshall Plan had not been without its impact upon the Cold War and upon the domestic situation in countries with sizeable Communist populations. Virtual civil war had broken out between the Communist parties of France and Italy and the governments from which their represntatives had been dismissed. Goodwill toward Russia which had been built up in the West during the war, was destroyed. In all this Stalin may have been neither surprised nor disappointed. The Cold War most closely resembled the conditions of tension and conflict which he regarded as the natural relationship between "socialist" and "imperialist" states, and it solved the problem of justifying to himself and to the Russian people the crushing burden of repression and exploitation throughout the Soviet empire. If anyone's prophecy had been fulfilled it was Stalin's. The American prophecy of isolation and a return to normalcy, the European prophecy of peace and security—both had been shattered. Only Stalin's prophecy that peaceful coexistence with the capitalist West was not realizable had been borne out by events.

It should not be presumed that Soviet policy followed a planned and foreseen line of development undeterred and unaffected by Western action. The immediate effect of American moves in Europe was to increase the momentum of the Cold War and to produce a withering reaction from the Soviet side. Certainly some of the worst excesses of the Cold War might have been avoided had American authorities understood that part of the motivation for Soviet attitudes lay in weakness and fear of the outside world. But the insight was lacking, and Stalin had done absolutely nothing to ease the suspicion that the Kremlin was exploiting the chaos in the West and waiting for the inevitable crisis to occur.

Action and reaction were almost simultaneous: the Cominform was set up to defeat Western strategy; the West went ahead to create an embryonic West German state; an ill-disguised Communist putsch thrust Czechoslovakia behind the Iron Curtain; five European democracies entered into the Brussels pact, and the United States announced plans to associate itself with it; the Soviet Union imposed the Berlin blockade; the government of Chiang Kai-shek was dissolving in the Communist tide.

As if to add intensity, a bizarre event now occurred: Communist Yugoslavia, which had so long seemed to outdo the Kremlin in its hostility toward the West, suddenly broke away from the Eastern bloc in a dramatic rupture. What had happened was that Stalin, fearful of any forces independent of his personal domination, had been working for some time to insinuate his control over the Yugoslav secret police and party apparatus. Rather than lose his own power and perhaps suffer the fate of other Communist leaders who had provoked Stalin's suspicion, Tito had chosen to assert his independence before it was too late. On June 28, 1948, as the West was being shut out of Berlin, Yugoslavia was being expelled from the Cominform with the ominous threat that enough "healthy" elements remained in the Yugoslav Communist Party to cause Tito to recant or to replace him. There was a strong belief in the West that Stalin would sooner or later attempt to use force against Yugoslavia. The uncertainty only added to the tension.

Each side—East and West—was now determined to use whatever means it had to weaken the other. Every point on the globe was now viewed as a potential battleground on which winning, or avoiding defeat, was the most important goal. Compromises were not possible. The struggle, no longer over concrete issues, was now a contest of will and determination to show which was the stronger system. Each of the important moves which Stalin had made in 1948 had strengthened those forces in the West which supported a vigorous policy of containment. The common theme on both sides of the Atlantic had become the need to organize for defense, and the repeated evidence of Soviet pressure gave these proposals an impetus which, in America at least, they would otherwise never have had.

Acheson's views too had changed in the intervening months. With the darkening prospects for peace, whatever detachment he had felt earlier about the Soviet Union had been replaced by a deep conviction that the Kremlin was testing the West. A comparison of Acheson's speeches between August 1945 and January 1947 with those made between January 1947 and his return to office in January 1949 shows a clear shift. In the earlier period Acheson had used words like "delay," "oppose," "block," "hinder," and "obstruct" to describe Soviet behavior; after January 1947 words like "pressure," "force," control," "exploit," "subvert," and "destroy" occur with increasing frequency. There was a marked deepening of pessimism and a belief that only resolution and steadfastness would see us through the crisis.

. . . there is no formula which will remove the difficulties which confront us. Dangers and difficulties are with us *not* because the right policy or the right action eludes us, but from the very nature of the situation we face. The idea that there is a right policy or a right action which will remove them and make all well is based upon the unspoken assumption that we could control the present situation if only we knew how.[8]

This speech is one of Acheson's most interesting statements because it marked a development in his thinking that would dominate his performance as Secretary of State. We were prone to fail, he said, not because we were failing to do the right thing but because the situation defied any reasonable solution. Grim and malevolent forces were abroad in the world which defied our efforts to deal with them in generous and reasonable terms. It meant that we must be even more calm and resolute in our deliberations. The situation was not beyond our ability to master it provided we showed the appropriate will and resolution.

It is often argued that men like Acheson were the instigators of the Cold War—that consciously or unconsciously they had created a Frankenstein monster in order to abet the interests and power needs of the capitalist class. Yet much of the record suggests that they were reacting in the hope of avoiding the worst. Had Acheson been able to see that the Cold War had acquired a dynamic of its own, that it was feeding upon each side's reaction or overreaction to the other, he might have acted differently. Instead Acheson's view was dominated by the deadly logic of the struggle. Should the Soviets succeed in closing the West out of Berlin or in cowing Western Europe into submission, the consequences seemed too deadly to be anything but intentionally malevolent.

The North Atlantic Treaty and European Diplomacy

The foremost issue besides the Berlin blockade which Acheson had to deal with when he became Secretary was the negotiation of the North Atlantic Treaty. Eight months earlier, in the wake of the Czech coup, the Administration had proposed that America associate itself with the newly formed Brussels Treaty. As chairman of the Foreign Relations Committee, Senator Vandenberg had brought forth a resolution that was so vague and cloudy as to be almost meaningless. The crucial paragraphs declared that the American government would foster "the progressive development of regional and other collective arrangements for individual and collective self-defense" and should promote "association of the United States, by constitutional process, with such regional and other collective arrangements as are based on continuous and effective self-help and mutual aid, and as affect its national security."

Acheson, of course, had much more precise views of American responsibility and of what the next steps should be. He based these on conclusions he had arrived at while still Undersecretary. Postwar tension with the Soviet Union, he believed, was due to the vacuum and disequilibrium left in the wake of the war. Germany and Japan, which traditionally maintained the equipoise, had been destroyed, and except for America, all the forces that traditionally contributed to the equipoise were either shattered

or in the grip of revolution. Only the United States could to some extent
right the balance, but American power was no substitute for local power.
Besides, the economic and political weakness which still persisted in
Europe bred low morale and defeatism. Nations can play their proper
role only if they are healthy, strong, and united. Acheson was increasingly
convinced that the answer to the Communist challenge lay in the restoration of the nation–state system to something of its former structure and
political substance.

To restore the world to its natural system of order and equilibrium
required that not only France, Britain, and all of America's other allies
be helped to regain their economic strength and independence, but that
Germany, Japan, and Italy be brought back into the balance too. Scarcely
four years after the war's end it was still rather shocking to advocate
giving Germany or Japan back their former positions in world affairs. But
to Acheson it seemed the only solution. The United States could not continue to carry the entire burden of containment; the American people
would not put up with it and neither would the Germans nor the Japanese—or anyone else for that matter. The existence of a void in the heart
of Europe would be a permanent source of instability and tension.

Others had thought about bringing Germany and Japan back into the
balance, but no one thought about it as consciously and cold-bloodedly
as Dean Acheson. In his memoirs Acheson wrote of what he thought at
the time:

To me . . . Western Europe and the United States could not contain the
Soviet Union and suppress Germany and Japan at the same time. Our best
hope was to make these former enemies *willing* and *strong* supporters of a
free-world structure. Germany should be welcomed into Western Europe, not
kept in limbo outside . . . relegated to maneuvering between the Soviet Union
and the allies. . . .[9]

How to bring it about was the question. Here logic had an answer. All
the major European states wanted to regain mastery over their destinies.
Why not make the price of helping Britain and France their acquiescence
in the return of economic and political power to Germany?* Acheson
regarded the pursuit of agreement with Russia a case of putting the cart
before the horse. In the first place, the Russians had shown that they
weren't interested in agreement for agreement's sake; their concern was
to gain their own ends or to frustrate Western goals. The proper sequence
was to restore the world to something approaching its former basic structure and equilibrium; then the East–West conflict would take on a different shape and meaning. Since the security and stability of Western Europe

---

* The case of Japan was less complicated but the United States executed essentially the same maneuver.

Young Dean Acheson and his mother on the way to Europe.

A serious school portrait of Dean Acheson.

A cornet player in the Groton School Band (seated at left).

Opposite top: An ensign, 1918–19.

Right: Family man in the 1920s. Acheson with two of his children.

Alice and Dean Acheson in the 1930s.

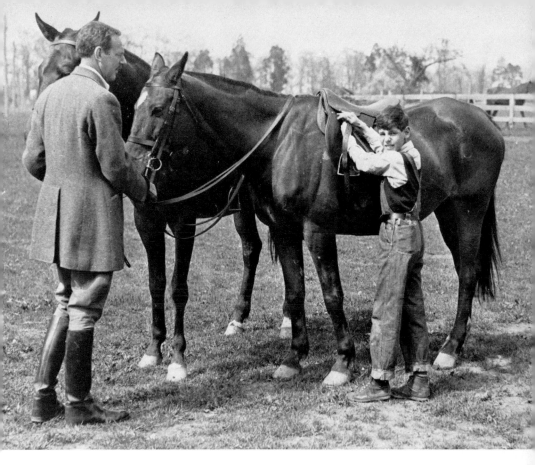

Above: Acheson giving his son, David, a riding lesson. Below: Dean Acheson with
Felix Frankfurter at the hearings on Frankfurter's nomination to the Supreme Court.
January, 1939.

An early photo of Acheson with Andrei Gromyko at the conference setting up the United Nations Relief and Rehabilitation Agency (UNRRA). November 11, 1943. The others are T. T. Tsiang, the Chinese delegate, and Colonel John J. Lewellin of the United Kingdom.

The American Delegation to the Bretton Woods Conference, 1944, including Henry Morgenthau, Jr., Secretary of the Treasury and head of the delegation, seated in the easy chair; Acheson standing third from the left; Fred Vinson (then a Congressman) on Acheson's right.

A vacation in the Canadian Rockies after service as Undersecretary. Acheson (center) with Ray Atherton, Canadian Ambassador, and the Park Director. Jasper Park. Summer, 1947.

Acheson as Vice Chairman of Hoover Commission. 1947–1948. Seated next to Truman are Herbert Hoover and Joseph P. Kennedy. Standing (left to right) Arthur A. Flemming, James K. Pollock, Dean Acheson, and James Rowe, Jr.

Dean Acheson at hearings on his nomination as Secretary of State. January, 1949.

could not be obtained in agreement with the Russians, it would have to be obtained without the Russians. Russia would always be a competitive factor in Europe's struggle to maintain its security and political relations; let it, however, be a competitive factor in a strong and healthy Europe. Precisely because Germany held the key to the balance between East and West, the Kremlin had proven unwilling to forego domination of Germany—if not of the whole of Germany then of East Germany. Acheson was convinced, in turn, that only if the resources of the Western zones of Germany could be built up and added to the power of the Atlantic bloc would Europe succeed in overcoming its essential vulnerability in the face of the Soviet monolith.

While other statesmen, such as George Kennan, hoped to see America and Russia out of Europe, Acheson knew that the United States had had an interest in Europe that extended back through two wars. This interest consisted of seeing that Europe was not dominated by a hegemonial power and of maintaining some form of peace among the European states. Europe had been traditionally racked by internecine wars into which America had twice been drawn. It was in fact these quarrels which had produced Europe's present sad state. Acheson could not forget that even if the Soviet threat did not exist, the United States would still have a stake in avoiding a recurrence of Franco–German hostilities.

Until Acheson took over, the premise of United States policy had been that the loss of West Germany would represent an unacceptable defeat. Acheson's view of the German place in European strategy went considerably beyond that. "Stated boldly, the policy of the United States under Acheson's direction was to press for the maximum development of German power as a counterpoise to the Soviet Union. . . ."[10] It was no longer sufficient that Germany merely survive; its economic and military potential had to be put to active use and existing restraints upon German power removed. True, it could not be done all at once. As Gaddis Smith remarks: "The French and to some degree all the peoples of Western Europe including some thoughtful Germans feared a precipitous revival of German power for understandable reasons."[11] Circumstances favorable to Germany's revival would have to be created; nothing must be permitted to obstruct that goal. Acheson's insistence that the North Atlantic Treaty must be more than a paper pledge became clear in light of his effort to reassure Europe, and in particular the French, that a reconstituted Germany would not be permitted to get out of control.

Acheson's logic also meant giving to the North Atlantic Treaty a shape and thrust which had not been evident in the early stages of negotiation. The paper promises of the Vandenberg resolution were no longer acceptable. The European governments now wanted, as did Acheson, a commitment that the United States would automatically come to their assistance militarily should they be attacked. As the French Premier Henri Queuille told an American reporter in a much quoted statement:

We know that once Western Europe was occupied, America would again come to our aid and eventually we would again be liberated. But the process would be terrible. The next time you probably would be liberating a corpse. . . . The real frontier of Western Europe which must be defended must be moved well beyond the actual frontiers, because once the geographic frontiers of these countries are crossed it will be too late for America to save very much. Even fifteen days after the invasion will be too late.[12]

More was at stake in the calculations of European governments than just security.

To Britain and France, faced with the three-fold problem of achieving military security in Europe and protecting their overseas holdings while regaining their economic strength and meeting the new demands for social welfare programs . . . America's formal political guarantee and her accompanying military and economic assistance seemed the only means of avoiding chronic overcommitment and of recovering great power status.[13]

Whatever scruples Americans might have about the alliance being used as a vehicle for these "extra" purposes, they were the sort of calculations European statesmen were accustomed to making in setting the terms of their collaboration. Besides, the United States had an interest of its own in an alliance that would be more than merely legal and symbolic in nature. Unless the political divisions and weaknesses within Europe could be overcome, the treaty would really not accomplish very much. The French were still as concerned about the Germans as they were about the Russians. If the United States hoped to relax French distrust of the Germans, the French would have to have the reassurance of a long-term American commitment to European peace and security—a commitment which would serve as a hedge not just against Russia but, equally, against a resurgence of German militarism. As Acheson told Vandenberg and Connally in asking for the strongest possible guarantee, "A pact of this sort would materially help in securing a realistic consideration of Germany."

There were already in existence two conceptions of the alliance in Washington—one largely political, the other envisioning a much more comprehensive military and political collaboration. Kennan was the principal exponent of the political conception. By contrast the military planners were already thinking of the United States stake in European defense; and while civilians like Acheson did not necessarily envision the alliance as an instrument for constructing the full-scale integration of Europe, they sensed its utility for getting the Europeans, particularly France and Germany, to bury their quarrels and collaborate in producing a stronger, more unified front to the Russians. For these various reasons the treaty had to be more than just a perfunctory commitment or the Europeans would be reluctant to join it.

Vandenberg, however, merely favored American participation in some form of cooperative defense arrangement; he had been unwilling to accept the principle of a clear and unreserved advance commitment. On the one hand Vandenberg argued that the "pledges of the Pact must be unmistakeable;" [14] on the other hand he insisted that America's allies should understand that "we cannot commit ourselves to go to war automatically," precisely what they were most insistent upon.

Isolationists in the Senate wanted as minimal a commitment as possible. They were still not prepared to accede to a marriage between military obligations and national policy; such was not in the American tradition. They were still not prepared to accept the principle that the effective conduct of foreign policy might require the giving of a virtually automatic commitment to go to war on behalf of allies as a condition of their becoming allies. They were averse to the political and bargaining component of alliance diplomacy, preferring the relative safety and unambiguity of a limited legal commitment with the constitutional provision that only the Congress could declare a state of war. The conflict over the North Atlantic Treaty posed for the first time in an acute form the relationship between policy and power, between political ends and military means, which America in its isolation had never really had to face. The needs of the treaty also challenged for the first time the neat, clear distinction that the Constitution posed between a state of peace and a state of war. The enlarged political purposes with which the United States was becoming involved required a new role for military power. How that new role was defined would be enormously important. For the preservation of its security the United States could no longer trust the traditional means of minimal involvement, minimal military means, improvisation, and the divorce of military considerations from national policy. Many of the same senators who wanted a stronger stand against Communism were also dead set against automatic commitments and entangling alliances. Instead of the debate being about the appropriate relationship of military power to policy, it took the form of a struggle over Congress's right to declare war.

Unlike his predecessors, Acheson did not believe that this conflict could any longer be blurred. Either the United States accepted the implications of great power and alliance diplomacy or it would fail to achieve its goals. As the person responsible for pushing America into this new and fettered role in world politics, Acheson was bound to make many enemies.

As a result of the gap between what the Vandenberg resolution offered and what the Europeans would accept, negotiations had reached a stalemate when Acheson took over. The two basic principles which had been agreed upon between Robert Lovett, Undersecretary of State, and the European ambassadors with whom he was negotiating were (1) that an armed attack upon one should be regarded as an armed attack upon all, and (2) that each nation "should take military or other action forthwith." But the latter provision had not been agreed to by the Senate conferees, and it still left up in the air the constitutional principle that the United States could act only after Congress had declared a state of war to exist.

Acheson met privately with Tom Connally (D–Tex.) and Vandenberg on February 5, 1949. (This was still an era when the Executive had neither usurped, nor the Senate abandoned, its foreign-policy prerogatives.) Acheson assured them that he did not intend to confront them with a fait accompli, but he needed time to find a formula acceptable to the Europeans that would not violate the Senate's war-making power. Normally the Secretary of State can count on the support of the chairman of the Foreign Relations Committee, especially if he is of the President's own party. Unfortunately, Connally, who had replaced Vandenberg as chairman in the wake of the Democrats' 1948 victory, was resentful of Vandenberg's reputation and apprehensive lest he appear in the eyes of the Senate to have bartered away Congress's war powers. Touchy and jaundiced by what he considered the one-sidedness of the treaty, Connally was not prepared to give Acheson the backing he needed.

Clearly Acheson hoped that the Senate would accept a formula in which the Congress's war-making power was not explicitly stated, but, fortunately or unfortunately, a public debate on so sensitive an issue could not be avoided. On February 14 Senator Forrest Donnell (R–Mo.) stood up on the floor of the Senate and claimed that, regardless of the care with which the American obligation was defined, the very assumption that an attack upon one member represented an attack upon all constituted a moral obligation upon the United States which inevitably abridged the constitutional duty of the Congress.

Senator Donnell's statement produced just the stampede Acheson had wished to avoid. Connally immediately announced that he would not vote for any such provision: "I feel . . . that the Senate Committee on Foreign Relations would not approve or adopt any form of language in an international agreement which would commit us to go to war when some other country in Europe might be attacked. We are not responsible for the disagreements which may arise in the countries of Europe"—as if two wars had not demonstrated that the security of Europe and the security of the United States were inseparable.[15] The following day Connally further impaired Acheson's ability to negotiate by revealing to the press the wording of Article 5, which contained the provision that an attack upon one is an attack upon all; he even began to agitate for a "no automatic war" clause.[16]

The next day Vandenberg and Connally again met privately with Acheson. Instead of taking counsel on how the damage could most effectively be remedied, both senators vehemently insisted that it be made clear in Article 5 that there was no obligation, moral or otherwise, to go to war. Connally preferred repudiating the mutual obligation clause in favor of "an attack on one would be regarded as a threat to the peace of all." Vandenberg merely wanted the word "military" omitted so as to reduce the American commitment to an innocuous obligation "to take such action as it deems necessary . . . to restore and maintain the security of the North Atlantic area."

Acheson was much perplexed. These were the Senate foreign-policy leaders. Both had knowingly embarked upon alliance diplomacy; both were intimately aware cf the anxious state of European opinion. Yet now, instead of trying to master the situation, they were more concerned about how to evade the burdens of leadership. In a press conference on February 16 Acheson reaffirmed his conviction that the terms of the treaty could be reconciled with the constitutional right of Congress to declare a state of war and stated that he would meet with the full Senate Committee on Foreign Relations. In a press conference the next day, Truman made a special attempt to imply that all of the major policy provisions of the North Atlantic Treaty were derived from the Vandenberg resolution, thereby placing the Senate under some obligation to assume its responsibilities.[17]

Further inroads were avoided by the meeting of Acheson with the Committee on Foreign Relations on February 18. At this meeting he circulated a "top secret" draft of the treaty. In order to get around the automaticity implied by the obligation to "take military or other action forthwith," Acheson proposed a formula that incorporated Vandenberg's qualifying phraseology without eliminating the European emphasis upon immediate military response. The final draft of Article 5 was a masterpiece of legal legerdemain, but one which was still bound to rankle:

The Parties agree that an armed attack against one or more of them in Europe or North America shall be considered an attack against them all; and consequently they agree that, if such an armed attack occurs, each of them, in exercise of the right of individual or collective self-defense recognized by Article 51 of the Charter of the United Nations, will assist the Party or Parties so attacked by taking forthwith, individually and in concert with the other Parties, such action as it deems necessary, including the use of armed force, to restore and maintain the security of the North Atlantic area.

Did this mean, senators and newspapermen wanted to know, that America had assumed a moral commitment that transcended the constitutional process by which the nation went to war (i.e., by a vote of the Congress meeting in joint session), or did it mean that the decision to go to war was still subject to constitutional processes and, therefore, that the obligation was not as absolute as the Europeans were being led to believe? One false step in answering this question and Acheson would find the rug pulled out from under him. Acheson's answer was that

> . . . the necessity of acting as a nation in the manner the Constitution provided did *not* mean either that in some undefined way the nation would act "automatically" *or* that legislators could act properly under "the law of the land"—in this case, the treaty—by *going contrary to its provisions*. No power but their own sense of right could force them to do their part in enabling the nation to keep its lawful promise, but that did not affect either the lawfulness or the meaning of the promise.[18]

It was what Acheson's enemies would call a sophist's answer, but no one has yet been able to parse more accurately the conundrums raised by the working of the American system. Senators didn't like it. They liked even less being told that as soon as the treaty was ratified it would be followed by a request from the Administration for a military aid appropriation in excess of one billion dollars.

Acheson announced the terms of the treaty on March 18. It still had to be approved by the Foreign Relations Committee and ratified by the Senate, a process that would require additional months of strenuous debate. Meanwhile, a meeting of Atlantic foreign ministers to sign the treaty was convened for April 4, 1949, in Washington.

The meetings at which the treaty was signed were held against the background of knowledge that the Berlin blockade was about to be lifted, and they were a brilliant success. Discussion of the German question led to sweeping agreements on the part of the French Foreign Minister Robert Schuman and British Foreign Minister Ernest Bevin. Acheson was entranced by such splendid fellows. When they went to see Truman, Bevin and Schuman assured him that everything was in top form. There emerged from these meetings a sense of satisfaction verging on euphoria. And why not, when Bevin and Schuman were the lucky recipients of an American alliance in advance of war. But if the treaty was now signed, it was not yet ratified by the Senate, where support was by no means automatic.

The Treaty Before the Senate

This was still an age when Senate ratification was not a foregone conclusion and when a Secretary of State not only had to inform but to convince a sufficient number of doubters to secure the necessary two-thirds majority. The Senate really debated the treaty and Acheson had to fight every step of the way. By incorporating the obligation to take *action forthwith*, the treaty had assured the automatic opposition of the Republican isolationists led by Robert Taft. Even John Foster Dulles, whom Governor Thomas E. Dewey had appointed interim senator following the death of Robert Wagner, appeared to have serious reservations. On March 19 Dulles, the leading foreign policy spokesman after Vandenberg, issued a lengthy statement. He warned the negotiators to avoid all commitments that might be construed by the Soviet government as "bringing United States military might" directly to Russia's Scandinavian border. He cautioned against permitting "military judgments" to dominate national policy. "It would," he concluded, "involve a high tribute to Soviet leaders to assume that, under these circumstances, they would exercise more self-control than would our people under comparable circumstances, as, for example, if the Soviet Union had military arrangements with a country at our border." [19]

Isolationist statements had one thread in common besides their obvious partisan skein. They raised the specter of large-scale economic and military involvement in European security. James Reston summarized a few of the isolationist misgivings in his column of April 3, 1949: "Senators W. F. George (D–Ga.) and R. A. Taft (R–Ohio) fear higher taxes and deficit spending almost as much as they distrust the Russians." [20] Reston pointed up the inherent dilemma in the foreign-policy position of the Taft wing of the Republican Party: on the one hand they demanded an increasingly hard line in American relations with the Soviet Union, and on the other hand they were reluctant to accept the necessary commitments to implement effective deterrence. In the face of this dilemma they grasped for legalistic formulas devoid of substantive commitment.

This was the evasive strategy which Acheson had to scotch when he came before the Senate Committee on Foreign Relations on April 27. In refuting the senatorial critics of the treaty, Acheson sought as much to educate them as to beat down their arguments. Time and again Acheson impressed upon his audience the need to judge the treaty in light of the actual requirements of America's own security. In his prepared remarks to the committee, Acheson directed attention to the inescapable fact that twice in this century all-out armed attacks upon Europe had necessitated American intervention. The unambiguous nature of the record of past experience, Acheson explained, ought to leave no doubt that the alternative to another repetition of this cycle of aggression and painful liberation lay in accepting the treaty. [21]

Acheson was unable to comprehend how anyone—once the interdependence of European and American security was admitted—could fail to recognize that the action required of America "might or might not include the use of armed force. . . ." [22] At the same time, an American guarantee would act as a deterrent against any ill-advised Soviet action and restore European self-confidence.

Acheson was forthright in telling the senators that ratification of the treaty alone was not enough. The Administration also planned to ask for a billion-dollar program of immediate military assistance to Europe. While ratification did *not* obligate a senator to vote the military-aid program, nevertheless if he accepted the treaty he was honor bound to give the aid program most serious and honest consideration. Acheson told the committee:

The pact does not bind the Congress to reach that same conclusion [as the Executive], for it does not dictate the conclusion of honest judgment. It does preclude repudiation of the principle or of the obligation of making that honest judgment. Thus, if you ratify the pact, it cannot be said that there is no obligation to help [with military aid]. There is an obligation to help, but the extent, the manner, and the timing is up to the honest judgment of the parties.[23]

In the course of questioning by the committee members, Acheson continued to impress upon the senators that it was not enough to examine the relationship of the treaty to constitutional procedures or to parochial American interests. They must view the treaty in the light of the overall requirements of North Atlantic security. Time and again Acheson reminded his audience that the defense of the whole North Atlantic area was inseparably linked to the security interest of the United States.

Under dogged questioning by Senators Forrest Donnell and Arthur V. Watkins (R–Utah), who had been given unprecedented permission to sit with the committee in order to interrogate him, Acheson was forced to reiterate the underlying political and strategic realities of American security in order to focus the debate on the real problem. There seemed no limit to the tactical dodges of the treaty's senatorial foes. It seemed utterly incomprehensible to Acheson that in the face of a problem which every member present recognized to exist, so many arguments could be raised to defeat and undermine United States purpose and will. Annoyed by the irrelevance of many of the questions, Acheson could barely conceal his exasperation. At one point Senator Donnell asked, "I would like to know why it is that this document is called the North Atlantic Treaty. What is the reason for that?" Acheson, with barely controlled sarcasm, replied: "It has to do with the defense of the North Atlantic area. Obviously that does not mean that you are defending water. This is not a treaty that has to do with water and not with land. It has to do with that area of the world which is concerned in the North Atlantic, and that means those countries which border on it or border on countries which border on it." [24]

In spite of his efforts to avoid giving the impression that ratification of the treaty would set fixed and final limits to America's obligations, Acheson let down his guard in one decisive exchange. In response to the blunt probing of Senator Bourke Hickenlooper (R–Iowa), who asked whether "we are going to be expected to send substantial numbers of troops over there as a more or less permanent contribution to the development of these countries' capacity to resist," Acheson replied: "The answer to that question, Senator, is a clear and absolute 'No.' " [25]

This was precisely the type of categorical statement binding future action which Acheson was usually careful to avoid. Senator Hickenlooper, deeply apprehensive about the advisability of the United States joining a peacetime military alliance, had asked his question in an obvious attempt to circumscribe the extent of America's involvement in the future defense plans for Western Europe. The categorical quality of Acheson's response must have sounded reassuring beyond Hickenlooper's immediate expectations. All the greater therefore was his bitterness two years later when Acheson was to reappear before the same committee to inform the Senate of the President's decision to dispatch four additional divisions of United States troops to Europe. To a man such as Hickenlooper, accustomed to viewing international affairs as isolated incidents, each compartmentalized and divorced from the other, Acheson's statement at the time of the North Atlantic Treaty hearings appeared as an irrevocable policy statement governing for all future time the engagement of American troops in Europe. The incompatible perspectives from which the two men viewed the international arena inevitably gave rise to the most basic misunderstanding. Later on, when Acheson came before the same committee to testify about the "troops to Europe" question, his earlier categorical statement was held up as an example of perfidy.

After hearings which lasted several weeks, the committee recommended the treaty to the full Senate. There, after some futile attempts by Senators Taft, Wherry, and Watkins to have it amended, it was approved on July 21 by a vote of 83 to 13. However, with ratification of the treaty Vandenberg felt freed of the obligation which he had assumed a year earlier when he sponsored the Vandenberg Resolution. He would be far less supportive of the next phase of Acheson policy to build up the North Atlantic community—the Administration's request for a $1.4 billion military assistance program which Acheson had warned would be forthcoming.

Lifting the Berlin Blockade

Meanwhile significant changes had been occurring on the diplomatic front. When Acheson took office the Berlin blockade was still in effect. But shortly thereafter, on January 31, in an exchange with an American journalist, Kingsbury Smith, Stalin had revealed an interesting omission in his terms for lifting the blockade. Stalin had omitted any reference to rescinding the currency reform which had taken place in West Berlin as a precondition for ending the blockade. On the advice of his Soviet and Berlin advisers, Acheson instructed Philip C. Jessup, America's representative at the United Nations, to explore the significance of the omission with Jakob Malik, the chief Soviet delegate. After a lengthy period of secret diplomatic exchanges, the Soviets agreed on March 21 that they would be willing to lift the blockade if the United States agreed to convene another four-power foreign ministers' conference on the subject of Germany. Provided it was not allowed to interfere with the progress then under way toward the creation of an independent West German government, this did not seem too high a price to pay, and on May 4 agreement was reached lifting the blockade on May 12 as a prelude to convening the Council of Foreign Ministers in Paris May 22. This agreement meant that as much progress as possible would need to be made in conjunction with the other two Western occupation powers toward agreeing on terms for an independent West German state beforehand.

The meeting in April of the European foreign ministers to sign the North Atlantic Treaty gave Acheson just the opportunity he wanted. As Gaddis Smith says, "Acheson's first meeting with Schuman and Bevin established a pattern of cooperation which was one of the most satisfying aspects of his experience as Secretary of State, second only to his relationship with President Truman. Acheson, Schuman, and Bevin had their differences, but candor, trust, honesty, and a common devotion to the strength and unity of the Atlantic community made compromise easy." [26] What won over the Europeans was the awareness that here was an American statesman who was as good as his word, who would buck the American Senate to get what he wanted, and who could approach common problems from their point of view. His sense of the gravity of dealing with other nations inspired his highest skills and instincts. The result was that the more successful he was in getting his way with Congress, the more persuasive he was with foreign statesmen. Gradually a connection became established and recognized between what you did for Acheson and what he did for you. It was like a reciprocating engine, so sure and certain became the interconnection.

Schuman was a Catholic, a native of Lorraine, and a leader of the Mouvement Républicain Populaire, the most promising of the postwar French parties. As a Lorrainer he was particularly conscious of the tragedy of Franco–German enmity and was determined to do whatever he reasonably could as a Frenchman to bury the quarrels of the past and put relations on a footing of trust and of amity. This outlook fitted in perfectly with Acheson's belief that only if Germany were welcomed back into the community of nations would Europe regain its strength and security.

Once Schuman was convinced that French security needs would get a considerate hearing, he was much freer to follow Acheson's German plans because of his own commitment to Franco–German reconciliation. In this instance he readily agreed to the immediate constitution of a new German government for the three Western zones, subject only to the continued exercise of allied control over West Germany's foreign and military affairs. To match the new status of the West German republic, the allied military occupation was to be ended and the allies were to be represented by civilian high commissioners. Giving the Germans the right of self-government was a watershed in postwar European policy; it created a new status for Germany and meant that henceforth the world would have to deal with the Germans as an independent entity. This development would unleash a favorable attitude among the Germans and hopefully give them an incentive to join actively with the West in resisting Soviet pressure.

The Council of Foreign Ministers: Paris, May 1949

While arrangements for an independent Germany and the struggle over the North Atlantic Treaty ratification were going on, Acheson also had to prepare for the Paris meeting of the Council of Foreign Ministers scheduled for May 22. At stake was the question of whether the Soviet Union and the Western powers could agree on a treaty that would guarantee Germany as a completely independent entity. Acheson did not believe that either side could afford to give up its part of Germany, and he was prepared to accept the division of Europe rather than lose the German contribution to Western strength and unity. Contrary to Acheson's view, the Policy Planning Staff led by George Kennan was considerably more concerned about the long-run consequences of a divided Germany for the peace and stability of Europe. Four years earlier, in the summer of 1945, Kennan had declared that

the idea of a Germany run jointly with the Russians is a chimera. . . . We have no choice but to lead our section of Germany—the section of which we and the British have accepted responsibility—to a form of independence so prosperous, so secure, so superior, that the East cannot threaten it. . . . Admittedly, this is dismemberment. But dismemberment is already a fact, by virtue of the Oder–Neisse line. . . . Better a dismembered Germany in which the West, at least, can act as a buffer to the forces of totalitarianism than a united Germany which again brings these forces to the North Sea.[27]

Now Kennan was coming round to the view that to accept a divided Germany was a folly from which the world might never recover. The moody and pessimistic Kennan feared the evil that would come from a divided Germany: "the fight would be on for fair; the division of Germany, and with it the division of Europe itself would tend to congeal and to become more difficult of removal with the passage of time." [28] Haunted by this specter Kennan had proposed to General Marshall that the Policy Planning Staff have another look at U.S. policy before accepting the division of Germany as final. The staff's conclusions, known as Plan A, called for a penultimate effort to reach agreement with Russia for a new four-power arrangement to run Germany. The entrance into operation of new control machinery would be followed by the early election of a provisional government for all of Germany. Simultaneously, military government would cease and allied forces would be withdrawn to garrison areas on the periphery of Germany. The thrust of Plan A reflected Kennan's conviction that much of the trouble sprang from the presence of Soviet and American forces facing each other in the heart of Europe; if they could somehow be gotten out, there would be more hope for a peaceful solution to the German problem. "Something along the lines of Plan A, even if not immediately acceptable to the Russians (and we did not suppose that it would be), would at least serve to hold open the door for an eventual peaceful withdrawal of the Russians from the heart of Germany. Unless this door was held open . . . the Russians might not feel able to withdraw even if a time should come when they would like to." Meanwhile our position in Berlin "could never be a comfortable one, and the people of the Western sectors . . . would be living constantly on the edge of an abyss. . . ." [29] Over and against Kennan's view that the United States should continue to work for the reunification of Germany must be put that of Charles Bohlen, America's other ranking Soviet specialist. Bohlen, who was also advising Acheson, did not believe that the Russians could be persuaded to withdraw their forces from East Germany. "It would mean the destruction of their entire position and all their real hopes for Germany." [30]

There is no need to doubt the logic which led Kennan to his deep pessimism. The preoccupation of his superiors, Marshall and Lovett, with the North Atlantic Treaty had also aroused within him considerable despair. That treaty "addressed itself to what was *not* the main danger. . . . To a certain extent we had to indulge [the European desire for an alliance]. . . . But it behooved us to bear in mind that the need for alliances and rearmament in Western Europe *was primarily a subjective one,* arising from the failure of the Western Europeans to understand correctly their own position."* Kennan's mystical belief that he knew best what

---

* George F. Kennan, *Memoirs: 1925–1950* (Boston: Little, Brown, 1967), p. 433. Emphasis added. Kennan was very distrustful of the British and French view of the German problem and saw the "progressive discarding of all possibilities which might really have led to something like unification of Germany under allied blessing" as due to the failure of the British and French even more than Acheson to see the German problem in "dynamic terms." *FR:1949,* III, pp. 889–890.

was good for other people was a facet of his personality soon to grate on Acheson. Looked at from the viewpoint of a Secretary of State, the European request for a guarantee pact, soon to be accompanied by a clamor for arms, had to be viewed as an objective reality. It had to be assumed that other nations knew what they wanted and why. And on a personal level Acheson was much more prepared than Kennan to live with the dark and perverse side of man's nature without becoming hopelessly discouraged by it. No one promised man an easy time on this earth. Man is born to struggle and make the best of his plight without being led to false hopes and illusions.

Aside from the fact that the Kremlin had shown no real intent to negotiate on any terms which would be acceptable to the West, Acheson could not take Kennan's proposal seriously. On a practical level, it would sow doubt in European minds and deal a setback to American strategy for a revivified Europe. When details, somewhat garbled, of the Kennan Plan became known in European capitals, it did arouse alarm and hostility.[31] Generally treated scathingly, it died before it had the least chance of serious consideration. Of course it was precisely the kind of proposal which should have been made by the Kremlin had it had its wits about it. Seven years later Kennan would renew his proposal for disengagement; this time it would be seconded by Polish Foreign Minister Rapacki. Neither would be successful.

Acheson did not hold that agreement with Russia on a unified control system for Germany was the necessary goal of United States foreign policy.* The obstacle to resolving tensions with Russia was that the West

---

* FR:1949, III, Acheson to Douglas (ambassador to the United Kingdom), "An Approach to the CFM":

1) Our major premise is that our concern is with the future of Europe and not with Germany as a problem by itself. We are concerned with the integration of Germany into a free and democratic Europe. We have made and are making progress to this end with the part of Germany which we control and we shall not jeopardize this progress by seeking a unified Germany as in itself good. If we can integrate a greater part of Germany than we now control under conditions which help and do not retard what we are now doing, we favor that; but, only if the circumstances are right.

2) Just as the unification of Germany is not an end in itself, so the division of Germany is not an end in itself. If, for instance, Russian troops were unilaterally withdrawn, we would not attempt—as an end in itself—by force to keep Eastern and Western Germany apart. Again the test is whether the unification can be achieved under conditions which help and do not retard the unification of free Europe.

3) Similarly, the presence of Russian troops in East Germany is not desirable. It is undesirable. So we do not seek to have these troops remain because their presence insures a divided Germany. We seek to have these troops withdraw as

had not re-established the international system in its necessary structure and balance. Europe needed to recover its strength and unity before Russia could be successfully persuaded to regulate its relations with Europe, and Germany was a part of that essential Europe which had to be restored before relations with Russia would normalize themselves. It was the West's good fortune to have within its sphere the greater and more industrialized part of Germany—the motor, so to speak, of Europe. Consequently the prospect of integrating a peaceful West Germany into Western Europe was not to be lightly dismissed as perhaps a better alternative than seeing Germany once again driven to maneuver neurotically between the Soviet Union and the West. Except for the portion of the Social Democrats led by Kurt Schumacher, the West Germans themselves preferred to be integrated into the West. °

The Berlin blockade had been aimed at exploiting the military weakness of the Western position in Europe. Lifting the blockade did not mean that the Kremlin had changed its goals. No concessions that the West might make would satisfy the Soviet desire for control over Germany on its own terms. Concessions would only weaken the Western position without satisfying the Soviet requirements. The British government and even the French were in total agreement with Acheson on that. On May 2, 1949, Bevin wired Acheson as follows:

It would be wrong and dangerous to assume that Russia's long-term policy had changed or that she is no longer working for the communisation of all Germany as agreed with the satellite governments in the Warsaw communique of June, 1948. As a safeguard against Soviet manoeuvres during the coming negotiations we would do well to keep continually in mind that, after losing an important battle—but only a battle—in Germany, Russia is now suing for

---

far as possible, and we seek to have rights of passage and the presence of Soviet troops in satellite states ended.

4) Here again the price which may be asked for the withdrawal of Russian troops may well be too high. The withdrawal of American and British troops from Germany would be too high a price. The net result of the withdrawal of all troops from Germany would do harm to our objectives and to the progress we have made toward them. So such a proposal would not be accepted, regardless of the propaganda consequences. The task would be to minimize and possibly reverse the propaganda advantage.

° Even Kennan reports how anxious West Germans were to end their pariah status and come in out of the cold. "'If an attempt was now made,'" one German told Kennan, "'to reunite the Soviet zone with the rest of Germany, a civil war would ensue worse than that which had taken place in Spain. Neither the USSR nor the Western powers would be able to see their friends defeated. . . . We should, therefore, make a virtue of necessity and cling to the split Germany as the only hope for a consolidation of Western Europe. A reunited Germany would probably be indigestible in Europe. . . .' He said this with regret, as one who had been born a German." Quoted in Kennan, op. cit., p. 457.

an armistice in order to gain time though not yet for peace. It seems, therefore, important to ensure that any Soviet offer which may now materialise is regarded by the press and public opinion with the utmost circumspection even if the Berlin blockade is lifted.*

The French were of a similar mind.**

Acheson believed that it was precisely because of Western military weakness that the Kremlin had felt confident in risking the brinksmanship implicit in the blockade.[32] Acheson did not believe the struggle was over phantoms. It was not necessary for Soviet armies to sweep to the Channel for the West to be defeated; had the blockade succeeded, European morale would have been so undermined that a victory for Soviet influence would have occurred just as surely as if Soviet armies had been in action. The struggle was not over phantom armies; it was over Germany.

Acheson did not believe that there was any compromise possible on Germany. Both sides had mutually incompatible and irreconcilable interests in Germany. The Soviet Union had employed threats and pressure to prevent the West from consolidating its position. He did not believe that lifting the blockade meant the end of Soviet strategy; the greatest conceivable danger would be for the West to assume that there existed some concessions which, if made, would satisfy the Kremlin. The only concessions that would satisfy the Kremlin would be a capitulation to Soviet demands; anything less than that would only undermine the progress already made without securing any corresponding Soviet concessions. Challenged by Senator Claude Pepper (D–Fla.) at an executive

---

* *FR:1949*, III, p. 862; Bevin to Acheson:

The Foreign Office feels that the principal difficulty is to decide whether the time is yet ripe to press for the re-unification of Germany. We are committed to such unification. We cannot therefore publicly oppose it. But we and the United States Government are both also committed to the establishment of a democratic government in Germany. It seems, therefore, of vital importance, particularly after what has happened in Eastern Europe, that unification should only take place if we can ensure the establishment and maintenance of the necessary safeguards. Assuming that these safeguards could be formulated on paper, it is difficult at present to see how the Russians could be expected to accept them or, if they did so, how we could possibly ensure their full implementation throughout Germany.

** *Ibid.*, p. 878; Bruce to Acheson:

Unification of Germany. All agreed unification was desirable under proper conditions. French specified primary conditions as (1) extension of Bonn Constitution and (2) free elections. French suggested Soviet reaction to such proposal might be purely negative or might be to propose new constituent assembly and new elections for all Germany. It was agreed that we could not delay in any way contemplated carrying out of Bonn Constitution while new machinery for unified Germany was being established.

session of the Senate on May 19, Acheson was about as adamant as anyone could be on the question of offering concessions to the Soviet Union in the hopes of finding some way out of the German impasse. Pepper asked if it was not possible to negotiate on the basis of recognition of Russian "rights." Acheson replied:

It is not a question of rights. The most dangerous thing in the world we can do is to again enter into any agreement which depends for its execution upon Russian cooperation and Russian goodwill. It is not only an impossibility [to reach agreement under present conditions] but it is a danger of such scope that we should not even consider it. The only agreement that you can enter into with the Russians are agreements which do certain things. One is to recognize facts. Secondly [agreements which] are as automatically operating as possible, so there is no opportunity [for the Soviets] to confuse or quibble about it. When you can get arrangements of that sort surely we will go ahead and make them.[33]

The first meeting of the conference, sometimes called the Palais Rose conference after the marble edifice in which it was held, convened on May 22. The Soviet Union was represented by its Minister of Foreign Affairs, Andrei Vyshinky.

What Vyshinksy had to propose at the start of the meetings was such a return to the past that it is hard to disagree with Acheson's prediction that the conference would be nothing more than a propaganda exercise. If Stalin really feared that the Western states were in the process of setting up "their" West German state, and that German rearmament would follow, now if ever was the time for him to offer a counterproposal, something which the French at least would have found difficult to resist. Instead there was not the least deviation from the position that Molotov had proposed two years earlier: (1) the establishment of a quadripartite body to control the Ruhr, (2) the restoration to its former position of the Allied Control Council, and (3) the creation out of existing German economic bodies of a German State Council which would assume full administrative responsibility subject to the Allied Control Council. Vyshinsky's unyielding position only served to bear out Acheson's belief that neither side could afford to give way to the other. Having survived the Berlin blockade and come out of it more united on Germany than ever, it was hardly possible that the West would accept Vyshinsky's terms and revert to a state of affairs which they had rejected two years earlier as one-sided and unreliable.[34]

The rigidity and emptiness of the Soviet offer was such that Acheson had an easy time keeping his French and British allies with him. In effect the conference did little more than ratify the existing deadlock in which the two sides found themselves. The Soviets could not go forward; and the Western powers would not go backward. A few points of agreement, however, were reached. It was agreed that neither side would reimpose the blockade or the counterblockade and that the occupation authorities would consult together in Berlin on matters of trade, transportation, and common administrative problems. Progress was also made toward an Austrian peace treaty, but appearances were deceiving; despite major agreement on terms, the treaty would not be signed until 1955, when Stalin's successors made it part of their détente offensive of that year.

One lesson Acheson drew from the conference may have been unfortunate: he now held a deepening conviction that Soviet diplomacy was not amenable to persuasion or compromise, and that the situation in which each side found itself pointed in one direction only—that of competition in which the worst would only be avoided if the West was better prepared. Here is what Acheson had to say about the conference upon his return to Washington:

It is in the progress that has been achieved in the restoration of Western Europe that you should look for the explanation of what happened at Paris. It has been the success of the cooperative efforts in Western Europe to which the United States has so greatly contributed in the last two years that made this meeting of the Council of Foreign Ministers different from its predecessors. It was those programs, plus the magnificent success, courage, and performance of the airlift which, in the first place, brought about the lifting of the blockade, and in the second place, brought about the situation which emerged from Paris. In other words, these conferences from now on seem to me to be like the steam gauge on a boiler. . . . They indicate the pressure which has been built up. They indicate the various gains and losses in position which have taken place between the meetings, and I think that the recording of this Conference is that the position of the West has grown greatly in strength, and that the position of the Soviet Union in regard to the struggle for the soul of Europe has changed from the offensive to the defensive.[35]

This peculiarly mechanistic view of the future of Soviet–American relations left little room for negotiations or for the chance that Soviet policy might change or mellow. Preoccupied as he was by the immediate problems facing the West, Acheson seems not to have considered what might be done to modify Soviet behavior once the West had regained its strength. Herein lies the principal strength but also the principal weakness of Acheson's statecraft. Thanks to Stalin's crude threats, Acheson was free to concentrate single-mindedly upon organizing the Atlantic community and restoring some degree of manageability to the non–Communist portion of the international system. But this same view led him to ignore the potential for change in the Kremlin and, later, to minimize the divergences that existed within the Communist camp. However vital it may have been to build up Western strength and unity, Acheson seems to have let his rather mechanistic view of the political struggle dominate his thinking. We get a later expression of it when he remarked that Soviet foreign policy is like a river: you can deflect it, you can contain it, but it's going to flow. It was a weakness of Acheson's statecraft that such a perspective did not allow sufficiently for the very changes which the build-up of Western strength and unity under Acheson's aegis would bring about in Soviet foreign policy.

Passage of the European Military Assistance Bill

If East–West diplomacy was henceforth to be little more than a gauge of who was winning, Acheson knew that a lot still had to be done, for if the pressure in the Western part of the boiler was to be maintained, far more progress would have to be registered in mobilizing Western unity, strength, and cooperation than had been achieved so far. The Palais Rose conference was over. The North Atlantic Treaty was ratified. Now the important military aid bill had to be achieved. Before the Congress was the Administration's request for $1.4 billion dollars.

In order to understand the theme of the debate into which presentation of the Military Assistance Program (MAP) plunged Acheson and Vandenberg, it is necessary to review Acheson's understanding of the requirements for gaining a solution to the European security dilemma. On the one hand, the existing European forces were inadequate to deter any type of military aggression; on the other hand, they were adequate to serve as a nucleus around which a viable defense force could be constituted. Until Europe's economic recovery had become self-sustaining and the individual national economies capable of supporting their own military forces, it was incumbent upon the United States to supply the military assistance which would make an immediate contribution to the European defense posture. According to Acheson, without the sense of security which this improved defense posture would bring, European economic recovery would be defeated and no workable scheme for the defense of Western Europe by the European nations could be realized. It was precisely upon the anticipated capacity of the European states eventually to provide for their own security that the long-run success of NATO depended.

The inseparability of the treaty and military assistance in Acheson's mind led him to propose that the one be accompanied by the other.[36] "For a time Congress wanted that, and then they didn't want it; that was too much; that was too complicated, and therefore they wanted to get through with the Treaty first, and then they would take this matter up." [37]

This concern with attempting to provide the elements of both an immediate and a long-range solution to the problem of the European defense capability should not be construed as implying the existence of an overall strategic concept. Acheson felt that that could come later. What seemed important to him at this juncture was simply that something be done. As he was fond of saying in this regard: "We must start somewhere." [38]

The initial sum requested bore no relationship to any strategic concept. As one of Acheson's lieutenants, Paul Nitze, later put it, the sum requested "would be useful as an initial stage toward a real military defense; it would be useful as an initial stage toward a lesser target of a respectable military force which would have political repercussions, and therefore one ought to go forward at least with this program which was within the limits of what one could foresee as being politically and economically in the realm of the possible." [39] This was the basically pragmatic and situational approach with which Acheson presented the program to the Congress.

But now, Vandenberg, freed from the obligation he had assumed a year earlier when he sponsored the Vandenberg Resolution, endeavored to call a halt to the deepening American involvement in Europe's security dilemma. Vandenberg took the view that "the great value of the pact was in its 'potentials.'" Writing to James P. Warburg, he declared:

My concept of it is the maintenance and integration of this nucleus [of nine European divisions] around which the potentials of tomorrow if necessary can be swiftly organized. . . . I do not believe there is any middle ground between this concept which still depends chiefly upon potentials and the complete rearmament which would turn Western Europe and America into an armed camp. . . . It seems to me that we must choose between "potentials" and "forces-in-being." I chose "potentials." [40]

Another argument he advanced to postpone action on a major military aid appropriation at this time was that the Administration request had been prepared outside the Council set up by the North Atlantic Treaty for determining the implementation of the pact. Any recommendation to the Senate for military assistance to Europe, Vandenberg declared, ought to come after the North Atlantic Treaty Council had had the opportunity to determine what was strategically necessary. [41] This was precisely the sort of formalistic reasoning against which Acheson could be expected to react impatiently. Vandenberg engaged Acheson in a series of sharp debates beginning with an executive session of the joint Foreign Relations and Armed Services Committees on August 2, 1949.

Acheson was not a man who compromised easily. Unnecessary compromise diluted one's purpose and led one away from one's goals. He held his opinions tenaciously and with a vividness of purpose that was very much part of his personality.

Acheson took up Vandenberg's criticisms one by one, in each case adducing the substance of the problem with which the MAP was designed to cope. To the argument that by providing for "potentials" the North Atlantic Treaty was sufficient as it stood, Acheson reminded his listeners: "We must never forget that we are dealing not with abstractions, but with people. Our allies in Western Europe are human beings with human hopes and fears." [42] Merely signing a treaty does not deter the temptation of war, particularly if an aggressor calculates that he can get away with it. "It is not intended that there should be maintained in Western Europe forces in being capable of defending all Europe. . . . But, it is essential . . . that there be maintained . . . forces sufficient to convince any would-be aggressor that he would not by quick marches gain easy victories." [43]

In the course of questioning, Acheson made explicit his determination to act upon the requirements of the situation and not to pursue the politically expedient course of yielding to the intense desires of Senator Vandenberg that military aid be put off for a year.

Viewed as a problem, the question of arming Europe permitted three possible solutions. One would have been based upon the premises of the Vandenberg proposal consisting of an "attitude" toward commitment with little or no substantive military support:

Senator Vandenberg: Under all existing circumstance, I take it you would resist the idea that our responsibility *at the moment* is to proceed in good faith *to indicate our intention* to furnish such arms *as we deem appropriate* under the terms of the pact?
Secretary Acheson: . . . I think that you gain no advantage in dealing with the forces with which we are dealing by merely taking attitudes. Attitudes do not impress. [44]

The second alternative, that of endeavoring to transform Europe into an armed camp, Acheson rejected because it was manifestly impossible for the United States to match the Soviet Union; therefore any such undertaking would be based upon an unreal appraisal of the possibilities of action.

Secretary Acheson: . . . The Russian forces are at the present time so much greater than anybody else's that there can be no question about a race to catch up with the Russians, for that can never be done. What one must have in mind, so far as any aggressor is concerned, is that there should be sufficient forces in western Europe to hold until added strength can be brought into play. . . . [45]

The third alternative, that of constructing a limited military deterrent, Acheson chose because it corresponded to the requirements of the situation and because it was a feasible course of action.

Senator Russell: So that at the very best we are buying a pig in a poke by committing ourselves to this program.

Secretary Acheson: The point is, we are confronted *with a situation,* and the question is, to what extent do the people want to remedy the weakness of western Europe? [46]

While most of Acheson's comments were directly related to defining the need for military assistance in terms of its immediate consequences, he was under no illusion that all the consequences were purely military in nature. In the course of the hearings and floor action, several sizeable cuts reduced the appropriation from $1.4 billion to $1 billion. In addition, Senators Dulles and Vandenberg attempted to regulate expenditure of the aid appropriation by tying the MAP to what they called "the integrated plan for the defense of Europe." [47] Vandenberg and Dulles seemed to feel that "the important thing was to have a strategic plan, and if you had a strategic plan then you could go ahead with an arms program, but if you didn't have a strategic plan then you shouldn't go ahead with an arms program." [48] The law was therefore revised so that it severely limited the manner in which the Executive could make use of the funds. One hundred million dollars was made available for immediate use, while the remaining funds were to be withheld until NATO could produce a strategic plan which would be approved by the President. Acheson remarked "that this attempt by the Congress to make the money contingent on doing something, made it contingent on something which had no relation whatever to the wisdom or unwisdom of the use of the money, because it was quite impossible to get a strategic plan, in the sense of a carefully worked out war plan. . . ." [49] He was aware that today's consequences would provide the facts and conditions for tomorrow's action; and while his arguments for the MAP were relevant in terms of their immediate effectiveness in securing passage of the program, the policy had also been cast with an eye to consideration of the future and its only dimly perceived consequences. Without the MAP, the next step in the more general policy of European recovery could not be taken because there would be only Vandenberg's "potentials" and no substance around which to coalesce.[50]

Final passage of the Military Assistance Program was probably helped by the President's announcement on September 23, 1949, that the Soviet Union had successfully tested a nuclear device. Impelled by the loss of America's nuclear monopoly, solid majorities in both houses approved the bill in less than a week, cutting the original request by only $100 million. Nevertheless the intensity of the opposition provides strong evidence for the proposition that it was less Acheson's personality or role that stirred up antagonism to him than it was his unrelenting espousal of an alliance diplomacy viewed with fear and loathing by a Congress that espoused anti–Communism but did not want to accept any obligation.

CHAPTER

10

STRATEGIC DECISIONS: FALL, 1949

IF THE PASSAGE of the Military Assistance Program was made easier by the news that the Soviet Union had exploded a nuclear device, nothing else was. Up until September 1949 American diplomacy had rested on the confident assumption that if worst came to worst the United States could always count on its atomic monopoly. Europeans and Americans alike assumed that Russia would hesitate to risk war or press home an advantage knowing that the Americans in extremis could always resort to an atomic counterattack. Such confidence had led to less-than-adequate strategic planning. Despite the creation of the National Security Council and the formation of the Joint Chiefs of Staff, there had been no real coordination of military strategy and planning.

Truman, who had come to the Presidency convinced from his Truman Committee experience that the military services had "unquestionably squandered billions of dollars," was skeptical of the military and annually compressed military spending to fit within a balanced budget. His method involved substracting all anticipated expenditures of the civilian government from anticipated revenues, the remainder then being made available to the military services. As a result, any relationship between America's foreign-policy goals and its military strategy was purely coincidental.

None of the four principal elements of such policies—diplomatic, foreign economic aid, military, and budgetary—could be put together with each other without great difficulty. The military spokesmen and those people in the Military Establishment, the White House, and the Bureau of the Budget whose particular frame of reference was budgetary considerations had little confidence in each other.[1]

Confronted by such an uncertain budgetary situation, each of the military services adopted whatever strategy promised to maximize its share of the budget at the expense of the others.

Truman's method of setting the military budget invited all kinds of trouble. It had already ruined relations between Truman and James V. Forrestal, the first Secretary of Defense. It had also led to some spectacular battles between the Air Force and the Navy over which should have the primary mission of delivering atomic weapons should war break out. Fearing that its role would be eclipsed if it did not possess the means of delivering an atomic bomb, the Navy proposed to build a supercarrier from which attacks could be launched with accuracy against Soviet targets. To accomplish its end, the Navy sought to discredit the Air Force's B-36 bomber, and the struggle produced an incredible donnybrook which was a disgrace to everyone concerned. So bitter were the exchanges between the Navy and the Air Force about which could do the best job of putting the Soviet Union out of action that Truman had to urge Acheson to deliver some reassuring word to the Russians lest they begin to believe that the United States had in mind some future plan for attacking Russia.

Equally deleterious, if less scandalous, was the deformation that limiting the budget in such an artificial manner imposed upon strategic planning. Given a choice between spending money on ground forces or on air power, the American people and the Congress had given the preference to air power. Against Truman's opposition, the Congress had appropriated funds for a 70-group Air Force; these funds Truman in effect impounded in order to avoid upsetting either the budgetary or the strategic balance among the services.[2] Still, arbitrarily limiting the budget and impounding funds did not change America's essential reliance upon air power and the atomic bomb for its strategic defense, nor did they solve the problem of inadequate strategy planning. In the absence of sufficient manpower, places that would later come to have political importance, like Korea, were left exposed to the temptation of a Soviet-inspired attack. American strategy was little more than a replica of World War II: primary reliance was upon air power to attack Russia should war occur; meanwhile in due time ground forces would be mobilized which would presumably be available to liberate Europe after it had been conquered. This strategy had already been thrown into doubt by the signing of the North Atlantic Treaty and by the European expectation that Europe would be defended *in Europe* by American forces from the moment war broke out.

No one had ever successfully tackled the problem of coordinating American strategy and diplomacy. Until Acheson came along no one cared or dared to examine the political significance and risk involved in permitting the military budget to be determined in such an arbitrary way. The barriers between the President and the military would have to be broken down along with the barriers between the State Department and the

Pentagon and between the military services. Acheson's ascendancy within the Administration stemmed in part at least from his success in breaking down those watertight compartments and in winning over both President Truman and the Joint Chiefs of Staff under General Bradley to a unified political and military concept of strategy. It was upon the unexpected reef of this unity that MacArthur was to run aground when he failed to recognize to what extent strategy had become a joint product of both political and military planning.

Knowledge that the Soviet Union had set off a nuclear explosion reached Washington in early September 1949. By September 14 the report had been confirmed, and President Truman made the news public on Friday, September 23. Although the public took the announcement in stride, the shock within the Joint Atomic Energy Committee of the Congress, headed by Brien McMahon (D–Conn.), and within the scientific and military communities was considerable.[3] Almost immediately sides formed within these communities for and against the development by the United States of a hydrogen bomb, the so-called "Super," which, if successful, would possess a much greater destructive power than the A-bomb.

The Atomic Energy Commission consisted of five men appointed by the President. David Lilienthal was chairman; the other members were retired Admiral Lewis Strauss, Henry Smyth, Sumner Pike, and Gordon Dean. They were advised by a group of leading nuclear scientists called the General Advisory Committee (GAC) whose chairman was J. Robert Oppenheimer, one of the men most responsible for developing the atomic bomb during World War II. Unusually sensitive to the moral dilemma posed by use of such weapons of mass destruction, the members of the GAC recommended against the immediate development of the Super on the immediate grounds that it would interfere with existing programs, but their ultimate concern was moral. GAC also raised questions in its report about the wisdom of America's complete reliance on weapons of mass destruction as an instrument of foreign policy—the same question that was disturbing Acheson.

The five-man Atomic Energy Commission divided on the scientists' report. David Lilienthal and, to a somewhat lesser extent, Pike and Smyth shared the opinion of Oppenheimer and the General Advisory Committee that the government should not begin development of the Super. Gordon Dean and especially Lewis Strauss, the other two members, believed that development of the Super represented the single most necessary and effective response to the threat posed by the Soviet Union. They reflected the views of a powerful group of scientists, including Edward Teller, Ernest O. Lawrence, Luis W. Alvarez, and others, who feared that American security would be jeopardized unless the Administration moved to develop the H-bomb. This group was quickly reinforced by support from Senator McMahon and the Joint Atomic Energy Committee, which quickly let Truman know in no uncertain terms that unless he went ahead with plans for developing the Super he would face all-out public opposition from the Joint Atomic Energy Committee of the Congress. This was a point of view that the President could not lightly disregard.

Meanwhile, Acheson had charged the Policy Planning Staff and George Kennan in particular with responsibility for recommending on the consequences for United States foreign policy of the Soviet atomic explosion. Some consideration was being given at the time to reopening negotiations for international control of atomic energy, and the relation of the H-bomb to that naturally came into the picture.

Kennan, depressed by the seeming lack of attention which his views were getting, asked to be relieved and to withdraw from the State Department entirely at the end of June of the following year. Kennan is doubtless right in believing that Acheson saw him "only as an individual— as one, in fact, of a group of individuals whom he had around him and with whom he liked to explore ideas. . . ." Acheson did not attribute to Kennan's role as director of the Policy Planning Staff the significance Kennan thought it should have.* Kennan is also correct in believing that his views, brooding and philosophic as they often were, seemed less and less relevant to the day-to-day and month-to-month problems with which the department was wrestling. As Acheson had said of Kennan's 1946 cable, its analytic and prophetic quality were brilliant but his recommendations "were of no help," ** by which he meant of no practical help. In fairness to Kennan, and indicative of the attraction Acheson had for men of his caliber, Kennan's leave-taking gave cause for more remorse than recrimination. After his departure, Kennan wrote that his "affection and admiration" for Acheson were so strong "that they would even withstand the public controversy of ensuing years." [4]

At bottom their disagreement was as much philosophic as operational.

---

* George F. Kennan, *Memoirs, 1925–1950* (Boston: Little, Brown, 1967), p. 450. "The thought of consulting the staff as an institution and conceding to it, as did General Marshall, a margin of confidence within which he was willing to respect its opinions even when that opinion did not fully coincide with his own. . . . All this would have been strange to him [Acheson]." *Ibid.*

** Acheson, *Present at the Creation* (New York: Norton, 1969), p. 151, Kennan goes on to say that Acheson was "sometimes amused, sometimes appalled, usually interested [by Kennan's oral contributions]; but there were times when I felt like a court jester, expected to enliven discussion, privileged to say the shocking things, valued as an intellectual gadfly on the hides of slower colleagues, but not to be taken seriously when it came to the final, responsible decisions of policy." Kennan, *op cit.*, p. 450.

Operationally Kennan felt that Acheson's instruction to clear Policy Planning Staff papers with the assistant secretaries, instead of having them go direct and undiluted by day-to-day bureaucratic considerations to the Secretary, undercut the usefulness of the staff as a source of long-range, independent advice. The problem of blending daily operations with long-run prognostications, often at variance with each other, is one which has never been successfully resolved. But as Kennan admitted a few days later in a diary entry, his differences with Acheson were also philosophic and substantive, and he was losing his influence as much for these reasons as for differences about organizational matters.

The heart of the difficulty lies in the fact that my concept of the manner in which our diplomatic effort should be conducted is not shared by any of the other senior officials of the department. . . . Even if he [Acheson] shared my views, he would not be able to find others who did; and lacking such others he would have to operate through people whose philosophy of foreign affairs would necessarily be a different one. The fact of the matter is that this operation cannot be unified and given real purpose or direction unless a firm theoretical groundwork has been laid to back up whatever policy is pursued . . . [and] through an intensive education effort directed toward public opinion. . . .[5]

The problem now was that Acheson's theoretical framework and Kennan's were at odds. Kennan was still hoping that efforts might still be made to re-examine in a most fundamental way the assumptions of United States policy vis-à-vis Russia in an effort to find points of agreement and negotiation. Acheson, on the other hand, had determined that such hopes were evanescent and that only a long and patient effort at building up Western strength could deter the Soviet Union from untoward adventures and bring it to its senses.

How different from Kennan's were Acheson's ideas? Twice that autumn Acheson had occasion to comment upon the problems facing American foreign policy as he understood them. On October 20 he addressed the annual Al Smith dinner in New York City. Quite apart from the problem of the Soviet Union, Acheson told his audience, there were innumerable problems left over from the war that involved an American responsibility. Within the world and within each nation were many stresses and strains, and "what a nation should do, if it were one person with one will and one mind, is often very different from what it actually can do, and does do, when those in charge of government resolve the multiplicity of thrusts into a single decision." The statesman must know the limitations

of the power of his own country and the limitations of his own position within it. . . . American assistance to other nations is always marginal assistance. The issue turns primarily upon their own will and effort. . . . We cannot direct or control; we cannot make a world, as God did, out of chaos. There are some, apparently, who think that we should do this, and in less than six days! *

Then, as if in response to Kennan's belief that the State Department could somehow impose its will upon American society, Acheson had the following to say:

So within our minds and within the government, the Department of State cannot think of itself as an institution apart, in monopolistic control of an isolated field of activity. . . .[6]

It must work in harmony with the other departments and branches of government.

It must be close to the American people, constantly reporting the facts without which informed judgment or criticism cannot be made. It must not be afraid to tell the truth when that is painful and unpleasant, as it was in the China White Paper. It must not be afraid to recommend and fight for courses which are hard and long when any other course would be a deception and a fraud. . . . We do not ask, any more than Al Smith did, that this relationship be one of blind and unquestioning acceptance of all we think and do. When people agree with us, we want their support; when they do not agree with us, we want their frank and constructive criticism.

In either case, whether they agree or disagree with what we are doing, we hope they will regard us as ordinary American people, trying our best to do a job in a highly complicated set of circumstances, and to do it in a way which Al Smith would have understood and approved.[7]

Later that autumn Acheson came over to the National War College to introduce George Kennan and took advantage of the occasion to address his thoughts to the nature of the struggle with Russia.

Today you hear much talk of absolutes also. You hear people say that two systems as different as ours and that of the Russians cannot exist in the same world. That is an absolute. It is followed up, for instance, by a statement that one is good and one is evil, and good and evil cannot exist in the world. If you think about that for a moment, the silliness of it is apparent. Good and evil have existed in this world since Adam and Eve went out of the Garden of Eden.

The proper search is for limited ends which soon enough educate us in the complexities of the tasks which face us. That is what all of us must learn to do in the United States: to limit objectives, to get ourselves away from the search for the absolute, to find out what is within our powers, to find out how it can be done with the materials at our disposal.[8]

---

* This contrasts nicely with the title of his book *Present at the Creation* and it marks the humility he felt at the time with his later magisterial view of what he and the Administration had accomplished. Address at the Al Smith dinner, New York City, October 20, 1949.

Speaking to his audience, primarily high military officers, Acheson continued,

. . . one of the most destructive ways to go at the task which you have before you, and which I have before me, is to go at it emotionally. If you start thinking about your opponent in terms of intense bitterness your mind is deflected. We must respect our opponents. We must understand that for a long, long period of time they will continue to believe as they do, and that for a long, long period of time we will both inhabit this spinning ball in the great void of the universe.[9]

This did not mean that Acheson chose to ignore the moral differences that existed between communism and the Western emphasis upon the freedom and dignity of the individual as *Time* and *Life* accused him of doing. Nor did it mean that he had gone to the other extreme and was the cynical advocate of a power struggle verging on nihilism. It simply meant that he did not agree that the conflict could be resolved by a resort to war.

The theoretical foundations of American policy were already settled in Acheson's mind. The problem now was to bring about their execution and realization. Admittedly, Acheson's philosophy left little room for the subtleties of diplomatic maneuver and for change within the Kremlin, but unlike Kennan Acheson did not believe that the potential for such developments existed under Stalin. The cultivation of potential, in which Kennan believed, would risk exploitation by Stalin and would expose the unity and perseverance of the Western powers. Stalin did not have to reckon with public opinion; Western statesmen did. The age of cabinet diplomacy and of compromise based upon subtle calculations of national interest and national power, for which Kennan so patently longed, had been eclipsed for Acheson by evidence that modern dictators were not bound by any respect for legitimate limits to their state's power. Secondly, success against the revolutionary and ideological challenge posed by dictators could only be realized if the West could offer something in its place, and that required economic and political sacrifices on the part of a democratic people that could not be had unless they were convinced of their essential necessity and rightness.

Despite their differences, Kennan agreed to stay on an additional year as counselor to the department and in that capacity to make his advice available to Acheson. Among the issues on which Kennan, as a departing member of the Policy Planning Staff, was asked to comment was the issue of the hydrogen bomb. It was an issue on which his philosophic differences with Acheson were to emerge in the strongest possible light and in a manner painful and disturbing to both men. Kennan admits that his moral abhorrence of the bomb stirred him deeply, and he threw himself into the analysis with as deep and moral a passion as he had ever given to any subject.

In the meantime, pressure had been building up during October and early November within the Atomic Energy Commission and the Joint Atomic Energy Committee for a recommendation about the H-bomb. The atmosphere was becoming supercharged by the belief on the part of those who favored development that those who opposed it were letting moral scruples and personal feelings prejudice their judgment. On November 1, Lilienthal came to see Acheson. While not as morally anguished as the GAC scientists by the idea of the Super, Lilienthal generally favored the viewpoint of those who were prepared to foreswear development pending what the Russians might decide to do. Like Acheson, he was also disturbed by the Administration's seeming overreliance on the atomic bomb as its first line of defense. Immediately after his talk with Lilienthal, Acheson met with the Policy Planning Staff which was now thoroughly conversant with "the far-reaching consequences of the even broader decision that now faced the President." * R. Gordon Arneson of the Policy Planning Staff was now assigned to examine the implications for U.S. policy of developing or not developing the H-bomb. In his report to Acheson later in December, Arneson would find little reason to believe that the Soviet Union would not press ahead with the Super, and he judged that sole possession of the H-bomb by the Soviet Union "would cause severe damage not only to our military posture but to our foreign policy position." **

Meanwhile, in order to resolve the conflict that was now boiling up between Strauss, Teller, McMahon, and others in the pro-bomb group and Lilienthal, Oppenheimer, and others opposed to its immediate development, on November 10 Truman appointed a special committee consisting of Louis Johnson, Lilienthal, and Acheson to advise him "whether and in what manner the United States should undertake the development and possible production of 'super' atomic weapons [and] . . . whether and when any publicity should be given to the matter." These circumstances gave Acheson his opportunity to make the issue of America's military and strategic preparedness a matter of deliberation at the highest level. Lilienthal continued to want to postpone research on the H-bomb pending review of the foreign and military strategies, including the possibility of

---

* Acheson, *Present at the Creation, op. cit.,* p. 346. The Policy Planning Staff was now headed by Paul Nitze, a former Wall Streeter but long-time specialist in strategic and foreign-policy matters.

** Richard G. Hewlett and Francis Duncan, *A History of the United States Atomic Energy Commission,* Vol. II, *Atomic Shield: 1947–1952* (University Park: Pennsylvania State University Press, 1969), p. 403. This enormously important decision is discussed in complete detail in the Hewlett and Duncan study (pp. 369–409) entitled *Atomic Shield,* which is Volume II of the official history of the Atomic Energy Commission and which contains surprisingly frank and detailed analyses of the entire range of atomic decisions.

reopening discussion of international control of atomic energy. Louis Johnson favored a crash program to develop the H-bomb, in part because he favored the policy of more "bang for the buck" and in part in the hope of short-circuiting Acheson's review of the strategic policies and military spending.

Any delay in developing the H-bomb could only be justified if there were still some chance of negotiating an agreement for international control of atomic weapons. As counsel, Kennan too had been studying the implications for American foreign policy of the merit of trying once more for atomic negotiations. Kennan, together with some others, worked on the problem over the final weeks of 1949. Unlike the members of the Policy Planning Staff, Kennan came out against developing the H-bomb. He reasoned that either the United States had to take seriously its professions about desiring to see atomic weapons abolished, and therefore had to ban them from consideration in the development of its strategic doctrine as proof that America had no intention of initiating their use in any military encounter, or the United States ought frankly to recognize that it was basing its defense posture on the first-strike use of atomic weapons, "regardless of whether they had been or might be used against us in any major military encounter." * Kennan concluded his report with an eloquent plea that, before the United States government proceeded to the development of the hydrogen bomb, it re-examine "the whole principle of the 'first use' of atomic weapons or any other of the weapons of mass destruction," and he made clear that his voice would be raised most decisively in the councils of government against the principle of "first use" and against developing the H-bomb.[10] Acheson was getting advice of a similar nature from others—principally Oppenheimer, whom he continued to respect greatly.

Of Kennan's advice, Acheson remarked:

Kennan warned me not to get involved; not to commit myself or the country to development of the H-Bomb. He wrote a long memo urging that we let the Russians assume the moral odium and responsibility for its initiation. I told Kennan if that was his view he ought to resign from the Foreign Service and go out and preach his Quaker gospel but not push it within the Department. He had no right being in the Service if he was not willing to face the questions as an issue to be decided in the interests of the American people under a sense of responsibility. I then spoke to Oppenheimer but he refused to say any more than that he did not believe it to be technically feasible. As part of our responsibility to the American people we had to open that door not only because

---

* George F. Kennan, *Memoirs: 1925–1950* (Boston: Little, Brown, 1967), pp. 472–473. This "either–or" kind of reasoning has its own fuzziness because retaining the bomb does not require that it be used on a first-strike basis regardless of whether it has or has not been used against us.

we knew that the Russians would open it sooner or later, but because those are the kinds of problems with which man must live. Science cannot be willed away.[11]

Acheson stated that his decision to ignore Kennan's advice and to join in recommending to the President that the Administration investigate the H-bomb lay in his conviction that the American people simply "would not tolerate a policy of delaying nuclear research while we sought for further ways of reaching accommodation with the Russians. . . ." [12] It seems more likely that Acheson himself had little interest or confidence in reaching agreement and that, under the circumstances, to delay would be to open the Administration to the most serious kinds of charges of policy dereliction. This decision was also one of the few on which Truman would have already made up his mind on the basis of a gut belief that America should not foreswear any advantage in such a critical matter. Acheson probably sensed that to challenge the President's judgment on this matter would be not only futile but undesirable. Better wisdom would be to get the President to support a thoroughgoing reappraisal of the country's overreliance upon nuclear weapons. But Acheson was certainly aware of the larger moral and philosophic issues raised by the H-bomb. In his memoirs, he wrote that the broader issues

evoked a great deal of moral fervor. . . . Enough evil had been brought into human life, it was argued by men of the highest standing in science, education, and government, through the development of atomic weapons without adding the superhorror of thermonuclear ones. . . . Those who shared this view were, I believed, not so much moved by the power of its logic (which I was never able to perceive—neither the maintenance of ignorance nor reliance on perpetual good will seemed to me a tenable policy) as by an immense distaste for what one of them, the purity of whose motive could not be doubted, described as "the whole rotten business." [13]

By the end of December Acheson had made his decision in favor of supporting development of the H-bomb. It still remained to secure the President's approval for a thoroughgoing reappraisal of United States strategy. Louis Johnson, who was also opposing Acheson's efforts to disentangle the United States from support of Chiang Kai-shek, did not want any such review because he sensed quite rightly that what Acheson was after would be disturbing on two counts: it would challenge the ceiling presently placed on military spending, with which Johnson was now publicly identified, and it might involve a challenge to Johnson's uneasy control of the Pentagon. The niceties of nuclear strategy and sound strategic doctrine did not particularly interest him. He was fighting a desperate struggle to meet Truman's budgetary limitations on military spending, and he had no desire to see the matter opened up to a full-scale review that might go against him. The bitter fight over the B-36 had left him battered and shaken in his authority. The pressures of the job had already helped to destroy one Secretary of Defense. Johnson had no desire to see whatever ambitions he nourished destroyed by any campaign originating with Acheson to increase defense spending. The seed of a bitter personal feud already existed which would lead eight months later to Johnson's tragic effort to betray Acheson in secret dealings with Senate Republicans and his dismissal from office. The last thing Louis Johnson wanted was to disturb the existing uneasy situation. Consequently Johnson favored building the H-bomb with no strings attached. Would it not continue to provide America with that added margin of security at no extra cost?

But Acheson knew what he wanted: he badly wanted the opportunity to open up existing strategic doctrine and budgetary limitations in favor of a more comprehensive and balanced military establishment—just what Johnson, the Secretary of Defense, wanted to avoid. What Johnson had failed to appreciate was that there could be no progress on the diplomatic front, and no guarantee against another Berlin-type threat, without a more balanced military strategy.

Meeting with Acheson on January 26, Lilienthal still hoped to enlist him in opposing the immediate development of the H-bomb on the grounds that a Presidential decision to go ahead with the Super would confirm a wrong policy and lend credence to the myth that weapons of destruction provided national security.[14] Acheson was discouraging. He admitted that "strategic bombing would be no more effective as an instrument of national policy than would preventive war. But the continuing Soviet threat and the collapse of the Nationalist government in China made it hard to counter the demand for bigger weapons." [15] The very next day Lilienthal would have to face hostile questioning from members of the Joint Atomic Energy Committee who were determined to know what was delaying the President's decision to go ahead with the Super. Acheson, already under attack, was hardly in a position to oppose the H-bomb publicly, even had he been convinced that it was unwise on policy grounds, which he did not. Instead, what Acheson wanted was also a part of what Lilienthal wanted—namely, a searching examination of the adequacy of America's military strategy in relation to its foreign policy.

When Acheson, Johnson, and Lilienthal and their subordinates met on January 31, 1950, it was a foregone conclusion that they would not recommend against development of the H-bomb. But by throwing his weight behind Lilienthal's call for a comprehensive re-examination of United States strategy, Acheson knew that he could frustrate Johnson's desire to just go ahead and make the bomb. Lilienthal had in mind the insanity that American security was based upon little more than acceptance of a headlong rush into war with nuclear weapons. Acheson was thinking beyond that to the question of what strategy could be developed to put in place of "first strike" that would also support America's alliance policy. Lilienthal's courageous plea for a sweeping re-examination provided Acheson with the opportunity to open up the question of the adequacy of existing military strategy and budget at the Presidential level. The logic of the situation favored Acheson. Without Acheson's support, Lilienthal had to forego his opposition to the H-bomb, and Johnson had to forego his opposition to re-examining America's military posture.

Having agreed that Lilienthal could make one more appeal to postpone the H-bomb decision until after the government had studied the wisdom of making nuclear weapons the nation's first line of defense, that afternoon the three men went to see Truman. Truman tried to let Lilienthal down lightly by observing that had so much excitement not been aroused over the issue, a quiet examination of the H-bomb might have been possible.[16] That same afternoon Truman announced to the public that the Administration planned to examine the feasibility of developing a hydrogen bomb. The President instructed the Secretaries of State and Defense to undertake a re-examination of "our objectives in peace and war and of the effect of objectives on our strategic plans, in light of the probable fission bomb capability and possible thermonuclear bomb capability of the Soviet Union."

This meant that the State Department's interest in re-examination now had the full backing of the President and of the National Security Council. A special interdepartmental committee was now constituted, consisting of Pentagon and State Department representatives, whose work eventually emerged as National Security Council Paper 68 (NSC-68). But if Acheson had secured his re-examination, Truman's announcement about American intentions to proceed with the development of the H-bomb set off a storm of objections which, by default, Acheson was going to have to counter.

Albert Einstein denounced the decision as leading to the militarization of American life, and twelve other eminent scientists asked for an understanding that "the United States should not be the first to use the new bomb." *

Knowing how many scientists shared Einstein's and Oppenheimer's view, Acheson had anticipated their criticism. What he had not expected was for Brien McMahon, who had lobbied most vociferously in favor of the H-bomb, to get up on the floor of the Senate and propose that the

---

* Quoted in Coral Bell, *Negotiation from Strength* (New York: Alfred A. Knopf, 1963), p. 8. It should not be overlooked that atomic scientist Harold Urey regretfully concluded that the hydrogen bomb should be developed and built and that Eleanor Roosevelt among other liberals supported the decision.

United States should offer to finance a five-year, worldwide Marshall Plan, involving the expenditure of $50 billion, as a quid pro quo for Soviet agreement on control of atomic energy. Acheson could scarcely believe his senses. This was the same McMahon who had conspired so intently with Admiral Strauss and the Lawrence–Teller group of scientists to push ahead with the H-bomb regardless of its implications for American foreign policy.[17] Only a month earlier McMahon had threatened to go public unless the President acquiesced to the Joint Atomic Energy Committee's insistence that nothing must be allowed to stand in the way of the United States acquiring the H-bomb. The Russians were not to be trusted they argued. "If we let Russia get the super first," McMahon concluded, "catastrophe becomes all but certain—whereas, if we get it first, there is a chance of saving ourselves." [18] At that time, Lilienthal's proposal for a new initiative had been howled down by the Joint Atomic Energy Committee as a form of appeasement bordering on lunacy. How could McMahon, who knew better than anyone else in the Senate the nature of the obstacles to reaching agreement on atomic control with the Russians, believe that such an offer would now bridge the gap between what the Soviet Union and the American Congress considered to be an acceptable control agreement?

No sooner had McMahon said his piece than Senator Millard E. Tydings, chairman of the Senate Armed Services Committee, suggested that the President should call a world disarmament conference. Coming in the wake of the decision to develop the H-bomb, and at a time when Acheson was concerned that the balance of power was swinging against America and that time was needed to redress it, Acheson felt obliged to answer these proposals directly. At a press conference on February 8, 1950, and a week later in a speech to the American Advertising Council, Acheson set forth the elements of what later became known as the "situations of strength" doctrine. It is sometimes contended that these two speeches were "merely pieces of diplomatic temporizing, official tranquilizers for a case of nuclear anxiety.[19] In fact, the ideas and concepts expressed in both speeches—total diplomacy and negotiation from strength—reflected his most considered views about the matter.

At the press conference, Acheson again sought to clarify the premises upon which the Administration's foreign policy rested. First of all, Acheson sought to dispel the notion that the Administration was consciously or unconsciously embarked upon a war policy. "War," Acheson declared, "cannot accomplish the purposes of democracy. It can only make the accomplishment of that more difficult and therefore with a democracy war can be resorted to only when it becomes necessary to protect the physical side of the state. . . ." [20] (The image of Acheson the cold warrior often obscures the fact that he was adamantly opposed to any consideration of war as an instrument of national policy. Later that spring, when he was being grilled by the Senate Foreign Relations Committee in executive session, Senator Henry Cabot Lodge, Jr., asked Acheson if it would not be possible that the United States would be justified in waging a preventive war against the Soviet Union while we still had the nuclear advantage. Acheson replied: "I think that [talk of preventive war] brings on us all the troubles that we seek to avoid, and in connection with whether it is or is not true that the passage of time steadily increases the power of the Soviet Union, that is a matter about which I think there is very great doubt." * So much for Acheson as a warmonger.)

While Acheson dismissed war as an unsatisfactory instrument of American policy, he warned that the United States could not escape the reality of Soviet competition for positions which were essential to the security of the West. The situation in which the Soviet Union found itself prompted its expansionist tendencies. "To ask them [the Soviet government] not to fish and to say we will have an agreement that you won't fish is like trying to deal with a force of nature. You can't argue with a river, it is going to flow. You can dam it up, you can put it to useful purposes, you can deflect it, but you can't argue with it."

Acheson declared:

If we could reach our goal by agreement that would be highly desirable and the simplest and the easiest way to do it. But I think that four years of experience have brought us the realization that it is not possible. . . . Agreements reached with the Soviet Government are useful when those agreements register facts or a situation which exists, and . . . they are not useful when they are merely agreements which do not register the existing fact.

The great purposefulness of the Soviet Government has been directed towards exploiting the weaknesses of the non–Communist world. So it has been our basic policy to build situations which will extend the area of possible agreement, that is to create strength instead of the weakness which exists in many quarters. * *

Of this statement to the press, TRB (columnist Richard L. Strout) wrote in the *New Republic* of February 20: "It was evident that this was an answer to McMahon and Tydings. It was a firm, powerful, and grim declaration, brilliantly delivered. It tied in with the decision to make the

---

* Executive Session, *Review of the World Situation*, hearings before the Senate Committee on Foreign Relations, p. 173. Acheson went on to say that he believed that after discussions with General Bradley about the military implications for the long run there was a great deal to be said against the idea that time increases Soviet power.

* * Acheson concluded by warning that the United States "should be careful to see that our self-examination does not go to the point where it becomes self-reproach. Because that attitude of mind is one which is apt to bring paralysis in the field of action where action is necessary."

H-Bomb. It offered a picture of inability to deal with the Russians on anything but the plane of power. But here again . . . it was almost wholly
negative." This, Acheson knew, was the dilemma in educating Americans
to courses of action they did not like. The right-wing weeklies represented
by *Time* and *U.S. News and World Report* thought Acheson's speeches
were negative too, but in the opposite direction in that they did not go
far enough in challenging the Soviet Union and actively working for the
liberation of the Russian or Chinese people. David Lawrence writing in
the *U.S. News and World Report* of February 17, 1950 had this to say:

He has proposed that we wait vigilantly as we increase our strength and, by
deploying our military and economic influence, strive to render a third world
war less likely. This is an age-old doctrine. History proves that at best it merely
means a time between war. . . . An oppressed people need a goal—a hope. The
Russian people are the victims of oppression. Their salvation must come from
within and from without. It is our duty to furnish that hope . . . [instead of
accepting Acheson's static view]. We can organize the free people of the
world in a crusade of help to the Russian people. . . .[21]

Determined to make his point, Acheson returned to the same theme in
an address on February 16 to the American Advertising Council. Today
we are engaged in a struggle that is just as crucial to the continued existence of our way of life as the struggle against Nazism, he told Council
members.[22]

. . . but we are clearly not focusing our total resources on the winning of that
struggle.
    For one thing we have never taken the general activities of our country—
which mean governmental activities—as seriously as we should in time of
peace. We have regarded them with a good-natured tolerance expressed in the
phrase, "well politics is politics." We have thought of politics as a legitimate
field for trying to promote special interests. . . . Moreover while we have recognized that there were foreign claims upon us which our self-interest demanded
that we attend to, we have not thought of them as being in the same category
of importance as our own domestic business. Americans have put too much
confidence in the goodness of human nature and in the belief that "somehow
or other there was an answer to our problem if only we were smart enough to
figure it out."
    Then, too, it has been hard for us to convince ourselves that human nature
is not pretty much the same the world over. We hear it said that if we could
only get Harry Truman to "get his feet under the same table"—that is the
phrase used—with Joe Stalin, we would be able to iron out any international
difficulty. Our own experience with people in our own communities has been
such that it has seemed to us that good intentions must in the long run
prevail—and if one proposition didn't meet with acceptance, all we had to do
was to think up a better one.

There has been an attitude on the part of some that if things went too far we might have to "call their bluff" and possibly have a showdown.

These are some of the things that I meant when I referred to "total diplomacy." It means that all branches of the government must work closely together. Congress and the Departments of Defense, Treasury, Agriculture, and Commerce, the Interior Department with its responsibility for our national resources, and the others, all have roles to play that are just as important in our relations with other people as the role of the Department of State.[23]

Obviously how one viewed Acheson's prescriptions depended on whether or not one agreed with his assessment of the Soviet Union. Acheson did not believe that war was inevitable; quite the contrary. But neither did he believe that the other side was interested in reaching agreements except on terms favorable to its objectives; Russia would be constrained only by the existence of circumstances that would inhibit it from achieving those objectives.

There was absolutely no evidence that anything had changed in Soviet intentions. A new and more terrible purge of Eastern European leaders was under way. A worldwide propaganda campaign designed to create a frenzy of hatred among people both within and without the Soviet Union was about to be launched. No new note of moderation or tolerance had been struck by the Kremlin. No follow-up to the agreements reached on a peace treaty with Austria had been forthcoming. By not the slightest sign did the Kremlin indicate that it was interested in improving relations with the West. On the other hand it is highly unlikely that the Kremlin would have unleashed an anti–Western propaganda campaign had it really believed that the United States was either ready or determined to start a war.[24]

That autumn the Policy Planning Staff attempted to trace out the implications of the fall of China and the Soviet A-bomb for American policy, as well as the requirements involved in the defense of Europe for which America was now essentially responsible. A review of Soviet economic capabilities indicated that the Soviet capacity for military deployment would grow rapidly in the ensuing years.

Despite the signing of the North Atlantic Treaty and the advances made in the status of West Germany, the Kremlin probably did not yet feel constrained to view the American preparations as a significant threat. What was there to threaten them with? The United States had always had the atomic bomb, had permitted its production to languish, and had never once threatened its use. NATO was as yet nothing but an unarmed collection of dispirited allies.[25] The only thing the Russians might have feared enough to make them reasonable was German rearmament. Yet German rearmament, while contained, in the classic phrase of *Le Monde*, "like an embryo" in the NATO egg, was still a long way off and not likely to be realized unless something occurred to radically change the West European attitudes. The Kremlin could have at any time nipped European and eventual German rearmament in the bud by making even the most modest kind of gesture to the French, Dutch, British, and even the Germans themselves, along the lines of a reunified and disarmed Germany. Such past Soviet moves as the Berlin blockade had done much to eliminate any possible pro–Soviet feeling in Western Europe and to foster the renaissance and reintegration of West Germany within the Western community. The fact that the Kremlin did not make such moves until after German rearmament had been proposed suggests that Stalin still did not consider a compromise offer on Germany seriously worth considering. Once against the obscurity and unpredictability of Soviet intentions provided Acheson with all the incentive and opportunity needed to seek what he considered the only sure basis on which to deal with the Kremlin: strength—military, economic, and political.

It appears that Stalin was still counting on the internal contradictions within the Atlantic alliance to give him opportunities, as yet unexploited, to divide the West and nullify American diplomacy. Ulam is probably right when he says that just because the Kremlin's decisions were largely hidden, "it would be a mistake to conclude that the Russians at this point were free of indecision or of the burden of their past policies, ready and able to present East Germany as a peace offering." [26] But even that would not have been needed had the Kremlin shown the least inkling that it considered the non–Communist opinion of France, Italy, or Germany worth bothering about. The option was not between holding on to East Germany and seeing West Germany rearmed or giving up East Germany, seeking an accommodation with the West, and risking trouble inside Eastern Europe. As we shall see, when in May 1950 Acheson proposed a more aggressive line toward Eastern Europe, Schuman and Bevin turned him down flat, and Adenauer was as yet far from exercising that hold over Western policy that he later acquired. Until the summer of 1950, the whole issue of the future direction Europe and West Germany would take still hung in the balance. There was still a profound longing in Europe to meet the Soviet halfway, to accept any compromise that could give a reasonable hope of security and independence from Soviet or Communist take-over. The isolationist opposition to rearmament and foreign involvement was still very powerful within the United States. It would be touch and go for another year yet, until Korea that is, whether the American people could be convinced to make the commitments that would turn NATO into a real military force. It is hard to see, therefore, how revisionists can argue that Soviet behavior was dictated by Acheson's aggressive diplomacy. Such a view absolves the Soviet Union of all guilt for the trend of events and relieves the Kremlin of all responsibility for failing to make certain gestures and concessions which, had they been forthcoming, might easily have changed the psychological climate and undercut Acheson's diplomacy completely. In the hope of winning all of Germany, the Kremlin at this critical moment gave every evidence of being willing to maintain tensions at a very high level and to continue to exploit Western vulnerabilities wherever they presented themselves. Under these circumstances, there was no assurance in Acheson's mind that the West would not be presented again with some fait accompli or action that it would not be in a position to withstand short of all-out war. The fall of China and the Soviet A-bomb added a whole new dimension to American strategic problems while radically increasing the already anxious state of American public opinion.

How to convince the President, the Congress, and the American people that, under the circumstances, a much larger and more comprehensive diplomatic and military effort was needed? While the Policy Planning Staff set about the task of determining just how much additional American resources would be needed, Acheson confronted the double task of extricating foreign policy from the wreckage of the past (China) and of overcoming the divisions and rancors born of the already existing involvement.

CHAPTER

11

THE FAR EAST: 1949–1950

ON JANUARY 21, 1949, the day Acheson was sworn in as Secretary of State, Chiang Kai-shek turned over the government of Nationalist China to General Li Tsung-jen and left the mainland to prepare a sanctuary for himself and his followers on Formosa. Communist armies, having defeated the Nationalists in Manchuria and north China, were poised along the Yangtze River. The fate to the south lay open, and it was only a matter of time before all of mainland China would be engulfed by the Communists. The Nationalist struggle had become hopeless.

Theoretically the alternatives before the Administration were either to defend the Yangtze with American armed forces or to withdraw from China. In practical terms there were no such alternatives because the United States was not militarily prepared to make a defensive effort. It was to take the Communists three months to regroup and train their armies for the crossing of the river; it would have taken the United States much longer to have prepared and dispatched a force sufficient to have defended all of south China.* Moreover, the Administration was in no position to alter its course at this late date. For two years past its calculations had been based on the assumption that Nationalist China was doomed and that nothing the United States "could have done within the reasonable limits of its capabilities could have changed that result." [1]

Practically, the fall of China could not leave the United States' position in the Far East unaffected. China was too vast and too important to the balance of power in the Far East for it to pass under Communist domination without posing a new and unsuspected range of problems for the

---

* With the outbreak of war in Korea eighteen months later, the United States showed that it could respond quickly to an aggression, but it was barely able to hold the Pusan perimeter and then only because it could bring air and sea power to bear upon the enemy's forces in a way which would not have been possible in a war waged across the land mass of China.

186

United States. To be sure, as long as Chiang Kai-shek's regime had endured, the Administration had been able to avoid confronting the consequences of a Communist take-over, but the new Secretary of State could not indulge this luxury any longer; he was now destined to reap all the disadvantages that had been created by the Administration's previous efforts to play down the significance of events in China.

The coincidence of Acheson's becoming Secretary of State on the day that Chiang Kai-shek resigned was more than symbolic. The onus for the collapse of the Nationalists would fall upon Acheson, and it would be incumbent upon him to construct a new American policy for Asia—one which would have to take into account the fact that the most important country in Asia had become part of the world Communist bloc. Acheson little suspected that this task would be enormously complicated by two things: first, by the Administration's previous failure to keep the American people adequately informed about the implications for the United States of Chiang Kai-shek's collapse; second, by the advantage which the Republican Party, deprived of victory in the 1948 Presidential contest, would seek to extract by blaming the Administration for the stunning defeat of Chiang Kai-shek's forces.

The questions we must ask ourselves are: How did Acheson's presence as Secretary of State influence the evolution of United States' policy toward China? How did Acheson define American interests in the Far East? How did he relate United States power and diplomacy to these interests? Were there serious deficiencies in the manner in which he envisaged the problems posed for the United States in the Far East, and how are we to account for these deficiencies?

It must be remembered that Acheson had never disagreed with the Administration's position that the situation in China was beyond redemption by any action which the United States might or ought to undertake. Acheson had shared Marshall's view that it would be wrong—wrong politically and wrong strategically—for the United States to intervene in a civil war on the side of a regime which not only lacked popular backing but was also inherently incapable of governing China. Whatever the shortcomings or criticisms of Acheson's initial point of view, it was hardly to be expected that he would change it at the very moment when Chiang Kai-shek was deserting the ship, so to speak.

Events only seemed to confirm the wisdom of the basic premise on which the State Department had been operating ever since the failure of the Marshall Mission in 1946. The task now was to prepare for the future, but even that did not appear urgent. The first and foremost task, as Acheson saw it, was to cut loose from the wreckage of the Nationalist regime. Rather than break openly with the Nationalist forces, Acheson anticipated that the process of dissociation would come about with the final collapse of the Nationalist regime on the mainland.

On February 3, 1949, the National Security Council recommended a halt in the shipment to China of the $60 million in military supplies that remained out of the $125-million special grant. Acheson strongly endorsed this recommendation on the grounds that, if sent, these supplies would simply fall into the hands of the rampaging Communists.

But when, on February 5, Truman told congressional leaders that he was ordering the stoppage of aid to China, those present, including Senator Vandenberg, were unanimously opposed. In Vandenberg's opinion, such action would substantiate the charge that "we are the ones who gave poor China the final push into disaster." He urged that "this blood must not be on our hands."* On February 7, impressed by the political risks, Truman informed Acheson of his decision to follow congressional advice and not suspend or embargo shipments to China. Acheson passed the word along with the admonition that "it is desirable that shipments be delayed where possible to do so without formal action." ** But it was clear that Congress would not look kindly on any open break with the Nationalist forces still in the field.

On February 7, fifty-one Republican congressmen addressed a letter to Truman demanding the appointment of a commission to make an immediate re-examination of the situation in China, and on February 15, Acheson agreed to the President's request that he meet with them. On the same day, the Chinese ambassador, Wellington Koo, requested a new United States commitment, including the dispatch of United States military personnel to support the Nationalist armies. This Acheson refused to consider.

On February 24, in defending Administration policy before the Repub-

---

* Arthur H. Vandenberg, Jr., ed., *The Private Papers of Senator Vandenberg* (Boston: Houghton Mifflin, 1952), pp. 530–531. The Chinese ambassador, V. K. Wellington Koo made pathetic efforts to secure a new United States commitment, including the dispatch of American military personnel on February 15, 1949. But that option if it had ever existed was long since past. Acheson had discussed China with Butterworth, Rusk, and Nitze during his first few days in office. They considered the situation to be so hopeless that Acheson preferred that all aid to China be discontinued forthwith. Acheson memo, minutes of meeting, January 13, 1949, Acheson Papers.

** Acheson memo of February 7, 1949, Acheson Papers. Specifically Acheson pointed out that Marshall's call for a coalition government in China had been in pursuance of a plan for ending hostilities put forth by the Nationalist government— a Chinese plan for an interim government of some sort pending normalization of the Chinese Communist role in China. The subsequent growth of the Chinese Nationalist insistence upon a solution by force had been countered by Marshall's insistence that such a solution was not within their power. Minutes of meeting, State Department, February 24, 1949.

lican congressmen, Acheson pointed out that the continuation of the United States aid would be unpopular because it would prolong a war which the Nationalist regime could no longer win; direct military advice could not help so discredited a regime. Acheson was expressing his own perplexity when he told the congressmen that he would not know what American policy ought to be "until the dust settled." More ominous was the encouragement that he gave the congressmen: do not, he told them, exaggerate the magnitude of America's reversal—China was not a modern, centralized state, and the Communists would almost certainly face as much difficulty in governing it as had the previous regimes.* While this statement is not to be taken entirely at face value, it betrays an understandable, albeit regrettable, tendency on Acheson's part to underestimate the Red Chinese, which was to have tragic consequences at the time of the Korean War. At the time, however, the low estimation that Acheson put upon China's potential weakened any sense of urgency he may have felt about the collapse of the Nationalist forces.

If Acheson thought, however, that the Administration might drop Chiang Kai-shek and initiate a new policy at its leisure, he was soon disabused. On February 25, Senator Pat McCarran, an anti–Administration Democrat from Nevada, introduced a bill to provide $1.5 billion in loans to the Nationalist government and to authorize American officers to direct the Nationalist armies still in the field. This was the first time that any senator had proposed using American forces to help stem the Communist advance, and the proposal marked the beginning of a systematic effort to defeat the policy recommendations of the Department of State by whatever means possible. In a letter to Tom Connally, chairman of the Foreign Relations Committee, Acheson flatly rejected the McCarran proposal, but he felt sufficiently concerned about the ability of the China bloc to wield an influence in the Senate that he made a conciliatory gesture. In order to assure passage of the European Recovery Program for fiscal year 1950, Acheson agreed to permit the unexpended portion of the China Aid Act of 1948 to be spent beyond the expiration date of April 2. On April 14 the Congress included in the bill on the European Recovery Program a provision extending the expiration date of the remaining $54 million until February 1950. After this action, any chance of extending early recognition to the Communist Chinese government was clearly compromised.

---

* H. Bradford Westerfield, *Foreign Policy and Party Politics* (New Haven: Yale University Press, 1955), p. 347. Specifically Acheson said: "We must not minimize but we must not exaggerate the magnitude of our reversal. China is not a modern, centralized state—China even under Communism cannot become a springboard for attack. The Communists face a morass in China. Until some of the dust and smoke of the disaster clear away we must wait and see where there is a foundation on which to build." Meeting, February 7, 1949.

Any indication of willingness on Acheson's part to accord recognition to Communist China would have clearly flouted the wishes of Congress." *

On April 21, Senator William Knowland (R–Cal.) submitted a concurrent resolution calling for an investigation of America's foreign policy in the Far East by a joint bipartisan committee of five senators and five congressmen. Although the Senate Foreign Relations Committee pigeonholed Knowland's resolution, this did not end the assault. On April 26, Senator Styles Bridges (R–N.H.), another convert to the Nationalist cause, called for a "full dress investigation by Congress of the State Department's position toward China." Bridges accused Acheson of "what might be called sabotage of the valiant efforts of the Chinese Nationalists to keep at least part of China free." [2]

As if to underline the difficulties which the Administration would face should it attempt to recognize Red China, on June 24 Vandenberg expressed the hope that there would be no consideration of recognition of a Communist government in China without complete preliminary contact and exploration of the matter with the Senate Foreign Relations Committee. On the same day Senator Knowland released a letter to President Truman, signed by sixteen Republican and six Democratic senators, asking him to make it clear that no recognition was presently contemplated. "Taking note of Congressional sentiments, Secretary Acheson sent a letter to Senator Connally on July 1, giving assurance that the Foreign Relations Committee would be consulted when the subject came up for decision." [3] The door was fast being shut on an important option which every government ought to have at its disposal—the right to recognize another government.

To justify the nonrecognition policy forced upon it by the Congress, the State Department claimed that Peking must first show its willingness to abide by international standards, which included respect for all commitments previously entered into by the Nationalists. Since Mao Tse-tung had warned the United States as early as February 1947 that the Communists had no intention of honoring Chiang Kai-shek's commitments, was Acheson wise in making adherence to them a precondition of United

---

* A few days after the fall of Nanking on April 24, a Communist official, Huang Hua, approached Ambassador John Leighton Stuart about the question of recognition. Stuart was in no position to discuss the matter with him other than to say that recognition could only be considered when the new government demonstrated that it had the acceptance of the Chinese people and the ability to maintain relations with other nations according to international standards. Quoted from Stuart, in Tang Tsou, *America's Failure in China: 1940–1950* (Chicago: University of Chicago Press, 1963), pp. 236–247. However, it does not seem likely that Peking seriously entertained the possibility of establishing normal diplomatic relations with the United States.

States recognition? Revolutionary regimes are notoriously lacking in tolerance for traditional forms, and their initial reaction upon entering into power is to reject all existing norms of interstate cooperation. Knowing this, one must question Acheson's wisdom. Despite the congressional injunctions against recognition, he was under no compulsion to attach conditions which would clearly inhibit and impede a later shift in policy.

In order to understand the magnitude of the difficulties which Acheson encountered in adapting American policy to the realities of the China situation, one must understand that he was up against the earlier, fatal decision of the Administration to follow a passive policy in the Far East.*

On the other hand it can be argued that for the Administration to have engaged the opposition in the Congress in a test of strength over the merits of China policy in the period 1947–1948 would have led to a complete breach between it and those Republican elements who were supporting bipartisanship in Europe but who would have been driven to support their pro-Chiang colleagues should the fate of China have been made a major policy issue. To have risked Congressional support for recovery of Europe in a political debate revolving around a country which was irretrievable and which was not vital to the security interests of the United States would have been irresponsible. It would appear that the Administration deliberately played down the controversy over China in order to assure itself of maximum support from moderate Republicans for its European policies. But this still left Acheson with the onerous task of reconstituting U.S. policy following the fall of mainland China to the Communists.

Until the moment Acheson assumed office nothing had been done to prepare public opinion for a great diplomatic defeat, and nothing had been done to lay the foundations of a new American policy for the Far East. "General Marshall," writes Tang Tsou, "left the thankless and perplexing task of disengagement from China to Dean G. Acheson . . . admitting the defeat of a policy would have been difficult for a nation under any circumstances. It was still more difficult when the policy had been surrounded by a cluster of myths and had remained the object of sentimental attachment, at least for a vociferous group of politicians." [4]

Truman's totally unexpected election victory constituted another reason why it would have been nearly impossible for the Administration

---

* The blame for this inactivity has been variously assigned. In part it was due to the preoccupation of the political leadership with Europe. But it also seems to have been caused in part by the disruption of the Far Eastern Division. John Carter Vincent had been sent off as minister to Switzerland to get him out of the China lobby's line of fire. No one had as yet been appointed to replace him, and those temporarily in charge seemed singularly indecisive and lacking in drive.

to have its China policy understood in rational terms. During the 1948 election campaign, the China lobby threw its weight behind the GOP in the hope that a Dewey victory would bring about a radical change in policy toward China. (Until then the China lobby had been careful not to attack members of the Democratic Administration publicly.) [5] With Dewey's defeat, however, only the most radical kind of pressure would suffice to recoup Chiang Kai-shek's position—it was not even clear that he could hang on to Formosa without United States military and financial aid. As luck would have it, a number of events during the preceding year—the Chinese Communist incarceration of Angus Ward, the Hiss trials, and other episodes—along with the shock of the loss of China itself, combined to sow suspicion and doubt in the minds of an essentially unin- formed public. The fact that the Republican Party and the lunatic right- wing fringe needed an issue to attack the Administration also played into the hands of the leaders of the China lobby. It did not take much to per- suade Judd, Bridges, Knowland, the Democratic maverick McCarran, and others who were already disposed to be critical of the Administration's China policy to mount an all-out attack. The fact that the China lobby's demogoguery extended to senators like Robert A. Taft (R–Ohio) and Alexander Smith (R–N.J.) showed that a lot of respectable people will say irresponsible things knowingly if the possibility of political gain is great enough. Partisanship in foreign policy, long pent up by the obliga- tions of bipartisanship, now erupted over China policy. The minister of the Chinese embassy seized upon the possibilities of the situation to recommend using the Congress as the best method to influence United States policy. On July 21, Dr. Ch'en Chih-mai sent the following message to Generalissimo Chiang Kai-shek:

As far as our activities in the United States are concerned, it seems that [while] we should cover the administration, as well as the legislative branch, we should especially strive for a closer relationship with the latter. There is no danger at all if our procedure strictly follows the laws of the United States, but Dr. Hu Shih [ambassador to the U.S.] is opposed to getting in touch with the legisla- tive branch. His opinion is off the beam.[6]

The possibilities afforded foreign governments to influence United States policies through Congress and the press are very great; but because they can backfire, most foreign governments employ such approaches with restraint. But the peculiar emotional impact which the loss of China was having on the American people, and the readiness with which they ac- cepted the most sensational and lurid charges, provided a favorable psychological and political environment for the Nationalist cause.

To understand why the campaign against the Administration's past handling of China policy gained ground with such amazing rapidity one must also understand the state of mind into which Americans were plunged by the loss of China.

China had long occupied a peculiarly sentimental and emotional place in American minds. China had been marked out as the field par excellence of American missionary endeavor; indeed, there was some vague idea in American minds that the United States had as its destiny to bring enlightenment to the Chinese. Small symbolic acts by the United States, such as the use of the Boxer indemnity money to sponsor scholarships for Chinese students, were magnified all out of proportion while the underlying forces in Chinese life were treated in a banal fashion or neglected altogether. The war years had heightened the emotional affinity of Americans for the Chinese, without producing any genuine comprehension of the social or economic realities facing them. A gulf existed between the sympathy which many Americans felt for China and the actual contribution which the United States had made to China's well-being. In a peculiar way, the warmth Americans felt for the Chinese became a substitute for everything else. Did not China have America's sympathy? Wasn't that enough? What more could it ask? A fundamental unreality characterized the relationship. Americans have generally found it hard to accept social forces as a convincing explanation of failure. A dominant aspect of the American character is to blame failure on sin or on some defect of moral character and to assume that "action" can easily reverse social and political trends whose courses were charted long ago.

The sentiments with which Americans had invested their attitude toward China made it impossible for them to think of the Chinese embracing Communism of their own volition and rejecting America in such a humiliating fashion. Having never understood the realities of the Chinese situation, they were wholly unprepared for the deluge of hate and vituperation which now descended upon them from Peking. Could the Chinese really feel this way? Were they too not simply the victims of some monstrous conspiracy?

In a brilliant stroke, the Nationalists (abetted by their American apologists) said, "Yes, we *have* been betrayed." Normally it is a risky business for a foreign government to accuse another of having betrayed it, but this is just what the Nationalist regime and its American minions did, and it worked perfectly. Nationalist allegations brazenly and skillfully insinuated into the debate by senators, by the Luce publications, and by unscrupulous editors served to confirm what emotionally many Americans wanted to believe and saw no reason to challenge. Hitler had made his point when he said that little lies won't do; only big lies will work.

The technique of the big lie was now perpetrated on the American people with stunning success. It took the mindless influence of the transmission belts of the mass media to put it across.* *Time* and *Life*, with weekly circulations of well over a million apiece, lashed the American people into a frenzy of self-hate and pity over the fall of China. But basically it could not have taken hold had it not been for the psychological receptivity of the American people and the determination of a small, articulate group of congressmen, senators, and editors to exploit the China issue as a means of destroying the Administration and putting into power an administration that would favor all-out aid to Chiang Kai-shek.

The China White Paper Controversy

In an effort to counteract the campaign against the Administration's China policy, Acheson proposed that the department prepare a thorough account of relations with Nationalist China, centering on the previous five years, and publish it when the collapse came. Later, Acheson as much as admitted that it was a futile gesture, although it seemed at the time the only way to overcome the ignorance of the American people. W. Walton Butterworth, Acting Assistant Secretary for the Far East, was assigned the task of preparing the volume with Dr. Philip C. Jessup, then ambassador-at-large, as editor-in-chief. The final document, the so-called China White Paper,[7] was an immense tome consisting of 409 pages, extended by annexed documents to 1,054 pages. Few people other than academics and China experts ever read the volume, although its publication in August 1949 was the occasion for a tremendous uproar on the part of critics of the Administration. As an exercise in public information, the China White Paper stands as a curious monument to Acheson's ambivalence about the capacity of the American people to understand the issues of foreign policy. To understand the China White Paper requires a college education and a commitment to reading public documents which few Americans outside the academic profession possess. As a fair, accurate, and scholarly presentation and analysis of the facts, it is something of a model among collections of secret and confidential documents. But as a means of explaining to Americans why their government should not be held responsible for the fall of Nationalist China, it left a great deal to be desired.

What else might Acheson have done? A crash effort might have been undertaken to establish the terms of a new policy for Asia, and the President could have gone to the country with a series of speeches. But because the strategic importance of China did not loom so large for Acheson

---

* Henry Luce had turned his journals *Time* and *Life* over to an unrelenting portrayal of all that was happening and had happened in China as unnecessary and the outcome of deceit and defeatism on the part of high State Department officials, including, or especially, Acheson and Marshall.

as that of the Near East and Western Europe, he preferred to take his time about developing the basis of a new Far Eastern policy. After all, the United States still controlled Japan and the island approaches to China, and there was no evidence that China would become a major threat.

With the Military Assistance Program to Europe in trouble, and sensing that the White Paper by itself would not suffice to disarm critics, the President, Acheson, and Connally agreed that the Administration should make an all-out effort to win senatorial support for the White Paper by inviting the Republican members of the Senate Foreign Relations Committee to participate in initiating a new Far Eastern policy. This was one reason why Acheson chose to proceed with caution in propounding a new policy for Asia. He hoped to associate the foreign affairs committees of the House and Senate with any new departure rather than risk thrusting it upon them and seeing it rejected. On July 18 Acheson sent Jessup a top-secret memorandum setting forth the policy of containing Communism in Asia and instructing him to draw up possible programs of action to achieve this purpose.[8] Acheson told Jessup of his desire "to make absolutely certain that we are neglecting no opportunity that would be within our capabilities to achieve the purpose of halting the spread of totalitarian communism in Asia."[9] Acheson saw Connally on the 19th and urged the absolute necessity for developing bipartisan support for the China White Paper and for the development of Far Eastern policy. Acheson further declared himself prepared to take up what was a tacit offer by Senator Vandenberg on the floor of the Senate for closer liaison between the Executive and the Congress on Far Eastern policy. Connally thought it a good idea "to get the Republicans in."

On July 22 Acheson had a long session with Vandenberg at the Wardman Park Hotel regarding China and the question of atomic sharing with Great Britain. Vandenberg expressed satisfaction with the Administration's willingness to take the Senate Foreign Relations Committee into its confidence concerning China policy, but not much else.

On July 25, in another move not unrelated to difficulties over China policies, Acheson tried to meet Connally's demands that the State Department loosen up its opposition to a loan to Franco's Spain and thereby take the pressure off him (Connally). In response to his importuning, Acheson explained that the department was no longer opposed to such a loan on political grounds, and early the next year Acheson approved an Export–Import Bank loan to Spain. But he made it clear to the Senate Foreign Relations Committee that he did not favor close relations with Franco for any reason:

In my opinion we should deal with complete correctness with Spain, but we should neither take action which is detrimental to her nor should we go out of our way to be favorable to her. The nature of the regime . . . is not one which you would like to see reproduced in other areas. Intimacy with Spain does not help you in the cold war. . . . In fact it causes you great difficulty. Is it of any great importance to us from a military point of view? That I think cannot be decided by looking at the map. . . . What one has to do is look at the nature of the [Franco] regime and look at its performance in the last war.°

On August 2, in a further effort to strengthen Acheson's hand with the moderates, the President concurred in Vandenberg's demand that the MAP legislation be rewritten so as to curb the President's powers. Despite these efforts to mollify Republican criticisms, the Administration's campaign to elicit bipartisan support for the China White Paper failed. No leading Republican came to its support.

Acheson's letter transmitting the document to the President was unfortunately phrased.[10] By claiming to prove that nothing that the United States "did or could have done within reasonable limits of its capabilities could have changed the results . . . ," Acheson appeared to be prejudging the case contained in the White Paper itself. His strong underlying tendency to state a judgment as a fact, however well grounded, once again provoked the kind of response that defeated his purpose. It was not a serious offense, but it grated upon a society more used to humility and deference from its officials. Walter Lippmann refused to accept "Acheson's claim that our China policy was essentially right, and that the result was beyond our control." He demanded an inquiry into the disastrous failure which would be "pursued in the manner of statesmen forming a policy rather than of a lawyer seeking a verdict for his client." [11]

Other accusations were even more extreme. General Hurley issued a statement calling the White Paper "a smooth alibi for the pro–Communists in the State Department who had engineered the overthrow of our ally, the Nationalist Government of the Republic of China, and aided in the Communist conquest of China." [12] On August 19, Congressman Judd charged the State Department with omitting sixteen documents and facts

---

° Hearings, Executive Session, Committee on Foreign Relations, U.S. Senate, 81st Congress, First and Second Sessions. On the matter of Spain Acheson took a forthright position. He felt that the United Nations Resolution of 1946 barring Spain from membership in the United Nations Organization and recommending that members of the United Nations should recall their ambassadors and their ministers plenipotentiary from Madrid had failed. On the other hand, Acheson told the press that Spain could not expect to be admitted to Western European organizations until it recognized certain "simple fundamental facts which cannot be obscured . . . that the foundation of liberty—individual liberty—is not in great phrases at all but in certain simple procedures and simple beliefs, and I should put first on the list of essentials for individual liberty the writ of habeas corpus and an independent judiciary." Dean Acheson, Press Release #349, May 11, 1949.

which would further support the charges made by the Administration's critics.[13]

In throwing their columns open to these attacks, the newspapers, including the *New York Times*, all but obliterated the intended effect of the China White Paper. Acheson vainly tried to counterattack. At his news conference on August 24, he issued a point-by-point refutation of Judd's charges, but all to no avail. Critics had no need to prove their allegations; given the receptivity of the public mind, they merely had to make them believable. The China White Paper was not discredited; it simply disappeared from sight in the swirl of charges prompted by its appearance. Like so many other facets of the State Department's handling of China policy, the issuance of the China White Paper badly misfired.

The irony of the White Paper is that it stressed how much the United States had done for China and placed the full blame for Communist victories and the withdrawal of United States aid on poor and inept leadership by the Nationalist government. Had Acheson been able to remind Americans that the United States had no just basis for intervening at all, some degree of sanity might have been brought into American thinking.

Nevertheless, Acheson's letter of transmittal contained an element of strategic thinking hitherto missing from China policy. Taking a leaf from the historical record, Acheson noted that the Communist leaders of China "have forsworn their Chinese heritage and have publicly announced their subservience to a foreign power, Russia, which during the last fifty years, under Czars and Communists alike, has been most assiduous in its efforts to extend its control in the Far East."* Sooner or later, he said, the Communists in Peking would have to choose between the interests of their own people or servitude to Moscow. The emergence of such a crisis "will necessarily be influenced by the degree to which the Chinese people come to recognize that the Communist regime serves not their interests but those of Soviet Russia and the manner in which, having become aware of the facts, they react to this foreign domination." [14]

There was some inclination on Acheson's part to believe that at such a point the Chinese people would turn against the regime, that "ultimately the profound civilization and the democratic individualism in China will reassert themselves and she will throw off the foreign yoke." **

---

* Russia still benefited from the legacy of Yalta which had given Russia special rights and a pre-eminent interest in Manchuria. Besides, the Communist leadership in Peking proclaimed its dependence upon Moscow. Whether this constituted subserviency remained to be seen. *United States Relations with China with Special Reference to the Period 1944–1949* (Washington, D.C.: Government Printing Office, August, 1949), p. xvi. Also known as the China White Paper.

** It was unfortunate that Acheson even let this pious note creep into his discourse. It has more the appearance of a sentimental residue from the past than of any

Rather than assume a posture of automatic hostility, Acheson took a hopeful position that the Communist assumption of power would not put up a
permanent bar to better relations. Unfortunately, it was a judgment based
more upon hope than on any profound knowledge of the Chinese situation.

What practical policy conclusions did Acheson draw from his strategic
assumptions?

What does this mean for us? It means something very significant. It means
that nothing we do and nothing we say must be allowed to obscure the reality
of this fact. . . . The only thing that can obscure it is the folly of ill-conceived
adventures on our part which easily could do so and I urge all who are thinking about these foolish adventures to remember that we must not be in the
unenviable position which the Russians have carved out for themselves. We
must not undertake to deflect from the Russians to ourselves the righteous
anger, and the wrath and the hatred of the Chinese people which *must* develop. . . .[15]

Although unstated, clearly what Acheson had in mind was the unwisdom
of continued American intervention in the Chinese civil war represented
by United States support for Chiang Kai-shek's regime on Formosa.

Besides fitting in with Acheson's strategic view that there was nothing
to gain and everything to lose from continuing to be involved in China's
civil war, there was a certain historic logic to Acheson's formulation of
the situation, although it was not one his critics were willing to concede. America had traditionally benefited from protecting China against
its more powerful neighbors. Usually, some weak government in Peking
was striving to defend itself against the depredations of more powerful
foreign invaders. This time, Acheson argued, it was the Russians, and
their imperialism took the form of native Chinese Communist leadership
in control of China itself. Sooner or later, however, China would reject
this new form of imperialism. Meanwhile, the United States should assume
the role of a disinterested spectator so as not to draw China's attention
away from its imperialist partner.

The Recognition Question

The logic of the premise was clear. More than ever the United States
had to disentangle itself from the Nationalist regime on Formosa. But that
was just what the China lobby did not want to have happen, and it would
be difficult to convince Americans that their interest lay in deliberately

---

realistic assessment of Chinese society. Mao Tse-tung appears to have taken it seriously "as an indication that the United States would continue to make trouble, placing her hope on the Chinese support of democratic individualism.'"

exposing Formosa to a Communist take-over: such subtle calculations were likely to be misunderstood in the face of rising anti-Communism. Traditionally, a decision to normalize relations with a newly established regime would also include recognition, but under the circumstances for the Administration to recognize Red China would have been even more painful than dissociating itself from the Nationalist regime. Fortunately for Acheson, but unfortunately for the development of Sino–American relations, the rulers of Red China at first indicated that they did not care to have American recognition. On July 1, 1949, Mao Tse-tung declared that China must ally herself "with the Soviet Union, with every New Democratic country, and with the proletariat and broad masses in all other countries." * In the same pronouncement, Mao made it unmistakably clear that China had no choice. According to China's experience, Mao wrote: "The Chinese people must lean either to the side of imperialism or to that of socialism. There can be no exception. There can be no sitting on the fence; there is no third road. We oppose Chiang Kai-shek's reactionary clique, which leans to the side of imperialism. . . . Neutrality is merely a camouflage; a third road does not exist." In "leaning to one side," Mao recognized that Communist China would need help from the outside. Help from the United States and Britain was ruled out because they would only grant aid to "ease their own crisis" rather than to "help the Chinese people." The only aid that Communist China could accept would have to

---

* Mao Tse-tung, *On People's Democratic Dictatorship* (Peking: Foreign Language Press, 1952), p. 10. Acheson's failure to normalize relations with the People's Republic of China was not an entirely American fault. Warren I. Cohen writes that there were actually two obstacles to diplomatic recognition of the Peking government. "The first was the strength of those Americans in public office and out who retained an emotional commitment to Chiang Kai-shek's China. . . . The second and by far the more serious obstacle to recognizing Mao's regime was the fact that Mao was not particularly anxious to come to terms with the United States, was indifferent to recognition, and was more interested in exploiting American hostility for domestic purposes." Warren I. Cohen, *America's Response to China* (New York: John Wiley & Sons, 1971). Acheson's views on recognition were succinctly summed up in secret testimony before the Senate Foreign Relations Committee on January 10, 1950. In response to Senators Smith, Hickenlooper, Wiley, and others, Acheson declared: "We have gotten into more trouble in South America and other places by linking recognition with approval or disapproval. It is an instrument as powerful as a popgun in trying to disapprove of somebody. It hurts the fellow who does not recognize much more than the person who is not recognized. It is of absolutely no use in trying to affect the internal operations of a government. For hundreds of years it never had any such aspect at all. It merely meant that you said, 'I recognize that this outfit over in this particular country runs the country,' and in accordance with diplomatic procedure we would receive a representative from them and they would receive a representative from us. You may hate their guts, but that is what it was in the past and that is what I think it should be in the future."

come from "the international revolutionary forces"—in other words, the Soviet Union.*

Nevertheless on October 8 the American Consul at Peking, O. Edmund Clubb, cabled Washington that "there seems good reason to believe Communist leaders truly desire American recognition and regularization [of] relations for both political and economic reasons. . . ." ** Acheson felt constrained by domestic pressures as well as by skepticism about Peking's real intentions from any precipitate act of recognition. He continued to believe that a decent regard for the opinion of the Chinese people as yet uncommitted to the Communist cause militated against precipitate recognition; this was probably an unfortunate and mistaken judgment if not a simple rationalization because there was no evidence that the Chinese people saw Communism as any worse and probably better than any possible alternative. In justice to the integrity of Clubb's reporting and to Acheson's reservations concerning the wisdom of recognition Clubb also reported that Chinese university students were being told by their professors that recognition could not alter the basic enmity between China and America and Americans would have to be treated accordingly.[16]

Acheson's decision to withhold recognition was not made lightly. It came only after extensive meetings with a group of China consultants brought in from private life and following two lengthy meetings (October 26th and 27th) with all the principal officers of the department including Dean Rusk, George Kennan, Walton Butterworth (Assistant Secretary for Far Eastern Affairs), Leighton Stuart (Ambassador to China), Ambassador Jessup, and Far Eastern specialists Raymond Hare, John Allison, Philip Sprouse, and John Paton Davies among others. The consensus of the group was against recognition but also against any effort "to detach Formosa from the Communist controlled mainland either by application

---

* Of these developments Warren I. Cohen writes: "Before long it was apparent that the Chinese Communists and Chiang's friends in America had entered into a symbiotic relationship, feeding off each other's hate, adding to the misery of men of good will throughout the world. Every abuse by Mao's men provided ammunition for those who sought to stiffen American opposition to Mao's government. Every statement by the likes of Senators William F. Knowland, Styles Bridges, and Kenneth Wherry facilitated Mao's anti–American campaign and led to new abuses." Cohen, *op. cit.*, pp. 201–202.

** *FR:1949*, IX, p. 106. Clubb repeated his advice favoring recognition in even more emphatic fashion on October 25, warning that "There has never before been exacted as prerequisite for recognition [of] China's various governments the position that new rule should have consent of governed. . . ." Clubb did admit that the Chinese Communist willingness to abide by international law, an important condition of Acheson's "go slow" policy, had still to be clarified especially with the American Consul in Mukden, Angus Ward, being held under house arrest. *Ibid.*, pp. 143–144.

of force" or by legal maneuvers, since such actions on our part "would outrage all Chinese elements" and inhibit the development of a Sino-Soviet schism.[17]

In any case, it was not recognition, but continued support for Chiang Kai-shek that Acheson regarded as the greatest obstacle to his strategy for deflecting Chinese wrath and hatred away from America and onto the Soviet Union. If withholding recognition of Peking, pending the fall of Formosa and some show of reasonableness on Peking's part, would quiet congressional criticism and ease the process of disengagement, would it not be worth the risk of worsening short-term Sino–American relations? To accept a lesser and, presumably, temporary disadvantage meant that we would win a greater and more permanent goal.

The Formosa Question

In mid–August, the swift onward march of the Communist forces seemed to indicate that the demise of the Nationalist government was close at hand. As one province after another fell to the Communists, the Nationalist government moved first to Canton, then to Chungking, then finally to Taipei, Formosa.* There Chiang Kai-shek prepared to resume the presidency of Nationalist China (which he did on March 1, 1950). But without United States military assistance, the Nationalist forces on Formosa were not expected to hold out. On August 4, 1949, Acheson sent a memorandum to the executive secretary of the National Security Council, stating that the fall of Formosa appeared probable and could not be prevented by political and economic measures alone. On August 16 the Joint Chiefs reaffirmed their previous views that "overt" military action to deny Formosa to the Communists would not be justified.[18]

Acheson undoubtedly anticipated that if he could hold on long enough Formosa would fall and thus relieve the United States of all further entanglement with Chiang and permit it to develop its Far Eastern policy in keeping with the realities. If, in the meantime, withholding recognition would relieve some of the domestic pressures and avoid throwing the moderate Republicans into the arms of the China bloc, then it was well worth it. Nothing in Acheson's behavior suggested that he was permanently and unalterably opposed either to recognition or to Red China's admission to the United Nations in place of the Nationalist regime.

Contrary to charges leveled by congressional critics, however, Acheson

---

* Acting President Li Tsung-jen did not himself lead the regime to the island. He flew to the United States during the winter of 1949 for treatment of an "illness." There he lived in New Jersey until 1965 when he returned to mainland China. The Peking regime welcomed his return as a propaganda victory. King C. Chen, *Vietnam and China, 1938–1954* (Princeton: Princeton University Press, 1969), p. 201.

tried to the very end to dissuade other countries from recognizing Red China. In part he genuinely believed that to present a united front would provide greater leverage on Peking to respect its obligations; in part he believed that for the Europeans to rush ahead would make a bad impression on Congress upon whom Marshall Plan aid depended for appropriations. On December 8 Ambassador Oliver Franks informed Acheson that the British Cabinet could be expected to take the decision to recognize Peking at its mid–December meeting. Far from indulging the British in any belief that United States recognition would follow, Acheson told Franks that as long as the Chinese Communists continued to consider themselves not an evolutionary but a revolutionary regime, and failed to give any reassuring evidence of how they intended to conduct themselves vis-à-vis the outer world, the United States was not inclined to extend them recognition. Hasty recognition, Acheson warned Franks, would confer no benefits on those who undertook it. Finally, as for the United States, it was important to bring Congress into the State Department's deliberations so that the problem would be fully talked out and the issues clarified.[19] Therefore the United States would not act hastily. Britain was free to act on its own if it so chose." *

India extended recognition on December 30 and Pakistan on January 5. On the same day Britain withdrew recognition from the Nationalist government and the next day accorded *de jure* recognition to the Communist government. A succession of recognitions followed until mid–January 1950, when Peking's seizure of French, Dutch, and American properties on January 14, and Mao's recognition of the Vietminh government of Ho Chi Minh on January 19, brought recognitions to a halt for a time and saved the United States from diplomatic isolation on the issue. These confiscations also had the effect of solidifying opposition to Peking's admission to the United Nations. Had the Chinese Communist regime held off from these acts, there was every possibility that its admission to the United Nations would not have been long delayed.**

---

* Acheson files, December 8, 1949; minutes of meeting between Acheson and Franks. Acheson went on to state that he recognized that "the views of states differ and each has to act upon its own immediate and long-term self-interest." On December 16, Bevin informed Acheson of a Cabinet decision to extend recognition in early January. Acheson in reply expressed his regret over the British decision and said that there was nothing he could add to the views previously expressed by him. Truman was more irate at the British for deserting the United States on the recognition issue. *Nomination of Jessup,* pp. 624–625, 907. Hearings, Senate Foreign Relations, 81st Congress, Second Session. *FR:1949,* IX, pp. 1–92.

** The USSR, India, Yugoslavia, Great Britain, and Norway already recognized the new Peking regime. France and Egypt were expected to follow suit. On January 19 Peking radio announced that the Chinese Communist government had decided to extend diplomatic recognition to the Vietminh government of Ho Chi Minh. The

If Acheson had hoped by withholding recognition to skirt the more critical issue of Formosa, he was mistaken. We have seen how the Administration was obliged to accept the extension of the China Aid Act of 1948 beyond its termination date of April 2 in order to insure the unobstructed passage of the European Aid Program. The Military Assistance Program of late summer gave the China bloc in the Congress another opportunity to pressure the Administration. Congressman James Richards (D–S.C.) had offered a resolution which would cut in half the $1.1 billion requested by the Administration for the NATO countries. With strong support from the China bloc headed by Judd, the Richards amendment passed the House by a vote of 209 to 151. A similar tactic was tried in the Senate. Once again the United States appeared to be tied to Chiang by a new program of military assistance. (Acheson managed, however, to shelve the spending of any of this money until December 29, at which time the National Security Council recommended against giving military assistance to the Formosa regime.)

Suddenly a new threat to his strategy arose. This time the pressure came not from congressional foes but from within the Administration itself. A feud was developing between Acheson and Louis Johnson, Secretary of Defense, which soon spread to conflict over the Far East. This time the issue was Formosa. On August 16 and again in September, the Joint Chiefs of Staff had reaffirmed their views that "overt" American military action to deny Formosa to the Communists would *not* be justified.* In September the Joint Chiefs of Staff advised Johnson that, in their opinion, the United States should not even send a military mission to Formosa for the purpose of ascertaining the facts.[20] Johnson now made a strong bid to have the Joint Chiefs reverse their findings on the grounds that their initial recommendation had been made under political pressure.**

Meanwhile, by mid–November the conclusions of the State Department study group on the Far East were beginning to surface. Based on

---

United States countered by recognizing the French puppet regimes of the Associated States of Indochina.

* In a memorandum dated August 26, General Albert Wedemeyer, Deputy Chief of Staff for Plans and Operations, had said as much when he suggested to George V. Allen, Assistant Secretary of State, that the latter might consider "information measures" to counter the ill effects of the fall of Formosa on the governments and peoples of the Western-oriented nations, particularly in the Far East. Wedemeyer's memorandum, *Current Position in the Far East,* p. 2371.

** Johnson's testimony, *Military Situation in the Far East,* Hearings before the Armed Services and Foreign Relations Committees, U.S. Senate, 82nd Congress, First Session, Part 3, p. 2577. According to Johnson's retrospective account, he felt that the Joint Chiefs' recommendation was made under political pressure and was influenced by political considerations. *Ibid.,* pp. 2664–2665.

their findings, as well as his own convictions, Acheson recommended to the President that the United States disengage completely from Chiang Kai-shek and thereby avoid diverting Peking's attention from its real antagonist—the Soviet Union. The President felt that Acheson's analysis was correct in the broad sense, but needing more general understanding, he asked to meet with the Jessup group upon their return from the Far East. Prompted by Johnson, the Joint Chiefs reversed their earlier position. Without finding Formosa vital to U.S. security, they now favored a fact-finding mission to Formosa. They also proposed that some military assistance should be given to the Nationalists. Having fairly well come to a decision, Truman was unlikely to change his mind as a result of this switch by the Joint Chiefs. Acheson too stuck to his original position that military aid would merely court further damage to the American position in the Far East.* Consequently, on December 27, Truman informed Johnson that while he would not argue about the military considerations "on political grounds he would decide with the State Department." [21] Having heard the President's decision, Johnson repaired for a mid-winter vacation to Florida, leaving the field to Acheson.

Congress and the Formosa Question

With the reconvening of Congress in January 1950 came a renewed assault upon the Administration's China policy, this time with the focus on Formosa. Precisely because the rejection of Chiang's regime had become a matter of principle with liberal Democrats, it was inevitable that this policy should become a principal target of Republican onslaughts. But in trying to avoid further attacks, Acheson hoped to enlist the members, Republican as well as Democratic, of the foreign-affairs committees of the Senate and the House. The policy he envisaged in his charge to Jessup of the previous July to draw up programs of action to contain Communism in Asia was now pretty clear. He sought to repair the strategic

---

* Acheson was also under heavy pressure from the British to put an end to Chiang's blockade of the China coast and his interference with foreign shipping entering Chinese ports. The British were also annoyed that the regime on Formosa still continued to supply itself by private purchases of military equipment. As evidence that Acheson's position was hardening even on Formosa, in the *aide memoire* from Franks it was noted that at the September meeting of the foreign ministers, Bevin had gotten the impression that the United States would take no practical steps to prevent Formosa from falling into Communist hands and that such an event was inevitable. For this reason continual supply of military aid to Chiang via private purchases *authorized by the State Department* raised questions in the British mind as to whether this would create a dangerous state of affairs. Acheson files, minutes of Acheson–Franks meeting, December 8, 1949.

damage occasioned by the fall of China by reconstituting Japan as a power in the Far East and by maintaining a policy of strong political and economic support to South Korea, Indonesia, and the Philippines.

The prospects for the success of such an appeal—never good—had been darkened by the attitude already adopted by Senator H. Alexander Smith (R–N.J.). With the absence of Vandenberg, ill with cancer, Senator Smith had assumed a key role on the Senate Foreign Relations Committee and, as chairman of the subcommittee on the Far East, Smith had gone to the Far East on a fact-finding mission. Far from returning with any new appreciation, he came back more than ever convinced that the United States had an obligation to preserve Formosa. On November 30 Smith expressed the view to Acheson that the United States ought to retain Formosa by military occupation if necessary.* Smith thought a United Nations Trusteeship might be established over the island.** He also urged that Acheson permit a combined subcommittee of the House and Senate foreign-affairs committees to accompany Jessup on his trip to the Far East slated for January of the new year. This Acheson refused to do, reminding Smith that the State Department preferred to prepare its recommendation for presentation to the *full* committee. In his report to the Foreign Relations Committe dated November 29, and in a news conference on December 1, Smith made his views known publicly. But unless Acheson could enlist the support of moderates like Smith, it was highly unlikely that he would be able to shut off the renewed attacks of his China critics.

What happened next was predictable. Taking advantage of the known split within the Administration over the question of military aid—Louis Johnson and the Joint Chiefs of Staff aligned against Truman and Acheson—Knowland proposed sending a military mission to Formosa.[22] But now something new was added to the China debate. Up until the end of the year, the traditional isolationist spokesmen of the Republican Party—men like Senator Taft—had not made their voices clearly heard on the China issue. They had refrained from taking forceful positions in support of Chiang because they had no hankering to see America involved in a war in China at a time when they were espousing disengagement in Europe. Now, however, with the China issue safely reduced to a question of whether or not the United States should defend Formosa, the leaders of

---

* Smith had originally made this recommendation to Acheson in a letter of November 4 in which he pleaded that the United States should "under no condition" allow Formosa to fall to the Chinese Communists.

** Symptomatic of the underlying convictions of the two men, neither could agree with the other's version of Chiang's behavior in going off to Formosa with China's treasury after he had resigned as president the previous January and turned the government over to Li Tsung-jen.

the Republican Party publicly joined the China bloc in urging that the Administration extend military backing to Chiang Kai-shek. On December 30 Senator Taft suggested in an interview that Formosa should be kept out of the hands of the Chinese Communists even if it were necessary to employ the United States Navy. Herbert Hoover, in a letter released by Senator Knowland on January 2, suggested that the United States should, if necessary, give the Nationalist government naval protection for Formosa and possibly Hainan Island.

Administration plans had been to consult with the Senate and House committees before publicly making known the Administration's plan to adopt a hands-off Formosa policy. But Knowland's campaign, aided and abetted by Taft and Hoover, made it difficult to wait without risking the discrediting of the Administration's decision in advance. On January 4, Acheson advised the President that he had best announce the new policy without waiting to consult with Congress. The next day Truman released a statement to the press in which he reaffirmed United States support of both the Cairo Declaration of December 1, 1943, and the Potsdam Declaration of July 26, 1945, which had promised the restoration of Formosa to China. He went on to say: "The United States Government will not pursue a course which will lead to involvement in the civil conflict in China. Similarly, the United States Government will not provide military aid or advice to Chinese forces on Formosa."

Having brought the pot to a boil, Knowland and Smith now asked to call upon Acheson. As chance would have it, their appointment was set for the morning of January 5, at the very time the Administration was announcing its policy on Formosa. Having forced the President into a premature announcement of policy, they were now coming by to persuade Acheson to rescind that policy. Acheson was polite but cool.

The situation, Acheson informed his visitors, allowed only two alternatives. Either the United States would fight if need be for the retention of the island or it must be prepared to accept what now appeared to be a real possibility of collapse. It was not in the interest of the American people to hazard a war over Formosa, and the mere statement of our intention to hold the island would defeat the general line we had been taking and the philosophy of self-determination we had been preaching. It would play right into the hands of the Russians.

Acheson admitted that he could take this view only because the Joint Chiefs deemed Formosa to be *not* of vital importance to the security of the United States. Acheson concluded the meeting by stating that inasmuch as Formosa was not of vital strategic importance more would be lost than gained by United States military action or aid leading to military involvement. Distasteful as it might be, the possibility of a Communist occupation had to be faced up to, and we must concede this possibility rather than compromise our entire position in the Far East.*

Knowland objected to all these points, particularly to the "spirit of defeatism" which he saw contained in certain passages of the State Department's information circular (the aforementioned Policy Information Paper of December 23, 1949).** Acheson rejected the inferences Knowland had drawn from the guidance paper, and reiterated that the possibility of the fall of Formosa had to be faced up to. The senator from California responded by informing Acheson that in all conscience he would have to acquaint the country with the fatal policy which Acheson was pursuing and which he would live to regret.

Senator Smith limited himself to warning Acheson that the Administration's failure to have consulted the Senate in advance might well affect his future support of bipartisanship. Acheson did not remind Smith that it was Knowland's campaign which had aborted any such constructive approach. That same afternoon the two protagonists—Acheson and Knowland—took their cases to the public—Acheson in a press conference and Knowland on the floor of the Senate. Acheson first made it clear that the Administration had intended to consult with members of both parties before any statement was made, but premature disclosures and attacks had made that impossible. In order to justify the decision to abandon Formosa, Acheson relied heavily upon moral and legal arguments. (He skirted the strategic justification for abandoning Formosa—in other words, the desire to avoid the appearance of interfering in China's affairs—because he could

---

* "We simply cannot afford by overt moves on our part, to place ourselves . . . in the same orbit of imperialistic design that Russia is following today. . . . Such action would be met with a sense of revulsion." Minutes of meeting, January 5, 1950. In testimony before the Senate Foreign Relations Committee on January 10 Acheson did not deny that it would be much better for Formosa not to be in unfriendly hands, but against that had to be weighed the political costs of the United States becoming involved in supporting Chiang Kai-shek. The notion of political costs made no impression on Senators Smith, Hickenlooper, and others. *Review of the World Situation: 1949–50*, Senate Foreign Relations Committee, Executive Session, 81st Congress, pp. 164–165.

** We get an even sharper exchange on this matter with Acheson's testimony before the Senate Foreign Relations Committee in executive session on January 10. Senator Smith repeated Knowland's question of who authorized such a paper. Acheson categorically rejected the thesis that the State Department had been mistaken in forewarning its personnel to be prepared for the possible fall of Formosa. It was not a policy statement, he said. "The misfortune of it was that some damned scoundrel gave it to the press." *Ibid.*, p. 166. Acheson was not opposed to the senators contesting a particular policy, but he objected to a conspiratorial interpretation being put upon a routine advisory to American embassies to prepare foreign opinion for the possible fall of Formosa and thereby minimize the impact upon American prestige.

not count on the American people to be as responsive to strategic calculations as they would be to moral and legal arguments.) "Contrary to the
amateurs of military strategy," * Acheson declared, the reasons for abandoning Formosa "are not in that area." The underlying factors had to do
"with the fundamental integrity of the United States and with maintaining
in the world the belief that when the United States takes a position it
sticks to that position and does not change it by reason of transitory expediency or advantage on its part." It had been agreed at Cairo and confirmed at Potsdam that Formosa was to be returned to China; the Nationalists had administered Formosa for four years and the United States did
not intend to step in now on the basis of a legal quibble and contend that,
since no treaty had been signed ratifying the return of Formosa to the
Chinese, the United States was free to treat it as a military trusteeship.

Such noble moralism, even if sincerely meant, was soon swallowed
up by the much more potent moralistic arguments used by the other side.**
That same afternoon, on the floor of the Senate, Senator Knowland bitterly
denounced the Administration's decision not to continue military assistance to Formosa and called for the appointment of General MacArthur as the "co-ordinator" of United States policy in the Far East. He was
joined by Senators Taft, Smith, and Joseph McCarthy in an all-out assault
upon Administration policy. Knowland spoke darkly of another Munich
in the making. Wherry, who could not have cared less about China, cited
British recognition of Peking as an "even more compelling reason for
cutting this ECA [European Cooperation Administration] spending to
support British socialism." †

There was one weakness in the China-bloc campaign, however. Many
Republicans who were content to see the Administration criticized were
also aware that any United States attempt to deny Formosa to the Communists involved a serious risk of war. When confronted with such a pos-

---

* This was a gratuitous slap at Taft: "I didn't know that Senator Taft was a military expert." *New York Times*, January 13, 1950, under the byline of Walter H.
Waggoner.

** At the same time Acheson was reassuring Congressman John Kee, chairman of
the House Foreign Affairs Committee, that, far from being militarily helpless, Chiang
possessed a considerable military potential on the island and that there was no possible way that the Communists on the mainland could achieve a military conquest by
invasion as they did not have landing barges. Even if Formosa did fall to the Communists by way of internal collapse, the United States would still exercise sea and air
control over the island.

† *Time* Magazine, Vol. LV, No. 3, Jan. 16, 1950. Of this campaign, Lippmann
wrote that the interventionists' proposals were an effort "to force our country into an
undeclared war, waged without allies, without objectives, and without hope of a decision"; a prophetic description of the Vietnam War two decades later. Quoted by
TRB (Richard Strout), "Washington Wire," *New Republic*, January 16, 1950.

sibility, timid critics like Senator H. Alexander Smith backed away from Knowland's firm stand. By military assistance, Smith explained, he did not mean "the sending of American troops to Formosa, but simply the establishment of a joint political authority and responsibility there between ourselves, the Nationalists, and the Formosan people." [23]

The redoubtable old Tom Connally now drove a sharp offensive into the Republican salients. He demanded to know if the Republicans really intended that American soldiers should die to defend Formosa. He challenged Republicans to "rise and tell the Senate and the country that 'I favor sending an army to Formosa.'" Needless to say, none rose.

I want to know, Connally demanded, who the Senators are, and I shall revive the question from time to time, who want to plunge this country not directly, but possibly, into World War III, in the name of Formosa, but principally in the name of a bitter attack upon the President of the United States and upon the Department of State.[24]

Republican senators recoiled in horror. Knowland protested that he had never "advocated sending American troops to occupy Formosa." Only Taft held fast to his position that if the United States made clear its intention to defend Formosa there would be no Communist attempts at an invasion.*

Acheson's Perimeter Speech

The new Asian policy which the Administration had planned to reveal in consultation with the congressional committees now had to be revealed publicly. Acheson determined to take the offensive. He would make in an address to the National Press Club, scheduled for January 12, an important statement of Far Eastern policy. Scrapping the speech that had been prepared for him by his aides, Acheson retired to his Georgetown home, where he put in the better part of a day writing a new one.[25] The speech has been described as "one of the most brilliant as well as the most controversial speeches ever made by Secretary Acheson." [26] It is known chiefly for the famous passage in which Acheson failed to include South Korea within the American defense perimeter in the Far East. To deal with the military threat posed by the Communist bloc, which in his opinion was "not the most immediate" menace, Acheson

---

* In November Taft, Knowland, and Smith had urged on Acheson that the Seventh Fleet be moved into the Formosa Straits. R. M. Freeland, *The Truman Doctrine and the Origins of McCarthyism* (New York: Schocken Books, 1974), p. 341. Contrary to the myth that Taft was not a war-minded interventionist, Taft later favored a blockade of China, bombing of Manchuria, and use of Chiang's troops in diversionary raids in South China. Robert A. Divine, *Foreign Policy and U. S. Presidential Elections.* (New York: New Viewpoints, 1974), pp. 9–10.

drew a defensive perimeter in the Western Pacific which must and would be held by the United States. This defensive perimeter included the Aleutian Islands, Japan, Okinawa, and the Philippine Islands. It did not include South Korea or Formosa. This was the same defensive perimeter that MacArthur had described in a speech a year earlier (March 1949); and, as Acheson later admitted to his chagrin, it showed the dangers of relying upon military position papers for the presentation of anything as subtle as diplomacy.

In focusing upon Acheson's failure to include South Korea within the United States defense perimeter, it is often overlooked that Acheson was very explicit about the importance with which the United States viewed the security of South Korea. Not only did he list South Korea together with Japan as the two Asian nations in which the United States had a vital interest (by contrast with those of Southeast Asia where Acheson indicated no clear-cut American interest), but he also made the point that should an attack occur on nations outside the defense perimeter, "their resistance would spark the commitment of the entire civilized world acting under the Charter of the United Nations." * And the Charter, Acheson reminded his listeners, "has not proven itself a weak reed to lean upon for any people who were determined to protect their independence against external aggression."

At the time of the speech the importance of the passage defining America's defense perimeter in the Far East was ignored by everyone except the South Korean ambassador, John Myun Chang. On January 27, the ambassador expressed the appreciation of President Rhee and the Korean

* Dean Acheson, "Crisis in Asia—An Examination of U.S. Policy," Department of State *Bulletin*, Vol. XXII, No. 551, January 23, 1950, p. 116. As if to emphasize the importance of Korea, Acheson said:

We have given that nation great help in getting itself established. We are asking the Congress to continue that help until it is firmly established, and that legislation is now pending before the Congress. The idea that we should scrap all of that, that we should stop halfway through the achievement of the establishment of this country, seems to me to be the most utter defeatism and utter madness in our interests in Asia. But there our responsibilities are more direct and our opportunities more clear. When you move to the south, you find that our opportunity is much slighter and that our responsibilities, except in the Philippines and there indirectly, are very small. . . .

Department of State *Bulletin*, Vol. 22, Part 1, January–March 1950, January 23, 1950, p. 117. In responding to a question by Senator Knowland in Senate Foreign Relations hearings on January 13, Acheson first thought that if South Korea was attacked the United States would not undertake to defend it by military force, but if under the UN Charter action were taken, "we would take our part in that, but probably it would not be taken because they [meaning Russia] would veto it." *Review of the World Situation, op. cit.*, p. 191.

National Assembly for the Secretary's remarks regarding Korea [27] and for Acheson's letter of January 20 to President Truman restating the vital importance of the Korean Aid Bill (House Republicans had defeated it the previous day).* Unfortunately, the State Department never seems to have used this message to fend off the charges that it was Acheson's failure to include South Korea that triggered the attack six months later.

Pointing out that nationalism, as the symbol of freedom both from foreign domination and from poverty, was the most powerful force in Asia, Acheson asserted that the interests of the United States had been parallel to the interests of the people of Asia. Historically the United States had always been opposed to the control of China by a foreign power and in favor of the independence of all Asiatic countries. It must not desert that policy now. For Acheson, the contrast between Russian imperialism and America's traditional friendship for China provided the basic justification for the Administration's decision not to continue to intervene in the Chinese civil war and not to defend Formosa. Reverting to the theme of his letter of transmittal to the China White Paper, Acheson warned:

We must not undertake to deflect from the Russians to ourselves the righteous anger, and the wrath, and the hatred of the Chinese people which must develop. It would be folly to deflect it to ourselves. We must take the position we have always taken—that anyone who violates the integrity of China is the enemy of China and is acting contrary to our interests.[28]

Acheson was right in focusing upon the inherent potential for resentment of the Chinese against the Russians, but he went too far with his constant emphasis on Peking's subservience to Moscow. This interpretation not only revealed his own limited understanding of the indigenous nature of the Communist regime in China, but it put him at a disadvantage. If the Chinese Communists were only puppets of Moscow, critics wanted to know, why not work for their overthrow by supporting Chiang again? Louis Halle has suggested in *The Cold War as History* that the whole approach of the West in stressing China's dependence on Russia at this time was "something akin to the operation of a self-fulfilling prophecy." [29]

With obvious reference to the negotiations then going on in Moscow between Stalin and the Chinese Communist leaders, Acheson observed:

---

* "It was the Republicans who loudly demanded that something be done. Then last week, to the amazement of everybody, House Republicans teamed up with Southern Democracts and New York's Communist-line Vito Marcantonio to defeat a $60-million installment of economic aid for Korea. The vote was 192 to 191"—a good indication that Republicans were playing politics with the Asian situation. *Time*, Vol. LV, No. 5, Jan. 30, 1950.

The Soviet Union is detaching the northern provinces from China and is at-taching them to the Soviet Union. This process is complete in Outer Mongolia. It is nearly complete in Manchuria, and I am sure that in Inner Mongolia and in Sinkiang there are very happy reports coming from Soviet agents.[*]

Contrary to Acheson's assumptions, the Moscow deliberations between Stalin and Mao, announced with the conscious intent of burying any divisive territorial issues between them, included the renunciation by Stalin of most of the concessions extracted from the Nationalist government under the Yalta agreements. The wisdom Stalin displayed at this time in not attempting to hold on to Chinese territory only confirmed the importance of the point which Acheson was trying to make: namely, that the United States should avoid putting itself in the position of seeming to thwart Chinese nationalism.

By contrast, for all the virtue of his emphasis upon nationalism as the dominant force in Asia, Acheson was not particularly equipped to understand the fanatical and dogmatic form which it was taking in China. It does not seem to have occurred to Acheson until it was too late that the new regime in Peking might well represent the deepest and most significant interests of the Chinese people, who, stung by the humiliating collapse of their ancient civilization, were motivated to find in the hated foreigners the explanation for their century of trauma. Revolutionary governments are seldom reasonable, especially toward those who have opposed them in their struggle for power. Only superficially acquainted with the humiliations and agonies of the Chinese people and with the solidity of their peasant base, Acheson consistently underrated the strength of the indigenous support for the militancy of the new regime. The possibility that China, even more than Russia, might have profound reasons for hating the capitalist West seems to have been minimized in Acheson's thinking by his own essentially ethnocentric and strategic view of the situation.

Mao had already made known in any number of ways that in relations between revolutionaries and "reactionaries" he did not believe it made any difference whether one was provocative or not. The United States was an evil and noxious form of society, the elimination of which had an important moral claim upon China's revolutionary ardor. Furthermore, clear-cut and provocative behavior vis-à-vis the United States served Mao's purpose of "raising our own morale while deflating the enemy's prestige." [30]

---

[*] Acheson, "Crisis in Asia," p. 116. Discussing China policy before the Senate Foreign Relations Committee (October 12, 1949), Acheson had this to say: "The Chinese Government is really a tool of Russian imperialism in China that gives us our fundamental starting point in our relations with China." He later reiterated his belief that Russia was annexing or extending a sphere of influence over northern China.

Laudable, therefore, as Acheson's emphasis upon dissociation from Chiang and respect for China's national integrity happened to be, it was based upon an essentially Western-oriented concept of the basis for mutual respect between powers, and it paid insufficient attention to the historical experience which lay behind China's xenophobia. Acheson's seeming reasonableness reflected the relatively satisfactory state of American experience, but not that of China—a failing to which America, as the leading status-quo power, was, and is, peculiarly prone.

The Truman Administration continued to recognize and extend economic aid to Chiang Kai-shek long after Acheson had stated that it was unwise to do so. Furthermore, it was hard to tell which was the real American policy toward Peking—that of Acheson and the Truman Administration or that of its critics. Certainly American views of the meaning of events in China were as contorted and strained as those of Mao and Chou En-lai, and Acheson was paying a fearful price for his efforts to straighten them out. Nevertheless, by his emphasis upon the need to respect China's national pride and territorial integrity, Acheson was essentially right. Had he stuck to that precept, the United States might have been spared the fatal encounter with China a year later on the snowy wastelands of North Korea.

Another thing missing from Acheson's analysis of the situation was the serious potential for an eventual armed clash between the Chinese Communists and the United States. Given Acheson's estimate of the limitations of Chinese military power and his own desire to avoid such a conflict, the possibility of war did not seem to have figured as a factor in his campaign to dissociate the United States from the regime on Formosa. Yet, as Tsou points out: "Without foreknowledge of the seriousness of a possible Sino–American clash, the very real and ever present difficulties involved in a policy of prompt disengagement could not have been overcome." [31] This was the Achilles heel of Acheson's China policy all along—the optimistically low estimate of China's willingness to assert its national interest by resort to war if necessary; a low estimate of the potential for war generally in Asia.* Yet the Administration's failure to dissociate itself from Formosa and its policy of sustaining the Nationalist government** reinforced Mao's already distorted view of the United States, and the United States' policy of limited assistance failed to impress on him Amer-

---

* "But it is a mistake, I think, in considering Pacific and Far Eastern problems to become obsessed with military considerations. Important as they are, there are other problems that press, and these other problems are not capable of solution through military means." Acheson, "Crisis in Asia," p. 116.

** The United States recognized the French puppet regimes of Vietnam, Laos, and Cambodia on February 7, 1950, creating another point of conflict with Peking which had already extended recognition to Ho Chi Minh.

ican strength and determination. Ever since publication of the White Paper, Mao had characterized the United States as a "paper tiger." He had heaped scorn and contempt on the United States as a "neurotic upstart" among the imperialist powers for being so naive as to publish the record of America's assistance to the bumbling and futile Nationalist regime. After that, how could anyone take America seriously? Just as Acheson seriously underestimated Red China's willingness to risk war, so Mao's preconceptions inhibited him from appreciating American power and tenacity.

The second part of Acheson's address to the National Press Club set forth his policy assumptions toward the rest of Asia. Identifying the principal force sweeping over Asia as nationalism, Acheson indicated that American aid should be extended only when it could be effective, which depended upon adequate support of the recipient government by its people. This self-restraining ordinance, which one might call the doctrine of the missing component (meaning that the United States should not intervene where it cannot supply the missing component of popular support),* was not entirely consistent with his instructions to the Jessup study group: "make absolutely certain that we are neglecting no opportunity that would be within our capabilities to achieve the purpose of halting the spread of communism in Asia." Since Acheson did not consider military intervention or defense of Southeast Asia among America's existing capabilities, there was no inherent contradiction between his instructions to Jessup and what he was saying to the National Press Club; but to the extent that no technique had yet been found for halting the spread of Communism without some form of United States intervention, Acheson's admonition that the United States must not become involved in support of governments which lacked a popular following must be viewed more as a cautionary ideal than as a practical guide. The fact of the matter was that the search for a policy toward Southeast Asia had become more acute with the fall of China. Already Acheson was giving consideration to French requests for military assistance to their puppet regime in Indochina against the Vietminh.

If any interpretation is to be made of Acheson's reasoning at this point, it is that he could not come to terms with the possibility that Communism might be the only bona fide and legitimate expression of nationalism in certain parts of Asia—as it was in China and as it had become in Vietnam.

---

* Freeland, *op. cit.*, pp. 342–343. The *New Republic*, too, interpreted Acheson's analysis to mean that he did not intend to extend the Truman Doctrine to Asia. It would have been nice if this had been possible, but as we now know he was wrestling with the problem America has never solved: how to stop Communism in Asia without becoming the backer of hopeless and inefficient regimes lacking in popular sup-

Once the Yalta settlement, with its rough distribution of spheres of influence and its premise of a non–Communist China, began to break down, it became strategically and politically necessary for the United States to establish new limits to the Communist sphere or risk finding itself with an unmanageable situation both overseas and at home. And Acheson had still not figured out how to do that. Could a balance of power analogous to that in Europe be established, or was some other strategy more in keeping with the unsettled political condition of the region more appropriate? Acheson had still not decided because so much remained ambiguous.

As a practical matter of domestic politics, the Administration could not afford to lose any more ground in Asia; while trying to avoid direct conflict, the best it could hope to do was to hold out the hope that the Communist victory in China was not the final chapter. From a strategic point of view, the weakness of most of the newly emerging governments of Southeast Asia made a French defeat in Indochina unacceptable. Here, too, the only practical choice seemed to be to support the French while attempting to help the neighboring countries to build up their long-term potential to survive. But it would certainly be wrong to see in Acheson's speech of January 12 the threat of encirclement and containment of China. As the speech indicated, Acheson was proposing a defensive perimeter in which United States involvement with Taiwan was specifically disclaimed.

The problem Acheson now faced was how to rally support in congressional circles for this new departure in China policy. He called Vandenberg on January 18 to offer to work out something with regard to the extension of economic aid to Formosa. The same day he notified Vandenberg and Congressmen James Kee and Charles Eaton of his recommendation to the President that the United States change its attitude toward Spain. He reported that the United States was prepared to support repeal of the April 1946 resolution in the United Nations whereby members would once again be free to exchange ambassadors and ministers with Spain as they wished. Acheson hoped this would meet the trend of thinking in the House and Senate committees. On January 19 he ordered the release to the press of a letter to four Catholic congressmen announcing this new element in policy vis-à-vis Spain.

January 19 was an eventful day. Trygve Lie came by to express his high satisfaction with the President's and Acheson's statements on Formosa and for Acheson's Press Club speech.* That same day, too, on a vote in the House Republicans, by a margin of 5 to 1, rejected the Administra-

---

* It was agreed that Communist seizures of *official* United States and European property made admission of Peking to the United Nations "along the previously expected pattern" more conjectural.

tion's Korean Aid Bill.* Congressman Judd, a long-time critic of the Administration's China policy, was aghast. Judd remonstrated with his fellow Republicans not to defeat Korean aid merely out of pique at the Administration's China policy, but to no avail.

Acheson really had to get busy now. He saw Vandenberg, suffering the initial stages of a fatal illness, at his apartment on January 21. Vandenberg expressed shock at what the House Republicans had done. Acheson now agreed to additionally extend the time limit for expenditure of the funds under the China Aid Act of 1948 from June 30, 1950, to June 30, 1951. Vandenberg agreed to discuss this concession with Knowland and Smith with an eye to easing their opposition to the Administration's China policy. This in turn enabled the Administration to reverse the adverse vote in the House on the Korean Aid Bill. Despite a new attack upon the China policy which sprang up around McCarthyism, Acheson succeeded in limiting the United States commitment to Nationalist China to the unexpended portion of economic aid funds. All efforts to reopen the question of military aid to Formosa were short-circuited.

Despite the limitations on what Acheson could do in the way of reestablishing diplomatic relations with the new Communist government in China, the door was never closed on such an eventuality.** When the question of admission of Red China to the United Nations came up for the first time in January 1950, the United States representatives took the position that a decision as to which government was entitled to China's seat depended upon the question of recognition, but they also indicated that the United States would view the issue as a procedural one and would accept any Security Council decision made by a majority of its members. The vote on January 13 was six to three against seating the Chinese Communists (the United States and five others voting against, the United Kingdom and Norway abstaining). Thereupon the Soviet Union began its United Nations boycott. Thereafter the United States

---

* In a debate on the floor, Representative John Vorys (R–Ohio) took the position that in the absense of a comprehensive and sound program for the Far East, economic aid to Korea was money down the "rat hole." Robert Chipperfield (R–Ill.) argued that the loss of China rendered South Korea indefensible. Representative Donald Jackson (R–Cal.) asked: "What kind of policy for the Far East would put economic aid into Korea, which bears no relationship to our national defense, and at the same time refuse a request to put aid into Formosa?"

** Acheson had gone out of his way in September 1949 speaking about recognition policy toward Latin American governments to stress that recognition did not constitute a judgment on the government's origins or policies. The primary consideration behind the act of recognition was that "We are all on the same planet and must do business with each other." There is value, he added, in keeping open "a channel of communication with the country involved." Department of State *Bulletin*, Vol. 21, September 26, 1949, pp. 463–464.

made certain that there could not be, for the time being, a majority in favor of the admission of Peking in place of the Nationalists.

But now a new and far more ominous crisis emerged, one which would dwarf and subsume the crisis over China policy. On January 25 Acheson made his ill-omened statement that he would not turn his back on Alger Hiss, and on February 7 a junior senator from Wisconsin named Joseph McCarthy, trekking the political trail for a campaign issue, struck gold.

CHAPTER

12

SPRING, 1950: A NEW CRISIS

ACHESON BEGAN THE year 1950 with certain decisions—Formosa, the H-bomb—that clearly needed explaining to the American people. The fall of China and the Soviet's newly achieved nuclear capability had added to the growing hysteria over the "Red menace," and Acheson knew that if nothing were done to reassure the country, the public mood could turn much worse. "Rarely," the New Republic declared, "has the mood of public opinion been so unprepared for the actions that America must take." [1] Ultimately, the nation could only be reassured if the Administration succeeded in stabilizing the situation. But in order to stabilize the situation and compensate for the fall of China and the Soviet A-bomb, the American people would have to be persuaded to support new and higher levels of defense spending and learn to live with the vicissitudes of international affairs. The inroads which Republican critics had already made on public confidence in the Administration's China policy, combined with what might happen should the United States suffer additional setbacks, worried Acheson, as naturally it should have. Clearly, the Administration had to make a better effort at explaining the complicated nature of the situation in which America found itself. Americans were not accustomed to a diplomacy that was neither peace nor war. Either the United States was not threatened and it was at peace, or it was threatened and it went to war. Anything else was confusing and smacked of pusillanimity.

What was needed was a Franklin D. Roosevelt who could go to the people in a fireside chat and explain complex matters in a persuasive and reassuring way. Unfortunately, Truman was no Roosevelt, and besides, there was no inclination on Truman's part to take the lead at this time. The task and the speeches went by default to Acheson.*

---

* There was much talk in the news weeklies that Truman was leaving it to Acheson to carry the ball, and attention was focused on him as never before. They might

If by his speeches of that winter Acheson had hoped to induce sober understanding in the American people, he undid it all with his statement of January 25, 1950, that he would not turn his back on Alger Hiss. Every war brutalizes the spirit of tolerance in society, and the Cold War was no exception. However much Acheson may have wanted to preserve the civilized amenities, the outcry over Hiss showed that he could not arouse the country to struggle against Soviet imperialism with one hand and expect to extend human sympathy to Alger Hiss with the other.

Alger Hiss had been a high State Department official until 1947, when he left government service to become president of the Carnegie Endowment for International Peace. In 1948 he was accused before the House Un-American Activities Committee by Whittaker Chambers of having committed acts of espionage on behalf of a Communist espionage network in Washington in the 1930s. When Chambers's charges became public, the political community divided between those who disliked and distrusted New Dealers and who were sure that Hiss was guilty as accused and those who could not give credibility to accusations against a person of Hiss's standing. In order to defend his innocence, Hiss brought a libel suit against Chambers. Many prominent people, including John Foster Dulles, testified as character witnesses for Hiss. Acheson, who was *not* that close a friend or associate, was not one of them. Alger Hiss's first trial resulted in a hung jury in July 1949. On January 21, 1950, the jury in the second trial found Hiss guilty of perjury. Hiss's conviction presented Acheson with a genuine problem of conscience.

On the morning of January 25 Acheson closeted himself in his office. He had come to the decision that he could not be true to himself and still remain silent about Alger Hiss. He had not been asked to testify as a character witness. But now with everything collapsing around the Hiss family, he did not feel he could simply ignore the tragedy. That morning at breakfast he told his wife that what he was going to say was going to change their lives; it would be a great deal worse than she might realize. Her view was the same as Acheson's: it would be cowardly not to say something.[2] The quality of life is bound up with personal relationships. What kind of civilization would exist if men were not true to each other, if personal relations had no meaning and no enduring quality beyond what expedient benefit came of using one another?

Even more compelling was the question of obligation raised by his conscience. He had known Alger Hiss—not as intimately as others—but known him nonetheless. Did he owe it to his conscience to acknowledge

not have shared the same opinion, but *Time, U.S. News and World Report,* and the *New Republic* all agreed that "Today in Washington there is only one Administration official who puts on a good show. It is Dean Acheson." TRB (Richard Strout), *New Republic,* February 6, 1950.

that he had known this man, had called his brother friend, or did he take the expedient way out and assume that nothing was owing to their previous relationship? How did one judge these matters? The answer was clear to Acheson. If there was the least doubt, one took the course that would erase doubt. Precisely where the temptation to evade is the greatest, there the duty to conscience is the greatest. The very ease with which he might have evaded the issue, by simply letting it pass, positively propelled Acheson to acknowledge their relationship as two human beings.

At a news conference that afternoon, Acheson had no trouble finding questioners to ask him how he felt about Hiss's conviction. He carefully prefaced his remarks by noting that: "Mr. Hiss's case is before the courts and I think it would be highly improper for me to discuss the legal aspects of the case or the evidence or anything to do with the case. I take it the purpose of your questions was to bring something other than that out of me." Then he continued:

I should like to make it clear to you that, whatever the outcome of any appeal which Mr. Hiss or his lawyer may take in this case, I do not intend to turn my back on Alger Hiss. I think every person who has known Alger Hiss or has served with him at any time has upon his conscience the very serious task of deciding what his attitude is and what his conduct should be. That must be done by each person in the light of his own standards and his own principles. For me there is very little doubt of those standards or those principles. I think they were stated for us a very long time ago. They were stated on the Mount of Olives and if you are interested in seeing them you will find them in the Twenty-fifth Chapter of the Gospel according to St. Matthew, beginning at Verse 34.[3]

Acheson then quoted verses 34 to 46 of Matthew 25. Bets were taken at the Washington headquarters of the *New York Times* that the *Times* would not run the entire Biblical passage. It did, but who was interested in what the Bible had to say?

Acheson's statement as reported in the press completed the imprisoning image of conspiracy and somehow furnished proof for many minds that China had been sold out. Had he intended to do so, Acheson could not have dealt the cause of his policy a greater blow.

A roar of indignation rose from Capitol Hill and echoed across many of the nation's editorial pages. . . . Nixon [declared] "Disgusting. . . . Here he is serving notice in advance that he will not accept the decision of the Supreme Court." . . . Arends declared that Acheson's continued presence in the cabinet was "an affront to the nation." . . . Knowland said he would move to withhold State Department appropriations. . . . Georgia's James C. David . . . "How long can Americans be expected to show respect for Acheson when he hugs to his bosom those who have betrayed their country?" [4]

And so it went. No Democrat in Congress raised his voice in rebuttal. To defend Acheson would be to defend Alger Hiss. Of the major newspapers, only the *New York Herald Tribune* thought that Acheson's statement "was as courageous as it was Christian." Many deplored the public consequences of speaking out on an issue of private conscience. Judgments of the appropriateness of Acheson's statement varied even among his associates. Frankfurter wrote in a letter to Geoffrey Persons that Acheson's statement counteracted the "notion that conscience is something a public man checks in the cloakroom of prudence." [5] Others like Paul Nitze and Carlton Savage, members of the Policy Planning Staff, regretted that he had said anything at all or had said it in such peculiarly ambiguous terms.[6] James Reston observed that had Acheson employed a term more in the American idiom like "I won't kick the man when he's down," he might have been better understood.* Acheson subsequently admitted that had he listened to his advisers he might have chosen a somewhat better phrase than "I do not intend to turn my back on Alger Hiss."

Following his declaration, he went immediately to the White House and proffered his resignation to Truman. With characteristic loyalty Truman told Acheson to calm down and forget about it.**

What does the Hiss statement tell us about the gulf between Acheson's world and that of the average American? To a man of Acheson's education and patrician background, it was entirely possible to distinguish between personal honor and *raison d'état*. It was entirely possible for him to believe that a statesman could defend the interests of his nation against its enemies and still show compassion for a fellow being implicated in Communist-conspiracy charges. These were civilized sentiments with which it would appear churlish to disagree. There was only one flaw. Was it to be expected that the average American, ill educated to understand the nuances of civility and emotionally disturbed by the situation, would understand Acheson's motives? Acheson's was the gesture of a sensitive conscience, but it was singularly ill-conceived given the fevered state to which the Cold War had already pushed the American people. For all of his understanding and admiration of the Puritan conscience, Acheson may have forgotten that theirs was a singularly bloody-minded age in which conscience was a matter of religious principle and one man's salva-

---

* Personal interview with James Reston, Washington, D. C. Arthur Krock summed it up when he noted: "Mr. Acheson should weigh the effects of what his conscience as a man might prompt him to say or do against the consequences of these on the great public duty he has accepted." *Time,* Vol. LV, No. 6, Feb. 6, 1950.

** Reportedly, Truman reminded Acheson that he had just returned from the funeral for Boss Pendergast, and what kind of a hypocrite would he be holding Acheson's judgment against him?

tion was another man's damnation. Similarly, within postwar American society, the stresses and strains of the struggle against Communism abroad were beginning to produce a Manichean reflex at home. Few Americans were educated to draw a distinction between opposition to Communism abroad and tolerance for people suspected of Communism or fellow-traveling tendencies at home. Given their educational attainments and the demagoguery in the press and the Congress, how could they?

Acheson does not seem to have understood how deeply and emotionally the Cold War had effected Americans. What was for him a challenging exercise in statecraft, the chance to exercise his highest powers of reason against a skillful opponent, was to the average American a troublesome and diabolic affair. Under the successive shocks of the Cold War, Americans were "bewildered, anxious, and suspicious as 1950 rolled in. Responsible spokesmen saw the nation drifting toward disaster, through ineptitude if not through deliberate betrayal. In the Far East we were reaping the bitter harvest of our failure or inability to settle on any steady, coherent policy." [7] Exposure had followed exposure of Communist infiltrators in high places and sensitive posts. The Amerasia case, the Igor Gouzenko spy-ring disclosures in Canada, the Wadleigh case, the Hiss case, the Gubitchev–Coplon case being tried in New York that spring were all weighing on American minds. And the Fuchs case was about to break with the arrest by British authorities of the German-born, British-naturalized scientist for passing atomic secrets to the Russians while working at Los Alamos.

In the midst of all this, word came out of Washington of a fierce controversy among America's atomic scientists over both the utility and the morality of constructing the theoretically possible hydrogen, or "hell-bomb," with intimations that some of the physicists were motivated less by love of humanity than by an urge to help the Communist cause.[8]

Nothing like this had ever happened to Americans before. Is it any wonder that they were shocked to hear the Secretary of State, Dean Acheson, a figure already tarnished through guilt by association, say that he would not turn his back on Alger Hiss? Although letters to the State Department initially applauded Acheson, the political effect of his statement was devastating.

The fallout from the Hiss statement was only the beginning. On February 9, 1950, barely two weeks after Acheson's remarks, Joseph McCarthy, a relatively unknown Republican senator from Wisconsin, wheeling through Wheeling, West Virginia, on a Lincoln's Day speaking engagement, charged that there were 205 known Communists still in the Department of State. Until he made his sensational charges, McCarthy was a nobody in the Senate. He had been there for four years and, except for some publicity surrounding his investigation into the legitimacy of the military trial that had been meted out to some Germans found guilty of the massacre of American prisoners during the Battle of the Bulge, McCarthy had made only a negative impression on most of his fellow senators. Precisely because his record was so barren of positive achievements, McCarthy had been casting about for some issue on which to build his forthcoming re-election campaign.

Sometime in early 1950 he appears to have been made privy to a report by Robert E. Lee, an investigator for the House Un-American Affairs Committee who had been taking notes on the files of 108 past, present, and prospective State Department employees on whom the FBI had turned up some alleged security questions. Truman ordered that such security files not be made available, but not before Lee had succeeded in preparing a report which had been passed along to other congressional committees. One of these had come into McCarthy's hands, and he seized upon it as evidence that the government's security program was being sabotaged, either by laxity or conscious design.

It is quite conceivable that McCarthy really believed that the notes of the raw data contained in Lee's report constituted evidence of grave weaknesses in the State Department's internal security system. One does not need to believe that McCarthy himself was evil to understand how, coming from his background, he should fall on the security issue with all the zeal of a true believer. As his biographer says, if one understands the man, one can understand the force and style with which he prosecuted the issue. He had all the cocksureness of a man "who thinks in black and white, blind to indiscriminate hues; he had the poorly educated man's repugnance for intellectuals and 'fancy-pants effetes'; he had the savage directness, truculence, and scorn of compromise of the uncouth American who has never been socialized to what it takes to get ahead in polite society." [9] Although there were others who had exploited the Communism issue before McCarthy, only the qualities that marked McCarthy as an outsider can explain the vicious and dogged simplicity of his attack. But precisely because his blunt, slashing accusations reflected the exasperation many Americans felt—that Communists were being mollycoddled while Americans were being humiliated—what in the normal course of events would have been put down to a fit of lunacy struck a powerful response in the country at large. It is not too much to say that McCarthyism was born of the existence of two nations in the country—one highly educated and able to understand the complexities of foreign affairs, the elite so to speak; the other uneducated, smarting with a sense of powerlessness and clinging to its Americanism as a badge of loyalty in a period of desperate upheaval.

Being an outsider, or free-booter as one biographer calls him, Mc-

Carthy was all the more effective because he suffered no inhibitions in making whatever charges came to his mind, and he was largely impervious to criticism or setbacks. If something he had said was demonstrated to be untrue, McCarthy would either argue that the whole story was not known or that the facts were being obfuscated and misrepresented by his opponents. No ordinary politician would have been able to sustain the clobbering McCarthy took, any more than a person less extraordinary than Acheson would have been able to take the clobbering he took. As Gaddis Smith so aptly observes: "The unsavory phenomenon of McCarthyism called forth in Acheson the stoic traits he so admired in his own father. 'Much in life could not be affected or mitigated, and hence borne. Borne without complaint, because complaints were a bore and a nuisance to others and undermined the serenity essential to endurance.' " [10] But above all McCarthyism cannot be understood apart from the state of the American psychology. "Had not a situation—a climate of dread and distrust—been created over a long period of time, McCarthy's words would have lighted no fires of resentment; they would have been pointless." [11]

Half unknowingly, half unavoidably, the Truman Administration's presentation of the Cold War to the American people had led to this psychology of fear and frustration.* The nation was being wrenched out of its traditional isolationism at painful psychological costs. Those who

---

* Athan Theoharis and other scholars blame Truman (and Acheson) for sowing the seeds of McCarthyism with their own Cold War policies and anti–Communist rhetoric. There is inevitably some truth in this because one could not conduct a policy of containment and mobilize the American people without emphasizing the actual or potential threat posed by the USSR. But the validity of the charge that Communist hysteria was created knowingly and with malice aforethought can only be judged in the context of whether one believes that there really was a Soviet threat to Western Europe and that the Truman Administration spoke and acted knowing there was none. Theoharis does not go all the way in making this argument, although other revisionist historians do and, basing their research on various interpretations, have judged the Truman Administration responsible for starting the Cold War. It is also true that Truman and other Administration figures employed anti–Communist rhetoric in their 1948 attacks on Henry Wallace and in defending the Administration's record against accusations of being soft on Russia. But one must balance this off against Wallacite criticisms and Republican attacks upon the Truman Administration. It is only if one really believes, as Theoharis apparently does, that "the Democratic leadership's own red-baiting did not differ substantially from McCarthyite tactics" (Athan Theoharis, *Seeds of Repression* [Chicago: Quadrangle Books, 1971], p. 167) that one can really argue that nothing distinguished the attempts at dealing rationally with the problem of external and internal security threats from the utterly indiscriminate attacks of the McCarthyites. There is also a stange insensitivity on the part of revisionist critics to the problems and psychology of popular opinion and of democratic politics which refuses to recognize how the Truman Administration, finding itself on the defensive, might be led to fight back by stressing to the American people what it had done to legitimately look to the security of the nation.

were against foreign involvement, those who were fed up with twenty years of Democratic rule, and those who out of a perverted sense of reason and honor were dissatisfied with half measures in dealing with Communism were not above exploiting those fears and frustrations. The success of McCarthyism was to give life to a host of ex–Communists who, rising from the garbage heaps of American politics, would fix themselves like witches and warlocks in the Walpurgis Night of postwar American experience.

Naturally, Acheson figured very prominently in McCarthy's lurid accounts of how card-carrying Communists were still nesting cosily in the State Department. It was Acheson who as Undersecretary, McCarthy charged, reinstated John Stewart Service after he had been forced to resign in connection with the Amerasia case. Acheson had not only reinstated him but "placed him in charge of all placements and promotions." Next McCarthy resurrected the old Berle charge that Acheson had dismissed the wartime allegations against Hiss. Finally, he charged Acheson, "this pompous diplomat in striped pants with a phony British accent," with having refused to "turn his back" on the convicted traitor Alger Hiss and with being the official most responsible for the continued presence of known Communists within the department.*

In Salt Lake City, reacting to State Department disavowals, McCarthy challenged Acheson to call him that night at the Utah Hotel, and he would gladly give him the names of those "57 card carrying Communists. . . ." (It had been 205; it was now 57.)** However phoney to those in the know, such bravura episodes lent an air of plausibility to McCarthy's charges. Many educated people, including newspaper editors, stung by years of frustration and yearning to do something about the "Commies," were ready to believe McCarthy's charges—or if not believe them, then at least use them as a stick to get back at those in high places who seemed less patriotic because they did not take immediate and drastic action to get rid of alleged security risks. At least here was somebody willing to explain why the Communist states had gotten away with so much for so long in terms which made sense to people unaccustomed to dealing with

---

* Lately Thomas, *When Even Angels Wept—The Senator Joseph McCarthy Affair—A Story Without a Hero* (New York: William Morrow, 1973), pp. 84–98. These were only the mildest of McCarthy's epithets. As he slipped into high gear he fueled his attacks with the most extreme smears and innuendos. Acheson had little choice but to stick to the high road.

** The 205 figure is more understandable that that of 57. In a letter of July 26, 1946, then Secretary of State Byrnes explained that of 3,000 wartime employees transferred into the State Department, a loyalty screening committee had recommended that 284 be denied permanent employment and of these, as of that date, 79 had been discharged. That left 205 presumably on the payroll.

the complexities of international politics and even less accustomed to standing still while events held their sway. The very recklessness and brazenness of McCarthy's charges, which made it difficult for the knowledgeable to believe that his words could be given credence, gave them an air of plausibility to simpler minds or to minds outraged by what they regarded as the spectacle of high officials reinstating or defending men charged with service to a foreign power.

Acheson was not alone in being the object of McCarthy's attacks, but his role as Secretary of State and his personal style made him the principal target. By once again drawing public attention to the Hiss connection, Acheson had exposed himself far more directly than anyone else in public life to precisely the situation that McCarthy was attacking. Acheson was also the prime target of those who disagreed with his foreign policy. By sheer force of will and logic, Acheson had imposed on the Congress and on the country a level of international responsibility that was utterly anathematic to the isolationists. At the same time, he had just successfully defended a policy of disengagement from the forces of Chiang Kai-shek that outraged backers of the Nationalist regime.

For the first few days, McCarthy's charges did not receive much attention. (The *New York Times* did not report the affair until three days after the Wheeling speech.) Meanwhile McCarthy had continued to Salt Lake City and Reno. As he went, he picked up more public attention. When the State Department and leading Democrats, including the President, challenged McCarthy's veracity, he merely shifted onto them the onus of explaining the truth or falsehood of his charges. As his biographer remarks: "raising on a poor hand was McCarthy's way of playing the game." [12]

By the end of McCarthy's speaking campaign in the West, public attention had reached crash proportions. On February 20, true to his promise that he would carry his case to the floor of the Senate, McCarthy met the challenge of the Democrats. The session, lasting six or eight hours, soon degenerated into a nightmarish performance, with McCarthy unable to produce a coherent account of his evidence and his critics badgering him for specific names and evidence. The initial reaction of those most partial to what McCarthy had to say was one of disappointment. Militant anti–Communists already in the field were dismayed. Republican congressional leaders were generally reluctant to go out on a limb for "Tailgunner" Joe.* The reaction of the general public, however, was quite different. McCarthyism took hold with frightening speed. Reckless

---

* McCarthy had run for the Senate on his World War II record which had been falsely embellished by his claim of having served as a tailgunner. Taft initially thought McCarthy was out of his mind. Thomas, *When Even Angels Wept*, p. 119.

and even lunatic though McCarthy's charges were when delivered, they came through in the press as being serious and even well founded.* Coming on top of the Klaus Fuchs and Judith Coplon espionage cases and Acheson's statement about Hiss, many Americans were prepared to believe that a conspiracy really existed. The country was gripped by one of those periodic American crises of confidence in which a form of hysteria gains the upper hand.

Acheson took the situation very seriously. After all, the State Department was the center of the controversy and Acheson had not helped matters at all. He now took the first opportunity available to him to explain the Hiss statement. Appearing before a Senate Appropriations Subcommittee on February 28, he gave an explanatory account of his motivation. Acheson first admitted that his statement could give people grounds for questioning his fitness for the office of Secretary of State. He then gave what must be taken as the central explanation for a statement which he knew, even before he made it, risked destroying his effectiveness with the public.

One must be true to the things by which one lives. The counsels of discretion and cowardice are appealing. The safe course is to avoid situations which are disagreeable and dangerous. Such a course might get one by the issues of the moment, but it has bitter and evil consequences. In the long days and years which stretch beyond that moment of decision, one must live with one's self; and the consequences of living with a decision which one knows has sprung from timidity and cowardice go to the roots of one's life. It is not merely a question of peace of mind, although that is vital; it is a matter of integrity of character.[13]

He went on to deny that what he had said

could carry to any fair mind the implication that I was condoning the offenses with which Mr. Hiss was charged and of which he had been convicted. . . . But for the benefit of those who would create doubt where none existed, I will accept the humiliation of stating what should be obvious: That I did not and do not condone in any way the offenses charged, whether committed by a friend or by a total stranger, and that I would never knowingly tolerate any disloyal person in the Department of State.[14]

Amidst the din outside, Acheson's explanation hardly penetrated beyond the walls of the Senate chamber. It was all too easy to associate

---

* The press at this time presented all newsworthy statements as though they were facts on the assumption that if they were not true other facts would come along to correct them. Thus charge after charge was headlined in leading newspapers as if they were the gospel truth; thus, headlines like: "JESSUP PAL OF REDS—McCARTHY" (Washington *Times Herald*), "LATTIMORE NAMED BY BUDENZ AS RED." Later the press was to appreciate the service it had performed in keeping McCarthyism alive.

Acheson's words on behalf of Hiss with the concessions allegedly made to Stalin at Yalta, with the fall of China, and with all the frustrations and sacrifices which seemed to have been America's lot since V–J Day. The American people were suffering a major crisis of confidence.

The impact which these attacks, which were to continue for the rest of his career as Secretary, had upon Acheson's private life is characteristic. Archibald MacLeish went down to Washington rather frequently when Acheson was Secretary and stayed with the Achesons. His bedroom was near Acheson's bathroom and MacLeish would wake up to hear Acheson shaving while listening to Fulton Lewis's diatribes against him. "I remember him turning on the seven-thirty news while he shaved and listening to Fulton Lewis, all the while whistling away. It was during this period that Dean's intellectual arrogance became a great strength." Dean would come home from the department outwardly unperturbed by events; he would have a drink and discuss the events of the day as if he hadn't a care in the world.*

Outwardly the person who suffered most was Mrs. Acheson. The attacks took their worst toll with her. Acheson tried to get her to stop reading the columnists but it was not easy.

Not in its entire history had the American people felt themselves so desperately on the defensive. The atmosphere of mutual distrust, in which everyone was conscious of having to prove his anti–Communism, was bound to limit the scope of debate and of speculation about the international situation.

In an effort to counter McCarthy, the Democratic Policy Committee and the Democratic Conference moved with alacrity to have his charges investigated. A subcommittee of the Senate Foreign Relations Committee was impaneled, chaired by Tydings and consisting of Democrats Green and McMahon and Republicans Hickenlooper and Lodge. The members of the Tydings Committee had little experience with investigating such vague charges as McCarthy had raised and were unfortunate in the temperamental nature of their chairman. Moreover, the President and Democratic leaders expected the committee to get rid of McCarthy's unwelcome accusations as quickly as possible. Under this pressure the committee did not hire a staff, as later investigatory committees would

---

* Personal interview with Archibald MacLeish, Conway, Massachusetts, July 2, 1964. Acheson insisted that they must simply refuse to read what was being said, to ignore it completely or it would destroy them, and that is what they did. He and Mrs. Acheson would occasionally encounter newsmen and columnists who were attacking Acheson or not presenting his side of the case at parties. They would sidle away either out of embarrassment or so as not to be seen with Acheson. Personal interview with Mrs. Dean Acheson, Washington, D. C., February 21, 1975.

do, to conduct the hearings in a manner that would minimize the charge of whitewash.

The Tydings Committee hearings began on March 7; in their midst Acheson journeyed to California. There, in speeches to the University of California at Berkeley, on March 16, and to the Commonwealth Club in San Francisco, Acheson endeavored to continue the experiment in foreign-policy education begun two months earlier. Acheson began his Berkeley address by sharply underscoring the evil nature of the Communist system and its malevolent intentions. "We can see no moral compromise with the contrary [antidemocratic] theses of international communism: that the end justifies the means, that any and all methods are permissible, and that the dignity of the human individual is of no importance as against the interest of the State." Nevertheless, he carefully refrained from espousing the goal of a moral crusade:

Yet it does not follow from this that the two systems, theirs and ours, cannot exist concurrently in this world. Good and evil can and do exist concurrently in the whole great realm of human life. They exist within every individual, within every nation, and within every human group. The struggle between good and evil cannot be confined to governments. That struggle will go on, as it always has, in the wider theater of the human spirit itself.[15]

But although it was possible for the Soviet and American systems to coexist peacefully, he continued, it was up to the Soviet leaders to co-operate in seven areas of difference, "which must be . . . reconciled if the two systems are to live together . . . in reasonable security." [16] This is a very important listing because it marked a definition of America's objectives which went somewhat beyond mere containment and reflected the first clear statement of Acheson's terms for ending the Cold War. The Soviet leaders must:

(1) permit the unification of Germany, Austria, and Korea under governments chosen by free elections;
(2) refrain from the use of force . . . in maintaining regimes in satellite countries;
(3) cease their policy of walk-out in the United Nations;
(4) cooperate in seeking realistic and effective control of atomic energy and the limitation of armaments;
(5) refrain from using the Communist organization as a tool to submerge established governments;
(6) treat the official representatives of all foreign countries according to accepted codes of international law; and
(7) desist from distorting to the Russian people the picture of the Western world.[17]

In effect, point two went beyond containment to demand of the Soviet Union the liquidation of its sphere of influence in Eastern Europe, something which Acheson must have known the Soviets could never accept. Nevertheless, it formalized Acheson's belief that normalization of international relations depended upon a Soviet withdrawal to within its traditional frontiers, and was again to find expression in his efforts later that spring at the Western Foreign Ministers' Conference to get Bevin and Schuman to make the liberation of Eastern Europe one of the objectives of Western foreign policy. They turned aside this aspiration, but it does suggest the strength of Acheson's conviction that only a complete withdrawal of the Soviet presence in Europe would suffice, and it helps to explain his assumption that the West must be prepared for a long struggle.

Even if Russia could not accept all of these terms, the acceptance of some would have signified to Acheson Russia's readiness to abandon its apparent hostility to the West and to work positively for peaceful co-existence. As the *New York Times* observed editorially, the terms were a demand for the "abandonment of the Communist program of world revolution and a reversal of policies which the Soviets have pursued during and since the war." Yet, continued the *New York Times*, "this is the only program on which we can negotiate without betraying the principles for which we stand and abandoning the nations which have placed their trust in us." [18]

To build up his listeners' self-confidence and offset the corrosive influence of McCarthyism, Acheson ended his speech by dwelling upon the positive things America had going for it in the struggle against Communism: "a burning and fighting faith in our institutions . . . ," the capacity to communicate the idea of freedom to the whole world, and the capacity "to create a better material life for ourselves and for other people in many parts of the world." [19]

The immediate impact was positive. Even *Time* and *Life* gave their grudging approval, although they continued to doubt that Acheson had the necessary confidence in Americanism as a fighting faith to make it triumphant. ("Mr. Acheson has great virtues but they do not include a confident belief in America.") * Predictably the *New Republic* was more circumspect, although in the opposite direction. It noted that "Acheson's

---

* "With the exception of Paul Hoffman no other official of the Truman Administration has gone to such lengths to spell out the substance, the background, and the meaning of public policy. Certainly no other Secretary of State in recent times has tried so often and *so well* to let the public in on the nature of policy and the reasons why he, the Secretary, thinks and acts as he does. On three occasions in the past six weeks Mr. Acheson has explained United States foreign policy as it is and as he believes it should be in statements which are *models of official expression in a democracy.*" Editorial, *Life*, March 20, 1950, p. 40. Emphasis added.

California speech-making tour is a new attempt to 'sell' him and Administration foreign policy to the public. . . ." [20] It admitted that Acheson had "made an able review of many aspects of the Cold War, and some of his attacks on Soviet Russia were telling ones." But it was difficult to see, the *New Republic* concluded, "how our relations to the U.S.S.R., or to any other nation were advanced in the slightest. . . ." [21] Accurate but negative was TRB's comment. "So far as it went it was realistic. A moral chasm yawns between Russia and America. . . ." [22]

The *U.S. News and World Report* felt that Acheson was doing the job of "getting the American people back on the track in their attitude toward the outside world," but that he was making a mistake in thinking that he could reason with the common man. "He doesn't know the man in the street as well as he might. He wants to reason with him, to go back logically and 'educate' him when the American public hasn't the time to sit down quietly and be educated." [23]

Perhaps the following comment by the editors of *Life* Magazine best conveys the Luce empire's pseudointellectual response to Acheson's speeches. It is alien to the American temper, *Life* told its readers, to find a Secretary of State who does not share the average American's morbidity about security—to find a Secretary of State who is not only concerned with "the nature of freedom's enemy but with the ways and faults of free society as it exists in the United States . . . The faculty of criticism can be dangerous as well as useful; it can carry its possessors to the point of fundamental non-confidence in the systems which they critically examine and defend. . . . [24] The net impression conveyed by Acheson's speeches, *Life* concluded, "is that American Society, as it exists, functions, 'thinks' today is in the Secretary's innermost opinion neither strong enough nor good enough to meet the Communist threat." [25] One can only conclude that what was held against Acheson was that his reasoning did not produce the kind of emotionally ideological answers which the publisher of *Life* wanted. For Acheson to point out the difficulties and dilemmas facing United States foreign policy undercut Henry Luce's belief that this was to be the American century. Hard analysis was unacceptable to *Time* and *Life* because it put in doubt the simple nostrums with which Luce operated. Since there was no basis for Americans to have doubts about the wisdom or virtue of their cause, something must be wrong with Mr. Acheson's character and personality to be complicating matters so much. Not only does he think too much, but he is aristocratic, *Life* commented. "His aristocracy is of the mind, and it conditions all that he is and does." [26] It made Acheson a Hamlet, given to introspection, unable to admit a traitor (Hiss) when he knew one. Could a man who suffered "the tortures of soul and mind that any man of intelligence and self-perception must undergo in the Secretary's job" have confidence in America? [27] Obviously not. Such a person could only be a stranger to good Americans.

Whatever good Acheson's speeches may have done, the headlines were all Joe McCarthy's, and whatever hope the Tydings Committee hearings may have held out of seeing McCarthy's charges aired and removed from the public limelight were soon to vanish before the persistence of both the man and the issue. No sooner had the committee convened than McCarthy began to produce names, some old, some new to the public: John Stewart Service, Dorothy Kenyon, Haldore Hansen, Stephen Brunauer, Owen Lattimore, and Philip C. Jessup.

His charges, such as those against Dorothy Kenyon, were often vulnerable to stunning setbacks, but no matter; as Senator Taft told McCarthy: "If one case doesn't work, try another." [28] As he continued to plod doggedly through his list, shock waves from the hinterland began to reassure his Republican colleagues that, right or wrong, McCarthy had a tremendous issue. On March 22 the Republican leadership formally endorsed McCarthy's cause.[29]

The Tydings Committee did not handle the investigation at all well. Instead of paving a cool, methodical course which might have convinced at least some observers of the objectivity of its Democratic members, Tydings let it become a forum for trying Joe McCarthy, and in that kind of contest McCarthy stood to win. One inconclusive confrontation after another occurred—Lattimore, Jessup—with McCarthy each time better prepared to exploit the weaknesses of the committee as a final forum to prove or disprove his charges. Because Truman would not agree to give the committee access to the confidential loyalty files of the eighty-one State Department employees accused of Communism, the committee was vulnerable to McCarthy's charge that the investigation was merely a whitewash designed to get the State Department off the hook. While Acheson did not normally approve of congressional committees being given access to confidential personnel files, he was confident that in this case doing so would do more good than harm. Unfortunately, the Justice Department and the FBI, both of which had all along contributed their share to the anti–Communist hysteria, recommended against opening the files to the committee on the grounds that the President would have "to reverse his earlier [March 1948] Executive Order denying Congressional Committees access to the loyalty files. . . ." [30] Truman sought to regain the initiative by ordering the Loyalty Review Board to study the files and report its findings to him. But this did no good because McCarthy immediately denounced Truman's gesture as an attempt to cover up executive error. In the end, Truman was obliged to authorize the committee members to look over a summary of the personnel files prepared by J. Edgar Hoover, but that still did not satisfy McCarthy because it still excluded committee members from access to the raw data in the FBI files. When

J. Edgar Hoover testified before the committee that the files were intact and that nothing in them indicated that those currently employed by the State Department constituted security risks, even that did not satisfy McCarthy or allay the suspicions which his accusations had reinforced in the public mind.

What was Acheson's record on the security issue? It is certainly true, as one writer observes, that "Acheson's moral austerity, his passionate sense of privacy and his civil libertarianism granted highest respect to the individual," [31] but did this mean that he neglected the significance of personnel loyalty and security within the State Department? The two security chiefs appointed by Acheson were John Peurifoy, who served from 1947 to 1950, and Carlisle Humelsine, who served from 1950 to the end of Acheson's tenure as Secretary of State. In line with his practice of delegating as much responsibility as possible to his subordinates, Acheson delegated to Peurifoy and Humelsine chief responsibility for security matters. Both men were highly sensitive to the security issue and both enjoyed good standing with the appropriate committees of Congress. In 1947 Peurifoy commissioned an FBI survey of State's Division of Security and Investigations that, according to Richard Loss, "proved to be the most impartial and thorough review of personnel security under Acheson." [32] Despite the FBI's recommendations, the State Department may not have done all that it might have done to perfect the training of its security personnel, but this does not prove that the State Department's security system under Acheson was inadequate.

The most publicized cases involved charges against Foreign Service officers whose judgment, not whose loyalty, was at issue. Among such cases were those of John Carter Vincent, John Stewart Service, Philip C. Jessup, and later O. Edmund Clubb. Executive Order 9835 (1947) established departmental review boards to remove persons "if reasonable grounds exist for belief that the persons involved are disloyal to the United States." Executive Order 10241 (1951) transferred the burden of proof from the government to the accused employee by making grounds for dismissal any "reasonable doubt as to the loyalty of the person involved." Of the loyalty or security worthiness of Vincent and Clubb, Loyalty Review Boards had found a "reasonable doubt" (not always unanimously). In both cases Acheson, who was convinced that the charges were ill-founded, ordered review boards. Upon review both men were cleared of the charges against them with Acheson concurring. But in both cases, as well as others, their careers had been blighted and they ended by resigning (Vincent resigned under pressure from Dulles in 1953).

Some employees did resign and some were dismissed for alcoholism, homosexuality, or other reasons which made them potential security risks. Of the China hands only John Stewart Service was dismissed by Acheson when a Loyalty Review Board (a government-wide and not a State Department board) found his implication in the Amerasia case grounds for "reasonable doubt as to his loyalty." Had Adrian Fisher, the department's regular legal adviser and a man close to Acheson, been available, it is possible that he would have advised against Service's dismissal on grounds that the decision was not binding. But no one else was dismissed or forced out for disloyalty when in fact the charges against him were that he had taken a controversial position in some past delicate and now controversial situation.* Contrary to the popular impression, no department employee was either accused or found guilty of espionage or any other security charge during Acheson's tenure as Secretary of State. It has been argued that since a more politically effective personnel security program (meaning effective with his critics in the press and on the Hill) was indispensable to reassuring the country about his loyalty and that of the State Department, Acheson should have been more active, like Dulles, in using the security system to get rid of personnel whose political judgments or past associations, not their loyalty, were under attack, or in classifying the several hundred employees released or forced out as security risks. This Acheson declined to do.

Acheson endeavored to undo the McCarthyite damage as best he could. Publicly, he attempted to appeal to the country's spirit of reason and fair play. Just two days after McCarthy had won resounding applause from the American Society of Newspaper Editors, Acheson went before the same group. Disregarding his pledge never to insult his listener's intelligence, Acheson launched into a forty-minute blast at McCarthy and his method of fighting subversion. In a despairing effort to bring the editors to their senses, he catalogued the reputations of the men who were currently serving under him in the State Department. He detailed their character and loyalty as well as the courage and steadfastness of those Foreign Service officers serving in the field in the hope that their work might blow away the miasma of mistrust and doubt that engulfed the department. He ended with an appeal to their professional integrity:

I don't ask you for sympathy. I don't ask you for help. You are in a worse situation than I am. I and my associates are only the intended victims of this mad and vicious operation. But you, unhappily, you by reason of your calling, are participants. You are unwilling participants, disgusted participants, but, nevertheless, participants, and your position is far more serious than mine.

---

* Acheson, *Present at the Creation*, pp. 710–712. See also Thomas, *op. cit.*, p. 92. Acheson recognized that Service had been guilty of a serious indiscretion in the Amerasia incident and accepted the findings of the President's Loyalty Review Board accordingly, but he considered the charges against the other men to be luridly exaggerated by the temper of the times.

As I leave this filthy business, and I hope never to speak of it again, I should like to leave in your minds the words of John Donne . . .

Any man's death diminishes me, because I am involved in mankind.

And, therefore, never send to know for whom the bell tolls;

It tolls for thee.[33]

Although he got a standing ovation, his confidence in their help was perhaps better conveyed by the sentiment he expressed later: "As I sat down, it was with a hope that here and there among those rows of white, and possibly stuffed, shirtfronts a conscience pricked." He was quite right not to count on the press, for its headlines continued to blare forth McCarthy's accusations, and its columns and editorials continued to treat what he said as newsworthy and therefore fit to be enshrined as truth in the eyes of the reader.

Behind the scenes another effort was under way to limit the damage McCarthy was doing. The burden of Acheson's statement about Hiss had fallen upon the State Department's congressional liaison team under the direction of Jack McFall. McFall had made it clear that for the liaison team to fight back against McCarthy would imperil its legislative effectiveness and sacrifice the bipartisanship which was considered more vital than ever. The lead was taken, therefore, by Adrian Fisher, legal adviser to the department and, like Acheson, a former Brandeis law clerk, who created a special group of people in and out of government to investigate and refute McCarthy's charges. Within the department besides Fisher, the group included Carlisle Humelsine, John Peurifoy, and G. W. Foster, Jr.; Fisher's reserves outside the department included John Carroll, congressional liaison for the President, Governor Thomas E. Dewey, Senators Lister Hill, Brien McMahon, and John Sparkman, and Representative Chet Holifield. These men were willing to go to bat for Acheson on an informal basis with such members of the Senate and the House as they could influence. Fisher also organized a campaign to reply to McCarthy's charges through critiques of his evidence privately distributed to friendly senators and through the private release of anti–McCarthy broadsides called *McCarthy Says—the Facts.*[34] It was the work of this group that explains the ostentatious support that Governor Dewey extended Acheson during that terrible spring, and it may explain why Governor Earl Warren swung around from support of McCarthy's charges to repudiation of them. The Fisher group provided supporters with accurate rebuttals to McCarthy, raised the level of debate over the security issue, and headed off ill-informed criticism before it reached the public.

Obviously the need to reknit the bipartisan ties was greater than ever. With Vandenberg ill and Dulles smarting from his defeat in the New York senatorial race, something had to be done to restore bipartisanship.

On March 25 the ailing Vandenberg made his last great contribution.

He published a letter to Paul Hoffman, director of the Economic Co-operation Administration, in which he reaffirmed the virtue of "unpartisanship" in foreign affairs. Then, on March 29, he wrote directly to Acheson. In his letter, Vandenberg noted the difficulty of maintaining bipartisanship when he himself, the ranking Republican senator on the Foreign Relations Committee, was too ill to participate. He recommended that Acheson's best chances lay in occasional meetings with the four active Republican members of the Senate committee and with the four ranking Republican members of the House Committee on Foreign Affairs. This was not easy to arrange because Tom Connally, the new chairman of the Senate committee, was morbidly sensitive of his prerogative to be consulted first and foremost.

An obvious move in the direction of restoring bipartisanship—at least with the internationalist wing of the Republican Party—would be to reappoint Dulles to some prominent State Department post. Vandenberg wrote Acheson again on March 31 recommending just that. The prior appointment of John Sherman Cooper, former Republican senator from Kentucky, as adviser to Acheson, had given rise to speculation that Dulles was being passed over. It is certainly true that Dulles was *persona non grata* with Truman, whose Fair Deal views he had attacked in the course of his campaign against Herbert Lehman. But being a political realist, Truman was soon persuaded of the wisdom of bringing Dulles back into the fold. For a while Dulles played coy, adducing the criticism to which he would be subjected by fellow Republicans should he accept anything less than the most influential kind of post. In the end, however, he was convinced that his appointment with the rank of ambassador-at-large assured him of a role that would be a most serious and weighty one in the department.

Thomas E. Dewey, the unsuccessful Republican Presidential candidate in 1944 and 1948, also threw his weight behind efforts to re-establish bipartisanship. In a speech delivered at Princeton on April 9 Dewey attacked "sections of the Republican Party. . . . Politics should 'stop at the water's edge,' and if it does not do so soon, I doubt if we will long own the water's edge."

At about the same time Dewey came prominently into Acheson's mind as the successor to Ambassador Lewis Douglas at the Court of St. James's. Acheson journeyed to New York and met privately with Dewey, but the latter would not accept the appointment. Nevertheless, the approach to Dewey is indicative of the lengths to which Acheson and the President were willing to go in order to rescue foreign policy from the destructive assaults of McCarthy and Taft.

Truman's activities on behalf of Acheson were further extended. On March 26 and again on April 14, Truman appealed to his old colleague

Styles Bridges to cease and desist from his more extreme attacks upon the Secretary of State.[35] (The New Hampshire senator bore a personal grudge against Acheson for some aspersion cast by Acheson, word of which had gotten back to him.) Although Bridges was one of McCarthy's most powerful backers in the "get Acheson" campaign of that spring, the President hoped that a personal meeting of the two men would at least ease their quarrel. Truman brought Acheson and Bridges together at Blair House on April 17. The meeting was very cordial. Acheson expressed regret for any insult. It was agreed that Acheson would confer with Bridges about meeting with some senior Republicans following the next session of the Senate Foreign Relations Committee. The Blair House conversation led to the issuance of a statement endorsing the virtues of bipartisanship.

Naturally, the Taft wing of the Republican Party viewed these efforts with the gravest misgivings. "They emphasized that Dulles himself had never been elected to any public office and that his political patrons Dewey and Vandenberg were no longer in a position to exercise much party leadership either." The significance of this jibe was to put the Administration on warning that naming Dulles to a high State Department post was no guarantee against Republican attacks on foreign policy. The Bridges meeting brought an even severer reaction because "Republicans who were most hostile to Administration foreign policy were afraid that their growing ranks would be splintered if Bridges deserted." [36]

The next day Senator Tom Connally helped Republican critics of bipartisanship out a bit. Connally demanded to know whether Truman and Acheson still intended to employ the traditional avenue of communication with the Senate on foreign-policy matters. With that question, Connally left Truman and Acheson little room for consulting with Republicans outside the duly constituted channels.

By one of those ironies of which history is so fond, the very spring Acheson set out to educate the American people on the complexities of foreign policy witnessed one of the greatest assaults on intelligence and reason to which the republic had ever been exposed. Acheson's campaign to create a sense of urgency in the face of the Soviet challenge and his calls for "total diplomacy," in which everything Americans said and did would have a bearing on the struggle, misfired. Paradoxically, the McCarthyite movement was born as much as anything out of the strain to which the volatile American democracy had already been put by the Cold War. In spurring the American public, the Congress, and allied governments to even higher peaks of effort, Acheson was bound to add significantly to the very strains that were producing McCarthyism, and in a broader sense, Acheson did not seem to have appreciated how incompatible with the delicate balance of the American psychology were his calls for greater struggle. Had America been at war, as in 1917 and 1942, all the divisive forces aroused by this unaccustomed travail would have been swept away in one all-consuming crusade. But that was precisely Acheson's problem. He was asking Americans to gird up as if they were actually at war without the catharsis of war itself. Few American statesmen have confronted such an unenviable situation. A President of Roosevelt's magnetic talents might have brought it off, but Truman was no Roosevelt.

CHAPTER

13

THE FIRST FRUIT OF ALLIANCE DIPLOMACY:
FROM BRITISH DEVALUATION
TO THE SCHUMAN PLAN

THE LEVEL OF world problems was growing exponentially due to the inter-
action between two distinct sets of problems. In Acheson's own words:
"One set of problems arises from the conduct in international affairs
of the Soviet Union . . . seeking to extend its dominion where its
grasp and reach coincide. . . ." The second set "are the problems,
economic, social, political, which would arise, as in Europe, from the dis-
ruptions of war and changed relationships with other parts of the world—
as in Asia, from a great awakening of peoples to a new revulsion against
acceptance of poverty and hunger and to a consciousness of national independence." [1] Together they were threatening to doom America's mastery
before it had even been established.

Everywhere Acheson turned in the fall of 1949, he found the United
States severely restricted in its ability to influence international events.
A skirmish had been won the previous spring with the lifting of the Berlin
blockade, but only by the narrowest and most fortunate of margins. No
new accretion of Western power had occurred. To the Communist conquest of China had been added the Soviet atomic explosion of that
August. The Soviet Union was orchestrating an increasingly menacing
campaign against Yugoslavia, accompanied by widespread purges within
the other satellites. Progress on the Austrian peace treaty—which had
seemed quite hopeful in the summer—suddenly bogged down. No significant new release of energy seemed forthcoming in Europe. The magnificent success of the Marshall Plan had had little effect on Europe's
worst weaknesses; if anything, the old divisive forces of nationalism were
reasserting themselves.

239

For Europe, where Acheson pinned his greatest hopes for establishing mastery over threatening world forces, the situation was proving especially intractable. Superficially, the embitterment which characterized Anglo–American and Anglo–French relations that summer could be traced to economic causes, but peering deeper one could see beneath the turbulent surface of European diplomacy the clashing currents of nationalism.

The American recession in the spring of 1949 had sharply reduced British exports to the dollar markets, thereby worsening Britain's chronic dollar shortage. Out of desperation, the Labour government had been driven to consider the humiliating expedient of devaluing the pound sterling. To be forced to this, after years of struggle to overcome the country's economic failings, was almost more than the Labour government could bear.*

But British resentment was fueled by something more basic than the dollar gap. An implicit condition of the Marshall Plan had been that the European nations would strive for economic integration. The European Recovery Program had been practically sold to the American people as an economic mission to redeem Europe from nationalistic folly. Paul Hoffman, high priest of this religion, had that year received particularly powerful sanction from Congress to convert the unbelievers to the gospel of the American mass market, lest they earn the ire of the following year's congressional budget-cutters. The American people and the Congress had their hearts set on a dramatic resurrection of Europe and were not interested in British opposition.

Whatever the merits of Hoffman's campaign—and in the abstract they were many—the British Labour government regarded it as a pernicious attempt to dictate Britain's national interest. Having just come back from the brink of economic collapse, and weak though Britain was, the Labour government had no intention of sacrificing its national independence and the economic advantages of the sterling bloc upon the altar of European integration.** Nor could the British avoid associating the ordeal of monetary devaluation with Hoffman's campaign. Had not Hoffman always argued for free convertibility which precipitated the run on the British

---

* Sir Stafford Cripps, Chancellor of the Exchequer, "had been much shaken by having to submit to the devaluation of the pound in September 1949. And he had been much wounded by accusations, from Churchill and many minor figures, of dishonesty. For he had repeatedly denied, right up to the day when devaluation was actually announced, that it was even contemplated." Hugh Dalton, *Memoirs: 1945–60* (London: Muller, 1962), pp. 337–338.

** Acheson understood that they had quite enough to do just to keep the sterling zone functioning without adding to the burdens of the London money market the accumulated payments deficit of Europe.

pound in 1947? Was he not always pointing an accusatory finger at the British pound as an example of an overvalued currency?

Anglo–American financial talks had been set for Washington in September 1949, and as the date drew near, Ambassador Lewis Douglas urged Acheson to "go easy on the British, who will be feeling desperate." [2] The United States, Douglas warned, must try to prevent any outburst of ideological differences and any suspicion that the United States was seeking to bring about the downfall of the present Labour government. Unfortunately, the United States' position was at best an embarrassing one. If Britain took the obvious course and devalued—which American authorities by and large regarded as inevitable—it would be sure to damage the interest of other European countries which would blame the United States for tolerating Britain's violation of the International Monetary Fund ban upon unsanctioned devaluations. Under the circumstances, Secretary of the Treasury John Snyder preferred that the United States take an absolutely hands-off position in the financial talks. Snyder's reasoning was, as Acheson put it, "that even to discuss devaluation both incurred a commitment to underwrite the result, and made us an accessory to a possible outbreak of financial hostilities. . . ." [3] Acheson himself took the opposite view—that while it was up to the British to decide such a matter for themselves, there was no reason why the United States should not consult with them and, once the decision was taken, smooth over its adverse consequences upon the other European partners. Above all, the United States must not allow the British devaluation to become the cause of destructive competition among its allies. This was not easy to do. The decision to devalue had been taken before the British delegation even left London, but the "quantum" (the amount by which to devalue) had not been decided when the British arrived in Washington on September 6. That was a decision in many ways as crucial as the devaluation itself. Devaluation marked another nail in the coffin of Britain's centuries-old economic domination—one which they had sacrificed a great deal to avoid. George Kennan felt that the American negotiators, headed by John Snyder, showed shocking callousness toward the British, but Acheson, who shared Kennan's concern, recognized that there was nothing the United States could do until the British had made their decision. The United States could not afford to appear either to be forcing Britain's hand or to be conniving with Britain in disregard of the French and other European economies. "The United States delegation sat around grave but not saying a word. They persisted in this course until we British made up our minds what to do. Once we made up our minds the dam broke so to speak and a whole lot of other decisions flowed naturally." [4] Thus was one of the great decisions of postwar finance diplomacy achieved; a generation earlier a similar one had wrecked the London Economic Conference and helped precipitate the economic nationalism of the 1930s.

The British devaluation, coming as it did in the midst of Anglo–American financial talks, triggered a wave of anti–American criticism in Europe. French ambassador Henri Bonnet seized upon the move as evidence of the existence or re-establishment of a "special relationship" between the United States and Britain and the Commonwealth at the expense of the Atlantic Community and of European economic integration. And indeed the British immediately began showing an increased reluctance to commit themselves to the European Payments Union, the next step in European economic integration. Fortunately, Acheson was able to allay the worst effects of this outburst in direct conversations with French Foreign Minister Robert Schuman.

Meeting together at the Western Foreign Ministers' Conference in New York later in September, Acheson was able to reassure Schuman that all talk of a special Anglo–American relationship was unfounded. Schuman accepted Acheson's explanation with his usual goodwill and dismissed Bonnet's charge as a product of his own government's nervousness and uneasiness—emotions France had every right to feel, for as a consequence of the British devaluation of the pound, the French government had to follow suit. This led to a rise in the level of French domestic prices, a widening of the gap between wage levels and living costs, and a sharpening of the struggle for existence on the part of French people and government alike. On October 5, the fall of the Queuille government, partly as a consequence of worsening economic conditions, precipitated a prolonged period of crisis and instability in France. Schuman, fortunately retained the post of foreign minister in the new Bidault Cabinet. Nevertheless, devaluation could not help but undermine French confidence in the Fourth Republic.

In spite of Acheson's opposition within the Administration to his program, Hoffman persisted in his campaign to have the Economic Cooperation Act (ECA) for 1949 contain a statement calling for progress toward European economic integration. The United States Congress obliged by inserting such an amendment in that year's appropriation.

Part of the trouble was that what Hoffman meant by economic integration and what others thought he meant were two quite different things. Hoffman meant an unimpeded flow of men, goods, and money (currency and capital). He feared the creation of nationalist economic blocs such as occurred between wars. Hoffman was actually thinking less in political and federal terms than in economic terms when he called for European integration. But the British feared that even to accept convertibility and an end to other controls would involve risks and would undermine the sterling bloc. The French were staunch advocates of the Hoffman gospel because it fitted into their diplomacy. According to British Ambassador Sir Oliver Franks:

One problem all the way through which Acheson . . . understood and which Hoffman didn't, was that all the countries of Europe were identical in one sense but that Britain was different in another sense. By that I mean that the British pound was the exchange currency for a host of extra-European countries—Egypt, India, etc. Hoffman's concept was too inadequate in the currency sense. So a three-way dialogue went on among Hoffman, Dean, and myself in which Hoffman never really understood or believed this crucial difference.[5]

On October 21, in the wake of congressional action, British Ambassador Franks appealed to Acheson to refrain from putting pressure on the British to enter any deeper into French schemes for linking the European economies, as it would only lead to recrimination within the Labour government. Acheson agreed to do his best. Nevertheless, Acheson could not go to the President and insist that Hoffman be dissuaded from forcing the issue because the Administration itself was committed to European integration both in principle and as a condition for obtaining future ECA funds. On October 31, speaking to the Organization for European Economic Cooperation (OEEC) council in Paris, Hoffman delivered himself of the judgment that only by accepting economic integration could Western Europe move toward a "more dynamic expanding economy. . . . The substance of such integration would be the formation of a single large market. . . ."[6] Hoffman gave his European listeners the impression that unless genuine progress was made, the United States Congress might discontinue aid after 1950. Acheson was angry.

Acheson did not approve of this hectoring, especially since it was very unlikely to accomplish its objective and it threatened to upset American diplomacy. Upon his return from Europe, Hoffman failed to enlist Acheson's support for the delivery of a thinly disguised ultimatum to the Europeans. At a meeting on November 3 with Hoffman, Acheson rejected his argument that ECA appropriation would be doomed unless Europe made substantial progress toward integration. Acheson reiterated his opinion that it was unwise to attempt to force the European states to abdicate their sovereignty: "It is extremely difficult on a democratic and voluntary basis to overcome a couple of thousand years of history. . . . We must not put ourselves in a position of even appearing to subvert authority in any of these friendly countries with which we work."[7] Acheson preferred progress along lines of freeing trade, introducing competition, and widening markets. Laying down ultimatums would only rebound against the ECA and American diplomacy.

Much as Acheson had feared, Hoffman's campaign to bring about economic unity prompted an equally determined British campaign to secure formal recognition of its so-called "special relationship" to the United States. George Kennan had returned that summer from a mission to Europe with a view that the United States could not hope to deal simultaneously with the congeries of European relationships, and that Europe had more cohesive forces within itself than any part of Europe— Britain excepted—could have with the United States. As an outcome of his observations, Kennan contributed the idea that it would be unwise to try to force the British into a uniform and equal relationship with France, Germany, and the other continental countries. Britain's relationship with the Commonwealth and its essentially insular relationship to the continent justified a position of independence for Britain between the United States and the continent. While the State Department did not take a hard and fast position, it seems clear that Acheson's opposition to Hoffman reflects in part Kennan's influence and in part his own predisposition not to force solutions upon an unwilling partner. It seemed perfectly clear to Acheson that a special relationship *did* exist between Britain and the United States and that it formed the very heart of that worldwide order which the United States was trying to hold together. But it was something, Acheson felt, which the British, like the Americans, ought to realize and act upon instinctively, and which above all ought not to be given any formal status in American diplomacy.

Unfortunately, the British were so disturbed by Hoffman's campaign that they acted out of character and attempted to put this subtle political relationship in writing. When Acheson arrived in London in November 1949 for the foreign ministers' meeting, he discovered that the agenda actually listed a paper drawn up by Roger Makins entitled "Special Relationship between the United States and Great Britain." "I was shocked, horrified, and overwhelmed to discover that there was a paper which spelled out this common law marriage in a way which I thought would utterly destroy us if it were ever known, either to our allies or to anybody in the United States." [8] Acheson had an awkward time getting it off the agenda. Nevertheless, the British had made their point; thereafter it was tacitly understood that while Britain would play its part on the continent, it had a special position in the world which justified its standing aloof from continental integration.

But that was not enough for the British. Were Britain to be confronted by an actual union of the continental powers, where would its much vaunted independence get it? Unless the formation of a possible continental bloc of such overwhelming economic and political potential could be avoided, it would only be a matter of time before Britain found itself confronted by a formidable competitor. The British lost no time in trying to capitalize upon tacit acceptance of its special relationship to subvert the Organization for European Economic Cooperation. When in the course of the conference the question arose of how Canadian–American cooperation with the continent was to be channeled, the British called for a new mechanism outside of OEEC. Acheson immediatly drew the line and insisted that North American relations continue to be expressed through OEEC so as not to discourage the continental federationists grouped around that body.

That winter of 1949–1950 saw an additional strain put upon United States–European relations. The British mounted a concerted effort to defeat Belgian Foreign Minister Paul Henri Spaak's candidacy for the secretaryship of the OEEC. The British were not so much opposed to Spaak personally as to the cause which he embodied: a strong secretariat with executive authority for OEEC, and for freeing up currency exchange, convertibility, and so forth. British skepticism about such matters stemmed from their experience with the loan which they received from the United States in 1946.

Former Ambassador Franks summed up the British attitude:

What had gone wrong with that loan, where had it gone? When we got it Dalton had said, "Now we're going to honor our commitments." Gold and dollars flowed out to Belgium, Argentina, and a score of countries to whom Britain owed war-incurred trading debts. That experiment in freeing up trade and currency had been disastrous for us. Britain had almost gone bankrupt. Britain was worried as hell that if asked to go into EPU [the Europe Payments Union] and free up its currency, how soon and how quickly would it be bankrupt and forced to devalue again? The United Kingdom was caught. Great strides in liberalizing meant taking ventures which you couldn't know whether Britain could stand or not. People in London were nervous. The United Kingdom, unlike Belgium, is a world economic power which was threatened with being driven into a European situation whose imperatives were not entirely compatible with Britain's obligations as a world economic power.

Spaak was the symbol of the importance which Europeans and Americans attach to the Secretariat of OEEC. He was also viewed as standing for the realization of Hoffman's mission. . . .

. . . Spaak was a big fish. If he was appointed Secretary of OEEC, you would automatically begin to create an American-style executive in the office. Britain preferred power to reside in the council of members. That is why we opposed Spaak's candidacy.[9]

On January 20 Ambassador Franks sought to enlist Acheson in opposing Spaak, ostensibly out of pique over an article Spaak had written critical of the British but actually out of determination to nip Spaak's candidacy before he could use his position with OEEC as a device to promote economic integration. Acheson rebuffed Ambassador Franks. He made it clear that the United States would not permit Britain's "special relationship" to become an instrument for wrecking European integration and thereby defeating the American interest in a strong, unified, and prosperous continent.

In essence, Acheson let Ambassador Franks know that while Britain had a right to set its own policy, and the United States would not try to coerce it into joining the movement toward European economic union, Britain had no right to defeat any effort which the continental governments were inclined to make. If the United States had any hope of restoring Germany to its traditional power position in Europe, it depended upon convincing Frenchmen that a reconstituted Germany would not pose a mortal threat to France. The only possibility of winning French confidence on this count would be through the creation of a European framework strong enough to house the German dynamo. The future orientation of Germany, too, was at stake. For these reasons Acheson rejected and rebuked all British efforts to obstruct the emergence of a European economic unity.

The Genesis of the Schuman Plan

That same summer, Konrad Adenauer, the first chancellor of the new German Federal Republic, had written Foreign Minister Robert Schuman, asking him to consider exchanging an end to the dismantling of German factories in return for the internationalizing of the mammoth Thyssen steel mills at Hamborn. Among the advantages of such a deal, Adenauer cited the benefit that would accrue to Franco–German relations and to the Christian Democratic cause in Germany. "I believe," Adenauer continued, "that such a spirit of cooperation concerning the most important steel mill in Europe would constitute the seed of international cooperation in the far vaster domain of coal and steel, which would be highly advantageous from the viewpoint of Franco–German understanding."

Nothing came of this remarkable proposal at the time because Acheson managed to secure French and British agreement that same autumn to remove the Thyssen steel mill, along with six other steel mills and eleven synthetic oil and rubber plants, from the dismantling and reparations list. Destruction of the I. G. Farben chemical works was also halted. Only the existing 11.1-million-ton ceiling on German steel production was retained, together with the prohibitions and restrictions on industries that had a potential for war.

In order to allay French sensitivity about these concessions, the Bonn government was instructed to undertake four specific obligations:

(1) It agreed to apply for full membership in the International Ruhr Authority, on the understanding that its admission would not be subject to any "special conditions."

(2) It affirmed its earnest intention to "maintain the demilitarization of the Federal territory," to endeavor "by all means in its power to prevent the re-creation of Armed Forces of any kind," and to cooperate fully in the work of the Military Security Board.

(3) It professed determination to conduct its affairs according to the principles of freedom, tolerance, and humanity, to eradicate all traces of Nazism from German life and institutions, to prevent revival of totalitarianism "in this or any form," and to liberalize its governmental structure and exclude authoritarianism.

(4) It promised to take legislative action in the field of decartelization and monopolistic practices, in accordance with decisions of the High Commission under the Occupation Statute.[10]

Acheson could not have secured acceptance of these concessions to German recovery had France not been willing to go along. People forget that there was nothing inevitable about the Franco–German rapprochement or about the formation of the Schuman Plan and the Common Market. One authority writes that a deceptive impression of inevitability "came to characterize Germany's advance toward equal status and its participation in the defense of Western Europe" that was not justified by relationships at the time.[11]

In fact, four years after the war, the obstacles in the way of a successful resolution of Franco–German differences . . . were very great. . . . France, while moving away from its earlier policy of dismemberment, had not yet arrived at the policy of close union with Germany. The establishment of a Saar Republic with separate membership in the Council of Europe on March 3, 1950, amounted to a continuation of the former [French] policy.[12]

It would be wrong, however, to attribute Acheson's success solely to American pressure and French impotence. It took a great deal of political courage on Schuman's part to agree to such concessions. Time and again Schuman risked his political life in order that progress be made on German matters. Acheson was fortunate indeed that throughout his tenure as Secretary of State the French foreign office was largely in the hands of an individual singularly sympathetic to European reconciliation, the sincerity of whose convictions many times carried the French government and the French Assembly against their own predilections. According to one of his political adversaries, Schuman was "a dry and mediocre speaker, but, meditative and tenacious, his honesty ended by convincing everyone." [13]

Time after time Schuman got the French National Assembly to accede to concessions on Germany which it had previously resolved to oppose. This record of success came to an abrupt end when Dulles became Secretary of State, and it cannot, therefore, be attributed entirely to French weakness. Unlike Dulles, Acheson consistently managed to strike a responsive chord in his dealings with the French leadership. He consistently sought to advance American interests within a framework of European interests; thus the American zeal for German recovery was synchronized with the French desire to allay Franco–German rivalry and establish a European community. Where direct and open opposition could not be avoided—as over the German rearmament in 1950—Acheson waited for the French themselves to come up with a solution rather than forcing one upon them.

A strong case exists for those who argue that France's capitulations on Germany were forced upon her by America's superior power. But it would be wrong to ignore entirely the subtle personal relationship which Acheson established with Schuman and Bevin and, to a lesser but nonetheless significant degree, with Adenauer. To begin with, Acheson's intellectual prowess and imperturbable demeanor inspired confidence. When men are ringed by a sea of uncertainty and incipient chaos, an enormous premium goes to whichever of the company manifests the decision and energy to master events.

The statesmen of Europe had been struggling for over three decades to control Europe's fate. They had not yet succeeded. Suddenly there appeared in their midst a person whose confidence had not been undermined, who came fresh to the fray with an enormous energy and capacity for reasoning and organizing. Acheson still had unbounded confidence that by the steady application of intelligence and self-discipline, European civilization had a fighting chance to master its destiny. He had "the quality that Thucydides admired in Themistocles: the ability, by some hidden force of mind or character, to fasten immediately, after short deliberation, upon what was needed in a given situation." [14] Not only did he impart to European statesmen a faith in themselves, but he had an uncanny knack for resolving internecine quarrels and finding solutions to immediate and pressing concerns. Gordon Craig has written of Bismarck that,

in addition to [his] professional or technical skills, Bismarck possessed certain qualities of mind and personality which, in his Berlin years, impressed his co-workers and seemed to them to contribute to the success of his statecraft. He was a man of unfailing courtesy and great charm and, on occasion, could be witty and even genial; . . .[15]

His description, while actually more true of Acheson than of Bismarck, makes an important point: the personal buoyancy and graciousness which a statesman brings to negotiations can make all the difference between success and failure in dealing with his partners.

European statesmen were also impressed by the firmness with which Acheson dealt with the great leviathan of American public opinion and especially with the Congress. For years Europeans had been inured to the most outrageous reversals in American policy. They had learned from painful experience that it took an unusual American statesman to control the massive shifts in American popular thought which sprang up with all the suddenness and ferocity of a tropical storm, leaving a trail of twisted plans and wrecked policies in its wake. They were now amazed to find a strong hand at the helm of American statecraft, a Secretary of State who did not panic or yield when the winds began to howl in the canyons of American public opinion.

Not only did Acheson produce the first European military alliance in time of peace, but he fought for and won from the American Congress additional billions in economic and military aid. How could European statesmen not help but be impressed? Here at last was an American statesman upon whom they could count, upon whom they could lean. It was also known that he had an extraordinarily solid relationship with the President. And finally, he was not above intermingling America's security plans with Europe's. The appeal of Acheson's qualities to Bevin, Schuman, and other sorely tried European statesmen was bound to be enormous. They were persuaded to rely upon his solutions, even when they went against long-standing prejudices, because his were the only ones likely to succeed. Their trust was also inspired by the friendship and solicitousness with which Acheson graced their relationships. A thoroughly personal camaraderie enveloped Acheson's relations with his European counterparts. Concourse was sealed by a personal friendship which if not on quite the heroic scale as that between Roosevelt and Churchill was fully as intimate and compelling. After all, given the opportunity, men cast in the lonely role of responsibility for their country's foreign policy are bound to drift toward each other and draw what warmth they can from their common endeavors.

How utterly dependent Schuman was upon Acheson can be gleaned from the fact that Schuman was so surrounded by intrigue that he had to rely upon the American Embassy in Paris to forward certain crucial messages to Acheson rather than transmit them through the French Foreign Office.

This does not mean that Acheson's decisions were always right, but they had a certain reasonableness and proportion about them which they certainly would not have had, had they been derived from a priori postulates of doctrinaire realism. They had about them the spirit of life and reason and hope which engaged the response and willpower of the sorely divided nations of Western Europe and beyond. In the midst of their sufferings and anxiety, Acheson neither preached nor frightened by insisting upon rigid moral "principles, categories, supposed necessities"; rather, he encouraged a spirit of confidence by "looking towards last things, fruits, consequences, facts." [16] He acted in terms of problems and solutions, of real and immediate dangers, and of ways of overcoming them. By so doing he contributed to freeing the minds and wills of Europeans. He offered them true ideas in the sense that the ideas made a concrete difference in the actual lives of people. He did not insist upon any absolute correspondence of their thought to an equally absolute (but a priori) reality or require that they think unconditionally—as did Dulles, his successor. The political value of such pragmatically determined decision-making was immense. It created movements in the European experience which were worthwhile because they led toward "other movements which it will be worthwhile to have been led to," such as European cooperation and federation. The breath of life was pumped into the spectral vision of an economically and politically federated Europe. The powerful appeal of Communism and neutralism was countered by rekindling the vision of the role an independent and united Europe might once again play in world politics. These moves may have been made in reaction to initiatives taken by the Communists, but we now know that because of them Europe became a healthy, revitalized, and prosperous weight in the balance of world affairs.

By undertaking to solve their problems in terms which Europeans could understand, rather than in narrow national-interest terms, Acheson established the moral and political ascendancy of America in Europe in a way which force and browbeating could never have achieved. By the style of his actions Acheson became the guarantor, if not the *auctor,* of the European and North Atlantic communities. By resisting the course of expediency and of pseudomorality and cynicism, he was able to inspire confidence in Europeans of the rightness of American action. By setting them the example, by answering "for the rightness of the action" and "for the certainty that it will yield good fruit to the man who undertakes it," [17] Acheson became the inspiration for actions taken, if not freely, at least in the knowledge that any other alternative was hopeless.

Out of this hospitable environment came one of the most revolutionary innovations of the twentieth century—the European Coal and Steel Community, first known as the Schuman Plan. Such a plan would not have stood a chance had Acheson not opposed British attempts to sabotage it.

In recalling the precise circumstances that surrounded the unveiling of the Schuman Plan, Acheson revealed the warmth and affection which he held for its author. Acheson first learned of the Schuman Plan when en route to the London meeting of the NATO Council in May 1950. He stopped first in Paris for informal talks with the French to reassure them that there was nothing the British and Americans were talking about that they did not already know.[18] On the drive in from Orly, Ambassador David Bruce informed Acheson that Schuman had requested an immediate Sunday afternoon appointment at the ambassador's residence. Bruce and Acheson were puzzled by the urgency implied by such a request. As Acheson recalled the occasion:

After a few words of greeting and appreciation of my coming to Paris, Schuman began to expound what later became known as the "Schuman Plan," so breathtaking a step toward the unification of Western Europe that at first I did not grasp it. The whole French–German production of coal and steel would be placed under a joint high authority, with an organization open to the participation of other European nations. Schuman implored us to treat what he was about to tell us in the greatest confidence, not to speak to any of our colleagues about it, not to send cables, or to have memoranda transcribed. For he had discussed the proposal only with the Premier and one or two members of the Cabinet. The next step would be to consult the whole Cabinet, and, if it approved, then to make some public statement, perhaps in the Chamber of Deputies. After that, France's neighbors would be approached. As he talked, we caught his enthusiasm and the breadth of his thought, the rebirth of Europe, which, as an entity, had been in eclipse since the Reformation.[19]

As in so many happenings of Acheson's four years in office, the actual event was not so significant as the implications which were borne within the seed of the idea. In and of itself the idea of the Franco–German Coal and Steel Community constituted a turning point in European history, for with its achievement the processes leading to European economic integration were finally set in motion. We can well imagine what must have appealed to Acheson as he listened to Schuman. Before him stood a European expounding a scheme characterized at once by great vision and practicality. One had to go back almost two decades—to the Europe of Aristide Briand and Paul Boncour—to find the last time a French statesman had propounded a plan for an integrated European community. There had been a good deal of talk and planning in postwar Europe about the ultimate necessity for Europe to unify. The statesmen and political leaders, however, had been too busy with more mundane matters, such as economic recovery and national survival, to take any serious interest in unification beyond that required of them in planning the European Recovery Program.

And now, here suddenly was an initiative of a vast and most promising sort from the European side. Acheson was struck by the paradox that so sweeping and imaginative an idea should be brought forth by a minister of the most unstable and, in a sense, moribund government in Europe. However, it is not hard to see that the inspiration for Schuman's proposal lay in his cognizance that France was not succeeding in solving its most desperate domestic problems, and that the renaissance of Germany would most assuredly overshadow whatever success France might achieve in regaining national power and prestige. Like many European Catholics,

Schuman had long considered European federation the only solution to national rivalries. He was seconded in these ideas by Jean Monnet, who had helped plan France's postwar recovery and had the technician's vision of a Europe harnessed from the Elbe to the Pyrenees and from the North Sea to the Adriatic. There was also a subtle element of European chauvinism and anti–Americanism in their ideas. As long as Europe remained divided into national entities, it would have no possibility of matching the power represented by the Soviet Union and the Anglo–Saxon world; Europe would either have to unify itself or see its divisions exploited to the advantage of one side or the other. Ever since assuming his post at the Foreign Ministry on July 26, 1948, Schuman had been steadily made aware of France's inability to influence events in Germany, or elsewhere, due to the debilitating internal French weaknesses. As a German-speaking Lorrainer imbued with a historic sense of the atavistic nature of Franco–German conflict, it was perhaps easier for Schuman than for others to reconcile himself to the realization of French interest within an indissoluble Franco–German union. Whatever Schuman's precise motives in putting forward his proposal, Acheson seized upon their implications for the resolution of the European security problem. So much of the stalemate and deadlock into which NATO had fallen stemmed from a lack of French confidence, which threatened to deepen as the necessity for the restoration of Germany's power became fully evident. Acheson saw in the Schuman proposal the political and psychological means for easing French anxiety, as well as the basis for a new departure in his quest for a viable and manageable European security system.

It should not be assumed, however, that all elements of French opinion were reassured by the uncertain perspectives opened up by Schuman's proposal. In the first place, it apparently originated in the fertile technocratic brain of Jean Monnet, long an advocate of "practical" schemes for European integration. Monnet's American associations had alerted him to the advantages of large-scale national and international business organization. He, like Schuman, was close enough to the American administrators of the European Recovery Program to grasp the feasibility of integrating the Franco–German coal and steel industries before German ascendancy became formalized. From the technocrats' point of view this must have appeared as a splendid answer to the economic and political problems raised by German recovery. Whether or not the idea of integrating the European coal and steel industries was specifically Schuman's, it appealed to him as a practical step toward realization of a long-standing personal interest in Franco–German unity and in meeting sentiment for a European federal union which had been rife in his own party, the Mouvement Républicaine Populaire, ever since the end of World War II.

These circumstances enabled Schuman to keep the proposal confidential, knowledege of it being limited to Acheson and a few French officials until May 8, when it was unveiled before the French Council of Ministers. Cabinet discussion of the proposal at the May 8 meeting was perfunctory, in part because practical knowledge about the significance of the plan was lacking. A similar ambiguity and lack of knowledge surrounded the plan when later it came before the French Assembly for discussion and ratification. A French authority writes: "Apart from twenty or thirty deputies and senators with sufficient general knowledge to form an opinion on the Plan, few grasped its meaning. . . ." [20]

Schuman announced his plan on May 9, just prior to his departure for the Foreign Ministers' Conference in London, where his proposal would receive a cool reception from the press and from the Foreign Office. Immediately sensing the threat to Britain's economic position implied by such a potent combination of French and German resources, the Labour government's reaction was one of thinly veiled hostility. When the three foreign ministers met for the first time in private following Schuman's announcement, Acheson found himself and Schuman both facing Bevin's ire at the French fait accompli. Bevin accused them of having conspired behind Britain's back to formulate a plan which deeply involved British interests. Before Schuman could reply, Acheson interposed that it was purely fortuitous that he should have gone to Paris on May 7, and should thereby have come to know about the hitherto confidential French proposal. Acheson cut off Bevin's indignant outburst by reminding him that only the previous September the British had kept all but two or three high American officials in the dark about their plans to devalue the pound sterling. The French, Acheson pointed out, had acquiesced in the necessity for British secrecy at that time.

As in other instances, Acheson found that the price of advancing the viability and manageability of one aspect of the European situation meant the creation of sharp resentments elsewhere. It was of the utmost importance in these circumstances that the American government be able to play the role of the honest broker, and this was more possible now because both Schuman and Bevin respected Acheson's integrity in these interpersonal relations.

Although it could not be seen at the time, the Schuman Plan bore within it the seed of a much more comprehensive and tightly knit union of the European states. Meanwhile, immediate progress would still have to depend upon negotiation among the NATO allies for increases in their military forces and a common strategy. These began in a series of tripartite meetings involving Bevin, Acheson, and Schuman. Despite European desire for an American military guarantee, there still existed a widespread longing in Europe for the Cold War simply to go away. Given the painful ambivalence in which France found itself trapped—between fear of the Soviets and remembrance of the Germans—it was Foreign Minister Schuman who was most often torn between longing for new initiatives toward Russia and a desire for more United States backing both in Europe and in Indochina and North Africa. In an effort to clarify objectives, Acheson had come to the meetings with a State Department brief entitled "Fundamental Common Objectives." The idea was to gain the adherence of America's allies to a common understanding, which would in turn facilitate their agreement on what was to be done. Among the terms (paraphrased) which Acheson succeeded in having accepted were the following:

A. (1) Soviet leaders consider themselves engaged in an irreconcilable struggle against all non–Communist countries,
   (2) their basic strategy is to exert constant pressure wherever non–Communist capacity or will to resist is limited,
   (3) the free world contains many weak spots against which the Kremlin is exerting heavy pressure and which the West cannot afford to lose.
B. It is essential for the West to:
   (1) prevent extension of Soviet Communist domination by direct or indirect aggression or subversion,
   (2) regain and retain the psychological initiative,
   (3) organize the resources of the Western allies to ensure that any Soviet attempt to subjugate the world by armed aggression would be defeated.
C. In order to accomplish these objectives the West must:
   (1) build the necessary economic strength for increased defense and at the same time realize normal improvements in the standard of life,
   (2) build faith in freedom into a dynamic force,
   (3) review constantly problems of common concern, and
   (4) sustain and stiffen the wills of the people even at some sacrifice, to build up the necessary military and economic strength for their ultimate security.[21]

In line with Acheson's own thinking, it was agreed that broad negotiations with the Soviet were undesirable at the time because neither side would yield on fundamentals. Broader negotiations might be necessary because of public pressure for at least one more effort at a general settlement; but in event that such negotiations were held, the Western powers would have to be prepared to demonstrate that their reasonable position on the issues was unacceptable to the Soviets, thus debunking Soviet peace propaganda.[22]

D. If negotiations were necessary, the following problems would have to be discussed:
   (1) control of atomic energy and international regulation of all forms of armaments and armed forces,
   (2) general settlement of problems with respect to Germany, Austria, and Japan to be considered concurrently with (1) above if practicable,
   (3) China and Southeast Asia,
   (4) implementation of Yalta agreements,
   (5) human rights,
   (6) peaceful settlement of disputes through the UN,
   (7) Cominform activities outside the Soviet sphere, and
   (8) the Iron Curtain.[23]

The paper also recognized that the Soviets would probably present embarrassing counterproposals for discussion with the West and stated that the West would presumably wish to feel assured that they were in a position to deal with such proposals.

In the actual meetings Acheson appears to have gotten Bevin and Schuman to accept the following terms for their future collaboration:

   (1) recognition of the dangers and threats to the peace from the Soviet Union of the present situation,
   (2) the need to proceed immediately to increase their military strength,
   (3) the need to create the economic foundations for a European military program,
   (4) the need to bring the productive capacity of Germany into this effort,
   (5) the need to prevent further erosion by Communism in the Far East, and
   (6) the need to evolve institutions to aid in attaining these objectives.[24]

It was agreed to hold off on admitting Peking to the United Nations on the grounds that it would increase the capacity for Communist trouble-making in Southeast Asia. It was also agreed that a democratic and economically sound Germany should move quickly to take its place in the European Community, and as an immediate gauge to the Germans, Chancellor Adenauer was notified that it was the allies' understanding that an attack on NATO forces in Germany would constitute an armed attack within the meaning of Article 5 of the North Atlantic Treaty, thereby extending to Germany the same protection that NATO gave to America's other allies.

The only objective on which America's partners failed to go as far as Acheson wanted was in calling for the eventual withdrawal of Soviet forces from Eastern Europe. Acheson did not consider liberation of Eastern Europe a practical possibility, but he wanted to keep the issue before the eyes of the world.[25] The need to bolster Yugoslavia was agreed to, however, and the need should the occasion arise to furnish Tito with various military supplies in the event of a Soviet attack was also agreed to.

Finally, the three foreign ministers agreed to refrain from supplying arms to Israel or the Arab states for purposes of aggression. Whatever degree of common and constructive interest this agreement intended, it did not long outlast Acheson's departure from office.

When the question of implementing these objectives in the form of a tangible military strategy came before the larger meeting of the NATO Council, Acheson saw just how far the West was from having a credible, coordinated program.

In retrospect, the spring of 1950 witnessed the emergence and growth of lines of policy, inspired either directly or indirectly by Acheson, all directed toward mobilizing the economic, military, and political resources of the Atlantic Community. Because these policies had for their ultimate end the enhancement of European strength and security, it was becoming apparent that all were converging on the great, unresolved issue of German rearmament. Until then all Western strategies had floundered on the question of whether the defense of Europe was to be made at the Elbe or the Rhine. The strategists shocked the political leaders by their insistence that in either case massive military forces far exceeding those presently available were absolutely indispensable to any coherent strategy. As this realization came home to the civilian planners and statesmen, the appeal of German rearmament as the solution to the dilemma became ever greater. But resistance to German rearmament, not only in France, but in the United States, Britain, Italy, and West Germany as well, continued to preclude its active consideration; and as 1950 headed toward mid-year, Acheson was in no position to foresee its eventual acceptance. That would have to await the onset of the Korean War which renewed the sense of desperation and panic in Europe.

Nevertheless, the initiative and energy with which Acheson developed successive policy lines—no one of which gave any immediate hope of perfectly resolving the problems facing Europe—were indicative of Acheson's conviction that when faced with any given political situation there was more to be achieved by reasoned action than by inaction, hesitancy, and vacillation.

In the context of the European situation, action of the sort inaugurated by the organization of NATO and military assistance had the advantage of meeting the opponent's thrust from a dynamic rather than a flat-footed posture. It had the second advantage of engaging America's partners in a common endeavor whereby their attitudes and reflexes could be subtly conditioned to acting in terms of the total good rather than a parochially defined national good. Thirdly, the purposefulness of action, as opposed to the purposelessness of inaction, would dissipate the pangs of fear and anxiety and impart a positive quality to the European psychological and political environment. And finally, Acheson could be sure that in spite of unpopular reactions to American initiatives in France and elsewhere, the French government and bourgeoisie had certain profound dependencies upon the United States which outweighed the marginal loss of popularity that would come from acquiescing in German rearmament at the proper psychological moment. No bourgeois, no matter how dissatisfied with American policy, could ignore the presence of large Communist forces within his country or the indispensable role of American economic and military assistance to the preservation of French national existence.

Acheson's diplomacy that year was not limited to just Western Europe. In June 1948, Tito had wrenched Yugoslavia out of the Soviet orbit in a convulsive effort to save himself from Stalin's all-consuming paranoia. For that act of lese majesty, Stalin ordered Yugoslavia expelled from the Cominform, and the Kremlin embarked on a systematic war of nerves to break Tito's resistance. Acheson quickly recognized the split between Yugoslavia and Moscow as a precedent that ought to be supported. The problem was how to overcome the ideological resistance that existed within the Pentagon and the Congress to aiding a Communist state. At the same time Acheson had to be tactful and not offend Yugoslavia's spirit of resolute independence and ideological zeal. In order to extend essential economic assistance to Belgrade, Acheson first had to overcome Louis Johnson's objections. The issue happened to be whether the transfer of a steel finishing mill to Yugoslavia would be a threat to the national security. Johnson and the Pentagon said it would; Acheson argued that it would not, declaring that to keep Yugoslavia out of Soviet hands was really in the interests of national security. Truman backed Acheson on the issue. But getting a subsequent loan and military aid out of the Congress was a much more difficult matter. The President made a quiet appeal to the Congress on November 29, 1950, for the enactment of special legislation to take care of Yugoslavia's pressing food needs. In subsequent months, that and other legislation was gotten through Congress despite frequent attempts by the opposition to tie it to a grant to the Nationalist Government on Taiwan.

Improvement of relations with Yugoslavia enabled Acheson to broach the question of Trieste. At first Italian and Yugoslav claims seemed as far apart as ever, and both sides expected American backing as a condition of their continued friendship with Washington. Premier Alcide De Gasperi insisted that Italian public opinion would not tolerate the existence of any Italians living in the Trieste region under Yugoslav rule. Acheson persisted, suggesting that De Gasperi might get a reasonable settlement in secret negotiations with Tito rather than posturing in public. Although agreement had still not been reached when Acheson left office two years later, the two sides were much closer to a settlement, and the issue at least had been gotten out of the headlines. Once again Acheson had succeeded in winning over the opposing sides by winning support from Congress for their other vital interests. By overcoming ideological hostility to aiding Tito, Acheson succeeded in preserving Yugoslavia as an independent entity and warding off Soviet threats to its existence. It did not hurt Acheson's efforts that he had established a relationship of trust and confidence with De Gasperi by supporting Italy's membership in the North Atlantic Treaty Organization.

CHAPTER

14

FAR EAST POLICY ON THE EVE OF KOREA

ANOTHER ARENA in which Acheson felt the compelling need for progress that spring was in the Far East and Southeast Asia. As long as it had appeared that China would function as a more or less independent, sovereign power—as had been envisaged at Yalta—no great urgency seemed to attach to the security of American interests in that part of the world. But now that China had become Communist, the area suddenly seemed more vulnerable to Communist penetration than it had previously appeared. Not only did the fall of China represent a victory for the Communist side, but it created for the first time the reality of a Communist state bordering on the great Asian littoral stretching from Japan in the north to India in the south.

Vietnam

Up until the end of 1949, American foreign policy had indulged in pressuring the British, the Dutch, and the French to grant independence to their Asian colonies. Independence was assumed to be the natural and inevitable destiny of Asia, and America looked to nationalism as the best bulwark against Communism.

In Indochina, however, the situation was complicated by the official American view of Ho Chi Minh. As early as December 1946, in advising the American representative what position to take in the struggle between the French and Ho Chi Minh, Acheson cabled as follows:

Assume you will see Ho in Hanoi and offer the following summary [of] our [Department of State] thinking as guide.
Keep in mind Ho's clear record as an agent [of] international communism,

259

absence [of] evidence of recantation Moscow affiliation, confused political situation France and support Ho receiving from French Communist Party.[*]

In May 1949, when the question arose as to whether Ho could be considered a potential Tito, Acheson admitted as a theoretical possibility that any area beyond the reach of the Soviet Army could establish a national Communist state on the pattern of Yugoslavia, but he argued the exception in the case of Asia.

Question whether Ho as much nationalist as Commie *is irrelevant* [emphasis added]. All Stalinists in colonial areas are nationalists. With achievement of national aims (i.e., independence) their objective necessarily becomes subordination [of their] state to Commie purposes and ruthless extermination not only opposition groups. . . .[1]

Even if Acheson had been willing to recognize the Titoist potential in the Ho Chi Minh situation, could he have accepted the risks involved in recognizing him? It must be remembered, as the author of the *Pentagon Papers* narrates, that for America to have accepted Ho Chi Minh,

would have involved perspicacity and risk. As clear as national or neutral or independent Communism may seem today, it was a blurred vision in 1947–1948. Even with the benefit of seeing Tito successfully assert his independence it would have been hard for Washington to make the leap from there to an analogy in Asia. Recourse to "national communism" in Vietnam as an ultimate bulwark against China . . . would have called for perspicacity unique in U.S. history. The risk was there too. The reality of Ho's strength could have worked seriously against U.S. interests as well as against Chinese Communist interests. Ho's well-known leadership and drive . . . could have produced a dangerous period of Vietnamese expansionism. Ho always considered his leadership to extend to Indochina as a whole. . . . It could have been the domino theory with Ho instead of Mao.[2]

Given these considerations at a time when the collapse of China was already sending shock waves through the American body politic, Acheson believed that the most prudent course was to continue to support the French while attempting to build up the neighboring states.

By the time Acheson became Secretary of State, the French and Vietnamese had been at war for two years. In order to bolster their appeal to

---

[*] As a matter of fact Ho was receiving embarrassingly little support from the French Communist Party at the time. According to the *Pentagon Papers*, the French Communists "were not prepared to press the case for Vietnamese independence at the cost of votes in France." *United States–Vietnam Relations: 1945–1967.* Department of Defense edition for the House Armed Services Committee, (Washington, D. C.: U.S. Government Printing Office, 1971), Part I, Section I, p. A-32, hereinafter referred to as *Pentagon Papers*, DOD edition.

Vietamese nationalists, the French had been obliged to enter into a series of accords (the March 6, 1949, or Elysée, Accords) designed to bring back Bao Dai as emperor and to bring about the establishment of Vietnam, Laos, and Cambodia as associated (and autonomous) states within the French Union. These measures were conceded by Paris without any intention whatsoever of giving up French rulership. To get Paris to go further, Acheson indicated that the United States would be prepared to recognize the Bao Dai government and to give it economic aid and military supplies *as soon as* the French ratified the Elysée agreements whereby Vietnam would acquire *de jure* autonomy within the French Union; that is, Acheson did not want to recognize Bao Dai until he could be viewed as a genuine nationalist leader.*

It has been argued in retrospect that "We really should have pushed the French [to grant autonomy] right after the Elysée agreements of March 1949.[3] And it is quite conceivable that Acheson might have put more pressure on the French than he did, and as he did upon the Dutch in the case of Indonesia, but as we know now from America's own sad experience in Vietnam, the passions and political interests aroused in such a war are very difficult to deal with, especially when they involve another country's affairs. Then too there was the specter of another Asian state becoming Communist and the impact that would have upon American opinion. Whether or not the decision to support the Bao Dai experiment was sound or moral, it appeared to be the only alternative, and the only way to make it succeed, or at least to give it a fig leaf of legitimacy, was by persuading the French to execute the Elysée Accords, finally ratified in January 1950.

Until the Communists took power in Peking, Acheson's interest in Indochina, as in all of Southeast Asia, generally had been only nominal. In addition to verbal support for the nationalist movements toward independence, it included little more than technological assistance under Point 4. By the end of 1949, however, his concern was acquiring a more urgent character. As part of the general review of Asian policy instituted that autumn under the direction of Philip C. Jessup, the conviction began to emerge in Acheson's mind that the United States would have to be more active in supporting nationalism and containing Communism if more countries were not to fall.[4] His instructions to Jessup were "to make abso-

---

* The French finally persuaded the emperor to return from self-imposed exile in return for the promise to recognize the independence of Vietnam and for arrangements to unify all of Vietnam, South as well as North, under Vietnamese administration, but Bao Dai's regime was so corrupt and unsavory that Nhu Dinh Diem and other more respectable Vietnamese figures would not deign to join it.

lutely certain that [we] are neglecting no opportunity that would be within our capabilities to achieve the purpose of halting the spread of totalitarian communism in Asia." *

The new urgency with which Acheson viewed the situation found expression in National Security Staff Paper NSC 48/2, approved by President Truman on December 31, 1949, as part of an overall review of Asian policy. The paper recommended that the United States should continue to employ its influence to end colonialism in Asia and bring about the strengthening of nationalism, but it also included the premise that "it is now clear that southeast Asia is the target for a coordinated offensive directed by the Kremlin." [5] The United States, the study went on to say, should act to develop and strengthen the security of the area from Communist external aggression or internal subversion by providing "political, economic, and military assistance and advice where needed to supplement the resistance of other governments *in and out* of the area which are more directly concerned." [6] Acheson was even conjecturing that if the French effort in Indochina collapsed the United States might find itself compelled to intervene in their place. It was not a pleasant thought, but it was what underlay his final decision to give the French what political and military support they needed to keep going. In the light of hindsight it may be argued that Acheson took an excessively exaggerated view of the Communist threat to Southeast Asia, but as Jessup remarked of his meetings with American diplomats in Bangkok in mid–February, all believed in the "very critically strategic importance of the whole Southeastern Asia area," and "the possibility of an invasion by the Chinese Communist armies was in these times constantly considered a danger." [7] And Raymond Aron observed that "the notion that the various Communist parties at that time were receiving and following similar instructions from Moscow was true, or nearly so. The presentation of a worldwide conspiracy, its threats woven in Moscow and stretching throughout the world, was never so close to reality as in the last years of Stalinism." [8] But quite apart from Stalinism, Acheson was primarily concerned with the impact a Communist victory in Indochina would have upon the uncertain situation in Asia and on opinion at home.

By a kind of symmetry, changes occurring in United States policy vis-à-vis Indochina that winter were being matched by changes in relations between Ho Chi Minh and the two great Communist states. One of the

---

* Acheson to Jessup. Top-secret memorandum, July 18, 1949. Reprinted in *Nomination of Jessup.* Senate Foreign Relations Committee, p. 603. On October 12, 1949, in an executive session with the Senate Foreign Relations Committee, Acheson was still of the opinion that "We will get nowhere, I think, by supporting the French as a colonial power against Indo-China." Quoted in Philip C. Jessup, *The Birth of Nations* (New York: Columbia University Press, 1974), p. 170.

first fruits of the summit meeting between Stalin and Mao that took place in Moscow from December 1949 to February 1950 was the decision to recognize Ho Chi Minh's government. Peking announced its recognition of Hanoi on January 18 and Moscow on January 30. Such immediate recognition could only appear as a blow to the French, and it confirmed, as far as that was needed, Acheson's belief that Soviet strategy was focusing on Asia and that Ho was one of its agents. The Soviet and Chinese recognitions, Acheson said, "should remove any illusion as to the 'nationalist' nature of Ho Chi Minh's aims and reveal Ho in his true colors as the mortal enemy of native independence in Indochina." *

Prompted perhaps by the impact that this new situation was likely to have on both Vietnamese and world opinion, the French Assembly on January 29 finally approved legislation giving autonomy to the state of Vietnam within the French Union. Any hope Acheson may have had of getting Paris to move ahead with creating truly independent regimes for Laos, Cambodia, and Vietnam were dashed by Paris's next move.** Taking advantage of the favorable turn in United States policy, the French Foreign Office now reported that, the French position in Vietnam being very grave, France was considering recognizing the regime in Peking as a means of "getting a line" on Ho Chi Minh, and would do so *unless* France could get military help from the United States equal in significance to that with which China was reputedly supplying Ho! Paris also made clear that it had no intention of granting any additional independence to the Bao Dai regime; and Jessup met first sullen and then open hostility from French authorities when he spoke of the "independence" of the Associated States without adding the qualification "within the French Union." 9

Taking advantage of the French ratification of the Elysée agreements according autonomy to the Associated States, Acheson worked hard all that spring—with Nehru, with Carlos P. Romulo, the Philippine ambassador, and with other Asian leaders—to secure their recognition of the Associated States, but to little avail. He informed Ambassador Bonnet on

---

* *Pentagon Papers*, DOD edition, *op. cit.*, p. A-49. Philip C. Jessup, who was Acheson's special ambassador on mission and in Vietnam at the time, remarks that "he would not now agree that the Kremlin's recognition of Ho proved that he was not a nationalist, the sense being that he was a Communist stooge." Jessup, *op. cit.*, p. 182. But unfortunately neither Jessup nor anyone else with the possible exception of Kennan disagreed with Acheson *at the time.*

** Typical of the situation that Acheson faced was an exchange with Ambassador Bonnet on February 16, 1950. Acheson reflected to Bonnet that "he was extremely fearful in the absence of some further action on the part of the French that the reluctance of the Asiatic powers to recognize the Associated States would persist." Bonnet suavely replied, "How unfortunate for the belief to grow in the minds of the Vietnamese that they had not achieved in fact a very high degree of independence. . . ."

March 13 that it was difficult to secure such recognition because the Asians did not seem convinced of French good faith, to which Bonnet replied that it was difficult for the French government to ask Frenchmen to give up their lives in Indochina if they could not feel that they were doing it for France or the French Union.[10]

Having concluded that American strategy should not sustain the loss of Indochina, Acheson was now prepared to treat the French effort as a legitimate part of containment, whether or not additional concessions to Bao Dai were forthcoming, for a new element had entered Acheson's thinking. What if the French buckled or were defeated? Who would replace them? The loss of Vietnam would be like opening a cork on a bottle. Communism would flood out all over Southeast Asia, and militarily America was in no position to react.

When Acheson appeared before the Senate Foreign Relations Committee with Jessup in March 1950 to report on the latter's trip to Asia, Acheson explained the difficulty of providing military equipment for both the French and the Vietnamese forces.

We want to be very careful in what we do for the Indo-Chinese that we do not substitute for what the French are doing. . . . We do not want to get into a position where the French say, "You take over; we aren't able to go ahead on this." *We want the French to stay there* [emphasis added]. . . . The Commonwealth have got to really carry their burdens in Burma, the French have got to carry theirs in Indochina, and we are willing to help, but not to substitute for them.[11]

So while negotiations continued to dither along about how far the department could push the French without being accused of trying to drive a wedge between France and its Associated States,[12] Acheson was already viewing the French as playing an indispensable role in Vietnam, one which we would do well not to undermine lest we be handed the hot potato. Acheson was saying that there were limits to American power and that we had better not create vacuums which we ourselves were not in a position to fill. That was an important shift. Hitherto the United States had worked for independence; now Acheson was saying that if the colonial powers were not encouraged to retain their responsibility, then the area would collapse. "The United States can't take it over and we can't allow them to walk out on us. We need every bit of help that we can possibly get." [13]

This position puts quite a different significance on U.S. support for the French than is customarily recognized. Far from wanting the French out of Indochina, Acheson was now rather desperately concerned should the French, like the British, pull out. To underscore his concern, Acheson returned to it again: ". . . what we want to do, as I said, is to get them to see that they cannot turn the problem over to us. They are in there, and they have to go in there deeper and stay as long as anybody stays. We want more participation from the dominions. . . . We are not the people who have responsibility there. . . ." [14] Acheson showed here a striking recognition of the strategic situation that would confront us in 1954 after France admitted defeat. Unlike Dulles, Acheson had no illusions about the United States being able to fill the vacuum in Southeast Asia. It is only partly true to say, therefore, that Acheson felt constrained from exerting more pressure on Paris to liberalize its treatment of the Associated States out of fear of upsetting French concessions concerning Germany. Such concessions were important and, in the context of the fragile political situation in France, almost any additional pressure upon Schuman was bound to be seized upon by the Gaullists (and the Communists) as evidence of American interference in French affairs. But it must be kept in mind that, rightly or wrongly, Acheson now viewed Indochina as part of a worldwide struggle in which the French were bearing a heavy burden. The new emphasis was quickly evident. A new study group, sent to Vietnam under R. Allen Griffin, recommended in favor of military and technical assistance. In April, the Joint Chiefs of Staff recommended in favor of military assistance. On May 1, 1950, President Truman approved of a $10-million military assistance item for Indochina.

On May 7, the day Acheson learned of the Schuman coal and steel proposal, he also cabled the State Department to start the flow of American military supplies to Indochina. It was not a quid pro quo because, of course, Acheson had already made that decision; it was more of a token of America's desire to cooperate wherever the interests of the two countries could be mutually and constructively advanced. It did not mean the end of Acheson's effort to get the French to turn over a larger share of responsibility to the Vietnamese; that struggle never ceased,* but it had to take second place to the critical strategic demands that Acheson felt the West faced in Asia. Little did he reckon that within six weeks the full weight of that burden would come crushing down upon the United States when the North Koreans attacked across the 38th parallel in Korea. All his anxieties about the unprepared state of Western defenses in Asia would be fully confirmed.

Japan

Another point in Asia at which Acheson was determinedly striving for progress in the spring of 1950 was Japan. In February 1948, George Kennan had recommended that the United States should

---

* Acheson's subsequent efforts to persuade the French to give independence to Vietnam are discussed in Chapter 20.

devise policies toward Japan which would assure the security of that country from Communist penetration and domination as well as from military attack by the Soviet Union and would permit Japan's economic potential to become once again an important force in the affairs of the area, conducive to peace and stability.[15]

It was Kennan's view, similar to ideas he held about the desirability of neutralizing Germany, that a new, stable Japan could eventually be neutralized as part of a Soviet–American understanding; but in the absence of any essential trust or desire for such agreement on either side, Kennan's views were no more likely to prevail on Japan than they had on Germany.

By the time Acheson took over as Secretary in January 1949, the logic in favor of restoring Japan as a makeweight to the Communist conquest of China was compelling. In fact the existence of Japan under U.S. control was viewed by Acheson as easing significantly the dislocation caused by the passing of China into the Soviet orbit. As long as the United States retained Japan, it could view with a certain amount of equanimity what was happening on the Chinese mainland.

Acheson had no intention of rearming Japan; rather, Japan would be encouraged to regain its economic and political independence to the extent necessary "to preserve what remained of the Yalta status quo." [16] Specifically, the appropriate strategy seemed to be to put an end to the state of war still existing between Japan and the wartime victors "and then to conclude a military alliance with Japan, enabling the United States to keep its forces on Japanese soil more or less indefinitely. This would perpetuate the existing situation, but it would also mark a departure in that the way would now be opened to Japan's eventually becoming a power, thus cooperating with the United States to maintain what was left of the Yalta balance rather than being a passive captive of the system." [17]

Why was a treaty needed at all? First, to end the occupation status so as to restore Japan to its full place in the international community, and secondly, to put U.S. relations with Japan on a more normal basis. Since it would be difficult to achieve such an arrangement and also include Russia and Communist China in the conference, a great deal of attention had to be given to how the matter of a peace treaty for Japan could be ararnged. Acheson raised it for the first time with British Foreign Minister Bevin in September 1949, and both men agreed on the urgent need for such a treaty. But before Acheson could go any further into it with America's wartime allies or the Japanese, he first had to gain acceptance for his strategy from General MacArthur and from the Pentagon, which did not want to yield up the military advantages of the occupation status. Acheson argued that the occupation relationship was bound to deteriorate and that the Japanese could not be encouraged to assume an active responsibility for their own destiny without having their independence re-stored to them. The military, including MacArthur, proposed that Japan be given back its political and economic sovereignty while remaining mili-tarily occupied. At a meeting in the department on April 24, 1950, be-tween Acheson, Louis Johnson, General Omar Bradley, and the other military chiefs, Acheson tried to reason with them. He argued that a Pentagon proposal that the State Department negotiate political and eco-nomic terms of peace while leaving the military occupation unchanged was unrealistic. It was the State Department's view, Acheson explained, that under the guise of guaranteeing Japan's security (there was no ques-tion of rearming Japan) a treaty signed by friendly powers would afford ample reason for maintaining United States military bases and rights necessary to defend Japan against aggression. A security treaty embody-ing such arrangements would be signed with Japan simultaneously with the coming into effect of the peace treaty. The Joint Chiefs of Staff reg-istered their opposition on the exaggerated grounds that such a treaty meant abrogating all of America's rights and pulling out of both Japan and Okinawa.[18] Louis Johnson opposed the strategy on the ground that existing Communist exploitation of popular feelings against granting bases would succeed in defeating them. Acheson tried to explain that it was precisely because the recent Sino–Soviet agreement called for a peace treaty with Japan that the United States could not afford to be caught flat-footed. MacArthur was reported opposed to such a treaty on the grounds that it would reduce United States forces to token size, and since it was "only a propaganda move" he did not see that it was necessary. All efforts, Acheson explained, would be made to secure what the United States needed militarily, "but please for the military not to demand more than was needed." All to no avail. Johnson and the Joint Chiefs rejected Acheson's reasoning and proposed a moratorium on the subject until July 1 pending discussions with MacArthur.

It is argued that,

viewed from Moscow, these trends in United States policy might have seemed exactly as events in China were impressing American officials in Washington. The proposed peace treaty with Japan without Soviet and Chinese Communist participation and public discussions about the desirability of resurrecting Jap-anese power might well have struck the Russian leaders as evidence that the United States was pursuing a policy calculated to alter the Yalta status quo by encouraging the resurgence of Japanese militarism and imperialism.[19]

Against this so-called hostile trend in United States policy must be set the withdrawal of American forces from South Korea without any as-surance of a balance between the armies of the two Koreas and the virtual absence in Japan of American ground forces capable of threatening anyone. (When the test came in Korea, the United States would suffer a period of humiliating defeats.) Also against this thesis must be set the very deliberate effort Acheson had made to detach America from any provocative alliances with Chiang Kai-shek on Formosa.* This gesture, made at enormous domestic political cost by the Administration, can hardly be considered part of a strategy of militarism and imperialism. So-called "trends" were not trends at all. Acheson's proposed peace treaty was equally designed to end a vacuum by restoring to the Japanese a stake in preserving the status quo in East Asia, which had been badly upset by the Communist assumption of power in China. Neither then nor later did Acheson intend to restore Japanese military power. What he could not afford to do was to permit Japan to become a pawn in a further extension of Soviet influence. Unfortunately he was too late in taking the necessary precautions against a genuine military threat—that of Soviet-inspired aggression against South Korea.** As we have seen, Acheson had defined America's defense perimeter in such a way as to make clear that the United States did not intend to threaten either Russia or mainland China, and it is hard to imagine Japan at such an early stage in its postwar recovery constituting a threat. What Acheson had failed to anticipate was that the other side would employ aggression to exploit the vacuum that existed in South Korea and the shock that it would represent to the still fragile Asian balance. It seems more realistic to see that attack as a

---

* After examining the record, one scholar wrote that both the Chinese and the American governments on the eve of Korea were seeking to consolidate their political positions in Asia, "but neither government was avowedly seeking an international confrontation despite their ideological differences . . . both governments were apparently working toward a détente prior to the war. Within the framework of the Asian balance of power, their policies were subtly geared toward coexistence. . . ." Unfortunately the Korean War was destined to shatter this promising easing of tensions for which Acheson was striving. G. H. Poteat, *Strategic Intelligence and National Security: A Case Study of the Korean War* (Ph.D. dissertation, Washington University, December 1973), p. 23.

** The allegation that the prospect of an American security treaty with Japan prompted the Soviets to support the North Korean attack is badly undercut by Khrushchev's memoirs. Khrushchev reports that Kim Il-sung proposed the invasion and that Stalin saw no reason not to give him all the support necessary. "In my opinion, no real Communist would have tried to dissuade Kim Il-sung from his compelling desire to liberate.South Korea from Syngman Rhee and from reactionary American influence. To have done so would have contradicted the Communist view of the world. I don't condemn Stalin for encouraging Kim. On the contrary, I would have made the same decision myself if I had been in his place." Nikita S. Khrushchev, *Khrushchev Remembers* (New York: Bantam Books, 1970), p. 401. Later, of course, when Kim Il-sung failed to conquer South Korea and the Americans intervened, Stalin cagily liquidated Soviet involvement. *Ibid.,* p. 404.

product of Stalin's opportunistic calculations than of any real and present response to the danger of a Japanese–American alliance.

The U.S. defensive perimeter in the Pacific had been established so as to conform to what military power was available. The estimate that we had, Acheson told the Senate Foreign Relations Committee on January 13, 1950, was "that South Korea could now take care of any trouble that was started solely by North Korea, but it could not take care of any invasion which was either started by the Chinese Communists or powerfully supported by them or by the Soviet Union." [20] Had the United States the forces, it might have been able to give South Korea more support, but as it stood, Acheson told the senators, we could only hope to take action through the United Nations. While the situation in Korea was becoming more tense (upon return from his study mission to Asia, Ambassador Jessup warned both publicly and in private that the Cold War was in fact becoming a hot war in Korea), there was very little Washington could do, and it was relying upon the assurance by American military advisers in Seoul that, if attacked, the South Korean army would be able to defend itself. Unfortunately, about this time the Soviet Union began supplying Kim Il-sung with the material requisite to an attack. [21] In a sense, South Korea had been neutralized as a buffer between the Soviet and American spheres in East Asia. Had it been permitted to remain in that status, the Cold War might never have taken the extreme turn that it did.

In Acheson's campaign that spring to gain the backing of the Europeans, the Congress, and the American people for a larger military commitment to undergird the strategy of balancing or containing Communist expansion, Korea had not figured very prominently. Still, the fate that was about to overtake Korea seems to justify what he feared might happen in Europe or Yugoslavia or Iran or Japan should the United States fail to cover its defensive commitments with an adequate military base. It has been argued that the situation of South Korea was unique—that the United States had failed to make clear its intention to defend Korea and that the triumph of Communist forces on the mainland made the fate of Korea a foregone conclusion. It has also been argued that U.S. moves in Japan prompted a Soviet pre-emptive action. Judging from Khrushchev's testimony, it was American moves that were essentially defensive and consolidationist in the face of a Soviet willingness to risk aggression in Korea and elsewhere. [22] However, the most meticulous and authoritative study shows that the North Koreans were strongly motivated to eliminate the anti–Communist regime in South Korea and that they were armed, trained, and closely advised by Soviet military officers. [23] The fact that Acheson and his advisers may have failed to adequately assess the Communist temptation to seize a relatively unguarded pawn hardly exculpates

Moscow and Pyongyang from a blatant act of aggression. Had Acheson stressed the American commitment to South Korea he would have drawn attacks from his critics, "and why not defend Formosa, too?" and found himself forced to compromise his policy of disengaging America from involvement in the Chinese civil war.

Contrary to Kennan's strictures against the militarization of American diplomacy, the opportunism exemplified by the North Korean aggression was precisely the type of situation against which Acheson did not think a political or purely moral commitment would suffice to deter Communist probes. Nor did the Europeans, who more than ever after the onset of the Korean War insisted that the tangible presence of American troops was indispensable to their security. It must be remembered that it was not apparent in 1950 what has been argued since: that before his death Stalin was preparing to alter the Soviet policy in the direction of moderation.[24] It seems more likely that it was the outcome of U.S. intervention in Korea and the subsequent stimulous the Korean War gave to American and European military preparations and political cooperation that had more to do with the moderating of Soviet foreign policy by 1952. Stalin's intentions were still a riddle wrapped in an enigma.

NSC 68

The other component of Acheson's campaign to beef up the credibility of America's commitments was National Security Council Paper No. 68— NSC 68. One may remember that on January 31, 1950, as part of his decision authorizing the development of the H-bomb, and with a view to minimizing the nation's dependence on atomic weapons should war occur, Truman had also instructed the Secretaries of State and Defense to undertake a re-examination of American diplomatic objectives and of the effect of pursuing those objectives upon our strategic plans. Acheson had immediately appointed a State Department team consisting of Paul Nitze and George Kennan to meet with representatives of the Secretary of Defense and of the Joint Chiefs of Staff. A split immediately emerged between Nitze and Kennan over the interpretation to be put upon Soviet intentions and capabilities. Kennan did not believe that the Soviet leadership had any real intention of risking war with the United States. Even their probing actions, Kennan argued, were likely to remain at a submilitary level.* Nitze and the others placed greater weight on Russia's

---

* Kennan sums up this debate as follows. My views conflicted, furthermore, with the highly inflated estimates of Russian conventional military strength that had already become ingrained . . . in the official assessment of NATO needs, and with the resulting belief on our part that we could never meet the Russians successfully on nonnuclear ground. They conflicted finally with the growing tendency in Washington . . .

potential military capabilities. By 1954, they estimated, the Soviet Union would have not just a nuclear capability but a capability for both general and piecemeal aggression, any one of which could undermine the alliance and weaken the American and European will to resist unless something was done to offset it. Even if the Soviet Union had no intention of risking all-out war, it still confronted the United States with the challenge of limited and indirect aggression.

Charles Bohlen, the other ranking Soviet expert, was in Paris at this time, and for a while Acheson considered bringing him back to participate in the deliberations.[25] When Bohlen saw the NSC 68 paper later, he expressed the same reservations as Kennan against viewing Soviet policy as anything more than a determination to spread the Communist system throughout the world. Like Kennan, Bohlen was convinced that the Soviet Union, as far as its actions went, was largely motivated by its interests as a national state. By contrast with Kennan, however, Bohlen was gratified by the basic recommendation "that American military power be increased so as to be more commensurate with commitments forced on us in the world."[26] He also felt in reading NSC 68 that there was absolutely no chance that its recommendations for huge increases in military spending would be adopted by the Congress.[27]

Acheson, who took satisfaction that the NSC 68 deliberations were the most searching ever devoted to the relationship between diplomacy and strategy, became somewhat exasperated with the debate. Kennan, Acheson wrote later, argued that Stalin placed the survival of the regime and "communism in one country" ahead of world revolution or world conquest. "We did not dissent from this," Acheson writes, "but pointed out that, assuming the proper semantic adjustment, the effect of their point bore on the degree of risk of all-out war which the Soviet Government would run in probing a weak spot for concessions. Granted that they might not go as recklessly far as the Japanese . . . the difference seemed to me more theoretical than real in devising courses necessary to eliminate the weak spots which so tempted Moscow to probe our resolution and that of our allies."[28] Little did Acheson suspect how soon events in Korea would test that hypothesis.

Kennan also objected to the notion of reducing "vast and infinitely complex considerations" into a manageable paper, "cleared" by superiors and serviceable as an easily communicable design of American means and objectives. As a professional diplomat, Kennan rightly feared that such a

---

to base our own plans and calculations solely on the *capabilities* of a potential adversary, assuming him to be desirous of doing anything he could to bring injury to us, and to exclude from consideration, as something unsusceptible to exact determination, the whole question of the adversary's real *intentions. Memoirs, op. cit.,* p. 501. Emphasis added.

paper was likely to introduce into policy-making "a new rigidity that limits flexible response to unexpected developments and thus affects future developments as well." [29] Kennan feared that too much emphasis on the military side would damage the possibilities of a diplomatic ending of the Cold War. Unlike Kennan, Acheson did not agree that the requirements of modern diplomacy could ignore the military and strategic dimension. Even if Soviet capabilities at the moment were at an all-time low, they were scheduled to grow very rapidly, partly in response to NATO, partly in response to the greater availability of resources after the lean postwar years. Besides, if our allies were to be confident of our intention to defend them, alliance diplomacy required a greater level of preparation in time of peace. Kennan tended to dismiss the current demands of America's European allies as those of self-serving importunists.[30] In Asia, as in Europe, Kennan had his mind on an overall East–West settlement which would reduce Soviet pressures and European demands upon the United States—a settlement the basis of which Acheson simply could not see.

In the end Kennan's positions were brushed aside and the final recommendations reflected Acheson's view that if the United States was to achieve a balance between commitments and capabilities a much larger military appropriation would be needed. In the words of one of NSC 68's principal authors, it recommended "an immediate and large-scale build-up in our military and general strength and that of our allies with the intention of righting the power balance and in the hope that through means *other than all-out war* [emphasis added] we could induce a change in the nature of the Soviet system." [31] Although these recommendations were accepted by the President as the basis for discussion and went on the agenda of the National Security Council as NSC Paper No. 68, there was practically no expectation that the spending levels envisaged would ever be approved. Had the Korean War not occurred, it seems quite likely that the enormous military increases called for in NSC 68 would have remained a dead letter.

As in the case of his Asian strategy, Acheson was hoping to establish some basis for American foreign policy that would enable it to hold until such time as the Soviet Union might show evidence of easing its pressure on the West. Little did Acheson imagine that the very kind of aggression against which NSC 68 was designed to function would make possible its implementation. Had there been no aggression in Korea, there would have been no $30-billion nor even a $20-billion military budget. A ceiling of $15 or $18 billion would have been more likely.

CHAPTER

15

THE KOREAN WAR

SATURDAY, JUNE 24, 1950, President Truman was vacationing at his home in Independence, Missouri. Acheson was at his farm in Maryland. Secretary of Defense Johnson and General Bradley, chairman of the Joint Chiefs of Staff, were just returning from an inspection trip to the Far East. Although danger signals had been flashing all spring along the 38th parallel in Korea, few believed that war was really imminent. Korea was, to be sure, on the list of danger spots along with Berlin, Turkey, and Iran, "but not among the favorites." * Korea had also been included among the countries studied in connection with NSC 68. But it was only in light of the North Korean assault that roared out of the predawn in the faraway Land of the Morning Calm that Acheson and his advisers recognized the adverse political reverberations that would follow should South Korea be lost. Suddenly America's strategic and political stake in Korea was emblazoned across the horizon. Just as the Soviet gambit had been delicately modulated to exploit the political chips left uncovered by the unsuspecting Americans, so Acheson sensed the bitter choice which faced the United States—either to acquiesce in the North Korean aggression or give a credible demonstration of America's determination to resist aggression and uphold the principle of collective security.

As the decision-makers gathered in Washington the next day, it became apparent that the most significant feature of their reaction was the emotional quality of their dedication to "no appeasement." The most meaningful international experiences of Acheson's generation had been the failure of the League of Nations and the Japanese march into Manchuria. The stigma, but even more the lesson, of Munich was too recent

---

* Acheson, *Present at the Creation* (New York: Norton, 1969), p. 405. Yet Korea presented the one situation in which the Soviet Union could most safely risk aggression by proxy. North Koreans attacking South Koreans could be characterized as a civil war which one could well imagine would have considerable appeal to the Kremlin.

to be forgotten by the generation that had witnessed the bitter fruit of appeasement. No member of a Western democracy who had lived through the moral nightmare and felt the stultifying shame of impotence as the dictators marched into one hapless nation after another could escape the comparison with Korea. If America was in a far better position to react than Britain and France had been in 1938, it was because American society was more united in its attitude toward the Soviet Union. There was overwhelming agreement among the majority of all classes that the Soviet Union represented a moral, political, and military threat to what America stood for. The *New Republic*, the *Nation*, and the *Progressive*, all of which had been lukewarm to Acheson's Cold War policies, swung in behind the Administration's decision to resist aggression. Even Henry Wallace quit the Progressive Party saying, "I am on the side of my country and the United Nations." * Some wanted to go further than others in meeting that threat and some preferred to retreat into a "fortress America" strategy, but virtually all Americans shared a distrust of Soviet intentions and a revulsion against aggression. Few Americans doubted that what was happening in Korea was a particularly open and brutal form of aggression. They were not alone. Bohlen reports that when told of the American decision to intervene, Foreign Minister Schuman's eyes filled with tears. "Thank God," he said, "this will not be a repetition of the past." [1]

Then, too, as a status quo power confronted by unprecedented levels of change, the United States had made it a point of national interest that it would not accept violent change imposed from without.** Had Communist probing taken a more ambiguous form, the American reaction might not have been so swift. But direct aggression across a frontier was bound to evoke an almost instinctive reaction of horror. As one participant in the week's deliberations put it: "The real basis of the Korean decision had almost nothing to do with Korea. It had to do with aggression." [2]

At this moment of stress other expressions of moral righteousness came surging forth. On the night of the first Blair House meeting, Glenn Paige reports, President Truman sat on a window seat and said softly: "We can't let the UN down." Acheson, less awe-stricken and less given to incanta-

---

* Alonzo L. Hamby, *Beyond the New Deal: Harry S. Truman and American Liberalism* (New York: Columbia University Press, 1973), pp. 404–405. "By August, Wallace was expressing his willingness to use the atomic bomb if the battlefield situation necessitated it. By November, he was advocating a large-scale American rearmament program, bitterly condemning the USSR, and abandoning his earlier support of the admission of Red China to the U.N." Quoted in Hamby, p. 405.

** This condition of United States foreign policy had been set forth in the Truman Doctrine. "The world is not static and the status quo is not sacred. But we cannot allow changes in the status quo in violation of the charter of the United Nations by methods such as coercion, or by such subterfuges as political infiltration."

Acheson with America's key European representatives. May, 1949. Averell Harriman, European head of E.C.A.; Dean Acheson; John McCloy, U.S. High Commissioner in Germany; David Bruce, U.S. Ambassador to France.

Foreign Ministers Conference, Paris, May, 1949. Robert Schuman, French Foreign Minister; Andrei Vishinsky, Soviet Foreign Minister; Dean Acheson; and British Foreign Secretary Ernest Bevin. At a dinner given by French President Vincent Auriol.

George F. Kennan (left) and members of the Policy Planning Staff. 1948–1949.

Acheson conversing with a Soviet Commandant at Berlin.

Weekend Retreat: Alice and Dean Acheson relaxing on the lawn of their farm "Harewood," in Sandy Springs, Md.

Each cultivated a garden at "Harewood" in a spirit of friendly competition. Here Dean admires his wife's success.

Dean Acheson found in furniture-making a satisfying outlet for his love of practical work and a revivifying break from his duties as Secretary of State.

Maintaining effective relations with key Congressional figures was as important as keeping up good relations with foreign powers. President Truman signs the foreign military aid bill, July 27, 1950, while Senator Millard Tydings (Md.); Acheson; William Foster, Deputy ECA Administrator; E. T. Dickinson, Assistant to Joint Secretaries of Defense; Senator Tom Connally (Tex.); and Senator Alexander Wiley (Wis.) look on.

The American delegation at the United Nations, gathered for a planning session on September 18, 1950, with only Acheson absent: (left to right) Henry Cabot Lodge, Jr.; Mrs. Eleanor Roosevelt; Warren Austin; John J. Sparkman; and John Foster Dulles. Behind them, the alternate delegates, left to right, are: John Hickerson, Assistant Secretary of State; Ernest A. Gross; Benjamin V. Cohen; Mrs. Edith Sampson; and John C. Ross.

Acheson with Special Ambassador Philip C. Jessup.

German rearmament meant difficult negotiations with the French in Washington, D.C., October 12, 1950. From left to right: Dean Acheson; Maurice Petsche, French Finance Minister; George C. Marshall, Secretary of Defense; Jules Moch, French Defense Minister; and John Snyder, Secretary of the Treasury.

President Truman and Acheson conferring upon his return from the Brussels meeting of the NATO Council, December 21, 1950.

General Dwight D. Eisenhower, newly designated Commander of NATO forces, confers with Acheson, January 4, 1951.

With Mrs. Franklin D. Roosevelt, member of the American Delegation to the United Nations.

Acheson en route to a Foreign Ministers conference with some of his principal lieutenants. Left to right: George Perkins, Assistant Secretary, European Affairs; Philip C. Jessup; Acheson; Senator John Sherman Cooper (R–Ky.), bipartisan representative.

ACME PHOTO

UNITED PRESS—ACME PHOTO

Left: Dean and Alice Acheson on a brief Mediterranean cruise aboard the S.S. Independence en route to a 1951 Foreign Ministers meeting.

Above: Acheson presiding over the signing of the Japanese Peace Treaty by Shigeru Yoshida, Prime Minister of Japan. San Francisco, September 10, 1951.

Right: John Foster Dulles and Dean Acheson testifying before the Senate Foreign Relations Committee on the Japanese Peace Treaty and the Pacific Defense Treaties. January 21, 1952.

Acheson signs the Japanese Security Treaty in the presence of John Foster Dulles and (left to right) Senators John Sparkman (Ala.), Alexander Smith (N.J.), Bourke Hickenlooper (Iowa), Abraham Ribicoff (Conn.), and Alexander Wiley (Wis.).

Anglo-American Meeting. Washington, D.C., January, 1952. Seated, left to right: Sir Anthony Eden, British Foreign Minister; Sir Winston Churchill; President Truman; Acheson; John R. Snyder, Secretary of the Treasury; Robert A. Lovett, Secretary of Defense. Standing, left to right: Ambassador Walter Gifford; General Omar N. Bradley; Sir Oliver Franks; Lord Cherwell; Lord Ismay; and Averell Harriman.

Sir Oliver Franks, the British Ambassador, and Dean Acheson.

President Truman greeting Acheson upon his return from the Lisbon meeting of the NATO Council, February 27, 1952.

A bit of friendly repartee as President Truman presents Acheson with his Cabinet chair.

The elder statesman. A meeting in the White House with President Lyndon B. Johnson and his principal advisers. Seated beside Acheson are George Ball and Dean Rusk. Across from Rusk is Charles Bohlen.

tions, had already made up his mind about a number of things even before the conferees met. On that Saturday evening, when word had barely begun to filter in, on the President's authorization he had instructed the American delegate to convene an emergency meeting of the United Nations Security Council for the next day to take up the invasion of the Republic of Korea by the armed forces of North Korea. It is argued that Acheson's resort to the United Nations was largely adventitious given his anti–UN bias.[3] If both Dean Rusk (Assistant Secretary for the Far East and former Assistant Secretary for United Nations Affairs) and John Hickerson (Assistant Secretary for United Nations Affairs) had not been present at the State Department that evening, Acheson might never have taken the United Nations route. This hypothesis seems to rest upon an erroneous notion of Acheson's skepticism about the United Nations and a sad underestimation of his ability to perceive the advantages of proceeding through it. The United Nations cannot be a substitute for power, but in this instance Acheson expected the United States to provide the power; all he wanted was UN sanction.

Like other American officials, Acheson had little doubt that the Soviet leaders must have given the North Koreans the go-ahead signal, a point of view shared by both of America's top-ranking Soviet experts, Kennan and Bohlen.[4] He shared the consensus that the Soviet Union was using its Korean satellite as a pawn and was probably not ready itself to risk a global war. He viewed the attack as either a probing operation, designed to exploit a soft spot, or a diversionary action, designed to tie down American forces, that might be followed by moves at other critical points around the periphery of the Soviet bloc.[5]

In the past, Acheson had always insisted that the United States must not put itself in the position of provoking war with the Russians. No American interest, Acheson argued, justified getting into a shooting war with the Soviet Union. In the quietness of his office that Sunday afternoon Acheson had it in his power to alter that perspective. Instead, Acheson chose to stick to his strategic perspective and avoid branding the Soviets as the authors of the tragic drama unfolding in faraway Korea.*

---

* "This whole idea that war is inevitable," he told Charles Collingwood in an interview that summer, "seems to me to be completely wrong and very vicious. I remember looking back over the history of the United States not long ago and reading the terrible things that were said in the 1850s about the irrepressible conflict. It's talk like that, talk of an irrepressible conflict, talk about war being inevitable which tends to make it so. War isn't inevitable. It doesn't have to come. If we go ahead doing the things which we have to do here then we have our best chance for peace." Television interview of Dean Acheson by Charles Collingwood, Edward R. Murrow, Bancroft Griffing, September 10, 1950. State Department Release #922, September 8, 1950.

Without waiting for the evening's deliberations, Acheson had the department send off to Moscow a note asking the Soviet government to disavow its "responsibility for this unprovoked and irresponsible act," * and to use its influence to bring about a withdrawal of North Korean forces. The note was also deliberately designed to relieve the Soviets of any immediate concern about a possible confrontation with the United States. In their reply of June 29, far from being threatening, the Soviets spoke only of the "impermissibility of interference of foreign powers in the internal affairs of Korea." [6] On Sunday evening at the first Blair House meeting to discuss the matter, Truman expressed the view that Soviet leaders were gambling that the United States would do nothing in Korea, and therefore expected to achieve a victory by default; ** nevertheless, he was inclined to agree with Acheson that nothing ought to be done to provoke the Russians into a war.

Thus from the very outset it was agreed that the utmost caution ought to be exercised in any operations against North Korea which might have as their consequence the bringing of the Soviet Union into the war or tempting them to attack somewhere else. Similarly, on June 27, at a conference with the congressional leaders convened by the President, Acheson pointed out that the USSR had carefully not committed itself as yet and that we were avoiding publicly engaging Soviet prestige at this time. By deciding to treat the North Korean aggression as a local war, by limiting its definition of the *casus belli* to a proxy adversary, Acheson established the Cold War precedent for fighting limited war in lieu of general war.†

Knowing how dreadfully weak and vulnerable the non–Communist forces were at practically every point around the periphery of the Communist bloc, Acheson's desire that nothing be done to trigger an unde-

---

* Although dispatched on June 25, it was not delivered until June 27. There is no clear explanation for the delay. Glenn D. Paige, *The Korean Decision* (New York: Free Press, 1968), p. 127, fn. 83. The note carefully avoided charging the Soviet Union with direct complicity in launching the North Korean invasion.

** Harry S Truman, *Memoirs*, Vol II, *Years of Trial and Hope* (Garden City, N.Y.: Doubleday, 1956), p. 335. Some measure of the seriousness of the crisis which gripped the decision-makers: "Although their estimates of Soviet intentions at this time did not bring them to the firm conclusion that World War III was imminent, nevertheless [they] did consider [that Soviet moves] at other critical points [might be imminent]. Paige, *op. cit.*, pp. 133-134.

† Again in a memorandum to Paul Nitze outlining his views on the future course to be followed in Korea, Acheson proposed to limit the operation to the 38th parallel. "As to widening the theater of operations by attacks on Chinese territory generally— as against attacks on forces coming in—I should think this unwise as an invitation to the Russians to join the Chinese under their treaty. . . ." The principal source from which the danger of general war came was Russia, which explains why Acheson was so insistent upon doing nothing which would provoke a Soviet riposte.

sired response from the Soviet Union was accepted by everyone, including the military chiefs. As General Bradley later told the Senate committee investigating the relief of MacArthur, "We accepted a limited challenge . . . with the hopes that it would be limited to Korea and would not develop into a world war." *

Unfortunately, the hostility which could not be projected against the Soviet Union seemed now, by some psychological mechanism, to be transferred to Red China, and the distinction between China and the general phenomenon of Communist aggression became blurred. As a result, Peking, which may not have even been aware of the impending aggression (Khrushchev says it was) and for whom it may have constituted an undesirable event, became the object of renewed American distrust and hostility. Acheson seems not to have been aware of the extent to which his judgments about Red China may have begun to suffer from the general lack of precision in distinguishing between China and the actual perpetrators of the aggression in Korea.

As part of the phenomenon, Acheson was almost immediately under pressure to bring the island outpost of Formosa within the American defense perimeter.** That the decision to defend Formosa was now conjoined in Acheson's mind with the fact of aggression in Korea is evident in the statement he prepared for Truman announcing the decision to put the Seventh Fleet in the Formosa Straits.

The attack upon Korea makes it plain beyond all doubt that Communism has passed beyond the use of subversion to conquer independent nations and will now use armed invasion and war. It has defied the orders of the Security Council of the United Nations issued to preserve international peace and security. In these circumstances the occupation of Formosa by Communist forces would be a direct threat to the security of the Pacific area and to the United States forces performing their lawful and necessary fuctions in that area. Accordingly I have ordered the Seventh Fleet to prevent any attack upon Formosa.

---

* General Omar N. Bradley, *Hearings to Conduct an Inquiry into the Military Situation in the Far East,* Senate Committees on the Armed Services and Foreign Relations, 82nd Congress, 1st Session, Part II, p. 1070 (hereinafter referred to as the *MacArthur Hearings*). By the same token, General Bradley also shared the civilian point of view that the Soviet move in Korea was a "softening-up operation" the first stop on a "timetable" of aggressions the final destination of which, if uninterrupted, would be World War III. *Ibid.,* Part II, pp. 896, 942, 971.

** The military case for interposing the Seventh Fleet was conjoined in Acheson's mind with the criticism he would face should the Administration decide to defend the Korean peninsula with American forces and *not* do anything about Formosa. "Once the United States decided to defend South Korea, which had also been placed beyond the 'defensive perimeter,' it would be increasingly difficult to explain why Taiwan should not be defended." Warren I. Cohen, *America's Response to China* (New York: John Wiley & Sons, 1971), p. 202.

As corollary of this action I am calling upon the Chinese Government on Formosa to cease all air and sea operations against the mainland. The Seventh Fleet will see that this is done. The determination of the future status of Formosa must await the restoration of security in the Pacific, a peace settlement with Japan, or consideration by the United Nations.

If Acheson had hoped to avoid antagonizing the People's Republic of China (PRC) by limiting the American role to that of neutralizing the Straits, the final sentence could scarcely have been reassuring to Peking because it called for an international settlement of the Formosa issue, whereas in the past the American position had been that the issue was strictly related to the internal affairs of China. In point of fact, Acheson's view of the strategic importance of Formosa had been shifted by Korea. Both in a conversation with Norwegian Ambassador Wilhelm Morgenstierne (June 30) and in a letter to Paul Nitze outlining his views on Korea and Formosa (July 12), Acheson declared that for the longer run there was no alternative to garrisoning and supporting a reoccupied South Korea and holding on to Formosa as long as "(1) we wish to maintain our present or better our position in the Pacific . . . and (2) as long the Chinese and Soviets are a militant menace there."[7]

The last line of Truman's statement took the fate of Formosa out of the limbo to which it had been consigned by his statement of January 5 and now made it dependent on a series of conditions unlikely ever to be worked out in a way satisfactory to Peking. Consequently, if the new Formosa policy met the test of consensus at home, it brought an understandable roar of indignation from Peking to which Acheson seems to have paid insufficient attention.

Within twenty-four hours of the Truman statement, Foreign Minister Chou En-lai denounced the move as armed aggression against the territory of China in total violation of the United Nations Charter.[*]

Instead of treating Chou's statement in the light of what the United States had just done to the status of Formosa, Acheson reported that the State Department considered the Chinese Communist statement to be tantamount to a declaration of war.[8]

Mao was even more vehement a few days later:

American aggression cannot but evoke widespread determined resistance on the part of Asian People. . . . [Truman] has broken every international agreement

---

[*] Alan Whiting, *China Crosses the Yalu: The Decision to Enter the Korean War* (New York: Macmillan, 1960). The United Nations was getting a good workout from both sides. The symmetry is worth noting. Since Acheson knew that the United Nations would not approve of the Formosa Straits decision, it was not presented to the Security Council for approval. Red China, which had tacitly spurned the UN, was now invoking its principles.

by the United States that it would not interfere in the internal political affairs of China. . . . Imperialism has a bold front but is empty within because it does not have the support of the people. People of China and peoples of the world arise! Prepare thoroughly! Defeat every provocation of American imperialism.[9]

As usual the implications from the Chinese point of view did not register sufficiently with Acheson. The intricacies of American domestic policies that had led Truman and Acheson to present their Korea–Formosa package could not be appreciated in Peking, "where there was undoubtedly great bitterness at the fact that they were being punished for this action by the Soviets and their satellite." [10]

Once the hands-off policy had been reversed, it was very difficult to limit American involvement with the Chiang regime. On July 27, at the instigation of the Joint Chiefs, the Administration agreed to grant military aid to the Chinese Nationalists "for defensive purposes," and it was agreed that a military survey team under General MacArthur's command should be sent to Formosa to survey its military needs. It was carefully stipulated, at Acheson's insistence, that MacArthur not go in person.[11] There then occurred MacArthur's first breach of instructions. Without the least hint or by-your-leave, MacArthur undertook to go personally to Formosa, thereby giving Chiang Kai-shek an opportunity to embarrass the Administration before its allies in the United Nations by announcing that "the foundation . . . for Sino–American military cooperation has been laid." * This was the beginning of MacArthur's career of insubordination. Instead of nipping it in the bud by reprimanding the Supreme Commander, the Administration dispatched Averell Harriman to Tokyo in the forlorn hope of winning MacArthur over to an appreciation of the Truman–Acheson policy. Far from accomplishing that, it merely raised MacArthur's status to that of a virtual policy-maker on co-equal terms with the President and his advisers in Washington and provided the Republicans with a hero and spokesman.

The nature of Acheson's role within the inner circle of those men who advised President Truman in his ultimate decision to commit American armies to battle was characteristically decisive. Acheson exercised a unique influence upon the decision taken by invariably coming to each Blair House meeting with the only well-ordered set of recommendations. At the first meeting Acheson advanced the following suggestions for consideration by the conference: (1) that General MacArthur be authorized

---

* Memo, Acheson to Truman, meeting, August 3, 1950. Acheson Papers. The President indicated that he had not approved of MacArthur's going. Acheson Papers. By August 3 Acheson once again reverted to the need to avoid interference with development of long-run Sino–Soviet quarrels, "the need for circumspection on Formosa, and the need to avoid having the admission of the PRC come before the UN where it would arouse American opinion against our allies."

to furnish the South Koreans with military equipment over and above that already authorized under the Mutual Defense Assistance Program; (2) that American airplanes be employed to cover the evacuation of the American women and children from Inchon; (3) that the Air Force be authorized to destroy North Korean tanks and airplanes interfering with the evacuation; (4) that it be considered what further assistance might be given to Korea pursuant to the Security Council resolution just passed or to any subsequent resolution; and (5) that the Seventh Fleet be ordered to prevent a Chinese Communist invasion of Formosa as well as prevent an expedition by the Chinese Nationalists against the mainland. The decisions of the Sunday-night Blair House conference involved some form of action or deliberation on the basis of all five of Acheson's recommendations.

The following Monday was taken up with intensive consultations between Acheson and his advisers, including Assistant Secretaries Webb, Rusk, Matthews, and Hickerson, Ambassador Jessup, and Counselor Kennan. At 3:50 P.M. Acheson joined the President at the White House for the purpose of hearing an urgent appeal from the Korean ambassador, John M. Chang. The remainder of the afternoon Acheson used to think through his position in the light of the rapidly deteriorating situation.

At the second Blair House conference on the evening of June 26, Acheson made five more recommendations for decision by the President. These proposals were as follows: (1) that the navy and air force be instructed to give the fullest possible support to the South Korean forces and that such support be limited to the area south of the 38th parallel; (2) that orders be issued to the Seventh Fleet to prevent an attack upon Formosa, that the Chinese Nationalist government be told to desist from operations against the mainland, and that the Fleet be ordered to secure the compliance of the latter; (3) that American forces in the Philippines be strengthened and that increased military assistance be rendered to the Philippine government; (4) that military assistance to Indochina be accelerated and that a military mission be sent there to advise in stiffening its defenses; and (5) that our ambassador to the UN, Warren B. Austin, be instructed to report any action taken under the above recommendations to the United Nations.

Meanwhile, the process of informing the public and securing the support of America's allies went forward at a steady pace. On June 25 the United Nations Security Council called upon the North Koreans to withdraw from South Korea; on June 27 (with the Soviet delegation still boycotting the UN) the Security Council called on its members to assist South Korea against the North; and on July 7 a joint United Nations military command under General MacArthur was established for purposes of repelling the aggression in Korea.

The development of recommendations and plans went forward at a steady pace with Acheson, supported by his staff, providing most of the evaluations and alternatives on which decisions were ultimately based. The decisions were the President's alone, but the entire decisional process involving the President, the Congress, the American public, the United Nations, allies and neutrals was conducted by Acheson. Even the issue for which he is most often criticized—the failure to secure a Congressional resolution of approval—was considered. Except for the decision to introduce the Seventh Fleet into the Formosa Straits it is hard to fault the deliberation with which the decisions were made, given the speed with which the North Koreans were advancing southward.

The ultimate decision to commit United States troops to the Korean fighting was made by Truman alone at 5:00 A.M. on the morning of June 30 upon receipt of an urgent request from General MacArthur to be allowed to do so. Later the same morning, Truman's advisors, including Acheson, endorsed the President's decision to give General MacArthur ". . . full authority to use the troops under his command."

One of the most criticized aspects of the President's course of action was his failure to secure congressional approval for the American intervention. "To have gone to Congress for a joint resolution or the Senate [sic] for a declaration of war would have been an easy exercise . . . a careful declaration of support by Congress, a joint resolution, would have preserved the constitutional prerogatives of legislative and executive." [12] At the time only a few senators (Kem, Taft, Watkins) questioned the President's decision not to ask for a congressional resolution approving his actions which he believed were consonant with his authority under the UN Charter. Most Republican senators (Saltonstall, Smith, Knowland, Morse, Lodge, and others) joined in unequivocal expressions of support.* Paige states that Acheson reportedly urged the President not to seek a congressional resolution authorizing or approving of the decision to intervene, but offers no evidence for his statement.[13] In point of fact, Acheson did recommend that the President "go before the Congress . . . to a joint session on the Korean situation. This report to the Congress to be followed by a Joint Resolution approving of the action taken in Korea." [14] Acheson even presented a draft resolution proposing that the Congress commend the action taken "by the United States rather than action by the President." [15] Truman was in agreement, but he was dissuaded from it by Senator Scott Lucas, the Democratic leader, on the grounds that "things were now going along well. The President had very properly done what he had to do." Congress was not in session, Lucas

---

* Paige, *op. cit.*, pp. 196–197. Most Republican critics were still attacking Acheson for not having done enough in the past.

argued; only Taft and Wherry had voiced the view that Congress should be consulted. "Many members had suggested to him [Lucas] that the President keep away from Congress and avoid debate." [16] It was then agreed that it would be enough if Truman simply reported his actions to the Congress and addressed the American people. Acheson reserved his judgment, although he later observed that he had refrained from pushing the resolution because he shared the view that "the thing to do was to get on and do what had to be done as quickly and effectively as you could, and if you stopped to analyze what you were doing, you immobilized yourself and [tried] to answer a lot of questions which were unanswerable. All you did was to weaken and confuse your will and not get anywhere." [17] In retrospect it is unfortunate that Acheson did not insist that the President seek a congressional resolution. The reassuring consensus that had been there in the early weeks of the crisis began to crumble, and Republicans could hold it against the Administration that it had not secured a declaration of war.[18]

The next critical political question that summer was whether MacArthur should be authorized to cross the 38th parallel and, if successful in annihilating the North Korean army, whether the United Nations Command should proceed to the unification of all of Korea. On July 31 the Joint Chiefs of Staff proffered a meticulous set of assumptions on which MacArthur, as the UN commander, should be directed to cross the parallel, defeat the enemy's forces, and unify the whole of Korea. The Department of State was divided on the issue: the Far Eastern Division under Dean Rusk and John Allison urged that a crossing not be precluded; the Policy Planning Staff led by Nitze and influenced by Kennan took the opposite view. Kennan, shocked by the Joint Chiefs' views,[19] prepared a memorandum urging that Acheson recognize that the balance of forces in the area militated against the United States trying to unify the peninsula. Korea could not maintain its independence against its more powerful neighbors and, the Soviet Union being the most powerful, Korea was bound to revert sooner or later to Soviet hegemony. Although like Acheson's Kennan's attention was focused on the Soviet, not the Chinese, capacity to dominate, Acheson dismissed Kennan's views as unrealistic.

First Acheson dismissed the issue of the 38th parallel: "Until the actual military situation developed further, no one could say where the necessity for flexibility in tactics ended and embarkation upon a new strategic purpose began. One conclusion was clear: no arbitrary prohibition against crossing the parallel should be imposed." [20] Next Acheson let his desire to maximize American gains and get the Korean problem off the agenda lure him into a belief that unificaion of all of Korea was well within the legal and military (ignoring the political) possibilities of the situation, provided the Chinese did not intervene. The UN resolution of June 27 recommending that members "furnish such assistance to the Republic of Korea as may be necessary to repel the armed attack and restore peace and security in the area" was now construed to mean something more than a return to the status quo *ante bellum;* it was now construed to mean that the UN Command was authorized to end the principal obstacle to peace and security in the area—the division of Korea into a northern half and a southern half. Thus caught by the logic of abstract reasoning and propelled by the desire to get something accomplished, Acheson acquiesced in the decision to make Korean unification a goal of American policy. Henceforth the seriousness with which Acheson viewed the danger of Soviet or Chinese intervention would run parallel with a delusive belief that Korea could be unified without provoking such an intervention. Confidence hinged on nothing more than the conviction that, the North Koreans once defeated, "chances were believed good that neither Russian nor Chinese troops would intervene." [21]

The next contretemps with MacArthur came on August 26 when a speech that the general had written for the annual encampment of the Veterans of Foreign Wars was printed in the *U.S. News and World Report.* In this speech MacArthur publicly challenged the Administration's foreign policy:

Nothing could be more fallacious than the threadbare argument by those who advocate appeasement and defeatism in the Pacific that if we defend Formosa we alienate continental Asia. Those who speak thus do not understand the Orient. They do not grasp that it is the pattern of oriental psychology to respect and follow aggressive, resolute and dynamic leadership. . . . To pursue any other course [than to hold Formosa] would be to turn over the fruits of our Pacific victory to a potential enemy. It would shift any future battle area 5,000 miles eastward to the coasts of the American continents. . . .[22]

Understandably, the speech had not been cleared by the President since it was nothing less than an all-out attack upon the cautionary assumptions of Administration foreign policy.* First, Truman gave serious thought to relieving MacArthur of command and replacing him with General Omar Bradley. Then "to avoid the appearance of a demotion," since he had "no desire to hurt General MacArthur personally," Truman ordered MacArthur to withdraw the speech.[23] In not replacing MacArthur as commander of UN forces in Korea, Truman was making a disastrous error that would come back to haunt him. Republicans immediately rallied to MacArthur and further reinforced him in his megalomania and in his career of insubordination. Neither Acheson nor Truman ever really

---

* The purple prose aside, the strategic importance which the Administration now attached to Formosa was not that much different from MacArthur's view.

came to grips with the implications for their policy of the policy which MacArthur wanted. The reports that Harriman had brought back of the general's wildly anti–Communist views and his known paranoia and pathologic hostility to the leadership in Washington did not seem to have given Acheson pause to consider whether this person was to be trusted with the delicate and controversial mission of unifying Korea. Instead of studying this great rival and threat to his policies, Acheson contented himself with dismissing MacArthur as an egomaniac and leaving it to Truman, a much humbler man, to define the policy and authority relationship.* What seems to have happened is that Acheson, perceiving Truman's commitment to the general, did not choose to challenge the confidence being placed in MacArthur. Put off by MacArthur's "incredible arrogance and vanity," [24] and unable to grasp the depth of MacArthur's messianic Asian anti–Communism except in terms of repulsion, Acheson tended to assume that MacArthur was someone else's responsibility— either the Pentagon's or the President's. This was tragic because Acheson was the only one in the Administration with the perspicacity and will-power to have challenged the general. Instead, when Truman later decided to fly for a rendezvous with MacArthur at Wake Island, Acheson disdained to go along, as much out of a refusal to kowtow to the emperor of the East as out of the press of business elsewhere.

Inasmuch as the war was being fought for a limited and essentially political purpose, Acheson's refusal was a fatal derogation of the states-man's responsibility. It meant another divorce in an operation already and increasingly bifurcated in its military and political components. De-spite his admonishments against the artificiality of a military viewpoint as distinct from a political viewpoint, the operation in Korea tended in-creasingly to become a military operation partly because, in the absence of a strong hand, the American command system tends to let the military generate its own rationale for the conduct of operations which often run counter to the objectives and criteria for political success.

It is often said that a nation's foreign policy is the expression of deep underlying economic and psychological forces. General MacArthur was in many ways the incarnation of the Asian thrust in American foreign policy. His father had crowned his own career with his appointment as the military chief of the newly conquered Philippines, and MacArthur

---

* "If we had been able to peer into MacArthur's mind, we should have been infinitely more cautious than we were a few weeks later in giving him his instruc-tions." Acheson, *Present at the Creation, op. cit.*, p. 424. But MacArthur had never hidden his fundamental antipathy toward both Truman and Acheson. Kennan warned Acheson on several occasions that the ascendancy which MacArthur had gained over the conduct of Asian policy and over the public mind was so abnormal as to be a constant source of danger to rational policy.

himself had gained epic stature as the result of his escape from beleagured Bataan, his triumphant return across the Pacific, and his apotheosis as the ruler of a conquered Japan.

By contrast, Acheson's pre–Korean Far Eastern policy represented an attempt to break with the pre-existing romantic image of American destiny in the region and establish a new image in keeping with political and strategic realities of the mid-twentieth century. Because that effort had already provoked one deep and divisive debate within the nation, one would have expected Acheson to be doubly on guard against its recurrence. Yet on September 15, the day of MacArthur's brilliant landing at Inchon and the defeat of the North Korean forces in the south, Mac-Arthur was informed by the Joint Chiefs of Staff that he might conduct military operations behind the 38th parallel; "If there was no indication or threat of entry of Soviet or Chinese Communist elements. . . . [MacArthur] was to extend his operations north of the parallel and to make plans for the occupation of North Korea. . . . No ground operations were to take place north of the parallel in the event of Soviet or Chinese Communist entry." [25] These instructions were spelled out in another directive on September 27 warning him that "in the event of the open or covert employment of major Soviet units south of the 38th parallel, you will assume the defense, make no move to aggravate the situation and report to Washington. You should take the same action in event your forces are operating north of the 38th parallel, and major Soviet units are openly employed." Later Chinese forces were added to this injunction.

On September 28 Acheson was called back from New York, where he was presenting the Uniting for Peace Resolution to the United Nations and struggling to secure European approval for German rearmament, to review Korean policy with Truman and General Marshall, the new Secretary of Defense. One outcome of the Veterans of Foreign Wars fiasco had been Louis Johnson's reluctance to send MacArthur the message of reprimand, word of which got back to Truman. Johnson subsequently made the mistake of conniving with Senator Taft for Acheson's ouster, and when this too became known to the President, Truman asked for Johnson's resignation.[26] In his place Truman appointed General Marshall, but only after a bitter Senate fight which saw Republican extremists rally behind Senator Jenner's excoriating attack upon Marshall's loyalty and patriotism as a means of renewing their attack upon the Roosevelt–Truman record in foreign policy. The attack of the McCarthyites or, as Acheson called them, "the primitives," was by no means limited to Acheson. It extended to anyone, even George C. Marshall, who had had to do with recent American foreign policy. Essentially, a group of Midwestern and Western Republicans who were still isolationist in their sentiments had resolved their frustration by alleging that there existed a Communist conspiracy plotting to deny America the victories to which its strength and virtue entitled it. Hence anyone who had served either Roosevelt or Truman was suspect.

Truman, Marshall, and Acheson reviewed the previous day's instructions which, according to Acheson, seemed "excellently contrived to create a strong military position from which to exploit the possibilities of the North Korean defeat—either to insure the South by a strong defensive line . . . or, if . . . the Chinese did not intervene, to move toward the UN goal of a united, free, and independent Korea." [27] Unfortunately, on the same day Marshall sent MacArthur an "eyes only" telegram saying, "We want you to feel unhampered tactically and strategically to proceed north of the 38th parallel." Later MacArthur was able to point to this message as justification for continuing operations after the Chinese had made their presence known. On October 7 the UN General Assembly with little opposition (47 to 5 with 7 abstentions) recommended the taking of "all appropriate steps" toward a unified government of Korea. This vote was generally understood as sanctioning the military occupation of the North and gives some indication of the degree of support that the United States had for the operation. On October 8 Truman approved new instructions from the Joint Chiefs to MacArthur, warning him:

In the light of the possible intervention of Chinese Communist forces in North Korea the following amplification of our directive [of September 27] is forwarded for your guidance:

Hereafter in the event of open or covert employment anywhere in Korea of major Chinese Communist units, without prior announcement, you should continue the action as long as, *in your judgment,* action by forces now under your control offers a reasonable chance of success [emphasis added].*

Meanwhile, on October 1 Chou En-lai again warned that the PRC "would not stand aside" should North Korea be invaded,[28] and on or about October 14, as Truman was flying to Wake Island for his meeting with MacArthur, elements of the Chinese armies began crossing the Yalu and marching south. At Wake MacArthur assured Truman that Chinese Communist intervention was either unlikely or would be easily handled. Truman appears to have in no way qualified MacArthur's belief that his unalterable mission was to unify all of Korea. Furthermore, by virtue of a directive from the Joint Chiefs of Staff quoted above, it had been left to MacArthur's *judgment* to determine whether or not unification could be successfully pursued with the forces at his disposal. About the only contribution Acheson made to the Wake Island meeting was a memo-

---

* Harry S Truman, *Memoirs,* vol. 2, Years of Trial and Hope (New York: Doubleday, 1956), p. 362. There is no indication in Truman's account that Acheson participated or concurred in this new directive to MacArthur.

randum to Jessup, who was traveling with the President, criticizing a draft of a speech Truman was to give at San Francisco following his return from Wake and ordering deleted all reference to Korean events as a victory.

. . . the whole idea of victory should be taken out. We should not be talking about victory. This is out of keeping in the U.N. There are no victors or vanquished in this kind of situation, only an adjudication. The only victor is peace. . . .To talk in terms of victory makes this too much of a U.S.–U.S.S.R. conflict. This part of the speech should be done with great restraint, should be sober, somber, with a sense of responsibility.

Acheson also objected to the speech's "hammering away at the theme of communist imperialism in this way. Not only stale and uninteresting but dangerous in the present situation." [29]

Now began a series of events in which the ungovernable MacArthur, taking advantage of the authority and discretion handed to him by a negligent administration, brought his armies to the brink of destruction and the administration to the brink of disaster.

Within a week of his return from the Wake Island conference, MacArthur authorized his field commanders to use *any and all* ground forces at their command in order to capture all of North Korea. On October 25, MacArthur's headquarters erased the limitation that the Joint Chiefs had imposed upon the use of non–Korean forces in the approaches to the Yalu. The Joint Chiefs warned MacArthur that his order was "not in consonance" with their directive of September 27.[30] In reply MacArthur referred to General Marshall's message "to feel unhampered" and justified his action as militarily necessary to relieve the Republic of Korea (ROK) forces which were now encountering Chinese forces.[31]

No sooner had ROK forces begun their advance in the direction of the Yalu than they were pinned down and routed by remarkably effective operations which could only be coming from entirely new armies.[32] While the full extent of Chinese intervention was still unknown, General Walton Walker interpreted the stiff resistance that his ROK forces were encountering as evidence "that China was in deadly earnest" and he advised strongly against a hasty advance to the Yalu. With a gap of fifty to seventy miles between his Eighth Army on the west side of the peninsula and Almond's Tenth (Marine) Corps on the east, elementary military tactics dictated extreme caution until a link-up could provide accurate intelligence of what lay between the two forces. The Joint Chiefs were generally aware of these dangers, but hesitated to challenge MacArthur's authority and did not broach the subject with either the President or his civilian advisers.

But even if Acheson was not *au courant* with the military deficiencies and risks of MacArthur's strategy, the latter's decision to advance to the Yalu was already evoking demands from him that were clearly not consonant with the political and military limitations which Acheson had assigned to the operations. For example, it had been understood that under no circumstances was the United States Command to bomb the bridges or power complex over the Yalu connecting North Korea and Manchuria. Consonant with this limitation, on November 7 the United Nations interim Committee on Korea had declared that the United Nations troops would "fully support" (meaning respect) the Manchurian frontier; three days later a six-power resolution introduced into the Security Council reaffirmed that the United Nations would hold the frontier "inviolate" and "would fully protect Chinese and Korean interests in the frontier zone." [33]

Yet on November 6 Acheson succeeded only at the very last minute in halting a bombing mission to take out the bridge across the Yalu River from Sinuiju (Korea) to Antung (Manchuria) ordered by MacArthur. As there still seemed to be no serious and immediate threat to American forces, the President vetoed the mission and MacArthur was ordered not to attack targets within five miles of the Manchurian border. But two days later Truman succumbed to MacArthur's protests that failure to destroy the bridges would endanger his command. On November 8 the Far East Air Command knocked out the two three-thousand-foot spans, "although of course most of the Chinese Communist troops were already in Korea by this time." *

Acheson had another opportunity on November 9 to call a halt to MacArthur's offensive on the grounds that it was endangering the nation's political and strategic interests. MacArthur had just announced a final great offensive which would carry the United Nations Command to the Yalu. At the November 9 meeting of the National Security Council, General Bradley explained that the United Nations *"could hold its present positions* in Korea but beyond that, any advance would entail the possibility of the need for decisions by the United States for attacking Manchurian bases." ** The threat to Acheson's policy of definite but limited and controlled risks from MacArthur's grandiose designs was now posed in political terms: either MacArthur's offensive must be halted forthwith

---

* David Rees, *Korea: The Limited War* (New York: St. Martin's Press, 1964), p. 131. This was not the first time Acheson acted to limit actions near the frontiers. Minutes of meeting, Acheson and Lovett, October 10, and Acheson and Finletter, October 12. Acheson Papers.

** Documents, Princeton File. The Princeton File is a transcript of a seminar that was held by Acheson and his principal lieutenants after his retirement from office. It constitutes a combination debriefing and analysis of his decisions as Secretary of State. (Emphasis added.)

or face the military necessity of having to extend operations into Manchuria. Acheson's suggestion of a twenty-mile demilitarized zone was the only discussion of Chinese interests, and it is notable that nothing was done about it.

It has been argued by Richard Neustadt, a White House aide to Truman, that Acheson hesitated to oppose MacArthur's offensive out of scruple at appearing to trespass into the field of military operations. But given the terms in which Bradley posed the alternatives, one can scarcely contend that Acheson would not have been on solid political grounds in opposing the offensive.

As if to underscore the likelihood that MacArthur would sooner or later have to have recourse to bombing Manchuria, Secretary of Defense Marshall "pointed out . . . that our eastern front in Korea was widely dispersed and thinly spread and that this represented an added risk. . . . Bradley replied that of course General MacArthur had done this in order to carry out his directive that he was to occupy the whole country and hold elections." [34] Acheson did ask "if there was any line that was better from a military point of view than the present one, and Bradley replied that . . . the farther back . . . the easier it would be to maintain . . . however, he realized that any backward movement . . . might lose us the South Koreans' will to fight." [35] Since this was a political judgment, here again Acheson was offered an opening to reconsider the merits of the offensive from the viewpoint of America's political objectives. It could hardly be seriously argued that South Korean morale would have fallen so much as to outweigh the risks of war with Red China. Instead of all these discouraging statements becoming the basis for a serious reconsideration of Chinese intentions and of the risks implicit in MacArthur's offensive, Acheson let the occasion pass. He seized upon a statement by Bradley that "if the Chinese desired only to set up a buffer area . . . negotiations might be fruitful" [36] and offered forthwith to look into that possibility.

Truman, who had to miss this meeting, records Acheson's summation of the Council's views:

[Acheson] pointed out that it was agreed that General MacArthur's directives should not now be changed and he should be free to do what he could in a military way, but without bombing Manchuria. At the same time, the State Department would seek ways to find out whether negotiations with the Chinese Communist were possible. . . .[37]

Whatever prompted Acheson to think that he might try for a diplomatic understanding with Peking while MacArthur was left free "to do what he could in a military way"? It had not previously been assumed that ending the war would depend upon negotiations with Peking. All calculations up to this point had been made on the assumption that the

Chinese did not intend to intervene, but if they did the United Nations would be able to break off military operations, repair to a good defensible line, and await developments. Now that the Chinese had indicated that they were not bluffing, there was no reason for Acheson not to assume that they meant what they had said all along—that they intended to evict the United Nations Command from all of North Korea and that in some sense they had the means to do it. Besides, as Acheson told Truman, "the trouble with any such proposal for negotiations . . . would be that the Communists would insist on all foreign troops leaving Korea, and thus abandoning Korea to the Communists." [38] Nevertheless he now permitted himself to believe that Chinese intervention could be parried diplomatically by negotiations for a ten-mile buffer zone south of the Yalu.

All evidence suggests that the participants in the meeting of November 9 knew that the military situation was uncertain and, depending upon Chinese strength, could quickly become desperate. Acheson had been told that unless the Chinese were weak and willing to accept a buffer zone the military situation might become so desperate as to necessitate bombing bases in Manchuria. Now, if ever, would have been the time for Acheson to have notified the President that both the political and the military risks far outweighed the advantages of continuing the advance northward. Instead, the issue as it reached President Truman "wore a diplomatic face which fatally obscured the military risk, a reversal in effect of late September's situation." [39]

Why did Acheson not call for a re-examination of the political risks which he had a perfect right and duty to do? Neustadt suggests that Acheson, already under fire for his Far Eastern policy, was reluctant to appear to meddle in military strategy. "In immediate terms the risk was 'military'; if it justified reversing the commander in the field, then the Joint Chiefs must make the judgment and tell Truman." [*] But if that was the case Acheson never should have fostered the idea that it might be possible to reach an accommodation for some form of buffer zone.

Thanks to Neustadt and others, a myth has been fostered that Acheson felt constrained by his role as Secretary of State and by his reluctance to bring down upon the Administration the obloquy that would follow should MacArthur's offensive be called off. [**] It is true that Acheson could

---

[*] Richard E. Neustadt, *Presidential Power* (New York: John Wiley, 1960), p. 139. But, as we have indicated, the immediate risk was not only "military"; it was "political" as well.

[**] Neustadt goes to an extreme when he writes that "for Cabinet members and for military chiefs, a decision to go to the President is something like a government's decision to go to war; it is not something done each day on every issue." *Ibid.*, p. 140. When the issue happened to be one of the gravest kind, involving the likelihood of war with China, Neustadt's seems a strange explanation for keeping the President ignorant of the risks and no justification whatsoever unless we are to assume that the

not help but be influenced to some extent by the obvious price which both he and the President would pay should it become known that he had been instrumental in denying MacArthur "total victory." MacArthur had made it clear that if his command were ordered back he would regard it as an act of appeasement, a defeat for the West, and a scuttling of United Nations objectives.

Despite these considerations it would be a mistake to believe that Acheson was a convinced opponent of MacArthur's campaign, constrained to silence by virtue of his civilian role or by political expediency. Quite to the contrary, in confidential meetings with his staff and in conferences with Marshall and Bradley in the absence of the President at which Acheson might have made known his reservation without intruding upon military policy, Acheson does not seem to have expressed any serious misgivings about the consequences of Chinese intervention. For example, at a meeting of Acheson and his staff on the morning of November 21, Acheson noted the confusion in MacArthur's authorizations. On a straight military basis, Acheson noted, MacArthur was authorized to pursue the enemy forces north of the 38th parallel and destroy them as a military force. If China intervened he was to pursue the mission until it was evident he could not succeed. Acheson felt that *no one should change this part of the directive* until MacArthur had had a chance to "probe" the situation, but there was no attempt to define what was meant by "probe" or to arrive at any conclusions on the basis of alternative outcomes. Acheson noted the concern which China and Russia might experience over the use of Korea as a route to Manchuria, but he doubted that the Communists believed the United States would use Korea in that way. Their fear might relate, he said, "to propaganda on the rearmament of Japan. . . . This might lead you to believe that there is more sensitivity here than the intelligence reports lead one to believe." * This observation does not appear to have led to any significant revision of his thinking, however. Acheson's concluding observations accepted by implication the possibility of Chinese intervention.

If MacArthur is successful in repelling Chinese intervention and ROK takes over tension may ease, but if Chinese Communist forces cannot be destroyed and strong resistance is met there and we find ourselves with a long struggle on our hands we must turn to negotiation and their [Chinese] sensitivity becomes even more important.[40]

President is the equivalent of the prewar Japanese emperor. Unfortunately, it seems to be true that in this instance the President was not kept informed, with what consequences we all know.

* Documentation, Princeton Seminar. Minutes, meeting in Department of State, November 21, 1950. Acheson Papers. Note that it is on the basis of a sensitivity to *Japan,* not to the American advance, that Peking might react.

Secondly, Acheson showed very little knowledge or concern about MacArthur's actual military dispositions. That afternoon (November 21) when Acheson, Marshall, Bradley, and their advisers met at the Pentagon, attention was mainly centered on the modalities by which a buffer zone would come into being between the United Nations Command and the Chinese along the Manchurian border. But the unreality of this discussion for bringing the war to an end should have been enough to make Acheson wonder about the feasibility of the campaign itself. Discussion at the meeting went as follows: should the United Nations attempt to negotiate a buffer zone or simply make an announcement of intent to practice self-restraint? General Marshall preferred a political announcement of intent *following* MacArthur's success.[41] Acheson stressed the need for finding a way of terminating Chinese intervention in the war should it occur. The concept of a buffer zone based upon the high ground along the Yalu was finally agreed upon, with Acheson envisaging a demarcation line accepted tacitly by the Chinese and ratified by negotiation.

There was something strangely unreal and inconclusive about this meeting. Reputedly the principal participants had been laboring for weeks under the dread of Chinese involvement; now it was simply taken for granted that, whatever happened, MacArthur's offensive would be a success and hostilities would end with the Chinese accepting some form of demarcation line between the UN Command and the Manchurian frontier.* Far from revealing great anxiety or trepidation about MacArthur's advance to the Yalu, Acheson seems to have shared the prevailing confidence.

In light of the minutes of the meeting cited above and of what we know about Acheson, it seems hard to believe that he felt constrained by his role as Secretary of State or by considerations of domestic politics from revealing any deep concern he may have had about MacArthur's campaign. This was not the time for Acheson, Marshall, and the Joint Chiefs of Staff to engage in some kind of Gaston-and-Alphonse routine about who would be the first to break the news to the President that his commander in Korea was a dangerous plunger whose judgment could no longer be trusted.**

---

* The estimated presence of some 100,000 frontline Chinese troops (there were actually 300,000) together with 40,000 guerrillas in the rear of the United Nations Command does not seem to have dampened the confidence with which the American high command plotted the final stage of the war. Large though the United Nations Command seemed (377,000 men), it actually consisted of only 100,000 frontline strength, which (as General Marshall noted) was already stretched thin and about to become even more dispersed as it fanned out toward the Yalu.

** It is also part of the myth that MacArthur's northward advance prompted trepidation and concern in allied chancelleries. "From their forward positions on the

Acheson's misjudgment, which he shared with all the other participants, seems to have derived from wishful thinking. "Such a lack of realism is not at all rare. Psychologists have noted a general disposition in individuals to exaggerate gratifying features of one's environment and to overrate the probability of desirable events. . . ." [42] Acheson still clung to the rather benign view of Peking's motives and capabilities that had all along conditioned his thinking. He had hardly entered, if at all, into Peking's frame of reference. Having first adopted a prudent policy toward Peking, he failed to adhere to it when the temptation to unify Korea became too great. While aware that there was a certain level of risk in attempting to unify Korea, he completely underestimated the incentive which China would have to protect its flank against a powerful foe to whom it imputed only the worst and most aggressive of intentions.

Secondly, Acheson was not well informed on the deficiencies of the military situation. The Joint Chiefs of Staff were rightly concerned about MacArthur's strategic dispositions, but their concern reached Acheson only in a muted form. MacArthur's violation of orders and his refusal to be guided or even influenced by recommendations from the Joint Chiefs was essentially unknown to Acheson. The Joint Chiefs knew that MacArthur's forces were spread dangerously thin and that their disposition was faulty in the extreme, but they were too intimidated and bamboozled by MacArthur to express their concern in an unequivocal or decisive fashion.* As a result, they put the best face possible upon the situation and let Acheson and presumably the President think that all was well.

The meeting at the Pentagon on November 21 was the Administration's last chance to stop MacArthur. On November 24 MacArthur launched his "end-the-war" offensive. Hardly had the advance begun when the United

---

Chongchou River to the Cabinet office in Whitehall, all were keeping their fingers crossed and hoping that the worst would not happen." David Rees, *Korea: The Limited War* (London: Macmillan, 1964), p. 146. This seems to overrate the prevalent concern in foreign capitals. According to British Ambassador Sir Oliver Franks, "We did not perceive the crossing of the 38th parallel or the later November offensive as installments of MacArthurism. . . . No one really thought the Chinese would come in— I shouldn't say no one, but really one didn't consider it likely. Everybody thought the war was going well. MacArthur was in the process of ending the whole thing. If he was going beyond the limits set for him was it all that bad? That was the prevalent British view." Personal interview, Worcester College, Oxford, June 27, 1964. In fairness, Rees does note that "like Truman and Acheson, Attlee and Bevin did not think that the objective of a united Korea would provoke a massive Chinese counteraction" (p. 147).

* Bradley admits that MacArthur's stature was so great that the Joint Chiefs of Staff felt literally incapacitated to deal with him. Personal interview, Department of Defense, April 25, 1963. When Truman finally decided to remove MacArthur, neither Marshall nor Bradley had difficulty convincing themselves that MacArthur had violated orders on countless occasions and should have been removed much earlier.

Nations Command was struck by the full fury of the Chinese armies massed in the mountains. Within two days the advance which MacArthur had launched with such high hopes had become a defeat and within four days a total rout.

There is a refreshing candor in Acheson's subsequent statements about his and others' responsibility for misjudging Chinese intentions. "They really fooled us when it comes right down to it, didn't they?" asked Senator Saltonstall of Acheson in the course of the MacArthur Hearings. "Yes, sir." [43]

Why was this not apparent to Acheson at the time? All previous experience forewarned that China would not willingly tolerate the presence of hostile armies in its backyard. The United States had not hesitated to resist aggression eight thousand miles from its shores; why should China not be expected to react to MacArthur's hostile campaign in similar fashion? The explanation seems to lie in the pervasive American tendency, shared by Acheson and his critics alike, to believe that somehow the canons of international politics are suspended when it comes to China. We have already indicated that China invoked in Acheson an image which was quite at variance with the facts and quite at variance with the way Acheson conducted diplomacy when he was dealing with the Soviet Union. Acheson's image of the Peking regime was that of a docile puppet of Moscow without a will of its own.

Had Acheson stuck to his initial position that nothing required we go beyond restoring the status quo *ante bellum*, there would have been no need to engage the Chinese in a new test of strength. Lured by the desire to achieve a positive accomplishment, Acheson ended by undoing all his carefully contrived handiwork. Not only was the nation plunged into a new and interminable war but his farsighted efforts of the previous year to disentangle America from the Chinese civil war and put America's relations with the PRC on a more rational basis were utterly destroyed. It is also true, as Gaddis Smith observes, that Acheson "did as much as anyone in Washington to curb MacArthur's provocative words and tactics." [44] But by extending the war to the North, Acheson put his policy at the mercy of the military operations over which in the final analysis he could not exercise much control. Even if someone other than MacArthur had been in command of UN forces, it was a mistake to rely upon the military instrument under such politically delicate circumstances. Acheson was the first American statesman to practice the notion that there were limits to the use of war as an instrument of national policy; yet until it was too late he failed to recognize that those limits were at the 38th parallel.

CHAPTER

16

FROM DEFEAT TO RECOVERY:
THE RELIEF OF MACARTHUR

THE ADMINISTRATION was now caught in a terrible three-way squeeze. If disaster overtook American arms in Korea, it would be under the greatest pressure to extend the war against China by aerial and naval bombardment. If this occurred, America would lose the support of its allies; yet if it failed to extend the war, the Administration would come under even stronger attack from its domestic critics.

The most harrowing pressure came, of course, from the battlefront where the United Nations' armies were suddenly confronted by the threat of annihilation in the wintry passes of faraway Korea. Armies which two weeks earlier MacArthur had described as all but irresistible were now found to be "mentally fatigued and physically battered." Everywhere the magnitude and swiftness of the Chinese appearance had the effect of creating panic.

The President met the National Security Council at 3:00 P.M. November 28 in the first of a grim series of meetings at which the basic policy for the new situation was hammered out. ". . . General Bradley and the Chiefs of Staff had been in session all the day before, examining the situation, and they felt that while it was serious they were doubtful that it was as much a catastrophe as our newspapers were leading us to believe." [1]

General Bradley then reported that despite the danger posed by the presence of some 300 bombers on nearby Manchurian airfields, the Joint Chiefs "did not believe that General MacArthur should be authorized to bomb airfields in Manchuria." [2]

Bradley agreed with Marshall that the United States should go along with the United Nations, "even if going along with the United Nations meant some difficult problems for us." [3] And both agreed that it would be disastrous for the United States to be pulled into a general war with China, either alone or with the United Nations.

Speaking against the background of intelligence estimates, which once again adduced a greater-than-ever Soviet willingness to risk general war, Acheson strongly endorsed the idea of finding some way to end the war in Korea as quickly as possible and restoring some balance to America's worldwide defensive posture. The United States could afford neither to accuse the Soviet Union of fomenting aggression in Korea nor to precipitate Soviet intervention by bombing Manchurian airfields. "We had banked our entire foreign policy on the idea of keeping Russia contained. . . . If we allow the Russians now to trap us inside *their* perimeter, however, we would run the risk of being sucked into a bottomless pit." [4] The only solution, Acheson concluded, was to find a line which the UN Command could hold, and hold it; then, as soon as possible, to turn that line over to ROK troops and restore the American strategic initiative in Europe.

Over the weekend of December 2, the news from Korea became more and more ominous.* Acheson was also having trouble with America's allies at the United Nations who were panic-stricken by events in Korea. To crown the situation, Truman inadvertently informed his press conference on Friday (December 1) that the use of the A-bomb was always under active consideration, at which remark Prime Minister Attlee announced to a hushed and anxious House of Commons that he was leaving for Washington immediately to insist that America consult with its allies prior to any such decision.

By the weekend of December 2–3 the options facing the Administration were very grave indeed. Now as never before the situation called forth Acheson's best qualities. The danger to MacArthur's Korean command was so great that either or both of two courses of action might well have to be taken: the United States might have to sue for an armistice and accept a humiliating withdrawal from Korea, or, if in the course of retreat and evacuation the Tenth Corps should come under attack by Communist bombers, the United States would be obliged to risk general war by bombing China's Manchurian bases.[5] Either course appeared disastrous—the first because it would be such a mortifying defeat; the second because it was assumed that China and Russia desired such an extension of the war. Bombing China's Manchurian bases would, at the very least, bitterly divide America from its allies and break open the entire United

---

* Memo of meeting. Joint Chiefs Conference Room, Pentagon, 8:30 A.M., December 1, 1950. Marshall, Acheson, Bradley, and staffs. It was agreed that the United States would bomb Manchuria only in the event that American forces were threatened with annihilation. Meanwhile, Acheson solicited military agreement for a cease-fire on the 38th parallel.

Nations operation in Korea. It was agreed among the President, Acheson, Marshall, and Bradley that if General Lawton Collins (who was leaving immediately for Tokyo) deemed it necessary to the security and safe evacuation of the Tenth Corps to bomb the Manchurian bases from whence attack was coming, then MacArthur should so decide. In order to avoid the risk of a general war with Russia, however, the United States should not take such action either for the purpose of holding Korea or for retaliation against the Chinese. In the meantime the State Department was given approval to seek a cease-fire either by direct or indirect nego-tiations with General Wu, the Red Chinese delegate at the UN, or through countries having diplomatic representatives at Peking.* Expecta-tions of anything coming of this initiative were virtually nil because it was assumed that Peking would doubtless demand the evacuation of all of Korea, a seat in the United Nations, abandonment of Formosa, and a place at the Foreign Ministers' Conference on a Japanese peace treaty. In that case American strategy would have to be to regroup and to hold militarily in Korea to the bitter end.

A profound resolution was distilled out of the meetings of that week-end. Made up in part of desperation, in part of hope, and in part of Ache-son's belief that action—action of any sort—would be better than no action, the realization had materialized that America's best political advantage lay in a fighting retreat on the model of Dunkirk. A show of weakness at this point, according to Soviet specialists Kennan and Bohlen, would only excite Communist appetites, whereas a retreat on the Dunkirk model would create a psychological climate favorable to the United States and would be better received than if the United States first evacuated its forces and then resorted to attacks on China. At a meeting of Acheson with his aides on December 4 it was decided that the Administration was being deliberately infected by a spirit of defeatism emanating from MacArthur's headquarters in Tokyo. Kennan, Rusk, and Matthews were delegated to call on Marshall and make known their view that the situa-tion could be saved if less attention were paid to MacArthur's gloomy reports and more emphasis put upon recovering America's combat capa-bility. For the first time the idea of replacing MacArthur was broached.[6]

As a consequence of these dispositions, the Administration was primed for decision. On December 3 MacArthur confronted the Administration

---

* Wu had arrived in response to a Security Council invitation to Peking of No-vember 8 to discuss a cease-fire. Acheson's instructions to Ambassador Austin and Ambassador Gross at the UN were: (1) Chinese intervention might bring develop-ments of unparalleled destruction, (2) unless brought to a halt the UN would be crippled, (3) Chinese allegations could be resolved but not while the fighting con-tinued, (4) try to arrange a cease-fire ending hostilities and disengaging United States forces.

with an imperative demand for new, positive, and immediate forms of action. The grisly alternative he posed, should no new action be forthcoming, left nothing to the imagination: "Steady attrition leading to final destruction could reasonably be contemplated." Truman quickly approved a reply by the Joint Chiefs of Staff which said: "We consider that the preservation of your forces is now the primary consideration. Consolidation of forces into beachheads is concurred in." [7] Subsequently on December 29 the Joint Chiefs directed MacArthur to defend his forces in successive positions, and, "subject to the safety of your troops as your primary consideration," to make an advanced determination of the last reasonable opportunity for an orderly evacuation.[8] It was added, however, that a successful resistance to Chinese–North Korean aggression at some position in Korea and a deflation of the military and political prestige of the Chinese Communists would be of great importance to our national interest, if they could be accomplished without incurring serious losses.[9]

Prime Minister Attlee arrived in Washington on December 4. He was extremely anxious about America's intentions in Korea and determined to straighten things out. Had not events in Korea proved the British right in criticizing America's refusal to recognize the Peking regime and accede to its claims in the Far East? Well, now was the opportune time to set Far Eastern policy on its proper course.

As a result of this attitude, Attlee's first meeting with Truman the afternoon of December 4 did not go very well. Attlee proceeded to inform the President and his advisers that they had no choice but to negotiate with Peking. He made no secret of his belief that such negotiations would involve Formosa, a seat for the People's Republic in the UN, and recognition of the Peking government.

Truman was ready to assure Attlee that the United States had no intention of getting embroiled in a war against the Chinese mainland. "Regarding the question of all-out war against China [Truman reports in his *Memoirs*] Acheson assured the British conferees that there were 'not many of the President's advisers who would urge him to follow that course.'" [10]

The United States was equally determined not to take concessions under duress or to evacuate Korea unless forced to do so by the threat of military annihilation. Acheson and Truman agreed with Attlee that it might well be true that the defense of Korea was hopeless and that, unless the United States indicated a willingness to negotiate with Communist China, the war in Korea might go on until the UN forces were driven into the sea or until the American clamor for all-out war against Red China became irresistible. Nevertheless, America's obligation to the South Koreans and, above all, the United States government's obligation to avoid sowing panic and defeatism among its own people demanded that the Chinese challenge be met and contained in Korea. Acheson was only too aware of the bitterness that would ensue among the American people to let pass Attlee's remark that "nothing would be more dangerous than for the Asians to split away from us." Breaking in, Acheson said, "Weakening the U.S. would be definitely more dangerous." As for negotiating with the Chinese Communists, " 'My own guess is that it wouldn't work,' the Secretary continued. 'All we might get would be time, but never enough time to do any good. Just enough time to divide our people bitterly. Just enough time to lose our moral strength.' " [11]

The question for Acheson was no longer how extremist opinion would react, but how the vast pool of moderate opinion in America would react failing the adoption of the proper course of action. In this context, Acheson sought to point out to the British that there could not be one foreign policy for Europe and another for the Far East; there could not be one response to small aggressions and an entirely different response to big aggressions. A policy of such schizophrenic proportions would lead to a derangement of public opinion. The American people would not understand why such heavy expenditures and commitments were necessary in Europe if the same enemy was yielded to in Asia; they expected their government to be consistent.[12]

Acheson also pointed out to Attlee that surrender in Korea on Communist terms would have repercussions far beyond Korea and Formosa. The shock to Japan and the Philippines of American acquiescence in Chinese and Soviet hegemony would be such that even the island chain upon which both agreed United States security depended might be lost. A surrender that would lose to America all the fruits of the Pacific war would be unendurable to American public opinion.

Stirred by the arrival of Attlee at such a crucial juncture, twenty-four Republican senators supported a resolution by Senator James P. Kem (R–Mo.) demanding to be informed about "secret commitments" which they believed Truman and Acheson were making to the British. British influence was viewed as part of the conspiracy to sell America out to the Communists.[13] They might have been surprised to learn that power has its own reasons: whereas a month later Taft would be calling for the evacuation of Korea in a typical isolationist gesture, at that moment the Administration was rejecting British efforts in the same direction. In order to bend the British to the Administration's will, Acheson avoided any dramatic showdown. The British wanted to narrow the diplomatic gap by focusing upon the large, long-run differences of attitude toward Red China which separated London and Washington. That was just what Acheson did not want to do. The difference in British and American long-run views on Far Eastern policy were, at that moment at least, fundamentally antithetical and virtually unbridgeable. Any attempt to reach agreement, Acheson knew, would only end in demonstrating how far apart they really were.

Rather than try to bridge the gap at the point of widest separation, Acheson insisted that they stick to that which divided them the least— namely, what was to be done in the United Nations and in the field, pending some evidence of Communist willingness to negotiate. In the end Acheson succeeded in assuring Attlee that the United States would not use the A-bomb without consulting the British, and the British in turn agreed to bury for the moment their demand that the United Nations capitulate to Peking and the PRC be admitted forthwith to the UN.[14]

In Korea unmitigated disaster continued to overwhelm the UN forces. The situation at the UN in New York was equally grim. On December 14 the General Assembly adopted an Indian-sponsored resolution calling for the establishment of a three-nation committee to determine the basis on which a satisfactory cease-fire in Korea could be arranged and to make recommendation to the General Assembly as soon as possible.[15]

The Peking regime, through Chou En-lai, responded to the cease-fire committee's efforts on December 23 by rejecting the UN overture on the grounds that it embodied the U.S. strategy "to first obtain a cease-fire and later negotiate." Undaunted, the cease-fire committee prepared a state- ment of principles as a basis for negotiations "subsequent to the envisaged establishment of a cease-fire." [16] While the United States continued to support these prolonged efforts, domestic criticism was now such that the State Department had to let it be known that the whole question of the American public's support of the UN was at stake in the action, or in- action, of the General Assembly on the question of Chinese intervention in Korea. Acheson sensed that China's uncooperative attitude would sooner or later force the UN to brand it the aggressor in Korea; before that could happen he would have to wait out the futile efforts of the Asian states to negotiate a cease-fire.

Acheson was deeply angered by the failure of the General Assembly to rally to the side of the Korean command. Although making all allow- ances for the failures of judgment on the part of MacArthur's command, there was no excuse for adding to the humiliating spectacle. However much Acheson privately deplored the efforts of the Asians, and even of the British and Canadians, to appease Red China's aggression, he accepted the necessity of letting it work itself out within the United Nations. Nothing that happened in the UN would affect the immediate outcome in Korea until the military rout was halted. And the United States would only disrupt the Atlantic alliance by prematurely attempting to impose its policy of condemning Red China. On December 17 Acheson had to fly to Brussels for a critical meeting of the NATO Foreign Ministers' Council to inform the Europeans that the President intended to nominate General

Dwight D. Eisenhower as supreme commander of NATO and to secure their agreement to new defense plans including the rearmament of Germany.

It is some measure of the peculiar difficulties Acheson faced that on December 15 the Republicans in the House and Senate, meeting separately, voted in the House unanimously and in the Senate 20 to 5 that Acheson had lost the confidence of the country and should be removed from office. While Acheson negotiated in Brussels, the United States Senate debated and defeated, 47 to 29, a resolution asking the President for his removal and the appointment of a successor.

The campaign to "get Acheson" had been building up all fall. His conduct of Far Eastern policy had been a prime campaign issue for the Republicans. Following his speech to the Governors' Conference in mid-1950, a resolution endorsing Acheson and American foreign policy was rejected. Even an expression of thanks for his appearance encountered Republican opposition. At the same time *Life, Time,* and other journals had been giving their readers the impression that occult and mysterious forces were defeating America's invincibility in Asia. Who was holding back on the use of Chiang Kai-shek's armies in Korea? Acheson. Who was denying MacArthur his opportunity to attack beyond the Yalu and give America the victory it so richly deserved? Acheson. MacArthur's courage was contrasted with the character of the leaders at home who were "obsessed by fears." Although *Time* grudgingly recognized that "so far Acheson is against a deal with the Reds," it feared that his desire to conciliate the allies would undermine America's moral will to resist the Red menace. "We must realize that we are in a war to the bitter end," *Life* trumpeted, "and it will not be over until one side or the other conquers completely." Any talk of negotiations or settlement is "defeatism."

The Republican action was like waving the bloody shirt in front of the President, whose esteem for Acheson and his political instincts was aroused. Contemptuously comparing the requests for Acheson's dismissal to those made upon Lincoln to expel Seward, Truman left no one in doubt that as long as he was President Acheson would remain in office.

Meanwhile, the evacuation of the Tenth Corps from the Hamhung–Hungnam beachhead—which had begun on December 11—was completed on December 25. This remarkable operation, which included the withdrawal of 105,000 troops, 100,000 refugees, 17,500 vehicles, and 350,000 tons of equipment and supplies through the mountain passes of North Korea, had been a complete success, in great measure because the Chinese Communists had refrained from using their airpower. Instead, the Chinese were about to launch their first great offensive aimed at the conquest of all Korea.

On December 26 MacArthur asked Washington for more divisions and for authority to use Chinese Nationalist divisions, warning that he could not hold without them. Conditions still appeared so critical on December 29 that MacArthur again informed the Joint Chiefs of Staff that unless his command was permitted to (1) blockade the coast of China; (2) destroy, through naval gunfire and aerial bombardment, China's industrial capacity; (3) secure appropriate reinforcements from the Nationalist garrison on Formosa; and (4) release the Nationalist troops there for diversionary action against the Chinese mainland, it would be necessary to pull back the UN defense lines to the Pusan beachhead for final evacuation.

Once again the Administration considered and rejected MacArthur's program for retaliation against China. Acheson pointed out that blockade would require British consent, that Chinese troops on Formosa were more important where they were, and that unless the Communists attacked U.S. forces outside of Korea the United States had no cause to extend the war against China proper. Meanwhile, General Walton Walker, who had been killed in an accident on December 23, was replaced as commander of the Eighth Army by Lieutenant General Matthew Ridgway, who immediately started touring the battlefield telling his beaten armies that they were going to stay in Korea and fight.

For a time, however, the momentum of the first great Communist offensive aimed at China's conquest of all of Korea was too great to be denied. On January 2, 1951, Ridgway ordered the evacuation of Seoul and retreat to the Pyongtaek–Samchok line about seventy miles below the parallel.

As long as MacArthur remained supreme commander, neither the Joint Chiefs nor the President could ignore his right to warn about the dangers of continuing on a course of military operations that he believed would eventually lead to the destruction of his command. On the other hand, by improperly painting the situation in such desperate and hopeless colors, MacArthur was bringing great pressure to bear upon the Administration, and the Joint Chiefs in particular, to accept the loss of Korea as the price of their refusal to attack China.

On January 10 MacArthur sent the Joint Chiefs another gloomy message. He insisted that limiting the war to Korea would "eventually render untenable the military position of the command in Korea." The only basis upon which he could accept responsibility for the destruction of his command was that of overriding political strategy. "Under the extraordinary limitations and conditions imposed upon the command in Korea . . . its military position is untenable, but it can hold, if overriding political considerations so dictate, for any length of time up to its complete destruction." [17]

MacArthur's messages were little more than a continuation of his earlier campaign to involve the United States in a war with Communist China. However endangered his armies might be, they were certainly not going to be saved by bombing Red China or introducing Nationalist troops into an already chaotic situation. MacArthur was still intent on playing out his mad dream that the future of the world would be settled in Asia. "The lands touching the Pacific with their billions of inhabitants will determine the course of history in the next ten thousand years." [18]

MacArthur's intent, pure and simple, was to redeem his own colossal failure on the Yalu by involving the United States in a new war against China. That honest soldier Bradley sniffed MacArthur's latest missive suspiciously. The commander's message clearly called for something more than a routine military directive. According to Bradley, the State Department proposed to incorporate certain political reasons into the military directive, but the Joint Chiefs objected to that.[19] It ended up in a discussion at the White House with the President in which the decision was made that the military part of the directive would be pulled and sent by itself while the State Department would prepare with the President a letter on the political issues to be sent separately.[20] The military directive simply instructed MacArthur to defend in successive positions, to stay in Korea as long as possible, with the understanding that the security of his troops was paramount.[21]

The political part of the message was drawn up by Acheson in the form of a personal letter from the President to MacArthur. Truman presented not just one but ten purposes that would be served by continued military resistance in Korea, presumably in the hope that what one argument might not do ten would. Truman also explained why the United States could not afford to separate itself from its allies in the United Nations or get bogged down in a wider war in Asia.

Our course of action at this time should be such as to consolidate the great majority of the United Nations. This majority is not merely part of the organization but is also the nations whom we would desperately need to count on as allies in the event the Soviet Union moves against us. Further, pending the build-up of our national strength, we must act with great prudence in so far as extending the area of hostilities is concerned. Steps which might in themselves be fully justified and which might lend some assistance to the campaign in Korea would not be beneficial if they thereby involved Japan or Western Europe in large-scale hostilities.[22]

Truman ended his letter by praising MacArthur's splendid leadership and superb performance. It is evident that the purpose of the letter was to set the weight of the Administration's logic before MacArthur in the hope that he would be responsive. Of the President's letter to MacArthur, one author has written, "there was greatness in that message, if only in its patience and in its sincere attempt to clarify a difficult situation for a military commander who was himself difficult." * Nevertheless, the men in Washington were still counting on their own logic, and not taking sufficient account of MacArthur's logic. His frustrations were nurtured by a well-developed belief that opposition to his strategy was part of a vast conspiracy fostered by Communist appeasers and Anglophiles ever ready to put the interests of a declining empire ahead of the challenge to a virile America to redeem Asia from Communism. No letter, however sincerely couched, was likely to sway him.

It was also decided to send Generals Collins and Vandenberg to Korea to check the military situation for themselves. "This visit and the President's message with its emphasis on the importance of continuing the fight in Korea both betray an Administration belief that MacArthur had perhaps deliberately exaggerated the desperateness of the military situation in order to win approval of his own strategic program." [23]

Fortunately for the Administration things now began to look up. On January 17 the Chinese advance was halted and Ridgway began laying plans for offensive operations that would soon carry the United Nations Command back to the 38th parallel. The contingency which MacArthur had not foreseen—the failure of a major Chinese Communist breakthrough—and the unexpected success of Ridgway's counteroffensive deprived the Far Eastern commander of the dreadful alternatives upon which he had hoped to hang the Administration—defeat or an Asian war.

With the passing of the military initiative to the United Nations Command, MacArthur knew that he had lost any chance which he might have had for levering the Administration into an all-out war. So long as it did not face the ultimate disaster of being hurled off the peninsula, the Administration would stick to its decision to fight a limited war in Korea. Truman and Acheson might suffer the slings of public outrage but there would be no chance of getting them to accept MacArthur's strategy. A week after receiving Truman's letter, MacArthur capitulated to the inevitable. On January 20 he flew from Tokyo to Taegu and there announced, "No one is going to throw us into the sea." It would not be his last announcement.

Troubles at Home

The heat was still on the Administration from another direction. As yet no progress had been made in securing a United Nations condemnation of the Chinese intervention, for the majority of the members were still unable to bring themselves to the point of condemning Peking as an

---

* Robert Leckie, *Conflict: The History of the Korean War, 1950–1953* (New York: Avon, 1962), p. 217.

aggressor. The State Department had sent telegrams to its diplomatic missions in thirty countries, including Britain and France, setting forth the view of the United States on what the United Nations could do to meet the Chinese Communist aggression in Korea. UN Ambassador Austin, speaking at Atlantic City on January 9, 1951, urged a strong, united position featuring the condemnation and the taking of collective measures against Peking. Nevertheless, on January 11 Lester Pearson of Canada, on behalf of the cease-fire group, presented a statement of five new principles for cease-fire to the Political and Security Committee. In addition to a renewed plea for a cease-fire, the proposal called for reunification of Korea on UN principles, the withdrawal of all foreign troops, and the establishment of "an appropriate body" on which would be represented the United States, the USSR, *and* the People's Republic of China, to settle Far Eastern problems, including those of Formosa and UN representation of the PRC. The State Department was given only a few hours to decide how it would vote on this bitterly divisive proposal. Despite the odium he knew would be incurred, Acheson recommended to the President that the United States delegation vote *for* the resolution as a gesture of solidarity with the spirit and processes of the United Nations. And on January 13 the General Assembly, by a vote of 50 to 7, with the United States voting affirmatively, supported the five-point cease-fire resolution proposed by the UN Political and Security Committee.

Senator Taft led the attack on the Administration's support for the resolution by declaring that it was a "shocking step" toward appeasement. He said, quite characteristically, "I would rather retire from Korea entirely and retain a free hand in rejecting Communist China as a member of the UN and the complete exclusion of the Chinese Communists from Formosa." In order to allay criticism of a vote the purpose of which, had his critics been acting in good faith, they would have recognized or at least kept quiet about, Acheson had to issue a statement.

The [cease-fire] proposal . . . was founded on two principal attitudes. One was the belief of many members that the Chinese Communists might still be prevailed upon to cease their defiance of the UN. While we did not share this belief we recognized that it was sincerely held by many members. The second attitude was that, even though there might be little prospect of success in the approach to Peiping, the UN should leave no stone unturned in its efforts to find a peaceful solution. Holders of each view believed and stated to us that opposition or abstention by the U.S. would destroy any possibility of success which the proposal might have. . . . It has been our goal to so act as to maintain the unity of the free nations against aggression which has marked the UN actions in Korea. Accordingly, we voted for the resolution to demonstrate our adherence to these basic principles even though we did not share the beliefs of other members . . . that it would achieve its purpose.[24]

Acheson went on to point out that far from committing us to any position regarding Formosa or Chinese representation in the UN, it merely obliged the United States to discuss these questions "in the future under proper circumstances."

Acheson later recognized that the resolution involved the risk, mainly domestic, of appearing to acquiesce in Peking's claims in conection with a cease-fire, but it was a risk which he felt the United States had to run if it was to win unqualified support for its resolution condemning Communist China as an aggressor in Korea. Moreover, if the United States hoped to keep its allies united and influence their behavior on other matters vital to American foreign policy, Acheson knew he must respect their commitment to the United Nations. By refusing to break with the United Nations, in spite of the domestic advantages of doing so, Acheson acknowledged a commitment to the political universe which those who called for a "go it alone" policy did not. Despite his limited faith in the UN, Acheson could not close his eyes to its reality as a part of a system of international relations which had to be supported in its entirety.

The success of Acheson's position is reflected in Canadian Foreign Minister Lester Pearson's observation. "I felt that the new United States position was extremely valuable and that it would be tragic if it were rudely rebuffed by the Chinese." [25] Unfortunately the People's Republic damaged its position by treating the resolutions offered by Canada and the neutralists led by India with contempt on the grounds that all efforts by the Untied Nations to mediate the conflict were illegitimate since the U.N. was itself a party to the struggle in Korea. Unfortunately it was only after Peking rejected the U.N. cease-fire proposal on January 17 that it proposed via the Indian government a more reasonable alternative, namely a peace in two stages—first, a cease-fire for a limited time period, followed by a conference to discuss all of the Far East issues outstanding.[26]

As Acheson had predicted, Peking rejected the cease-fire proposal on January 17. And the United States, acting alone, now submitted its draft resolution branding Peking an aggressor and calling upon the UN membership to support collective action to meet this aggression by, among other things, withholding assistance to the aggressors in Korea.

Many statesmen, including Britain's Attlee and, of course, India's Nehru, continued to espouse a "go slow" policy and spoke of "keeping the door to peace open by not passing such a resolution." The Senate acted in a contrary sense by adopting two resolutions, the first calling upon the UN to condemn the Peking regime as an aggressor and the second opposing admission of Communist China to the UN. After several days of lengthy debate the Political and Security Committee (not the Security Council) adopted the U.S. resolution 44 to 7 (Burma, India, and the Soviet bloc) with 8 abstentions (Afghanistan, Egypt, Indonesia, Pakistan, Sweden, Syria, Yemen, and Yugoslavia). On February 1 the General Assembly adopted the aggressor resolution with all delegations voting as they had in the Political and Security Committee.[27] Although the resolution passed, it lacked the support of the neutral states and further alienated the People's Republic of China; yet the failure of the U.N. to adopt such a resolution—"to pronounce moral judgment" as Ambassador Warren Austin put it in the debate—would have had a terrible impact on domestic political opinion.

The long-drawn-out battle to secure UN condemnation of mainland China's intervention was only tangentially related to developments in Korea. It neither limited nor advanced the immediate outcome of issues on that far-off peninsula, although it gave ammunition to those domestic critics who chose to exploit the so-called spectacle of the United States voting to consider admitting the Peoples' Republic while Americans died in Korea. Its importance lay in the influence which the outcome of the diplomatic struggle would have upon domestic and international attitudes.

In running the gauntlet of cease-fire resolutions in the United Nations, the Administration engaged in one of the oldest operations known to diplomacy. The circumstances surrounding Chinese intervention had provoked a rebellion against American leadership of the United Nations operation in Korea. Many members felt that Peking ought to be given its due and that it was the United States that stood as the obstacle to peace by depriving Communist China of her "rights" to be represented in the United Nations and to govern Formosa. The terrifying possibility of the war extending to the whole of the Far East intensified these pressures all along the line. At the same time the Administration was being raked from its other flank by Republican cries of appeasement. On the face of it, all Peking had to do was keep the military pressure on in Korea until America's ties with her allies and with the UN snapped. Sooner or later the Administration would be driven to choose between either its domestic critics, who supported MacArthur's strategy, or its allies. The only way the Administration had of escaping from this excruciating trap was by accepting the "form" of negotiations while denying the "substance" of concessions. But even this was not easy to do, because the Administration's domestic critics were ideologically opposed to acceptance even of the form, while the Asian bloc had to be convinced that there *was* real substance. In these circumstances the Administration chose to adhere to the position that while it was willing to settle questions by peaceful means, the United Nations would be betraying its own highest trust if it permitted decisions to be forced upon it under the coercive influence of an aggressive action. By going along in principle with the successive cease-fire resolutions, Acheson succeeded in having included in each of them the condition that a cease-fire must precede negotiations. As Acheson explained it, "The whole basis of the United Nations Charter is that we settle questions by peaceful means. We are required to go before the United Nations Organization and discuss questions. We are not called upon to agree. We are not called upon to give up our position on anything that we regard as some basic interest." [28] But by accepting the rules of the game and by giving the impression that the United States was willing to cooperate with its allies in seeking a speedy termination of hostilities, the Administration skillfully forced upon the UN negotiators acceptance of terms which Acheson knew Peking could only accept at the price of giving up its own ambitions.

By rejecting the final cease-fire resolution, Peking incurred the onus for blocking settlement of the war. The United States could now press ahead with its resolution condemning Communist China as an aggressor. Precisely because the Asian critics of American leadership had been given their chance and failed, the diplomatic consensus in the UN shifted to the United States, and India's desperate attempts to block action were brushed aside. The American resolution which now passed with an overwhelming majority called upon "all states and authorities to continue to lend every assistance to the United Nations' action in Korea." It would be some time, however, before the UN brought itself to consider the application of sanctions. As Spanier remarks: "The inclination to take a favorable view of Communist China's 'legitimate' demands could not be erased overnight by a formal resolution. . . . Nor could the fear that the United States was tugging at the leash of a major war be dampened quickly. . . ." [29] Nevertheless, Acheson's policy, brutal though the punishment had been at the time, succeeded at least in preserving the form of allied unity and in restoring the initiative to the State Department both at home and abroad.

Unfortunately, this maneuver, carried out under exceedingly adverse circumstances, was far from decisive. Under the terms of the Uniting for Peace Resolution the General Assembly could do no more than recommend military sanctions against the People's Republic of China. From a constitutional standpoint only a decision by the Security Council could require members to impose sanctions (under article 25) and such action could be blocked by a Soviet veto. Consequently the UN vote did not confront Peking with decisive military sanctions and left the war to drag on. It also gave MacArthur and his domestic allies ammunition with which to lambast the Administration.

Despite the many disadvantages, Acheson knew that the Administration had achieved the best arrangement it could hope to obtain. To have kept the existing support for UN operations pasted together was no mean achievement. The department had no intention of letting MacArthur destroy the delicate balances achieved by some irreparable act of folly in Korea. When MacArthur's action threatened to disintegrate NATO and open the floodgates of Asian hostility, the Administration felt compelled to bring about his removal. Perhaps they recognized that, having achieved as much as they did in the intervening months, they were now in a position to remove MacArthur once and for all.

New Troubles with MacArthur

It took the closest coordination of State and Defense decisions throughout February and March to keep MacArthur in line, and even then they did not always succeed. MacArthur had already asked publicly three times to bomb what he now called "the privileged sanctuary of Manchuria." [30] On February 16 the Administration gave MacArthur further evidence of its determination to shelve any more ambitious plans he might still be contemplating when Secretary Marshall announced that the Administration intended to send four divisions to reinforce General Eisenhower's NATO command in Europe. On February 21 MacArthur was informed that "he still might not bomb Rashin, an important Chinese Communist supply center in Korea near the Soviet border." [*] On March 12, his armies having regained the 38th parallel, Ridgway declared, contrary to MacArthur, that having done so constituted a "tremendous victory" for the United Nations. On that assumption the Administration began preparation of a Presidential announcement "that, with the clearing of the bulk of South Korea of aggression" the United Nations was "now preparing to discuss conditions of settlement in Korea." [31] But before announcing American (and United Nations) terms for a cease-fire, Acheson felt obliged to ask the Joint Chiefs to request of MacArthur what freedom of action he would require for the next few weeks "to provide a security for UN forces and maintain contact with [the] enemy," should a cease-fire be entered into.[32] The next to the last round in the Administration's running battle with MacArthur was about to begin.

Sensing that any hope he might still have had of securing support for extending the war would fade in the light of the United Nations' call for a cease-fire, MacArthur beat the President to the punch with his own pronunciamento on March 24. Whereas Truman had intended to broach the possibility of a cease-fire with China in concilatory tones, MacArthur's

---

[*] Trumbull Higgins, *Korea and the Fall of MacArthur: A Précis in Limited War* (New York: Oxford University Press, 1960), p. 105. Minutes. Acheson to Marshall, February 19. MacArthur now wished to reopen an issue discussed and settled by the President on September 11, 1950. Rashin was only seventeen miles from the Soviet border. Communications could be disrupted further south. The gains were not commensurate to the risks. Marshall agreed.

message constituted a virtual ultimatum to a far-from-defeated enemy. It began with a lengthy exposition of contempt for the Chinese military effort, followed by the assertion that the People's Republic "has been shown its complete inability to accomplish by force of arms the conquest of Korea"; it warned that a decision of the United Nations "to depart from its tolerant effort to contain the war to the area of Korea . . . would doom Red China to imminent military collapse," and concluded with Mac-Arthur's haughty offer to meet with the enemy's commander-in-chief on the battlefield.[33] Just as the United States refused to negotiate under duress, MacArthur knew that Peking could hardly be expected to negotiate under this ultimatumlike pronunciamento. Truman's message, which was never delivered, had as one of its purposes—should it have been rejected—to clear the ground for possible enlargement of operations against the Chinese by "convincing our allies that the former were unwilling to settle for the status quo *ante bellum*." [34] If the United States made a genuine offer to negotiate and it was rejected then it would be in a position to rally support for operations directly against China. "In Mr. Acheson's graphic explanation, a Presidential statement was now impossible since the field of negotiations 'had been occupied' by General Mac-Arthur." [35]

Truman determined then and there to recall MacArthur. By intervening in the highest political and diplomatic processes in such a way as to defeat the President's policy, MacArthur had crossed a line which, for all his ebullient esteem for American military heroes, Truman could not ignore. "By this act MacArthur left me no choice—I could no longer tolerate his insubordination." [36] Before announcing his decision, however, the President determined to consult with his military and civilian advisers. Several of these had met late the previous night (March 23) at Acheson's home. Robert Lovett, then Undersecretary of Defense, upon receipt of knowledge of MacArthur's ultimatum, had come by accompanied by Assistant Secretary of State Dean Rusk and two others. Lovett's immediate annoyance and anger apparently prompted him to argue that MacArthur should be removed and removed at once. Since that appeared unlikely, as an immediate solution Acheson proposed that MacArthur be enjoined to make no more statements of any sort whatever. As a result, when Acheson, Lovett, and Rusk met with the President the next day at 11:30 A.M. they had no trouble agreeing that MacArthur's statement violated the directive of December 5, "requiring that all public statements be cleared with any department concerned." * Following the

---

* The Joint Chiefs discussed MacArthur's insubordination for an hour that morning. In light of their directive of December 5, 1950, to MacArthur specifically requiring him to clear any statements relating to political matters, they agreed that anyone

meeting, instructions were sent to MacArthur reminding him of his responsibility under that order and directing him, in the unlikely event of a cease-fire proposal from the other side, to refer it to the Joint Chiefs of Staff for instructions.

The next incident occurred thirteen days later, on April 5. Congressman Joseph Martin (R–Mass.) released a letter from General MacArthur in which MacArthur again criticized the strategy of limited war and the decision not to employ Nationalist troops. He also condemned European diplomats for waging a war of words while the Communists waged real war on the battlefield where the victory over Communism would have to be won or lost. The day following the release of MacArthur's letter, the President met with Acheson, Marshall, Harriman, and Bradley. Acheson agreed with Harriman and Bradley that MacArthur should be recalled; but, like Marshall, Acheson also advised caution, saying: "If you relieve MacArthur, you will have the biggest fight of your Administration!" [37] Acheson also advised something which was to be of inestimable importance in light of later efforts by the Administration's critics to show that Truman and his civilian advisers had relieved MacArthur in opposition to or without the concurrence of the military. Acheson urged the President to recognize that, whatever he did here, "he would have to do [it] with the unanimous support of all his military and civilian advisers; if he acted without the real support of the Chiefs of Staff and General Marshall, greater trouble was likely to occur; even graver trouble than if he didn't act at all, . . . if this removal took place it should be with a completely united front, with no cracks whatever." [38] In line with his recommendation, Acheson urged that the whole matter "should be thought about very carefully, over the weekend, and the decision should be made by the President on Monday, since there was no need for doing it before then." [39] The next morning, April 7, a Saturday, the same group was again summoned to the President's office in the White House and the matter was discussed further. "The President then requested General Marshall and General Bradley to get the Chiefs of Staff together and get their views and be prepared to come back on Monday with the views of everybody for a final decision." [40]

However, on Sunday morning the President summoned Acheson to Blair House again, and he and the President discussed the matter for some time alone. Finally, on Monday morning at 9:00 A.M. the four advisers—Acheson, Marshall, Bradley, and Harriman—met with the Presi-

---

other than MacArthur would have been relieved at once. The Joint Chiefs recognized the startling and potentially adverse results of his relief but "they do not believe they can let it slide. They are thinking of a reprimand." Lovett to Acheson, March 24, 1951. Acheson Papers.

dent to hear the decision of the military. The Joint Chiefs of Staff were of the unanimous opinion that MacArthur should be relieved.[41] Of course, "whether any such judgment could be purely military is another matter." *

When Harry Truman decided to relieve MacArthur of his Far Eastern commands, he knew, in his own words, that "I was in for the fight of my life." The stuffing was going to be torn out of the Administration.

A Democratic administration was now going to pay the price for having built MacArthur up for so many years and for contributing to his emergence as an independent political power in the Far East. Over the years millions of Americans had come to identify MacArthur with the authoritative expression of American policy in the Orient. The success which had attended his proconsulship in Japan had burnished with luster the legend that had come to surround him. For Americans burdened by world responsibility to which they were not accustomed, MacArthur's masterful handling of the Japanese stood out in distinct relief. His public relations to this end had left nothing to be desired. The absence of any effective allied or Russian check upon his performance and the propensity of the Administration to let MacArthur run his own show enabled him to become a political power in his own right, a general who, while often seconded for Presidential office, had kept himself free of political tarnish. Truman's respect for this formidable political figure had long restrained him from making a decisive issue of MacArthur's repeated acts of disrespect and disobedience. A point had been finally reached, however, where the Administration could no longer allow itself to tolerate MacArthur's machinations. MacArthur not only struck at the bases of United States foreign policy but also propounded confusion at home and abroad as to who was actually running the United States government.

Nevertheless, while pushed to the brink, Truman had continuously refrained from a decisive break. That came, as we have seen, only when MacArthur committed the most heinous of all political and constitutional sins by writing a letter to House Republican Leader Joseph Martin, who made it public, in which he attacked the Administration's policies and cast aspersions upon the President's capacity in the conduct of foreign affairs. In Truman's own words:

The second paragraph of this letter was in itself enough of a challenge to existing national policy. MacArthur had been fully informed as to the reason why the employment of Chinese Nationalist forces was ruled out. He himself, only eight months earlier, had endorsed the merit of this decision. Later, when he

---

* Higgins, *op. cit.*, p. 118. Not all the Chiefs based their decision on MacArthur's alleged "insubordination." Several chose to see his removal as essential because of his "incompatability" with the Administration's conduct of the war.

had changed his position and reopened the subject, he had again been advised that this was part of the over-all policy on which the President had decided. So, in praising Mr. Martin's logic and traditional attitude, he was in effect saying that my policy was without logic and violated tradition.[42]

By acting as he did, MacArthur demonstrated that he was no longer content to influence policy from the inside; he was now prepared to connive openly with the Republicans—nominally isolationist but now backing MacArthur's strategy for war with China—at the destruction of the President's authority and of the Administration's political life. Under these circumstances MacArthur's letter to Martin represented his last affront to the Administration. Republicans were delighted. Herbert Hoover wired MacArthur to "fly home as quickly as possible before Truman and Marshall and their propagandists can smear you." [43] If Truman had not acted at this point, he would have risked abrogating all pretense of authority and control over foreign policy. Of the seriousness of the crisis Acheson later reminisced:

It would be clear to everybody that not only had we created here an absolutely impossible situation in which we could not conduct our relations with our allies, we could not conduct the military policy and the political policy in Korea which the government decided to conduct, because of MacArthur's defiance; but this was even graver than that, because a man with great popular support in the country, with great military reputation, great authority in the Congress, was defying the authority of the President of the United States himself. And this seemed to me to go to the very root of democratic government, it was threatening the control over the military by the President and the whole civil side of the government. It seemed to me that we were in the presence of the gravest constitutional crisis that perhaps the U.S. had ever faced, and I say that quite seriously and not in any oratorical sense. I think it is quite as serious as any of the crises which were faced during the Reconstruction Period after the Civil War, and might have completely overthrown the constitutional system.[44]

The decision to relieve MacArthur was Truman's alone; however, in terms of policy, the decision had for its prime consequence the removal of Acheson's only formidable opponent to keeping the war in Korea limited. Whatever else might follow, it was certain that unless the Republicans succeeded in bringing about his removal as Secretary of State, Acheson's Far Eastern policy would be the unchallenged and operative policy; * for as the hearings on MacArthur's dismissal were to make clear, both Marshall and the Joint Chiefs were in essential agreement with Acheson's thinking and were content to accept his logic for containing the war to the Korean peninsula.

---

* Ridgway, while not always in agreement with Acheson and the Joint Chiefs, nevertheless meticulously adhered to the orders sent him.

By an unhappy coincidence, Acheson had scheduled a long-standing conference with Senators Styles Bridges (R–N.H.) and Pat McCarran (D–Nev.) for the afternoon of April 10 at the very time when the orders relieving MacArthur were enroute to Secretary of the Army Frank Pace, on tour at Pusan. Bridges and McCarran were two of the Administration's meanest critics, men for whom the political style of the grudge fighter came naturally and who bore little love for Acheson.

I got up there [to Capitol Hill, Acheson reported] and we had a little talk of a general nature, . . . then McCarran said he was very glad that they had this appointment at this time, because there was great feeling throughout the country which he knew all about—and great feeling in the Congress that Mac-Arthur was right and he was a very important person and he hoped the President wouldn't do anything headstrong or undesirable about this, because if the President got into a row with MacArthur the President was sure to lose, so he wanted me to be sure to tell him [the President] he had to go easy on this. Well, of course the decision to relieve MacArthur had been made the day before and the orders relieving him were on their way to Pusan at the time I had this meeting, and quite clearly I couldn't say anything about it. So I listened and said that I knew the President was always interested in having the views of these two distinguished senators and that I would transmit them in due course. This led to a renewal of our estrangement, my estrangement with the senators was even more bitter then than it had been before, because they accused me of misleading them on this [because] I obviously knew about this and didn't tell them. Which was quite true. I knew this was a desperate situation, but there I was and there was nothing I could do about it.[45]

MacArthur's return on April 17 was the signal for one of the greatest orgies of mass adulation known to American history. Millions followed with rising expectation MacArthur's dramatic return to shores he had not seen for over fifteen years. Given the aura of greatness which surrounded his accomplishments in the intervening decade and a half, it was inevitable that his triumphal entry should be touched by messianic overtones. Of MacArthur's address to the Congress, Representative Dewey Short intoned: "We heard God speak here today, God in the flesh, the voice of God." Calls for Truman's impeachment and for Acheson's dismissal were heard everywhere.[46] Not everyone took such an adulatory view. While no one in Congress publicly held back from inviting MacArthur to address the Congress, here and there Democrats did their best to let some of the air out of MacArthur's bubble.

Representative Adolf Sabath, Democrat of Illinois and chairman of the Rules Committee, for a time insisted upon trying to load the invitation. Sabath announced that the Rules Committee was going "to consider the concurrent resolution giving General of the Army, Douglas MacArthur, an opportunity to address the joint meeting of the Senate and House to explain and give his reasons for failure to comply with the orders of his superiors and in disregarding the instructions of the President, the Commander-in-Chief." [47] Sabath's irreverent views were not allowed to prevail. However, the Democrats did succeed in having the occasion of MacArthur's address to Congress designated as a joint meeting rather than a joint session in order to make the point that his appearance was less a formal state function than a courtesy to a distinguished hero of the republic.[48]

Whatever his own intentions may have been, MacArthur was far too valuable a piece of political property to be allowed to fade away. While he continued his triumphant tour of American cities, the stage was set in Washington by congressional Republicans to press home their indictment of the Administration's Far Eastern policy. By virtue of his relief, it was now possible to lay out for the public record the general's case against the Administration in a far more dramatic and, Republicans hoped, telling fashion than was possible when MacArthur had had to conduct himself with some degree of circumspection. Republican as well as Democratic foes of the Administration looked forward to nailing Acheson with the responsibility for everything that had gone wrong in the Far East. The complete success of their plans was put in jeopardy from the outset by the sequence in which the witnesses were to be heard. Instead of Acheson following MacArthur in such a fashion as to pit the two protagonists, it was arranged that Generals Marshall, Bradley, Collins, and Vandenberg and Admiral Sherman should testify for the Administration before Acheson. This interposition of prestigious testimony from the Joint Chiefs of Staff did a little to mute the attack on Acheson.

Long before the critics got to Acheson they were taken aback to find that the Joint Chiefs, far from agreeing with MacArthur, were fundamentally opposed to his strategy for extending the war. By his testimony of May 3, 4, and 5, MacArthur had given the Republicans every indication that they would find the Joint Chiefs in basic agreement with him. Had he not said that "nothing I can recall" suggested disagreement between his views and those of the Joint Chiefs? Had he not declared that their views "coincided almost identically with my own beliefs in the matter . . ."? He had then gone on to pay his respects to the Joint Chiefs: "I want to say that the relationships between the Joint Chiefs of Staff and myself have been admirable. All members are personal friends of mine. I hold them individually and collectively in the greatest esteem. If there has been friction between us, I am not aware of it." [49] Great was Republican disappointment when the testimony of the Joint Chiefs revealed fundamental support of the Administration. Far from asserting that the war could be terminated by an assault upon China, the Joint Chiefs felt that this would be an act of the greatest danger, and suggested that the existing military strength of the United States was not sufficient to withstand a possible Soviet intervention. Korea, Bradley declared, "must be looked upon with proper perspective. . . . We have recommended against enlarging the war. The course of action often described as a 'limited war' with Red China would increase the risk we are running in engaging too much of our power in an area that is not the critical strategic prize . . . this strategy would involve us in the wrong war, at the wrong place, at the wrong time, and with the wrong enemy." [50]

Nevertheless, as the chief Administration witness, Acheson came under a most ferocious assault. While the interrogation of other witnesses, with the possible exception of Marshall, was restricted to the general issue under scrutiny, the interrogation of Acheson surged back and forth over the entire range of United States foreign policy. Because the circumstances surrounding the hearings were so conducive to the arraignment of the Administration, Republicans took license to strike wherever possible. Acheson was their obvious target, for his role as architect of the Administration's Far Eastern policy and as intercessor on behalf of the European and Asian states made him a perfect scapegoat for all Republican feelings of dissatisfaction. Acheson was called to the witness stand on Friday, June 1, and did not complete his testimony until Saturday, June 9. In comparison to MacArthur's testimony, which ran to 317 pages, Acheson filled 624 pages of the hearings.* One might wonder how questions concerning (1) possible loan to Mexico for development of its oil resources, (2) an oil crisis in Iran, (3) the family connection between Assistant Secretary of State George McGhee and the petroleum engineer de Golyer, (4) admission of German scientists to the United States, (5) a unilateral aid treaty between the United States and Turkey, and (6) soybean speculation could have any bearing upon the military situation in the Far East. Acheson's patience was frequently strained.

Nevertheless, the hearings gave Acheson a major opportunity to explain the Administration policy while it had the benefit of public attention focused upon it. He dealt at length with the danger of getting bogged down in a strategically useless war, and of the risks involved in extending the war to China—the Soviet Union might feel obliged by its security treaty with Peking to intervene and America would most certainly lose the support of its allies. Twice during the hearings Acheson spelled out for the benefit of Peking and Moscow America's terms for an armistice: if the United States could get an assurance that hostilities would not be renewed against South Korea, the United States was willing to accept a

---

* This does not include the several hundred pages of documents which Acheson was obliged to submit as appendices to his testimony.

cease-fire at or near the 38th parallel and agree to remove foreign troops from Korea, both Chinese and United Nations.[51]

Acheson was also able to point to strategic and political factors which MacArthur and his Republican supporters all too readily discounted. By succeeding in driving the Chinese back to the 38th parallel, Acheson could claim that extension of the war was unnecessary because Communist imperialism had been contained and denied the fruits of its aggression. True, the war had not been brought to an end, but its continuation on a small front was more to the advantage of the UN forces than to the Chinese. From extending the war, we could gain nothing except larger casualty lists with no guarantee of victory. Punishing the mainland of China would only involve us in a larger war with the risk of Soviet intervention under their treaty of alliance. Furthermore, it would wreck America's alliance system and defeat the principle of collective security.

We cannot expect that our collective security system will long survive if we take steps which unnecessarily and dangerously expose the people who are in the system with us. . . .

The power of our coalition to deter an attack depends in part upon the will and mutual confidence of our partners. If we, by the measures proposed, were to weaken that effort, particularly in the North Atlantic area, we would be jeopardizing the security of an area which is vital to our own national security.[52]

As to MacArthur's complaint that victory could not be won by limiting the war to Korea, Acheson had this to say:

It doesn't make any difference exactly where the fighting may end. The point is, is a settlement going to be made or is it not going to be made where the Chinese will not have the will and the desire to come back in and fight again? If the forces were pushed back to the Yalu River in accordance with your hypothesis here, if installations behind that were attacked, then their tack would be to recreate them or find some substitute for them. The important element in bringing this thing to a stable end would be to change the will to do this.[53]

Acheson could see no reason why this change in the Chinese will to aggression could not just as well be brought about in Korea rather than on the mainland itself.

If the time comes when the Chinese have thoroughly convinced themselves by the repeated failures that they cannot accomplish their purpose of driving the United Nations troops out of Korea, then it seems to me that the way is open for some sort of a settlement in Korea which can be accepted on the basis of mutually known strengths.[54]

How else do you end wars, Acheson asked his senatorial critics, if not by stalemate? Even total victories and unconditional surrenders do not change the underlying balance of forces. Wars are essentially interludes in the unceasing process by which nations test their relative political strengths. They accomplish nothing worthwhile. Unless the United States intended to wage a war of extermination against Red China, the necessary balance could be established in Korea.

What I am talking about is the defeat of the Chinese effort, and when the Chinese know that they are defeated and have suffered as they have suffered in the last two attacks, then I think their purpose changes and, as their purpose changes, you get a possibility of a settlement.[55]

Negotiations in Korea

Acheson's testimony was not a very hopeful note on which to end, but it completed the Administration's defense of its Far Eastern policy. Seldom had the issues of foreign policy been so critically aired. It seemed to serve its purpose because the steam went out of MacArthur's campaign and the American people showed themselves more ready than before to accept the Administration's explanation for its handling of the Korean War. Still, it was destined to drag on tragically for two more years.

In an effort to renew the American cease-fire offer that had been so abruptly short-circuited by MacArthur, Acheson asked Kennan, who was on a leave of absence at Princeton, if he would see UN Ambassador Jacob Malik unofficially and inform the Russians that we were interested neither in a confrontation nor in continuing the war. If they had any suggestions about how the conflict might be ended, the United States would be open to them.

Kennan quietly arranged to see Malik at his summer house on Long Island and relayed Acheson's message. Predictably, Malik could not give an immediate answer, but when the two men met again on June 5 Malik was able to inform Kennan that the Soviet government also wanted a peaceful settlement in Korea and as rapidly as possible.[56] Not being a party to the war, the Soviet government could not appropriately take part in discussions of a cease-fire, but Malik's personal advice was to approach the North Koreans and Chinese. To help things along, Malik announced in the course of a UN radio program on June 23 that the Korean conflict could be settled, and as a first step "discussions should be started between the belligerents for a cease-fire and an armistice providing for the mutual withdrawal of forces from the 38th parallel."

After some preliminary deliberations, armistice negotiations were begun between the military authorities, first at Kaesong and later at Panmunjom. Convinced that the prospects for a long-run political settlement of the Korean situation were dim, Acheson and his advisers were determined to hold out for a cease-fire with which the United States and

South Korea could live. This led to an insistence that the armistice line must be the existing battle line along the 38th parallel rather than the parallel itself. The United States also would not accept the Communist demand for withdrawal of all foreign troops after an armistice on the grounds that an armistice was not a final settlement, and pending such a settlement the Seoul regime had to have the assurance of an American or UN presence. Thirdly, Acheson insisted on a thorough postarmistice inspection system to discourage North Korea from renewing its attack upon the South. When after months of wrangling it became apparent that the United Nations negotiators were not going to get a postarmistice political settlement, Acheson agreed to settle for simple cease-fire, but that was all the more reason, he believed, to hold on to the most favorable defensive line. The other side agreed to that on November 27, 1951.

Unfortunately, a new and most intractable problem presented itself in the form of Communist prisoners of war who did not want to be repatriated. For the Communist side this posed a serious problem of prestige and morale. Without the example in Korea of forcible repatriation, other Communist soldiers might be tempted to surrender. At the same time the American military feared that unless all Communist prisoners were returned, the Communist side would refuse to repatriate UN/Americans POWs. Clearly, there was a delicate balance between the humanitarian impulse not to forcibly repatriate Communists to face the same uncertain and perhaps tragic fate as had been met by many Russian soldiers at the war's end in Europe and the desire to get an armistice and secure the release of American and other UN troops held by the enemy. In the end Acheson opted for the difficult task of trying to find some alternative to forcible repatriation acceptable to the other side. Over a period of a year, all kinds of proposals for various face-saving forms of voluntary repatriation were proposed, but none was ever found acceptable to the other side.

The only way in which the United States might have budged the Chinese would have been either by renewing the ground offensive against the North, which would have incurred heavy casualties and necessitated lifting "our self-imposed ban on attacks on the enemy sanctuary north of the Yalu," [57] or by direct bombing and blockade of China with the possibility of Russian intervention. The latter option was considered as part of a study to determine if some idea was being overlooked which might break the deadlock at Panmunjom. Neither Acheson nor America's allies with whom the bombing and blockade option was discussed considered it acceptable on either strategic or political grounds. Acheson himself was more than ever determined not to escalate or extend the war if he could help it. A massive new offensive could only increase losses while providing no assurance that the prospects for a settlement would improve. Better, thought Acheson, to continue to concentrate America's effort along the narrow waist of Korea where America's fire power gave us a distinct advantage. Secondly, a new offensive either against North Korea or against China directly would divide us from our allies at a critical time when we were about to achieve the rearmament of Western Europe, including West Germany. Acheson raised the notion of bombing or blockading over and over again with America's principal allies only to be rebuffed. The British agreed to consider the bombing of Manchuria as one of the means of holding China to an armistice agreement but balked at the idea of a naval blockade. Short of a unilateral ultimatum such as Eisenhower would send to Peking in 1953, there was nothing Acheson could do to break the deadlock.

The Democratic Party paid heavily for the Administration's refusal to resort to more drastic and potentially more disastrous measures. The Republicans led by Taft charged Acheson with appeasement for agreeing to negotiate at all and constantly called for a much bigger war including the use of Chiang Kai-shek's forces against the mainland.[58] But who in the end is to say that Acheson's decision to make the best of a difficult and often tragic situation was not the best policy? The Administration had gambled once with disastrous results; it was not prepared to gamble again at risk of damaging our policy elsewhere. Moreover the outlook of human beings the world over was changing. An action which at the height of the Chinese offensive might have been acceptable was not acceptable in light of a situation in which there was no longer any real threat to United Nations forces.

Reversal of China Policy

Aside from the killing and destruction, the greatest loss of the Korean War was Acheson's China policy. Our invasion of the North and the subsequent Chinese intervention killed off all hope of Sino–American relations developing in a reasonable, nonhostile manner. The new American policy toward the Peking government was defined by Dean Rusk, Assistant Secretary of State for the Far East, in May 1951. "We can tell our friends in China that the United States will not acquiesce in the degradation which is being forced on them. We do not recognize the authorities in Peiping for what they pretend to be. The Peiping regime may be a colonial Russian Government—a Slavic Manchukuo on a large scale. It is not the Government of China. It does not pass the first test. It is not Chinese." [59] Thus was interred Acheson's earlier policy of trying to establish a modus vivendi for peaceful coexistence with the new regime in

Peking. Six days after Rusk spoke Truman declared it American intention to support "the Chinese armies on Formosa to help keep that island out of Communist hands." [60] While not publicly disavowing previous policy—"To build these statements into far-reaching conclusions of involvement in the Chinese civil war is not justified"—Acheson had completely reversed himself on Formosa. He now took the position that Formosa should be denied "to any regime aligned with or dominated by the USSR" (meaning mainland China), and that "a Korean armistice and satisfactory settlement [of the Korean War] would not in themselves suffice to indicate Chinese Communist non-alignment with the USSR and non-aggressive intent. . . ." [61] For this reason, knowing how it would only divide America from its allies, Acheson did not want Formosa to be included on any agenda to be discussed in postarmistice negotiations ending the Korean War. For the same reason he did not want Chinese Nationalist troops employed in Korea because that too would link the issues. In this Acheson's diplomacy was successful: he successfully avoided having the new American policy toward Formosa linked to Korea or debated in the United Nations.

The reasoning behind Acheson's policy was not so much that the fall of Formosa would result in the island's being turned into a strategic threat to the United States but that Formosa should not be yielded up under pressure until such time as Peking showed some inclination to accept the status quo in the Far East. In effect Acheson now extended to mainland China the same strategic assumptions he applied to the Soviet Union. Until Peking changed its strategy, there was no point in trying to make concessions to induce negotiations. Only when a favorable relationship of forces had been established would Peking be willing to alter its behavior; only at that point might the future of Formosa be reopened. In the meantime the United States would view the Chinese refusal to negotiate a cease-fire in Korea as evidence of a basically hostile intent the United States could do little to change.

Asked by Churchill at their meeting in Washington in January 1952 his prognosis for the future of Sino–American relations, Acheson responded that "the United States no longer felt, as it had in January 1950, that there was any real possibility of inducing Chinese Titoism in the foreseeable future." [62] Acheson expressed the view that "policy toward China had to be pragmatic, i.e., to deal with situations as they were."

Except for MacArthur in Korea and the Pentagon's insistence upon German rearmament, the military had generally adhered to civilian wishes in foreign-policy matters. But beginning in 1952 Acheson encountered an increased tendency on the part of the military to engage in actions that were not consistent with policy. Now there was heavy pressure from the military to employ Nationalist forces in Korea and to unleash Chiang Kai-shek's forces for raids on the mainland.*

Acheson regarded such requests as frivolous and pernicious since we could do just as well by arming South Koreans, and to involve the Chinese in Korea would only alienate our other allies and make negotiations at Panmunjom that much more difficult. Here there was a certain continuity with his earlier view that the United States must not make the situation any worse than it already was. But the longer the war dragged on, the greater the pressure from the Pentagon became to secure its resolution by expanding the war against China.[63] When Acheson expressed the view that "policy toward China had to be pragmatic," [64] he meant that he wanted to do nothing that would weaken America's position as leader of the United Nations Command or complicate negotiations at Panmunjom. Pragmatic also meant securing advance agreement with one's allies about what should be done should negotiations at Panmunjom break down or should the Chinese unleash a great new offensive in Korea. Much of his diplomacy with the British during 1951 and 1952 was taken up in trying to persuade Britain of the need, should the occasion arise, to put into effect a blockade of the Chinese coast and, if need be, to bomb Chinese military targets in retaliation for a renewed offensive in Korea or should Chinese troops enter the Indochina war. The subject was first broached with Herbert Morrison in September 1951 and continued to be a staple of Anglo–American diplomacy to the end of Acheson's tenure.[65] He took it up again with Churchill and Eden at their Washington meeting in January 1952. Despite his most persuasive efforts, Acheson never quite succeeded in getting the British to agree. They were "nervous as ever over the ramifications of the threat or actual use of force directly against China," and they "did not share Acheson's confidence that the allies could simultaneously bomb China and avoid war with the Soviet Union." [66]

The pressure continued. On July 23 Acheson had to complain to Secretary of Defense Lovett against an unauthorized naval air show of force off the coast of China by planes under the command of Admiral Arthur

---

* Position Paper. Additional economic measures against Communist China and North Korea, October 31, 1951. Memo. Acheson, Lovett, Admiral Fechteler, Admiral Libbey, September 17, 1952. On April 11, 1952, the director of the CIA drew Acheson's attention to a memo of questions and answers in which Chiang Kai-shek stated that Nationalist forces "shall be able to occupy an important strategic point in South China and hold it. Subsequently more points may be secured. . . . Chiang believes 90% of the mainland population will support him if action is taken soon . . . no need for U.S. or U.N. *ground* forces on the mainland." (Memo. Merrill to director, CIA, April 11, 1952. Emphasis added.) Fortunately, U.S. military had the intelligence to recognize that Chiang's forces were far from prepared for any such undertaking.

Radford, Commander in Chief of the Pacific Theater.* The navy also had to be warned against participation in a NATO exercise involving the Danish island of Bornholm on the grounds of its proximity in the Baltic to the Soviet Union. But the biggest eruption of the military into policy-making came in the form of military opposition to Acheson's new cease-fire proposal in Korea: that the United Nations offer an armistice on the basis of the exchange of the 83,000 UN prisoners in Communist hands for the 12,000 UN-held Chinese POWs who wished to be repatriated. This exchange would leave the question of prisoners not wishing to be re-patriated to future negotiations following the signing of a cease-fire. In terms very reminiscent of the stubborn refusal by the Joint Chiefs of Staff to agree to a prolonged bombing halt in Vietnam, the military objected because such a proposal would indicate a weakening in the UN Com-mand's negotiating posture, and "it would permit the Communists to use the period of post-armistice negotiations for a military build-up to renew hostilities in the absence of a solution to the POW problem. Defense be-lieves that the best hope of a truce lies in continued and increasing mili-tary pressure on the Communists. . . ." [67]

Acheson reminded the military that at the time of MacArthur's ad-vance to the Yalu the Joint Chiefs of Staff (JCS) and the State Depart-ment had been against doing what MacArthur proposed, but they had been ignored by the commander in the field with disastrous results. "In the present case the preponderance of military opinion both in the field and among the JCS . . . in Washington is against the political advice of the State Department that a further effort should be made to propose a new formula which the Chinese negotiators might be able to accept." Acheson did not feel confident that the Chinese would accept the new proposal, but felt it ought to be tried. Despite these arguments, Acheson was overruled by the President; the military view prevailed.[68]

Peace Treaty with Japan

Another element of Acheson's Far Eastern policy on the eve of Korea had been to sign a peace treaty with Japan ending the occupation and restoring Japan's status as a sovereign entity. Acheson held that it would be better to anticipate the recrudescence of Japanese nationalism and end the occupation before it had outrun its usefulness. By restoring self-government to Japan, Acheson also intended to win Japanese support in

---

* Memo, Acheson to Lovett, July 23, 1952. Acheson Papers. The next day Secre-tary of the Navy Kimball added his braggadocio to that of Radford in a speech to a Chicago audience. As expected, such talk aroused anxieties among America's allies. The proposal for a show of force off the Chinese mainland had been vetoed by Acheson on February 12, 1952.

the Cold War and establish Japan as the anchor of American policy in Asia, offsetting the powerful currents set in motion by the Communist conquest of China. He had been opposed in these plans by the military, both in Washington and Tokyo, who preferred not to lose their privileged status under the occupation.

The onset of the Korean War prompted Truman to overrule the military opposition. He ordered negotiation of such a treaty to go forward. The actual negotiation of the treaty had been turned over to John Foster Dulles, who had been reinstated in the department in April 1950 as a gesture to bipartisanship. The treaty involved a number of difficult issues.

In order to short-circuit Soviet obstructionism, negotiation had to be conducted in private on a bilateral basis. A conference would be convened merely to sign the treaty. Dulles consulted with Malik at the United Nations, but knowing it could do nothing to influence the outcome, Moscow contented itself with a diplomatic and propaganda barrage.

Another issue of the negotiation involved a decision about which government would sign for China—the one in Peking or the one on Formosa. Acheson decided that neither would be invited. The issue was tricky because the British recognized Peking and wanted the matter of which Chinese government Japan would recognize held in abeyance until after the treaty had come into effect; then Tokyo could decide for itself. The United States Senate, however, insisted that Tokyo's preference for the regime on Formosa be known beforehand as a condition of ratification. To meet the latter demand, Dulles secured from Japanese Prime Minister Shigeru Yoshida an understanding of Japan's intent to recognize the Chiang Kai-shek regime. But not content to let Yoshida's assurances speak for themselves, fifty-six senators signed a letter warning Truman that should Japan recognize any government other than that on Formosa ratification would be in trouble. Fearing that without stronger assurances the Senate might reject the treaty, Dulles requested a letter from Yoshida stating Japan's intention of establishing diplomatic relations with Taipei and not with Peking. "Through an oversight, Eden and Churchill were not informed at the time of the Yoshida letter," [69] perhaps because it foreclosed any possibility of Japan recognizing the government in Peking. When the letter was released on January 16, Eden felt betrayed. Once again Acheson apologized and did his best to heal the rift. "Discussion of the incident ended, but a residue of suspicion remained on Eden's part, especially against Dulles for what he considered a devious trick." [70] The British, who were strongly opposed to Acheson's efforts to draw a line against dealings with the People's Republic of China, were doubly bitter at having their expectation that Tokyo might establish diplomatic and commercial relations with Peking so crudely overturned.

The conference was convened for September 5, 1951, in San Francisco.

Truman insisted that Acheson preside; he did, "with a slick but iron parliamentary hand, stifling debate before the Russians appeared to understand what was happening." [71] And because television was for the first time covering a major international conference, the country got a chance to see Dean Acheson sternly putting the Soviet and Polish delegates in their places and presiding in a masterful and decisive fashion over an American diplomatic triumph, such as it was.

By restoring Japanese independence and signing a mutual security treaty establishing Japan as an American ally, Acheson completed his effort to stabilize the balance in Asia that had been upset by the Communist victory in China. The United States had been looking for a new equilibrium when it was overtaken by events on June 25, 1950. Just as it was indispensable not to give up South Korea without a fight, so now Acheson felt that the abandonment of Formosa would "signify a lack of will, determination, and confidence to bolster up the structure of Asian–Pacific relations which had begun to be redefined by the United States after the fall of China to the Communists." [72] By authorizing MacArthur to advance into North Korea, Acheson had sought to challenge a situation that clearly lay within the Sino–Soviet sphere. That had been a mistake. But elsewhere in Asia the tide had not turned against the United States, and Acheson was determined not to let those gray areas pass out of American control without an effort. The defensive shell in the Far East was too thin to let any other holes be punched in it. Acheson may have attributed too much Soviet design and strategic intent to events in Asia, but there is no reason to doubt the sincerity of his conviction that new setbacks in Asia would undermine conditions elsewhere. Whether out of personality or out of the statesman's prudential wisdom, Acheson was profoundly convinced that the West was skirting disaster should it not reinforce the dikes wherever they were threatened. Whether he exaggerated them or not, the shock of events first in Europe and now in Asia stirred his deepest concern lest events get out of control.

Because of his concern that Communist gains in Asia would rebound to the benefit of Moscow and carry the contingent danger of undermining the as yet fragile independence of Japan and the states of Southeast Asia, Acheson chose to view Chinese attitudes as a threat essentially inimical to the peace and security of the entire area. Had the war in Korea not happened, this change in Acheson's attitude toward Peking might not have occurred. But having happened in a way most painful to America, the events caused Acheson to view Chinese intentions as essentially hostile to American interests; therefore he felt justified in applying the same strategic reasoning in Asia toward China as he had adopted in Europe toward Russia—namely, that the only possible basis for peace and security against Communist states lay in opposing them with situations of strength.

In an immediate sense Acheson's diplomacy was a success, for he had succeeded in stemming aggression in Korea and establishing American strength in Japan and Formosa. (The Treaty of Mutual Security, signed with Japan on September 8, 1951, provided that the United States would have the right to maintain armed forces in Japan and its vicinity.)

However, since a policy of refusing to recognize the government in Peking and of defending Formosa reinvolved the United States in the Chinese civil war, the policy was somewhat more complicated than Acheson's strategy for containing Russia in Europe. The United States was now officially hostile toward the regime on the mainland and stood in a position of frustrating China's nationalist aspirations—something Acheson had sought to avoid doing prior to the outbreak of the Korean War. This in turn had adverse consequences for the long-run success of Acheson's diplomacy because it militated against China's acceptance of situations of strength and of a status quo that appeared manifestly inimical to China's legitimate aspirations. In his preoccupation with the immediate danger, Acheson locked American policy into an essentially untenable position toward mainland China that would sooner or later have to be altered. Containment and situations of strength were likely to work in deterring a state like the USSR because it was essentially satisfied with the status quo; it was not likely to deter a state whose essential legitimacy was being denied. That was the flaw in Acheson's application of containment to Asia. Its foundations were too rigidly fixed to conditions that were essentially illegitimate and therefore unstable.

17

GERMAN REARMAMENT AND THE
"GREAT DEBATE"

THE KOREAN ATTACK sharpened Acheson's conviction that the West could never be secure until it could deal with the Soviet Union from situations of strength. Believing that the basic cause of international tension lay in the lack of any real desire or intention on the part of the Soviet Union to reach basic agreements, Acheson decided that a change in Soviet attitudes could be brought about only by the development of Western power so impressive that the Kremlin would have no alternative but to cease and desist out of inability to upset the international balance.

Acheson had been urging Western rearmament since discovery of the Soviet A-bomb in September 1949, but not until the Korean attack was there an opportunity to adopt it as a principal goal of American policy. On July 20, 1950, Acheson instructed Charles Spofford, the newly appointed American representative to the NATO Standing Group and Council of Deputies, that the Administration was prepared to ask for $4 to $6 billion in additional military assistance provided that "the other NATO countries are prepared to go forward promptly with the necessary measures to implement their own rearmament programs." [1] In return for a European commitment to drastically reorient its economy toward preparedness, the United States was prepared to extend Marshall Plan aid beyond 1952. [*]

Acheson would have much preferred that the question of German rearmament be held off until the groundwork for European rearmament had been laid. On July 31 he told Truman:

---

[*] Memo. Acheson to Johnson, July 20, 1950. The President approved this over Louis Johnson's opposition. Meeting, Acheson, Truman, Johnson, July 21. Acheson Papers.

The question was not whether but how Germany should be brought into the general defensive plan without disrupting everything else we were doing and without putting Germany into a position to act as the balance of power in Europe. I said we were thinking along the lines of a European army or a North Atlantic army . . . made up in part of national contingents . . . who would act under a central European or North Atlantic command. . . . Germans might then be enlisted in a European army which would not be subject to the orders of Bonn but of decisions taken within the North Atlantic Treaty.[2]

On August 9, Charles Spofford flew back to Washington to report to Acheson that without a substantial commitment of U.S. ground combat forces to be permanently stationed in Europe, NATO was in danger of losing its forward momentum and falling into desuetude. French terms for increased French effort in support of NATO also suggested stationing additional U.S. forces in Europe under a unified command. "Spurred by the French, prodded by the JCS and impelled by its own recognition of the need to reinvigorate NATO, the State Department moved hastily toward definite proposals to place before the North Atlantic Council meeting, now only a few weeks away."[3]

The need to move more American troops to Europe was discussed between Acheson and Truman on August 10 with the recognition that it might result in "strong differences of opinion with the Defense Establishment."[4] On August 21 Acheson reported that Truman was "disturbed by talk about rearming Germany which he felt to be quite impossible outside of a European Defense Force."[5] By coincidence on August 23 French Ambassador Bonnet remarked to Acheson that Germany's role would be easier to accept once West European forces were strengthened.[6]

By mid–August the State Department set before the Pentagon a proposal for continued financial aid to Europe combined with the dispatch of four to six divisions to reinforce American ground forces in Europe. These were to form part of an integrated NATO force under a supreme commander—presumably an American. The moment the State Department asked the Pentagon to consider sending additional U.S. troops to Europe, the Pentagon acquired a voice in United States policy on that subject. The Joint Chiefs were presented with a lever whereby they would be able to secure their long-standing objective of German rearmament.

The irreconcilable conflicts in the Defense and State Department views about European rearmament seem to have come to a head on August 28 when Truman designated Acheson and Johnson to work out an appropriate solution. Acheson was still arguing that gaining support for German rearmament would take time and that to precipitate a demand might well damage relations with France. Unfortunately, the Joint Chiefs of Staff insisted that should the Russians attack, the totally inadequate strength of the forces then contemplated for NATO "would condemn the American commander and his troops to complete disaster." [7] Acheson appears to have discussed the situation *au fond* with General Bradley on August 30 and to have given in to the military point of view: German rearmament must be part of any plan to send American forces to Europe.[*]

There could be only a few days between a final decision and the scheduled opening of the Foreign Ministers' Meeting on September 12. Not to have held off on the decision meant that there would be no time for prior consultation with our allies before the recommendation would be sprung on them. "In these circumstances, the abrupt demand for German rearmament could only assume the character of an ultimatum." [8] Robert McGeehan suggests that two considerations weighed in Acheson's decision to include German rearmament in his recommendations. First, that it was an election year and the Administration was "under severe domestic political attack to press the Europeans to do more at once for their own defense." [**] Secondly, and perhaps more important in Acheson's mind, was the knowledge that "an immediate attempt to get German rearmament under way would have the dual advantage of commencing what . . . would of necessity be a long process." [9] McGeehan aside, it is also possible that Acheson may have wanted to avoid a conflict with General Bradley and the Joint Chiefs at a time when relations were already difficult. He had still not reached that point in his relations with Bradley where he could persuade him to look at issues from the political viewpoint. In any event, the JCS insisted that the recommendations must be submitted and accepted as a whole. A written agreement was finally produced and approved by Truman on September 8 which "bound [American] reinforcements, a supreme commander and German rearmament closely together in a 'single package' . . . which in the eyes of the JCS" meant the formation of German units as "divisions directly incorporated in the NATO forces." [†] The President approved the new policy on Sep-

---

[*] Memo of conversation, Bradley and Acheson, August 30. Acheson Papers. Upon informing his staff of the decision, Acheson added for good measure that he was "serious about protecting against the regeneration of the 'old German power.'" Memo, Acheson to staff, August 30.

[**] Robert McGeehan, *The German Rearmament Question: American Diplomacy and European Defense After World War II* (Urbana: University of Illinois Press, 1971), p. 47. In early September Acheson received a personal letter from John McCloy, U.S. high commissioner in Germany, urging him to tell the French that American public opinion was "getting damn delicate too" and where would they be if the Soviets attacked and "American troops got pushed around without German troops to help them."

[†] Acheson has subsequently written that everything about it "was wrong: the plan itself, the attempt to bring it forward without preparation," and his own decision to do so. Acheson, *Sketches from Life of Great Men I Have Known* (New York:

tember 9, and word that Acheson intended to present the question of German rearmament was wired to Bevin and Schuman as they were about to depart for New York.

Although news reports and rumors had made known beforehand what Acheson intended to say, it nevertheless came as a bombshell. It seemed unreal that the United States should propose to rearm the Germans just five years after a great war fought to destroy the might of German arms forever. Nor had the Europeans anticipated that the package would be so tightly tied together. The French high commissioner, André François-Poncet, who was present, gives the following impression:

I remember seeing Acheson in action for the first time at the Waldorf–Astoria meeting in September 1950. He announced in solemn and grave tones the historic significance of the decision the United States had taken to break with the Monroe Doctrine. He moved from a declaration of America's acceptance of defense of the free world to announce the decision to authorize Germany to rearm and to make Germany a military ally. "Are you in agreement?" he concluded. All [Belgium, Italy, the Netherlands, Canada, Luxembourg, Denmark, Norway, Portugal, and Iceland] answered "yes" except Bevin and Schuman. Schuman said "no." He was troubled. His refusal caused a sensation. Acheson was manifestly discontent. . . . It was an incredibly difficult situation for Schuman. . . .[10]

Before Bevin could accept, which he did the next day, he had to call London. This was the first time witnesses remember ever seeing Bevin worried enough to call Attlee to determine whether he would back him or not. "All Britons were bound to ask themselves: What has this fifty years been about if we are now to rearm the Germans? There was no question in Bevin's mind about the virtue of the proposal; the uncertainty lay about the political viability of the idea in Britain. Bevin damn well wasn't going to make the decision on his own." [11]

Any hope Acheson had of once more moving Schuman by an appeal to their common interests and common bonds was doomed to disppointment. Some indication of the unexpectedly stubborn opposition which Schuman showed at this time is recorded in the words of his colleague, French Minister of Defense Jules Moch:

The reaction of Robert Schuman was more firm than I had expected. . . . His attitude [toward the American proposal] was beyond reproach. . . . He *held*

Harper, 1961), pp. 26–41. Acheson felt he had no choice in the matter, especially since it would be impossible to suppress knowledge of the recent decision. Now, if ever, he had to count upon his diplomatic skills to get him through.

his own against Acheson in the course of conversations on September 13th and 14th.*

"He told Acheson in private that even if he were to agree with the American demand his government would not support him, and even if it did the National Assembly would not support the government." [12] Thus opened one of the largest and most tenaciously fought duels in the annals of American diplomacy.

Sir Oliver Franks, the then British ambassador to the United States, felt that German rearmament was one of the few occasions when the United States government reached a decision and felt it had to prevail. "You simply could not set up a viable defense of Western Europe without the Germans, and Acheson was determined to attain a viable defense. . . . Schuman was made to feel the full extent of France's isolation" as Acheson rallied everyone around the American decision except the French. The French were left alone and isolated and made to understand that at the forthcoming meeting of the defense ministers in October the United States would "formally move plans for the establishment of a German army." [13]

Unable at the time to budge the French delegation beyond the point of recognizing that "Germany should be enabled to contribute to the build-up of the defense of Western Europe," the conference went on to agree on the creation "at the earliest possible date of an integrated force under a Supreme Commander." [14] Meanwhile, the United States would make no additional contribution of American ground forces pending a resolution of the German question.

Once it became clear that Schuman was not going to give in, deliberations were put off until September 22 when the Big Three foreign ministers were due to get together with their defense ministers.

The sudden replacement of Louis Johnson by Marshall as Secretary of Defense on September 12 introduced an element of flexibility into the American position, but the French position was stiffened by the arrival of Jules Moch, whose son had been tortured and garroted by the Nazis and who was fervently opposed to German rearmament. What the American government now wanted, Acheson told the meeting of the French, British, and American ministers on September 21, was merely a decision *in principle* on the participation of German units. It need not even be a public announcement. Without it, Acheson warned, he could not guarantee what

---

* Jules Moch, *Histoire du rearmament allemand depuis 1950* (Paris: Laffont, 1965), p. 47, emphasis added; a fascinating and authoritative account of the struggle over German rearmament by a first hand participant. Moch admitted that one of the most telling appeals to a Frenchman was that the United States had for the first time made clear its intention to defend Europe in Europe and not simply let its commitment rest with a guarantee, as the French said, "to liberate a dead corpse." *Ibid.*, p. 56.

the reaction of Congress would be to the Administration's request for European military assistance.

By now the French Cabinet had had time to examine Acheson's proposal, and it was unanimously hostile not only to immediate German rearmament but even to an immediate declaration accepting it in principle.[15] Moch now argued that not until the twenty divisions France had promised to produce (ten in 1951, ten in 1952) were completely rearmed should any consideration be given to rearming German units. Acheson recognized that at the root of the disagreement lay the differences in national experience and national feeling about the Germans. But having put his hand to the plow, he was determined not to turn back. He again warned Schuman and Moch that neither he nor Marshall nor President Truman could guarantee military aid and troops to Europe unless France acquiesced. The French refused to budge, and once again Acheson had to agree to put the issue over to their next meeting, warning that: "If, in October, the French government notifies us that it is irrevocably opposed to German rearmament, we shall have to consider our whole plan and look for another solution." [16] As McGeehan remarks, this showed that Acheson recognized that "France did have a veto on the German rearmament question, but it [was] suggested that if Paris exercised this [veto] then the price might be the loss of the other elements of the package which the French had so long desired." [17] As Acheson later wrote, "the Pentagon's plan had been tried on and produced a Donnybrook, in which many heads were broken and tempers and time lost." [18]

By now the French government was feeling the weakness of its position and the consequences of American pressure. The French could not possibly meet the costs of the war in Vietnam and their NATO commitments without American financial and military assistance. Contrary to official reports, the war in Indochina was not going at all well. On October 3 the evacuation of the French post of Cao Bang had been decided, and a relief column was sent to meet the forces abandoning the post. On October 8 both were surrounded and decimated by the Vietminh (three-fourths of the 3,500 officers and men were made prisoners).[19] To top off the evidence of France's weakness, if any was needed, Acheson noted in his meeting with the French and American finance ministers on October 17 that of the ten new divisions France hoped to raise in the course of 1951, nine would have to be equipped with American materiel and only one with French.

The French were in a tight spot. Schuman returned to Paris in a disturbed state of mind. Meanwhile, the French Cabinet, guided by the ideas of Jean Monnet, had come up with a plan for a European army. "In outline terms the French cabinet proposed that the question of German rearmament be solved by merging European armed forces into a single army which would include Germans . . . and a European minister of defense. . . ." [20] As McGeehan says, the French proposal, known as the Pleven Plan, made German rearmament virtually dependent on the coming into existence of a politically unified Europe. By separating the timetable of German rearmament from that of European rearmament via NATO, the French assured that "considerable time would pass before a German in uniform would appear—and if he did, he would not be in a German but a European uniform." [21] It was a characteristically astute move. "Acheson's urgings had compelled Paris 'to pull a rabbit from a hat quickly,' and since the magician in both cases was the same [Monnet], it was 'little wonder that Pleven's animal was a close relative of Schuman's lapin.'" [22]

The French Assembly gave the plan its endorsement, 343 votes to 225, but specified that there must be no German national army and no German general staff. Acheson's initial reaction was to view the Pleven Plan for what it seemed—a plan designed to obfuscate and delay rather than advance German rearmament.[*] His statement acknowledging the proposal was distinctly cool:

> The United States Government welcomes the initiative taken by the French Government in proposing a method for organizing armed forces in Western Europe, including those of Western Germany. . . . This represents a further approach toward the objective of bringing the common interests of the free nations of Europe more closely together within the North Atlantic Community. This proposal . . . deserves and requires further study. . . .[23]

This was a far cry from the enthusiasm with which Acheson had greeted the Schuman Plan six months earlier. But it did not mean that Acheson was not already reconsidering his options. He simply urged Henri Bonnet that the French not "become too rigid on the schedule for transforming Germany into a participant." [24]

By November 7 Acheson was wondering whether the Pleven Plan reflected the deepest elements of French feelings or the personal feelings of Moch. In any case, would a U.S. formula that was window dressing suffice for the French or would they really insist on a formula that included the basic elements of the sort raised in the Pleven Plan? Acheson was now determined not to let the Pleven Plan stand in the way of the other part of the package—namely, the establishment of a unified NATO force under an American commander. The deadlock had moved to London where the NATO deputies were wrestling over the question of when

---

[*] ". . . a politically impossible and militarily unfeasible subterfuge for preventing German rearmament," Acheson later called it, "designed for infinite delay." Dean Acheson, *Present at the Creation* (New York: W. W. Norton & Company, Inc., 1969), p. 457.

and in what form German units might be integrated. An indication of the easing of Acheson's position was his statement on November 15, 1950, recognizing that the question of German rearmament must be "dealt with soberly and quietly without getting exasperated because everyone does not see the problem in exactly the same way. We must find a solution which can be acceptable to all. . . . It is our judgment here that time is most important, that if this strength can be built up quickly then many dangers can be averted which would not be averted if too much time has to be occupied with preliminary adjustments." [25] This and other unequivocal statements by U.S. officials to the effect that a new national German army would not be created opened the way to the search for some kind of alternative.

On December 6 Acheson cleared with Lovett and the JCS an understanding that we would simply act on the assumption that the French had accepted German rearmament in some form and that we go ahead with German participation while still working on the question of a European army. This meant that agreement had been reached to separate the issue of rearming Germany from the sending of additional U.S. divisions and an American commander of NATO.

The letter Schuman wanted from us for use with his Cabinet, Acheson explained to Bradley, would say that if the French would agree to separate the question of raising German contingents from the long-range problems of the European army and political integration, and would additionally agree not to make the latter a condition of the former, then we would help them on the long-range matters.[26] Acheson acknowledged that the British would object (to letting the French idea of a European army prevail), but the only way to handle British objections was by stating that the United States was prepared to appoint a Supreme Commander provided we could solve the problem of immediate German contingents.* Bradley acquiesced. The very next day (December 7) the French Cabinet sent instructions to Hervé Alphand, the French NATO deputy, to the effect that "France *would* [emphasis added] consent to the raising of German units ('combat teams') of 5,000 to 6,000 men," [27] but at the same time Alphand was to state that by so doing "France did *not* renounce its commitment to the actual initiation of . . . the Pleven Plan." [28] So it is not true to say that Acheson long remained frozen in his opposition to French diplomacy. By early December the ugly crisis in Franco–American relations that had been created by adoption of the Pentagon package had been buried.

---

* Memo of meeting. Acheson to Bradley, December 6, 1950. Acheson Papers. The British opposition was based on their desire that the long-range plan for an integrated European army fail, and they were against the United States jumping in to promote its success.

Acheson was now anxious that the German problem be subordinated to the immediate issue of organizing NATO. In deciding to allow the ingredients of the original package proposals to be separated, the United States withdrew its ultimatum that German rearmament had to be agreed to if the other elements were to be forthcoming, and thereby took the step which meant that NATO could be properly launched. "It had been more important all along that an integrated force under a single commander be established than that the Federal Republic, a defeated, politically occupied, and psychologically ambivalent country be pushed into raising troops." [29]

The way was now cleared for the meeting of the NATO Council in Brussels on December 18–19 to agree to the American proposal for the appointment of General Eisenhower as Supreme Commander and for the creation of a combined NATO army. The French had dropped their opposition in principle to an eventual German contribution; they were still holding out for the European army as the basis for solving it. The face-saving nature of the agreement was also such that it permitted Acheson to avoid the charge in Congress that our European allies were not doing enough.

The deadlock over the issue had also shown Acheson how many politically complex problems had to be cleared up before either the allies or the Germans could even begin to reach an agreement on German rearmament. The Germans, for example, had made it clear that they would agree to rearmament only on terms of complete sovereignty and equality, something that had not been anticipated when the package deal had been so hastily concocted. Acheson now recognized that until Germany's neighbors were reassured, it would be unwise to indulge the Germans in excessive demands which, under the circumstances, would be totally unacceptable to the former victims of German aggression. A lengthy period of negotiations between the allies and the government at Bonn was not only necessary but might even be salutary in reassuring and persuading the Europeans of Germany's trustworthiness.*

---

* Acheson to Lovett, December 15, 1950. "The crux of the matter is not the French but the Germans. If the Germans do not want to fight how are we going to hold east of the Rhine?" Lovett felt that the Germans should be disabused of the notion that they were in command of a bargaining position, that we should ease up on saying how important they were so as to make them want to get in. Acheson agreed that we must forget about Adenauer for a while and get on with other problems. *Ibid.* Acheson expressed the same idea the next day on the eve of his departure for Brussels (Memo, Brussels Meeting: Acheson, Pace, Collins, Gruenther, et al., December 19, 1950. Acheson Papers) a point of view repeated to the President on January 5, 1951. Memo, Acheson to Truman. "We should proceed with integration and let the rearmament of Germany follow as a normal part of this process. Acheson Papers.

Consequently two distinct but interrelated processes now got under way. On February 15, 1951, the French convened a meeting of all the European members of NATO to begin negotiations for the creation of a European Defense Community. Acheson was still without much confidence in it, and it would be another six months before he would become a convert and throw the full, but not necessarily decisive, weight of American diplomatic support behind it. The other process would go on in Bonn where the high commissioners were designated to negotiate with Adenauer the modalities for ending the allied occupation and bringing German military forces into being.

These moves had not been without their effect on Soviet policy, which "had been galvanized into a series of diplomatic countermeasures: the Prague conference of East European foreign ministers, protests to the three Western capitals, a proposal for a four-power foreign ministers' conference and a note to the British and French on December 15 attacking the proposed rearmament of West Germany as a violation of the Anglo–Soviet and Franco–Soviet treaties." [30] Communist strategy worldwide, but especially in Korea, remained so unrelentingly hostile that Moscow had little chance of influencing the basic momentum of Western policy. Acheson felt sufficiently confident about Western unity that the position paper for the Brussels meeting accepted the desirability of talking with the Soviets but only on a basis which conceded no advantage in advance to the USSR.[31] Acheson stressed that no one must be afraid to talk with the Soviets.

However, we cannot permit anything to emerge from a conference (1) which would increase the possibility of the Soviet Union's gaining control of Western Germany; (2) which would prohibit or limit the right of a unified Germany or Western Germany to join the West and contribute to Western European defense; (3) which would limit our freedom of action to carry out the Brussels decision with regard to Germany. . . .[32]

It was difficult, Acheson concluded, to think of anything the Soviets could propose which we could accept, but no Soviet proposal should be allowed to divide the allies or upset the West Germans.

Had Soviet policy shown the least flexibility, it might have brought Acheson's diplomacy to naught, but as it was the Soviet Union was willing neither to relax its grip on East Germany nor to ease its menace to the West in other ways. On the contrary, Stalin was embarked upon a new "peace" offensive designed to threaten the West in the futile hope of discouraging Western unity. Had Stalin adopted a somewhat less threatening policy, Acheson's diplomacy was sufficiently fragile that it might have been dealt a setback.

The "Great Debate"

A great debate sprang up in the wake of Truman's formal announcement on December 19 (informally it had been known since early September) that additional U.S. military forces were to be sent to Europe as part of a NATO army. Republicans insisted that Truman had no power to order such an action without the consent of Congress. The call for greater consultation had been a frequent one ever since the Republicans had emerged victorious from the November elections, but as Acheson pointed out in his testimony, he had consulted with Congress over and over again:

The matter of sending troops to Europe is not a new matter, not at all. You speak as though for the first time in your knowledge this question had been broached. That is not the case. The President made this statement on the 9th of September. That is a long time ago. Within a few days of that statement I appeared before you in your committee, before I went to New York, and went all over this matter with you. I appeared before your committee when I came back from the meeting of the Council in New York and went all over it all again. I appeared before your committee when I came back from Brussels, and I am anxious and eager to appear at any time and discuss any of these questions with you.[33]

Nevertheless, Republicans, believing that the November elections had given them a mandate, were determined to press home their attack against Acheson's foreign policy.

Instead of there being fifty-four Democrats and forty-two Republicans in the Senate there were now forty-nine Democrats and forty-seven Republicans. Several Democrats who had been prominently identified with the Truman–Acheson foreign policy—Tydings of Maryland and Scott Lucas of Illinois—had gone down to defeat; in California Richard Nixon had defeated encumbent Senator Helen Gahagan Douglas and in Ohio Robert Taft, running against an inept and unimpressive opponent, had turned the efforts of the labor unions to defeat him into a political triumph. Elsewhere Taft allies had triumphed handily over the Democrats: Eugene Millikan (R–Colo.), Homer Capehart (R–Ind.), Bourke Hickenlooper (R–Iowa), and Pat McCarran (a Nevada Democrat but no friend of Acheson's) had all been re-elected. Victory rekindled Taft's hopes of winning the Republican Presidential nomination in 1952 and convinced him that Republican attacks upon the Administration should not be confined to domestic politics. The Republican Party had the opportunity and the moral obligation to return America to its traditional foreign-policy principles of isolationism. For a decade Taft had stood in a minority position—sometimes virtually alone—in condemning the Democratic Party's commitment to international involvement and power politics. Now the chance had risen to vindicate his opposition.

Because of Vandenberg, Taft had until now found it difficult to fight the Democrats in their postwar addiction to internationalism. He had never really agreed with Vandenberg and had rarely supported his recommendations in foreign affairs, looking upon him as a doubtful kind of Republican, one who had gone soft in the head as a consequence of his conversion to internationalism. Furthermore, neither Taft nor his fellow mountain-state and Midwestern Republicans felt anything but antipathy to the bipartisan policy of economic and military assistance to Europe. Taft's intensely partisan cast of mind made him scoff at bipartisanship; there was something illogical about a practice which inhibited the opposition from opposing. But as long as Vandenberg lived, Taft felt bound to respect the proprietary role which Vandenberg had assumed in leading the Republican Party in foreign affairs. Now, with Vandenberg removed from the scene, Taft saw the road clear to deliver a major challenge.

Taft was genuinely convinced that no external power could really threaten America. The threat to America came from the insidious efforts of Democratic administrations to involve America in the toils of European wars. Democrats were fatally attracted by some alien or aberrant strain to the belief that America had a responsibility to involve itself in saving the world. It was part of their preference for "statism," militarism and centralized government at home. So deep had the isolationist paranoia become that there were even charges that America's failures in foreign policy were not natural but the result of some occult conspiracy, masterminded by Acheson. "The so-called conspiracy theory, the idea that Korea was but one link in a chain of events that stretched backward at least to Yalta, was one that gained wide credulity before the Inchon invasion." [34] MacArthur's stunning defeat in Korea and the Administration's refusal to let him bomb China gave powerful credence to the belief that there was a conspiracy afoot to deny America victory and hand it over to the Communists. "It all fits into a pattern," Senator George Malone (R–Nev.) proclaimed, ". . . we deliberately lose Manchuria, China, Korea and Berlin. . . ." [35] Acheson was portrayed as the arch conspirator. His "great and persuasive intellectual powers" were viewed as giving him an ascendancy over Truman and over foreign policy that made them subservient to his manipulations. He was assigned enormous diabolic powers. Acheson, Senator Wherry declared, "holds the destiny of the world in his hands." "Mr. Acheson pulls the strings, and the dummies nod their heads." He was, another Senator declared, "the very heart of the octopus itself" which was strangling and deceiving the American people.

Senator Jenner had attacked General Marshall in terms of conspiracy too, and upon the recall of General MacArthur Jenner would charge that "this country today is in the hands of a secret inner coterie which is directed by agents of the Soviet Union. We must cut this whole cancerous conspiracy out of our Government at once [applause from the public gallery]. Our only recourse is to impeach President Truman and find out who is the secret invisible government which has so cleverly led our country down the road to destruction." Jenner was not alone among his Republican colleagues in holding these views, and they also found wide acceptance with the American people, frustrated and embittered by the war in Korea. There existed a widespread view that America must go all out to defeat its enemies and at the same time have as little to do with the rest of the world as possible.

Acheson understood these attitudes and did not think much could be done about them. Asked by Charles Collingwood about the charge that he was responsible for the failure of American policy in Asia, Acheson had this to say:

Well, I think the first answer is that they flatter themselves and me and all Americans in saying that the troubles which now exist in the Far East are a failure of American policy. That results from the belief that Americans are all-powerful and that anything that they want to do happens and if things go wrong it must be some American mistake. That isn't the case in Asia at all.[36]

The "great debate" was also prompted by Taft's recognition that if he was to win the Presdential nomination in 1952, he must seek to impress his own foreign-policy views upon the Republican Party and, by so doing, establish his authority in an area from which he had been excluded by Vandenberg's pre-eminence. If he was going to be President, he would not want to have his hands irrevocably bound by additional commitments to Europe; therefore, the sooner he arrested the Administration policy in its course, the easier it would be two years hence to run for the Presidency and to take over the reins of government. If he allowed the consolidation of the Acheson–Truman foreign policy to continue, he would have the very devil of a time extricating himself from the fetters of the alliance. This is what Taft meant when he confided to W. S. White, "I am charged with moving in on foreign policy; the truth is that foreign policy has moved in on me." [37]

In a press interview given in Cincinnati on November 10 Taft called for a fundamental re-examination of the scope, methods, and character of American aid to Europe. Taft wondered how large a land army was really needed to defend America's shores and questioned the value of NATO. "Is Europe our first line of defense? Is it defensible at all?" And what were the Europeans contributing? It was really just a bit of preliminary trumpeting on Taft's part which Acheson might well have ignored. Instead he seized upon Taft's talk of re-examination to deliver a bitterly sarcastic attack. It was not worded in a personal way but no one could ignore that he was scoring off an old enemy.

"I don't want this word [re-examination] to fool us," Acheson began. "We need to look at this re-examinist and see what kind of a person he really is." He went on:

Now, it's possible that a re-examinist might be a farmer that goes out every morning and pulls up all his crops to see how they have done during the night. It might be that that is what it means. Or it might be that this kind of a re-examinist is someone who comes down to breakfast in the morning and looks at his wife or at her husband and says, "Do I really love that man or woman? How did I ever turn up here with her or him?" Or he can put on his hat and go down to the office and look around and say, "Am I really in this business? Are these my partners? How did I get mixed up with these people? I wonder if I shouldn't have been an atomic scientist after all?" Is that what it means? When we re-examine, does it mean that we are like the sound navigator who, on a long flight or a long voyage, checks his course by the sun and stars every day? Or does it mean that the navigator says, "How did I ever get started on this? Do I really want to take this trip after all?" [38]

Acheson was the virtuoso of this kind of attack. But was it really necessary to refute Taft's logic by making him out to be a silly ass? Taft would have his revenge.

The decision to send troops to Europe was particularly galling because it came at a time of deepening anger at our European allies for failure to support us adequately in Korea and at the UN. Consequently, while ostensibly a debate over which branch of the government should have the final say on sending troops to Europe, it was really a debate on whether or not the United States should revert to isolationism. The opening salvos were exchanged in the midst of the Truman–Attlee talks which Attlee had demanded as an outgrowth of Truman's ill-considered remarks about possible use of the A-bomb in Korea. It may be remembered that Republicans had moved a resolution demanding to know if the Administration had entered into any secret agreement with the British. No sooner had that charge been beaten back than resolutions were voted by the House and Senate Republicans, meeting in caucus, demanding Acheson's ouster as Secretary. The Senate debated and defeated that resolution 47 to 29 on a strong party-line vote. Despite this initial skirmishing, the debate really dates from December 20, 1950, on which day former–President Hoover delivered a major address in which he asserted that "no more American men and materiel should be sent to Europe until the free peoples of that continent had turned their territories into an impregnable fortress." Hoover argued that the United States could not hope to sustain a land defense of Europe under present circumstances, that the existing military costs would bankrupt the United States, and that the wisest solution would be for the United States to build up its air and naval forces "so as to overwhelm Russia in case of attack." [39]

We cannot stop a sudden Communist avalanche over the Continent of Europe with any present contemplated land armies. The only way I see to handle such a global situation is in the air force of such range that we can reach our targets from air bases more remote than the continental pact countries, possibly even from the U.S.[40]

This of course was *not* the problem to which Administration policy in Europe was addressed. The Administration had never claimed that NATO could match a Soviet land thrust. The most Acheson hoped for was that if war actually came, then the NATO land forces in conjunction with U.S. strategic air forces might contain the Soviet thrust east of the Rhine. The United States, Acheson argued, must seek to make credible its determination to defend Europe by establishing balanced forces. These need not be equal or anywhere near equal to those of the Soviet Union, but they must be part of a coherent strategy and sufficiently large to establish the credibility of U.S. determination in the eyes of a potential aggressor.

The logic of the Hoover analysis, however, was seductive. The United States could not hope to match the Soviet Union in a land war. "We can, without any measure of doubt, with our own air and naval forces, hold the Atlantic and Pacific Oceans with one frontier on Britain (if she wishes to cooperate), the other on Japan, Formosa, and the Philippines." Europeans need not feel bereft of security; the United States cannot make a great army but it can make a great navy and air force, Hoover reassured his listeners, and if it does that "there will be no mistake about where we stand or what we can do." [41]

Once let Hoover's seductive simplicity become established in the popular mind and there was no telling where it would lead. Immediately upon his return from Brussels on December 22 Acheson sailed into Hoover's analysis. No time was lost in providing Administration supporters with a point-by-point refutation. What was the purpose, Acheson demanded, in propounding a doctrine which would have for its immediate consequence an invitation to the Soviets to try their hand at seizing Europe? Since American bombers could not reach Russia from the continental United States, would we not be giving up the bases in Europe indispensable to the utilization of American air power? Finally, would not the loss of Europe place at Russia's disposal economic power and military resources vastly superior to that available to America? With that rejoinder the debate hung fire until January 5, 1951, when Taft made a speech in the Senate based essentially on Hooverian premises and logic.

Taft reiterated Hoover's major thesis that America's most effective contribution to European security should take the form of air and naval power based in the United States and Britain.

What I object to is undertaking to fight that battle [against Communism] primarily on the vast land areas of the continent of Europe or the continent of

Asia where we are at the greatest possible disadvantage. . . . We could not have a better lesson than has been taught us in Korea.[42]

Secondly, there were serious limits "to our economic and manpower capacity." Additional taxes would require controls, and additional manpower drafts would take men out of needed production. A reliance on air and naval power, on the other hand, would avoid such requirements. To Acheson's concern for the survival of democracy, Taft had a ready response: "An indefinite surrender of liberty such as would be required by an all-out war program in time of peace might mean the final and complete destruction of those liberties which it is the very purpose of the preparation to protect." At the same time Taft supported MacArthur's call for all-out war against Communist China and rejected the Administration's view that it would lead us to war not only with China but with Russia.*

To a country wearied with the war in Korea and fed up with its allies, these words had a ready appeal. Many Americans felt strongly that the Europeans were not making a sufficient effort, and that America would only be making a sucker of itself to carry their burden as well as its own. The natural role was for the United States to provide air and naval support—let the Europeans take care of the ground forces. The additional danger of this appeal lay in the fact that many senators and congressmen who might normally have been expected to support Administration foreign policy were disturbed by what they considered to be the lack of any assurance that the Administration knew what it was doing. The challenge to the Administration was formidable, especially if it could be couched in language that limited the President's power and sowed doubts in

---

* The Republican Party determination to press for MacArthur's strategy of a land war in Asia took the form of a resolution (Senate Joint Resolution 62) declaring war on North Korea and China. The Republican resolution never came up for a vote, but it is a startling example of the extreme contradiction besetting Republican foreign policy—isolation in Europe, all-out war in Asia. Ronald J. Caridi, *The Korean War and American Politics: The Republican Party as a Case Study* (Philadelphia: University of Pennsylvania Press, 1968), pp. 156–157. Some of Taft's other proposals were equally contradictory. He proposed that if the Soviet Union would not accept amendments to the United Nations Charter designed to create "an ideal organization," then the United States should seek the dissolution of the United Nations and the formation of a new organization which "could be an effective weapon for peace." Acheson could only wonder what Taft had in mind by "a new organization" if not a NATO-type alliance; yet it was precisely against the presumed costs of NATO that Taft's strictures were directed. This contradiction was topped in the next paragraph of Taft's speech by the recommendation that within this new organization "our first consideration must be defense of America. . . ." Did Taft really believe that an organization with such an exclusive goal would rally other nations to its support?

European minds of America's willingness to share the burden and stay the course.

On January 8, Senator Kenneth Wherry, still Acheson's nemesis, presented the following resolution as a direct challenge to the President's authority:

Resolved, that it is the sense of the Senate that no ground forces of the United States should be assigned to duty in the European area for the purpose of the North Atlantic Treaty pending the formulation of a policy with respect thereto by the Congress.

The fact that the President had taken the country into the disastrous Korean War without congressional approval was now held up as a warning against letting a similar decision occur in connection with troops to Europe.

Another critic, Senator Arthur Watkins (R–Utah), had this to say:

The President is waging war in Korea. It is an undeclared war into which the United States has been taken by the unilateral action of the President without consulting the Congress. . . . If the President is now permitted to order American armies into Europe without consulting Congress, we will wake up . . . and find that we have again been taken into all-out large-scale war on the order of the President in violation of the spirit as well as the letter of the Constitution.*

After much pulling and hauling, the Administration finally succeeded in persuading the Senate Foreign Relations Committee to report the resolution out in a more moderate form:

. . . it is the sense of the Senate that, in the interests of sound constitutional processes, and of national unity and understanding, Congressional approval should be obtained of any policy requiring the assignment of American troops abroad when such assignment is in implementation of article 3 of the North Atlantic Treaty; and the Senate hereby approves of the present plans of the President and of the Joint Chiefs of Staff to send four additional divisions of ground forces to Western Europe.[43]

It is popular to trace the origins of the Vietnam War back to some mythical usurpation of constitutional power that occurred under Truman and Acheson. But that is just not the case. Truman and Acheson objected strenuously to this resolution, but their objections took the form of debating, not circumventing it. Prompted by the unexpected opposition that

---

* *Congressional Record,* January 22, 1951, p. 537. As Caridi points out, this attitude was supported by the Gallup Poll published on April 3. Asked whether they thought Congress or the President should have the right to limit the number of troops sent to Europe: Congress—58 percent; President—31 percent; Both—1 percent; and No Opinion—10 percent. Caridi, *op. cit.,* p. 129.

sending troops to Europe was encountering, Acheson made another of his periodic efforts to get through to Congress. He had the support of the House Foreign Affairs Committee and of most of the members of the Senate Foreign Relations and Armed Services committees. What he needed were the moderates in both parties. His files for that winter and spring are filled with memos of meetings with senators and calls to be returned cultivating their support. On March 16, in response to Senator William Benton's (D–Conn.) urgings that the department make an even greater effort to improve its relations with Congress, Acheson ordered his staff to go all out in improving relations on "an intelligent and sound basis." *

The hearings before the Senate Foreign Relations and Armed Services committees lasted a month. In order to strengthen the appeal of their air-power strategy the Taft–Hoover forces had to make the strongest case possible against the feasibility of NATO strategy. Over and over Taft made two assertions about the Administration's European strategy which were simply not true but were good debating points. The first was that the troops-to-Europe policy aimed at building an army to a point "where it could perhaps defeat a Russian army" and that "the control of the Eurasian continent would require a quadrupling of the expense for the army. . . . I believe a study of the figures will show that the program recommended by the President is at the very limit or beyond our economic capacity. Yet this program only contemplates an American land army of 24 divisions, obviously insufficient to control the land mass in Europe and Asia." [44] Acheson readily admitted that measured by the standard of what it would take to defeat the Red Army in a land war NATO was not sufficient but he submitted that defeating Russia was not NATO's purpose.

Our first purpose—and this is something we need to make absolutely clear to our friends in Europe—is to deter aggressors from attacking Europe. Our primary concern is not how to win a war after it gets started, *but how to prevent it. . . .*[45]

The Taft–Hoover forces argued that the Soviet acquisition of an atomic capability made Europe strategically both more vulnerable and less important. If war came, the European ports would be under direct nuclear attack and Europe would become a vast graveyard for the whole NATO army. Acheson held that the Soviet possession of an atomic capability made it all the more imperative that the United States be able to defend

---

* Memo of meeting, March 16, 1951. Acheson, Fisher, Webb, Humelsine. Acheson Papers. Acheson found that a minor concession or two to Franco's Spain without the least approval for the regime was sufficient to rally Catholic Democrats and southern "cotton state" senators for support on more critical issues.

its vital interests in Europe without having to depend upon the atomic bomb:

. . . the best use we can make of our present advantage in retaliatory air power, is to move ahead under this protective shield to build the balanced collective forces in Western Europe that will continue to deter aggression after our atomic advantage has been diminished. . . .

Some have asked why we need to do this—why can't we continue to rely on the deterrent force of our retaliatory air power, and our reserve power elsewhere. Some have argued that this European defense force cannot possibly be made large enough to be effective, while others have argued that this European defense force would be so great a threat to the Soviet Union that it would be provocative. These concerns, although contradictory of each other, have led to a common line of reasoning—that we should *not* move ahead with our European allies in building a defense force in Western Europe.[46]

As Acheson saw it, the missing component which could make the situation manageable was a far more limited one than that described by his critics because the real problem, and not the one compounded of their fears and hallucinations, was a far more limited one. All that the United States was being asked to do was to provide some more tangible deterrent.

A limited deterrent force in Europe would assure that the Soviet Union could not use its satellites for indirect aggression. "In the absence of defense forces in being, satellites might be used for such disguised aggression in the hope that they could get away with it, since the free nations could respond only with weapons of all-out general war, or not at all." [47]

To the argument that whatever the NATO powers might do they could not hope to match the forces available to a potential aggressor, Acheson replied, "The difficulty with this argument is that it considers the European defense forces in isolation, as a sole weapon, instead of considering these forces as a vital adjunct to the other deterrent forces available," in other words, United States nuclear power.[48]

The Taft forces also insisted that the Europeans were capable of providing for their own defense, that they were sponging off of America, and that if and when they provided for their own defense, then some form of American commitment might be useful. Such a contribution, they said, ". . . never ought to be a key point in *our strictly military* strategy. And the initiative should be theirs and *not* ours." [49] Acheson countered this with a favorite theme: "Our allies are building their forces *now;* the time for our contribution is *now* [emphasis added]. If each [of us] should wait to appraise its partners' efforts before determining its own, the result would be as disastrous as it would be obvious." [50]

When debate turned to the constitutionality of the President's power, Acheson simply argued that it was within the Executive's authority to send troops to Europe.[51] Much of the steam was taken out of that issue, however, when the Administration made known that it intended to send only four divisions to join the two already there. The opposition was to some extent appeased, but there was still enough resistance to support passage, 49 to 43, of the McClellan Amendment which stated that "it is the sense of the Senate that no troops in addition to such four divisions should be sent to Western Europe in implementation of the North Atlantic Treaty without further Senatorial approval." [52] Acheson was opposed to that on grounds that it set an unconstitutional limitation upon the President's authority, but since it did not interfere with existing plans, it hardly mattered.

Two days after passing the McClellan Amendment, the Senate voted 69 to 21 in favor of Resolution 99 approving in principle the dispatch to Europe of the American forces.

The amendment limiting the authorization to four divisions was undoubtedly the key to the program's passage. (Half the Republican senators—Taft among them—voted for it.) The immediate result was to reassure Europe of the steadfastness of the American commitment and to strengthen European diplomatic momentum. This in turn dashed any expectation Moscow may have had of dividing America from its European allies. When the deputy foreign ministers convened in Paris on March 5 to discuss the issues of East–West tension, the Soviets, having no new proposals of their own, confronted a united Western delegation. Instead of exploiting the strains of the Korean War, Gromyko pushed the propaganda aspect until the conference finally adjourned on June 21.

But at home the setback to the isolationist campaign undoubtedly contributed to the rancor and ferocity of Republican attacks upon Acheson for the relief of MacArthur and added to the vehemence of their determination "to get him" if at all possible. The strategy of building up Europe and limiting the war in Korea was so clearly Acheson's strategy that their entire fire would be used to show that Acheson was practicing appeasement in Asia while spending the country into bankruptcy at home.

18

DIPLOMACY, 1951

ONCE THE DEBATE was concluded, Acheson could turn his attention back to Europe and the implications of the Pleven Plan: a European army in a European defense community. Neither by intellect nor temperament was Acheson sympathetic to plans for European unity, especially when they threatened to interfere with or delay the realization of his more immediate objective: the rearming of Germany. Acheson did not have much confidence in European unity as an end in itself. Like de Gaulle he did not believe that there existed a European psychology sufficient to support the weight of European political federation; unlike de Gaulle Acheson believed that such a psychology would develop out of actions taken in common over time. But there was no chance to avoid diplomatic involvement in such plans once French Foreign Minister Robert Schuman called for a conference to determine upon the formation of a European army and a European ministry of defense.

The conference opened in Paris on February 15, 1951. France, Belgium, Italy, Luxembourg, and the West German Republic attended as full members; representatives of the United States, Canada, Denmark, Norway, the Netherlands, Portugal, and Great Britain were present as observers. The French plan envisaged the creation of a single European army and air force under the command of NATO, but administered and financed by the members of the European Defense Community (EDC). The plan remained unsatisfactory to NATO military planners insofar as it retained the restrictive notion that national units should not exceed combat team size of 6,000 men and that two or three different national teams should be combined to comprise the European army division.*

At the same time Acheson had taken the precaution of initiating nego-

---

* Even this was an advance upon the original French proposals to integrate national units at the company level.

tiations for German rearmament directly between the three Western high commissioners and the authorities of the German federal government. These negotiations, held at Petersberg near the West German capital of Bonn, went on simultaneously with those being held at Paris on EDC under French auspices, and served as a constant reminder to the French that the Americans were determined to move ahead with German rearmament and that France had better reach a decision concerning EDC if it hoped to exert any control at all.

That spring Acheson became disturbed by the direction which EDC negotiations were taking. Schuman had initially rejected the argument that Europe should be united politically and economically before the attempt was made to integrate the armies. But it soon became apparent that the French, in endeavoring to take account of every contingency which might arise, were thereby making the draft treaty for a European Defense Community peculiarly complicated. Acheson was willing to accept whatever degree of integration was necessary to regulate and coordinate the activities of the national military formations under EDC, but he was against letting EDC, by the extension and elaboration of its functions, become the instrument for the virtual economic and political integration of Europe. Acheson's aim was to restrict the integrative functions of EDC to the bare minimum necessary to achieve German rearmament.

Word from Paris that General Eisenhower and Ambassador David Bruce were themselves stressing the broader integrative role of EDC fairly made him bristle. He had some disparaging remarks that spring for what he scathingly called the Bruce "cult" of federation. Fortunately, this may have been a time when he was especially well served by his lieutenants in Europe. They were closer to the scene and more aware that there was no simple solution to the German problem. Part of the much larger issue of burying a century of Franco–German enmity, the German problem could not be resolved apart from the assurance that Germany "would never again use her power to turn on her Western neighbors." [1] Even John J. McCloy, U.S. high commissioner in Germany and a staunch advocate of German rearmament, had come to admit that it could only be brought about within a framework of European institutions. Acheson also had to confront the fact that unless some progress on German rearmament was being made, congressional elements hostile to America's military commitment to Europe would again become active. As a result, Acheson decided that since he had no choice, he had better swing American support behind EDC and push it as far as possible. At a meeting with his staff on June 21 he stressed that "a number of dragging forces are behind us—the French elections, British Cabinet instability, domestic turmoil—and unless we provide the initiative in getting the solution to an apparently insoluble problem, the effect on the international situation, including the Soviets, is likely to be disastrous." [2]

As Supreme Commander of NATO, Eisenhower was now authorized to give public support for the principle of integration and to push for speedy adoption of EDC; High Commissioner McCloy announced on his return to Europe in July that the Petersberg Plan for German rearmament should be integrated into the European army proposals. Acheson now calculated that if he could sell the Europeans and the French in particular on the logic of EDC as a means of avoiding the dangers associated in European minds with German rearmament, then the other problems— German sovereignty, occupation costs, etc.—might well fall into place. Acheson put these thoughts in a mid–July memorandum that became the basis for all subsequent action.[3] Acheson stressed the need to go forward simultaneously with the European defense force idea, restoration of German sovereignty, and the training of German troops. American objectives were to get started on German forces as early as possible and not to let the European army idea impede the build-up of Eisenhower's NATO forces.

Before progress could be made on EDC, however, Acheson saw that something had to be done to solve Europe's rapidly worsening economic situation and, in particular, to redeem the French budget from collapse.

The Economic Crisis Confronting NATO in the Summer of 1951

The onset of the Korean War had given rise almost immediately to another crisis within NATO—that of financing the greatly augmented defense effort that each country had undertaken.

Before the war Americans took the idea of economic assistance to Europe in stride; immediately after its outbreak attitudes changed. Americans reasoned that if they had to make a big military effort, then the Europeans ought to forego further economic assistance and share the burden by themselves making a greater military effort. The onset of the Korean War was an excuse for many Americans to assume that everyone would have to carry an "equal" burden and that if they didn't they were shirking their responsibilities. Taft's statement that before the United States contributed any additional troops the Europeans ought to provide for their own military security, even if it meant a cut in their living standards, was typical of the new mood. There was little inclination among Americans to understand that for European states to undertake a greater military effort required them to import more raw materials and to devote a much higher proportion of their national resources to war production and away from vital exports. Nor did Americans understand that under such circumstances Europe would need more, not less, aid from the United States. How else could it hope to balance its payments?

Acheson fought one sharp engagement over this issue as early as July 1950 when the State Department had determined that in light of the drastic reorientation of the European economy occasioned by the war the Marshall Plan ought to be extended beyond 1952. Secretary of Defense Louis A. Johnson had sharply attacked such an extension, arguing that the entire military assistance program ought to be transferred to the Pentagon. Acheson succeeded in enlisting Averell Harriman's support at the White House to have the Marshall Plan extended and to have control over the military aid program remain in the State Department.[*]

America's European partners quickly understood what was expected of them. At the NATO Defense and Finance Ministers'. meeting of October 1950, the European states volunteered to undertake considerable increases in their defense effort and set to work with a will and determination. The average proportion of gross national product spent on defense rose from less than 5 percent in 1950 to 8 percent, with Britain and France undertaking increases on the order of 9.6 percent and 9.3 percent respectively. The European military effort became much greater in every category. Italian strength on the Brenner–Trieste front rose to seven divisions in 1951 and nine in 1952. The number of tactical aircraft in Europe increased from four hundred at the end of 1949 to one thousand in April 1951 and to four thousand by the end of 1952.[4]

In spite of their willingness to make a substantial contribution to the European defense effort, the French soon found the demands upon their military resources simply too great.[**] Their promise at the October meeting to re-equip five existing divisions and create fifteen completely new divisions remained an empty commitment. The claims upon French resources at this time were staggering. On the basis of a still only partially recovered economy, France was also endeavoring to fight a full-scale war: hundreds of millions of dollars and an entire generation of French professional soldiers were being poured into Indochina. After a full year of

---

[*] Memo of meeting, July 21, 1951. Truman, Acheson, Johnson, Harriman. Acheson Papers. This marked the increasing reliance that Acheson would have upon Harriman to make good his grand design for NATO. From his positions first in the White House and then as director of the Mutual Security Administration, Harriman would provide Acheson with invaluable support.

[**] The French projected military outlays for 1951 three times that of 1950, a figure that the minister of finance and M. Moch admitted France could not possibly finance alone. Therefore, they were asking the United States for an additional billion dollars for military expenditure and help with an anticipated balance-of-payments deficit of $2.4 billion.

preparations there were still fewer than eighteen divisions on the Central European Front; these included six American, four British, and five Benelux divisions, but only three French. French preoccupation with its colonial wars meant that the French were effectively absent from Europe.

For the Western defense effort to have succeeded under these circumstances would have required a degree of economic discipline and cooperation equivalent to that attained during World War II. The increased demand for raw materials should have been approached on a cooperative basis, but in the absence of a Combined Purchasing Board such as existed in World War II each NATO partner attempted to meet its raw material requirements on an individual and competitive basis. Since there was not enough to go around, competition merely succeeded in driving up the prices. This was especially painful for the European states which depended to a proportionaly greater degree than the United States upon importation of raw materials and foodstuffs to survive.

The magnitude of the economic effort which would be required had not been immediately apparent at the outset of the Korean War. The ambiguity which characterized the Korean War in its initial stages—police action or major war—inhibited the Truman Administration from recognizing the major consequences which would flow from it. It was assumed that the necessary economic adjustments could be made without declaring a state of national emergency and without interrupting the essentially peacetime character of the national and international economy. It was not until December 16 that Truman declared a state of national emergency; by that time much of the economic damage had already been done.

Economic Nationalism as a Factor

Instead of promoting interallied cooperation, the onset of the Korean War was a signal to a great many Americans to ignore the experience of the immediate past and revert to an aggressively nationalistic approach more akin to the era of the thirties than to the immediate postwar period of economic cooperation. Within the Administration the shift from recovery to rearmament provoked a steady crisis between those officials like Paul Hoffman, chief of the European Recovery Program, who still felt that the United States should not let rearmament interfere with the recovery aspect, and those who felt that the military and political pressures on the budget necessitated curtailment of America's contribution to economic recovery. Acheson stood somewhere in between. He was determined to employ the shock of the Korean War to elicit a much greater military effort both at home and abroad. At the same time he recognized (probably not enough, however) the interdependence of Europe's military effort and the successful completion of economic recovery. By opposing

Louis Johnson's efforts to curtail the extension of the Marshall Plan in July 1950, Acheson had recognized that the defense effort would require more, not less, American financial assistance.*

While the pace of the rearmament program was not supposed to halt European recovery, nevertheless higher taxes, sharp inflation, balance-of-payments troubles, and (in some instances) lowered real income were generating a crisis for the governments in power. By the summer of 1951 it was clear that the economic crisis in Europe was weakening European support for American policy in Korea and impairing the unity of the alliance.**

---

* The Korean War was also a signal to forces in the Congress to embark upon a course of renewed economic nationalism. For several years sentiment had been building up against Administration campaigns to liberalize trade policies as well as against foreign aid programs. In part these sentiments were nourished by the traditional protectionist proclivities of some sections and industries of the country and in part by congressional resentment at having international economic policy removed from their hands for so long. The Korean War afforded an opportunity and a rationale to reverse the processes of the previous decade and to return to good old-fashioned economic self-interest as the basis of U.S. trade and commercial policy.

At a time when the Korean War was putting its strain upon the European economy, the United States Congress voted: (1) to reinstate the famous "peril point" provision, (2) to limit the importation of perishable farm commodities under certain conditions, (3) to require the withdrawal of trade concessions to members of the Soviet bloc, and (4) to insist on the inclusion of an escape clause in all trade agreements to which the United States was a party. As if these weren't enough, it also enacted the so-called "cheese amendment" to the Defense Production Act establishing import quotas on dairy products from Canada, Norway, Denmark, and the Netherlands. And without adequate examination of the net costs and advantages, Congress passed the Kem Amendment and the Battle Act, both of which provided that any country exporting strategic commodities to the Soviet bloc would suffer the loss of all U.S. economic, financial, and military aid. Given the hysteria whipped up by Senator McCarthy, an exaggerated importance was attributed to East–West trade in helping the Communist economies with the result that the Administration was constantly under pressure from Congress to punish its allies who transgressed these laws. The Europeans regarded it as an infringement on their sovereignty to have the United States Congress dictate what they could and could not sell to the Communist bloc. The issue, a constant thorn in Acheson's side, was capable of arousing passions in Congress and in Europe out of all proportion. As Acheson said to van Roijen, the Netherlands ambassador, regarding the Kem Amendment: "It's a race between education and irritation on the Hill." Memo of meeting. Acheson and van Roijen. June 20, 1951.

** The consequences of the British rearmament contributed to a crisis within the Labour government. Aneurin Bevan, passed over for the post of foreign minister upon the death of Bevin, resigned from the Cabinet with a bitter blast at the government for allegedly sacrificing the welfare program to rearmament. In his House of Commons speech Bevan explicitly cited "the failure on the part of the American Government to inject the arms programme into the economy slowly enough" as one of the reasons for his resigning.

What was needed was a mechanism to coordinate the defense expenditures of the NATO members with the military planning being done at Supreme Headquarters Allied Powers Europe (SHAPE) and to offset the criticisms of those in America who argued that the Europeans were not doing enough. Acheson held meetings in July and August with Harriman, Paul Nitze, and Charles Bohlen to discuss ways and means of easing the European economic crisis and at the same time coordinate the competing demands upon the national budgets of the various NATO members before disaster engulfed the whole enterprise.

The Temporary Council Committee

By a fortuitous stroke Schuman and René Mayer (French finance minister) arrived in Washington in September with a proposal for a small committee to bring rearmament more into line with capabilities. Acheson saw in this the mechanism to deal with the economic crisis confronting the alliance and it was adopted at the Ottawa meeting of NATO. The purpose of the Temporary Council Committee (TCC) was twofold: to reassure Europeans about America's concern for their economic problems and at the same time to obtain from them a clear and authoritative statement of their economic and military capabilities. Acheson and Harriman believed that both these purposes could be achieved by a thoroughgoing canvas of the national economies and budgets of all the NATO members. Those who were not doing enough would have to show cause why, so that they could be assisted more intelligently. In effect what Acheson hoped to do with TCC was to have an organ of NATO break through the traditional barriers of each member's national sovereignty and make authoritative recommendations concerning the allocation and improved utilization of their economic, financial, and military resources.

Such an evaluation would also serve to bring the military planners in the Pentagon and at SHAPE back to earth. The Medium Term Defense Plan, upon which strategic planning was based, had been drawn up almost entirely without reference to the economic capabilities of the NATO members. It called for extremely high force levels based upon a strategic plan for containing a Soviet thrust east of the Rhine (the so-called Forward Strategy). In spite of the obvious inability of Europe to achieve the goals envisaged for it, the Joint Chiefs of Staff and NATO military planners in Europe continued to talk and act as though they

---

An interesting account of this crisis, in which the author writes, "In retrospect it seems clear that Bevan's play for power in the spring of 1951 was just as much an appeal to British neutralism as Taft's campaign was to American neo-isolationism," appears in David Rees, *Korea: The Limited War* (New York: St. Martin's Press, 1964), pp. 233–242.

were attainable. The TCC was designed to change all that.

The idea for such a committee to coordinate defense preparations came just in time. The pressures which had been building up in the European economies and parliaments over the costs of the Korean defense effort hung like a dark cloud over the forthcoming meeting of the NATO powers at Ottawa in September. It was with considerable sense of relief that the British and French foreign ministers learned of the proposed creation of TCC. Such a proposal meant that Herbert Morrison, the new British foreign minister, and Schuman could look forward to the Ottawa Conference without nagging concern that their economies were likely to buckle under the strain of rearmament.

When the idea of a Temporary Council Committee was first broached at Ottawa, the smaller powers resented that they had not been consulted beforehand and insisted that all NATO members must be represented on it. Since this would have defeated its purpose from several points of view, Acheson finally got them to agree that while all NATO members would constitute the Temporary Council Committee, its Executive Bureau, which would do the actual investigation and evaluation, would consist of only the Big Three—Britain, France, and the United States. The Executive Bureau consisted of Averell Harriman for the United States, Edwin Plowden for Britain and Jean Monnet for France, known as the Three Wise Men.* It worked in a rather ingenious way.

The TCC was given carte blanche to examine each member's economic and fiscal resources and to redirect the allocation of its resources. It could not only tell each member the total amount it ought to put into its military budget but what to do with it. The result was that the TCC ended by redirecting the military effort of the NATO members according to overall criteria rather than letting each nation be its own judge of its military contribution. More than that, in the exercise of its terms of reference the TCC successfully involved itself in such vital political questions as the length of the draft, the investment and import program, and the rations and housing policy of each member. Never before had such intimate coordination and direction of twelve countries' economic and political life been attained in time of peace.**

The French budget posed the greatest problem to the Three Wise

---

* To assist them in their work a staff was set up. The American staffers included General McNarney, Abe Lincoln, and Lincoln Gordon, the latter having worked with the European Recovery Program for the better part of four years.

** It was not an entirely happy solution because, as Alexander Werth suggests, the opinion grew that "military expenditure could not be decided upon by the French Assembly without NATO coming to a decision first. All this was depressing and a little humiliating."

Men because Georges Bidault, the French defense minister, wanted both to prosecute the war vigorously in Indochina and fully match the proposed German forces in Europe. For France to achieve these targets would have required a minimum of $1 billion from the United States, a sum which the Administration could not realistically hope to promise. The French were unwilling to pare down their force targets to a level within their financial and economic capacity; and unfortunately the amount that the Administration had or thought it could make available ($500 to $600 million) was to be cut back in the spring of 1952 by the Congress.*

The TCC operation represented a considerable development and extension of alliance diplomacy in the direction of balancing Europe's military spending against the need to protect its economic recovery and social gains. It converted a potentially chaotic situation into a basically orderly one. TCC achieved a crystallization of the willingness of the European states to do what they could within reason. Probably for the first time in history an alliance was invested with the authority to delve into the financial and budgetary affairs of each member and on that basis to set budgetary and military targets for each.**

As a result of Acheson's acceptance of EDC and the timely creation of TCC, the obstacles to German and European rearmament were at least partially cleared away, or so one would have thought. But on the critical central issues progress was still agonizingly slow. To meet the complaints of Eisenhower and General Alfred M. Gruenther concerning the slowness of German rearmament, Acheson had decided to push the Petersberg contractual agreements providing for German rearmament with Morrison and Schuman on their arrival in Washington and press for the recruitment of German soldiers by November 1.[5] In the course of their Washington meetings in September Acheson apparently persuaded Schuman to agree to have recruitment of German soldiers begin November 1,

---

* Of the $7.9 billion requested by the President in January 1952 for foreign economic and military assistance, the French were counting on from $650 to $750 million in military assistance. When foreign economic and military assistance was cut by Congress to $6 billion in July and it was found that *only* $525 million could be spared for France, the French charged Acheson with bad faith. The fact that much of the money was being used to finance a war in Indochina in a way which Acheson had never approved and which even Foreign Minister Schuman agreed was hopeless made no difference.

** This meant that these nations had to submit their entire fiscal system to the examination of people outside their governments and this affected not only their military budget but other parts of their budget because if you had some sort of limit, as you increased the military, you might decrease something else." Princeton Seminar File, December 13, 1953.

only to have the French Foreign Office later deny that any such decision
had been reached.*

Acheson, impatient, found it hard to understand why the French
could not see the advantage that would accrue from accepting EDC as a
military scheme. Was it not intended that the main forces of EDC, including the German divisions, would serve under French Marshal Juin on the
Central Sector? Why could not the French have the sense to seize upon a
once-in-a-lifetime chance to subordinate the Germany army to a European
military command guaranteed and underwritten by the United States and
Great Britain?

Meanwhile, despite his impatience, the elaboration of the all–European
political institutions that would presumably govern the European army
was slowly going forward at Paris and at meetings of the foreign ministers of the six interested governments at Strasbourg. Essentially these
plans called for the establishment of an executive authority on a collegial
basis, an assembly, a council of ministers, a defense commissioner, a court
of justice, and a common military budget for the European Defense Community. By the year's end Acheson was wondering where the Europeanizing would end and the defense begin.

Rome Meeting, NATO Council

When the NATO Council met next in Rome (November 24–28), Acheson confronted more disturbing evidence of the cul de sac into which
EDC was gradually driving German rearmament. The Benelux countries
were becoming dissatisfied with the federalist nature of the authority
that the political institutions being elaborated under the aegis of EDC
were assuming and the degree to which control over their military forces
was becoming vested in a military high command dominated by France
and Germany!

Dirk Stikker, the Netherlands foreign minister, and Paul Van Zeeland,
the Belgian, confessed to Acheson that they were having second thoughts
about fusing their countries' military forces with EDC and having their
economies subjected to the derangements besetting the French and Italian
economies. So bitter was the atmosphere at Rome that Eden thought EDC
might be doomed.[6] Fortunately, Acheson managed to surmount the crisis
by judicious pressure on the French and Italians to relax their federalist

---

* Memo, Acheson, Schuman, Bonnet, September 6, 1951. Acheson Papers. In
fact, upon his return to Paris, Schuman announced on October 25, 1951, that a European army could only function under a European *political* authority. This was a step
backward. Robert McGeehan, *The German Rearmament Question: American Diplomacy and European Defense After World War II* (Urbana: University of Illinois Press,
1971), pp. 150–151.

positions. In private Acheson set Schuman a deadline for French passage of EDC and acceptance of the German contractuals that would bring an end to German occupation, restore German sovereignty, and open the way to German rearmament. But the great hurdles were still ahead. The British in the meantime had elected a Conservative government headed by Winston Churchill with Anthony Eden as foreign minister. In direct contradiction to his out-of-office stance in favor of British membership in some form of European federation, Churchill was now taking potshots at EDC. Acheson returned from the Rome conference determined to squelch this not-so-subtle British opposition to EDC. Churchill and Eden were due to arrive in Washington early in January 1952; he would tackle them then.

Relations with the New British Government

The Conservative leaders, who were accustomed to a good press in the United States, arrived in Washington on January 7, 1952, determined to reassert the "special relationship" which British governments claimed with the United States.* Churchill did not hesitate to reveal his conviction that the Labourites Morrison and Attlee had let the United States run away with the ball, and he and Eden were determined to put the British stamp back upon European diplomacy.

Given the harmful effects which Churchill's utterances were having on EDC, it is not at all surprising that the Churchill–Eden visit to Washington was not a love feast. True, the special relationship which Britain claimed with the United States still retained a certain significance. Churchill enjoyed an immense personal prestige—so much so that his new-found disagreement with the tough anti–Communist line which was enjoying such a vogue in America was deliberately overlooked.** It was taken for granted that the British and Americans, like cousins, could have

---

* André Fontaine writes that Churchill's "dream would have been to re-establish the Anglo–American directorate which he had created during the war with Roosevelt." *Histoire de la guerre froid*, Vol. II (Paris: Fayard, 1967), p. 60.

** From being the herald of the Cold War that he was in 1946, Churchill had become after 1950 a leading exponent of prudence and conciliation vis-à-vis the Soviet Union, but it would not do to see him as entirely a dove. In talks with U.S. officials Churchill remarked that "the central factor in Soviet policy was fear; the USSR feared our friendship more than our enmity. Churchill hoped that the growing strength of the West would reverse this so that they would fear our enmity more than our friendship and would be led to seek our friendship." Acheson merely hoped that present policy was correct, "namely not to create forces beyond our capacity but to create sufficient force to make any action by the Soviet Union in Europe too dangerous to be attempted." Minutes. Truman, Churchill, January 8, 1952.

amicable falling-outs.* But the visit also had its bitter, tense moments precisely because the two governments were distinctly at odds on crucial issues. The Conservatives, who had been out of office for six years, were to an astonishing degree out of touch with the imperatives of American policy and *played down* the Communist threat, except where British interests were directly affected.** Churchill was still thinking in terms of spheres of influence with the United States receiving British support in the Far East and the United Kingdom having American backing in the Middle East.† The fact that Britain feared and did not want any form of European integration to succeed reinforced Churchill's partiality for what General de Gaulle was later to call a "union of fatherlands," that is to say, a union in which the national governments, not supranational institutions, determine policy. Churchill's and Eden's stubborn preoccupation with the threat to British interests in Iran and Egypt seemed perverse to Truman and Acheson, preoccupied as they were with the political and military threat of Soviet Communism. This did not inhibit a certain amount of swapping—for instance, of British support for the United States in the Far East in return for Washington's support for the United Kingdom in Iran and in Egypt. But Churchill's scoffing attitude toward EDC was definitely unwelcome. Truman, Acheson, and other Administration figures went out of their way to be nice and jolly with Sir Winston but they bore down hard on poor Eden.‡ At their very first meeting Acheson warned Eden rather forcefully that in solving the problem of German rearmament no ready alternative to EDC existed, and that contrary to what Britain might think, the American intention of maintaining troops in Europe depended upon making EDC effective. Acheson pointed out that congres-

---

* There were also many good moments. In the course of one dinner Churchill had Lord Cherwell get out his slide rule and calculate the depth to which the alcoholic beverages he (Churchill) had consumed in a lifetime would rise in the room. Churchill was quite disappointed to learn that it only came to two or three feet—it was, after all, a rather large room. Churchill also had the unusual honor of being invited to address a joint session of Congress. All in all there was a family quality to Churchill's and Eden's visit, including its unusual duration, which lasted almost two weeks.

** The ill-fated Suez expedition gives evidence that Eden never really learned that the national interests of the European states had to take second place to America's global interests or else.

† He reaffirmed the Attlee–Morrison commitment of the previous spring to permit UN action "not confined to Korea" in event of heavy air attacks against UN forces from Chinese bases.

‡ Acheson's exhaustion and edginess got so much the better of him at one dinner meeting that he insulted Eden by bluntly informing him that it was his [Eden's] inability to divorce the foreign-policy aspects of the Iranian oil dispute from the business and technical that was prolonging the crisis with Mossadegh. Letter, Acheson to Pearson (Foreign Minister, Canada), January 23, 1952. Acheson Papers.

sional legislation clearly committed the United States to support for EDC and that the Congress would not be happy if EDC failed. As usual, British resistance to Europeanizing took practical forms. The British wanted NATO headquarters to remain in London where it would be under the observant eye of the Foreign Office. In justification the British claimed that London was the linchpin of NATO because it joined the North Atlantic area to Western Europe. Acheson would hear nothing of it. He was now pulling out all stops in an effort to help the continental governments over the last hurdles facing EDC. It would be politically and psychologically important to the French government to have NATO headquarters adjacent to Eisenhower's military headquarters at Fontainbleau. Since the British were not being asked to make major sacrifices, the prizes had to go where they would do the most good. The important area for action was on the continent of Europe, and Acheson knew that he would be more successful in getting EDC through the French Assembly if NATO were located in Paris.*

Midway through their Washington visit the British delegation journeyed to Ottawa for talks with the Canadians. Acheson took advantage of his strong personal ties with Lester Pearson, Canadian foreign minister, to ask him to steer Churchill and Eden into desirable channels. This Pearson did to the best of his ability.[7] Their Canadian visit seems to have helped convince Churchill and Eden that their expectations of reversing the American government on any of the controversial issues were far-fetched. They returned to Washington far more conciliatory, and the final communiqué read: "Our two Governments will continue to give full support to the efforts now being made to establish a European Defense Community, and will lend all assistance in their power in bringing it to

---

* Characteristically Churchill's main concern was with the North Atlantic Naval Command. The previous February (1951) an American admiral had been appointed to the Supreme Command of NATO forces in the North Atlantic. The only sop to British pride was the appointment of a British deputy to the American commander and of a British admiral to command the Eastern Atlantic area. The Labour government which had accepted these appointments had been roundly denounced by the opposition in the House on April 19, and Churchill had come to office determined to reassert British primacy in the North Atlantic sphere of naval affairs. Churchill's convulsive efforts in the course of the Washington meetings to have undone the appointment of an American as Supreme Naval Commander in the North Atlantic was literally the last gasp of a declining naval power. It was fitting that it should be Churchill; and Truman remarked that it was very difficult to deny the ex–First Sea Lord and former Naval Person his fondest wish. But even if it had wished to humor the old boy, the American government had to concern itself with the political repercussions which would follow within the Pentagon and within the Congress from any decision to reverse itself. At their last meeting Acheson managed to convince Churchill to leave the matter as it was rather than obstruct the operation of the command.

fruition. We believe that this is the best means of bringing a democratic Germany as a full and equal partner into a purely defensive organization for European security. . . ." This was progress of sorts, but it was barely sufficient to neutralize the other disintegrative forces at work on EDC, and there was still no agreement with the British to move NATO headquarters to Paris. In fact, on January 28 Ambassador Franks dropped by the State Department with yet another message from Eden insisting upon the absolute necessity of NATO headquarters remaining in London.

Meanwhile, the situation in Paris that winter was going from bad to worse. The nearer the date of the Lisbon NATO meeting came, at which presumably France would have to agree to both EDC and the German contractuals, the more desperate and febrile French political maneuvers seemed to become. Unable to extricate themselves from a scheme of their own devising, the French Cabinet was engaged in a last-minute series of obstructionist maneuvers.

In spite of every concession to ease French concern and increase the benefits that France stood to gain by approving EDC,* Ambassador Henri Bonnet complained to Acheson that Adenaur ought *not* to be invited to the Big Three foreign ministers' meeting set for London as a prelude to the larger NATO meeting in Lisbon. The French were obviously hoping that if Adenauer could be kept from attending the London meeting (set for mid–February), perhaps the last-minute agreements would *not* be reached, Lisbon would turn out to be another Rome (where little positive was accomplished), and the French would be off the hook for another six months. Bonnet also argued that the West German government had still not settled (1) the financial contribution which Germany would make to EDC, and (2) the matter of the limitations which Germany would accept on the production of armaments.** Acheson turned Bonnet's objections by pointing out that the conference had been called by Eden; hence it was up to Eden to decide who was to be invited. Then, dryly, Acheson agreed that the matters raised by Bonnet and still under discussion at Bonn *ought* to be settled speedily.

While the representatives of the EDC countries met in Paris on Janu-

---

* On January 28 Acheson told Franks that "the important area for action was on the continent of Europe and that we could more successfully accomplish the task if NATO was located in Paris than if it were located in London" and that was that. Memo, January 28, 1952.

** Memo of meeting. Acheson, Bonnet (French ambassador), February 2, 1952. Philip Jessup suggests that there was a definite group in the Quai d'Orsay (French Foreign Office) who, to offset American insistence on getting German forces in the field, had convinced themselves that the Soviet threat was not as real as the Americans said it was. Personal interview with Jessup, Acheson's ambassador-at-large, New York City, June 22, 1960.

ary 26 and 27 in a last desperate effort to reconcile the differences still outstanding on the European Army Plan, important progress was made; but the German representatives, feeling the hot breath of public opinion on their necks, declared that their country could not agree to be a member of EDC and at the same time not be a member of NATO. The French government in the meantime had injected a new element into the debate by appointing a diplomatic mission to the Saar.* On February 1, in connection with this French maneuver, Adenauer declared that "in wide circles in Germany faith has been shaken whether France seriously desires a genuine partnership with the Federal Republic, such as is essential as the foundation of a defense community."

In spite of these incidents, debate in the German parliament led only to a series of limiting resolutions. These were acceptable to the Adenauer government because they were not substantively at odds with the Petersberg Agreements. The final resolution passed by the Bundestag provided that: (1) the sovereignty of the Federal Republic must be complete, except in certain instances such as Berlin; (2) the West German government must be permitted to decide which Allied occupation measures should be retained; (3) no action be taken prejudicial to a future treaty of peace; (4) all discriminatory organs, such as the Military Security Board, must be abolished; (5) all controls on industry must be lifted; (6) Germany must make only one financial defense contribution, which would include relief to refugees as well as to the support of allied troops in Germany; (7) German labor and guard units in the service of the occupation powers must be eliminated; (8) disputes must be referred to neutral arbitration; and (9) Berlin must be more closely linked with the Bonn government. On February 8 the Bundestag approved all these resolutions by a vote of 204 to 156.[8]

Debate in the French Parliament

The agonized state of French political opinion on the eve of the Lisbon Conference was evidenced by the debate in the Assembly. Before the new government of Edgar Faure could secure a parlous vote of confidence, it had to make concessions to the Socialists—concessions which carried the treaty back to an earlier stage in its development and marked a definite erosion in parliamentary support for EDC. Things were going backward rather than forward.

On the same day as the Bundestag passed its resolution, Foreign Minister Schuman promised the French National Assembly that "there would

---

* The Pleven government fell on January 8 and was succeeded on January 18 by a new government under Edgar Faure. Schuman remained as foreign minister.

be no autonomous German units in the European defense forces," and that defense arrangements would be handled in Germany by a civilian organization, the authority of which would be limited to recruiting, to administration of reserves, and to certain political problems. He emphasized that U.S. support for the proposed army had been obtained on condition that there would be no delay in the organization of a defense contribution from Western Germany. Schuman concluded by pointing out that if EDC was not approved, the United States would insist on some other form of German participation in the defense of Western Europe.

During the course of the debate, which demonstrated that many French deputies were not confident that the plan offered sufficient guarantees against the revival of German militarism, a number of opposition motions were tabled.

Together the compromise amendments constituted a formidable roadblock to eventual agreement on the issues still dividing the French from the Americans, British, and Germans. A number of them, such as those calling for recognition of France's military burden in Indochina and requiring that French contingents in Europe must be equal, at all times, to those of any other member of the community, were capable of being regarded as bargaining counters and therefore susceptible to adjustment. Others, such as that restricting NATO membership to states without territorial claims, deliberately discriminated against the Federal Republic; while still others, such as conditions placed upon the recruitment of national units and calling for more formal U.S. and British guarantees against possible rupture of EDC by the Germans, were out of the question. In fact, the joining of a demand for the formation of a supranational political power and for participation by the United Kingdom involved a fundamental contradiction. The British were not going to contribute to the consolidation of a united Europe to which they were fundamentally opposed. The French could either have a genuinely integrated defense community or a British guarantee; they could not have both.

After lengthy and often emotional debate, the French Assembly finally passed a vote of confidence in the Faure ministry 326 to 276. The strength of French reservations was open to two interpretations. Either it could be taken at its face value as denoting such a fundamental change of attitude toward EDC on the part of the French that some alternative had better be found, or it could be assumed that much of the French opposition would be dispelled by the gradual achievement of compromises and by the assiduous application of American funds to places where the French budget was hurting. Acheson believed that there was no alternative to EDC; therefore, he had to assume that French fears and suspicions would be dispelled as the various parts of the agreements began to function satisfactorily.* But even if Acheson had imagined how the French opposition to EDC would grow in succeeding months, it is doubtful if he would have felt that there was any alternative.

Prelude to Lisbon: The London Meeting, Adenauer in Attendance

When Acheson arrived in London on February 14 (he had arrived a few days early to attend the funeral of George VI), the EDC debates were still being heard in Bonn and Paris. On the 17th the three foreign ministers, joined by Adenauer (over French objections), got down to their penultimate negotiations before Lisbon. Acheson's talents as a negotiator were once again taxed to the fullest. There were five main problems that still had to be negotiated. The first was how Germany was to have a voice in NATO while a fight was avoided on the issue of formally admitting the Federal Republic, which the French had made quite clear they would not tolerate. The answer, worked out at London and agreed to by Schuman at Lisbon, was to have two councils: one a council of the European army nations, all of whom were members of NATO except Germany— the other was the NATO Council. Whenever a question affecting German participation arose, Germany had a right to call a meeting of the two councils. Any NATO member who felt that a question affected its political stability or territorial integrity could also call a joint meeting. Practically, this meant that Germany had the opportunity to sit with the NATO Council on the entire range of NATO matters without actually being a member.

A second problem was that of meeting the French demand for a more concrete Anglo–American guarantee of EDC. A three-power communiqué stated that the British and U.S. foreign ministers had "declared their abiding interest in the establishment and integrity of the European defense community and, in association with the foreign minister of France, studied means by which their governments could support and cooperate with the community." It also said that "these subjects will be matters of continuing consultation between the three and between their governments in order to find appropriate means of giving the community the desired cooperation and support."

A third problem concerned the distribution of the German financial contribution. Hitherto Germany had been obliged to bear a heavy share of Allied occupation costs. Everything from maid service in the homes of

---

* In the meantime he would endeavor to supply successive French governments with American financial and military aid in the paradoxical hope that the most demoralizing aspects of their dependence on the United States would be overcome.

Allied military personnel to the costs of a large number of Germans employed in services connected with the Allied military establishments in Germany were paid for by the Bonn government. If Germany was to be treated as a self-respecting ally, these occupation charges would have to be abrogated. It was agreed that as a participating member of EDC the German government would be assessed an annual sum to support the military forces, including the German forces envisaged for EDC. In fact, the German government wanted as much as possible of their contribution to EDC to go for their own military units and as little as necessary to go for supporting the other forces.

The financial position of France was especially complicated because the French would be part of EDC and at the same time part of NATO. The French could not expect to continue to draw down occupation costs at Germany's expense and at the same time have the French forces assigned to EDC partly financed out of Germany's EDC assessment. A special committee of the NATO Council estimated that West Germany could devote 11.25 billion marks (about $2.7 billion) to military defense. Adenauer indicated that despite any reservations which his finance minister might have, that figure was acceptable to him even though it did not take into account the special burden of Berlin or the costs connected with the presence of nine million refugees in West Germany. The British, who had a direct stake in having Germany continue to pay for a sizeable portion of the occupation costs and to contribute as largely as possible to the collective defense effort, now began to dig in their heels. They knew that once EDC went into operation, they would get no further contribution from Germany toward maintenance of their army of occupation.

Another highly controversial issue revolved around the question of what military production rights Germany was to have. After all, the Germans had only recently been deprived of much of their direct military potential and forbidden ever again to engage in arms production. But Acheson was determined that Germany should not be denied certain lines of military production if they were important to the Western defense effort as a whole. Here, too, the French put up a spirited opposition which was not easily broken down. In the end the German government voluntarily agreed to refrain from aircraft production subject to discussion with the Western powers. Munitions production was also subject to a complicated system whereby the production of explosives for everybody in the EDC would be subject to the control of an agency of the EDC, and such production should not take place in areas defined as exposed or forward areas (in other words, a definition that included most of Germany). As a result France, provided it could get the support of one other member of the EDC agency, would enjoy a virtual veto over the production of explosives in Germany.

Finally, Eden was as adamant as ever against moving NATO headquarters and the offices of the OEEC to Paris. Acheson again had to say
no. Yet in spite of all their disagreements, Acheson succeeded in having
the French, British, and Germans agree to far-reaching compromises on
all the issues and problems under discussion. As Gaddis Smith remarks:
"For the first time in a year real progress was made—in defining the constitutional relationship of EDC to NATO, levels of expenditure, and limitations on the kind of arms Germany would produce." [9] But it did little
to render EDC and German rearmament acceptable on other than the
governmental level.

In spite of the obvious gap between the agreements reached on the
principal questions at London and the conditions set forth in the motion
before the French Assembly, Schuman agreed to proceed. On February 17
he told Guy Mollet, leader of the Socialist opposition, that nothing final
had been decided. But it must have been clear to Mollet that Schuman
had gotten all he could hope to get by bargaining and that either the
French Assembly must pass the government motion or open up a parliamentary and diplomatic crisis at an unpropitious moment in the life of
the Fourth Republic.* Mollet was not about to risk that. As noted above,
in the vote that followed, the majority of the Socialist deputies were
persuaded to overlook the contradiction between what they were voting
and what the government had actually agreed to. The motion passed by
a quite narrow margin—with Communists and Gaullists providing most
of the opposition—on the night of February 19, thereby enabling Faure,
Schuman, and Bidault to proceed to Lisbon for the next stage of their
lugubrious task.

The NATO Conference at Lisbon, instead of being a mere pro forma
conference to ratify agreements worked out beforehand, turned out to
be a week-long work session. Acheson had to keep breathing purpose
and life into the affair. On the surface the conference seemed to involve
fitting and tying together an endless range of interconnected decisions.
"The whole operation," Acheson later remarked, "was like one of those
games where a dozen little shots have to be maneuvered into holes in a
cardboard field: the slightest jar in trying to get the last one in shakes
all the others out." [10] And on the face of it the value of the months of
work and negotiation which had gone before proved themselves out at
Lisbon. But on a deeper level a great many issues were left unresolved.
As McGeehan remarks, "Acheson's impression that 'the world that lay be-

---

* The combination of Communists and Gaullists elected in June 1951 made the
life of any French government precarious and highly dependent on the full support
of all the center parties.

fore us shone with hope,' was simply not supported by the realities of the moment." [11]

French opinion was still far from reconciled to German rearmament in any form, and the French government itself was clearly maneuvering to gain time. Had it presented the agreements to the French parliament in their existing form, they would have been defeated. In fact, on the same day that Acheson returned to Washington from Lisbon the Faure government was overthrown following his request for new taxes to implement the French obligation under the Lisbon program. Secondly, the United States had taken EDC over in a way that departed from original French intentions. In proclaiming the historic significance of EDC in burying Franco–German enmity, Harriman "noted that it would be closely associated with NATO, using language which indicated the transformation of the European army from a European to an American policy object. . . ." [12] McGeehan observes that the same conclusion was reached by a British study group.

Still are we to say that nothing had been accomplished? Diplomacy is always something of a gamble—a bet on an uncertain outcome, as Acheson would say. A statesman begins with some proximate goal; there is no guarantee he will achieve it. But if in the process of striving, he changes the situation in ways favorable to his general purpose, then it cannot be said that he has entirely failed. Sooner or later the future of Germany would have had to have been faced by the French. By exploiting the opportunity posed by the Korean War, Acheson had at least made it possible for the German problem to be considered at a time when both sides —Paris and Bonn—felt under some compulsion to bury their feud in the face of a new danger. Secondly, by placing France and the other European states under obligation to the United States for their economic recovery and security, Acheson obliged them to make concessions toward the common good that they might not otherwise have been willing to make. Thirdly, by creating evidence of solidarity and progress, Acheson strengthened his hand at home. Isolationists and critics were less successful in attacking a policy that showed consistent gains. The most eloquent testimony of all that something had changed came from the Soviet Union. Hardly had the Lisbon Conference adjourned than the Soviets sent a diplomatic note calling once again for a peace settlement for all of Germany.

CHAPTER

19

DUEL FOR EUROPE: THE SOVIET
DIPLOMATIC NOTE OF MARCH 10, 1952

UP UNTIL the Lisbon meeting the pieces had been moved around on the chessboard by diplomats. The decisions taken at Lisbon were, after all, agreements among a small group of men with whom Acheson enjoyed an uncommonly high degree of loyalty and confidence. Now the results of Lisbon had to be exposed to the batterings of national legislatures and of public opinion in the various countries before they could be ratified. Acheson hoped that the agreements themselves would carry conviction, thereby helping to shape a favorable attitude among the peoples involved. Unfortunately, now that a degree of détente had been engendered, the Europeans and their governments alike were prone to discount the necessity for what had, a few years earlier, appeared as an absolute imperative. But people losing their sense of urgency was no excuse for the leading stateman of the leading power to abdicate his responsibility. A statesman was obliged to act upon what risks the future might hold, not on transient moods of the moment. Furthermore, EDC and NATO were not ends in and of themselves; they happened to be the issues on which the contest with Russia had become focused. Their realization would be as important to the outcome of the Cold War as Stalingrad and Midway had been to the outcome the hot war. If they were realized, a hot war would become less likely because the opportunity for aggrandizement would be markedly reduced.

Acheson had likened the Lisbon Agreements to the game of coaxing shot into cardboard holes; it could hardly be expected that the agreements would all stay in place once exposed to the buffeting of national passions and domestic politics. To succeed, the agreements would have to be cushioned against shock from a number of directions simultaneously: from the East in the form of new Soviet overtures to negotiate; from a new outbreak of Franco–German rivalry; and from the vicissitudes of domestic politics among the political parties of Germany, France, Britain, Italy, and the Low Countries.

The first shock came, naturally enough, from the Soviet Union. The Kremlin was sufficiently impressed by the progress realized at Lisbon to embark upon a powerful new diplomatic offensive. Hitherto Soviet offers to negotiate a German settlement had always insisted upon a completely disarmed Germany. But the prospect of West German rearmament and European unity produced a completely new Soviet card designed to trump the American strategy: in a diplomatic note to the three Western powers on March 10, 1952, the Soviet proposed "discussion of a peace treaty for Germany on the basis of a unified and independent Germany *with a national army,* on the condition that Germany be neutralized and all foreign troops withdrawn [emphasis added]." [1] The note held out to the Germans the prospect of unity and access to Eastern markets, on the condition that Germany not become involved with the EDC—that is, not to be bound by any alliance directed against a state which had fought against Germany in World War II.

The Soviet note was designed to stir up popular opposition to German rearmament in France and Britain, while simultaneously offering Germany, if united and neutralized, a national military establishment considerably more independent than the one projected under EDC. It offered, as French Foreign Minister Schuman remarked, something to every group of Germans, and especially to the embattled socialists who had all along opposed integration with the West on the grounds that it would make more difficult, if not impossible, the eventual reunification of Germany and deprive the Federal Republic of its bargaining power vis-à-vis the Soviet Union. Its pressure upon Adenauer was bound to be intense, as British Foreign Secretary Eden well understood. The British, he wrote, "must respond in such a way as to help the Government of the Federal Republic meet opposition criticism. Fortunately the proposal for a national German army with national sources of military equipment and without control has alerted French distrust. Properly handled this could strengthen support in Germany for a controlled German rearmament with EDC." [2]

Acheson, of course, was in no way seduced by Moscow's note. To begin with, the Soviet offer did not go nearly so far as he believed necessary if there was to be any real chance of peace and security in Europe. Germany was only a preliminary issue; the security of Western Europe could not be realized until all Soviet forces were withdrawn from Eastern Europe. Acheson expressed his view of the situation in a series of off-the-record meetings with newsmen that spring: "One of the greatest dangers to peace is the presence of Russians in the heart of Europe." The

Russians would not release their control over Eastern Germany, and therefore it would be a false notion that there could be "a neutral band in an armed Europe." *

Acheson also had to face the question of whether the Soviet note of March 10, 1952, constituted a genuine "negotiating bid" or was merely a "delaying bid" designed to stall and disrupt the carefully contrived arrangements agreed to at Lisbon. Marshall Shulman writes that the "ambiguity of the Soviet note does not offer much support for the interpretation that the Soviet Union seriously entertained the possibility of reunification on any terms. That would have jeopardized the Soviet position in East Germany, where a force-draft program for the 'construction of socialism' was then in preparation." **

To Acheson the distinction between "negotiating bid" and "delaying bid" really mattered very little because either way it would produce unacceptable results in terms of what Acheson really believed essential to the long-run regulation of East–West relations. Any inclination to take the Soviet offer seriously would destroy the very structure which had prompted Russia to propose negotiations in the first place. Once the Lisbon Agreements were disrupted, there would no longer be any reason for Russia to negotiate for a reunited Germany. The West would be back where it had begun in 1947, with no chance of achieving its objectives.

Furthermore, any form of reunification not on Western terms would also deprive NATO of West German troop commitments and thereby weaken the structure of containment. The balance of American and West German interest weighed in favor of continuing to build situations of strength in anticipation of influencing Soviet behavior and bringing about German reunification on Western terms. It was not thought desirable to chance negotiations that would risk putting a neutral Germany at the mercy of Soviet military pressure and political subversion. Aden-

---

* Memo of backgrounder. Acheson to Joseph Evans (*Wall Street Journal*) and Don McNeil (*The Pathfinder*), Monday, March 26, 1952. Acheson Papers. When asked if he meant Soviet withdrawal from Eastern Europe as well as Western Europe, "the Secretary replied that he did. He did not mean, he said, that satellites would cease to be satellites. This might well be, but the presence of Soviet forces 100 miles from the Rhine is the source of trouble and these would have to be withdrawn." Memo of backgrounder. Acheson, Shulman, Drummond, Kuh, Bancroft, March 27, 1952. Acheson Papers.

** Marshall D. Shulman, *Stalin's Foreign Policy Reappraised* (Cambridge, Mass.: Harvard University Press, 1963), p. 194. Ulam writes: "From what we know of Stalin's foreign policy, we must conclude that only an extremely urgent danger would have made him surrender a Soviet territorial conquest, which East Germany was in fact." But whether the prospect of German rearmament constituted such an urgent danger remains a moot question. Adam Ulam, *Expansion and Coexistence* (New York: Praeger, 1968), p. 537.

auer, too, was politically committed to European and Atlantic integration and did not care to weaken American support or risk a Soviet–American deal at West Germany's expense. For these and other equally compelling reasons, the question of whether the Soviet note was a "bargaining bid" or simply a "delaying bid" was one that had to be explored but not at the risk of breaking up the Western alliance. "It has," Acheson wrote Truman on March 11, "the usual apparent hooks in it. It is shrewdly drafted to appeal primarily to the Germans but also to impressionable opinion generally, and it seems clear that we would be ill-advised . . . to turn it down out of hand." [3] Nevertheless, given the troubled state of French and West German opinion, the Soviet offer was too shrewdly conceived to lend itself to easy dismissal. There was the issue in a nutshell. How could the Soviet thrust be parried? Acheson recognized that he could not simply condemn the idea of a German national army. What if EDC should fail to secure French ratification? The Western reply could not afford to be too flatly on record as opposing the formation of an out-and-out German national army. At the same time if the Soviet note succeeded in delaying EDC and the German contractuals beyond 1952, "the Soviet Union could be fairly confident that the proposals themselves were dead." [4]

Since Acheson did not wish to slow down or disrupt the progress of the Lisbon Agreements, the Western reply to the Soviet note was deliberately designed to pose the issue in terms that the Soviet Union was least likely to be willing to accept—namely, free, UN-inspected elections throughout Germany as a prior condition for the creation of an all-German government to negotiate a peace treaty. "Such a Government can only be set up on the basis of free elections in the Federal Republic, the Soviet zone of occupation, and Berlin." [5] Since free elections in East Germany would lead to a repudiation of Communism and could have for its only outcome depriving the Soviet Union of its influence, the Western proposal was likely to be unacceptable, and the Western powers of course knew it. But to insist on anything less than free elections, Acheson feared, would be seen as a capitulation and undermine West German support.

In line with their commitment to Adenauer, the Western reply also took exception to the Soviet statement that the territory of Germany was determined by frontiers laid down by the decisions of the Potsdam conference. As for the creation of German national land, air, and sea forces, the Soviet proposal represented a step backward which might jeopardize the emergence in Europe of a new era in which international relations would be based on cooperation and not on rivalry and distrust.[6] This was a good opening counterthrust, but it by no means put an end to the Soviet diplomatic campaign.

Nor did the Western reply succeed in allaying Chancellor Adenauer's domestic critics, who took the occasion to mount a powerful campaign against the Western orientation of German foreign policy. Adenauer started out bravely enough by scoring the Soviet proposal as merely a delaying tactic. But the Soviet proposal raised doubts in German minds about the adequacy of Adenauer's assurance that the Western schemes for collective defense constituted the best means of forcing Moscow to accept German reunification. Over Adenauer's opposition, the Bundestag adopted the following resolution on April 3, 1952:

In the exchange of notes between the Soviet Union and the three western Powers . . . the Bundestag sees an important contribution towards the clarification of the premises essential for the attainment of this objective [reunification of Germany]. . . .

The Bundestag asks the Federal government to approach the occupying powers with a view to the holding of free elections for a National Assembly for the whole of Germany. . . .

A second Soviet note of April 9 so inflated German hopes that the Russians might really be serious that the pressure on Adenauer became additionally intense. Adenauer's inflexible opposition and skepticism about the Soviet offer now began to arouse uneasiness even within his own party. Germans began to question the advisability of rushing into EDC and other agreements which might deprive West Germany of influence on Soviet policy for an indefinite future.

Meanwhile, the Lisbon arrangements took a shock from yet another direction. In anticipation of the Lisbon negotiations, the German Federal Bundestag, in a resolution of February 8, had declared itself firmly opposed to French attempts to prejudge the political disposition of the Saar before conclusion of a peace treaty in which the political fate of the Saar would be finally settled. In early March the Adenauer government suddenly projected the fate of the Saar into the forefront of Franco–German relations by asking that conditions in the Saar be discussed at the forthcoming meeting of the European Council of Ministers.

Upon the defeat of Hitler's Germany, France had annexed the Saar but had been persuaded to give the Saarlanders a regime based upon political autonomy and economic attachment to France. At the time of the signing of the European Coal and Steel Community (April 18, 1951), France had agreed that the fate of the Saar would be left to the signing of the peace treaty with Germany. But in direct opposition to this course, the French had recently gone ahead with the appointment of a French ambassador to the Saar and with plans for elections in which parties hostile to French policy (German, naturally) were excluded from participation. These decisions by no means sealed the fate of the Saar, but Germans were incensed.

On March 12, Acheson, who had hoped to see the future of the Saar settled by quiet diplomacy, took to task Federal Secretary of State Walter Hallstein for submitting the Saar issue to the Council of Europe.[7] Adenaur appears to have been using the Council simply as a gambit to force the French to negotiate; either that or Acheson's blistering admonishment had its effect. In any event, following conversations with Schuman on March 19, Adenauer agreed to withdraw his memorandum to the members of the Council. But further negotiations between the French and German statemen only led to charges of appeasement at home and bad faith on the other side. Try as everyone might, the decisive issue of the Saar could not be gotten off the European scene. Public emotions were deeply aroused on both sides of the Rhine. The German parliament insisted that the Saar was exclusively German territory and that France had no legal right to dispose of it without German consent; the French government, having had to make heartbreaking concessions on so many other fronts, was determined to use what bargaining power it had left to maintain its hold upon the coal basin of the Saar.

Unable to contain the eruption of German nationalism in the Bundestag debate of March 23, Adenauer sought to drain it off the next day by declaring himself in favor of Four Power discussions with the Soviet Union. At the same time he rejected both the neutralization of Germany and the Oder–Neisse line and insisted that "the first object of further exchanges with Moscow must be to extract a definite offer of unity in freedom which had not so far been made."

In France, meanwhile, the reaction against EDC was becoming harder and harder to mollify. As the project to contain a rearmed Germany within the European Defense force came nearer and nearer to decision, French opinion began to lash about. Led by Charles de Gaulle, nationalist opponents of the French government launched an explosive assault upon the European Defense Community which they charged with being nothing but an Anglo–American plan to betray French sovereignty and reduce France to the status of a third-rate power dominated by Germany.

Despite such attacks, the political forces within France working in favor of EDC and accommodation with Germany were still very strong. Besides the Mouvement Républicain Populaire represented by Schuman, they included Guy Mollet, the Socialist leader, and important elements within the Radical Party. In addition, American commitments to help France in Indochina and in balancing its budget carried great weight with parts of the bureaucracy, the army, and the financial interests of France. Jean Monnet, an important intermediary, saw Acheson in Washington on May 6 and assured him that he had just spoken to Hervé Alphand in Paris and that negotiations on EDC and the contractual agreements with Germany were going forward in a favorable atmosphere, and that agreements would soon be initiated.[8] Monnet remarked that he was not worried about the German contribution to EDC or about an eventual agreement with Germany on other matters. Rather, like Schuman, Monnet expressed grave concern about Indochina, where the burden was becoming too much for France to carry alone. Monnet agreed with Acheson that the solution lay in accelerating and intensifying the training of a Vietnamese national army. But neither was very optimistic that even that would be enough.

Clearly, American diplomacy could still count upon the existence of a strong current of French political opinion dedicated to the realization of EDC provided that the United States gave France relief in Indochina and diplomatic support in North Africa.* Nevertheless it was hard to predict what might happen when EDC came before the Assembly for ratification. The Schuman–Monnet forces might be far less effective in public than they were behind the scenes.

To rally opinion the French government next asked for a formal United States commitment to EDC which would take the form of a guarantee against a withdrawal of West Germany from the Defense Community. Had the Truman Administration been able to accord the French government this assurance, EDC might well have secured the support necessary for its ratification by the French Assembly. Unfortunately, the American commitment to internationalism—which had begun with the Truman Doctrine and continued with the Marshall Plan, NATO, and the Korean War—was losing its political attractiveness at home. A reaction had set in, prompted in part by a sense of frustration that an easy victory over Communism was not forthcoming and in part by the inroads of Mc-Carthyism. With the 1952 Presidential elections approaching, Truman was fast becoming a lame duck and could no longer hope to rally support for new initiatives.

These circumstances clearly limited the nation's diplomacy at a time when an American commitment to guarantee the integrity of EDC might have carried it to realization. Just when another surge of internationalism and resolution was most in demand, Truman had to notify Acheson that no guarantee requiring congressional approval was possible. The revolution in American foreign policy was short-circuited at the point in history at which European unity had come closest to realization. Success or fail-

---

* In talking to the French about their colonial problems, Acheson drew a sharp distinction between the French position in Indochina and in North Africa. In the case of Indochina, France had done about as much as it could be expected to do in transferring responsibility for government to the Associated States. Unfortunately, the native rulers in the Associated States had shown themselves inefficient and unwilling to govern. As for North Africa, Acheson warned the French that they were too slow and unduly influenced by vested interests in introducing reforms in the local administration.

ure now seemed to depend exclusively upon Acheson's skillful use of the tools of diplomacy and on whatever monies Congress might vote that spring for economic and military assistance.

Eden now made a helpful contribution. Using the broad discretion which British foreign ministers enjoy, Eden was willing to give EDC the guarantee which Acheson could not. In response to a request by the six continental members, Eden indicated that Her Majesty's government "would be willing to conclude an agreement with the Community [EDC] in the sense desired by the Conference [the Six Powers]." Eden informed the continental six that his government would be willing to sign a treaty with the European Defense Community, extending to it the same guarantee which Britain had undertaken under Article 4 of the Brussels Treaty four years earlier. "The effect of the British proposal is that the Brussels Treaty commitment to provide automatic military assistance in event of attack, will in future apply as between the U.K. and *the EDC as a whole* [emphasis added]." [9] Eden also reiterated the British government's intention to associate the U.K. as closely as possible with the EDC in all stages of its political and military development. These stirring and heartening words gave French leaders confidence. But not for long. British assurances were still not an Anglo–American guarantee. On April 16, in still another effort to move French acceptance of EDC, Acheson announced that the United States would be seriously concerned at any independent action likely to undermine the Defense Community (meaning any future German withdrawal from EDC). Still the French Assembly and Cabinet balked. The prospect of German rearmament was no longer a rational issue for the French; "the question now turns more on human emotions than on hard reasoning." [10] Negotiations in Bonn between Adenauer and the allied high commissioners were lasting as long as seventeen hours a day as objection after objection issued from Paris. Even after he had arrived in Bonn, Acheson was not sure the treaties would be signed. Schuman arrived from Paris "obviously tired, nervous, and depressed" [11] and unsure of his control over the situation in Paris. In order to meet the penultimate French demand for guarantees should Germany ever seek to evade its membership in EDC, the Anglo–American commitment for support for EDC was reworded so that the United States and Britain would regard as a threat to their own security any action which threatened the unity or integrity of EDC (meaning a German withdrawal) and in such case would consult to meet that contingency. Acheson also agreed that the Senate would be asked to consider the extension of Article 4 (binding members to consult together should one or more believe its security to be threatened) of the North Atlantic Treaty to West Germany *after* the formation of the Defense Community and after the conclusion of the contractual agreements between West Germany and the United States, Great Britain, and France.[12]

Another complicated set of negotiations, having as their crux the degree to which sovereignty would revert to the German Federal Republic, was being carried on regarding the conditions under which the allies would exercise an ultimate disposition over German affairs pending the signing of a peace treaty. Despite a last-minute fit of French nervousness, both sets of issues were successfully resolved when Acheson, Eden, and Schuman met with Adenauer in Bonn on May 24. Despite yet another Soviet note designed to delay the negotiations, the contractual agreements ending the occupation and restoring sovereignty to the Federal Republic were signed on May 26 clearing the way for EDC.

From Bonn Acheson flew to Paris for the official signing of the European Defense Community treaty. There he experienced firsthand the angry temper of French opposition. There, in the course of a private session with French President Vincent Auriol, Auriol bitterly decried both EDC and the contractual agreements. Auriol's outburst was the expression at the highest level of the bitterness being more and more openly vented in the French press: France alone knows Germany; France alone has suffered; the Germans are always the same; the great danger in Europe is not the Soviet Union but Germany. To which Acheson could only reply: "But what is the alternative? Can Germany be kept in a state of permanent inferiority? Had not that been tried with miserable results after World War I? Better that the West take its chances with a healthy, revived West Germany than let such a formidable people drift in a slough of self-pity and despondency." *

Ironically, a similarly hostile welcome awaited Acheson's return to Washington. Instead of congratulating him upon his success, Senator Hickenlooper wanted to know what happened "between Friday, when the French seemed rather adamant that they would not at least for the present sign this document [the German contractuals] and on Monday [when] they were satisfied that their rights were being safeguarded." Were any special assurances given to the French? At another point, H. Alexander Smith asked: "then you are prepared to say that no additional economic aid or military aid or further help to Indochina—no promises of that kind or no assurances were given to France as an inducement to sign this treaty?" [13]

Although the signing of the contractual accords with West Germany

---

* Princeton Seminar Transcript, March 14, 1954, Reel 7, Track 1, p. 11. Acheson was to repeat the same argument with much greater success a month later to a meeting of the British–American Parliamentary Group. London, June 26, 1952.

and the European Defense Community treaty represented big steps forward, their ultimate ratification was still not assured. As we have seen, still another Soviet diplomatic offensive had been timed to coincide with the Western ministers' meetings at Bonn and Paris. On May 24—by which date Russian hopes of preventing the signing of contractual agreements and the European Defense treaty must have died—yet a third Soviet note was delivered to the three Western foreign ministers, this time accusing them of trying to avoid the conclusion of a German peace treaty and renewing Moscow's bid for direct negotiation. It must be noted that this flurry of notes was accompanied by the most intense anti–American campaign of the postwar period. In giving the President his impressions of the situation, George Kennan, who was the American ambassador to the USSR, emphasized the extent to which "The Soviet Government has lost contact with the West. It is almost as if no diplomatic relation existed at all." If, however, we could continue to resist Soviet pressures successfully, Kennan believed, "they may change their attitude and thus make possible a slow and gradual solution of some of the outstanding problems." * This is just what Acheson was trying to do.

The Soviet missive could be neither defeated nor blunted in reaching its target. The French political situation was beginning to burst asunder. Try as Acheson did to keep France from breaking ranks on the issue of negotiation, on June 11 the French Cabinet declared in favor of quadripartite negotiations on German rearmament. The French Cabinet's espousal of four-power talks was dictated as much by domestic political opposition to EDC as by any expectation that Soviet agreement would be forthcoming on Germany, but the third Soviet note provided a good pretext. Acheson knew that once engaged in negotiations, there would be virtually no possibility of French ratification of EDC or of the contractuals. Therefore, unless he succeeded in demonstrating as quickly as possible that the Soviet position was a delusion and convincing his Western conferees of its unacceptability, he risked losing everything that had been gained at Lisbon. How to rally his colleagues and provide them with an acceptable escape from their domestic critics and tormentors? The Big Three Foreign Ministers' Conference was set for June 27. As a preliminary the American and British delegations met in London to coordinate their views in anticipation of rallying Adenauer and Schuman.

When Acheson and Eden met on June 24, they quickly agreed that

---

* Letter from Ambassador Kennan to President Truman, August 11, 1952. Acheson Papers. This change of attitude on the part of the Soviets must be made manifest in their behavior and until it had been made manifest, Kennan advised that the United States should leave the USSR strictly alone. What we need, Kennan said, were not rare and intermittent conversations with Stalin but orders from Stalin to his officials which will improve relations on all levels of contact. *Ibid.*

neither the Bundestag nor the French National Assembly was likely to ratify either the EDC treaty or the German contractuals until the Soviet position had been explored. They also agreed that no meeting with the Soviet Union should take place until after September, in order to avoid embarrassing Adenauer in his struggle to sell the Western package to the German parliament. In the interim, Acheson saw no objection to agreeing to meet with the Soviets over the question of an electoral commission to oversee all-German elections, because he was convinced the Russians would soon be forced to reveal that they were not prepared to give up East Germany (which would be the outcome of free elections). But such a meeting must not enter into discussion of the status of the future all-German government. Acceptance of free elections must come before discussion of an all-German government. If the Soviet Union succeeded in creating the impression that unification might be realized through a direct East and West German negotiation, then any hope of committing West Germany to the EDC would be postponed indefinitely.[14]

Acheson acknowledged that he must get Schuman aside and persuade him that the West German demands regarding the Saar must not be allowed to become the occasion for a breach—at least not until after German ratification of the EDC-contractual package. This was vital. It was also recognized that certain members of the French Foreign Office who were coming over to London with Schuman were opposed to both EDC and German policy. If they learned that Acheson was deliberately limiting the terms for negotiation with Russia in order to short-circuit the Soviet initiative and facilitate the ratification of EDC and the contractuals, they would certainly make it known to hostile groups in the French Assembly. Therefore a confidential agreement with Schuman was absolutely indispensable. In return for Schuman's cooperation, the United States would do its best to support the French position on Tunisia and Morocco, provided France had one. Even an inadequate reform program for North Africa would be better than none; but the way France was going, the United States would be lucky to get even that. As an added incentive to French opinion, Peking would be warned that the American reaction to any intervention Red China might undertake against Vietnam would *not* be confined to Indochina. It was arranged for Eden to let it be known to Peking, through the British chargé d'affaires, that the United States would meet such intervention along the lines of a blockade of the China coast combined with air attacks designed to upset the economy of mainland China.

Schuman, René Massigli (French ambassador in London), de Latournelle, and Roger Seydoux joined the meetings with Acheson and Eden in London on June 27. A compromise was struck between Adenauer's desire that no Big Four Foreign Ministers' Conference to discuss Germany be held lest German opinion become distracted, and French Cabinet pressure for a meeting with Soviet representatives to discuss a rather broad agenda.[15] Once let the Germans be stampeded by the possibility of unity on condition that they forswear their links with the West and German public opinion would pay no attention to the risks entailed in Soviet insistence on going back to the Potsdam agreement. The only safeguard Acheson could see against distraction and let-down was to limit the agenda of any conference with the Soviets to discussion of an impartial commission to conduct an all-German election. Such a limited agenda would reveal soon enough whether the Soviets had undergone a genuine change of policy. Schuman, however, feared that any conference which did not include a discussion of a possible all-German government and a reversion to the Potsdam agreements would not provide a sufficiently convincing demonstration of Soviet intransigence to reconcile the French Assembly to ratification of EDC. Schuman held out strongly for broadening the agenda, even if discussion of the role of an all-German government were conditioned upon progress of the impartial commission and free elections.[16]

The two statesmen discussed the issue in private. The years of friendship and the sense of common purpose upon which Acheson had founded his European diplomacy once again enabled him to win Schuman to his side. It is true that a statesman's definition of the national interest and the attention which he must pay to public opinions are highly important matters if he is to stay in office. But these imperatives are always filtered through the fine mesh of personal preferences and of relationships which exist between one statesman and another. Acheson had helped see France over many a bad patch in its struggle to recover from the war and regain its international equilibrium. Because of their past, and because of what Acheson held out for the future, Schuman was persuaded to accept Acheson's wish that the West agree to negotiate *only* upon the issue of all-German free elections—and that was the gist of the Western reply sent on July 10. There was still no assurance that the French Assembly would ratify EDC or accept German rearmament; nevertheless the agreement to hold a Four Power Foreign Ministers' Conference on Germany in the autumn enabled Schuman to return to France in a somewhat stronger position vis-à-vis the critics of his European policy.

Much as Acheson had anticipated, the Soviets responded to the carefully couched Western note of July 10 in a negative manner. The proposals for an impartial commission of inquiry and for conditions for free elections were denounced by the Kremlin as an insult to the German people "for whom elections were being prepared as if they were a backward people." The unacceptable nature of the Soviet reply sealed the fate of a four-power conference. Acheson confided to J. W. Beyen, the Netherlands' foreign minister, that, "considering the damage the Soviets could have done, I thought we had come off extraordinarily well. They could have agreed to talks and then broken them off, leaving us in a very difficult spot." [17]

Insofar as diplomacy could operate, Acheson had used it to brilliant account. But his effort was not sufficient. No French government felt sure enough of itself to seek parliamentary ratification of the European Defense Community that year or the next. Acheson recognized that he was working against time and had predicted privately that if the Soviets succeeded in delaying EDC and German contractual agreements beyond 1952, "the Soviet Union could be fairly confident that the proposals themselves were dead." [18] French ratification of EDC was delayed beyond 1952 and was eventually defeated in 1954, by which time the temper and spirit of American diplomacy vis-à-vis Europe had undergone a fundamental change at the hands of John Foster Dulles.

EDC represented an attempt to achieve an American national end by imposing a form of supranationalism on others. The same motive of national egoism that led the United States to attempt it made France oppose it. For this very reason Acheson had initially opposed tying German rearmament to EDC and did so only reluctantly when it became apparent that the French government of the day would accept no other arrangement. But just as American nationalism inhibited President Truman from extending a formal guarantee to EDC, so in time French nationalism rebelled at the prospect of France's subordination to EDC. The lesson of EDC was that you cannot expect others to do what you won't do yourself. Had that lesson been learned, the United States might have viewed its own goals in Europe more objectively, and might thereby have avoided substituting the chimera of a unified Europe subordinate to American strategy for the reality of a Europe of nation-states, each with its own ego and its own national interests.

Perhaps the United States was unrealistic in its attempt to create a politically bona fide Atlantic community. By past standards it was a most ambitious undertaking. Not even the Communist world has been able to retain its unity. But the failure of American diplomacy to gain its ends in 1952 exemplifies the gap between the illusions of a people inspired by abstract notions and the limited means available to their government when it comes to putting those ideas into practice even on a limited scale.

What was the purpose of Acheson's even attempting to pursue such a complicated diplomacy? What was it all about? In what sense can one say that Acheson succeeded or failed in his diplomacy? To answer that, one must ask what international relations is all about. It is in the nature of international relations for each state to strive for an order favorable to its security and interests. The precise expression of that striving will vary with the values and perceptions of statesmen and with the conditions of the international system they inherit. The risk of facing a military show-down under adverse conditions is fundamentally unacceptable to peoples and governments alike. International relations is the struggle by which statesmen impose some measure of order and predictability on their relations and on the political system itself. There is never any final resolu-tion of this struggle. The effort itself is part of the process by which the system is constantly being brought into an approximate equilibrium and by which the fear of falling victim to the other side is constantly allayed. The art of diplomacy is the avoidance of war, and the avoidance of war is the end.

The world that American diplomacy inherited in 1945 was dominated by two conditions—the total breakdown of the prewar international sys-tem and complete uncertainty about Soviet motives and intentions. Under the circumstances, Acheson's effort to reconstitute a shattered system took on a compulsive character. Acheson's diplomacy involved the twofold process of exploiting the threat in order to overcome the threat and to reconstitute the chaotic and demoralized Western state system.

The conditions of international order are as much psychological and political as they are economic and strategic. Just by working to attain his goals, Acheson assured the reconstitution of the psychological and polit-ical conditions of order in Western Europe and, indirectly, in Africa and Asia where the European states were in the traumatic process of liquidat-ing their empires. By defining goals and helping to make available the means to their realization, Acheson's diplomacy inspired psychological and political changes in Europe absolutely essential to its recovery and to the defeat of the forces of disunity and despair which in the final anal-ysis Russia was counting upon more than anything else to realize its ends.

Economic recovery of Europe was indispensable; the burying of past divisive quarrels was essential; the achievement of EDC and German re-armament while it would have been nice was not absolutely vital. The Soviet Union was not Hitler's Germany; Acheson knew that. Except at the onsets of the Berlin blockade and the Korean War, no sense of terror akin to that inspired by Hitler existed to justify or support the unlimited build-up of NATO; but some forces and some organized strategy were essential to deter the Kremlin and give Europeans the confidence that they were not helpless and alone should an attack materialize, and to help France overcome its fear and opposition to a reconstituted Germany.

On September 8, 1952, in a fitting salute to their six-year-old disagree-ment, Kennan sent a twenty-six-page dispatch from his post as ambas-sador in Moscow summing up his view that NATO had given American policy too military a cast. "Because the principal Soviet tactic was political warfare rather than military the Soviets expected our rational response would be in the political rather than the military sphere. . . ." [19] Acheson would argue that NATO was in the political sphere. It gave Europe the necessary assurance to recover and it established the community of relations between Europe and North America that discomfited the men in the Kremlin.

It is in this sense—of the confidence and unity imparted by a common purpose and endeavor—that Acheson's diplomacy must be measured. By employing diplomacy to unite the North Atlantic community and lay the basis of political order in Europe, Japan, and the Middle East, Acheson averted the decline that would most certainly have pitted Russia and America in a real war across the charnel house of Europe. Behind Acheson's concern with a Communist victory was the more primordial fear that the loss of Europe would have constituted such an upset to the balance of power that Americans would have seen no alternative other than resorting to arms as they had in World Wars I and II. In a sense Acheson's diplomatic moves and strategies were political substitutes for a war that was successfully averted. As in any human endeavor he had his successes and failures, but on the whole the prospect of an even worse outcome was averted.

Meanwhile, in Europe and Japan the whole scene was changing. Standards of living were rising and life was returning to normal. A great calm settled over Europe during 1952 and 1953, and with the death of Stalin all hopes were possible. The Communist parties of Western Europe were assuming a more normal, less menacing, role in political life; the longing many Europeans felt for détente was closer to realization precisely because the dangers that had seemed so real and menacing only two years earlier had begun to lift. Time had begun to work its will upon the Soviet Union as well. The violence of Soviet propaganda against the United States remained as great as ever (and vice versa, unfortunately); when the American ambassador, George Kennan, compared the similarity of conditions in Moscow to those which he had experienced while interned in Berlin during the early months of the war, he fell victim to the "hate America" campaign and was declared persona non grata. Still, the actions of the Soviet government had shifted considerably away from external threat and pressure to preoccupation with problems within the Soviet bloc and within Russia itself. Preparations for the Nineteenth Party Congress were under way and the maneuvering for succession to the aging dictator was already turning the attention of the Communist Party leadership inward. Inherent in these preoccupations were new international conditions and new diplomatic opportunities for the Republicans who were preparing for their succession.

CHAPTER

20

ACHESON AND THE COLONIAL PROBLEMS

French Indochina

THE OUTBREAK OF the Korean War had lent powerful support to Acheson's belief that a Communist conquest of Indochina would pose unacceptable dangers to the security and stability of Southeast Asia.* Contrary to the prevailing view that Indochina was important to Acheson only in the context of France's contribution to NATO, it was Acheson's belief that the fate of Indochina was important in its own right. His view continued to be shaped by his belief that no Communist-led nationalist movement could be anything but a puppet of Moscow or Peking and by his conviction—later called the domino theory—that a Communist victory in Indochina would lead to the collapse of all of Southeast Asia. Despite his earlier skepticism of French claims that they were fighting for Vietnamese independence, he had decided even before the onset of the Korean War that there was no substitute for the French effort in that part of the world until such time as the Vietnamese were able to produce their own resistance to Communism. Acheson never was able to surmount the contradiction between the real nature of the French effort, which was to restore colonialism, and his belief that Communism could only be defeated by according genuine autonomy to a government representative of

---

* NSC 64 (February 27, 1950) set forth the policy: "It is important to United States security interests that all practicable measures be taken to prevent further communist expansion in Southeast Asia. Indochina is a key area . . . and is under immediate threat." *United States–Vietnam Relations, 1945–1967*. Department of Defense edition. Book I, A-36. Only Kennan within the department disagreed with the view that Indochina was part of a worldwide Communist strategy, and he argued that France's efforts were hopeless and Paris should be encouraged to settle for a negotiated end to the war. Gaddis Smith, *Dean Acheson* (New York: Cooper Square Publishers, 1972), p. 316. Letter and paper regarding Far East–Kennan to Acheson, August 21, 1951.

Vietnamese nationalism. Perhaps if he had had better information about the real nature of the struggle occurring in Indochina he might, as Gaddis Smith observes, "have seen that the local Communists were largely moved by local goals and that there was no genuine nationalist alternative to the Vietminh." [1] The conviction that Ho Chi Minh was little more than an extension of Moscow or Peking made Acheson largely impervious to other policy alternatives. Even his usually discriminating language seemed to give way on the subject of the Vietminh to a primitive level of stereotype and cliché uncharacteristic of him: "Sino–Soviet dominated satellite," "Commie menace," "a new form of colony immeasurably worse than the old from which Vietnam has so recently separated itself [sic]." [2]

The outcome was to commit America to support of a cause that was hopelessly compromised by its colonialist nature. Despite the fact that the United States now began to pay a quarter and more of the costs of the war, Acheson found himself at the mercy of French leverage. The psychological advantage of the French bargaining position seems in retrospect extraordinary. While the United States paid an increasing share of the costs of the war, the French successfully resisted all efforts to make them give the Vietnamese more genuine independence. Military aid brought Acheson no leverage whatsoever; just the reverse—it served to indicate to French authorities that Washington was hooked and that they could do what they wanted. No wonder Acheson later said that the French had blackmailed us in Vietnam.* By attributing so much importance to an essentially false situation, Acheson had put himself in a position of supporting one of the worst causes in postwar French politics.

As a result Acheson found himself grasping at straws. When Bao Dai, the playboy emperor, was due to return as titular head of the Associated States of Vietnam, Acheson cabled the legation in Saigon to inform Bao Dai that Washington counted on him to make good the nationalist cause. Even assuming the French had any intention of letting him do so, Bao Dai had absolutely none of the qualities that would have enabled him to lead.

Later, when neither Bao Dai nor any other Vietnamese leader appeared able to generate nationalist support, Acheson attributed it to the Vietnamese themselves: "They seem to have a typically Eastern, fatalistic lack of interest in public support. So far as we can see France has already given them more autonomy than they have seen fit to use." [3] Only frustration could have led Acheson to accept that line of reasoning.

Frustration also fed Acheson's illusion that if only American advisers could replace the French, Vietnamese forces would soon prove effective

---

* Asked in an interview for the *New York Times Book Review* whether this was a fair interpretation of his views, Acheson replied: "Entirely fair. The French blackmailed us."

against the Vietminh. As Smith remarks, Acheson "believed that the French were incapacitated by character and the stigma of past imperialism from effective leadership of Vietnamese troops. He also believed that Americans possessed a unique capacity for working with the Asian people." [4] Here, too, the French were totally successful in preventing the American military mission from having anything to do with the training of the Vietnamese.

The Chinese intervention in Korea in December 1950 added a new element of urgency to Acheson's concern for Vietnam. China replaced the Soviet Union as the principal source of the perceived Communist threat in Southeast Asia. Since China actually bordered on Vietnam as well as on other states in the region, Acheson's concern about a possible Chinese intervention became more active. He now accepted the view expressed in NSC 124/2 (June 1952) that "the danger of an overt military attack against Southeast Asia is inherent in the existence of a hostile and aggressive Communist China." [5] NSC 124/2 was more explicit than any previous document in linking the loss of a single state of Southeast Asia to the stability of Europe and the security of the United States. "In the absence of effective and timely counter-reaction, the loss of any single country would probably lead to the relatively swift submission to or an alignment with communism by the remaining countries of this group." [6] Such an alignment would lead to the loss of the rest of Southeast Asia, would "endanger the stability and security of Europe," and "would render the U.S. position in the Pacific Island chain [including Japan] precarious."[7] Here was the domino theory in its purest form, and although Acheson may not have accepted its most sweeping projections, it certainly reflects the peculiar logic that dominated his judgments about Indochina.

Chinese actions in Korea further reinforced the French hold on Acheson's Indochina policy. When General de Lattre de Tassigny accompanied Schuman to Washington in September 1951, he publicly enunciated the French position that Korea and Indochina were part of the same war. Acheson and Truman were once again persuaded that the war was winnable, even though French doubts were growing. By 1952 Acheson found himself in the position of having to bolster up Schuman and Monnet about French prospects in Indochina.*

In January 1952, when Acheson proposed to Churchill and Eden the possibility of carrying the air war to China and cutting off ocean trade should there be no armistice in Korea or should the Chinese renew their

---

* Memo, Acheson to Monnet, May 6, 1952. Monnet expressed the view "that the present burden there was too much for France to carry and some solution had to be sought." Minutes. Acheson, Eden, London, June 26, 1952. Discussion of Indochina. "Schuman relatively defeatist."

offensive, the French immediately proposed that Indochina be included within the purview of this policy. Acheson resisted linking the two situations, agreeing only that the nature and extent of retaliatory action would have to follow an identifiable Chinese aggression. Nevertheless, short of bringing the Sino–Soviet pact into operation, he acceded to the French sufficiently to agree to discuss what action might be taken should Chinese forces intervene directly in Indochina.*

As Gaddis Smith remarks, "Indochina was by now the tightest knot in the tangle of issues binding Korea, Communist China, the Soviet Union, and the defense of western Europe." [8] When he asked the National Security Council on March 5, 1952, what the United States should do if the French asked for a direct American involvement as an alternative to their own withdrawal, the Joint Chiefs would only reply that that depended on a political assessment of the importance of Vietnam. Forced to consider that issue, Acheson "presented a broad strategy for consideration by the American military establishment, the French, and the British. . . ." [9] It called for recognition of the fact that the war could not be won without establishment of large, well-trained native armies which the United States stood ready to pay for and help train; that only air and naval action against China should be contemplated, and that the Chinese should be warned that not the destruction of their regime but their intervention was the motive for our action; and finally that while Southeast Asia should not be lost without a fight, "no American ground troops would be used in Indochina. There must be no more Koreas. To use ground forces again in Asia would be simply to fall into a communist trap. On this point Acheson enjoyed the full and enthusiastic support of the Joint Chiefs." [10] Acheson's efforts to have this policy adopted by the British and French at the June 1952 foreign ministers' meeting got nowhere. The British were fearful of getting into a war with China that might draw in the Soviet Union; the French, happy with an additional American commitment, "remained opposed to the idea of American training missions in Indochina." [11]

As a result Acheson had the sense to rule out even for purposes of contingency planning the possibility that American ground forces might be employed should the French prove unable to sustain their effort. With the Korean experience before him, Acheson recognized how risky and dangerous any such undertaking could be, especially when Asia was a secondary front and not one on which the United States should be bogged

---

* On June 29, 1952, Schuman requested diplomatic ratification of a military understanding and creation of "a permanent military organization to concern itself with the whole of Southeast Asia." Memo, Acheson, Schuman, Eden, June 29, 1952. The next day Acheson rejected this request on the grounds that "it would be a mistake. . . ." Like so much else in the Indochina situation, the proposal was a forerunner of the American-sponsored South East Asia Treaty Organization.

down. Acheson's contingency planning, should Chinese intervention occur, was strictly limited to aerial strikes and a naval blockade—nothing more.* "It would be futile and a mistake," Acheson wrote, "to defend Indochina in Indochina . . . we could not have another Korea, we could not put ground forces into Indochina. We could take air and naval action, however. . . ." [12]

The Iranian Crisis: 1951–1954

At the beginning of the century, the Anglo–Iranian Oil Company had been granted a major oil concession in Iran (known then as Persia). Subsequently, the British government bought a major interest in the company; and although it continued to operate as a private firm, it was really under the indirect control of the directors appointed by the government in London. This fact is important because Churchill and Eden later tried to maintain the fiction that Anglo–Iranian Oil was a private company about whose pricing and royalty policies they could do nothing.

In 1950 the British still refused to pay the Iranians anything beyond a modest royalty (25 percent) at a time when the royalties paid by American companies to Arab regimes in the Persian Gulf had been steadily rising. In that same year, for example, the Arabian–American Oil Company (Aramco) signed an agreement with Saudi Arabia fixing royalties on a 50–50 basis. When news of this agreement reached Iranian Prime Minister Ali Razmara, he withdrew his support for the British supplement which now appeared additionally contemptible. (Two years before, the British offer of a supplement had been so niggardly that the Iranian parliament [the Majlis] had refused to ratify it, despite which the British continued pumping out the oil.)

A cabinet crisis opened on March 6, 1951, with the assassination of Razmara by a religious fanatic. In the melee the Majlis voted to nationalize the Anglo–Iranian Oil Company (AIOC) holdings at Abadan, and simultaneously Mohammed Mossadeq, who presided over the nationalization proceedings, emerged as a national hero and then as prime minister.

There then ensued a three-way struggle between Britain and Iran, and between Britain and Washington. The British immediately embargoed the export of Iranian oil in a determined effort to wreck Iran financially, something that Acheson dreaded would only lead to a Soviet take-over.

The Iranian crisis put the United States on the spot because both sides

---

* "US thinking is along lines of a blockade of the Chinese coast combined with air action designed to upset the economy of mainland China and designed to lessen will of Chinese Communists to continue aggression. . . . Action should be avoided in areas of acute sensitivity to the Soviet Union. . . ." Acheson, Schuman, Eden, June 26, 1952.

were bound to be suspicious of American activities. The British, however, were still more suspicious because, given America's reputation for anti-colonialism, they were generally convinced that Acheson was ready to sell them out. And to the extent that Acheson believed that the AIOC should accept the nationalization as a fait accompli and settle for the right to manage the oil field and market the oil on a 50–50 profit basis, British suspicions were justified—especially because Conservative and Socialist governments alike viewed Iranian oil as vitally important to their economy and considered it absolutely indispensable that Britain regain its rights in totality. Since the British also had it within their power to seize the Abadan oil fields by force and make a mess of things generally, Acheson had constantly to maneuver around British resistance without either losing the Iranians or driving the British to desperation as Dulles did at the time of the Suez crisis.

Acheson's views were first expressed in a telegram to London and Teheran on March 15, 1951. ". . . We recognize the right of sovereign states to nationalize provided there is just compensation . . . although our Ambassador believes that the problem must be considered a British one . . . we have advised [our] Embassy London of our hope that the UK will take no major step with regard to the problem without consulting with us. . . ." [13] Acheson viewed the problem exclusively with two criteria in mind. Iranian nationalism was untainted by Communism and should therefore be supported; secondly, unless the issue was settled peaceably, Iran would be thrown into turmoil opening the door to Soviet penetration.

On April 27 Acheson pointed out to Franks that if Britain took a hard line in bucking the nationalist movement, "one risks its immediately being captured by the USSR." He stressed the need for practical judgment. "The question of ownership," Acheson argued, was irrelevant "so long as the British manage it and get 50% profits." [14] Franks responded that Americans were "overly impressed by the apparent unity and power of the nationalist movement. The British saw discord and factionalism. They accused the United States of favoring appeasement in the Middle East— just as the United States accused the British of favoring the appeasement of Communist China. . . . Nitze suggested that the British placed too much importance on Iran's organizational weakness while ignoring the psychological force of nationalism. He also said there was a difference between appeasing a movement that was solidly communist and in trying to prevent a regime from becoming irrevocably hostile." [15] These were essentially the perspectives from which each side would spend the next three years calibrating policy—and never quite succeeding.

In Teheran, too, each side's perceptions of the situation varied and added to the complications. The American ambassador, Henry F. Grady, felt strongly that Acheson had not sufficiently supported him earlier in his efforts to secure an Export–Import Bank loan for Iran. Grady also believed that the State Department policy toward the crisis was far too pro–British.[16] The result was a running feud between Grady and the department in which Grady, who considered the British to be the principal offenders, grew impatient with Acheson's efforts to appear even-handed. Grady was soon replaced by Loy Henderson, but before that happened Grady made clear his opinion that everything must be done to strengthen Mossadeq's hand as the best assurance against chaos and Communism: ". . . It would be a mistake to assume that he [Mossadeq] has not Iranian people behind him almost 100%. He has become to the Iranian people a Gandhi. They feel he is fighting for Iranian independence from British domination and they will make any sacrifice to support him." [17] The British ambassador, Francis M. Shephard, characteristically viewed the Iranian government's action as a bit of Middle Eastern cheek, nothing more than the demogoguery of reactionary cliques masquerading as nationalists. Later on, stung by the damage being done by such contradictory reporting, Acheson insisted that British and American authorities reach some joint assessments rather than cabling in such wildly conflicting reports of the same situation.[18]

Since Acheson did not have the same rapport with the new British foreign minister, Herbert Morrison, as he had had with Bevin, he had to step lightly or risk stepping on a badly inflamed British ego. Clearly, a great deal depended on Franks. Franks had a more detached and realistic view of the situation than the interests impinging on the Cabinet in London; yet, because of his friendship with Acheson, he was able to present his government's views in the most convincing manner possible. Doubtless only the trust and friendship Acheson and Franks felt toward each other prevented a very bad situation from getting out of hand. Only an ambassador who sympathized with Acheson's problem could have accepted the criticisms Acheson had of His Majesty's government in the handling of the situation, especially after the Churchill government came into office, and only Acheson's respect for Franks permitted them to continue a constructive relationship amidst so much pig-headedness, bungling, and disagreement.

Acheson's first move (July 4, 1951) was to deploy Averell Harriman to Teheran as a special Presidential mediator.* Morrison acceded to this while arguing that American indulgence was an important factor in encouraging Mossadeq's intransigence. "I feel most strongly that what is wanted from you now is not an offer to mediate but a firm and categorical statement that it is up to Persia to accept and follow the recom-

---

* Memos, July 7, 11, 12, 1951. The British wanted the Harriman mission hedged against any appearance of condoning Iranian actions.

mendation of the ICJ [International Court of Justice]." * Harriman's mission met with little success other than to persuade the British to accept nationalization in principle, which was of no use without a willingness to negotiate the details of a new contractual relationship.** Instead, the British withdrew their technicians, thus closing down the Abadan refinery in the stubborn belief that the Iranians would have to give in sooner or later.

Attlee now wanted all-out American backing, which Acheson parried by arguing that the two countries' "mutual goal in Iran [would be] best obtained if U.S. influence is maintained by an open-minded approach . . . which cannot be maintained if U.S. endorses every step or recommendation of [the] United Kingdom." †

Dissuaded by the United States from using force against Iran, the British, over Acheson's objections, now decided to take their case to the UN Security Council. True to his modus operandi, Acheson first privately pressured the British into sponsoring a more acceptable resolution and then publicly gave it American backing, despite his reservations about the utility of the whole procedure. The British lost their case when the Security Council, too, decided it lacked jurisdiction, but Acheson had the fun of meeting Mossadeq, who had come to New York for the debates and, later, to Washington, where he entered the Walter Reed Hospital for some medical attention. Acheson found him quite the most delightful and amusing fellow he had met in a long time. Mossadeq's skinny, birdlike appearance was attended by a lachrymose nature. Acheson had never had to deal with a statesman who could dissolve into tears like some marvelous character from *Alice in Wonderland.* Years later he would recount with a pleasurable chuckle the comic relief of those meetings. Far from being put off, Acheson developed a personal partiality for Mossadeq that may have reinforced his more studied view that sooner or later Britain had to come to terms wtih him. In any case Acheson's view was a far cry from the later employment, under Dulles, of the CIA to "destabilize" Mossadeq's government.

With the coming of Churchill and Eden to office, Acheson sought to

---

* Morrison to Acheson, July 7, 1951. The ICJ disclaimed jurisdiction over the dispute, which disclaimer Americans saw more as a vindication of the Iranian than of the British position.

** Harriman's findings were not sympathetic to the British position, quite the contrary, but true to their understanding Acheson kept them under wraps.

† The U.S. Embassy in London had now joined in the call for a common front against Teheran. Gifford to Acheson: "we must either condemn Mossadeq for his continued irresponsibility or we will condone Mossadeq's actions by resolution which attaches no blame and treats both parties equally." October 1, 1951. By contrast, Ambassador Henderson in Teheran warned Acheson that if the U.S. continued to support the United Kingdom, "Iran will eventually be lost to the free world." October 1, 1951.

gain their approval for a modest amount of aid to Iran and for a renewal of Anglo–Iranian negotiations. But he got nowhere. Eden expressed the opinion that the "United Kingdom is unable to accept the American view that the only alternative to Mossadeq is communism . . . and that if Mossadeq should fall there is a real possibility that a more amenable government might folow." [19] Acheson wired back to Washington the view that the "same incompetents who allowed AIOC to lead the United Kingdom into disaster are still the source of United Kingdom policy," and that the British would prefer that Iran fall to Communism than that they set a precedent for other losses in the Middle East.[20]

Acheson was well primed for his January meeting with Churchill and Eden in Washington. Churchill immediately suggested a deal. Britain would help the United States with its great burden in the Pacific, and in turn Britain should be aided by the United States with respect to Britain's great burden in the Middle East. Acheson replied that the realities in the two theaters were somewhat different: in Asia Communism was on the march; in the Middle East the forces were nationalist, and the West still had some chance if it came to terms with it. He amused Churchill by suggesting that perfect mutual support and understanding on present policies would be akin to two people locked in a loving embrace in a rowboat about to go over Niagara Falls.

Churchill and Eden argued that the ouster of the Anglo–Iranian Oil Company had been due to the refusal of the United States to support strong measures. Acheson argued that it was due to the retrograde policies of the company and its failure to make concessions when Razmara was prime minister. Eden took refuge in the argument that since the company was privately owned it was not the responsibility of the Foreign Office to get involved with the practical details of prices, royalties, production, etc., and accused Mossadeq of being little more than a rug merchant who ought to be brushed aside as he deserved. With that Acheson exploded. It was the British who were behaving like a bunch of rug merchants, haggling over financial terms when they ought to be focusing on the bigger issue of how to resolve the crisis without impairing Britain's access to the oil. Eden's feelings were so bady hurt that Acheson had to tread easy for a few days.

In the end the British agreed to explore the possibility of using an International Bank loan to Iran as a means of reopening negotiations with Teheran.[21] Despite the sharpness of their disagreement, both sides at least knew where the other stood; and the British had not been humiliated in public by an outright American break with their position.

Failing to make any headway with Eden, Acheson decided America should adopt a lower profile in the controversy in the hope that it would force both sides to take new initiatives. This seemed to have some effect because at their meeting in London on June 24 Eden acknowledged that the United Kingdom was "now inclined to favor a long-term settlement of the oil question. This [might] best [be] achieved through a Management Agency under contract to the National Iranian Oil Company. . . ." [22] The situation remained deadlocked until July 16 when Mossadeq resigned and America's old friend Qavam took over. Washington now rushed to proffer Iran the economic aid that it had so long dangled before Mossadeq in the hope that he would modify his position. Mossadeq's resignation appears as a classic example of the principle *reculer pour mieux sauter*, because five days later the wily old fox was back in office again, stronger than ever.[23]

Despite the annoyance of the situation, the essential wisdom of American policy was being borne out. Contrary to British opinion, the oil embargo had not forced Teheran to capitulate, and contrary to American fears, Iran had not fallen under Soviet domination. The possibility that countries—even weak and impotent ones—have independent minds and wills of their own is a lesson from which American statecraft might have profited.

Acheson next proposed that Truman and Churchill should make an immediate approach to Mossadeq for a compromise settlement. The Acheson–Franks plan provided for an immediate grant of $10 million to Iran, the British to purchase the oil in storage, and the question of compensation for the nationalized British property to be submitted to arbitration.*

Once again Acheson condemned Eden's desire to have the validity of the nationalization itself submitted to arbitration. Acheson was very sharp in his remonstrations with Franks, who agreed that Acheson's points were well taken. The joint offer was made on August 30.** Since Mossadeq did not feel Iran owed Britain anything, he rejected the offer. Loath to let it go at that, Acheson and his advisers came up with a new plan that would reduce Britain's visibility in the future management of Iranian oil.† By now Robert Lovett and the Joint Chiefs were getting into the act. As a penultimate solution, Acheson proposed that a consortium of American

---

* Memo, Acheson, Franks, July 31, 1952. Negotiations for a more permanent arrangement for distributing Iranian oil should be undertaken. Memo, Acheson, Truman, July 31. Both agreed that the situation was critical. Emergency assistance was necessary.

** Minutes. Acheson, Franks, August 11, 1952. Acheson also made it clear that he had no intention of letting the AIOC board of directors pass on the plan.

† Henry Byroade, in charge of the Middle East section, had recommended on September 16 that the United States break with the United Kingdom and announce that it "can no longer attempt to discourage U.S. or other private concerns" from buying Iranian oil or helping to operate Iranian production. Memo from Byroade, September 16, 1952.

oil companies be formed with British participation to purchase Iran's oil. Unfortunately, this could only be done by getting the Department of Justice to modify its opposition to the formation of such a cartel arrangement. Although time had run out on Acheson before the plan could be broached with the British and Iranians, it was eventually adopted in 1954, but only after Mossadeq had been overthrown in a military coup abetted by the CIA.

Acheson employed the same modus operandi with the British in their dispute with Egypt over the future of the Sudan. In September 1951, Cairo rejected the proposal for a Middle East Defense Command as little more than a British pretext to prolong its military presence in Egypt and to deny Egypt full sovereignty over its national territory. In October Egypt unilaterally abrogated the 1936 treaty governing Britain's presence in Egypt and the 1899 condominion agreement governing the Sudan. The British retaliated with an oil embargo. Acheson tried to get Eden to lift the oil embargo and to dissuade the British from using force on the grounds that it would only add to the crisis without solving the problem. In late January 1952 Egyptian hatred of the British erupted in fighting between Egyptian forces and British troops in the Canal Zone and in anti–British rioting in Cairo. Again Acheson refused to be stampeded or pressured into supporting British military action. Since Egypt was not directly vulnerable to Soviet influence, Acheson had no compunction about letting the British stew in their own juice until such time as they chose to make the necessary concessions to Egyptian nationalism.

In July 1952 the corrupt regime of King Farouk was overthrown by a military coup. A set of officers under the nominal leadership of General Naguib (but actually led by Colonel Gamal Nasser) took over. Naguib immediately sought economic and military aid from Washington which Acheson was prepared to give provided a satisfactory solution could be found to the Suez and Sudanese problems. Meanwhile, Acheson continued to pressure the British behind the scenes. The Sudan question was eased when Naguib announced Cairo's support for Sudanese self-determination, but the Suez crisis lingered on.

In line with Acheson's effort to stabilize the Middle Eastern situation, he secured the acquiescence of the British and French in a tripartite agreement (May 1951) not to escalate the arms race in the Middle East by supplying either side with arms beyond agreed-upon limits. Thus the Arab–Israeli dispute was dampened down while the UN looked for solutions.

French North Africa

Acheson adopted much the same strategy in dealing with the French on North African matters as with the British on the Middle East: intense diplomatic pressure behind the scenes, moderation in public so as not to rupture Franco–American relations. Obviously not a very satisfactory modus operandi in view of Acheson's strong belief that nationalism offered the only possible alternative to Communism, and national independence the only alternative to chaos and war.

By 1951 the French protectorates of Tunisia and Morocco were demanding autonomy within the French Union. The Bey of Tunis and the sultan of Morocco were conservative figures striving to meet nationalist pressures from forces opposed to French rule. French settlers and businessmen were implanted in both countries, and the French government feared that autonomy would only lead to demands for independence and to the eventual liquidation of the French stake in the countries. As in Indochina, the French policy aimed at giving the appearance of reforms while keeping the lid on. Acheson argued that the French should carry out the minimal reforms necessary to neutralize the nationalist forces and enable France to preserve its essential role. "In order to settle the [nationalist] agitation and to bring about order and stability [Acheson] recommended a positive approach of taking the offensive by putting forward a program which was progressive and good, and which could be supported by public opinion." [24] The French were too aware or to afraid that once reform was initiated there was no telling where the situation would end. To let go on a steep incline usually resulted in disaster. Deliberations dragged on month after month, the French having no intention of making concessions and Acheson seeing no alternative but to keep applying pressure.

The French argued that they were moving as fast as French public opinion would permit, that the struggle against extremist elements in North Africa was against Communism everywhere, and that if the United States failed to support France, they saw no alternative to French withdrawal from the United Nations and abandonment of the Indochina operation in order to concentrate on North Africa. Either the United States cooperated with France actively in North Africa or the French government foresaw a serious effect on NATO and possibly even the defeat of EDC.[25] Acheson tried his best to resist this blackmail, and generally refused to back any French proposal or resolution that had not been cleared by the State Department and which in his view did not go far enough in the direction of meeting Tunisian and Moroccan demands.* He tied American support for the French position to concrete reforms.

---

* Memo, bipartite Foreign Ministers' Meeting with the French. Acheson, Jessup, Dunn, et al., May 28, 1952. As expected the British supported the French on the grounds that "Britain's own colonial position inextricably [was] involved with the precedent of Tunisia." Telegram, London, August 6, 1952.

On March 19, 1952, Acheson warned Bonnet that unless France provided evidence of Tunisian reforms the United States would probably vote to place Tunisia on the agenda of the United Nations; neither the United States nor France could any longer afford to ignore the force of nationalist opinion either in North Africa or in the rest of the world.*

The situation was complicated by the fact that North African affairs were handled by another ministry and not by the Ministry of Foreign Affairs under Schuman. The arrogance of the French associated with North African affairs did not make dealing with them very pleasant.** As in the case of Indochina, they felt they had the upper hand vis-à-vis the United States and did not hesitate to formulate their positions with utmost crudity: a form of revenge on the United States for its heavy-handedness on the issue of German rearmament. It must be recognized that French governments were at the mercy of the National Assembly on North Africa, and neither public opinion nor the political leaders were willing to acknowledge any right of foreign intervention.† French opinion was outraged when the United States joined with the Soviet Union and Arab–Asian bloc to vote against the French and place the items on the agenda.[26] Acheson did his best to ease the crisis by reminding Schuman that the United States intended to use its influence to secure a moderate and constructive discussion of Tunisia by speakers of the Arab–Asian group.[27] In keeping with his policy, Acheson refused to join in any public indictment of France. He also succeeded in enlisting Madame Pandit, among other Asian leaders, in adopting a policy of moderation on the issue.[28] In the end, Schuman, who had flown to New York to handle the crisis, agreed to make a full statement on Tunisia and Morocco to the General Assembly, and he and Acheson agreed to work for a resolution with which the French could live.[29] Because he had warned the French that America intended to vote against France unless reforms were forthcoming, Acheson escaped charges of bad faith. And as with so many other issues, by exercising a combination of pressure and restraint, Acheson may

---

* Telegrams to Paris, April 29, 1952, September 26, 1952, informing French of U.S. refusal to go along with French.

** "General Juin retorted that the Arabs represented nothing, that militarily they are zero, and that they are a false value owing their existence to the support of the U.S." Memo, Assistant Secretary George McGhee, General Juin, Counselor of the Embassy Daridan, etc. (no date).

† Telegram from Paris, October 7, 1952, rejecting UN competence on the handling of the Tunisian and the Moroccan items before the UN. Memo, Acheson, Luns, October 31, 1952. Luns, Netherlands foreign minister, noted that North Africa was so important to French public opinion that no French government could make concessions.

have actually succeeded in advancing many matters in the only practical way possible.*

Latin America

Acheson's attention to Africa, Latin America, and other assorted parts of the globe was perfunctory. In the absence of trouble he had little time to spare and even less inclination to become involved. They were not the principal arenas of postwar diplomacy and so long as their security was not threatened Acheson was content to let matters take their course. His interest in Latin America, as Gaddis Smith remarks, took the form of the sympathetic and paternalistic hope that they would continue developing "toward political maturity." His policy positions toward Latin America were essentially political and pragmatic in nature. Latin America received precious little economic assistance under Acheson, but Acheson also fought clear of appeals to Washington for arms on the grounds of alleged subversionary threats to Latin American security. Acheson did not engage in the insidious pretention that "arms advanced the cause of democracy or improved the standard of living of the poor." [30] On the contrary, he frankly acknowledged that the relationship was just the opposite: arms strengthened the "power of existing regimes, most of which were military dictatorships." [31] Some military aid went south of the border to placate the Pentagon, but its dollar value was insignificant and its impact on the region nil.

Generally Acheson refused to become exercised about acts of Latin American economic nationalism.[32] When Allen Dulles came by the department seeking the government's support in reopening Standard Oil's claims against Mexico's expropriations of the 1930s, Acheson warned Truman against giving Dulles any aid or comfort. When Bolivia nationalized its tin mines Acheson refused to intervene. "He told the Reconstruction Finance Corporation in July 1951 that the political repercussions of a

---

* In one of his lengthy reports to Truman which he wrote whenever he was away from Washington, Acheson summarized the situation: "For a while, the French had their backs up over an affirmative vote by us that the Political Committee take up the Tunis and Morocco items immediately following the debate on Korea. This vote was cast in a situation in which, according to our estimate, the outcome would have been the same however we voted. By so voting, we were able to pick up a little leverage with the Asian–African group which may enable us to moderate the debate when the items are discussed. We have talked to the French both here and in Paris, and I think their initial sharp reaction is subsiding. They are faced with such an unstable and inflamed political situation at home that they are having a very difficult time here, and are difficult for us to deal with as a consequence. . . ." Acheson to Truman, October 25, 1952.

suspension of tin purchases from Bolivia would be explosive." [33] He warned Latin Americans about nationalizing American companies because it might scare away foreign investors, but he "also agreed with Edward G. Miller, Jr., the Assistant Secretary for Inter-American Affairs, that sanctions such as withholding Export–Import Bank loans would play into the hands of extremists." [34] After the outbreak of the Korean War, when Latin American states took advantage of the demand for their raw materials to raise prices, Acheson accepted it with equanimity. "In March 1952 he agreed with the Secretary of Defense that a trade agreement favorable to Venezuelan oil was essential for national security—even if domestic American interests should suffer. In May 1952 he succeeded in preventing Congress from enacting a three-cents-a-pound tariff on tuna, a measure that would have been disastrous for Peru." * As Gaddis Smith observes, "Acheson contributed nothing memorable to the history of U.S.–Latin American relations," but it cannot be said that his policies of minimal involvement left relations any worse "than did the more activist policies of subsequent American administrations." [35]

---

* Gaddis Smith, *Dean Acheson* (Cooper Square Publishers, 1972), p. 360. Acheson to Truman, May 15, 1952. The Peruvian ambassador called. Acheson said he understood the Peruvian point of view and was sympathetic to it, and that they were doing their best to forestall its enactment.

CHAPTER

21

APPRAISAL

DEAN ACHESON's statecraft was rooted in a combination of intellectual pragmatism, guarded optimism about man's ability to overcome the worst threats to his fate, and an unshakable sense of right and wrong. He acquired his intellectual pragmatism from his training in law, and especially from his apprenticeship to Brandeis. Following his experience with Brandeis, no one was more determined to root policy in bedrock knowledge than Acheson. His intellectual assurance—what some saw as arrogance—sprang from his insistence upon the hard logic of facts which, when accumulated, had an effect similar to one of Holmes's "can't helps." "When I say that a thing is true I mean I cannot help believing it. I am stating an experience as to which there is no choice."

Intellectual pragmatism had the effect of reinforcing Acheson's implacable concern with realities and consequences. Acheson did not believe that American policy could be conducted on the assumption that there existed or that we could provide some moral principle that, if followed, would square us with world opinion and which would in itself determine events. He abhorred the danger of the United States becoming victim of a public diplomacy more concerned with images comprised of words and postures without regard to constructive achievement. He was relentless in his determination to root American policy in the possibilities that were inherent in human nature and in the nation-state system. He believed that more of a positive nature could be accomplished and the worst avoided if the statesman worked with the realities as he found them and did not become a prisoner of a priori moralistic, deterministic, idealistic, or Manichean images and states of mind.

Acheson's determination that man could overcome the limitations of his fate was more a fighting faith than any easy belief in man's perfectability. The problems the world faces, Acheson believed, "come pretty directly from the medium with which one works, the human animal himself." But he did not believe that man was a hapless prisoner of his instincts, fated to fight a mismatch with a destiny over which he had no control. There was no inconsistency for Acheson in recognizing that men suffered severe limitations in their ability to act wisely but at the same time in insisting that statesmen had it within their power to give shape and direction to their actions—always provided that they were not paralyzed by self-doubts or by commitment to stultifying doctrines of inaction or despair.* Acheson's faith in action sometimes led him perilously close to action for action's sake and to a denial of the legitimacy of self-doubts, but his faith in the efficacy of action was always under the considerable restraint of his pragmatism. Action must be rooted in knowledge, which included knowledge of man's nature and motives, both as a private and as a political being.

In keeping with his belief in man's ability to rescue himself from the worst outcomes that situations might hold, Acheson reserved his greatest admiration for those capable of accomplishing something worthwhile and lasting against the inertia and ingrained forces of society. His writings abound in encomiums for those whose imagination and industry he so much admired—Holmes, Brandeis, Stimson, Marshall. These were men—pre-eminently lawyers—whose actions were the product of rigorous intellectual training and application. His respect went to those who were effective; it did no good to have ideals or the right sentiments if they could not be realized in practice. And the practical realization lay in how successfully one grappled day in and day out with the stubborn realities. Being able to find a solution to a difficult problem was more creative than expounding upon it.

Hence the waning of his zeal for Wilson, the regaining of his admiration for Roosevelt, his reverencing of Holmes, Brandeis, and Marshall, his zeal for Truman, his reservations about Kennan and Stevenson, his lack of respect for Eisenhower. Anyone who has set himself to excel at a particularly difficult task is likely to judge and judge harshly those whom he thinks lack the necessary mettle to excel in a similar way. But Acheson saw no alternative if mankind was to make it.

Strange as it may seem, the popular image of Acheson as a social aristocrat and fashion plate belied a life of considerable austerity.

Sir Oliver Franks observes that "Acheson never allowed himself to forget the New England roots from which he sprung. His home life in Georgetown was far from ostentatious, and his life on the Sandy Springs farm downright austere. He took pride in doing hard, pioneering things.

---

* For a good example of the anathema with which Acheson held deterministic theories of society and history see "History as Literature" in Acheson, *Fragments of My Fleece* (New York: Norton, 1971).

He lacked the indispensable political gift of believing that every argument has an equally legitimate political pedigree." [1] The inspiration for Acheson's foreign policy was rooted in the belief that unless America took the lead in restoring the postwar world to some manageable order, freedom of conscience, and individual rights and freedom generally, would go down before the forces of despair and chaos unleashed by two wars and a worldwide depression. If one asks what vision of America inspired Acheson's diplomacy it was that of a society in which human progress is determined by and depends upon the ability of each man to develop in his capacity as a human being and not upon the will of some all-powerful religion or dictatorship. He did not believe that America had the mandate or power to change what existed in other countries, but he did believe that wherever still possible people should be given the same choice as Americans enjoyed. Meanwhile, as a practical matter of its own security and of the preservation of conditions essential to its political and economic system, the United States had a stake in containing the Soviet Union while fostering political change conducive to the emergence of self-reliant nations. Acheson was not unaware of the danger that inhered in an activist foreign policy. Intolerance and illiberalism were the unavoidable by-product at home of the situation in which America found itself, but he was confident that somehow it would be worked through. He believed that by keeping a clear and limited view of his objectives he did not run the risk of engaging in a crude form of realpolitik. Whether he succeeded or not is for the reader to decide.

Above all, Acheson had a sense of right and wrong by which he held himself accountable in his public as well as his private life. As the son of a prelate, the fact that he was not a believing Christian made it all the more necessary that he conduct his life by ethical standards. Just because choice in politics does not lend itself to an easy distinction between right and wrong, Acheson did not conclude that the distinction should be dismissed. Rules for behavior in the international sphere are properly different from those followed by the actor who acts for himself in situations where he can directly observe the consequences for people he knows personally. In international relations the statesman acts in a fiduciary role and must make judgments for a collectivity of people without being able to predict the outcome. This reversal makes the terms of the moral equation different, more difficult, but no less moral. Questions of conscience were real and immediate for Acheson as he demonstrated in the Hiss case; but he held himself accountable in the conduct of diplomacy as well. The ends of American policy did not justify employing any and all means. Much of the unpopularity of Acheson's policies with the American people could have been overcome had he been willing to ignore questions of right and wrong. But it was precisely because he did not and would not evade the ethical decisions that he was able to remain undiscouraged by the savagery of the attacks upon him for refusing to conduct American policy as a moral crusade.

Failures

The Far East. The collapse of his Far Eastern policy represents the most serious failure that can be charged against Acheson. Prior to the Korean attack, the Administration was feeling its way cautiously and with considerable restraint toward a policy for Asia that would balance America's strategic role against the new forces of nationalism and Communism that were active in the area. Acheson's Asian policy (which was also Truman's) consisted of accepting the Communist victory in China and disengaging completely from the Chinese Nationalists on Formosa while strengthening those Asian countries which were still outside the Communist orbit. Acheson recognized that in contrast to Europe, there was no hope of establishing a situation of strength in the form of an alliance or balance of power; but by strengthening the nationalist forces in Japan, the Philippines, and Indochina, Acheson hoped that the West might have some chance of neutralizing the ideological, but as yet not overwhelming military, strength of the Communists in the region—in other words, to help fill the potential vacuum left by the defeat of Japan and the liquidation of the colonial empires.

The argument that Acheson's failure to include South Korea within the American defense perimeter led to the attack does not take adequate account of the political context in which Acheson was operating, or of the delicate terms of the political balance that he was striving for. Part of the problem lay in the fact that prior to the Korean attack the Administration's containment policy had not been globalized. The military forces available to defend the Far East were limited and the commitments similarly limited. Nor did Acheson believe that the situation in the Far East lent itself to military containment in quite the same way as in Europe, where America's allies were potentially much stronger and more motivated to resist Communist aggression. Furthermore, the possibility of outright military aggression was simply not anticipated. As Alexander George observes: "Psychologically, as well as politically, it was difficult for the Truman Administration to be receptive to indicators that North Koreans might attempt to overrun South Korea," because a new commitment on behalf of South Korea was "politically inconceivable unless it extended also to the defense of Formosa." [2] Further, it was politically difficult to anticipate the idea of an attack endorsed by the Kremlin and at the same time to pursue a policy of détente vis-à-vis mainland China.

To have provided South Korea with a guarantee and not Formosa would have brought on a conflict with those who opposed his disengaging from Chiang Kai-shek and would also have been at odds with his hope of seeing the status quo in the Far East stabilized at a relatively low level of tension with the People's Republic of China. In light of the political complexities and the delicacy of the status quo that he was striving to establish, it is unpersuasive to argue that by not including Korea within the U.S. defensive perimeter Acheson invited the attack. It was the general state of Korean unpreparedness and the mildness with which Washington had reacted to the fall of mainland China—not the failure to provide a strong-enough guarantee—that tempted the Soviet-backed North Korean attack. There are no perfect solutions, nor can all contingencies be provided for, especially not when they run counter to other policy considerations.

The real damage that Acheson did to his Far Eastern policy, which led to its collapse, came in his failure to anticipate Peking's reaction to the American effort to eliminate the Communist state of North Korea. The Acheson failure to anticipate Chinese reactions began with the placing of the Seventh Fleet in the Formosan Straits and the announcement that the status of Formosa would have to await international action by the United Nations (or some other body) to which the People's Republic did not even belong. The fact that the United States had intervened in the Formosa Straits made it unlikely that Peking could be persuaded of Acheson's peaceful intentions when United Nations forces began invading North Korea. The tragedy continued with Acheson's failure to have Truman stanch the unending stream of aggressive statements by MacArthur and other Administration figures. Their barrage of hostility had the effect of undercutting Acheson's attempts to send reassuring signals to Peking which in any case could not redeem a bad policy.

Acheson might still have rescued the essentials of his policy despite the onset of the war had he not then chosen to unify all of Korea under Syngman Rhee. The explanation for this misjudgment resides in part in the activist's and pragmatist's temptation to take advantage of an opportunity to exploit the possibilities of a situation and in Acheson's continuing tendency to downgrade the motivation and capability of China to intervene in Korea. The restraint that marked Acheson's concern to avoid war with Russia was strangely absent from his concern about China.

The decision to invade North Korea, taken in an uncharacteristically haphazard fashion during the dauntingly busy September of 1950, effectively ended Acheson's policy of avoiding war with the People's Republic and of keeping the Far East a secondary theater of American foreign policy. It was doubly tragic because, as Richard Neustadt has noted, Truman and Acheson did not regard Korean unification as a vital or very important objective of U.S. policy. They entered into the decision without fully or clearly confronting the costs and risks should China intervene.

As in the case of the Vietnam War, the decision to cross the 38th parallel meant that control over policy passed to MacArthur and to the contingencies of the military struggle. As Alexander George remarks: "Instead of a well-defined, carefully considered policy determining the answers to questions of military strategy and tactics, grand strategy itself was being shaped by incremental decisions geared to the evolving battlefield situation." *

By his failure to end the war on the basis of the status quo *ante bellum*, Acheson not only promoted a war which he did not want, but he aroused in the American people an anti–Chinese feeling that, although not of his making, was to be an impediment for twenty years to the normalization of relations between the two great states.

The effect of the Chinese intervention was to throw Acheson's Far Eastern policy into a shambles and to weaken for a time the European alliance. It also contributed to the resurgence of isolationism with all that it implied for the role that Acheson had cast for American foreign policy.

Fortunately, neither Acheson nor Truman let the war in Korea become their personal crusade the way Lyndon Johnson did in Vietnam. Having gambled and lost, Acheson immediately recommended cutting American losses. To do otherwise, Acheson recognized, would be to risk all-out war with China—a war that Peking was more motivated to fight than America—in a theater that still remained of secondary strategic importance. With the so-called "lesson" of the loss of China fresh in his mind, Acheson still had the sense to recommend that the United States now limit its objectives in Korea and settle for a cease-fire, even if that meant incurring the odium of relieving MacArthur of his command and, with it, a further erosion of public support at home. By putting his influence resolutely against extension of the war, Acheson succeeded in avoiding a break with America's principal allies and in maintaining the United Nations as an effective support and legitimator of U.S. policy—not an unimportant political asset in the overall Cold War struggle.

Contrary to revisionist historians, Acheson's Indochina policy did not make future American military involvement inevitable. The subsequent easing of Sino–American hostilities and the signing of the Geneva accords settling the Indochina War gave Acheson's successors ample opportunity to find a more enduring basis for adjusting relations in Asia. The fact that

---

* Alexander George, *Deterrence in American Foreign Policy* (New York: Columbia University Press, 1974), p. 203. Admittedly, intelligence gave an inadequate representation and prediction of the range of Chinese motivations, but that does not alter the initial misjudgment in deciding to cross the 38th parallel and challenge the People's Republic in much the same way as the invasion of South Korea had appeared to challenge the American strategic situation in the region.

they did not cannot be blamed on Acheson. He had had the courage to refuse to get involved in a bigger war at a time when an apparent majority of the American people were in favor of one. That his successors lacked the courage to educate the public about the limits of American stakes and power in Asia when conditions were more favorable to such an effort, or to strive to end the tensions with mainland China instead of exacerbating them, says something about the difference in their political courage and strategic sense.

German Rearmament. From a narrowly diplomatic point of view, Acheson's inability to secure the rearmament of Germany must also be considered a failure. German rearmament got off to a bad start because, uncharacteristically, Acheson felt obliged to acquiesce in the Joint Chiefs of Staff demand that German rearmament be made an absolute and immediate condition for the dispatch of U.S. forces to bolster Europe's defenses and for the appointment of General Eisenhower as Supreme Commander of NATO forces. Acheson generally did not permit military or lesser bureaucratic forces to impose policy. By maintaining his role as sole foreign-policy architect and principal advisor to Truman, Acheson generally assured that whatever policy was adopted was relevant to the facts of the international situation itself, not just a compromise arrived at to solve a domestic political–bureaucratic conflict. In the case of German rearmament, however, Acheson's eagerness to make Germany a part of a unified military force overrode his political judgment, and he was never able to overcome French resistance to the rearmament.

Still, his effort was not without its long-term benefits. French opposition to German recovery was limited to the terms on which it should be permitted to rearm. In all other respects, the German Federal Republic was permitted to get off to a healthy start (unlike Weimar). The occupation ended; it was readmitted on equal terms to the Atlantic community of nations. In addition, by posing the issue of German rearmament, Acheson may have forced the French to translate their ideas for European federation into concrete proposals (if only to safeguard Europe against a resurgence of German nationalism).

Failure to Maintain a Strategic Perspective. Despite the sweeping language of the Truman Doctrine, the actual policies which Acheson adopted between 1947 and 1950 hardly justify description as an all-out effort to contain Communism everywhere. They were concentrated on Europe and were as much political and psychological as military. The geographical scope of the Cold War was expanding because of the Communist victories in China, but active containment in Asia was not envisaged in the form that it took in Europe because Acheson still hoped that Chinese and American stakes could be balanced without a large-scale military build-up. Nevertheless, the sweeping language of the Truman Doctrine and the unqualified proclamations of determination to resist Soviet expansion everywhere (which were largely designed to mobilize public support) had the effect of blurring Acheson's strategic distinction between vital and peripheral interests and between varieties of Communism. Thus his efforts to explain limited policies in limited terms did not succeed. Despite the China White Paper and his National Press Club speech critics demanded to know why, if it was vital to defend against Communism in Europe, was it not equally vital to go all out against Communism in Asia. The use of universalistic language to define the conflict with Russia not only blurred the strategic distinctions and limitations that Acheson clearly wished to preserve operationally but it also made it difficult for him to put into effect his policy of disentangling from Chiang Kai-shek and deflecting Chinese nationalism against the Kremlin.

Successes

Establishment of a Strategic Basis for Dealing with the USSR. By the time Acheson became Secretary of State, the West had not yet achieved a strategic basis for dealing with the USSR. Acting on the evidence, Acheson believed that it was impossible to negotiate the differences outstanding between Russia and the West without a fundamental change of attitude on the Soviet side; the only alternative was to take the competitive nature of the relationship for granted while striving to avoid the onset of war. Acheson did not believe that building up the unity and military strength of the West would necessarily increase the dangers of war; quite the contrary, he believed it provided the only realistic basis on which the Soviet Union would be likely to cease and desist from probing Western weaknesses. It called for careful calculation and restraint on America's part that no provocation be given while mobilizing the strength necessary to deter the Soviet Union from any expansionist enterprise. It can scarcely be maintained that Acheson exaggerated the Soviet threat or that he failed to see the situation from the other side when he put such stress upon the need to avoid war with the Soviet Union. It was not Acheson who believed in the inevitability of war; it was Stalin.

On the other hand, Acheson did not believe that the West could afford to allow its defenses to languish. Once he had examined the facts, Acheson was not one to shirk the logic of a situation; and the logic of the situation hardly permitted him to establish a containment policy that was not buttressed by alliances and military power.

That détente had to await Stalin's death and the succession to power of Malenkov and Khrushchev does not undercut the political appropriateness of Acheson's strategy. The fact that the Kremlin had to turn from an area of relative strength (Europe), where expansion entailed the risk of total war, to an area of greater vulnerability (Korea), where containment had scarcely begun to be applied and where the low risk of war was not an effective deterrent to aggression, strongly suggests that Acheson's strategy was the appropriate one. The fact that in the autumn of 1952 the Communist Party Congress in its last meeting before Stalin's death had to forge a new Communist policy—one that did not rely so much on constant pressure and the intimidation of military power and violent propaganda— also suggests that Acheson's was the right policy. The fact that negotiations did not immediately flow from Soviet recognition that a new relationship of forces had been achieved does not invalidate it. The record of Stalin's foreign policy affords no real evidence that any such potential for negotiation existed during Acheson's tenure in office. It had to await Stalin's death and for the men in the Kremlin to consider seriously the possibilities of détente based on the existing status quo.

European Diplomacy. Meanwhile, Acheson's approach enlisted the overwhelming support of the states of Western Europe. Never before in peacetime had sovereign entities achieved such a high degree of collaboration and policy integration. Not only was NATO endowed with a common army and a unified command, but its members demonstrated a remarkable ability to bury their differences in the search for solutions to their common problems. Unquestionably, this unity could not have been attained without the trust that Acheson engendered in his European partners.

Acheson's foreign policy was tempered both morally and politically by his strategic view of a universe in which not all things are possible. Since a nation's power is not unlimited and the claims upon it are complex and multifarious, the task of statecraft is to decide what is necessary and what is expendable. The statesman, Acheson wrote in September 1949, "must know . . . the limitations of the power of his own country and the limitations of his own position within it. In most cases a decision on policy and resultant action does not settle the matter under consideration. The action of others is more often than not the controlling factor." [3] We must think of ourselves—Acheson liked to quote Holmes—not as little gods outside the community of nations "but as ganglions within it—as less than it, and as gaining our significance from the beneficence of our function and effect within it." [4]

Acheson's strategic view of international politics had a strong appeal to America's allies, despite their many points of disagreement. To begin with, it was a pleasure for them to deal with an American statesman who was not a moralist. Secondly, it was possible to work with Acheson in the common idiom of national interest. Acheson understood that foreign statesmen could not agree to what was not acceptable to their own people (just as America could not salvage governments that did not enjoy the loyalty and support of their own people); bargains struck on the basis of mutuality of interest, Acheson knew, offered the best hope of receiving popular acceptance and of enduring (as NATO has endured) because they were rooted in each country's self-interest.

Thirdly, Acheson's success in establishing America's leadership of the Western alliance lay in his ability to carry the Congress and the American people with him. Some of his severest conflicts with Congress reflected his view that "what we do affects our friends abroad quite as much as it affects us. They must never have cause to believe that we have disregarded their dangers. They must always know that their problems are in the forefront of our judgments." [5] At the same time he refused to let friendship or sentiment blind him to the primacy of America's interests. Acheson shaped U.S. policy to take into account but never to substitute allied interests for American. Europeans understood this. When a rupture threatened, as over Korean policy or German rearmament, Acheson knew enough to draw back. Unlike later American statesmen who were excessively swayed by anti–Communist fanaticism, moralism, and the mentality of military planners, Acheson knew that the success of American diplomacy depended upon a suppleness in its relations with both its allies and with other states. Acheson saw in the views of America's allies a touchstone for his own judgment, and by paying attention to these views, he maintained the balance and political essence so essential to successful statecraft.

Unlike his successors Acheson differentiated among the various regions of the world on the basis of their strategic importance, calculating the risks and cost-effectiveness of undertaking action in one region as opposed to another. "It is not defeatism—on the contrary it is the beginnnig of victory—to arrive at a realistic recognition of the limitations of one's own strength. We will bring ourselves nothing but confusion by thinking that we are so strong that there is some way by which our government can determine what is to go on in every country everywhere." [6] By keeping the political dimension at the forefront of his calculations, Acheson not only gave the Kremlin a striking demonstration of Western unity, but succeeded in resolving many divisive issues facing the allies both in their relations with each other and in the liquidation of their empires.

In sum, Acheson's logic and sensitivity to the nature of international politics provided American foreign policy with a strategic basis (situations of strength) for meeting the Soviet strategy and with a method (diplomacy) for relating itself to the rest of the world that was neither moralistic nor isolationist but was based upon reciprocity and upon a sense of commuinty and responsibility toward other states.

Effectiveness with the United Nations. In spite of his reservations about the United Nations as an effective agency for maintaining peace and security, Acheson was consistently successful in winning support for America's position before the United Nations. It was not simply a matter of America having an automatic majority of allied and other anti–Communist states available to it. He recognized the political advantage of securing United Nations backing, and he appreciated the political value of the United Nations as an agency for strengthening the fabric of international relations and for mediating the growing number of conflicts between the European powers and their colonial territories. The United Nations symbolized the aspiration of people for a better and more orderly world; as he saw it, there was no inconsistency that could not be worked out between that and America's national interest.

Korea confronted Acheson with a hard, and inevitably controversial, choice about the nature of the UN. Korea posed a direct challenge to the original conception of the organization as well as to the legal and moral principles on which it had been founded. While it was clear that the North Korean resort to force contravened the Charter, it was less clear in terms of the Charter what response could be organized through the UN over Soviet objections. Acheson had to choose between a strict construction of the veto which supported the original design that force would not be used under the auspices of the UN against the wishes of a Permanent Member, and a creative construction which would allow the steps to be taken under the auspices of the UN to oppose the North Korean use of force, despite Soviet objections to such measures. The U.S. choice in the form of the Uniting for Peace Resolution, although controversial, was broadly supported by the membership, and, although our choice "soured" the People's Republic of China on the UN the alternative—noninvolvement of the UN—would have had far-reaching and potentially adverse domestic consequences.

Acheson's Relations with the American Public. Acheson's relations with the public and the Congress have often been characterized as a failure. In light of subsequent revelations of how the Johnson and Nixon administrations dealt with Congress and the American public, Acheson's record may be in for revision. Even the Eisenhower–Dulles and Kennedy administrations relied upon anti–Communism and national prestige in ways which short-circuited the meaningful education of the American people as responsible participants in the foreign-policy process. Acheson's attitude came nowhere near the Woodrow Wilson who declared that "there is no apparent contradiction between democracy and the concentration of authority or command in the hands of a few." * In spite of his frequent and sometimes open discouragement at his inability to communicate the complexities of international politics to the people and to the press, and in spite of his run-ins with certain congressional figures, Acheson treated the Congress and the public with respect, which is more than can be said for subsequent administrations. And far from failing in his relations with them, he achieved an honorable success. He may have overstated the case for the Truman Doctrine, as subsequently he may have overdrawn the magnitude of the Soviet threat in making his case for "total diplomacy" and NSC 68, but he employed neither deceit nor deliberate distortion in representing American foreign policy to the American people. To do so would have been personally and politically repugnant to him. As Gaddis Smith so emphatically remarks: "There was nothing secret about the Truman–Acheson foreign policy—as distinguished from some of the details of military planning and operations, intelligence gathering and covert activities. What Acheson said in his public speeches was no different, except in detail, from what he said in closed Congressional hearings, conversations with ambassadors, or secret NATO sessions." [7]

Acheson was Secretary at an extraordinarily difficult moment in American national life, a time when Americans were being asked to break with isolationism and accept a role of responsibility in world affairs and when the failure of the peace was bound to arouse a visceral reaction against Communism both at home and abroad. The vicissitudes and constraints imposed upon Americans by their exposure to international politics was galling in the extreme. Their general innocence about the workings of history left them unprepared for Communist victories in China and elsewhere, and in their hysteria over Communism they were inclined to see in the Hiss case and other episodes proof of a general conspiracy in high places that explained those victories more satisfactorily than did Acheson's statements.

In line with his philosophy, Acheson made an extraordinary effort to educate and inform the American people. And measured by his success in securing public approval for those policies that he considered indispensable to his strategy, and in resisting pressure for those courses of action that would have plunged America into war in Asia and under-

---

* Papers of Woodrow Wilson, vol. 7, ed. by A. S. Link (Princeton: Princeton University Press, 1966 et seq.), p. 81. The freedom of a democratic nation consists not in governing itself: for that it cannot do: but in making undictated choice of things it will accept and of the men it will follow. Ibid., p. 359.

mined the unity of the free world, Acheson's relations with the American public may well be viewed as a success.

Furthermore, in spite of his public frostiness and private contempt for much of the press, and his rather strict efforts to prevent leaks,* Acheson made a studied and largely successful effort to get along with the working press. In practice he influenced the press more than he thought and fared better than he might have expected.

Relations with Congress. Reputation has it that Acheson's relations with Congress were unsuccessful, a failure in fact, and that his *"personal relations with Congress were, in the opinion of most observers, abysmal."* [8] Now that we have lived through the Dulles, Rusk, and Kissinger eras, it is hard to recognize a Secretary of State whose relations with at least some part of the Congress have not been bad. Still, the question remains: were Acheson's relations all that bad or unsuccessful? Rosenau's and Stassen's studies have clearly demonstrated that the principal criticism of Acheson came almost exclusively from about fifteen Republican isolationists "whose personal beliefs were . . . so strongly opposed to the postwar extension of American commitments that they could not contain their discontent within the requirements of their party-role," but let it spill over into *ad hominem* attacks on Acheson far out of proportion to the personal feelings of the majority of the Senate toward him. "The absolute and fervent opposition expressed toward Acheson by isolationists is remarkable: They made seven cordial remarks and 1,268 hostile ones" [9] in the Senate over the four-year period of Acheson's secretaryship. These senators, led by McCarthy, Wherry, Kem, and Jenner, and their claque among the columnists and news weeklies created the principal image of a Secretary who was totally unsuccessful in his relations with Congress. Yet senators such a Knowland, Republican of California, and Smith, Republican of New Jersey, who were opposed only to his Far Eastern policies, were far more reserved in their criticism, and a Republican such as Wiley of Wisconsin, who supported Acheson on both his alliance and Far Eastern policies, was even more cordial. Acheson's relations with segments of Congress were acrimonious not because he personally could not get along with congressmen, but because his policies challenged both isolationism and the traditional control that Congress habitually exercised over foreign policy in peacetime. True, Acheson was prone to reveal a disdain for congressional ideas that a more cagy Secretary like John Foster Dulles would studiously avoid. But it is not true that Acheson was contemptuous of Congress itself or of its constitutional function to advise

---

* He made it a general rule that lower rankers in the Department of State were not to give interviews or backgrounders unless cleared by higher-ups.

and consent, to debate and amend. Few Cabinet officers in any administration spent more time (approximately 25 percent) testifying before congressional committees than did Acheson; few engaged in such open give and take; few dissembled as seldom if at all; and few had to fight as hard to persuade a majority of the correctness of Administration policy. Acheson enjoyed no automatic majorities fueled by the so-called military–industrial complex to rubber-stamp whatever the Executive wanted. Perhaps that is why so many of Acheson's policies met the test of time better than those of his successors. They had to be rooted in solid justifications.

Acheson may have begrudged the time given to Congress, but he never doubted the constitutional role of Congress to advise and consent, to debate and amend foreign policy. Compared with the subsequent self-deceits and self-abnegatory practices with which later Congresses abdicated their responsibility to criticize and influence foreign policy, the clash of wills which marked the Truman–Acheson relations provided Congress with an open invitation to challenge and criticize the major premises and components of policy.

Since the constitutional role of the Congress in foreign policy was respected throughout the Acheson period (with the partial exception of the entry into the Korean War) and Acheson was still able to secure passage of most of the legislation and treaties needed to sustain his foreign policy, his relations with Congress must be considered as something more than a qualified success.

Successful Control of the Bureaucracy. By and large Acheson successfully resisted the iniquities or dysfunctionalities of the decentralized, diffuse, competitive decision-making process of which the American Executive is so often presented as the model. His success in this direction was rooted first and foremost in the relationship between Truman and himself. Everyone knew that he and he alone had the President's confidence in foreign affairs. To be sure, Truman did not go along with Acheson on everything, but "No other department or agency competed seriously with State for control of foreign policy." [10] This does not mean that a range of views was not heard. Neither Acheson nor Truman had trouble listening to contrary advice.

Acheson earned the trust and confidence which Truman reposed in him and the Department of State by anticipating the President's needs and providing him promptly with comprehensive, well-reasoned advice. Acheson prepared meticulously for his meetings with Truman; he deployed all his persuasive powers with fact and logic so overwhelming that Truman rarely questioned them. "In the race with time," writes Smith, "which was the key to influence over the President, Acheson was unbeatable." [11]

Acheson's successful control over the bureaucracy, especially the military, also resided in his ability to impose a pre-eminently political character upon foreign policy—as opposed to military, foreign aid, ideological and anti-revolutionary, "Presidential," or covert and secretive styles. Acheson recognized, and was determined to act upon, the premise that foreign policy involves judgments that are fundamentally political in character: What are the limitations and possibilities of various situations? What are the mainsprings of human motives and aspirations, and especially the motives and interests of foreign peoples and leaders? (Here his singular blind spot was in not recognizing Communism as a legitimate expression of Asian nationalism.) So ambiguous and contingent are these matters that real accomplishments in international relations are not always apparent, and certainly not immediately. Politics involves the aligning of the vital will of another country to one's own national interest. Just as Holmes argued that "general propositions do not decide concrete cases" and that a decision "will depend on a judgment or an intuition more subtle than any articulate major premise," [12] so Acheson believed that foreign policy is always a matter of the next step. In spite of his emphasis on power, Acheson knew that the successful acquisition of a security interest or the successful strengthening of a favorable international environment were more often than not a psychological or a political matter, dependent as much upon the will and effectiveness of others as upon one's own will or effort, however necessary the latter might be. The containment of Russia, and even more the overcoming of Europe's own internal schisms, depended upon the support which America's allies could count on from their own people, and that in turn was a delicate and contingent matter which could not be forced.

By shaping policy according to a single comprehensive view of the proper political basis for adjusting relations among states—a view which Truman not only shared but acted upon—Acheson made possible the subordination of the competing parochial and bureaucratic interests to a single strategic design. As a consequence of their combined qualities, Acheson and Truman crafted a grand strategy for containing the Soviet Union and restoring a manageable international system. It is no small thing to meet so comprehensively the needs of an era such as theirs.

EPILOGUE: 1953–1971

OUT OF OFFICE Acheson continued to be preoccupied with the issues that had confronted him as Secretary of State: the staying power of the American republic in foreign affairs, the leadership of the alliance, the difficulty of leaders' knowing how to make a decision and sticking with it. "Now the capacity to decide," he wrote in an article in 1954, "is not a common attribute of mankind. It becomes increasingly rare as the difficulty of the problems increases. The choice becomes one between courses all of which are hard and dangerous. The 'right' one, if there is a right, is quite apt to be the most immediately difficult one." [1] It was not long before Acheson found ample evidence for his doubts about the Eisenhower administration. The drift and evasions he detected in the new administration's policy-making could, he feared, lead to the break-up of the alliance. He was disturbed that, as one writer has put it, "bluffing was so much [Dulles's] natural technique that the line between policy and theatrical threat was repeatedly effaced." [2] Acheson viewed with contempt Dulles's sulky departure from the Geneva Conference of 1954 on Indochina. He watched in helpless dismay as the Suez Crisis of 1956 engulfed America and its European allies in recrimination and disaster. He viewed Dulles's neglect and sacrifice of the Foreign Service as a national calamity because he believed that effective foreign policy could not be made with the Secretary separated from the day-to-day thinking and work of the department. Neither should diplomacy and military strategy be compartmentalized so that the left hand did not know what the right hand was doing.

He did not believe in the new strategic doctrine of massive retaliation because he knew that U.S. military strategy could not be separated from

the stakes Americans and other people had in avoiding a nuclear holo-
caust. He did not believe that America should try to control international
conflict by brandishing the threat of nuclear war.

His first public intervention into foreign policy after his retirement as
Secretary came on January 10, 1957, when the House Foreign Affairs
Committee asked him to testify on the Administration's joint resolution
relating to the Middle East (subsequently known as the Eisenhower
Doctrine).[3] In an attempt to limit the loss of Western influence in the
Middle East and to ensure the preservation of Western economic and
strategic interests in the area, the Administration asked Congress for
authority, first, to assist any nation in the area in the development of its
economic strength for purposes of its national independence and, second,
to employ American armed forces to secure and protect the territorial
integrity and independence of any state requesting such aid. The proposal
was designed more to stabilize the status quo and safeguard American oil
than to meet the rising nationalism and economic needs of the Arab
peoples. Acheson made two points in his testimony. First, Presidents
have the authority to employ the armed forces to protect the vital interests of the United States should an emergency arise, but the resolution in
question did not indicate why the President must have this specific congressional authority now, "when by the very nature of things the power
asked for must be shadowy and vague." In Acheson's mind deterrence
warnings should not be issued unless and until the government made a
policy decision that it would definitely act if the contingency in question
arose. Secondly, Acheson questioned the import of Dulles's testimony that
there was no likelihood of military force being employed outside the
region "unless it was quite apparent that what was happening was deliberately intended to be the beginning of the Third World War." This
sounded, Acheson said, "perilously like another approach to the brink,"
and Acheson did not believe that Congress should leave to the Executive
the final decision as to which Soviet act constituted the intent to begin
World War III and, by implication, the decision to resort to nuclear
weapons. Not for a single moment should the country be indulged in the
supreme illusion that nuclear weapons had made deterrence foolproof or
that their threatened use could manipulate the levers of history in a
chaotic and revolutionary age.[4] Such reckless bluffing would not be necessary if, as he recommended, the country were adequately equipped with
conventional forces. Acheson also objected to the implication in the resolution that the employment of American armed forces would be carried
out unilaterally and alone. He still did not believe that America could
look to the United Nations to form American policy, but neither was it
wise to reject in advance the possibility of acting collectively should the
need arise. What was needed, Acheson reasoned, was not more military

intervention but a long-term program for economic development and some effort to alleviate Western dependence on Middle Eastern oil. The United States had a large measure of responsibility for the situation created in the Middle East by the founding of Israel; "American responsibility requires getting established, underwriting, and supporting with force an international arrangement for preventing . . . raiding, as well as attacks either way, by taking over responsibility for such punishment . . . as might be necessary." [5] Prophetic admonishments but ones not likely to be acted upon by an administration preoccupied with short-run and unilateral actions.

Much as Acheson had surmised, the Eisenhower Doctrine failed as a policy. It stressed military policy over such economic and political issues as Arab nationalism; it constituted a misapplication of deterrence policy because it sought to prevent crises and threats in the area with the threat of U.S. military intervention against locally instigated subversion; and finally it used an exaggerated threat of Communism as a pretext for intervention to preserve essentially Western economic and strategic interests in the area.[6]

Where Acheson saw no room for flexibility was in America's European policy. The Soviet interest, still not in the status quo, was in forcing the Americans out of Berlin and West Germany as the first step toward undermining the security and stability of an area vital to America's survival as a free society. He therefore came down hard on George Kennan's proposal, advanced in a series of lectures over the BBC (the 1957) Reith Lectures), that the time and possibility might have come for both superpowers to disengage their forces from Europe and to agree to a disarmed and neutralized Germany. Kennan's lectures aroused a storm of controversy, and Kennan was probably correct when he remarked that no academic lecturer ever had a more dramatic impact on the political elites of Europe and America.

Kennan argued that we could never end the specter of competition and war in Europe unless the division of Europe was ended and Soviet and American forces were withdrawn behind their own borders. To probe the possibility of this, and thereby of normalizing European affairs, Kennan proposed that the West drop its insistence that an eventual all-German government be free to join NATO, and instead declare itself the partisan of a neutralized and essentially disarmed but unified Germany. While Kennan carefully couched his proposal against any naive or precipitate belief that such a settlement could be had either easily or on the basis of one-sided concessions, his speech raised issues that could not be broached in the context of the Cold War without putting the existing basis of policy into question in ways that might have unpredictable consequences, and it presumed that the balance of gains and disadvantages on both sides would be symmetrical and equal.

Kennan's proposals were highly regarded by some and widely attacked by others. Acheson criticized Kennan on two principal grounds in a *Foreign Affairs* article of April 1958.[7] First, Acheson argued that without the American connection—economic, military, and political—it would be difficult if not impossible for Europe to maintain an independent national life. It took the two together—Europe and America—to confront the Soviet challenge. Kennan had tried to anticipate this objection by declaring that it was time Europeans took responsibility for their own fate—that it was precisely their refusal to give up their dependence on America that was prolonging the abnormality of the situation. Second, Acheson argued that the Soviet Union was in no position to liquidate its control over Eastern Europe, as the Hungarian episode had shown, and that mutual withdrawal would advantage the Soviet Union both strategically and psychologically by ending the American guarantee and presence while leaving Communism and the Red Army as nearby presences. Should America withdraw, Acheson argued, a disoriented West Germany would become prey to a renewed Soviet political and psychological offensive designed to win what continued to be its long-sought objective—mastery of Germany. It was on the issue of what evidence Kennan could advance to prove that the Soviets would really liquidate their political as well as their military power in Eastern Europe that Acheson chastised Kennan's "disengagement" plan for its blend of illusion, isolationism, and faith in the "diplomacy of earlier centuries." [8] In his article Acheson adverted to a paradox that Kennan agreed to be the most telling argument against him when advanced by Raymond Aron in a Round Table held in Paris in January. Aron argued that an abnormal situation (the division of Europe) was less dangerous than an equivocal one (where no one knew where they stood). Acheson expressed the same paradox: "The jockeyings and tensions of the two parts of Germany, the unopposable threat of Russian power, the bribes which can be dangled before Germany by the Soviet . . . . these alone are enough to put an end to hope of a united and strong Europe, invigorated by Germany." [9] By contrast Acheson did not dissent from Kennan's second controversial point, that too much reliance was being put on atomic forces at the expense of conventional forces to assure the West a credible deterrent should the Kremlin renew its pressure on Berlin.

Acheson and the Second Berlin Crisis (1958–1961)

The "deadline crisis" began with a Soviet note of November 27, 1958, containing a six-month deadline by which time the division of Berlin had to be ended or else Russia would transfer authority over access to West Berlin to the East German Government (GDR). On January 10, 1959,

Moscow followed up its deadline ultimatum by offering a draft treaty for Germany that, like the proposal for Berlin, called for an independent, demilitarized, and neutralized Germany but with no provision for the reunification of Germany under free elections or on any other terms acceptable to the West. A number of motives prompted Khrushchev's determination to bring an end to the divided state of Berlin. The status of West Berlin was a challenge that offended and damaged East Germany. Berlin also offered the Kremlin a point of Western weakness and vulnerability that invited exploitation. According to Walter Lippmann, who interviewed Khrushchev in October 1958, Khrushchev linked the pressure on the West to change the status quo at Berlin as part of a worldwide "process of revolutionary change which is in progress. He wants us to recognize the revolution not only as it is but *as it is going to be.*" [10] As a good Communist, Khrushchev probably felt an injuction to exploit the favorable breakthrough in strategic weapons (Sputnik) in order to effect a favorable shift in the general political and diplomatic relationship of forces.

Much as Khrushchev anticipated, the deadline note drew a divided response from Western capitals. Despite the existence of NATO, conventional military strength had been allowed to decline to the point that it did not offer a credible deterrent short of a nuclear confrontation. In the face of the ultimatum, Dulles endeavored to put as limited and benign an interpretation on Soviet intentions as possible. But in opting for negotiations to meet the Soviet demands, Dulles did so not out of any conviction that an agreement could be reached satisfactory to both sides, but to ward off the danger of a deadline confrontation, a confrontation he genuinely feared.

Being a member of the Advisory Council of the Democratic National Committee now gave Acheson a platform from which to give his disagreement with the Administration's assumptions about Berlin policy a wider public airing than had hitherto been possible. In a position paper written for the Democratic National Committee, Acheson argued that the Soviet determination to change the Berlin regime had to be taken very seriously both because Khrushchev meant it much more seriously than the Eisenhower Administration did and because the alternatives were so forbidding. Either the West would be forced out of Berlin with incalculable damage to its unity and morale, or it would face a confrontation under desperate and potentially uncontrollable circumstances. Whatever course negotiation takes ". . . the Soviets must be convinced that we are genuinely determined to keep the traffic to Berlin open, at whatever risk, rather than abandon the people of Berlin and permit the whole Western position to crumble." [11] Now was the moment, Acheson warned the Administration, for an explicit statement of Western commitment before Khrushchev got out on a limb.

Because the Soviets enjoyed a missile advantage and because he believed America should avoid a nuclear confrontation if at all possible, Acheson proposed reducing reliance on our nuclear arsenal and beefing up conventional Western forces for an initial and extended non-nuclear response to Berlin contingencies. Only in this way would the West signal the seriousness of its will to resist, which must be part of its bargaining strategy and part of its fallback position. Acheson believed that it was dangerous to let Soviet expectations develop in a context of ambiguity that would end with a feeling of a personal deception and defeat for Khrushchev.

Eisenhower implicitly rejected the Acheson thesis by letting it be known that the United States did not intend to fight a conventional war over Berlin; presumably "massive retaliation remained the only significant possibility." [12] Among European leaders, Adenauer and de Gaulle agreed with Acheson's thesis that the short-run advantages of negotiating as if the Soviet threats did not constitute a fundamental challenge to Western positions did *not* outweigh the long-run dangers of failure of negotiations followed by an explosion. Prime Minister Macmillan tended to side with Eisenhower.

We all know what happened. The Eisenhower Administration invited Khrushchev to visit America and had a measure of success in postponing the crisis by agreeing to hold a summit meeting, scheduled for Paris in June 1960, to determine the future status of Berlin. As the implications of the Soviet demands came home to the Administration in the months following the President's meeting with Khrushchev, the American position became increasingly rigid. Then, on the eve of the summit, an American U–2 plane was shot down over Russia. The world leaders met under the tensions raised by the incident, and when Khrushchev demanded that Eisenhower either disown responsibility for the incident or apologize to the Soviet people, the conference collapsed. Relations were worse than ever. Only Khrushchev's decision to put off the Berlin crisis until Eisenhower's successor had been elected averted a catastrophe. "After the abortive summit, the Eisenhower Administration confronted a resurgence of Soviet diplomacy no longer restrained by summit expectations. In striving to put his own house in order Khrushchev adopted the arguments of his opposition and became outspokenly bellicose toward the United States. He responded to a standoff in the crisis maneuvering between East and West by switching to pressure tactics and verbal militance." *

No sooner had Kennedy assumed office than Khrushchev reopened

---

* Jack M. Schick, *The Berlin Crisis, 1958–1962* (Philadelphia: University of Pennsylvania Press, 1971), p. 128. Krushchev was now under more pressure than ever both from his domestic opponents and from Peking.

his campaign for a Berlin settlement that would end Western occupation. In March 1961 Khrushchev reminded the American ambassador of a Soviet *aide memoire* to Bonn insisting that the issue of Berlin be settled before the German elections scheduled for September—or else. Upon receipt of this warning, Kennedy immediately assigned Acheson to head a study group established for the purpose of coming up with a policy on Berlin. No time was to be wasted because at his meeting with Kennedy in Vienna in June, Khrushchev handed the President another *aide memoire* renewing the deadline crisis over Berlin.

Acheson carried over into the Kennedy era his fundamental belief that the security and salvation of the West depended upon maintaining a unified and resolute front in face of Soviet efforts to dislodge the West from its positions. He did not care to accept the proposition that Soviet missile developments and the much greater risk of nuclear war made some "give" in American policy necessary if that risk was to be minimized. This rigidity was to be evident in his policy recommendations on Berlin and, even more strongly, in his policy recommendations at the height of the Cuban Missile Crisis.

In preparing his recommendations, Acheson was more than ever convinced that there was little if any genuine intention on the Soviet part to negotiate a treaty that would protect the interests of both sides. On the face of it, there seemed no basis for compromise because the Soviets were determined to stop the flight of refugees from East Germany and there appeared to be no method for doing that short of incorporating West Berlin into the eastern zone. Thus it was essentially a conflict of wills. Acheson recommended arming and signaling the Kremlin by a rapid mobilization of American forces that the United States had no intention either of negotiating under duress or of backing down. "To offer negotiations or an image of flexibility," Acheson argued, "would encourage the Soviets to press for the greatest possible realization of their objectives which, since the West would have to fight at some not-very-distant point, would raise the danger of war." [13]

Kennedy accepted Acheson's definition of the seriousness of the threat and of the need to mobilize U.S. forces; but he did not rule out negotiations, and to this end he exempted "free access between East and West Berlin" from the list of Western interests which he considered vital. This omission became increasingly significant as the crisis mounted. Caught between the pressure from the East German government to stop the tide of East Germans fleeing westward and faced by American resolve not to quit Berlin short of war, Walter Ulbricht, the East German leader, was given permission to seal off East Berlin from West Berlin. On the night of August 12–13 the Berlin Wall began to go up. By demonstrating resolution, the West had limited its losses to the minimally unavoidable and dissuaded Khrushchev from persisting in a policy of forcing the West out of Berlin that ran the risk of nuclear confrontation. Although immediately followed by renewed Soviet nuclear tests and sabre rattling, the erection of the Wall marked the beginning of the end of Soviet efforts to dislodge the West from Berlin and to undo West Germany's integration with the West. Just as Acheson had argued in a speech in December 1958 that it was time for the West to stop trying to undo the settlement in the East and buckle down to defending what it had, so the Kremlin began to accept the status quo in the West as final also, but it was not to do so without one final test of wills.

The Cuban Missile Crisis

When the Cuban Missile Crisis began to develop on October 15, 1962, Kennedy asked Acheson, although a private citizen, to join the Executive Committee of the National Security Council to which the problem was assigned. Other members were Vice-President Johnson, Secretaries Rusk, McNamara, and Dillon, the Joint Chiefs of Staff, General Maxwell Taylor, George Ball, and Roswell Gilpatirck, Presidential Assistants Bundy, Sorensen, and O'Donnell, Soviet specialists Bohlen and Thompson, and finally the President's brother Robert Kennedy. The Cuban Missile Crisis, too, developed against a complicated strategic and political background involving evidence that the Soviet missile capability had been greatly overrated but that Khrushchev was still determined to achieve some kind of breakthrough that would exploit the world's revolutionary potential and restore his sagging prestige at home and in Peking. Conversely, Kennedy had shown himself determined to bolster U.S. military forces for the purpose of deterring highly desired Soviet initiatives. The Bay of Pigs fiasco had solidified Soviet–Cuban relations and provided Khrushchev with a highly prized opportunity to install Soviet intermediate-range ballistic missiles in a location where they could easily reach the continental United States. When the missiles were discovered, the emplacements were far along, and the question arose in Washington as to how to bring about their removal. Should a number of the missiles become operational in Cuba, they would serve to deter U.S. attacks while additional missiles were being installed. Whatever Soviet calculations of the chances of getting away with such a daring move and avoiding U.S. retaliation, they were woefully wrong. The fact that the emplacements were actually going on while Khrushchev and other Soviet representatives professed to have only peaceful, defensive intentions with regard to their Cuban arms buildup only added to the insecurity and apprehension about domestic repercussions that Kennedy felt. At the same time, the Soviet leader continued to talk in boastful terms of what the Soviet Union would do with its nuclear strength should anyone choose to defy it.

Among the alternatives discussed by the Executive Committee, Acheson favored an air attack, limited to the missile sites, designed to destroy the sites before they had a chance to become operational. The President, too, initially favored this course of action. When Kennedy informed Adlai Stevenson, then at the UN, of the missiles, he mentioned only two alternatives: "I suppose the alternatives are to go in by air and wipe them out, or to take other steps to render the weapons inoperable." [14] Acheson based his support for the so-called surgical strike on the premise that the missiles were fast becoming an acute danger. Once again, as at Berlin, it would not do to temporize until Khrushchev had accomplished his goal because then it might be too late. Once the Soviet Union had the capability of striking at the United States, Acheson argued, there was no telling what Khrushchev might do or what the American people's reaction might be to the news that nuclear missiles deployed in Cuba bracketed large portions of the United States.[15] That the Soviet leaders had had the temerity to put missiles in Cuba in the first place only added to Acheson's determination that they had to be gotten out and the quicker the better. (The possibility that the Russians must have felt a similar provocation from the American missiles positioned in neighborng Turkey and nearby Italy and West Germany was not considered until it was too late to remove them.)

Secondly, Acheson believed that a sudden air attack on non-populated areas of Cuba would not be likely to elicit a reflex attack on the United States, for that would risk the reciprocal destruction of the Soviet Union. The Kremlin had taken a highly calculated risk which, according to Acheson, had for its intent to threaten the United States; the sooner that threat was ended the better. Acheson later explained that given the choice between waiting until a blockade had worked, with the danger that some of the Soviet missiles might become operational, and doing something to short-circuit that development, he felt that the advantage lay with an immediate air strike. Acheson rejected Robert Kennedy's comparison between what his brother would be doing with what the Japanese had done at Pearl Harbor; Acheson later termed it a "thoroughly false and pejorative analogy." [16] As Acheson recalls, he pointed out to Robert Kennedy:

that at Pearl Harbor the Japanese without provocation or warning attacked our fleet thousands of miles from their shores. In the present situation the Soviet Union had installed missiles ninety miles from our coast—while denying they were doing so—offensive missiles that were capable of lethal injury to the United States.*

---

* Quoted in Graham Allison, *Essence of Decision* (Boston: Little, Brown, 1971), p. 203. One authority who agrees with Acheson writes that Kennedy's citing of Pearl Harbor is not very persuasive. "The Japanese surprise attack on Pearl Harbor in 1941

For a variety of more or less compelling reasons, not least of all the provocation that a physical attack upon Cuba might give Russia to seize Berlin, the President chose to rely upon the blockade. Acheson was invited to see Kennedy personally on Thursday, at which time the President made clear his intention not to risk an air strike, an option additionally compromised in his mind by the Air Force's inability to understand what was meant by a surgical air strike. On Monday, October 22, the President announced the institution of the blockade.

Acheson meanwhile had been dispatched to Paris where, bright and early on that same Monday morning, he informed de Gaulle of the situation. Initially, just as Acheson had warned, the blockade did not seem to produce the desired results fast enough; by mid-week Kennedy began planning for an all-out American invasion of Cuba. On Friday, however, Khrushchev appeared to be buckling, and on Friday night a secret letter in four sections arrived from Khrushchev agreeing to remove the missiles from Cuba under U.N. observation if the United States would remove the blockade and promise not to invade Cuba. Called to the State Department that evening by Rusk, Acheson still had his doubts that the Soviets would go through with the deal if the blockade was lifted. "I felt we were too eager to liquidate this thing," Acheson recalled. "So long as we had the thumbscrew on Khrushchev we should have given it another turn every day. We were too eager to make an agreement with the Russians. They had no business there in the first place." [17] Acheson held to the view that the Soviet Union had put its neck in the noose, and it should not be released until the Soviets had complied to the letter of the American demand. Thinking that they had made good the threat, the others (Rusk, Thompson, etc.) were ready to ease the pressure rather than risk failure by pushing Russia too hard or too far.

Much as Acheson suspected, Khrushchev's Friday night letter was superceded the very next morning by a message from the Kremlin asking that American missiles be removed from Turkey as a price of removing Soviet missiles from Cuba. With that, the contest of wills promised to continue indefinitely with each side getting more and more locked into its position.[18]

Incidents likely to be misunderstood or misinterpreted (an American U–2 was shot down over Cuba and another drifted over Siberia provoking the accusation from Khrushchev that Washington was being deliberately provocative) were now occurring with some frequency. Meanwhile, with the Soviets continuing to press ahead with construction of the missile

---

belonged to a strong international tradition. . . . It was infamous with Americans precisely because it was so successful." Geoffrey Blainey, *The Causes of War* (New York: The Free Press, 1973), p. 247, pp. 167–169.

sites, the possibility that an air strike might have to be launched as early as Tuesday again began to receive attention. For some reason it was now felt that an air strike alone would not do the job; it would have to be followed by an all-out land invasion! Time was running out.[19]

Only Robert Kennedy's ingenious proposal offered any hope: It was his idea to respond to Khrushchev's secret letter of Friday night (but ignore the Saturday morning demand) and offer to accept terms for liquidating the crisis that the Kremlin had not formally made. This message was accompanied by a warning that unless construction on the missile sites halted forthwith and the missiles rendered inoperable, the situation would "lead to an intensification of the Cuban Crisis and a grave risk to the peace of the world." [20]

The offer was delivered Saturday evening to Ambassador Dobrynin, who "gave it as his personal opinion that the Soviet leaders were so deeply committed they would have to reject the President's terms." [21] On Sunday morning, as the country waited the dread possibility of a nuclear war, Moscow radio began to broadcast Khrushchev's acceptance of the American ultimatum. The crisis began to abate.

In view of the tension and escalation of each side's stake in the confrontation, Acheson's idea of an air strike limited to destroying the missile sites cannot be dismissed. The Soviet Union had done as much in Hungary when its security interests were at stake. The attack might, however, have prompted some drastic Soviet retaliation, say at Berlin, which would have forced the decision for war upon the United States. Instead, the blockade and accompanying exchanges put that responsibility on the Soviet Union.

Acheson and the NATO Connection

Despite the disruptive factor introduced into NATO policy in the early sixties by General de Gaulle, Acheson did not despair of America's ability to transcend the crisis in its relations with Europe. He half-recognized the legitimacy of de Gaulle's complaints,[22] and even after de Gaulle vetoed Britain's entry into the Common Market, Acheson preferred that America avoid exacerbating relations with the French president.[23] Nevertheless, Acheson felt confident to the point of arrogance that America could use its immense power to bring de Gaulle into line.[24]

Unfortunately, when America's power soon revealed its limits, and one frustration after another attended American efforts to force de Gaulle back into line, Acheson's attitude gave way first to exasperation and then to anger. For the next three years, Acheson engaged actively both in a private capacity and as a consultant to the Department of State in searching for ways to overcome the crisis in America's relations with Europe and within NATO and to circumvent de Gaulle's aim of an independent role for France.

Acheson recognized that the problem facing NATO was a political one, and he proposed to overcome it by rekindling European fears of a renewed Soviet offensive.[25] Unfortunately the division of Europe had become a fact of life; contrary to Acheson's view, no one—not even the West Germans—really believed in German reunification. The real problem lay in the fact that however much the division and weakness of Europe remained a disturbing reality there were neither forces nor leaders sufficiently strong to overcome it, neither on Acheson's terms nor on de Gaulle's. The Berlin crisis and the Cuban Missile Crisis constituted a watershed in the Cold War. With the failure of those efforts, the Kremlin seemed to have exhausted, at least temporarily, its dynamism; and within a year Khrushchev would be gone, succeeded by a group of men far less dynamic and venturesome and faced with an increasingly vexatious problem in Peking. Is it any wonder that European governments, exhausted by their long retreat from empire and facing steadily rising economic demands, should prefer the status quo and the hypothetical danger of a renewed Soviet offensive to the arduous and politically unpopular task of matching Soviet power on the Central European front? Looked at from this angle, even de Gaulle's effort to stimulate French nationalism may be seen as a final unsuccessful effort to reactivate the French for a role neither they nor other Europeans were any longer willing to play. In fact, de Gaulle's proposed solution of the German problem, "an entente from the Atlantic to the Urals," seemed just as good as Acheson's idea of a reunification brought about by the superior attractive power of a revitalized NATO able to loosen the grip of the East German regime and meet any Soviet riposte.

Contrary to Acheson's belief, the real political problem, the one which aroused feelings of resentment and the one about which Europeans felt they could do something, was the question of continued American dominance of the alliance at a time when there was a perceived reduction in the Soviet threat. The European emphasis was on the unacceptability of automatic involvement in an American war and on the reduced reliability of the American nuclear commitment at a time when America itself had become vulnerable to a Soviet nuclear attack. The risks and costs of the alliance had gone up just when certainty about benefits had gone down. But the real issue was a nationalist reaction to American dominance (and not just in France) together with an emerging recognition that Europe and America were in many respects rivals as well as partners, not least of all in the burgeoning race for détente.

Europeans did not reject the alliance; they rejected continued American domination of it. However logical Acheson's proposed remedies might be in the abstract, they were largely irrelevant to the kinds of political currents with which European governments were preoccupied. Not even the Germans, whom Acheson sought to spur to assume the mantle of European leadership, were so committed to the American cause that they cared to risk the disadvantages of a break with France.[26]

Acheson recognized that a so-called technical or hardware solution to the strains confronting European–American relations would not do; only a new and more vital political relationship could overcome the political and psychological problems besetting the Europeans. In the official United States approach, however, emphasis was placed not so much on reaching a political understanding with the new currents of nationalism stirring in Europe, as on prescribing the actual weapons and strategy that the Europeans should have as a means of making them feel they were taking part in the nuclear deterrent. According to State Department orthodoxy, the credibility of the American nuclear deterrent would be enhanced in the minds of the European allies if they too had a finger on the trigger. This gave birth to the idea of a mixed manned nuclear fleet (known as MLF) in which joint European crews would man vessels equipped with nuclear-tipped missiles. At first Acheson was dubious. Whatever its merits (and they were few) MLF was a gimmick, and it was so patently inspired by the intent of embarrassing the French in their effort to achieve an independent nuclear strike force that it was downright embarrassing to America's European allies. Not only that but the MLF constituted an evasion of the real issue. Who would decide when the missiles were to be fired? The American President. Secondly, MLF was Lilliputian in comparison with the American strategic arsenal that would continue to remain under exclusive American management. For a while Acheson was sold on MLF, despite his recognition that there was no hardware solution to the political problems besetting NATO. When it became apparent, however, that all of the European governments were discomforted by the artificiality of MLF and by its patently anti–French bias, it was left to Acheson to kill it off. In his role as special consultant to the State Department on NATO questions, Acheson recommended that MLF be abandoned as too divisive, a recommendation which, to his credit, Lyndon Johnson was ready to accept.[27]

Acheson's positive efforts to rejuvenate NATO fell on barren soil because they were not made with the dominant political problem in mind; American efforts, and not just Acheson's, to stimulate increased European concern about a renewal of Soviet pressure were destined to get nowhere. Efforts to rekindle European integration, to shape a united Europe into the twin of an American pillar in a new Atlantic edifice, had but limited appeal. Acheson recognized that only a new political basis would meet the demands of the Europeans, but he shared the dominant American tendency to wish away all those issues on which European nationalism was increasingly sensitive—issues like equal access to advanced nuclear technology, to the prestige of sharing control of nuclear weapons, and so forth. Reversing his own long-standing call for the recognition of the primordial power of the nation-state in any realistic approach to world politics, Acheson now declaimed that "Nationality is of little importance compared with the breadth of vision, understanding of economic and political forces, ability to use technical help without being overpowered by it . . ." [28]—noble words but not likely to have an influence upon European governments preoccupied with national economic and social problems.

Acheson and the Vietnam War: 1965–1968

More than ever, Acheson saw contemporary events as a function of two decades during which America had met challenge after challenge to its foreign policy. If Acheson had not recognized the indigenous, nationalist character of Ho Chi Minh's movement earlier, he was unlikely to see it now. Attitudes and positions that had been taken out of desperation and uncertainty twenty years earlier had now been hardened into dogmatic reflexes. The more governments like those of Castro or Ho Chi Minh struggled to free themselves from the rigidities of the Soviet–American Cold War system, the more dangerous that insurrectionism appeared and the more determined American policy-makers were to do whatever necessary to preserve the status quo. Acheson, now over seventy, was as vulnerable to this mentality as anyone. The more stalemated the Cold War had become, the more determined Acheson had become that the stalemate could and should be broken. A vicious circle had been formed.

In his preoccupation with the unchanging nature of the Soviet regime and its machinations in various parts of the world, Acheson had lost some of his earlier capacity to be flexible and politically discriminating in his judgments. An all-out American war in Vietnam, which a decade or so earlier would have left him cold, was now accepted as a necessary and inevitable price of America's role in the world. The stakes in Vietnam, Acheson now felt, were very large, and the costs limited.

His contempt for doubts and questioning had hardened in direct proportion to his fear and frustration that the West was no longer taking the Soviet threat seriously enough. In an article entitled "The American Image Will Take Care of Itself," Acheson argued that America must not let itself be dissuaded by some mythical world opinion, often no more than the fulminations of newspaper writers in foreign capitals, from taking the tough decisions that were necessary if the worst was to be avoided. "Always do right," he quoted Mark Twain; "This will gratify some people and astonish the rest." [29] The more difficult America's task became, Acheson seemed to be saying, the less attention it should pay to world opinion. Defined Acheson's way, one could agree that world opinion was not something by which America should determine its course of action; but what Acheson caricatured and dismissed was a much more serious body of opinion, held by our allies including President de Gaulle, which perceived that in Vietnam America was in danger of bogging itself down in a hopeless struggle that would only weaken and distract America from the real problems.

Although a leading member of Johnson's council of foreign advisers, Acheson was not a member of any advisory group directly seized with the problem of Vietnam. But when the foreign policy group held a two-day briefing session in November 1965, Acheson was the designated spokesman. Although the group was principally occupied with Europe, Vietnam came up in the plenary session, and Acheson gave it as his view that the United States had to face up to the war and see it through.

In the autumn of 1967, Johnson convened a somewhat reconstituted foreign-policy advisory group at which the generally discouraging character of the Vietnam War was again discussed. Again Acheson took the position that the country had to stick it out.

Acheson's involvement became much more acute following the Tet offensive of January 31, 1968. In late February Johnson asked for Acheson's advice on Vietnam, and Acheson replied that he could not give good advice unless he interviewed the people most closely involved. He had lost faith in the objectivity of the briefers who customarily filled him in on the war situation, and with all due respect he informed Johnson that the "Joint Chiefs of Staff don't know what they are talking about." [30] Johnson was shocked, but he wanted Acheson's considered judgment; and since Acheson replied that he could not give it without access to the real facts, Johnson agreed that Acheson should be free to conduct a wide-ranging inquiry going beyond the canned briefings served up by the JCS, Rostow, and the CIA. Working with a small group of knowledgable people at the second and third echelon, Acheson soon amassed a volume of evidence that revealed the essentially hopeless and unwinnable character of the war. By now, too, the vastly disproportionate assignment of resources to Vietnam and the bad domestic situation were too obvious to be overlooked. At a luncheon alone with Johnson on March 15, Acheson informed the President that "he was being led down the garden path by the JCS, that what Westmoreland was attempting in Vietnam was simply not possible . . . [and that the President's own] recent speeches were quite unrealistic and believed by no one either at home or abroad." [31] Acheson expressed himself firmly and clearly against increased troop commitments and in favor of a leveling off and gradual reduction of U.S. forces.

Bitterly and grudgingly, Johnson's views on the war now began to change. General Westmoreland's request for an additional 200,000 men to "finish off" the enemy had prompted Clark Clifford, the new Secretary of Defense, to launch a searching review of the military situation facing America. Despite the recommendation of the Joint Chiefs of Staff that Westmoreland be given the additional forces, the civilian heads of the Pentagon began to balk. On March 22 Westmoreland was relieved of his command and assigned home to be Army Chief of Staff. Johnson convened a meeting of the Senior Advisory Group led by Acheson, and on March 25 their grand inquest began. At luncheon on the second day of the inquest, McGeorge Bundy summarized with appropriate shadings what he felt to be the views of the group. When the diehards objected to Bundy's summary, Acheson silenced them with the admonishment that it represented his own view and the view of the majority.[32] The President probed but failed to shake the bleak and pessimistic assessment of the Acheson group. The turning point had been reached in the Vietnam War so far as American involvement was concerned. But withdrawal could seriously begin only when the Presidential elections of that year were over.

There came to office in November an administration headed by Richard M. Nixon; it was without deep popular support and without roots in the traditional sources of American foreign-policy support. Henry Kissinger was just another little-known Harvard professor, not yet the famous figure that he was destined to become. Irony of ironies, it was to Dean Acheson, whom Nixon had earlier reviled as "the dean of Acheson's cowardly college of communist appeasers," that the new President turned for the symbol of continuity and integrity that seemed to be lacking. Acheson was visibly welcome around the Nixon White House. The danger was that in his continuing desire to serve the republic he not be used by Nixon and Kissinger for their own ends rather than for his own advice.

Under the British system, Acheson upon completion of his tenure as Secretary of State would have assumed his place in the House of Commons as a member of the loyal opposition. But when an American party loses the Presidency, it loses the experience and talents of individuals like Acheson by failing to afford them a regular and responsible forum from which to contribute to the life of the polis. The American system also deprives an Acheson of the workaday responsibility that comes from pulling in harness with the knowledge that someday you may again be called upon to form part of the governing team.

Deprived of an official role in political life, Acheson practiced law and poured his energies into a series of books and articles that won him a *succès d'estime* among the lay public as well as with the professional political scientist. *A Democrat Looks at His Party* (1955), *A Citizen Looks at Congress* (1957), *Power and Diplomacy* (1958), *Sketches from Life* (1961), and *Present at the Creation* (1969), and scores of articles and addresses permitted Acheson to fulfill his lifelong penchant to educate, as well as to keep his thoughts before the public. Free of official duties, he took a more active role than ever as a member of the Yale Corporation in supporting the young president, Alfred Whitney Griswold, in a program of educational reform and financial rejuvenation that put Yale once again in the forefront of American academic life.

Unlike many distinguished figures called to serve on presidential panels and to sign reports written by experts, Acheson was his own expert. At a time of dramatic change in strategic doctrines, when the think tanks in Santa Monica and Cambridge were producing new systems of logic to undergird American foreign policy, Acheson was keeping abreast of the younger men, and had no trouble assimilating their ideas and parlance. The difference between him and these new "experts" was that when called upon to advise Presidents Kennedy and Johnson, Acheson had the intellect and the stature to put the imprint of his own logic and conviction upon that advice.

By the time he was again called upon for advice and recommendations, Acheson had been out of touch with the Department of State's cable traffic and with the changes in the world that those cables represented. The power of his logic had worn grooves in his thinking about the Soviet Union. He was probably right in his suspicion that the eternal Russia of repression had to be dealt with at arm's length in the most guarded way, and that negotiations could only reduce the tension without overcoming the basic antipathy of the closed society for the open one. But by the same logic, it was hard for Acheson to accept the possibility that not every situation and not every challenge called for the same answers as they had fifteen years earlier. Still, most of what Acheson stood for in the final decade of his life was rooted in the logic and candor he had brought to Washington from New England fifty years earlier and which, unlike almost everyone else, he had never lost.

Behind his preoccupation with NATO and with keeping up America's defenses lay his conviction that the spirit of freedom and the chance for the world to evolve along nontotalitarian lines lay in preserving the strength and unity of the West. It is no doubt the case that Acheson's commitments were based on the ideals and values represented by Western civilization as it evolved out of the French Enlightenment and the English struggles for freedom of conscience. Certainly, much of the force with which Acheson imprinted his mark upon the history of the time sprang from the logic and integrity with which he lived up to the ideals of those two great movements in human history. In any event, much that went on in the rest of the world, while important to Acheson, was seen by him as secondary to the question of whether the West could achieve the unity and discipline needed to preserve itself in an age of revolution and totalitarianism.

In an America in which power was quite capable of corroding the integrity of the strongest man, Acheson stood out because he spoke and acted upon what his thought and conscience dictated. Perhaps the price of integrity in a public man is that we must hear from him things that we don't want to hear and recommendations that jar our wishful hopes that the world might become a pleasanter place. This as much as anything explains why Acheson was as much a controversial figure in the last decade of his life as he had been as Secretary of State, although to a different group of Americans.

Until the end he said what he believed, no matter who was hurt, including himself.[33]

NOTES

There are several abbreviations that appear often in the footnotes.

FR, followed by date and volume number, refers to *Foreign Relations of the United States* (U.S. Government Printing Office), yearly compilations of secret U.S. diplomatic memos and cables in multivolumes.

China White Paper refers to *United States Relations with China with Special Reference to the Period 1944-1949* (Washington, D.C.: Government Printing Office, August, 1949)

MacArthur Hearings refer to *Hearings to Conduct an Inquiry into the Military Situation in the Far East,* Senate Committees on Armed Services and Foreign Relations, 82nd Congress, 1st Session, Part II (Washington, D.C.: U.S. Government Printing Office, 1951).

For an explanation of the *Princeton Seminar Transcripts,* see Chapter 2, footnote 20.

The Acheson Papers are presently located at the Truman Library, Independence, Missouri.

Chapter 1

1. Interview with Joseph Lawton, Middletown, Connecticut, March 6, 1970.
2. Dean Acheson, *Morning and Noon* (Boston: Houghton Mifflin, 1965), p. 10.
3. Interview with Mrs. Helen Britten, Middletown, Connecticut, March 6, 1970.
4. Judge Ray S. Baldwin, *Reminiscences of Middletown.* Pamphlet No. 61, April 1969. The Middlesex County Historical Society.
5. Britten interview, *op. cit.*
6. Interview with Mrs. Dean Acheson, Washington, D.C., February 21, 1975.
7. Lawton interview, *op. cit.*
8. Alexander L. George and Julliette L. George, *Woodrow Wilson and Colonel House: A Personality Study* (New York: John Day, 1956).
9. Acheson, *Morning and Noon,* p. 10.
10. *Ibid.,* p. 13.
11. *Ibid.,* pp. 14-15.

12. *Ibid.*, p. 18.
13. *Ibid.*
14. *Ibid.*
15. *Ibid.*
16. Lawton interview, *op. cit.*
17. Letter from Henry H. Richards, alumni recorder to the author, April 27, 1962.
18. *Ibid.*
19. Wilmarth Lewis, *One Man's Education* (New York: Alfred A. Knopf, 1967), p. 95.
20. *Ibid.*
21. Interview with Archibald MacLeish, Conway, Massachusetts, July 3, 1964.
22. Interview with Dean Acheson, Washington, D. C., June 20, 1960.
23. Wilmarth Lewis, *One Man's Education*, p. 102.
24. *Ibid.*, p. 97.
25. *Felix Frankfurter Reminisces,* recorded in talks with Dr. Harlan B. Phillips (New York: Anchor Books, Doubleday, 1962), pp. 100-111.
26. MacLeish interview, *op. cit.*

Chapter 2

1. Oscar M. Perlmutter, "Acheson and American Foreign Policy: A Case Study in the Conduct of Foreign Affairs in a Mass Society" (Unpublished Ph.D. dissertation, University of Chicago, 1959).
2. Personal letter, Acheson to Alexander M. Bickel, December 7, 1955.
3. *Ibid.*
4. Interview with Dean Acheson, Washington, D.C., June 20, 1960.
5. Personal letter, Acheson to Charles Wyzanski, February 27, 1957.
6. Letter, Acheson to Bickel, December 7, 1955.
7. *Ibid.*
8. *Ibid.*
9. Interview with Felix Frankfurter, Washington, D.C., June 17, 1960.
10. Acheson, *Morning and Noon* (Boston: Houghton Mifflin, 1965), p. 87.
11. *Ibid.*
12. *Ibid.*
13. Frankfurter interview, *op. cit.*
14. *Ibid.*
15. *Ibid.*
16. *Ibid.*
17. Acheson, *Morning and Noon*, p. 159.
18. Letter from Dean Acheson to Mary Acheson Bundy, June 8, 1945, quoted in Dean Acheson, *Present at the Creation* (New York: W. W. Norton, 1969), pp. 107-108.
19. Dean Acheson, *A Democrat Looks at His Party* (New York: Harper & Brothers, 1955).
20. Acheson, Princeton Seminar Transcript, July 2, 1953. Following his retirement as Secretary of State, Mr. Acheson agreed to participate with his colleagues and associates in a debriefing. The debriefing took the form of a seminar held weekends 1953-1954 at the Institute for Advanced Studies in Princeton, New Jersey. The sessions, which lasted two days, were held every other month for nearly two years. A synopsis of events

for each policy and period was prepared by James Rosenau. These were then used by the group as the basis for Acheson's retrospective analysis accompanied by reference to documents and papers, and with accompanying comments by the other participants. The motives and circumstances of each decision were then analyzed. The transcript of the proceedings exceed 2000 pages. Among the participants were George F. Kennan, Paul Nitze, Philip Jessup, Robert Oppenheimer, Averell Harriman, Dean Rusk, and others. Hereinafter referred to as the Princeton Seminar Transcript.

21. Grace Tully, *F.D.R. My Boss* (New York: Scribner's, 1949), p. 178.
22. *Ibid.*
23. Acheson, Princeton Seminar Transcript, July 2, 1953.
24. Baltimore *Sun,* October 20, 1936.
25. *Ibid.*
26. Interview with Dean Acheson, Washington, D.C., April 2, 1963.
27. *Ibid.*

Chapter 3

1. Interview with Felix Frankfurter, Washington, D.C., June 17, 1960.
2. Interview with Howard C. Westwood, Washington, D.C., April 7, 1963.
3. Dean Acheson, "Roger Brooke Taney: Notes upon Judicial Self-Restraint." Address before the Maryland Bar Association, Atlantic City, New Jersey, July 4, 1936.
4. *Ibid.,* p. 12.
5. Norman Hapgood to F.D.R., July 7, 1936. PPT2278, Roosevelt Library.
6. Dean Acheson, "Some Social Factors in Legal Change." Address before the Law Club of Chicago, January 22, 1937, p. 8.
7. *Ibid.,* p. 9.
8. *Ibid.,* p. 16.
9. *Ibid.,* p. 17.
10. Dean Acheson, *A Democrat Looks at His Party* (New York: Harper & Brothers, 1955).
11. Dean Acheson, "Cardozo and the Problems of Governments," in the Proceedings of the Bar and Officers of the Supreme Court of the United States, November 26, 1938, p. 7.
12. *Ibid.,* p. 13.
13. *Ibid.,* p. 14.
14. *Ibid.,* p. 17.
15. *Ibid.,* p. 20.
16. Arthur M. Schlesinger, Jr., *The Politics of Upheaval* (Boston: Houghton Mifflin, 1960), p. 223.
17. Report of the Attorney General's Committee on Administrative Procedure.
18. *Ibid.*
19. *Ibid.*
20. *Ibid.*
21. Dean G. Acheson, "An American Attitude Toward Foreign Affairs," Speech at Yale University, New Haven, Conn., November 28, 1939.
22. *Ibid.,* p. 9.
23. *Ibid.,* p. 11.

24. William L. Langer and S. Everett Gleason. *The Challenge to Isolation,* Vol. I (New York: Harper & Brothers, 1952), p. 757.

25. Copy of a letter from Henry Stimson to C. C. Burlingham in Acheson's files.

26. Langer and Gleason, *Challenge to Isolation,* p. 761.

27. Remarks made by Dean Acheson over Station WBAL, Baltimore, Maryland, November 1, 1940.

28. *Ibid.*

Chapter 4

1. Dean Acheson, *Present at the Creation* (New York: W. W. Norton, 1969), p. 18.

2. *Ibid.,* p. 41.

3. For the complete story of Acheson's role in this operation, see Herbert Feis, *The Spanish Story: Franco and the Nations at War* (New York: Alfred A. Knopf, 1948), pp. 138-169.

4. *Ibid.,* p. 61.

5. *Foreign Relations of the United States, 1941,* Vol. III, p. 12. Hereinafter referred to by the initials FR. Compilations each year of secret U.S. diplomatic memos and cables in multivolumes.

6. Acheson, *Present at the Creation,* p. 30. Emphasis added.

7. Roy Harrod, *The Life of John Maynard Keynes* (London: Macmillan, 1951), p. 583.

8. Dean Acheson, "Random Harvest," Department of State *Bulletin,* June 16, 1946, p. 1047.

9. *Ibid.*

10. O. W. Holmes in *The Mind and Faith of Justice Holmes,* edited by Max Lerner (Boston: Little, Brown, 1943), p. 19.

11. Eugene Dooman testimony cited in Len Giovanitti and Fred Freed, *The Decision to Drop the Bomb* (New York: Coward, McCann, 1965), p. 93.

12. Acheson, *Present at the Creation,* p. 90.

13. *Ibid.,* p. 98.

14. Letter from Dean Acheson to Mary Acheson Bundy, June 21, 1945, in *Present at the Creation,* p. 108.

15. Acheson to Mary Acheson Bundy, June 7, 1947, *Ibid.*

16. *Ibid.,* p. 109.

17. *Ibid.,* p. 107.

Chapter 5

1. Dean Acheson, *Present at the Creation* (New York: W. W. Norton, 1969), p. 120.

2. I. F. Stone, "Shake-up in the State Department." *Nation,* Vol. 161, August 25, 1945, pp. 171-172.

3. *The New York Times,* Sept. 20, 1945, p. 1.

4. *Ibid.,* Sept. 26, 1945, "Connally Puts Limits on Acheson's Role."

5. Acheson, *Present at the Creation,* p. 237.

6. As quoted in Richard G. Hewlett and Oscar E. Anderson, Jr., *A History of the United States Atomic Energy Commission,* Vol. 1, *The New World,*

1939-1946 (University Park: Pennsylvania State University Press, 1962), pp. 455-456.

7. *Ibid.*, pp. 416, 423.

8. *Ibid.*, p. 417. See also John Lewis Gaddis, *The United States and the Origins of the Cold War 1941-1947* (New York: Columbia University Press, 1972), p. 251.

9. Walter Millis, ed., *The Forrestal Diaries* (New York: Viking Press, 1951), pp. 95-96. Also cited in Gaddis, *Origins of the Cold War*, p. 249.

10. Hewlett and Anderson, *The New World*, p. 424.

11. *Ibid.*, p. 426.

12. Memorandum, Acheson to Truman, September 25, 1945. *FR:1945*, II, pp. 48-50.

13. *Ibid.*

14. Gaddis, *Origins of the Cold War*, p. 252.

15. *The New York Times*, September 29, 1945.

16. Acheson, *Present at the Creation*, p. 125.

17. Dean Acheson, "The American People and Their State Department." Address to the Maryland Historical Society, Baltimore, Md., November 19, 1945.

18. *Ibid.*, p. 10.

19. For an analysis of the important bearing that cables from American diplomats in Moscow and in Eastern Europe were having, see David S. McLellan, "Who Fathered Containment?" *International Studies Quarterly*, Vol. 17, No. 2, June 1971, pp. 225-226; and Lynn E. Davis, *The Cold War Begins: Soviet American Conflict over Eastern Europe* (Princeton, N.J.: Princeton University Press, 1974), pp. 378-388.

20. Acting Secretary of State Acheson to Secretary of War Stimson, September 17, 1945. *FR:1945*, IV, pp. 493-494. See also Davis, *Cold War Begins*, pp. 365-368.

21. Department of State *Bulletin*, November 18, 1945, pp. 787-789; Acheson, *Present at the Creation*, pp. 130-131.

22. *Ibid.*

23. *Ibid.*

24. Davis, *Cold War Begins*, p. 388.

25. Hadley Arkes, *Bureaucracy, The Marshall Plan, and National Interest* (Princeton, N.J.: Princeton University Press, 1972), p. 20.

26. Hugh Dalton, *High Tide and After* (London: Muller, 1962), p. 82.

27. Hewlett and Anderson, *The New World*, p. 474. For details see Acheson to Byrnes, December 15, 1945, *FR:1945*, II, pp. 609-610; Byrnes to Acheson, December 17, 1945, *ibid.*, p. 609; Acheson to Byrnes, December 21, 1945, *ibid.*, pp. 709-710.

28. Hewlett and Anderson, *The New World*, p. 475. Emphasis added.

29. Gaddis, *Origins of the Cold War*, pp. 285-290.

30. Hewlett and Anderson, *The New World*, pp. 474-475.

31. I am indebted to Wilmarth Lewis for some suggestive comments along these lines. Personal interview, Farmington, Connecticut, March 7, 1970.

32. David E. Lilienthal, *The Journals of David E. Lilienthal*, Vol. II, *The Atomic Energy Years, 1948-1950* (New York: Harper & Row, 1964), p. 12.

33. Hewlett and Anderson, *The New World*, p. 539. See also Lilienthal, *The Atomic Energy Years*, pp. 15-17, for a similar sense of exhilarating accomplishment.

34. Letter of Transmittal. *A Report on International Control of Atomic Energy* (Washington, D.C.: Government Printing Office, 1946).

35. Lilienthal, *Journals,* Vol. II, p. 30.

36. Robert G. Gard, Jr., "Arms Control Policy Formulation and Negotiation: 1945-46" (Ph.D. dissertation, Harvard University, 1962), p. 359.

37. *Ibid.,* p. 360.

38. Acheson, *Present at the Creation,* p. 155.

39. Hewlett and Anderson, *The New World,* p. 571.

40. Lilienthal, *Journals,* Vol. II, p. 59.

41. John W. Spanier and Joseph L. Nogee, *The Politics of Disarmament* (New York: Praeger, 1962), pp. 62-63; James F. Byrnes, *Speaking Frankly* (New York: Harper & Brothers, 1947), pp. 270-271.

Chapter 6

1. *FR:1946,* VI, pp. 344-345.

2. Harry S Truman, *Memoirs,* Vol. I, *Years of Decision* (Garden City, N.Y.: Doubleday, 1955), p. 552.

3. *FR:1946,* VI, p. 695.

4. John Lewis Gaddis, *The United States and the Origins of the Cold War 1941-1947* (New York: Columbia University Press, 1972), pp. 300-301.

5. Dean Acheson, *Sketches from Life of Men I Have Known* (New York: Harper & Brothers, 1961), p. 62.

6. Dean Acheson, *Present at the Creation,* (New York: W. W. Norton, 1969), p. 151.

7. Gabriel Kolko, *The Politics of War: The World and United States Foreign Policy 1943-1945* (New York: Random House, 1968), p. 309.

8. *FR:1946,* VIII, p. 352.

9. *Ibid.,* p. 347.

10. *Ibid.,* VI, p. 736.

11. *Ibid.,* p. 347.

12. *Anglo-American Financial Agreement,* Hearings before the Committee on Banking and Currency, U.S. Senate, 79th Cong., 2nd Session, March 13, 1946.

13. David S. McLellan and Charles E. Woodhouse, "The Business Elite and Foreign Policy," *The Western Political Quarterly,* Vol. XIII, No. 1, March 1960, pp. 172-190.

14. *The New York Times,* April 23, 1946.

15. *The New York Times,* April 24, 1946.

16. *FR:1946,* VI, pp. 842-843; Luthinger to Clayton.

17. *Ibid.*

18. Acheson, *Present at the Creation,* p. 184.

19. *Ibid.*

20. James Reston, "The No. 1 No. 2 Man in Washington," *The New York Times Magazine,* March 25, 1946, p. 8.

21. Acheson, *Present at the Creation,* p. 129.

22. *FR:1946,* VII, p. 817.

23. *Ibid.,* pp. 816-817.

24. *Ibid.,* p. 821.

25. *Ibid.,* p. 826.

26. *Ibid.,* p. 836; Durbrow to Secretary of State.

27. *Ibid.*, pp. 830-833, 840-850.
28. *Ibid.*, pp. 841-842.
29. *Ibid.*, p. 841.
30. *Ibid.*
31. *Ibid.*, pp. 849-850.
32. *Ibid.*, pp. 843-844.
33. *Ibid.*, p. 848.
34. *Ibid.*, pp. 905-906; via War Department.
35. *Ibid.*, VII, pp. 857-858.
36. *Ibid.*, pp. 860-866.
37. *Ibid.*, p. 869.
38. Address, Madison Square Garden, New York, September 12, 1946. For an appraisal of Truman's carelessness and irresponsibility in this matter see Herbert Feis, *From Trust to Terror: The Onset of the Cold War, 1945-1950* (New York: W. W. Norton, 1970).

Chapter 7

1. Winston S. Churchill, *The Second World War,* Vol. VI, *Triumph and Tragedy* (Boston: Houghton Mifflin, 1953), p. 227.
2. The Varkiza Agreement of February 12, 1945.
3. *FR:1946,* VII, p. 91.
4. *Ibid.*, pp. 187-188.
5. *Ibid.*, p. 146; advice repeated in a cable of May 16, 1946.
6. *Ibid.*, p. 235.
7. Richard Powers, "Containment from Greece to Vietnam—and Back?" *Western Political Quarterly,* Vol. 22, December 1969, p. 849.
8. *FR:1946,* VII, pp. 210-213; Clayton to Byrnes.
9. *Ibid.*, pp. 223-224; Byrnes to the Acting Secretary of State.
10. *Ibid.*, p. 232.
11. *Ibid.*, pp. 502-503.
12. *Ibid.*, pp. 529-532; memo by State-War-Navy Coordinating Committee to Major General John H. Hildring.
13. *Ibid.*, pp. 240-245.
14. *Ibid.*, pp. 235-237; Acheson to MacVeagh. Also memorandum from Acheson to Venizelos, October 29, *ibid.*, pp. 250-255.
15. *Ibid.*, pp. 262-263. Acheson to MacVeagh based on decision of October 29, *FR:1946,* VII, p. 255.
16. *FR:1946,* VII, pp. 238-239.
17. *FR:1947,* V, pp. 17-22, 26-28.
18. *FR:1947,* V, pp. 29-31.
19. *FR:1947,* V, pp. 28-29.
20. *Ibid.*
21. Acheson, Princeton Seminar Transcript, July 2, 1953.
22. Joseph M. Jones, *The Fifteen Weeks* (New York: Viking Press, 1955), p. 139.
23. Seyom Brown in *The Faces of Power,* (New York: Columbia University Press, 1968), pp. 49-50, gives this as the verbatim version of Acheson's statement.
24. Gaddis Smith, *Dean Acheson* (New York: Cooper Square Publishers, 1972), p. 46.

25. Jones, *The Fifteen Weeks*, p. 145.
26. *Ibid.*, p. 155.
27. *The New York Times*, March 12, 1947.
28. Raymond Aron, *The Imperial Republic* (Englewood Cliffs, N.J.: Prentice-Hall, 1974), p. 27.
29. *Ibid.*, p. 44.

Chapter 8

1. Memorandum, British Embassy to Department of State.
2. *FR:1947*, III, pp. 197-198.
3. *Ibid.*, pp. 198-199.
4. *Ibid.*, p. 208.
5. *Ibid.*, p. 218.
6. Hadley Arkes, *Bureaucracy, The Marshall Plan, and National Interest* (Princeton, N.J.: Princeton University Press, 1972), p. 39.
7. *Ibid.*
8. Lucius Clay, *Decision in Germany* (Garden City, N.Y.: Doubleday, 1950), p. 174.
9. Department of State *Bulletin*, May 11, 1947, p. 919.
10. *FR:1947*, III, p. 221.
11. *Ibid.*
12. Acheson as quoted in Joseph M. Jones, *The Fifteen Weeks* (New York: Viking Press, 1955), pp. 252-253.
13. Arkes, *Bureaucracy*, pp. 53-54.
14. *Ibid.*, p. 54.
15. Jones, *The Fifteen Weeks*, pp. 208-210.
16. Quoted in McGeorge Bundy, *The Pattern of Responsibility* (Boston: Houghton Mifflin, 1952), pp. 48-49.
17. *Ibid.*
18. Jones, *The Fifteen Weeks*, p. 236.
19. These last two paragraphs are based upon a paraphrase of the account presented in Thomas G. Paterson, *Soviet-American Confrontation: Postwar Reconstruction and the Origins of the Cold War* (Baltimore, Md.: Johns Hopkins Press, 1972), pp. 211-212.
20. *FR:1947*, III, pp. 232-233.
21. Harry S Truman, *Memoirs*, Vol. I, *Years of Trial and Hope* (Garden City, N.Y.: Doubleday, 1956), p. 114.
22. Commencement address, Wesleyan University, Middletown, Conn., June 15, 1947.
23. Dean Acheson, *Present at the Creation* (New York: W. W. Norton, 1969), p. 241.
24. The matter has been penetratingly studied by Hadley Arkes in his book, *Bureaucracy, the Marshall Plan, and the National Interest*.
25. Gaddis Smith, *Dean Acheson* (New York: Cooper Square Publishers, 1972), p. 52.

Chapter 9

1. Nomination of Dean G. Acheson, Hearings before the Committee on Foreign Relations, January 13, 1949, pp. 6-7.

2. *Ibid.*, p. 9.
3. *Ibid.*
4. H. Bradford Westerfield, *Foreign Policy and Party Politics* (New Haven, Conn.: Yale University Press, 1955), p. 328.
5. Ronald J. Caridi, *The Korean War and American Politics: The Republican Party as a Case Study* (Philadelphia: University of Pennsylvania Press, 1969), p. 3.
6. Alexander de Conde, *The American Secretary of State* (New York: Praeger, 1962), p. 41.
7. Acheson, "The President and the Secretary of State," *The Secretary of State*, edited by Don Price (Englewood Cliffs, N.J.: Prentice-Hall, 1960), p. 37.
8. Speech of September 30, 1948, to the Michigan Bar Association.
9. Acheson, *Present at the Creation* (New York: W. W. Norton, 1969), p. 338. Emphasis added.
10. Gaddis Smith, *Dean Acheson* (New York: Cooper Square Publishers, 1972), p. 79.
11. *Ibid.*, p. 80.
12. Quoted in Robert Osgood, *NATO: The Entangling Alliance* (Chicago: University of Chicago Press, 1962), p. 37.
13. *Ibid.*, p. 31.
14. Arthur H. Vandenberg, Jr., ed., *The Private Papers of Senator Vandenberg* (Boston: Houghton Mifflin, 1952), p. 479.
15. Congressional Record, Vol. 95, Part 1, 81st Congress, First session, p. 1165.
16. *The New York Times,* February 16, 1949, p. 1.
17. *Ibid.,* February 18, 1949, p. 6.
18. Acheson, *Present at the Creation,* p. 283. Emphasis added.
19. *The New York Times,* March 20, 1949.
20. *Ibid.,* April 3, 1949.
21. North Atlantic Treaty, Hearings before the Committee on Foreign Relations, United States Senate, 81st Congress, First Session, April 27, 28, 29, May 2 and 3, 1949, p. 11.
22. *Ibid.*
23. *Ibid.*, p. 13.
24. *Ibid.*, p. 23.
25. *Ibid.*, p. 47.
26. Smith, *Dean Acheson,* p. 92.
27. George F. Kennan, *Memoirs: 1925-1950* (Boston: Little, Brown, 1967), p. 271.
28. *Ibid.*, p. 445.
29. *Ibid.*, p. 448.
30. Charles E. Bohlen, Princeton Seminar Transcript, July 9, 1953.
31. Charles E. Bohlen, *Witness to History: 1929-1969* (New York: W. W. Norton, 1973), pp. 285-286. FR:1949, III, pp. 874-875, 877-879.
32. Adam B. Ulam, *The Rivals: America and Russia Since World War Two* (New York: Viking Press, 1971), p. 151.
33. Review of the World Situation: 1949-1950. Hearings held in Executive Session before the Committee on Foreign Relations, United States Senate, May 19, 1949. Historical Series, p. 22.
34. The entire proceedings of the conference including Acheson's daily

résumés and evaluations to Truman are to be found in *FR:1949*, III, *Council of Foreign Ministers: Germany and Austria*, pp. 913-1065.
35. Smith, *Dean Acheson*, p. 103.
36. Notes of Secretary for Executive Session of Senate Foreign Relations Committee, April 21, 1949; on military assistance.
37. Acheson, Princeton Seminar Transcript, October 10, 1953.
38. Notes of Secretary, April 21, 1949, p. 5.
39. Acheson, Princeton Seminar Transcript, October 10, 1953.
40. Vandenberg, *Private Papers*, p. 511.
41. *Ibid.*, p. 508.
42. *Joint Hearings on S.2388 (Military Assistance Program)*, U. S. Senate, Committee on Foreign Relations and Committee on Armed Services, 81st Congress, First session, August 8, 9, 10, 11, 17, 18, and 19, 1949, p. 10.
43. *Ibid.*, p. 13.
44. *Ibid.*, p. 24. Emphasis added.
45. *Ibid.*, p. 27.
46. *Ibid.*, p. 26. Emphasis added.
47. Acheson, Princeton Seminar Transcript, October 10, 1953.
48. *Ibid.*
49. *Ibid.*
50. *Ibid.*

Chapter 10

1. Paul Y. Hammond, "N.S.C. 68: Prologue to Rearmament," in *Strategy, Politics and Defense Budgets* by Warner R. Schilling, Paul Y. Hammond, and Glen H. Snyder (New York: Columbia University Press, 1962), p. 276.
2. Richard F. Haynes, *The Awesome Power* (Baton Rouge: Louisiana State University Press, 1973), p. 124.
3. For a detailed account see Richard G. Hewlett and Francis Duncan, *A History of the United States Atomic Energy Commission*, Vol. II, *Atomic Shield: 1947-1952* (University Park: Pennsylvania State University Press, 1969), p. 368.
4. George F. Kennan, *Memoirs: 1925-1950* (Boston: Little, Brown, 1967), p. 466.
5. *Ibid.*, p. 468.
6. Dean Acheson, address at the Al Smith Dinner, New York City, October 20, 1949.
7. *Ibid.*
8. Remarks at the National War College, Washington, D. C., December 21, 1949.
9. *Ibid.*
10. Kennan, *Memoirs*, pp. 472-473.
11. Interview with Dean Acheson, Washington, D. C., April 9, 1963.
12. *Ibid.*
13. Acheson, *Present at the Creation* (New York: W. W. Norton, 1969), p. 346.
14. Hewlett and Duncan, *Atomic Shield*, p. 404.
15. *Ibid.*
16. *Ibid.*, p. 408.

17. *Ibid.*, pp. 386, 393-394.
18. *Ibid.*, pp. 393-394.
19. Coral Bell, *Negotiation from Strength* (New York: Alfred A. Knopf, 1963), p. 9.
20. Department of State *Bulletin*, February 20, 1950, pp. 272-274.
21. David Lawrence, "A Way to Peace," *U.S. News and World Report,* February 17, 1950, p. 5.
22. *The New York Times,* February 17, 1950, p. 1.
23. Department of State *Bulletin*, March 20, 1950, Vol. XXII, No. 559, pp. 427-429.
24. Adam B. Ulam, *Expansion and Coexistence: Soviet Foreign Policy 1917-1973*, 2nd ed. (New York: Praeger, 1974), p. 503.
25. Raymond Aron, *The Imperial Republic* (trans. by Frans Jellinek) (Englewood Cliffs, N.J.: Prentice-Hall, 1974), p. 42.
26. *Ibid.*, p. 507.

Chapter 11

1. U.S. Department of State, *United States Relations with China with Special Reference to the Period 1944-1949* (Washington, D.C.: Government Printing Office, August, 1949). Letter of transmittal dated March 15, 1949, pp. xv-xvi. Sometimes known as the China White Paper and hereinafter referred to as such.
2. *The New York Times,* April 27, 1949, p. 1.
3. Tang Tsou, *America's Failure in China: 1940-1945* (Chicago: University of Chicago Press, 1963), p. 515.
4. *Ibid.*, p. 494.
5. See Chen Chi-mai cables, "The China Lobby," *The Reporter*, Vol. 6, Nos. 8 and 9, April 15 and 29, 1952.
6. Message inserted in the *Congressional Record* by Wayne Morse of Oregon (*Congressional Record*, SCVIII, 82nd Congress, Second Session [1952], p. 3970).
7. The China White Paper is officially entitled *United States Relations with China with Special Reference to the Period 1944-1949* (Washington, D.C.: Government Printing Office, August, 1949).
8. Secretary Acheson's top-secret memorandum for Ambassador Jessup, July 18, 1949, as reprinted in *Nomination of Jessup*, p. 603. Hearings, Senate Foreign Relations, 81st Congress, Second Session.
9. *Ibid.*, pp. 603-604.
10. Letter of Transmittal, China White Paper, pp. xv-xvi.
11. Walter Lippmann, "The White Paper: The Chiang Stranglehold," September 12, 1949, as reprinted in *Commentaries on American Foreign Policy* (New York: American Institute of Pacific Relations, 1950), p. 7.
12. Quoted in Tsou, *America's Failure in China*, p. 509.
13. *Ibid.*
14. China White Paper, pp. xvi-xvii.
15. *Ibid.*
16. *FR:1949*, Vol. IX, p. 148.
17. *Ibid.*, pp. 160-161. Memorandum of decisions reached by consensus at the meetings with Secretary Acheson and the consultants on the Far East, November 2, 1949.

18. Tsou, *America's Failure in China,* p. 527.
19. Acheson files, December 8, 1949; minutes of meeting between Acheson and Franks.
20. Tsou, *America's Failure in China,* p. 528.
21. Johnson testimony, *Hearings to Conduct an Inquiry into the Military Situation in the Far East,* Hearings before the Armed Services and Foreign Relations Committees, U.S. Senate, 82nd Congress, First Session, Part 3, p. 2578.
22. *The New York Times,* December 31, 1949, p. 1.
23. Tsou, *America's Failure in China,* p. 533.
24. Quoted in Tsou, *ibid.,* p. 533.
25. Dean Acheson, "Crisis in Asia—An Examination of U.S. Policy," Department of State *Bulletin,* Vol. XXII, No. 551, January 23, 1950, pp. 111-118. The handwritten copy is retained among the Acheson Papers.
20. Tsou, *America's Failure in China,* p. 534.
27. Acheson Papers, Truman Library, Independence, Mo.
28. Acheson, "Crisis in Asia," p. 116.
29. Cited in Foster Rhea Dulles, *American Foreign Policy Toward Communist China, 1949-1969* (New York: Crowell, 1972), p. 68.
30. Mao Tse-tung, *On People's Democratic Dictatorship* (Peking: Foreign Language Press, 1952), p. 10.
31. Tsou, *America's Failure in China,* p. 549.

Chapter 12

1. Editorial, *New Republic,* January 16, 1950, Vol. 122, No. 3, p. 5.
2. Interview with Mrs. Dean Acheson, February 21, 1975.
3. *The New York Times,* January 26, 1950, p. 1.
4. *Time,* January 6, 1950, Vol. LV, No. 6, p. 11.
5. Acheson-Frankfurter correspondence, January 27, 1950; papers of Felix Frankfurter, Box I, Dean Acheson. Library of Congress.
6. Interview with Carlton Savage, Washington, D. C.
7. Lately Thomas, *When Even Angels Wept—The Senator Joseph McCarthy Affair—A Story Without a Hero* (New York: William Morrow, 1973), p. 82.
8. *Ibid.,* p. 81.
9. *Ibid.,* p. 98.
10. Gaddis Smith, *Dean Acheson* (New York: Cooper Square Publishers, 1972), p. 166.
11. Thomas, *When Even Angels Wept,* p. 163.
12. *Ibid.,* p. 102.
13. Quoted in Acheson, *Present at the Creation* (New York: W. W. Norton, 1969), p. 361. Statement by Acheson in response to questions at the hearings of the Senate Appropriations Committee, February 28, 1950. Press release No. 185.
14. *Ibid.*
15. Address, Berkeley, California, March 13, 1950. State Department Release No. 240, pp. 2-3.
16. *Ibid.,* p. 3.
17. *Ibid.,* pp. 3-6. This is an abbreviated résumé.
18. *The New York Times,* March 17, 1950, p. 1.

19. Address, Berkeley, California, March 13, 1950, p. 7.
20. TRB, *New Republic*, March 20, 1950, Vol. 122, No. 12, p. 4.
21. *Ibid.*, March 27, 1950, Vol. 122, No. 13, p. 3.
22. *Ibid.*
23. "Mr. Acheson's 'Total Diplomacy,' " *U.S. News and World Report*, March 24, 1950, p. 6.
24. *Life*, March 20, 1950, Vol. 28, p. 40.
25. *Ibid.*
26. *Ibid.*
27. *Ibid.*
28. An expression similar to this is reported in Thomas, *When Even Angels Wept*, p. 133.
29. H. Bradford Westerfield, *Foreign Policy and Party Politics* (New Haven, Conn.: Yale University Press, 1955), p. 372.
30. Athan Theoharis, *Seeds of Repression* (Chicago: Quadrangle, 1971), p. 163.
31. Richard Loss, *The Power of Experience: Secretary of State Dean Acheson as Political Executive*, unpublished manuscript.
32. *Ibid.*
33. Acheson, *Present at the Creation*, p. 368.
34. Again I am indebted for this information to Professor Richard Loss.
35. Letter from Truman to Bridges, March 26, 1950, published in Alan Harper, *The Politics of Loyalty* (Westport, Conn.: Greenwood, 1969), pp. 265-266. See also letter from Truman to Vandenberg, *ibid.*, pp. 268-269.
36. Westerfield, *Foreign Policy and Party Politics*, p. 378.

Chapter 13

1. Dean Acheson address to the Al Smith Dinner, New York City, October 20, 1949, p. 2.
2. Douglas to Acheson, August 15, 1949. Acheson Papers.
3. Dean Acheson, *Sketches from Life of Men I Have Known* (New York: Harper & Brothers, 1961), p. 18.
4. Hugh Dalton, *Memoirs: 1945-60* (London: Muller, 1962), p. 338.
5. Interview with Sir Oliver Franks, Oxford, England, June 27, 1964.
6. Richard Stebbins, *The United States in World Affairs: 1950* (New York: Council on Foreign Relations, 1951), p. 131.
7. McGeorge Bundy, ed., *The Pattern of Responsibility* (Boston: Houghton Mifflin, 1951), p. 57.
8. Acheson, Princeton Seminar Transcript, October 10, 1953.
9. Interview with Sir Oliver Franks, Oxford, England, June 27, 1964.
10. Stebbins, *United States in World Affairs*, pp. 213-214.
11. James L. Richardson, *Germany and the Atlantic Alliance* (Cambridge, Mass.: Harvard University Press, 1966), p. 15.
12. *Ibid.*
13. Quoted in Alfred Grosser, *La IVᵉ République et sa Politique Extérieur* (Paris: Armand Colin, 1961), p. 210.
14. Gordon A. Craig, *From Bismarck to Adenauer: Aspects of German State-craft* (Baltimore, Md.: Johns Hopkins University Press, 1958), pp. 14-15.
15. *Ibid.*

16. William James, *Pragmatism* (New York: Longmans, Green, 1943), pp. 201-205.
17. *Ibid.*
18. Acheson, Executive Session, "Consultation Prior to Foreign Ministers' Meeting," May 1, 1950, *Review of the World Situation, 1949-1950*, Committee on Foreign Relations, United States Senate, p. 286.
19. Acheson, *Sketches From Life*, pp. 36-37.
20. Bernard Lavergne, *Le Plan Schuman* (Paris: Plon, 1952), pp. 14-15.
21. "Fundamental Common Objectives," *London Foreign Ministers' Meetings*, May 1950. Document No. FMDB-20e.
22. Position Paper: "General Attitude toward the Soviet Union and Possible Negotiations," *London Foreign Ministers' Meetings*, May 1950. Document No. FMDB-21c.
23. *Ibid.*
24. Acheson, *Present at the Creation*, p. 394.
25. *London Foreign Ministers' Meetings*, Document MIN/TRE, F/Y.

Chapter 14

1. *United States-Vietnam Relations: 1945-1967.* Department of Defense edition for the House Armed Services Committee (Washington, D.C.: U.S. Government Printing Office, 1971), Part I, Section I, p. C-5. Hereinafter referred to as *Pentagon Papers*, DOD edition.
2. *Ibid.*, pp. C-6-7.
3. Edmund Gullion in *Pentagon Papers*, pp. A-29, 30.
4. Philip C. Jessup, *The Birth of Nations* (New York: Columbia University Press, 1974), pp. 167-168.
5. *Pentagon Papers*, Part II, p. A-46.
6. *Pentagon Papers*, Senator Gravel edition, Vol. I (Boston: Beacon Press, n.d.), p. 39. Emphasis added.
7. Jessup, *Birth of Nations*, pp. 189, 194.
8. Raymond Aron, *The Imperial Republic, The United States and the World 1945-1973* (Englewood Cliffs, N.J.: Prentice-Hall, 1974), p. 46.
9. Jessup, *Birth of Nations*, pp. 188-192. See also David Halberstam, *The Best and the Brightest* (New York: Random House, 1972), p. 335.
10. Minutes of meeting, March 13, 1950. Acheson Papers.
11. Acheson testifying before the Senate Foreign Relations Committee in executive session, March 29, 1950, 81st Congress, First and Second Sessions. In *Review of the World Situation: 1949-1950*, pp. 266-267.
12. Jessup, *Birth of Nations*, pp. 190-191.
13. Acheson testimony, May 1, 1950. *Review of the World Situation: 1949-1950*, p. 293.
14. *Ibid.*, p. 297.
15. Kennan, *Memoirs: 1925-1950* (Boston: Little, Brown, 1967), p. 381.
16. Akira Iriye, *The Cold War in Asia* (Englewood Cliffs, N.J.: Prentice-Hall, 1974), p. 174.
17. *Ibid.*, p. 174.
18. Minutes of meeting, April 24, 1950. Acheson Papers.
19. Iriye, *Cold War in Asia*, pp. 174-175.
20. Acheson, *Review of the World Situation*, p. 291.

21. Nikita S. Khrushchev, *Khrushchev Remembers* (New York: Bantam, 1970), p. 402.
22. *Ibid.*, pp. 401-402.
23. Alexander L. George and Richard Smoke, *Deterrence in American Foreign Policy* (New York: Columbia University Press, 1974), pp. 157-161.
24. See Marshall Shulman, *Stalin's Foreign Policy Reappraised* (Cambridge, Mass.: Harvard University Press, 1963), pp. 114-115, 123.
25. Charles E. Bohlen, *Witness to History: 1929-1967* (New York: W. W. Norton, 1973), p. 290.
26. *Ibid.*, p. 290.
27. *Ibid.*, p. 291.
28. Acheson, *Present at the Creation*, p. 753.
29. *Ibid.*, p. 347.
30. *FR:1949*, III, pp. 888-890.
31. Quoted in Samuel P. Huntington, *The Common Defense: Strategic Programs in National Politics* (New York: Columbia University Press, 1961), p. 51; from Paul H. Nitze, "The Need for a National Strategy" (Address, Army War College, Carlisle Barracks, Pennsylvania, August 21, 1958).

Chapter 15

1. Charles E. Bohlen, *Witness to History, 1929-1969* (New York: W. W. Norton, 1973), pp. 291-292.
2. Glenn D. Paige, *The Korean Decision* (New York: Free Press, 1968), p. 298.
3. *Ibid.*, p. 92. See also Joseph H. de Rivera, *The Psychological Dimension of Foreign Policy* (Columbus, Ohio: Charles E. Merrill, 1968), and Ernest R. May, *Lessons of the Past: The Use and Misuse of History in American Foreign Policy* (New York: Oxford University Press, 1973), p. 72.
4. Bohlen, *Witness to History*, pp. 294-295.
5. *Ibid.*, p. 533.
6. Denise Folliot, ed., *Documents on International Affairs, 1949-1950* (London: Oxford University Press, 1952), p. 637.
7. Acheson to Nitze, July 12, 1950. Acheson Papers.
8. Paige, *The Korean Decision*, p. 248.
9. *Ibid.*
10. Adam B. Ulam, *Expansion and Coexistence: Soviet Foreign Policy 1917-1967* (New York: Praeger, 1968), p. 522.
11. Memo, NSC meeting, July 27. Acheson Papers.
12. Robert H. Ferrell, "Dean Acheson," *The Review*, Indiana University (Winter 1973), pp. 19, 21.
13. Paige, *The Korean Decision*, pp. 196-197.
14. Memo of meeting at Blair House, July 3, 1950. President Truman, Acheson, Johnson, Bradley, Harriman, and Senator Scott Lucas (D-Ill.). Acheson Papers.
15. *Ibid.*
16. *Ibid.*
17. Princeton Seminar Transcript, February 13-14, 1954.

18. Ronald J. Caridi, *The Korean War and American Politics: The Republican Party as a Case Study* (Philadelphia: University of Pennsylvania Press, 1969), p. 54.
19. George Kennan, *Memoirs: 1925-1950* (Boston: Little, Brown, 1967), p. 522.
20. Acheson, *Present at the Creation*, p. 445.
21. *Ibid.*, p. 454.
22. *U.S. News and World Report*, September 1, 1950, pp. 32-34.
23. Truman, *Memoirs*, Vol. II, pp. 354-355.
24. Acheson, *Present at the Creation*, p. 424.
25. Truman, *Memoirs*, Vol. II, p. 359.
26. Caridi, *Korean War and American Politics*, p. 64.
27. Acheson, *Present at the Creation*, p. 453.
28. *The New York Times*, October 2, 1950, p. 3.
29. Memo, Marshall D. Shulman (Acheson aide) to Ambassador Jessup (with Presidential party) in the files of Charles Murphy, Truman Library, Independence, Missouri.
30. David Rees, *Korea: The Limited War* (London: Macmillan, 1964), p. 128.
31. Trumbull Higgins, *Korea and the Fall of MacArthur* (New York: Oxford University Press, 1960), p. 65.
32. S. L. A. Marshall, *The River and the Gauntlet* (New York: William Morrow, 1953). Marshall was operations analyst for the Eighth Army.
33. Rees, *Korea: The Limited War*, p. 133.
34. Princeton Seminar Transcript. See also Rees, *Korea: The Limited War*, p. 132.
35. Princeton Seminar Transcript. See also Martin Lichterman, *To the Yalu and Back* (Indianapolis: Bobbs-Merrill, 1963), p. 36.
36. Cited in Rees, *Korea: The Limited War*, pp. 131-132.
37. Truman, *Memoirs*, Vol. II, pp. 378-380; *Hearings to Conduct an Inquiry into the Military Situation in the Far East*, Senate Committees on the Armed Services and Foreign Relations, 82nd Congress, 1st Session, Part II (Washington, D.C.: U.S. Government Printing Office, 1951), pp. 619-620. Hereinafter referred to as the *MacArthur Hearings*.
38. Truman, *Memoirs*, Vol. II, 378-380.
39. Richard Neustadt, *Presidential Power: The Politics of Leadership* (New York: John Wiley, 1960), p. 137.
40. Meeting in Department of State, November 21, 1950. Acheson Papers.
41. Minutes of meeting in the Pentagon, 2:23 P.M., November 21, 1950. Acheson Papers.
42. Klaus Knorr, "Failures in National Intelligence Estimates: The Case of the Cuban Missiles," *World Politics*, XVI (1964), pp. 455-467.
43. MacArthur Hearings, p. 1835.
44. Gaddis Smith, *Dean Acheson* (New York: Cooper Square Publishers, 1972), p. 234.

Chapter 16

1. Minutes of NSC meeting, White House, November 28, 1950. Truman, Acheson, Marshall, Bradley and staffs, and Collins, Vandenberg, Sherman, Harriman, Secretary Snyder, Bedell Smith (CIA), and others.

2. *Ibid.*
3. *Ibid.*
4. *Ibid.*
5. Memo for meeting, Acheson to Truman, "Soviet Intentions in the Current Situation," December 2, 1950. Acheson Papers.
6. Minutes of meeting, Acheson, Rusk, Kennan, Matthews, December 4, 1950. Acheson Papers.
7. Lawton Collins, *War in Peacetime: The History and Lessons of Korea* (Boston: Houghton Mifflin, 1969), p. 229.
8. *Hearings to Conduct an Inquiry into the Military Situation in the Far East* [MacArthur Hearings], Senate Committees on Armed Services and Foreign Relations, 82nd Congress, 1st Session, Part II (Washington, D.C.: U.S. Government Printing Office, 1951), pp. 2179-2180.
9. *Ibid.*
10. Harry S Truman, *Memoirs*, Vol. II, *Years of Trial and Hope* (Garden City, N.Y.: Doubleday, 1956), p. 398.
11. *Ibid.*, p. 404.
12. *Ibid.*, p. 403.
13. Ronald J. Caridi, *The Korean War and American Politics: The Republican Party as a Case Study* (Philadelphia: University of Pennsylvania Press, 1968), p. 105.
14. Truman, *Memoirs*, Vol. II, p. 413.
15. M. D. Donelan and M. J. Grieve, *International Disputes Case Histories 1945-1970* (London: Europa Publications, 1975), p. 59.
16. *Ibid.*
17. Minutes of meeting, Acheson and Bradley, January 11, 1950. Acheson Papers.
18. Quoted in John W. Spanier, *The Truman-MacArthur Controversy and the Korean War* (Cambridge, Mass.: Harvard University Press, 1959), p. 67.
19. MacArthur Hearings, pp. 736-737.
20. Memo for the Record. Truman, Acheson, Marshall, Bradley, the Joint Chiefs, and others, January 12, 1950. Acheson Papers.
21. MacArthur Hearings, pp. 736-737.
22. Truman, *Memoirs*, Vol. II, p. 46.
23. Spanier, *The Truman-MacArthur Controversy*, p. 144.
24. Dean Acheson, press conference of January 17, 1951. Department of State *Bulletin*, January 29, 1951, pp. 164-165.
25. Lester B. Pearson, *Mike: The Memoirs of Lester B. Pearson*, edited by John A. Munro and Alex. I. Inglis (New York: Quadrangle, 1973), p. 167.
26. *Ibid.*, pp. 169-170.
27. U.N.G.A. Res. 478 (v), 1 February 1951.
28. Quoted in Spanier, *The Truman-MacArthur Controversy*, p. 193.
29. *Ibid.*, p. 196.
30. MacArthur Hearings, p. 571.
31. MacArthur Hearings, pp. 1214-1215, 3180; Truman, *Memoirs*, Vol. II, pp. 438-439.
32. Truman, *Memoirs*, Vol. II, pp. 438-439.
33. *Ibid.*, pp. 440-441.
34. Princeton Seminar Transcript, February 14, 1954, p. 5.

35. Trumbull Higgins, *Korea and the Fall of MacArthur: A Précis in Limited War* (New York: Oxford University Press, 1960), p. 110.
36. Truman, *Memoirs*, Vol. II, p. 442.
37. Higgins, *Korea and Fall of MacArthur*, p. 116; Acheson, *Present at the Creation* (New York: W. W. Norton, 1969), pp. 519-520.
38. Princeton Seminar Transcript, February 14, 1954, p. 7.
39. *Ibid.*, p. 1.
40. *Ibid.*
41. Higgins, *Korea and Fall of MacArthur*, p. 117.
42. Truman, *Memoirs*, Vol. II, p. 446.
43. Quoted in David Rees, *Korea: The Limited War* (London: Macmillan, 1964), p. 221.
44. Acheson, Princeton Seminar Transcript, February 13 and 14, 1954, p. 2.
45. Princetown Seminar Transcript, February 14, 1954, p. 3.
46. Rees, *Korea: The Limited War*, p. 227.
47. Richard H. Rovere and Arthur M. Schlesinger, Jr., *The General and the President* (New York: Farrar, Straus, and Young, 1951), p. 178.
48. *Ibid.*
49. *Ibid.*, p. 186.
50. MacArthur Hearings, pp. 730-732.
51. Acheson, *Present at the Creation*, p. 531.
52. MacArthur Hearings, p. 1859.
53. *Ibid.*, p. 1860.
54. *Ibid.*, p. 1761.
55. *Ibid.*
56. Acheson, *Present at the Creation*, p. 533.
57. Matthew Ridgway, quoted in Acheson, *Present at the Creation*, p. 651.
58. Caridi, *Korean War and American Politics*, pp. 190-198.
59. Quoted in Foster Rhea Dulles, *American Foreign Policy Toward Communist China: 1949-1969* (New York: Crowell, 1972), p. 112.
60. *Ibid.*
61. Position Paper endorsed by Acheson for the Washington Foreign Ministers Meeting, August 20, 1951. Also letter to Senator H. Alexander Smith, September 24, 1951. Reaffirmed in Department Cable to Manila, April 7, 1952.
62. Memo of dinner meeting at British Embassy. Churchill, Eden, Cherwell, Acheson, Lovett, Bradley. Sunday, January 6, 1952. Acheson Papers.
63. Brief for the President, September 23, 1952. Acheson Papers.
64. Minutes of conversation. Churchill, Truman, Acheson, and others, British Embassy, Washington, D. C., January 6, 1952. Acheson Papers.
65. Memo of meeting. Acheson, Harriman, Gifford, Jessup, Morrison, Franks, Pierson Dixon, Hugh Gaitskell, September 9, 1951. Acheson Papers.
66. Gaddis Smith, *Dean Acheson* (New York: Cooper Square Publishers, 1972), p. 328.
67. Memo of meeting. Acheson, Lovett, Admirals Fechteler and Libbey, September 17, 1952. Acheson Papers.
68. Memo of meeting. Truman, Acheson, Foster, Smith, Bradley, and others, September 24, 1952. Acheson Papers.
69. Smith, *Dean Acheson*, p. 297.

70. *Ibid.*, p. 298.
71. *Ibid.*, p. 295.
72. Akira Iriye, *The Cold War in Asia* (Englewood Cliffs, N. J.: Prentice-Hall, 1974), p. 178.

Chapter 17

1. Memo of meeting. Acheson to Johnson. Acheson, Nitze, Ohly, Spofford, July 20, 1950. Acheson Papers.
2. Minutes, meeting of Acheson with the President, July 21, 1950. Acheson Papers.
3. L. W. Martin, "The American Decision to Rearm Germany" (manuscript version). Published in *American Civil-Military Decisions*, edited by Harold Stein (Montgomery: University of Alabama Press, 1963), pp. 22, 27.
4. Memo of meeting. Acheson and Truman, August 10, 1950. Acheson Papers.
5. Memo of meeting. Acheson and Truman, August 21, 1950. Acheson Papers.
6. Memo of conversation, Acheson and Bonnet, August 23, 1950. Acheson Papers.
7. Martin, "The American Decision," p. 28.
8. Robert McGeehan, *The German Rearmament Question: American Diplomacy and European Defense After World War II* (Urbana: University of Illinois Press, 1971), p. 46.
9. *Ibid.*, p. 47.
10. Interview with André Francois-Poncet. Paris, June 20, 1964.
11. Interview with Sir Oliver Franks, Worcester College, Oxford, England, June 27, 1964.
12. Cited in McGeehan, *The German Rearmament Question*, p. 52.
13. Interview with Sir Oliver Franks, June 27, 1964. For the French sense of isolation, see Moch, *Histoire du réarmament allemand depuis 1950* (Paris: Laffont, 1965), p. 57.
14. Martin, "The American Decision," p. 33.
15. Moch, *Histoire du réarmament*, pp. 52-59.
16. *Ibid.*, pp. 77-78.
17. McGeehan, *The German Rearmament Question*, p. 60. I have relied upon McGeehan's study for some of the points cited.
18. Dean Acheson, *Sketches from Life of Men I Have Known* (New York: Harper & Brothers, 1961), pp. 26-27.
19. Moch, *Histoire du réarmament*, p. 109.
20. McGeehan, *The German Rearmament Question*, p. 64.
21. *Ibid.*, p. 66.
22. *Ibid.*, p. 63.
23. Department of State *Bulletin*, November 13, 1959, p. 777.
24. Memo, Acheson to Bonnet, October 25, 1950. Acheson Papers.
25. Department of State *Bulletin*, November 27, 1950, p. 854.
26. Memo of meeting. Acheson to Bradley, December 6, 1950. Acheson Papers.
27. McGeehan, *The German Rearmament Question*, pp. 84-85.
28. *Ibid.*, p. 85.

29. *Ibid.*, p. 90.
30. Marshall D. Shulman, *Stalin's Foreign Policy Reappraised* (Cambridge, Mass.: Harvard University Press, 1963), p. 169.
31. "Soviet Proposal for a Meeting of the Council of Foreign Ministers," December 17, 1950. Acheson Papers.
32. Minutes, Truman-Pleven meeting, January 30, 1951. Acheson Papers.
33. *Hearing on Assignment of Ground Forces of the United States to Duty in European Area.* Hearings before the Senate Foreign Relations and Armed Services Committees, 82nd Congress, 1st Session, February 1-28, 1950, p. 104.
34. Ronald J. Caridi, *The Korean War and American Politics: The Republican Party as a Case Study* (Philadelphia: University of Pennsylvania Press, 1968), p. 55.
35. *Congressional Record,* September 5, 1950, p. 14214.
36. Interview, September 10, 1950. State Department Press Release No. 922. Acheson Papers.
37. William S. White, *The Taft Story* (New York: Harper & Brothers, 1954), p. 150.
38. Quoted in McGeorge Bundy, ed., *The Pattern of Responsibility* (Boston: Houghton Mifflin, 1952), pp. 85-86.
39. *Vital Speeches,* January 1, 1951 (New York: The City Publishing Co., 1952), p. 166.
40. *Ibid.*
41. *Ibid.*
42. *Congressional Record,* January 5, 1951, p. 61.
43. *Congressional Record,* March 14, 1951, p. 2436.
44. *Congressional Record,* January 5, 1951, pp. 60-64. Caridi, *Korean War and American Politics,* pp. 134-139.
45. *Assignment of Ground Forces,* p. 78. Emphasis added.
46. *Ibid.*, p. 79.
47. *Ibid*
48. *Ibid.*, p. 80.
49. *Congressional Record,* January 5, 1951, 82nd Congress, 1st Session, pp. 54-61. Emphasis added.
50. Dean Acheson, *Present at the Creation* (New York: W. W. Norton, 1969), p. 495.
51. *Assignment of Ground Forces,* pp. 93-94.
52. *Congressional Record,* April 2, 1951, p. 3170.

Chapter 18

1. Dwight D. Eisenhower, *The White House Years: Mandate For Change, 1953-1956* (Garden City, N. Y.: Doubleday, 1963), p. 398.
2. Memo of meeting. Acheson, Marshall, Bradley, and staffs. June 21, 1951. Acheson Papers.
3. Memorandum entitled *German Rearmament and Problems of Defense of Europe.* Acheson Papers.
4. Coral Bell, *Negotiation from Strength* (New York: Alfred A. Knopf, 1963), pp. 48-58.
5. Memo of Cabinet meeting, July 1, 1951. Also of conversation, Acheson to Truman, August 6, 1951. Acheson Papers.

6. Anthony Eden, *Full Circle: The Memoirs of Anthony Eden* (London: Cassell, 1960), pp. 33-34.
7. Letter, Pearson to Acheson, January 15, 1952. Acheson Papers.
8. *The New York Times,* February 9, 1952.
9. Gaddis Smith, *Dean Acheson* (New York: Cooper Square Publishers, 1972), p. 259.
10. Dean Acheson, *Sketches from Life of Men I Have Known* (New York: Harper & Brothers, 1961), p. 48.
11. Robert McGeehan, *The German Rearmament Question: American Diplomacy and European Defense After World War II* (Urbana: University of Illinois Press, 1971), p. 197.
12. *Ibid.,* p. 196.

Chapter 19

1. Marshall D. Shulman, *Stalin's Foreign Policy Reappraised* (Cambridge, Mass.: Harvard University Press, 1963), p. 191.
2. Memo of meeting. Acheson, Franks. Telegram from Eden, March 13, 1952. Acheson Papers.
3. Letter, Acheson to Truman, March 11, 1952. Acheson Papers.
4. Acheson to Raymond Allen (Psychological Strategy Board), March 17, 1952. Acheson Papers.
5. Memo of meeting. Acheson, Franks to discuss Soviet note of March 10. March 13, 1952. Acheson Papers.
6. Letter from Acheson to Truman, March 21, 1952. Acheson Papers.
7. Minutes of meeting. Acheson, Walter Hallstein, March 12, 1952. Acheson Papers.
8. Memo of Conversation. Monnet, Acheson, May 6, 1952. Acheson Papers.
9. Sir Anthony Eden, *Full Circle: The Memoirs of Anthony Eden* (London: Cassell, 1960), pp. 50-51. The official text of the British offer is in Document T. 26, April 18, 1952, Information Office, British Embassy, Washington, D.C.
10. Bernard Lavergne, ed., *L'Année Politique, 1952* (Paris: Plon, 1953), pp. 327-329.
11. Acheson, *Present at the Creation* (New York: W. W. Norton, 1969), p. 644.
12. Acheson, *Present at the Creation,* p. 645.
13. Hearings, Committee on Foreign Relations, United States Senate, June 2, 1952, 82nd Congress, 2nd Session, p. 17.
14. Minutes, Anglo-American Ministerial Talks, London, June 24, 1952. Acheson, Eden, and others.
15. *Ibid.,* Acheson, Schuman, and Eden. London, June 27, 1952.
16. *Ibid.*
17. Minutes, Acheson, J. W. Beyen, J. H. von Roijen, September 23, 1952. Acheson Papers.
18. Minutes, Acheson, Raymond Allen (Director, Psychological Strategy). Acheson Papers.
19. Digest of Kennan's Dispatch, September 8, 1952. Acheson Papers.

Chapter 20

1. Gaddis Smith, *Dean Acheson* (New York: Cooper Square Publishers, 1972), p. 319.
2. Message, Acheson to Saigon Legation, October 18, 1950. *United States-Vietnam Relations, 1945-1967.* Department of Defense edition, Part I (Washington, D.C.: U.S. Government Printing Office, 1971), A-23, 24, 25.
3. Memo, Acheson to Stikker, April 3, 1952. The same point was made to the Australian Ambassador, April 15, 1952. Acheson Papers.
4. Smith, *Dean Acheson,* p. 321.
5. *United States-Vietnam Relations,* A-47.
6. *Ibid.*
7. *Ibid.,* A-48.
8. Smith, *Dean Acheson,* p. 324.
9. *Ibid.,* p. 326.
10. *Ibid.,* p. 327.
11. *Ibid.,* p. 328.
12. Memo, Acheson to Franks, June 17, 1952. Acheson Papers.
13. Telegram to London. "U.S. Views." Acheson to Embassy, London, March 15, 1951. Acheson Papers.
14. Memo, Acheson, Franks, Nitze, April 27, 1951. Acheson Papers.
15. Smith, *Dean Acheson,* p. 338.
16. Letter, July 16, 1951. Henry F. Grady to G. McGhee, Assistant Secretary for the Middle East. Henry F. Grady Papers, Truman Library.
17. Letter, July 20, 1951. Henry F. Grady to G. McGhee, Henry F. Grady Papers, Truman Library.
18. Memo, November 4, 1951. Cited in Dean Acheson, *Present at the Creation* (New York: W. W. Norton, 1969), p. 509.
19. Memo, Eden to Acheson, London, November 4, 1951. Acheson Papers.
20. Telegram, Acheson to State Department, Paris, November 10, 1951. Acheson Papers.
21. Message, Eden to Acheson, February 12, 1952. Acheson Papers.
22. Memo, ministerial talks, London, June 24, 1952. Acheson Papers.
23. Telegram to London, July 26, 1952. Acheson Papers.
24. Memo of Bipartite Foreign Ministers' Meeting. Acheson, Jessup, Dunn, Pinay, Pleven, Schuman, May 28, 1952. Acheson Papers.
25. Telegram from Paris. Memo of conversation with President V. Auriol and General Eisenhower, May 23, 1952. Acheson Papers.
26. Telegram from Paris, October 23, 1952. Dunn to Acheson. Embassy to Department of State. Acheson Papers.
27. Memo, Exchange of letters, Schuman and Acheson, October 28, 1952; November 3, 1952. Memo, Acheson, Madame Pandit, October 29. 1952. Acheson Papers.
28. Memo, Acheson, Madame Pandit (Indian ambassador), October 29, 1952. Acheson Papers.
29. Memo, Acheson, Jessup, Schuman, Hoppenot, Lacoste, November 8, 1952. Acheson Papers.
30. Smith, *Dean Acheson,* p. 359.
31. *Ibid.*
32. *Ibid.,* pp. 359-361.
33. *Ibid.,* p. 359.

34. *Ibid.*, p. 360.
35. *Ibid.*, pp. 360-361.

Chapter 21

1. Interview with Sir Oliver Franks, Worcester College, Oxford, England, June 27, 1964.
2. Alexander L. George and Richard Smoke, *Deterrence in American Foreign Policy* (New York: Columbia University Press, 1974), pp. 172-173.
3. Speech at War College, Washington, D.C., September 20, 1949.
4. Max Lerner, ed., *The Mind and Faith of Justice Holmes* (Boston: Little, Brown, 1943), p. 42.
5. "Success Has Its Problems Too." Address to Michigan Bar Association, September 30, 1948.
6. Speech in Washington, D.C., April 11, 1950.
7. Gaddis Smith, *Dean Acheson* (New York: Cooper Square Publishers, 1972), p. 237.
8. Frank J. Merli and Theodore A. Wilson, *Makers of American Diplomacy* (New York: Scribner's, 1974), p. 293. Emphasis added.
9. Glen H. Stassen, "Individual Preferences versus Role-Constraint in Policy-Making: Senatorial Responses to Secretaries Acheson and Dulles," *World Politics*, XXV, No. 1 (October 1972), p. 115. James Rosenau, "Private Preferences and Political Responsibilities: The Relative Potency of Individual and Role Variables in the Behavior of U.S. Senators," in J. David Singer, ed., *Quantitative International Politics* (New York: Free Press, 1968), pp. 17-50.
10. Smith, *Dean Acheson*, p. 392.
11. *Ibid.*, p. 394.
12. Julius J. Marke, ed., "Idealist Doubts," *The Holmes Reader* (Dobbs Ferry, N.Y.: Oceana, 1955), p. 42.

Epilogue

1. Dean Acheson, *This Vast External Realm* (New York: W. W. Norton, 1973), p. 201.
2. Bert Cochran, *Adlai Stevenson* (New York: Funk & Wagnalls, 1969), p. 252.
3. Statement by Dean Acheson, House Foreign Affairs Committee, January 10, 1957.
4. This felicitous phrase appears in Cochran, *Adlai Stevenson*, p. 190.
5. Acheson statement, January 10, 1957.
6. Alexander L. George and Richard Smoke, *Deterrence in American Foreign Policy* (New York: Columbia University Press, 1974), pp. 257-258.
7. Dean Acheson, "The Illusion of Disengagement," *Foreign Affairs*, 36 (2) (April, 1958), pp. 371-382.
8. *Ibid.*, p. 377.
9. *Ibid.*, p. 380.
10. Walter Lippmann, *The Communist World and Ours* (Boston: Little, Brown, 1959), p. 13. Emphasis added.
11. Dean Acheson, "Wishing Won't Hold Berlin," *Saturday Evening Post*, March 7, 1959, pp. 32-36.

12. Jack M. Schick, *The Berlin Crisis, 1958-1962* (Philadelphia: University of Pennsylvania Press, 1971), p. 51. Robert Slusser, *Berlin Crisis of 1961* (Baltimore: Johns Hopkins University Press, 1973), pp. 32-33.
13. George and Smoke, *Deterrence,* p. 434.
14. Quoted in Graham Allison, *Essence of Decision* (Boston: Little, Brown, 1971), p. 202.
15. *Ibid.,* pp. 198-199.
16. Dean Acheson, "Homage to Plain Dumb Luck," *Esquire,* February, 1969, p. 76.
17. Elie Abel, *The Missile Crisis* (New York: Bantam, 1966), p. 178.
18. *Ibid.*
19. *Ibid.,* p. 172.
20. *Ibid.,* p. 178.
21. *Ibid.*
22. Dean Acheson, "The Political and Economic Strands in Our Atlantic Alliance." Address at the United States Military Academy, West Point, December 5, 1962.
23. Dean Acheson, "Europe: Kaleidoscope or Clouded Crystal." Address at the University of California, Berkeley, March 13, 1963.
24. *Ibid.,* p. 2.
25. Statement by Dean Acheson, Institute of Strategic Studies, Fifth Annual Conference, Cambridge, England, September 10-13, 1963.
26. Dean Acheson, "Germany in the New Europe," Speech to German American Club, Bonn, Germany, October 18, 1963.
27. *The New York Times,* April 27, 1966.
28. Acheson, "Germany in the New Europe."
29. *The New York Times Magazine,* February 28, 1965.
30. Townsend Hoopes, *The Limits of Intervention* (New York: David McKay, 1973), p. 204.
31. *Ibid.,* p. 205.
32. *Ibid.,* pp. 216-217
33. James Reston, *The New York Times,* October 17, 1971, Section IV, p. 11.

INDEX